HUMAN SEXUALITY

SECOND EDITION

Human Sexuality

Physiological, Psychological, and Sociological Factors

SECOND EDITION

James Leslie McCary
University of Houston

D. Van Nostrand Company
New York   Cincinnati   Toronto   London   Melbourne

All illustrations except figures 1.1, 1.2, 6.8, 6.9, 7.6, 9.6, 9.7, 9.8, 9.11, and 20.2 by Vantage Art, Inc.

D. Van Nostrand Company Regional Offices:
New York   Cincinnati   Millbrae

D. Van Nostrand Company International Offices:
London   Toronto   Melbourne

Published by D. Van Nostrand Company
450 West 33rd Street, New York, N.Y. 10001

Published simultaneously in Canada by
Van Nostrand Reinhold Ltd.

10 9 8 7 6 5 4 3 2

Dedicated to that person
who wishes both to better understand
his own sexual needs and behavior
and to be more accepting of his neighbor
whose sexual attitudes and behavior
might be different from his own

PREFACE

Since the first edition of *Human Sexuality* appeared in 1967, significant changes have occurred in the sexual attitudes and behavior of Americans. Consequently, the nature of sex education too has shifted. In the meantime, new data, new concerns, and new possibilities have emerged. This edition attempts to be responsive to the present state of sex education by incorporating recent findings and areas of interest into essentially the same framework that readers of the first edition appear to have found useful.

Although the aim of this edition remains the exploration of physiological, psychological, and sociological factors in human sexuality, emphasis on the psychological and sociological has increased.

I have attempted to keep the text as readable as possible while providing sufficient detail so as to dispel much of the mystery and confusion enveloping this needlessly sensitive area. My object today is identical to that which first led me to undertake the writing of *Human Sexuality:* namely, to promote an informed acceptance of one's own sexuality and that of others, through a thorough examination of what is now understood about the subject. My own experience in the sex-education course that I teach and my conversations with many interested persons across the country continue to reaffirm the view that mature and healthy sexual attitudes and behavior rest on a firm foundation of accurate information presented honestly and directly.

It is my hope that this edition will prove useful to the many college, university, graduate, professional, and lay audiences which responded so gratifyingly to the first edition and that it may reach new audiences which are now coming into being.

No book can be readied for publication without the help of many people, and I have been fortunate to have the aid not only of long-time friends who assisted with the first edition but of new associates. Publication of this edition also gives me the opportunity to make amends for earlier prefatory oversights! Especially worthy of mention here is my friend and former student, Dr. James L. Henderson, now head of Counseling Services at the University of Mississippi, whose knowledge and insight contributed significantly to the chapter on venereal disease. I am also long overdue in expressing appreciation to D. Van Nostrand's Jack Skelley, who has been a good friend to the book and to me.

The present manuscript has been read for medical accuracy by my good friend Dr. Ralph Eichhorn, to whom I am indebted for working yet another time-consuming task into a heavy schedule. Dr. Gerhard Neubeck, himself a leader in the field of sex education, also reviewed the manuscript and made valuable suggestions. Special thanks are due to Mary Elizabeth Sieber, whose bibliographic and other skills have been invaluable to the second edition from start to finish.

Among those who have helped with both "generations" of the book is Ellen Brochstein, who has again facilitated the compiling, typing, and retyping of manuscript, as have Betty Stewart and Judy Barron. My secretaries—Carmen Perez, Eleanor Underhill, and Kay McBride—have been tremendously helpful, especially with library work and with my appointments calendar.

A source of continuing inspiration has been the opportunity to work with Elizabeth Miremont Smith, my editor. I find that I depend more and and more on her good judgment and outstanding abilities with each of our publications. As stated in the first edition, Mrs. Smith is a gentle soul whose energy and enthusiasm have a way of extracting extra effort from all who work with her. I am grateful for that influence and for her guidance, assistance, and hard work, all of which have been so vital to the life of this book.

The most rewarding aspect in the preparation of this edition has been the participation of my son, Stephen Paul McCary, who is a doctoral candidate in educational psychology at the University of Houston and who displays considerable interest and understanding in the field of sex education. Any father would, I think, be pleased by such a professional association. I am doubly pleased because of the caliber of man that I know Stephen to be, and because of the excellent research, comments, and writing with which he has strengthened this manuscript.

My wife LaVirle and I have grown up together during the 35 years of our marriage. She has made more contributions to my life, and to this book, than I can ever recount. Both of us know what those contributions have been, and that is what really matters.

James Leslie McCary

CONTENTS

ILLUSTRATIONS

PART ONE

BY WAY OF INTRODUCTION

1 WHY
SEX
EDUCATION?

Sex—so small a word, yet so explosive a subject. Even the most casual observer of the American scene can hardly have failed to notice the spotlight trained incessantly on this topic in very recent years. Both attitudes and behavior of the American public in matters of sex have undergone rapid and significant changes during the past decade—undoubtedly a mere prelude to future changes, or at least modifications (Davis, K. E.; Rubin o; Walsh).*

The late Ernie Pyle once said, "It ain't the things you don't know that make you a fool; it's the things you know that ain't so." People desperately want answers to sex-related problems. Knowledge about sex is so vital that they seek it from whatever sources are available, good or bad. When accurate information is not available, people will, in their naiveté, accept misinformation for truth. This is especially noticeable among the young. The failure of adults to discuss sex openly with young people has several unfortunate consequences. It endows sex with an undeservedly

*References to book-length sources are cited parenthetically in the text by author. For full documentation, see the Bibliography at the end of the text.

unrealistic, magical quality, thus reinforcing adolescent preoccupation with it. It clogs natural, legitimate sources of sex information, forcing young people to use clandestine and often warped sources to satisfy their quite normal curiosity.

The extent of sexual ignorance among people of all ages can be judged from the burgeoning sales of sex-oriented books and the patronage of X-rated films in recent years. Nothing by way of themes, variations, and gymnastics has been omitted from these erotic presentations in the name of good taste or accuracy—except the beauty, tenderness, consideration, and love essential to a lasting, committed sex relationship. Unfortunately, exposure to this material often leaves the reader or viewer more confused and unsure of himself than he was before. Distortions are internalized, becoming the forerunner of sexual anxiety, which in turn leads to self-defeating behavior, psychosomatic ailments, or sexual dysfunction (or all three) (Chernick and Chernick).

The primary cause of these lamentable circumstances is simple: adults in a position to instruct the young are all too often filled with shame and guilt about sex. They are themselves sexually ignorant or misinformed and painfully uncertain about what they truly believe to be acceptable sexual behavior. Compounding this ignorance and conflict is their reluctance to admit to these shortcomings.

How to rectify this state of affairs is *not* a simple matter. At present there is no clearly accepted or acceptable code of sexual ethics in our adult society (Rubin *h*). One might logically ask how young people can be reared in an atmosphere of healthy sexual attitudes when the adult population cannot reach a consensus on an acceptable sexual ethic. Adults will have to resolve their own warped and guilt-ridden sexual attitudes before the young in their charge can become educated rather than indoctrinated. Until that goal is reached, sexual conflict and misinformation are liable to be perpetuated from one generation to another.

Few authorities in human behavior would deny that sexual adjustment is prerequisite to an individual's maturation and successful adaptation to his environment. Indeed, history has demonstrated that the mental health of whole nations has been markedly influenced by the sexual attitudes and behavior of their citizenry—young and old, male and female alike. Scientific investigations and clinical observations have confirmed the premise that sexual adjustment is positively correlated with well-timed, ongoing, accurate sex education presented in a wholesome, guilt-free manner (Malcolm; Thornburg).

If afforded an adequate, timely sex education, today's young adults will be in a position to educate their own children adequately in sexual matters. Only in this way can the cycle of sexual ignorance and sexual anxiety be broken.

A HERITAGE OF CONFUSION

Laymen and scientists alike are too often strangely reluctant to accept scientific findings, or even to give unbiased examination to new data, in the field of human sexuality. When new investigations appear to lend support to time-honored prejudices, they are quickly accepted as being scientifically impeccable. However, when contemporary research fails to confirm cherished theories, the research tends to be discounted as suspect, its conclusions judged as being quite likely distorted by sample- and examiner-bias. Such suspicious attitudes have been seen in certain public reactions to the several works of the Alfred C. Kinsey investigators and to the work of William H. Masters and Virginia E. Johnson on the subject of human sexual response. The Kinsey workers were especially harassed.

> During the first year or two we were repeatedly warned of the dangers involved in the undertaking, and were threatened with specific trouble. There was some organized opposition, chiefly from a particular medical group. There were attempts by the medical association in one city to bring suit on the ground that we were practicing medicine without a license, police interference in two or three cities, investigation by a sheriff in one rural area, and attempts to persuade the University's administration to stop the study, or to prevent the publication of the results, or to dismiss the senior author from his university connection, or to establish a censorship over all publication emanating from the study (Kinsey *et al.* a).

A variety of social ills has been ascribed to the sex research of Masters and Johnson—from spreading venereal disease to pushing the nation toward the brink of moral disaster. The person holding tenuously but rigidly onto any value system becomes panic-stricken when it is challenged, flailing about in the attempt to protect his beliefs. Challenge to one's sexual or religious ethics (one typically rooted in the other) appears to cause the most vocal and violent reaction of all.

Psychologist Albert Ellis, in his two-volume survey of contemporary American attitudes on sex, love, marriage, and family relations (*The Folklore of Sex* and *The American Sexual Tragedy*), painstakingly examined stories, advertisements, books, magazines, newspapers, movies, and other mass communication media. His conclusion was that our woefully inadequate sex education, with the resulting neurotic repression and inhibition of normal sexual expression, has had a gravely deleterious effect on our lives and behavior.

The burgeoning sales of "girlie" magazines, the use of attractive women with seductive voices and voluptuous figures as modern-day hucksters to sell everything from shoe polish to salad dressing, the suggestive "adults-only" ads for many films—all these point up the manner in which our mishandled sexual drives are being expressed.

Evidence of displaced sexual drive exists in many unlikely places. Not many years ago, as an example, a department store owner of Birmingham, England, managed to quell the indignation of window shoppers inspecting his negligee-clad mannequins only by putting wedding rings on the mannequins' hands. This sort of prudery was matched in America by the Society for Indecency to Naked Animals (SINA), which fought to protect children from the sight of naked animals, particularly cattle, dogs, and cats (From the editor's scrapbook a).* The society advocated the clothing of animals, at least if they appear in public or are in the presence of children. And while SINA started out as a hoax, many do-gooders were ready to take up the cause by joining the organization and fighting for its principles.

It is not that the mass communication media have a strong effect upon our sexual or aggressive behavior (Kinsey *et al. b*); rather, they merely mirror our sexual anxieties. For instance, millions of Sunday School children have studied and know the gruesome details of a crucifixion, but not many youngsters play crucifixion games with their friends (Money *c*). Confusion begets confusion, and we find a disturbing conflict in our social order. We live in a culture that ostensibly condemns illicit sexual relationships, yet these very acts are depicted, by innuendo at least, as enticing and desirable in various advertisements (Calderone *d*).

Parents too often suppose that if their children do not know about sex they will avoid it, and will consequently lead a sexually unblemished life. Nothing could be further from the truth. For example, parents will frequently withhold information on contraception and venereal diseases altogther, or will recount only the dangers and shame of illegitimate pregnancy and VD, expecting thereby to keep their children from engaging in premarital coitus. Yet the Kinsey group found that only 44% of the unmarried women interviewed listed "fear of pregnancy" as a deterrent to premarital sexual intercourse, and only 14% listed "fear of venereal disease" as a deterrent (Kinsey *et al. c*). And among girls questioned in a more recent study, a mere 2% cited fear of VD as a deterrent (Robinson and King).

Before the modern, swiftly effective cures for venereal diseases were available and when these "social diseases" were greatly feared, people blithely had sex relations even with partners whose freedom from infection was not determined. One study of the correlation between fear of VD and its incidence showed that of psychologically normal men who had no fear of venereal infection, 15.4% contracted one of the diseases. Of those who had moderate fear, the percentage rose to 20.8%; and of those who had a very strong fear, 15.3% became infected (Rubin *e*).

One investigation revealed that the unmarried pregnant girls surveyed had received little or no sex education either from home or school. Their

*References to journal articles are cited parenthetically in the text by article title. For full documentation, see the Bibliography at the end of the text.

mothers, furthermore, either lacked proper sex knowledge themselves, or were unable or unwilling to give proper instruction to their daughters (Teen-age extramarital conception). However, adequate knowledge of contraception is no assurance that a girl will use a device should she engage in premarital coitus (Stiller *f*). Research in the 1970s (Teen-age sex) showed that of sexually active single girls, more than 75% claimed not to use contraceptives at all, or only occasionally—incredible, in view of the wide-spread use today of the birth-control pill and other contraceptive methods.

Girls who do not themselves take contraceptive precautions typically do not insist that their partners do so. This foolhardiness prevails despite the fact that half the boys and almost three-fourths of the girls have a real fear of pregnancy (Schofield *et al.*) Some girls with a strong religious back-ground think that premarital coitus in which contraceptives are used is more "sinful" than intercourse without contraceptive protection. This attitude appears to arise from the feeling that pregnancy resulting from premarital intercourse offers some atonement for their moral transgression (Pohlman). Curiously, many unwanted pregnancies occur among the reli-giously devout who, despite their determination to "refrain from sin," somehow lose control of their emotions and get swept into the act of sexual intercourse (Kinsey *et al. c*).

The disclosures of another study (Martinson) were even more sur-prising. Most of the 500 men questioned expressed reluctance to use what little knowledge of contraception they possessed because (1) they were too embarrassed to purchase the necessary items, or (2) making the pur-chase implicated their subsequent coital relationships as "planned sin." Fewer than 25% of the unwed mothers surveyed in the same study thought that it was acceptable to use contraceptives before marriage!

The World Health Organization states that ignorance, not knowledge, of sexual matters is the cause of "sexual misadventure" (Calderone *c*). The clinical experience of most psychotherapists and marriage counselors cer-tainly lends support to this viewpoint, as does the subsequent strife and heartbreak of parents and their children who become victims of "sexual misadventure." That parents possess not enough accurate information on sex may be true. But what they do have should be shared in an open and honest manner with their children, even if they find the task most difficult.

For parents who do not have accurate or adequate information, or who are actually afraid or ashamed to talk with their children about sex, there are other sources from which the children (and parents, for that matter) can get a sex education with a minimum of emotional stress. But even then the danger exists of unwittingly selecting an emotionally oriented, unscientific book or a counselor with his own problems (Ellis *p*). Until very recently, medical training rarely included much more about human sexuality than its reproductive aspects, leaving physicians as a whole largely ignorant and somewhat prudish about human sexuality (Calderone *g*;

Mathis a). Furthermore, the formal training of ministers and social scientists in marriage counseling has traditionally been poor (Ministers and sex). In recent years, however, medical schools, seminaries, and universities have, fortunately, begun reconstructing their coursework and training sessions in this area, significantly raising these professional levels of competence.

The impact on marriages of adequate early sex information can be judged from Clifford Kirkpatrick's analysis of the components of successful marital adjustment. The subjects of his survey ranked "adequate sex information in childhood" third in importance among the leading 10 factors considered fundamental to a successful marriage, falling behind only "happiness of parents' marriage" and "adequate length of acquaintanceship, courtship, and engagement."

Religion, Sex, and Marriage

It has been speculated that ancient man's need for religion developed from his discovery of various elements in the world with which he could not cope (severe weather, famine, etc.). To overcome these misfortunes, he conjured up a supreme being who had the power to solve problems that man could not solve for himself (Ellis h). To have the privilege of calling on his deity in time of danger, man had to pay a price—giving up pleasures, as well as remaining good and pure. He underwent a self-sacrificial process that was somehow supposed to please his god.

Through punishing himself in minor ways, man mystically transferred to his godhead the responsibility for the solution of difficulties beyond his capabilities. Needing his god's help, and recognizing the surpassing pleasure of sexual activity, man quite naturally made his sexuality a focal point in his efforts to please or appease the deity. In effect man might have said, on the one hand, "Protect and help me, and I shall sacrifice my sexuality for your

---

FIGURE 1.1 Sex Education. Copyright 1971, G.B. Trudeau. Distributed by Universal Press Syndicate.

DOONESBURY   by Garry Trudeau

protection"; and on the other hand, "I have sinned, I have been evil, and I offer the sacrifice of my sexuality in expiation for my sinfulness."

Few people in the position to judge would deny that probably the greatest detriment to the psychosexual health of mankind is certain rigid, puritanical, guilt-instilling religions. Protagonists of such religions have succeeded remarkably well in indoctrinating their followers in the belief that sex is dirty and animalistic, to be looked upon only as a necessary evil— with emphasis on the word *evil* (Duffy a). This attitude is best exemplified in the prudery of the Victorian era, when "decent" women, not daring to expect pleasure from the sexual act, endured it only because of their "duty" to their husbands.

Changes in attitudes toward sex and marriage reflective of changing needs, but often lagging behind them, have occurred throughout history. Early Israelite tribes permitted polygynous marriages, for example, and women were regarded as little more than chattels; marriages were primarily of legal rather than of religious concern. Some men were left without female partners as a result of polygyny, and a more equitable distribution of women became necessary. Thus was monogamy evolved.

Mosaic laws (detailed in the books of Leviticus, Deuteronomy, and, to a lesser degree, Exodus), which are the foundations of prevailing Judeo-Christian morality, were assumed to have divine inspiration. Gradually marriage, together with sex, came to be regarded as belonging to a sphere higher than simple legality. However, because of reinterpretation of Mosaic laws over the centuries, only vestiges of their original content remain within our culture's code. We would not think of buying servants or slaves today, and we certainly would not keep the wife and children of the servant while freeing the man, but these were acceptable practices in early Judaic tradition (Exodus 21). Present-day civil law prohibits marriage between close relatives, yet Abraham in good conscience married his half-sister Sarah (Genesis 20). Jacob, Abraham's grandson, would be arrested today for bigamy, yet in his day his having two wives was wholly permissible.

Much of the ancient interpretation of Mosaic laws—indeed, the necessity for the laws in the first place—was based on the need for larger and stronger tribes. From the philosophy that developed in conjunction with the Hebraic sex codes evolved a single justification for sexual expression—procreation. By extension, sexual activity for any other purpose became an act of perversion.

The rule that women were to be considered unclean and untouchable during the five days of menstruation and for two days afterwards (Leviticus 15) was undoubtedly based on the fact that these days were (and are) generally considered to be unfavorable for conception. Man should not, therefore, waste his sperm lest he be punished by God for not attempting to add to the strength of his tribe.

It also appears that the laws prohibiting bestiality and homosexuality, and the judgment that such sexual acts were much more reprehensible between men than between women, were based on the need not to waste precious sperm and thereby perhaps impede tribal growth. Since there is no loss of sperm in lesbianism, no such rigid prohibitions against it developed.

In prescientific times, the belief prevailed that females were imperfect males. Sperm were considered miniature men, women merely providing the "soil" in which the miniature men grew into maturity. The weaker sperm were thought to be deformed, therefore "growing into" girls. Thus the concept was formed that the female is inferior to males. Any "loss" of semen, whether through intercourse during the menstrual flow, *coitus interruptus* (premature withdrawal of penis before ejaculation), or masturbation, was therefore viewed as mass murder of hundreds of thousands of potential men (Haring).

Much has been said about Onan's "spilling his seed on the ground," as recorded in Genesis. This story involved Onan's being ordered by God to marry his deceased brother's wife, as was the custom, and to have children by her. Onan refused to do so, apparently employing *coitus interruptus* as a birth control method, because any children born of the union would have borne his brother's name and not his own. God was angered by Onan's defiance of His orders and struck him dead. The misinterpretations of this story have had severe repercussions on Western sexual stability over the centuries. Onanism somehow became enlarged to imply a method of birth control. Furthermore, some time during the seventeenth century the "spilling of seed" and masturbation became equated, masturbation thenceforth being condemned as gravely sinful.

The preferential position of men in patriarchal societies apparently influenced the unconscious mind of early lawmakers and the traditions emanating from their decrees. A typical example is the Old Testament assertion that when a woman gave birth to a male child she was "unclean" for 40 days, but when she gave birth to a female child she was "unclean" for 80 days (Leviticus 12). Traditionally, the temptations of the flesh have been attributed to women and their presence.

Women are portrayed not only as "second-class citizens" in some sections of the Old Testament but also as sexual temptresses. In Genesis 3, Adam and Eve succumb to temptation, and Eve is designated as the instigator of the evil act. Later, in Genesis 19, Lot and his daughters, who had survived the destruction of a sinful city, found themselves involved in incestuous relationships. Once more the onus for illicit sexuality was placed on the woman—the daughters—because they supposedly had given Lot sufficient wine to render him incapable of knowing what he was doing and had then seduced him.

Lot appears biblically absolved of any responsibility for the act. The account therefore has all the features of attempting to place on women the blame for illicit sex acts, and to portray them as vehicles of sin. But the story of Lot and his daughters is not convincing. If Lot was so drunk that he did not know what he was doing, the chances are that he could not have performed sexually anyway, because male sexual functioning is severely repressed by heavy intake of alcohol.

History other than biblical demonstrates the evolution—good and bad—of sexual ethics and behavior. Prior to the fourth century B.C., Western civilizations, notably the Greek city-states, regarded sex according to a "naturalistic" philosophy—as a pleasure to be enjoyed. Those even attempting to lead a celibate life were looked upon with pity. When Sparta overcame Athens, however, the Spartan philosophy of rigid self-discipline (which included avoidance of pleasure and luxury) almost destroyed the Greek culture that had espoused "naturalism."

Alexander the Great, in his phenomenal swath of world conquest in the third century B.C., opened up many avenues of ultimate cultural exchange. As a consequence, the "spiritualistic" attitudes of India, Egypt, and Mesopotamia filtered into the Western world and gained a strong foothold. Rather than being a pleasure, sexual desire was deemed an evil to be overcome by self-denial. Salvation of the soul could be aspired to only through suppression of fleshly pleasures. Celibacy was glorified. Sex thus fell under the pall of guilt and condemnation long before the advent of Christianity. But because the New Testament was written during the latter part of this period, it naturally was strongly influenced by the "spiritualistic" movement (Rizzo).

Contrary to common belief, Jesus himself had little to say on the subject of sex. The vast majority of sexual proscriptions associated with and attributed to Christianity are actually outgrowths of the thought and writings of later Christian theologians, and most of this moral theology was not actually propounded until long after Christ's death. Paul was probably the first Christian to speak out specifically on sexual morality. He emphasized the need for marriage as a means to avoid fornication, although he apparently considered sexual abstinence a more admirable goal in life (I Corinthians 6 and 7).

The writings of St. Augustine during the fourth century A.D. have probably had as much impact upon prevailing twentieth-century sexual attitudes as any other single force. In them he severely condemned premarital and extramarital sexual outlets, including bestiality, homosexuality, and, especially, masturbation. In time the Roman Catholic Church came to idealize celibacy, with the highest level of male achievement being total rejection of all life's pleasures, while women could expect to reach their greatest glory only through permanent virginity.

Virginity and purity have long been regarded as one and the same thing. The virgin birth of Jesus, the springing of Athena full grown from Zeus's forehead, and the atypical genesis of other deities are testimonials to that view (Anthony). It is therefore not difficult to understand why concepts of sex and sin (impurity) are so closely bonded, or how indulgence in sexual acts or even thoughts, in marriage or out, can easily produce feelings of guilt and emotional stress. When young people are given rigid proscriptions in sexual matters that are not counterbalanced with a rationale for sexual morality, then guilt must be relied upon to control sexual behavior. Young people incorporate these rules into their emotional makeup, but if and when the rules are broken, emotional stress often results.

Far too frequently the marriage ceremony does not serve as a conjurer's wand to eradicate the "thou-shalt-not" and "sex-is-dirty-and-should-be-avoided" attitudes handed down by parents and society. Believing that sex equals sin, many brides and grooms eventually suffer from such unfor-

FIGURE 1.2 Marriage. Used by permission from VOICES—*The Art and Science of Psychotherapy*, Vol. 1, No. 1: one of the Seven Ages of Man. Artist, John Severin.

tunate reactions as guilt, pain, frigidity, impotency, or premature ejaculation. These reactions persist long after the marriage ceremony, even when the couple on a conscious level regard sex as something permissible and enjoyable. It is expecting too much to think that sex can be transformed from something sullying into something ennobling by a mere recitation of the words of the marriage ceremony.

With the development of Christian and Judaic theology came the evolution of an ethical code governing marriage. Morally acceptable sexual activity was henceforth limited to the marriage bed and any deviation was considered sinful. When a moral code is unrealistic and stands as an unyielding obstacle in an individual's emotional pathway, some sort of suffering is almost inevitable. In any case, research findings in England give little comfort to those who believe that religious convictions alone are necessarily a deterrent to premarital sexuality: the atheists interviewed had had less sexual experience than either the Protestants or the Roman Catholics (British sex revolution).

An individual should examine unemotionally the many ramifications of any moral code—arriving at his own conclusions about the probable effects of various forms of sexual behavior on himself, his partner, and society. He will then be much more likely to manage his sexuality in a manner that is normal, healthy, and anxiety-free. When we as a society mature to the point that we no longer feel compelled to impose our personal biases on others, we will encounter and engender fewer emotional difficulties, including sexual ones. This tolerance of others is embodied in the Golden Rule, that farsighted and sensible guide to human behavior with its unequivocal emphasis on the equal rights of all men—"Therefore all things whatsoever ye would that men should do to you, do ye even so to them; for this is the law and the prophets" (Matthew 7:12).

Vestiges of rigidity and bigotry still permeate some religious groups. Fortunately for the mental health of society, however, outmoded religious dictates are increasingly being submitted to objective analysis, their validity being assessed according to their relevance to present-day circumstances of life.

Breaking the Bonds of Sexual Fascism

An extension of the Golden Rule is the granting of relative freedom of behavior in sexual matters—because there *are* individual differences in sexual drives and preferences. Perhaps this aspect of sex education would be better termed "sexual democracy" or "freedom from sexual fascism."

Albert Ellis, in his excellent discussion of sexual fascism (Ellis a), points out that some people arbitrarily evaluate certain sexual behavior—their own, of course—as being right and superior to other sexual behavior, and will go to great lengths in imposing their viewpoints on other people. An individual's failure to comply with these arbitrary standards is tantamount to his being an anti-Christ, a pervert, or a sexual inferior.

The sexual fascist neither understands nor cares that women respond to sex relations differently than men do; he simply expects women to employ and respond to the same sexual techniques that are successful with men. Such bigots live by the traditional double standard of morality for men and women. For example, girls must be virgins until marriage, while boys are allowed, even expected, to have many premarital experiences. Women are much more condemned for having children out of wedlock than the men who father the babies. This unfair dichotomy in values is an obvious outgrowth of the patriarchal customs of early biblical days.

It has long been recognized by mental-health authorities that a crucial factor in people's health and adjustment is the maintenance of "a reasonable degree of flexibility and freedom from fixation in the major aspects of their lives" (Ellis a). We do not expect all people to eat or even to like asparagus; and indeed we do not expect those who do eat asparagus to want to eat it all the time. When it comes to sex, however, the bigot's philosophy does not allow for any behavioral flexibility. Nor does it condone the experimentation that adds so much to the adventuresomeness and spice which the normal, sexually mature person incorporates into his sex life.

Any student of human sexual behavior soon recognizes the extreme difficulty of trying to define precisely what is, and what is not, sexual deviation. For instance, coitus accomplished in any position other than husband above wife is often in Western cultures condemned out of hand as deviant. By extension, such noncoital sexual activities as masturbation, petting, and oral-genital contact are viewed as perversions. Such rigidity poses a unique problem, however. For research findings indicate that masturbation is commonly practiced by most men and women, both single and married; that oral-genital contact occurs in most marriages in the upper socioeconomic-educational stratum of society; and that more than 50% of women prefer noncoital methods of stimulation to sexual intercourse and respond more intensely to them (Ellis a; Kinsey et al. a, c; Masters and Johnson n).

The man-above coital position is not widely assumed anywhere except in the United States and a few other countries. Among boys of Arab countries, masturbation is little practiced and is considered a less acceptable activity than homosexuality (Ellis b). These are only two examples of the significant differences in sexual behavior to be found among cultures.

No one is justified in saying that the sexual practices of one culture are proper and normal, while a different set of practices in another culture is improper and abnormal. It cannot be overemphasized that there are individual human differences that extend into every aspect of life, including expression of sexuality. Any valid program of sex education must take these differences into account. If the rights of others are to be respected, we must accept the existence of tastes and pleasures quite different from our own. No one has the moral (nor should he have the legal) right to force his ethical views on others, any more than his aesthetic or political views.

FACTS—AND ARGUMENTS—ABOUT SEX EDUCATION

When the Kinsey reports were published they merely confirmed what educators had long known—guilt feelings aroused by inadequate sex knowledge interfere with happy living, schoolwork, friendships, and future marital adjustment. Sound mental health and a mind receptive to learning tend to go together; worry and anxiety hamper learning to the fullest of one's potential (Poffenberger a). Persons who have received an appropriate sex education develop more adaptive defenses and are less anxious than those without one, since the latter tend to repress their anxiety by the maladaptive means of avoidance and denial (Wright and McCary).

Those persons who are highly knowledgeable in sexual matters are more capable of enjoying their sexual feelings and of deriving pleasure from all forms of sexual activity than are the less knowledgeable, who tend to restrain sexual impulses (Wright and McCary). This disparity is probably related to anxiety, which serves to inhibit freedom of sexual response: the greater the amount of accurate sex information, the less the anxiety (Barfield). Masters and Johnson's most recent work confirms that maladjustment and chronic invalidism among both men and women, when caused by sexual conflicts generated by sexual ignorance, are preventable through early, adequate sex information (Masters and Johnson p).

Specific physiological anomalies have been found to be related to sex education and to emotions. For example, most women who suffer from premenstrual tension and difficult menstruation have a background of parental discord. And they typically received their sex education from their mothers, who presented the information in a deprecating way (Medical science notes b).

Dr. David Mace, a former president of the Sex Information and Education Council of the U.S. (SIECUS) and the founder and long-time executive director of the American Association of Marriage and Family Counselors, has commented that "a child who has been able to learn the basic facts about sex, to feel natural and comfortable about them, to hear the subject presented without embarrassment by at least one trustworthy adult, and to participate in the discussion of the subject with other children in a healthy and wholesome manner is the child who is going to cope effectively with his own emerging sexual feelings and needs. . . . The idea of 'protecting' children from sexuality is . . . a myth, a *dangerous* myth" (Mace a). These observations support other research findings suggesting that an adequate sex education is an asset to general psychological adjustment (Barfield and McCary; McCary and Flake).

The American Social Health Association (Deschin a) conducted a careful study of the relationship between VD and sex education (or the lack of it) in a sampling of 600 teen-age VD patients. The Association's primary conclusion was that these young people critically needed a better education about sex in general and VD in particular.

A graphic demonstration of this premise was the introduction of a course entitled "Family Life Education" in two junior and two senior public high schools in Washington, D.C. in 1957–58. In one of these schools there had been 38 cases of gonorrhea the year before sex education was introduced. During the school year that sex education was first taught, there were 22 cases, and in the next, only 16. By contrast, in one of the high schools in the District not offering this course, there were 35 cases of gonorrhea in 1957-58 and 40 in the next year. Realizing what was happening, the administration of this high school then instituted a sex-education program. In one year's time the incidence of gonorrhea decreased by almost 50% (Levine).

Those Who Oppose Sex Education in the Schools— and Those Who Defend It

A common argument used by those opposing sex education is "look what happened in Sweden," where sex education has been offered in the schools on a broad basis since 1956. Opponents allege that Sweden's sex-education program has catapulted that country into world leadership in such social ills as suicide, promiscuity, divorce, illegitimate births, rape, and venereal disease. But allegation and fact stand in stark contradiction. As examples: although Sweden's suicide rate was the world's highest prior to 1956, it now ranks ninth. Its divorce rate is currently half that of the U.S. The number of rapes committed there is one of the lowest in the world— and a fraction (20%) of the number committed in the U.S. The incidence of VD is 2.5 times higher in this country than in Sweden. It is apparently true that the illegitimate-birth rate in Sweden is climbing, but so also has it been in the U.S. for the past 30 years (Sex and sin in Sweden; Swift).

Robert Welch, founder of the John Birch Society—probably the most powerful of the anti-sex-education groups—has called sex instruction a "filthy communist plot" (Quality Educational Development, Inc.). (This pronouncement is particularly curious in light of the accusation contained in Russia's *Pravda* that sex education is part of the "Western imperialistic, capitalistic plot"!) Welch has urged his group to organize "nationwide, intensive and angry and determined opposition" to sex education in the schools (Breasted).

A similarly reactionary position was stated, with rhetorical skill, by John Steinbacher of the Anaheim, California, *Bulletin:* "The Communist change agents are among us. Such a change agent is Dr. Benjamin Spock, whose changed young minds are now following him down the path of hatred of country, of love of America's enemies, and of assaulting all the institutions in our society. . . . The name of their diabolical game is sex education . . . that contains within it the germinal seeds of America's final downfall" (Breasted).

Yet a recent Gallup poll showed that more than 7 out of every 10 parents favor sex education as part of school curricula (Breasted). The premise that 71% of the U.S. population is bent upon destroying the country boggles the mind. Sex education in the schools is endorsed not only by the populace but also by some of the country's most prestigious organizations as well. As examples: the Interfaith Commission on Marriage and Family Life (consisting of the Synagogue Council of America, the U.S. Catholic Conference, and the National Council of Churches); the National Congress of Parents and Teachers; the American Medical Association; the YMCA and YWCA; and the U.S. Department of Health, Education, and Welfare. About the most charitable comment that one can make about many of the arguments of those violently opposed to sex education is that they are badly distorted.

Despite endorsement of public-school sex education by the majority, one cannot ignore certain parents' genuine concern that sex education might be presented in too dry and dehumanized a fashion in the classroom, or that there is "too much too soon," most particularly for primary-school children. And it must be conceded that not all teachers giving sex instruction are ideally equipped to teach the subject. Nevertheless, it is difficult to see how a meaningful, effective sex-education course can be constructed in a community in which the school administrators and teachers are harassed by a vociferous minority (not necessarily parents) whose motivations are, variously, concern, confusion, fear, ignorance, or cynical opportunism.

The question of public-school sex education is, however, becoming academic. Recent court rulings have decreed that sex education does not violate the constitutional rights of those parents who oppose it, and that a school district may conduct such programs in the promotion of public health, welfare, and morality (Sex in the news *f*).

An especially groundless argument against sex education, but a singularly dangerous one, is that human sexuality is a simple phenomenon that one learns naturally. Formal sex education is therefore seen as unnecessary because the presentation of factual information about sex might destroy its "mystery" and "sacredness," hence lessening one's future enjoyment of it (Vincent *k*).

The weakest but most frequently heard objection of sex-education opponents focuses on the Freudian concept of the sexual "latency period" in a child's development, which, generally speaking, lasts from the ages of 6 to 12. During this six-year period, according to Freudian theory, children push sex from their minds. To jolt the child out of sexual latency by giving him sex education too soon could do him great and permanent emotional damage.

The theory of "latency" is unproven, however; there is little evidence to support the contention that sex interest lies dormant during this period. By the age of 10, for example, about 55% to 60% of all boys and 80% of girls are sure they want to be married some day. By the age of 12, 65% to 70% of all boys and 90% or more of girls have arrived at this conclusion. Furthermore, about half of the boys and girls in these early age groups claim at some time that they are in love (Broderick *b*)!

Only a scant few of those professionals who do accept the latency-period concept believe that proper sex education will harm children between the ages of 6 and 12. Even if the theory had validity for children of Freud's late nineteenth-century Europe, it would by no means automatically apply to modern-day children in more sex-oriented America (Sex education and the "latency" period).

Of all the arguments against school sex education, perhaps the most valid concerns the qualifications of those teaching it. There are few institutions that train people specifically to teach this most sensitive subject. Indeed, many of those selected to teach sex-education courses receive no special training beforehand. Consequently, they are often forced to obtain much of the source material for their classes from popular magazines and newspapers. Because of personal embarrassment, some teachers conduct their course in a strained, mechanical manner, or perhaps discard material that might be really meaningful to their students (Dager and Harper; Dager *et al.*). There is considerable evidence, in fact, that many teen-agers are less sensitive and embarrassed about sex-related topics than their teachers are (Kirkendall *d*). Still other teachers mingle religious prejudice and personal guilt with their sex instruction, which probably does the student more harm than good.

Yet, whatever the personal shortcomings of those who teach sex education, the implied suggestion in many arguments against sex education is particularly insidious—namely, that the school teacher giving sex instruction is (or might be) an unethical, perhaps morally depraved creature intent upon seducing the innocent into paths of immorality. The fact is that any teacher's ethical values will inevitably filter into any subject that he or she teaches, whether it be sex education, mathematics, or literature.

Inadequate sex education is not limited to the public schools; private and parochial schools, colleges, universities, and medical schools often have equally ineffective programs. Here, too, the lack of instructors who are qualified and free of their own sexual conflicts is a major problem (Leif). Another is the fear, shared by teachers and school administrators alike, that they might arouse public criticism if they do construct a sex-education course of any depth (Kirkendall e).

Sources of Sex Information

An investigation (Barfield and McCary) into the sex-education background of 1100 college students, conducted on the campus of a major university in the South, revealed some curious relationships between the primary source of sex information and its accuracy. When physicians and ministers were the source of such information, there was no relationship, either negative or positive, between source and accuracy. What is more important, there was a significantly *negative* relationship between the main source and its accuracy when the source was either the student's peer group or his parents. The only significant *positive* relationship that emerged involved those students who had received their sex education in the formal atmosphere of a classroom, or who had read sex-information books of authenticated accuracy.

In one study (Gagnon a), an overwhelming majority of both the male and female respondents expressed a preference for parents as the primary source of sex information for the young. About 90% of the respondents indicated a preference for the mother as a major source; 80% indicated the father; 60%, the family doctor; 40%, the school; 25%, the church; 25%, books; 10%, siblings. Only 5% signified a preference for friends as a primary source. But preference and actuality contrasted rather sharply. In actual fact friends were the primary source of sex information for 53% of the male respondents and 35% of the women in this study. Mothers were a source for 46% of the women, but for only 18% of the men. Fathers were a source for 25% of the men, but almost no woman in the study had received any sex instruction from her father.

When mothers give sex instruction to their children, it is limited almost exclusively to the facts of menstruation and pregnancy. Details of sexual intercourse, prostitution, and contraception, as examples, are much more frequently learned from peer groups than from any other source (Gagnon a). School had been a source of sex information for only 8% of the adult men and 9% of the adult women surveyed in one study. But it had been a source for 38% of the adolescents (both boys and girls) surveyed, indicating that schools have assumed an increasingly important role in sex education during the past generation or so (Abelson *et al.*).

Even so, young people report dissatisfaction with the sex information available in both home and school. Parents, they feel, are frequently too embarrassed or uninformed to talk openly and meaningfully about sex, whereas information offered at school tends to be irrelevant, sketchy, or ill-timed. In the absence of timely, satisfactory information from preferred sources, young people are forced to turn to friends, books, and periodicals to find out what they want to know, although they realize that these sources are not always reliable.

In recent years the medical profession has increasingly recognized that physicians are in need of sex education and that the responsibility for providing it rests with the medical schools. Whereas a short time ago only three medical schools of the 110 in the U.S. included human sexuality in their curricula, 90 of them had done so by 1971 (Calderone g).

It has been shown that, during their first years of graduate study, medical students and law students have about the same fund of sex knowledge. Upon graduation, physicians are slightly better informed than lawyers, but only because of their knowledge about the human reproductive systems and about pregnancy. For example, less than 20% of the senior medical students interviewed in one study (Coombs b) knew what a patient meant when she said she was a practicing lesbian.

Nearly 50% of the students canvassed at a Philadelphia medical school not many years ago thought that masturbation could lead to mental illness—and 20% of the faculty members were of the same opinion (Greenbank). And many professional religious workers hold similar views. Thus, despite advances made in professional training in recent years, it appears that parents and young people cannot always rely upon practicing professionals such as physicians and clergy for the most up-to-date information about sexuality (Coombs b). And there is growing agreement that the place for that education should be the schools, beginning early and continuing through high school (Commission on Obscenity).

Whether sex education should be taught in our schools is actually a rather meaningless question, for sex education has always been taught in the schools, one way or another, and undoubtedly always will be. The real question is whether sex is to be taught in the schoolyard or the classroom (McCary d). Sex information, even when presented in the schoolroom, comes too late. By age 10, 69% of boys already know about pregnancy, 57% know about sexual intercourse, and 43% about masturbation. By age 14, almost all boys (92–100%) know about these topics; most of them also know about prostitution. The largest areas of ignorance concern menstruation (37%) and venereal diseases (57%) (Ramsey; Thornburg).

A recent study (Malcolm) of the sexual habits and accuracy of sex knowledge of women students at the University of North Carolina revealed that of the sexually active women, over 25% failed to answer *any* question correctly, only 59% answered half the questions correctly, and none answered all of them correctly. Of the less sexually active women, 80% answered half the questions correctly and 9% answered all correctly. The researchers were led to conclude that the more a woman knows about sexual matters, the more responsible she is in her sexual behavior.

Those who oppose sex education in the schools argue that the comparatively sterile setting of a classroom strips the subject of its moral and ethical connotations. The truth of the matter is, however, that the child learns about morality (and immorality) wherever he finds himself—in school no less than in the home or church. Civics and social-science studies, as well as courses in literature and history, are daily exercises in morality. Through the first two subjects the student learns of man's obligations to his society. The last two are historical and artistic demonstrations of the varying results of man's acceptance or denial of those obligations.

Parents concerned about their children's exposure to explicit sexual information would do well to ponder the findings contained in the Report of the President's Commission on Obscenity and Pornography. When parents are their children's major source of sex information, the youngsters are not likely to learn about sex through pornographic sources—or to use pornography in their later years, for that matter. One important study, involving 600 teen-agers, showed that if a youngster "obtained his sex knowledge from parents or adults with whom a positive identification exists, there appeared to be less tendency toward involvement in promiscuity" (Deschin *b*).

Those children whose primary source of sex information is friends are frequently exposed to pornography as part of their haphazard sex education (Elias). By age 15 approximately 50% of all boys and girls report having seen pictures of or having read about at least five or more different forms of sexual activity, including sexual intercourse, oral-genital activity, homosexual behavior, and sadomasochistic acts. Well over half of 35 state departments of education studied by the President's Commission reported the belief that sensible and effective sex education would reduce the students' interest in pornography (Quality Education Development, Inc.).

Despite what those who oppose sex education in the schools would have us believe, it has been shown that the incidence of premarital sexual activity does not increase following formal sex education. Indeed, marriage and the family courses in which specific sex information is presented have proved valuable in reducing the divorce rate and number of illegitimate pregnancies. Men who have taken such courses have significantly fewer divorces than those who have not, and the rate of premarital pregnancy is significantly lower among women who have had such courses than among those who have not (Quality Educational Development, Inc.).

Accurate sex information need not, of course, be obtained in a setting as formal as the schoolroom to be effective. In a recent study, young unmarried patients at the Yale University Hospital, who were pregnant for the first time and whose average age was 17, were separated into matched groups of equal numbers. One group was given instruction in the human reproductive systems and in birth control methods; the second group received no such instruction. Within a year, 57% of those in the latter group reappeared at the hospital, pregnant a second time. By contrast, only 7% of the group that had been given sex instruction had a second pregnancy before they married (Guttmacher *c;* Rubin *k*).

These findings suggest two things. First: no thoughtful educator would disagree with the argument that, if parents feel comfortable in their role as teacher, the home is the ideal setting for a child's sex education. Ideal and actuality have, unfortunately, proved to be poles apart. Parents are not, generally speaking, discharging their obligation to provide children with the accurate, timely sex instruction essential to the young people's future good mental health. Second: since the common source of much sex information today is the peer group, those peers should be properly educated, so that any information they pass on to the younger, more impressionable members of the group will be accurate (McCary *d*).

The President's Commission concluded that interest in sex is healthy and good, and that it begins very early and continues throughout life— although the vigor of a person's interest varies during his life cycle. The physiological and hormonal changes accompanying the onset of puberty, for instance, quicken sexual interest and render the youngster more sensitive to sexual stimuli than he ever was before (or probably ever will be again). It is vitally important at this stage of his development that he have an adequate fund of sex knowledge so that he can understand and accept himself, place his new experiences and feelings in proper perspective, and cope with his new feelings.

The recent introduction of sex-education programs into public-school curricula and the variance among these programs' goals and content make it virtually impossible to evaluate them at present. However, the contention is indisputable that the failure to receive a timely sex education makes children's and adolescents' growth into adequately functioning sexual adults considerably more difficult.

The Various Approaches to Sex Education

Approaches to sex education range from advocating the avoidance of sexual experiences altogether to openly approving complete sexual freedom (Johnson; Rubin *h*). At one extreme is the ostrichlike position that there should be no sex education at all. A problem not faced squarely, it is hoped, will quietly disappear. Sexual conflicts, unhappy marriages, premarital pregnancies, abortions, and a general anxiety in sexual matters are all sad testimony to the fallacy of this premise.

Next on the continuum of sex-education theories is the "thou-shalt-not" approach, which treats sexuality as a gift from God that is to be used solely for the purpose of procreation. Judged from such a viewpoint, sexuality used for any other reason becomes immoral, animalistic, and defiling. This approach, however, obviously denies the basic fact that man's biological sex drive will, one way or another, find expression. It is thus less than realistic and probably produces more conflict than the total ignorance imposed by the first theory. It is not an exaggeration to suggest that the guilt-ridden, moralistic patients crowding the offices of marriage counselors, ministers, and psychotherapists have largely been molded by the "thou-shalt-not" philosophy of sex education.

The next approach on the continuum is that the fledgling should be bombarded with facts. Sex is hereby stripped entirely of its veil of seclusiveness and is presented without any suggestion of its emotional content. Sex is treated merely as a physical drive, a subject to be discussed in terms of physiological data only and in a straightforward manner. What this approach ignores is the incontestable fact that sexual activity is far more meaningful when it takes place between people who love or at least admire one another than it is, say, in masturbation or when love or affection is absent.

At the far end of the continuum is a viewpoint that might be called "sexual anarchy." This theory of sex education urges the removal of all blocks to sexual freedom and would grant unrestrained license to any act that individual sexual needs and desires might dictate, the only qualification being that no hurt or injury befall others. Such permissiveness, of course, challenges the value of virginity and monogamy. It implies that sexual activity is a matter of fun and should be uninhibited by shame, guilt, tradition, or any code of morality.

To a degree, such a permissive sexual ethic has much to commend it because so many of our taboos are, in fact, senseless. However, man does not pass his days in isolation from his fellowman. He cannot therefore expect to defy openly and consistently the mores of society, especially those of such emotionally laden content, without encountering society's wrath. Since most of us are influenced—willingly or not, directly or indirectly, consciously or unconsciously—by our associates, it is wiser to conform fairly closely to expected patterns of behavior (at least insofar as others know). Otherwise we shall find ourselves reprimanded, rejected—or even jailed.

The safest solution would appear to be a course of compromise and selectiveness from among the various philosophies of sex education. Certain sexual needs should be permitted expression; dispassionate, accurate information about the physiological and psychological aspects of sex should be presented to all; and the Judeo-Christian traditions within which we live should be understood and dealt with sensibly in the framework of present-day society. Relative freedom of expression in sexual matters is justifiable because of individual differences in sexual preferences. There are few absolutes in this world, and only bigots establish an inflexible code of sexual morality. Generally speaking, the consequences of a given act upon the individual or society are the best criteria upon which to judge its morality (Kirkendall a).

The approach to sex education as set forth by the Sex Information and

Education Council of the U.S., in general, probably better meets the needs of young and old alike than that of any other published program. The objectives of SIECUS are these (Kirkendall e):

To provide the individual with an adequate knowledge of his own physical, mental, and emotional maturational functions as they relate to sex.

To eliminate fears and anxieties regarding the individual's sexual development and adjustments.

To develop objective and understanding attitudes, in the individual himself and toward others, regarding sex in all of its various manifestations.

To give the individual insight concerning his relationships to members of both sexes, and to help him understand his obligations and responsibilities to others.

To provide an appreciation of the positive good that wholesome human relations can bring to both the individual and the family group.

To build an understanding of the fact that ethical and moral values form the only rational basis for making decisions regarding one's behavior.

To provide enough knowledge about sexual abuse and aberration so that the individual can protect himself against exploitation and damage to his physical and mental health.

To provide an incentive to work for a society in which such evils as prostitution, illegitimacy, archaic sex laws, irrational sex-related fears, and sexual exploitation are nonexistent.

To provide the insight and the climate conducive to the individual's eventually utilizing his sexuality effectively and creatively in his roles as spouse, parent, community member, and citizen.

The Parent's Role in Sex Education

It is incumbent upon each individual to develop his own code of acceptable sexual behavior. Then he must decide how he is to present that ethic in the sex education of his children—an instructional process, incidentally, that begins at a far earlier age for the child than many suspect. The evidence is clear that sex education begins long before nursery school (Calderone e). It begins, in fact, with the first intimate mother-infant contact after birth.

Experiments have been conducted in which infant monkeys were raised in isolation, except for wire "mother substitutes," and were deprived of the usual early affectional relationships with the mother and other monkeys. The results demonstrated that without interaction with their own kind, the monkeys' behavior was disorganized and psychoticlike. They became so confused in what was expected of them by way of comportment that, even as physically mature animals, they could not copulate because they did not know how to assume coital positions (Harlow and Harlow a, b).

When terrycloth coverings were placed over the wire "mothers" so that the infant monkeys had a softer "mother" to which they could cling and cuddle up, they did not become so sexually disorganized. Furthermore, when the baby monkeys were allowed to play and to cuddle one another, they at least learned to copulate, even though the consummation was still far from normal because of the social and maternal deprivation. It is evident from these studies that the sexual training of these primates commenced at birth (Calderone e; Harlow and Harlow a, b).

Many factors significantly affect a child's emerging sexual attitudes and conduct: the way in which mothers and fathers love, fondle, and hold their infant; the soothing or harsh sound of their voices, which comes to be associated with love or with rejection and hostility; the feel of their skin; the smell of their bodies. Whether they realize it or whether it is their intention to do so, parents begin a child's sexual tutelage in the earliest days of his life. Even when parents avoid discussing sex altogether, the child nevertheless detects their attitudes—stressful or happy—through nonverbal communications (Calderone e). Some of the most crucial aspects of sex education are thus taught unconsciously (SIECUS). "Indeed, the way a boy's father lives, his self-esteem, and the way he treats his wife and children all constitute a boy's earliest sex education from his father" (Gadpaille a).

The only way our society is going to achieve proper sexual stability and mental health, which are undisputed requirements for maturity, is to instigate and persevere with a sound sex education for everyone. This goal means that those who are in a position to instruct must freely admit to what they do not know, at the same time teaching that which they know to be the truth. They must educate, not indoctrinate; teach facts, not fallacies; formulate a code of ethics, not preach asceticism; be objective, not subjective; be democratic, not autocratic; and seek knowledge, not emotionally biased constructs. This goal is difficult because most people have grown up in a culture which produces and espouses most or all of the negative agents in sexual ignorance and maladjustment. Richard Starnes in the *New York World Telegram and Sun* summed up this problem fairly well with his comment: "never in history has a nation talked so much about prudery from a basically horizontal position."

Hopefully, the material in this book will assist the reader toward a better knowledge of himself and his sexuality and will encourage him to prepare others for a healthy, well-adjusted sex life.

2 WHAT
I WOULD TELL
MY DAUGHTER
ABOUT
PREMARITAL SEX*

As a part of the course in Marriage and Family Life that I teach at the University of Houston, students ask frank questions about sex and receive equally frank and direct answers. One question that I am asked each semester is "What would you tell your daughter about premarital sex?" On one occasion, my answer was recorded, and a written transcript is presented here.

This question about one's daughter, I tell my students, is often directed at psychologists who talk on problems of sex. Most often it is meant to embarrass the psychologist, the questioner assuming that the psychologist will talk out of both sides of his mouth. That is, he might make certain liberal statements about sexual matters to the public, but when it comes to his own daughter, he will forget his academic views and become as rigid, demanding, and moralistic as the next father.

The question "What would you tell your daughter about premarital sex?" is one which cannot be answered with one short statement because a whole lifetime of living sets the stage for the answer. But let me at least give you some of my own thinking on the question that you raise.

*Reprinted by permission of Sexology magazine. ©Sexology Corp., 1966.

I will assume you mean a daughter who is roughly of your age—that is, college age. Basically, of course, there must be a healthy attitude toward sex in the home. If the parents are well adjusted in the area of sex, if they have a healthy attitude toward sex, then the children, also, will likely have healthy sexual attitudes and will, in general, react about sex in much the same manner as have the parents.

Parenthetically, I might add that the converse of this is also true—if the parents have an unhealthy attitude toward sex, if they are filled with guilt and repressions in this area, then their children are also likely to learn the same disturbed attitude and suffer from it throughout their lives.

I would want my daughter to know the biological and physiological sexual structure of the male and of the female, and I'd want her to know that males, for example, become sexually excited more easily than females do, and that they are excited by different stimuli and techniques than women are. I'd want her to know what these techniques are, so that she might avoid their use in many situations and also so that she could make use of them in appropriate situations.

I'd want consistency in all matters, if possible, but certainly I would want consistency in sexual matters in the home. I think that a parent has to be consistent within himself or herself in order to produce sane and predictable ideas in the daughter. A parent must feel at ease with his or her sexual ideas if he or she is to present the same sexual attitudes and approach day in and day out. A parent should come to his own conclusions as to what is proper before making a statement or revealing an attitude that his children may adopt.

I furthermore would wish that both parents would be consistent between themselves. That is, the mother and father should have consistent ideas about sex. The father should not make certain demands and present one set of ideas while the mother makes different demands and presents a different set of ideas.

Inconsistency can only produce confusion and insecurity within the child. If a child accepts the ideas of the father, frequently she feels guilty about not accepting the ideas of the mother. On the other hand, if she accepts the ideas of the mother, she feels guilt about rejecting the ideas of the father. The child should have to abide by a single set of rules and regulations, not a separate set with each parent.

Of equal importance with these points concerning consistency is the fact that the home should be somewhat consistent with the outside world. This goal is not always possible in sexual matters, because society is too varied in the demands that it makes of its members, depending upon what subculture and area one lives in. But my daughter must nevertheless understand what her own society expects and demands of her.

Therefore, I would want her to understand that there will be some inconsistencies between society's expectations and what she is taught in our home. She must understand the attitudes of bigots, the people whom Dr. Albert Ellis has called the sexual fascists. She must understand that these people disagree with any person who does not conform to their way of thinking, demanding, and behaving, and that they are ready to condemn and even persecute those who do not follow to the letter their unbending ideas.

I'd want her to know of methods and techniques of sexual outlet other than sexual intercourse, and I'd want her to know the values of these methods. I would want her to know that masturbation and petting are perfectly normal modes of behavior—that they can and will satisfy sexual urges, yet do not cause some of the same problems that result from sexual intercourse.

I would want my daughter—and my son, too, for that matter—to have a kind and fair attitude toward her fellowman. I'd want her to be ethical in all relationships, including sexual ones. There should be no cheating, no lying, no taking advantage of others. I'd want her to understand that, when her behavior in any way harms another person or herself, this behavior should be reconsidered because it is oftentimes truly evil.

I'd want her to understand that sex is a game for many boys and young men, and that she must be prepared for lies and trickery. Seduction is an ego boost for boys and men who feel sexually inferior. She must understand that boys get this attitude from a society which has a disturbed attitude toward sex, and that this behavior is not a personal thing directed toward her.

For these boys and emotionally disturbed men, seduction is designed to increase, albeit only momentarily, their ego strength. They are not necessarily after sex as such. When she finds men behaving in such a manner, she must understand that it is their problem, and she must deal with it accordingly.

I'd want her to understand the views of various religions and how the unwise use of some religious ideas and ideals can produce guilt and repressions. I'd also want her to understand guilt and repression; if she avoids sex, I'd want her to do so because of rational factors and not guilt. For guilt in this area, as in others, leads to many problems, and sexual conflicts resulting from guilt can be devastating.

If, with all this information, together with the attitudes and background of her home, she still decided on sexual intercourse, then I would certainly want her to know about and have access to contraceptive devices. I'd also want her informed on pregnancy and venereal diseases.

I'd want her to know that, basically, I think one is usually significantly better off if he or she avoids premarital sexual intercourse, especially in the teens, and uses masturbation or petting when sexual expression is necessary.

But, if she makes the other decision—that is, to have sexual intercourse before marriage—I would want her to know that, while I might think she has made a foolish mistake, no matter what she does along these lines, so long as she does not hurt herself or others, I am with her and my respect and love will not change. And I would hope—and I believe it would follow—that if she ever needed a friend, she would turn first to her father or mother and know that she would receive support from either of us.

These are the principles in which I believe and the ones by which I have reared my daughter, who is now happily married. I do not know whether or not she had premarital sexual intercourse—and, frankly, I couldn't care less. I respect and love her too much even to question her, although I could ask and she could answer without embarrassment to either of us.

I am pleased that she has an open and healthy attitude toward sex. She does not have the guilt, shame, or fear that causes sexual repressions which can later build to such an intense peak that they erupt into sexual or neurotic acting out. Because of her views on sex—among other things—she is likely to remain emotionally stable and healthy.

3 WHAT
I WOULD TELL
MY SON
ABOUT
PREMARITAL SEX*

Since my article "What I Would Tell My Daughter About Premarital Sex" first appeared, I have been asked many times what I would say to my son on this particularly vital subject. It would appear as if these questioners are so firmly enmeshed in the traditional double standard of sexual ethics, so long a plague in our society, that they cannot apply the same rules of human behavior and human decency equally to both sexes. A side effect of this double standard, at least as far as adolescents and young adults are concerned, seems to be a game in which a boy attempts every maneuver, trick, and "line" at his disposal to seduce a girl. The girl, on the other hand, must use every method, technique, and "gimmick" known to her in order to attract the boy and to entice him sexually, yet must stop short of sexual intercourse. If a boy seduces a girl, he "wins"; if a girl holds the boy's interest, but manages not to go beyond the mystical point that divides the "good" girls from the "bad" girls, she "wins."

Such games are obviously immature and foolish. An adherence to the double standard of sexual morality is so plainly unfair and downright immoral that it is surprising to find it continuing to exist in our supposedly

*Reprinted by permission of *Sexology* magazine. ©Sexology Corp., 1969.

enlightened time. But these sexual games *do* exist, even among college-age men and women to whom this article is primarily addressed. For a start, therefore, I hope my son will never forget that there is no place for the double standard in any honorable relationship.

As I said concerning my daughter, the answer to such a complex question as "What would you tell your child about premarital sex?" cannot be given in a brief statement—or in a lengthy article, for that matter—because "a whole lifetime of living sets the stage for the answer." I hope that my views on all aspects of human behavior have been made clear to my son through my own philosophy of life and the way I conduct myself with respect to other people. This approach, I feel, is certainly preferable to my having to *tell* him what to do. It has been my experience that most young people turn a deaf ear to authoritarian directions, and that little is therefore gained by preaching. This is not to say that open verbal communication between my son and me is not necessary at all times; such exchange of feelings and ideas is necessary for any wholesome relationship, and both of us can learn from such interactions. Furthermore, I am, after all, a parent first and a psychologist only secondarily. I am emotionally involved with my son and must guard against—as all parents must—"laying down the law," rather than teaching by example.

As with my daughter, I would want my son to know the physiological and psychological similarities and differences between the two sexes. He should know, for example, that young men between the ages of 17 and 21 have reached the height of their sex drive, and that there is a sound biological basis for their great interest in sex at this time. Girls of the same age, however, do not ordinarily have a strong physical need for sex— women typically reach the peak of their sexual drive when they are about 35 years old. Usually, therefore, if young girls *do* become involved sexually with a boy, they do so because of emotional rather than sexual needs. For instance, a girl may strive to "prove" her desirability and worth as a person through sex; or she may use sex to snare some boy who appeals to her; or she may attempt to shore up a faltering relationship with a boy through sex. Rarely does she enter into a sexual relationship because of sexual desire or need.

My son must be made to realize that an immature and maladjusted girl often can easily be persuaded that a deep emotional relationship exists between her and a boy when sex is involved—that they are in love—because of her rather desperate need for the security that mutual romantic feelings bring. It is his responsibility not only not to lead such a girl purposefully into this position, but also to avoid entering such a relationship if he thinks she is doing so for emotionally disturbed reasons.

Even if the girl has strong sexual needs and the passion of the moment urges her toward the act of sexual intercourse, I would want my son to recognize that he would be infinitely wiser and, in the long run, kinder to avoid it, at least for the time being. The negative attitude and frequently horrified reaction of the American public toward premarital sexual intercourse can easily bring to the surface feelings of guilt or shame in both a boy and girl if they do have intercourse before marriage. I would want him to understand that because of unforeseen circumstances—feelings of guilt, an unwanted pregnancy—it is ordinarily more beneficial to delay sexual intercourse until after marriage, especially if those involved are of high-school age. Any young man or woman who feels the need of sexual gratification along with the other benefits of a close, warm relationship before marriage should consider the advantages of mutual masturbation and petting. These acts can be quite satisfying, and do not carry with them many of the problems that sometimes follow sexual intercourse.

The elements basic to all successful human relationships, and perhaps most especially to the sexual one, are honesty, fairness, decency, kindness, respect, and an understanding and love of all mankind. If these great qualities are present and maintained, no relationship is likely to be harmful to the people involved.

This does not mean that deep and lasting love must necessarily exist before a satisfactory sexual relationship can be enjoyed. However, one would think that even before sexual desire develops, there should, in addition to physical attraction, at least be a fondness for the other person. I have always felt that one of the most immoral sex acts that people can involve themselves in takes place within marriage itself. I refer to those marriages in which one or both partners despise the other, yet they continue to have sexual intercourse. These people are putting sex on a totally physical basis, and it remains something of a mystery to me how they can function sexually—or even *want* to do so—under the circumstances. I hope that my son will always think enough of himself, to say nothing of placing proper value on his time, not to want even to share a cup of coffee with a girl whom he does not enjoy and like, much less to share so intimate an experience as sexual intercourse with her.

I want my son to evaluate any girl in whom he is interested as a total person—evaluate her according to what she is, does, and believes in, rather than according to whether she has or has not had sexual intercourse in the past, or will or will not have intercourse with him now. Certainly this philosophy implies that should any sort of sexual experience take place between a boy and his girl, he should maintain the same—if not more— respect for her afterwards as before. Furthermore, he should help the girl maintain her reputation in the community, which is so ready to frown on and criticize any girl who has sexual experiences, by keeping quiet about the sexual aspect of their relationship, by speaking favorably of her, and by continuing to treat her with respect and courtesy in public and in private.

It is not easy for a young man to learn and carry out the rules of decent behavior in mature sexual interactions if he has not had a home background in which the equality of all the family members' rights has been consistently maintained, regardless of age or sex. It is in the home that understanding, honesty, and respect for the rights of others in interpersonal relationships develop. It is here that the small boy learns to communicate openly and honestly with his mother and sisters, as well as with his father and brothers, and to observe the interactions of family members of the same or different sex. It is here that means of successful interaction with people outside the home, now and later, are developed. It is here that he learns that showing tender emotions—love, affection, acceptance, respect, forgiveness, and sensitivity—is not a sign of being a sissy or weakling, but that these emotions are in fact distinct signs of being strong and decent.

If the ethical standards of his home are rooted in the Golden Rule— "do unto others as you would have them do unto you"—the young man emerging into adulthood is far better equipped to establish and maintain healthy human relationships, sexual and otherwise. He will therefore not be unduly swayed by the immature bragging of other young men who, ignoring the rights and feelings of the girls involved, regard seduction as a measure of their masculinity and success as a person. Neither will he be influenced by their contempt or belittling attitude when he refuses to adopt similar neurotic patterns of behavior. He will not, furthermore, be unduly persuaded by a girl who is willing to have intercourse but would only use sex in an attempt to make their relationship into something it is not or cannot be. I would hope that my son will understand that these young people have emotional hang-ups that will grossly interfere with their development toward maturity; and that their sexual attitudes are indicators not of masculinity or feminine attractiveness, but, rather, of their feelings of inferiority and insecurity and in no way reflect on him.

Some boys and girls are, of course, emotionally mature at quite an early age, while some people at the age of 50 are not mature enough to make responsible judgments in sexual matters. However, not many girls before at least the age of 18 have the experience, knowledge, tutelage, or maturity to handle the responsibilities that go with premarital sexual intercourse. And a young man is not usually in a position to assume these responsibilities until he is about 20 or 21. After all, he is usually the one who encourages the act of sexual intercourse, yet he is the one whose reputation is least likely to be damaged by it, should it be discovered or should pregnancy result. The boy, therefore, has a greater responsibility than the girl to keep harm from befalling either of them.

Neither party, in my opinion, is likely to be damaged by premarital sexual intercourse—*if* they are believers in decency and fair play; *if* they have a mature, guilt-free attitude toward sex; *if* they have decided that they wish to go ahead only after a rational discussion, and not when they are caught up in the passion of sex play; and *if* they are mature enough to accept the responsibilities that go along with intercourse. Having made an affirmative decision—or actually before it is reached—my son should know about and have access to various contraceptive devices, and should use one faithfully to guard against a premarital pregnancy. He should, furthermore, know the signs, symptoms, and dangers of venereal diseases, and the necessity of taking every sensible precaution to avoid them.

Our society expects the male to be the tutor of the female in sexual matters. I would therefore want my son to be well versed in all aspects of sex, especially techniques, in order for him to give the girl as much pleasure and satisfaction as possible in whatever form of sexual relationship they might enter into. He should place her needs and satisfaction on a plane at least equal to his own. For when both partners take this approach, much greater fulfillment can be expected from all facets of the relationship.

These are the principles by which we reared our son, who is now a junior in college. He is a mature, sensitive young man whom we love, respect, and admire. Our relationship is not only that of parents and son; we are also close friends. I do not know what his sexual experiences have been, although he knows well my views on the matter and I know his, which are much the same as mine. His attitude and behavior toward his fellowman are honorable and decent; his attitude toward sex and toward women is equally mature and healthy. He is a man.

PART TWO
THE HUMAN SEXUAL SYSTEM

4 DEVELOPMENT OF THE MALE AND FEMALE GENITALIA

This and the chapters immediately following will constitute a foundation for understanding the physiology of human sexuality. And we shall return to physiological factors again and again throughout this book, in the belief that any truly informed inquiry into sexuality must encompass a thorough understanding of the "givens" of sexual functioning. For sexuality *is* greatly determined by our physiology, as well as by our psychology and our sociocultural conditioning. This discussion therefore begins with the development, differentiation, and functioning of the male and female sexual systems.

Although it is commonly held that men and women are vastly different creatures, the truth of the matter is they are quite similar. Martians, for instance, would undoubtedly be much perplexed in trying to detect the differences, because such externals as clothing and hairstyles are so often nearly identical. Generally speaking, the concept of a "typical male" and a "typical female" reflects more of customs and cultural attitudes than of actual anatomical differences.

Even the sexual systems, where the primary differences lie, are quite similar. From the early embryonic through the mature adult stages of human development, there is a marked likeness both in the structure and function of the male and female sexual systems. The completely developed *genitalia* (internal and external sexual, or reproductive, organs) of the adult man and woman maintain homologous (similar) but modified structures and have complementary functions. The most obvious of the original homologous structures are the male penis and female clitoris.

The two sexual systems are counterparts of one another more than they are different in development, structure, and function. Furthermore, Kinsey and his co-workers concluded from their monumental investigations into human sexual behavior that, "in spite of the widespread and oft-repeated emphasis on the supposed differences between female and male sexuality, we fail to find any anatomic or physiologic basis for such differences" (Kinsey *et al. c*).

The development of human sexual systems is quite complicated. The genitalia of both sexes originate from the same anatomical structure or cell mass. In the early days of the embryonic stage—the first eight weeks after conception—the reproductive system appears to be merely a genital thickening on the posterior outer layer (*epithelium*) of the embryonic body cavity. In a very young embryo there is no distinguishable difference between the two sexes in this thickening, and the sexual system is said to be in an indifferent, or undifferentiated, stage. In time the genital thickening or cell mass grows and the specific organs of the two sexual systems develop and become differentiated (structurally distinguishable). This differentiation, whether in the male or the female, results from a special chromosomal pattern that was established in the embryo at conception.

Each male sperm contains either one X (female) or one Y (male) chromosome. Sperm containing X- and Y-bearing chromosomes are, in a unique way, produced in exactly equal numbers. The male germ cell is the sex-determinant of the offspring, in that, of the 200 to 500 million sperm contained in an average ejaculate, only one will penetrate and fertilize the female ovum or egg. If an X-bearing sperm fertilizes the ovum, an XX, or female, child is conceived; a Y-bearing sperm will produce an XY, or male, child.

Development of the Internal Genitalia

In their early formative periods, the internal organs (*gonads* and *ducts*) of both sexes follow an identical course of development and are sexually indistinguishable. Most of the structures in the embryonic generative system either disappear, degenerate, or are replaced by new structures long before the end of fetal life. During the undifferentiated period, a genital gland (gonad) originates from the genital ridge that has developed from the early epithelial cell mass. As the gonad grows, it pulls away from the ridge and later partially forms the male or female sex structure.

The primitive genital ducts are exceptions to the process of early degeneration of the embryonic generative system. All embryos develop two systems of ducts, *wolffian* and *müllerian*, before ultimate sex is established. These ducts serve as forerunners of specific sexual development. The wolffian ducts will evolve into the male genital structure and the müllerian into the female genitalia.

The embryo of about six weeks possesses undifferentiated sex glands, plus both male and female genital ducts. The embryo's internal sexual transformation, first observable about six weeks after conception, starts with the differentiation of the gonads into male *testes* or female *ovaries*. The gonads produce procreative germ cells (the male *sperm* and the female *ova*) and are also involved in the hormonal interplay of the body. After maleness or femaleness has been established by the gonads' development, the ducts of the opposite sex for each embryo remain rudimentary or degenerate.

When the male embryo is four to six weeks old, a series of primordial tubules develop and grow, connecting with the wolffian (mesonephric) duct, which terminates in the urogenital sinus (opening). From this mesonephric network the male sex system is partially formed.

In the male, the *testicles* are the first sexual structures to develop from the genital ridge, eventually to become housed in an outpocketing of the body (the *scrotum*). Some of the mesonephric or wolffian ducts and tubules persist and grow to form another network of tubes called the *epididymis*. The epididymis is a swelling attached to each testicle; within it is a compactly wound tube, approximately 20 feet in length. The coiled tube is positioned at the side and top of the testicle, and serves to receive, house until maturity, and then convey the sperm to the *vas deferens,* a small connecting tube approximately 18 inches in length. The vas deferens takes a circuitous path from the epididymis of each testicle through the inguinal canal and into the abdominal cavity, where it connects with the *seminal vesicle* ("seed" reservoir) to form the ejaculatory duct.

The two seminal vesicles are pouchlike structures located behind the bladder and adjacent to the top of the prostate gland. The ejaculatory duct from each side passes through the prostate, opening into the urethra. The *prostate gland*, composed of muscular and glandular tissues, surrounds the upper portion of the urethra and is located between the bladder and base of the penis. The male *urethra*, a canal within the penis, conveys urine from the bladder and semen from the seminal vesicles. Within the prostate gland the connection is made—at a small elevation on the floor of the prostatic urethra known as the *verumontanum* or *prostatic utricle*—between the canal from the bladder and the genital ducts, which then continue as one tube through the length of the penis.

While the male genital-urethral system is in the process of formation, the müllerian ducts, for the most part, degenerate and disappear. The proximal ends, however, are preserved and become appendages to the testes

FIGURE 4.1 Internal male and female genitalia; development from undifferentiated into differentiated stage.

Undifferentiated

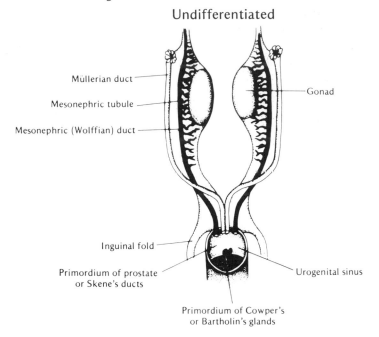

Müllerian duct

Mesonephric tubule

Mesonephric (Wolffian) duct

Gonad

Inguinal fold

Primordium of prostate or Skene's ducts

Urogenital sinus

Primordium of Cowper's or Bartholin's glands

Differentiated

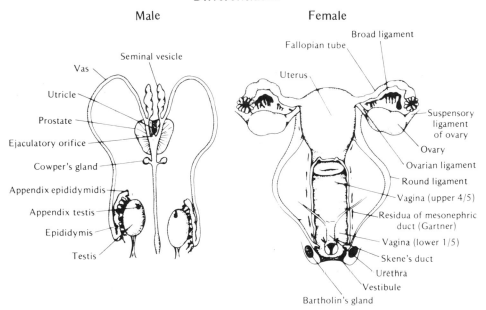

Male

Vas

Utricle

Prostate

Ejaculatory orifice

Cowper's gland

Appendix epididymidis

Appendix testis

Epididymis

Testis

Seminal vesicle

Female

Broad ligament

Fallopian tube

Uterus

Suspensory ligament of ovary

Ovary

Ovarian ligament

Round ligament

Vagina (upper 4/5)

Residua of mesonephric duct (Gartner)

Vagina (lower 1/5)

Skene's duct

Urethra

Vestibule

Bartholin's gland

(*appendix testes*), and the fused distal ends become a tiny pouch (*prostatic pouch*) in the floor of the prostatic portion of the urethra. The pouch is part of the elevated area, the verumontanum.

In the female embryo, the müllerian ducts follow the pattern of the wolffian ducts in appearance and development. The upper ends of these ducts become the uterine (*fallopian*) tubes, projections that grow eventually to cup over each ovary and in some way pick up each ovum as it is discharged from an ovary. In the embryo's seventh week, the müllerian ducts fuse and terminate in the urogenital sinus, forming the müllerian tubercle, which is destined to become the uterus (womb), the upper 80% of the vagina, and the hymen (maidenhead).

The *uterus,* a heavily muscled structure shaped somewhat like a flattened pear, is the organ in which the fetus develops. The uterus has a lateral-anterior opening on each side leading to the fallopian tubes, which are the passageways for transport of the ova from the ovaries and the structures in which fertilization takes place. In the female, the atrophied wolffian ducts are functionless. They form a tiny vestigial line, which is involuted in the roof of the vagina and runs parallel to the urethra.

Certain accessory genital glands are homologous in the male and female. For instance, the part of the sexual structure that becomes the prostate in the male becomes the *Skene's ducts* (para-urethral ducts) in the female. The part that develops into a woman's *Bartholin's glands*— major vestibular glands opening on the labia majora just within the vestibule of the vagina differentiates into a man's *Cowper's glands.* These glands secrete a precoital fluid that prepares the urethra for easy passage of the sperm. The Cowper's glands of the mature male are located just below the prostate, and each is about the size of a pea.

Development of the External Genitalia

The growth, development, and differentiation of the external genitalia of both sexes are similar to what has been described for the internal genitalia. In the male, the developing *penis* with its penile urethra parallels the development in the female of vagina, uterus, and intrauterine formations. The external genitalia are first defined at about the sixth week of embryonic formation, and for a period of another week or so they are indifferent in appearance. By the end of the seventh week the sex of the embryo becomes distinguishable by external characteristics. These first criteria for sexual distinction are not entirely reliable, however, and errors are sometimes made in distinguishing male from female at this early stage.

The external genitalia of male and female arise at a common site, located between the umbilical cord and the tail of the embryo. This site becomes the *genital tubercle*. It is at first an undifferentiated area, then becomes a phalluslike projection that eventually develops into the male or female external sexual organs. In about the fourth week of prenatal life, the front area of the genital tubercle begins to form a vertical groove. This groove produces a separation of the anal pit from the genital ridge, the separating area being known as the *primitive perineum*.

Two urethral folds or swellings *(labioscrotal swellings)* develop on the elevated margin (lateral and parallel) of the urethral groove, and differentiate into the female labia majora or into the male scrotal pouch. Although at the seventh embryonic week sex can be distinguished with a moderate degree of accuracy, there is about a three-week lag before the external genitals assume a really distinct form. Once begun, genital development is rapid, and by the fourth month the sex of the fetus is easily recognizable.

The male embryo reaches a definitive stage about the tenth week when the edges of the urethral groove fold and grow together. The previously open urogenital sinus is thus closed and transformed into a tubular urethra within the penis, the fused edge being referred to as the *penoscrotal raphe*. The evidence of this fusion appears in the adult male as a scar line on the underside of the penis, running from the anus to the *glans* (head of the penis). The penis, which has evolved from a phallic tubercle projection, elongates and grows rapidly. By the end of the third month the male urethra is fully formed. The *prepuce* (foreskin) develops over the glans of the penis simultaneously with the formation of the urethra. The outside opening of the urethra at the end of the penis is called the *penile meatus*.

The female external genitalia are less complicated, yet slower to develop than those of the male. A phalluslike tubercle projection slowly develops into the body and glans of the *clitoris*, the most sensitive organ in the female sexual system. The labioscrotal swelling becomes the *labia majora*, the outer protective lips of the vaginal region, and continues anteriorly to terminate in the *mons veneris*, or *mons pubis*, the fatty tissue on the upper exterior of the female genitalia.

In its early stages, the female urethral groove follows the same pattern of formation as the male's. However, the groove never closes to form a tube. Instead, part of it deepens to fashion the *vestibule*, the area surrounding and including the opening of the vagina. The urethral folds fail to unite in the female, and they gradually develop into the *labia minora*, the inner protective—and highly erogenous—lips of the vagina.

The female *urethra*, or bladder outlet, is homologous to the prostatic portion of the male urethra. It is just above the vagina, and both open into the vestibule. A prepuce or foreskin, often referred to as the *hood*, also develops over the glans of the clitoris. *Vulva* is a collective name used for the whole of the external female genitalia, as is the term *pudendum*, which derives from the Latin word *pudere*, "to be ashamed." The derivation of this word suggests the guilt and the psychological difficulties that too often become associated with anything sexual.

FIGURE 4.2 External male and female genitalia; development from undifferentiated into differentiated stage.

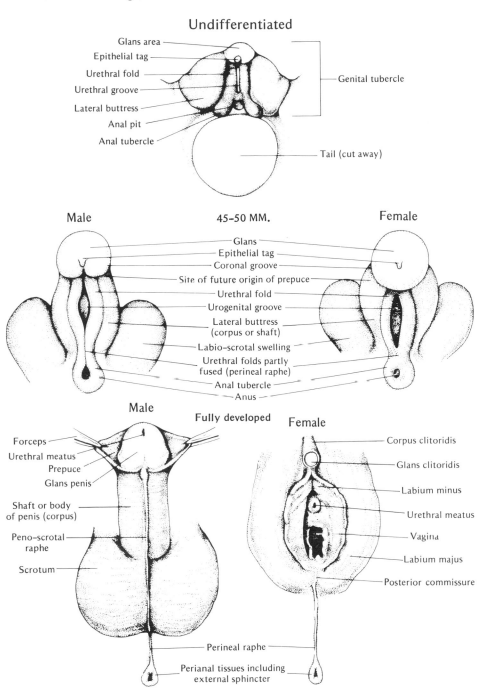

A peculiar and marked contrast exists in the differentiation of the male and female embryo. As has been said earlier, genetic sex is fixed at the time of fertilization. However, the sex genes do not exert their influence until about the fifth or sixth week of prenatal life, prior to which all embryos appear to be morphologically female.

In the genetically male embryo, the masculine sex tissue will develop under the stimulus of the male hormone *androgen.* Normal development of the male embryonic cell mass, then, depends upon the addition of androgen. If for any reason the male embryo is deprived of androgen, the primitive sex organs will differentiate into those of a female. In the female embryo, however, the opposite situation is *not* the case. No such hormonal addition is necessary, as the development of the female sexual structure occurs whether or not the female hormone estrogen is produced (Money e; Salzman a).

Since only the male embryo undergoes differentiation in its sex-developmental process, some biologists hold the belief that female, not male, is the primal sex. In those rare cases in which the male embryo is, for one reason or another, deprived of androgen, the external genitalia cannot differentiate into penis, foreskin, and scrotum (although the testes and other male internal accessory organs are present). Rather, they form homologous female sex organs: clitoris, clitoral hood, and the labia minora and majora. These androgen-deprived males are so feminized that at birth their genitals appear to be completely female; no abnormality is therefore suspected. The infant is assumed to be a girl and is reared as such, and the error may not be discovered until he reaches adolescence. ·

The analogue to this irregularity in the male is the female embryo who becomes masculinized under the influence of excessive androgen dosage, usually from a malfunctioning adrenal cortex or, in some cases, as a side effect of the synthetic progestins contained in injections given its mother to prevent miscarriage early in pregnancy. The result is a clitoris so enlarged that it is taken for a penis. If the genetic sex is discovered very early in the child's life, feminizing surgery and hormonal therapy can be instituted to assist in the correct sex-role assignment. If not discovered until the child's psychosexuality as a male has been firmly established, then corrective masculinizing surgery is probably indicated so that this sexual identity can be maintained (Money e; Salzman a).

The condition in which a person is genetically a male or a female, but has the outward appearance of the opposite sex (or of both sexes), is called *pseudohermaphroditism,* a subject discussed in Chapter 20, Sexual Diseases and Disorders.

Androgen deprivation or gonadal failure may occur in adult life or in infancy as well as in prenatal life. The more severe cases of androgen deprivation are classified as *primary*—i.e., of testicular origin—or *secondary,* in which the difficulties lie with the pituitary gland. Such conditions as destructive inflammatory diseases (mumps, syphilis, tuberculosis), X-ray irradiation, neoplasm, vitamin deficiency, and vascular disorders may restrict androgen production. The result is called *hypogonadism*.

If this uncommon disorder occurs during prepubertal life, the patient may never become potent or develop a sex drive. If the disorder occurs in adult life after the person has experienced normal sexual activity, he may experience a marked loss of sexual vigor, feel inadequate, and display a variety of symptoms indicative of depression. Treatment for hypogonadism is possible, however, and is frequently successful (Anderson, E. E.).

5 THE ROLE OF THE ENDOCRINE SYSTEM

The subject of sex has probably fascinated man since prehistoric times. Undoubtedly even primitive creatures recognized the external differences between male and female. Yet it has only been in very recent years that scientists have begun to understand more clearly the basic physiological differences between the sexes and the role of glands in influencing these differences.

The primary control in sexual maturation is the secretion of sex *hormones* (from the Greek *hormōn:* to arouse or set in motion). Hormones are chemical substances produced by the *endocrine glands,* which act rather like small chemical laboratories. They take materials from the bloodstream, convert them into hormones, and then secrete the hormones directly into the bloodstream for distribution throughout the body. Because hormones are secreted into the bloodstream without passing through any duct or canal, endocrine glands are also referred to as *ductless glands* or *glands of internal secretion.*

The brain also exerts a vital influence on the coordination (or dysfunction) of human emotions and sexual behavior. The *cortex* (forebrain) controls such superior functions as thought, memory, and ideation. It additionally controls motor impulse and action—in particular, voluntary behavior. In general, the higher the species of animal, the greater is the cortical involvement in his behavior, and *homo sapiens* has the most intricate cortex of all animal species.

The *mesencephalon* (midbrain), lying below the cortex, functions as the coordinating center of such behavior as feeding, sexual activity, and aggressive behavior. Within the midbrain lies the *hypothalamus,* which appears to function as a form of biological timing device. Interacting with the endocrine glands, it monitors and controls the onset of puberty, fertility cycles, and sexual arousal. Hormonal or electrical stimulation of the hypothalamus—whether natural or artificial—has a dramatic impact on emotional reaction, including sexual response. Clearly, then, well-coordinated interplay between the emotional impulses generated in the hypothalamus and the behavioral impulses generated by the cortex is essential to a well-ordered and satisfying sexual life (Barclay).

THE PHYSICAL CHANGES OF PUBESCENCE

The influence of hormones on the sexual system first becomes prominent during *puberty,* that stage of life at which sexual reproduction becomes possible and secondary sexual characteristics commence their development. It is directly preceded by a period of rapid change occurring just before the body reaches maturity known as *pubescence,* which is often referred to as the *pubic growth cycle.* The pubescent growth spurt, with its anatomical and sexual transformations, is the second period of accelerated growth in human development, the first having been in infancy. It is more of a transition than a state, more a becoming than being. Sexual glands mature, and physiological differences between the sexes become more marked. Body chemistry, as well as physical appearance and functioning, become more distinctively male and female in pubescence. As these differences widen, a girl becomes ready for womanhood and a boy for manhood.

There is no "typical" pubescence. Every boy and girl has his or her own periods of transition, and the range of individual differences is broad. Antecedents to puberty–pubescence appear later in boys than in girls, for whom development is more swift. Girls begin the rapid maturing process at about 10 to 12 years of age, approximately two years before boys do. The earlier development of girls gives them a temporary superiority over boys— physically, sexually, and socially. Most girls reach their full stature by their sixteenth year, while boys continue to grow in height until 18 or later.

Pubescence is a period of "sexual awakening," which is met with ambivalent reactions by both sexes. Attitudes, emotions, and interests change. Physical experimentation and new gratifications, such as masturbation, begin to occur or increase in frequency. A positive attitude toward one's biological sexual urge and condition, as well as an understanding of society's expectations for the newly emerging self, are essential to the emotional well-being of both sexes at this time. (Elaboration on the subject of sexual attitudes, both adolescent and adult, follows in later chapters, especially Chapters 15 and 16.)

Sexual Development in Girls

The first evidences of pubescence in a girl are changes that occur in the breasts; the small conical buds increase in size, and the nipples begin to project forward. A girl now becomes quite aware of breasts, not only because of the physical changes within her, but also because of the attitudes toward breast size held by our culture.

As development continues with the growth in size and sensitivity of breast tissue, the female body contour gradually rounds out and the pelvic area broadens. The bony structure of the pelvis widens, a growth of fatty pads develops on the hips, and the vaginal epithelium, or lining, thickens. There then appears soft, downy, rather colorless pubic hair, together with some axillary (underarm) hair growth. The pelvic hair thickens and coarsens, becoming curly and dark in color. It grows downward to the pubic area into the inverted triangular shape peculiar to women. With these bodily changes, and the unfolding of the classic feminine form, menstruation is imminent.

About two years after the breasts begin budding, and about one year after the appearance of pubic hair (at approximately 13 years of age), menstruation begins. The *menarche,* or beginning of menstrual functioning, is the first real indication that a girl is becoming a woman. She cannot bear a child until she starts *ovulation*—i.e., until the ovaries commence releasing mature ova—and this process usually does not take place until a year or so after menstruation first occurs. When a young girl's ovaries produce their first mature eggs, at about the age of 14, she has reached puberty.

There is considerable variation in the age at which girls reach the menarche because of individual differences in general health, developmental maturation, and heredity. In 1939, for example, at the unbelievable age of 5, a Peruvian girl gave birth to a normal, healthy son. (Fathered by a mentally retarded teen-age stepbrother, the baby was delivered by caesarean section.) In spite of the fact that the mother was so young, she was sexually mature, and physicians confirmed that she had menstruated since she was perhaps one month old. Cases are on record in which a girl became pregnant and produced a child without ever having menstruated. The explanation appears to be that the girl, contrary to the usual sequence of events, released a mature ovum just before she would have started menstruating, and the resulting pregnancy delayed menstruation until after delivery. Such cases are, of course, exceptional.

Female genital changes continue to occur from pubescence on into adolescence. The thickened pelvic hair continues to spread; the *mons pubis* (fatty pads just above the vulva) becomes prominent; the outer lips (*labia majora*) develop and become more fleshy, hiding the rest of the vulva, which is ordinarily visible during childhood; and the inner lips (*labia minora*) also develop and grow. The *Bartholin's glands,* which lie just to each side of the opening of the vagina, are now capable of secreting a fluid, especially during sexual excitement.

The clitoris rapidly develops its extensive system of blood vessels at this time. The vagina turns a deeper red color, and its mucous lining becomes thicker, remaining so until the *menopause,* or "change of life," when it reverts to the thinness of childhood. Vaginal secretions now become acid. The uterus, which begins to grow rapidly when a girl reaches age 10 or so, doubles in size by the eighteenth year (although the wombs of 60% of 15-year-old girls have already reached their adult size).

It is interesting to note that, because of the influence of the mother's hormonal secretions, the uterus of a female infant is larger at birth than it will be again until the ovaries start to produce hormones as a prelude to the menarche. Because of the abrupt withdrawal of maternal hormones at the time of birth, the infant's uterus shrinks within a few days after birth. Sometimes the change is significant enough to result in vaginal spotting or staining. Uterine size then remains constant until the ovaries begin their hormone production. Pregnancies will later increase the permanent size of the uterus slightly more.

When a girl is around 10, her ovaries begin to secrete female sex hormones (in particular, estrogen) and ovarian growth is rapid. At the time of the menarche, the ovaries are about one-third their adult size, reaching maximum size and weight by the time a woman is 19 or 20.

The age at which girls begin to menstruate has dropped sharply in the last few centuries (Sexual maturity and climate). In Germany, for example, the average age of menstrual onset was 16.6 years in 1795, but was only 14.5 years by 1920. In the United States in the late 1930s, the average age was 13.5, while data from the mid-1960s indicate a drop to 13 years. In all advanced countries, as a matter of fact, the average age at which the menarche occurs has been dropping about four months per decade (Money g). Some authorities conclude that approximately one-half of American girls become capable of bearing children between 12.5 and 14.5 years of age. There is recent evidence, however, that the age of puberty is now leveling off after many years of gradual decline (Sullivan, W.).

It has long been recognized that the average city dweller matured sexually at an earlier age than did rural inhabitants. The reason generally put forward has been that genetic factors were responsible: slower maturing rural people intermarried and faster maturing city dwellers intermarried. They tended not to meet and "cross marry," primarily because a lack of inexpensive transportation restricted social activities to one's own geographic areas. About a century ago, however, mass production of the bicycle allowed young men to widen their vistas in the search for a bride, resulting in a wider dissemination of the genes controlling earlier maturity.

Altitude is apparently related to growth and date of menarche. One study showed that girls from Denver, Colorado (5300 feet above sea level), averaged 7 pounds at birth and reached menarche at 13.1 years. A matched sampling of girls from Berkeley, California (sea level), averaged 7.5 pounds at birth and reached menarche at 12.8 years. The difference is thought to be caused by the oxygen-rare atmosphere of Denver's high altitude. The Denver girls lagged behind the Berkeley girls in weight throughout their early development, but the weight difference disappeared when they finally reached menarche (Sullivan, W.).

The prepuberty growth spurt and the menarche are thought to be precipitated by the body's having reached a critical weight, regardless of age or height. The growth spurt apparently begins when a girl's weight reaches an average of 68 pounds, and menarche when she weighs about 106 pounds (Sullivan, W.).

Because she is unaccustomed to it, a girl often feels insecure or inadequate in her new role as a sexually maturing person. She stands in critical need of support and guidance to help her view puberty as a normal, healthy process. She will face many problems and challenges during the next few years, not all of them sexual. If they are not dealt with properly during this crucial period, they can lead to emotional difficulties that will have adverse effects on later personal and marital adjustments.

Sexual Development in Boys

A boy's pubic growth curve lasts from 4 to 7 years and parallels that of a girl's but, as we have noted, lags behind hers by a year or two. Progress to and through puberty varies considerably from boy to boy; generally speaking, however, a boy's physiological maturation occurs later, moves more slowly, and continues longer than a girl's. His greater physical size does not develop until after puberty; in fact, boys of 13 are usually smaller than girls of the same age. Even so, boys of today are considerably better developed physically than in the past. For example, a 9-year-old boy today is 3.8 inches taller and 18.7 pounds heavier than a boy that age living in 1881 (Steinhaus). The most obvious changes, and the greatest variability in physical size and physiological development, are first observed in boys at the age of 12 or 13. The developmental transformation continues to or beyond their seventeenth year.

It might be noted that when today's boys and girls arrive at their full stature they are significantly taller and heavier than their grandparents were. But the degree of difference is somewhat less in adulthood than it is during childhood and adolescence. It is speculated that the difference is attributable to the fact that young people of today reach their prepubertal growth period earlier, that it proceeds at a faster rate than it did in the past, and that they therefore reach physical maturity earlier.

At the age of 11, a boy shows few outward signs of pubertal altera-tion. He may first blossom into a "fat period," often an antecedent to male pubescence. Penile erections occur spontaneously at this early age, but from various sources of stimulation, not all of which are sexual. By the age of 12, his penis and scrotum begin to show an increase in size, one of the earliest indicators of approaching puberty. Erections occur more often, but still spontaneously; while he might know about ejaculation, he has yet to experience it.

A boy's pubic hair commonly appears at the age of 13 or 14, follow-ing the spurt of genital growth by a year or so, although it sometimes becomes discernible as early as the twelfth year. For the average boy of 13 or 14, ejaculation is now possible. Secretion of sperm begins—a process parallel to ovulation in a girl, although neither sperm nor ova are yet nec-essarily mature. Growth of axillary and facial hair follows that of the pubic hair. Nocturnal emissions ("wet dreams") are now probable if a sexual out-let of another nature is not utilized.

A change in voice occurs about the fourteenth or fifteenth year (the voice of a mature man is usually about an octave lower than that of a mature woman). The average age at which a boy's voice changes has dropped over the years. For example, at the time of the eighteenth-century Bach Boys' Choir in Leipzig, the average age of voice change was 18; in London in 1959, by contrast, it was 13.3 years (Sullivan, W.). It is interesting to note in passing that, in Moscow during the wartime stresses of the early 1940s, the average height of 13-year-old boys dropped roughly 1 inch, probably because of substandard nutrition (Sullivan, W.). Adequate nutri-tion notwithstanding, many boys do not attain full stature and mature sexual development until they are of college age.

GLANDS AND HORMONES

Age alone is not responsible for the remarkable transformations that make boys and girls sexually mature. Indeed, there are some adult men and women who lack the proper primary or secondary sexual characteristics associated with full sexual capability. And, in contrast, boys and girls far short of their teens, who would not be considered adult by ordinary standards, have been known to have mature sexual organs and to show sexual behavior usually found only in adults—for example, fathering or giv-ing birth to babies.

FIGURE 5.1 Schematic representation of the functional relationships between the pituitary gland and the male and female gonads, showing the effect of hormonal secretion on the bodily parts and functions.

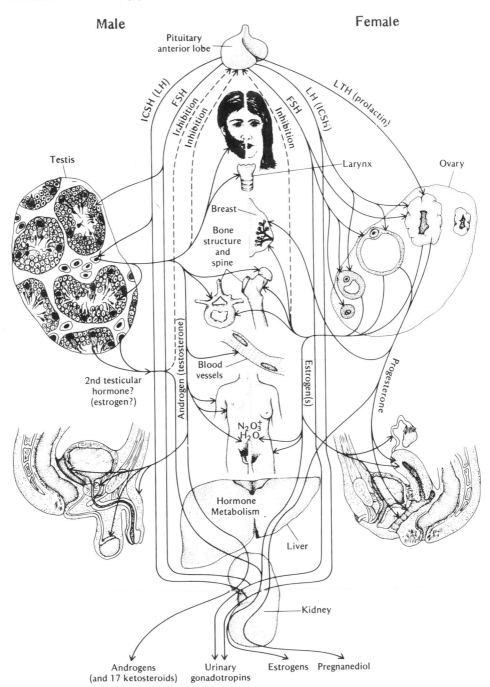

As was said earlier, sexual maturation (or the stunting of sexual development) is dependent upon sex hormones. The endocrine system is quite complex and contributes to many of the physiological functions and behavior patterns of humans. In this discussion, however, only those hormones that more or less directly influence sexual development and functioning will be considered.

The *pituitary gland,* located at the base of the brain, is about one-half the size of a thimble and contains three lobes: the anterior, the intermediary, and the posterior. The anterior pituitary lobe is known as the "master gland"; it serves as coordinator of the functions of all other endocrine glands and is therefore important to sexual growth and functioning. A properly functioning pituitary has a harmonizing influence on the other endocrine glands. If it functions abnormally, it can have a disturbing effect on any or all of them.

With regard to the male testes and the female ovaries, the anterior lobe of the pituitary gland specifically controls both the cytogenic (the beginning of a cell) function concerned with the production of sperm and ova and the endocrine secretory function (Lloyd). The anterior lobe secretes at least six hormones, three of which are directly related to gonadal function and are termed *gonadotropic.* They are: (1) the follicle-stimulating hormone (FSH); (2) the luteinizing hormone (LH) in the female, and its counterpart, the interstitial cell-stimulating hormone (ICSH) in the male; and (3) the luteotropic hormone (LTH), also called prolactin, which regulates the production of progesterone by the corpus luteum and prompts the secretion of milk by the mammary glands following childbirth (although it apparently plays no part in the development of the mammary glands themselves). These gonadotropic hormones exert great influence on the growth, development, and sexual activity of both males and females.

The gonads or sex glands (the ovaries in women, the testes in men), in addition to their other functions, produce sex hormones. On the basis of chemical and physiological differences, these hormones form three groups: the *estrogenic* hormone group and the *corpus luteum* hormone group (both female hormones), and the *androgenic* hormone group (male hormones). The action of these three hormonal groups differs greatly, although their chemical structure is quite similar. They are all classed as steroids and each is a natural substance that is a basic component of living cells. Once the sex hormones have been used by the body, they are broken down and eliminated, usually in the urine.

Hormonal Activity in the Female

Estrogen (from the Greek *estro-*: to produce mad desire) is the hormone responsible for stimulating the sexual urge in a female animal's reproductive organs during *estrus*, her mating period, which is also called *heat* or *rut*. In human females (who do not experience estrus), estrogen is essentially a growth hormone, highly important in controlling body structure, and in the development and functioning of genital organs. Estrogen also influences the menstrual cycle, especially its first half.

Humans and certain primates (e.g., apes and Old World monkeys) have similar menstrual cycles. Other mammals do not menstruate, although the estrous discharge resembles bleeding just as menstruation does. The production of large amounts of estrogen in these lower female animals heralds estrus, at which time ovulation has occurred or is about to. It is also the time when these animals are most receptive to copulation. Human females, however, typically experience the height of sexual desire just before or after menstruation, when estrogen levels are quite low, pointing up a major difference between female humans and mammals in the rhythm of their sexual receptiveness (Barclay).

Studies have shown that the physiological mechanisms controlling the sexual activity of male and female infrahuman mammals are different, although the sexual patterns of both sexes are ultimately governed by the central nervous system. In females, interest in and receptivity to sexual activity are the effect of hormonal influence on neural tissue, whereas in males sexual activity is triggered by the neural tissue itself, which depends upon hormonal action only to maintain its functioning (Lisk).

Estrogenic hormones in the human female, in addition to their role in reproductive functions, aid in (1) maintaining the normal size and function of the uterus, its tubes, and the vagina; (2) controlling the production of gonadotropic and other hormones by their action on the pituitary gland; (3) influencing the growth, development, and maintenance of the secondary sexual characteristics, such as distribution of fat; (4) maintaining the normal condition and function of nasal and oral mucous membranes; (5) influencing normal uterine contractions; (6) controlling the growth of breast-duct tissue; and (7) developing and maintaining physical and mental health in the mature, normal female.

The evidence is fairly conclusive that in the majority of women—unlike subhuman animals—hormones produced by the ovaries do not play a major role in regulating the sex drive. In one study approximately 90% of the women, who were under the age of 40, experienced no change in sexual desire and functioning after a bilateral ovariectomy. The hormones produced by the pituitary and adrenal glands appear to play a vastly more important role in women's sex drive. To demonstrate: one study of 30 women, from whom these last glands had been removed as part of the treatment for breast cancer, revealed that none had maintained their preoperative sex drive; in 84% of them, it had vanished completely (Reichlin). In the average woman, however, any temporary fluctuation in sexual responsiveness is apparently influenced more by emotional and physical factors than by hormonal conditions (Luttge).

Recent experimental research (Money b) has uncovered evidence that certain neural centers of the brain are directly affected by sex hormones. For example, female test animals show an intensification in smell acuity during certain stages of the estrous cycle. In female animals, body odors become much stronger during those days, which accounts for the attraction of male animals to them while they are in heat. Dense crowding of female mice can cause pseudopregnancies, a reaction that is prevented if their olfactory bulbs (organs sensitive to odors) are removed. Also, inseminated female mice will not become pregnant if they are made to smell the urine odor of a mature male mouse other than the one with which they have copulated (Parkes and Bruce).

Studies of humans have revealed that women have greater smell acuity than men, and that their olfactory sensitivity is greatest midway between menstrual periods when estrogen levels are the highest. Smell acuity decreases after an ovariectomy, but can be restored through administration of estrogen.

As a part of a girl's developmental process, either the pituitary gland begins to secrete more of its follicle-stimulating hormone (FSH), or the ovaries develop to the point where they become more sensitive than before to the already existing level of FSH secretion. A third view is that pubertal development is initiated by the maturing of cells within the hypothalamus rather than by changes in either the ovary or the pituitary, "as both these glands are capable of adult function at birth if properly stimulated" (Eastman and Hellman). Whatever the cause, FSH stimulates the growth of the immature ovaries and the *ovarian follicles* (small sacs, each containing an immature ovum), which, in turn, initiate the production of estrogen from the cells of the cavity lining of each follicle. Among its other effects, estrogen inhibits the pituitary's production of FSH and causes the lining of the uterus to thicken in the first half of the menstrual cycle. The luteinizing hormone (LH) plays a role in causing the follicles to secrete estrogen. In addition, when LH reaches a certain ratio in relation to FSH, it serves to trigger ovulation (Eastman and Hellman).

Hormonal Activity in Ovulation, Menstruation, and Pregnancy

When an egg is discharged from a follicle in ovulation, the remaining follicular cells multiply rapidly and fill the cavity of the follicle just ruptured. The new cell growth is yellow in color and is known as the *corpus luteum* (yellow body). Under the influence of the pituitary gland's luteotropic hormone (LTH), the corpus luteum begins to secrete *progesterone,* the second female hormone. (The corpus luteum also produces estrogen, but in a reduced amount compared with the production from the follicles.) The cells of the yellow body produce progesterone for about 13 days following the peak development of the cells that fill the follicular cavity after the discharge of the ovum.

If the ovum is not fertilized by about the twenty-seventh day after the first day of the previous menstrual period (14 days preceding ovulation, plus the 13 days just discussed), the corpus luteum begins to atrophy and its secretion of progesterone begins to wane. Progesterone is the reproduction hormone, of primary importance in preparing the lining of the uterus for implantation and in maintaining the pregnancy itself. When impregnation does not occur and progesterone is gradually withdrawn, the uterine lining begins to break down. The degeneration of the uterine tissue is the onset of the monthly flow of blood known as menstruation.

In the process of degeneration, the margin of the corpus luteum shrinks rapidly and loses its yellow color, and the lutein cells are replaced by connective tissue. After a few weeks only a small white body, the *corpus albicans*, remains in the space that was once the location of the follicle. This cessation of the secretion of progesterone, together with the decrease of estrogen, causes a new production of pituitary gonadotropins, which stimulate another crop of ovarian follicles. The ovulatory growth cycle commences anew.

If the ovum is fertilized, the corpus luteum does not degenerate. Rather, it continues to secrete progesterone, which keeps the endometrium or uterine lining sensitized and ready to implant the blastocyst, a stage of development of the fertilized ovum, and to develop the membranes needed for the survival of the egg.

In pregnancy, the bright yellow corpus luteum develops and grows until it may, at the peak of its progesterone production, occupy as much as half of the ovary (Netter). This endocrine tissue continues to function until about the fourth month of pregnancy. At that time the placenta takes over the necessary production of estrogen and progesterone and maintains this production for the remainder of gestation (the period of pregnancy).

Progesterone stimulates the secretion capabilities of the mammary glands of the pregnant woman, thus causing an enlargement of the breasts. A proper amount of progesterone is also necessary to inhibit premature uterine contractions. In fact, progesterone hormonal therapy is often prescribed by the physician when there is a danger of spontaneous abortion, especially during the tenth to sixteenth week of pregnancy when the threat of miscarriage is greatest. In a woman who is not pregnant, improper production of progesterone may produce dysmenorrhea, premenstrual tension, and similar gynecological problems.

It should be noted in any discussion of progesterone that modern birth control pills are effective because they contain the female hormones which inhibit the pituitary gonadotropins causing follicular growth and ovulation. (This subject will be treated more thoroughly in Chapter 14, Birth Control.)

The continued functioning of the corpus luteum during pregnancy is brought about by a special gonadotropic hormone produced not by the pituitary but by the placenta. (Without some hormonal stimulation, the corpus luteum would degenerate as described earlier.) During the very earliest days of a pregnancy—actually, from about the middle of the first month—the *chorionic villi* begin to secrete *chorionic gonadotropin,* a hormone that is excreted in the urine of the mother-to-be. (The chorionic villi are small fingerlike protrusions from the covering of the fertilized egg that form the tie between the egg and uterine wall and are the forerunner of the placenta.) Production of this hormone reaches a peak during the third month of pregnancy (Netter), then begins rapidly to decrease during the fourth and fifth months, gradually leveling off and stopping altogether by the end of pregnancy. It is the presence of this particular hormone in the urine that makes possible certain laboratory tests for pregnancy during the early days after conception. Its production starts about the twenty-fourth or twenty-fifth day of the menstrual cycle.

The amount of chorionic gonadotropin secreted initially by the chorionic villi is apparently so slight that biological tests designed to confirm pregnancy cannot detect its presence in the urine until about 10 days after the next menstrual period would normally have started. For this reason, laboratories usually refuse to run such a test for pregnancy until the menstrual period is about two weeks overdue.

A more recent test for pregnancy (Crawley et al.), not involving the use of animals but, rather, a process of agglutination, will show a reaction to the hormone within 1 to 14 days after menstruation should have commenced. The reliability of this test may be as high as 96%, depending upon the time elapsed since the missed period, and some forms of it require only 3 minutes to determine pregnancy (Science notes f). Still other pregnancy tests are purported to have a near 100% accuracy.

Hormonal Activity in the Male

The male sex hormone *testosterone* is produced in the testicles when the underlying developmental processes, including proper pituitary function, have occurred. A boy's testicles grow and develop rapidly in pubescence as a result of the pituitary gland's secretion of the follicle-stimulating hormone (FSH). In the male, FSH acts to stimulate the seminiferous tubules to begin the process of *spermatogenesis,* the formation and development of spermatozoa or sperm. This is not the complete story, however, because while the germinal cell layers of the tubules become active at the time of pubescence, mature spermatozoa do not develop without the presence of the interstitial cell-stimulating hormone (ICSH), which, it will be remembered, is the same as the luteinizing hormone (LH) in woman. Without ICSH, spermatogenesis does not go beyond the secondary spermatocyte stage (the second division and third stage of spermatogenesis).

The chief function of ICSH, however, appears to be the stimulation and maintenance of the interstitial (Leydig) cells of the testes in their production of the male gonadal (androgenic) hormone, testosterone (Lloyd). The male hormone is responsible for development and preservation of masculine secondary sexual characteristics, including facial and body hair, voice change, muscular and skeletal development, attraction to the opposite sex, and mental attitudes, as well as the development, size, and function of male accessory sex organs (seminal vesicles, prostate, penis, and scrotum).

Testosterone is furthermore associated with certain biologic conditions (Schering Corporation): (1) dryness and itching of the skin, (2) retention in the body of chlorides and water, (3) effectiveness of the circulation of the peripheral blood system, (4) size and function of the kidneys, (5) reactions of the nervous system, such as irritability and apprehension, as well as effective mental functioning, (6) inhibition of the development of peptic ulcers, since this disorder is thought to be related to disturbed pituitary–gonad interaction, and (7) certain forms of heart pain and disease.

Apparently a healthy male body produces a more than ample supply of sex hormones for adequate sexual functioning. In proof of this, men with only one testicle reveal no evidence of hormonal deficiency. Even in men whose ejaculate contains as little as 60% of the normal hormonal content, the existing hormones are sufficient to sustain a normal, satisfactory sex life (Raboch b; Weaver).

Perhaps sensing the special function of the testicles that we now identify as hormonal, men from early recorded history have been known to attempt to increase their sexual prowess by eating the testicles of a defeated enemy. Indeed, 4000 years ago tiger testicles were eaten by decrepit Chinese ancients, and in 1400 B.C., a Hindu doctor prescribed a diet of tiger testicles for men suffering from impotency (Rubin g).

As late as 1889, the renowned French physiologist Charles E. Brown-Sequard was evidently dissatisfied with his sexual vigor at the age of 72 and tried to outwit nature by injecting himself with extracts from the testicles of dogs. This famous scientist was apparently barking up the wrong tree, because despite the fact that he reported spectacular rejuvenation, any benefits he actually derived must surely have been the result of autosuggestion, for an injection of the extract from approximately 500 pounds of bull testicles would be needed to furnish what is considered an average dose of male sex hormones (Schering Corporation)! The one thing that Brown-Sequard did accomplish, however, was to stimulate a considerable amount of research in this area. Since his time, well-controlled experimentations with hormones have shown that we are physically, mentally, and emotionally dependent upon the action of our endocrine glands.

Male and female sex hormones are produced by both sexes—that is, a small amount of female sex hormones is to be found in the male, and a small amount of male sex hormones in the female. The source of the "opposite" hormones is not known definitely, although it is thought that the gonads and the adrenal glands are probably responsible. The urine of normal men and women will contain some of the "opposite" hormones.

Hormonal Imbalance and Hormonal Treatment

In adulthood an excessive amount of male hormones in a woman, and vice versa, can produce marked changes in secondary sexual characteristics. An imbalance in the natural hormonal state in an infant or growing child can produce deviations in primary sexual characteristics, as well as changes in the secondary characteristics. Hormonal therapy is often successful in adjusting the imbalance and, in turn, correcting or preventing associated problems.

Women who have developed cancer are often successfully treated with male hormones injected in an effort to reduce the rate of growth and the spread of the malignancy. Preliminary investigations indicate that it may be possible to reduce the death rate among men from heart attacks by as much as 50% in some instances when the female sex hormone estrogen is used in treatment. Estrogenic treatment, however, leaves the man with a decreased potency and sex drive, together with an enlargement of the breasts (Medical science notes a; Science notes a).

By contrast, androgen treatment of women serves to enhance the sex drive, although it also has certain masculinizing effects (e.g., encouraging the growth of facial hair). After puberty, however, male and female hormones exert no influence on the individual's masculinity or femininity in the course of psychosexual development. Hormones cannot therefore be used successfully as a therapeutic tool in changing the sexual proclivities and behavior of such people as homosexuals, transsexuals, and transvestites (Money e).

Other relationships between sex hormones and certain conditions of the body, including disease, have been detected (From the editor's scrapbook b). Apparently there exists a correlation between male hormones and glaucoma, a condition in which the pressure of the fluid in the eyeball increases, often sharply, and interferes with vision. Pregnancy has been observed to reduce this ocular pressure in women with glaucoma, while injections of male hormones increase it. Castration of male rabbits, as a further example of this relationship, lowers the pressure in their eyes.

It has also been reported that the sperm count of men suffering from acne is 33% lower than the average man's, and that the number of normally formed sperm is 10% lower, all three anomalies suggestive of hormonal imbalance (Science notes g). The fact that light has a stimulating effect on the reproductive organs of birds is used to economic advantage by farmers, who augment the egg production of their hens by increasing the intensity of light and the length of time that the birds are exposed to it.

6 THE MALE SEXUAL SYSTEM

THE MALE GENITALIA

The male gonads, the *testicles* (also called *testes*), develop as a pair in the abdominal cavity. As in many other mammals, a man's testicles descend shortly before or just after birth into the *scrotum* (or scrotal sac), a loose pouch of skin that is an outpocket of the abdominal cavity. During the seventh month of fetal life, the testes pass through the *inguinal canal*, a passageway leading from the abdominal cavity into the scrotal pouch. After the descent, this opening is usually sealed off by a growth of connective tissue, and the body cavity and scrotum are henceforth separated.

Any of a variety of factors may cause the testicles not to descend in due time into the scrotum, in which case endocrine or surgical assistance is needed. It has been estimated that up to 2% of males have undescended testicles at the time of birth, and that in about 7% of this group the testicles remain undescended at puberty (Garrett). Physicians generally agree that an undescended testicle should be dealt with by the time the boy is five or six years of age.

Occasionally the inguinal ring fails to close after the descent of the testicles around the time of birth. Or it reopens when the boy or man is older—because of strain, muscular tear, or some other reason—resulting in an inguinal hernia. Sometimes a loop of the intestine may slip through the ring and into the scrotal pouch. If it is caught there, it is possible that its blood supply may be cut off and an operation becomes necessary.

The testicles are ovoid bodies that vary in size but in the adult are usually about 1.5 inches long and about 1 inch in diameter (Steen and Montagu). The scrotum in which they are housed is supported by special muscles (*cremaster*) and tissues acting to regulate the temperature of the gonads. Ordinarily the scrotal temperature is slightly lower than that of the body itself. This lower temperature is necessary for the production of sperm. The supporting muscles and tissue act to contract the scrotum when the outside temperature is low, thus bringing the testicles closer to the warm body; they relax when the temperature is high, lowering the testicles away from the body. It is well known to most men that the scrotum shrivels, bringing the testes closer to the warm body, during cold showers, cold weather, and certain emotional conditions.

FIGURE 6.1 Schematic representation of the male pelvic region, showing organs of reproduction.

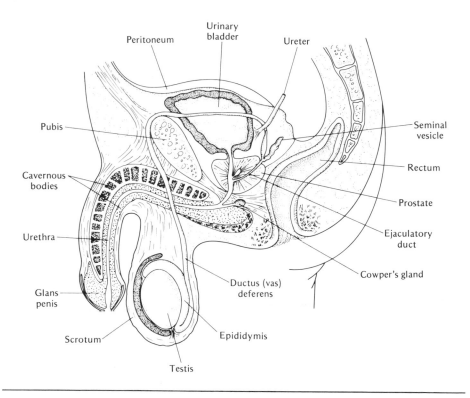

FIGURE 6.2 Schematic representation of the testicle.

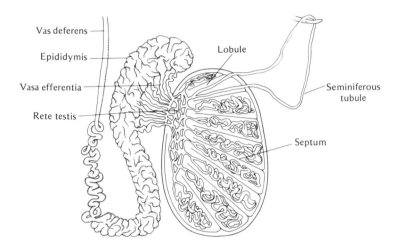

The arguments are time-honored that long hot baths, prolonged use of athletic supporters, high fever, and the like can cause infertility, especially in men with a low sperm count to start with. A 2°C to 3°C increase in temperature does in fact occasionally result in temporary sterility in men, but fertility returns after a short time. Also, there is little evidence of success in a man's taking prolonged hot baths as a contraceptive technique, as is done in some countries. Nevertheless, Dickinson has reported that heat which is tolerable to the hand can, in a 30-minute period, arrest the testicular manufacture of sperm for a period of weeks.

Each testicle has within it several hundred lobules (small divided areas), which contain, in turn, several winding and tightly coiled *seminiferous* (sperm-producing) *tubules* measuring from 1 to 2 feet each when uncoiled (Netter). The walls of the tubules are lined with germinal tissue. It is here that the production of sperm in the process of maturation known as *spermatogenesis*—a continuous process in man but a seasonal one in some animals—takes place (see pp. 69–72, this chapter).

The seminiferous tubules, some 1000 of them, meet at the corelike structure known as the *rete testis* (network of vessels in the testicle), located near the surface in the upper portion of the testicle. This meshwork of tubes, fibers, and vessels empties into approximately 10 to 15 efferent ducts (*vasa efferentia*) through which the sperm are moved by means of peristalsis (successive waves of contraction) to the *epididymis,* the chamber of maturation discussed earlier. Here the sperm may remain to ripen or mature for as long as six weeks, during which time they are nurtured by its lining. Those spermatozoa less fit to survive and to endure the long journey ahead are crowded toward the center of the tube, where they are less likely to live, and where they are absorbed. The epididymis thus serves also as a selection chamber.

Sperm are transported by ciliary action through the epididymis into a minute connecting duct, the *ductus deferens* or *vas deferens* (commonly called the *vas*). About 18 inches in length, this tiny tube originates at the small end of the epididymis and passes upward into the abdominal cavity. There it serves not only as a passageway for sperm but also as a storage place, particularly at its upper end where it broadens into an ampulla (dilated portion). The ampulla connects with the seminal vesicle at a juncture that opens into the prostate gland.

To assess the size of a sperm, one has only to consider that it must travel 500 times its length in order to progress 1 inch. This is equivalent to a man's swimming almost a mile (Story of the sperm).

The mature spermatozoa, or sperm—which, incidentally, were first identified under a microscope as early as 1677—have little motility until they mix with prostatic fluid to form the semen. Sperm are transported by the peristalsis and ciliary movements of the various tubes through which they pass into the two *seminal vesicles*—saclike structures that are about 4.5 inches long when stretched—which lie behind the bladder, in front of the rectum, and near the top of the prostate. The exact function of the seminal vesicles is much debated. Some scientists believe that they act only as storage compartments for spermatozoa. Others have suggested that they are glands specifically designed to produce a secretion that not only serves as a vehicle for the sperm but also activates the whiplike movements of their tails. (Following coital ejaculation these lashing movements propel the sperm in their migration from the vagina toward the fallopian tubes.)

Immediately below the bladder, surrounding its neck and the upper part of the urethra, lies the *prostate gland*. It is a firm body, weighing approximately two-thirds of an ounce, and is made up of partially muscular, partially glandular matter. The mature prostate is in a continual state of activity. Part of its secretion is voided with the urine, while the remainder makes up the greater portion of the ejaculatory fluid.

That part of the prostatic secretion discharged at the time of ejaculation is a highly alkaline, thin, milky fluid that contains many substances including proteins, calcium, citric acid, cholesterol, and various enzymes and acids (Mann). The alkalinity of the secretion apparently serves to allow the sperm to move through acid areas at a rapid pace, since, for example, acid in the vaginal fluid will easily destroy them if left in contact even for a short time.

The prostate surrounds the *ejaculatory ducts*, which partially house the semen until its discharge. The *semen* or *seminal fluid* is composed of spermatozoa and secretions from the epididymis, seminal vesicles, prostate

FIGURE 6.3 Schematic representation of the prostate gland, showing ejaculatory duct openings joining the urethra.

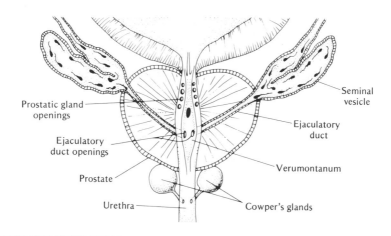

gland, and Cowper's (bulbo-urethral) glands. It should be pointed out that the substance of seminal fluid varies from man to man, and that variations in the fluid are to be expected in a single individual. Sometimes the fluid is thick and almost gelatinlike, while another time it will be thin and somewhat watery, the determinant being, generally, the frequency of the man's ejaculations. Semen coagulates shortly after ejaculation, but liquefies about 20 minutes later (Clark *j*).

The average amount of semen ejaculated is 4 cc, which weighs about 4 gr. Given the protein and fat contained in semen, the average ejaculate probably represents less than 36 calories. The evidence is therefore convincing that a normal discharge of semen cannot in any way "weaken" a man (Clark *m*).

The *Cowper's glands* are two pea-sized structures situated slightly below the prostate at each side of the base of the penis. Along with the seminal vesicles and prostate, they make up a man's accessory reproductive glands. During sexual excitement, the Cowper's glands secrete an alkaline fluid that lubricates and neutralizes the acidity of the urethra for easy and safe passage of the semen. This thin fluid can be observed at the opening of the glans of the penis during sexual excitement and before ejaculation. The fluid does not ordinarily contain spermatozoa, but some few sperm do occasionally make their way into the fluid. It is therefore possible for a woman to be made pregnant by penetration even if the man does not actually ejaculate. Many years ago the well-known sexologist Abraham Stone demonstrated the presence of sperm in 20% to 25% of the samples of precoital fluid examined (Stone).

Situated just below the Cowper's glands is the base of the *penis*, a cylindrical organ composed mostly of erectile tissue. In the adult male, the average penis is from 2.5 to 4 inches long when flaccid (limp), slightly over 1 inch in diameter, and about 3.5 inches in circumference. The size, of course, varies considerably from man to man. When in a state of tumescence (erection), the average penis extends 5.5 to 6.5 inches in length, and becomes 1.5 inches in diameter and about 4.5 inches in circumference. Again, the size of the erect penis shows considerable variation from man to man.

There is little relationship between the size of a flaccid penis and its size when erect. And there is less relationship between penile and general body size than exists between the dimensions of other organs and body size (Masters and Johnson *n*). The measurement of a perfectly functioning erect penis can vary from 2 inches in one man to 10 inches in another, but one is no less capable of coital performance than the other.

Men are often concerned about the dimensions of their penises because childhood experiences have conditioned them to associate an adult's larger penis with strength and masculinity. When a boy so conditioned grows up, he may well think that in order to be a man of sexual prowess he must have an inordinately large phallus. Yet, as will be seen later, a woman's vagina has few nerve endings. Aside from any psychological influences, therefore, the size of a man's penis has nothing to do with the pleasure experienced by either coital partner, or with the man's impregnating ability, unless there is some hormonal dysfunction. If a boy has a hormonal malfunction, then the size of his external sex organs may indeed be impaired (Wood).

The male hormone testosterone causes the penis to grow, the period of most rapid growth being usually between the ages of 11 and 14 years. If the testicles do not produce sufficient quantities of this hormone, the penis will remain small unless the boy receives hormonal therapy. But in a healthy and normal man, the size of the penis is fixed by heredity, and nothing can be done to make it larger.

Scientists at the Sexological Institute of Prague, Czechoslovakia, have recently investigated the relationship between penile size, male hormone functioning, and potency. Their sampling consisted of 34 adult male subjects, most of whom were aged 25 to 35, whose male hormone functioning had been deficient during the critical adolescent years of sexual development, and whose flaccid penile length was consequently under 2.2 inches. Through hormonal treatment their flaccid penile size was increased to normal size (2.4 inches to 4 inches) within a few months (Raboch a). Of the subject population of this study, potency disturbances rarely affected those men whose flaccid penis was shorter than 2.4 inches and narrower than 0.8 inch, further evidence that male impotence has very little to do with a small penis. One surprising incidental finding in this investigation was that the penises of both effeminate and noneffeminate homosexuals were larger in length and width than those of the control group of heterosexual men.

The erect penis is somewhat triangular (inverted) in shape because the shaft is made up of three cylindrical, spongy bodies composed of erectile tissue: two larger bodies on top, and one smaller body below. The two top bodies are known as the *corpora cavernosa penis*, and the single body below is called *corpus spongiosum* or *corpus cavernosum urethrae*. The lower body houses the urethral canal, which passes through the length of the penis. These three bodies are encircled, and the lower body separated from the upper two, by *Buck's fascia*. This is a band or sheet of tissue that is a continuation of the tissue joining the penis to the symphysis (connection juncture) of the pubic bone and the perineal and related muscles.

Throughout the penis, but especially at the top, both above and below Buck's fascia, are large arteries that feed blood to its spongy erectile tissue. As the spongy structures of the penis fill with blood, it becomes erect. The erection is lost when blood leaves the penis venously faster than it flows in through the arteries.

The *glans* (Latin: acorn) is the smooth conelike head, or distal end, of the penis. It is by far the most sexually sensitive and excitable part of a man's body. Its surface is filled with nerve endings, especially at the *corona*, the crownlike ridge at the back edge of the glans where the glans drops

---

FIGURE 6.4 Glans penis and foreskin, showing position of the frenum.

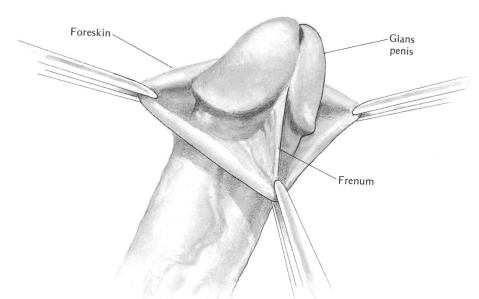

down to join the shaft of the penis. The corona, particularly at the frenum, is a primary source of sexual pleasure and excitement when stimulated properly. The glans is a continuation of the corpus cavernosum urethrae. At its tip end is a *meatus,* the external opening of the urethra.

The shaft of the penis is covered by a loose skin which is continuous with that of the scrotum. This looseness of the skin allows free movement and full erection when the penis elongates and enlarges as it becomes engorged with blood. Near the tip end of the penis, the skin is no longer attached to the organ directly, but encompasses the glans, usually hanging loosely. This fold of skin, which covers the glans but may be pulled back from it, is known as the *prepuce* or *foreskin.* It is attached to the glans on the glans' lower surface by a thin midline tissue called the *frenum.* For hygienic, functional, and, in certain instances, religious reasons a portion of the prepuce covering the glans is frequently removed surgically in a procedure known as *circumcision,* usually just after birth while the infant is still in the hospital.

Just behind the glans, under the corona and on each side of the frenum, are the *Tyson's glands.* They are modified sebaceous (suet-oily) glands, the secretions of which, together with cells shed from the glans and corona, form a smelly, cheeselike substance known as *smegma.* If the prepuce is tight over the glans, smegma may collect and emit a foul odor, and may act as a breeding ground for irritants and disease. Prevention of this condition is one of the main purposes of circumcision, although research showing an inverse relationship between circumcision and penile cancer makes circumcision even more important. In an investigation of the cases of penile cancer at one general hospital, the Catholics and Protestants, who comprised 67% of the hospital's patients, had 94% of the cases, whereas the Jewish 30% of the admissions had only 3% (Licklider). This study tends to support the belief that circumcision prevents accumulation of smegma, which apparently encourages penile cancer. (Penile cancer will be discussed further in Chapter 20.)

A surprisingly persistent myth in human sexuality is that of *penis captivus*—that humans can get "hung up" in sexual intercourse. This notion quite likely results from man's observing the behavior of animals and attributing the same possibility to himself. Dogs do get "hung up" because of the peculiar anatomical structure of the male dog's sexual organs. There is a bone in the animal's penis (*os penis*) that enables him to penetrate the bitch's vagina before full erection. With ensuing tumescence, the head of the penis fills the vaginal barrel and at the same time the walls of the bitch's vagina swell, all of which serves to "trap" the penis and prevent its withdrawal before ejaculation (Dengrove).

Most people have heard stories of couples who became locked together while copulating, the services of a physician being required before the penis could be released. The story is characteristically told as the truth

FIGURE 6.5 Representation of the penis, showing a collection of smegma.

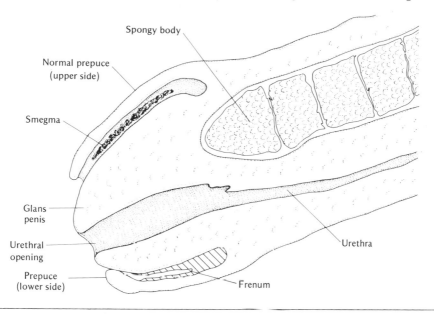

and as having happened to a friend (or to a friend of a friend), although no one has ever witnessed the phenomenon or experienced It. It is, of course, theoretically possible for a woman to experience sudden strong muscle spasms of the vagina (*vaginismus*) during sexual intercourse, and the vagina may momentarily tighten around her partner's penis. But even in these circumstances, the pain or fear the man would experience would cause loss of erection, permitting easy withdrawal of the penis. There are no scientifically verified cases of *penis captivus* among humans in modern medical literature (Dengrove).

MALE SEXUAL FUNCTIONING

Delivery of mature male germ cells into the female vagina is typically the culmination of three male functions: spermatogenesis—the process of sperm formation; erection of the penis to permit penetration of the vagina; and ejaculation—the expulsion of the male semen.

Spermatogenesis

The germinal tissue of the seminiferous tubules contains two types of cells: the *spermatogenic* cells, which eventually produce the mature sperm; and the *sustentacular* cells (cells of Sertoli), which nurture the sperm at various stages of development. The space between the tubules is filled with interstitial tissue that, when stimulated by the luteinizing hormone of the pituitary gland, produces the male sex hormone testosterone.

As a male matures, the seminiferous tubules come to contain at the inner periphery of each tubule an increasing number of cells known as *primitive spermatogonia*; these constitute the first stage of spermatogenesis. *Mitosis* (ordinary cell division) of the spermatogonia begins when a boy is

FIGURE 6.6 Representation of the human testis with seminiferous tubules, showing various stages of spermatogenesis. Interstitial cells, where male sex hormones are produced, are also shown.

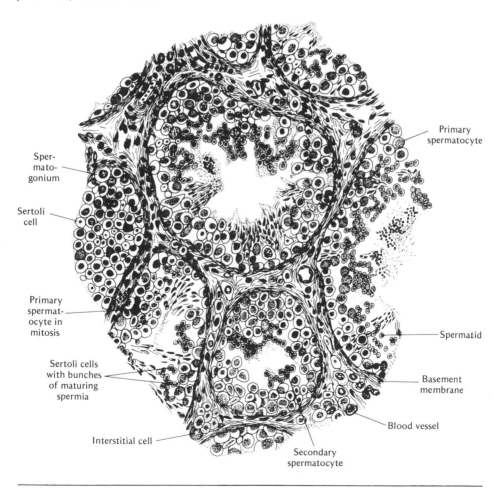

about 11—although the age varies considerably, as can be judged by the different times at which individual puberty is reached.

Through the unique process of mitosis, each spermatogonium divides and produces two daughter cells, both containing the full component of 46 chromosomes. One is another spermatogonium, which remains at the periphery of the tubule ready to split again, thus perpetuating formation of future spermatogonia. The other is a *primary spermatocyte*, which constitutes the next stage of spermatogenesis. The primary spermatocyte is a large cell that moves toward the center opening (or *lumen*) of the tubule. It undergoes meiotic cell division (*meiosis* or *reduction division*), producing two smaller *secondary spermatocytes*. In reduction division—primary spermatocyte to two secondary spermatocytes—the number of chromosomes in each cell is reduced to 23: 22 similar (*autosomal*) chromosomes plus an X chromosome in one secondary spermatocyte, and 22 similar chromosomes plus a Y in the other. X and Y sperm are thus produced in equal numbers.

These secondary spermatocytes immediately cleave or split by mitotic division into the last primitive germinal cells, the *spermatids,* the process of division progressing as the cells move from the periphery to the lumen. Spermatids begin to appear when a boy is approximately 12 (the lack of ICSH hormones until this time prohibiting development beyond the secondary spermatocyte cell), and the testes grow rapidly as a result of marked enlargement of the tubules. The intensity of the germinal activity increases as a boy advances to his mid-teens.

FIGURE 6.7   Schematic representation of a seminiferous tubule, showing the process of spermatogenesis.

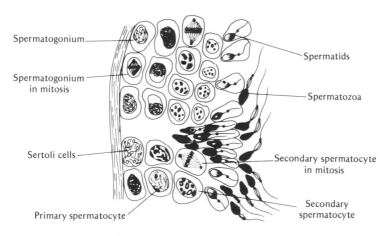

Spermatogonium

Spermatogonium in mitosis

Sertoli cells

Primary spermatocyte

Spermatids

Spermatozoa

Secondary spermatocyte in mitosis

Secondary spermatocyte

FIGURE 6.8 Microscopic view of sperm, showing the difference between X-bearing sperm (with larger, oval-shaped head) and Y-bearing sperm (with smaller head, longer tail). Photograph courtesy Dr. Landrum B. Shettles.

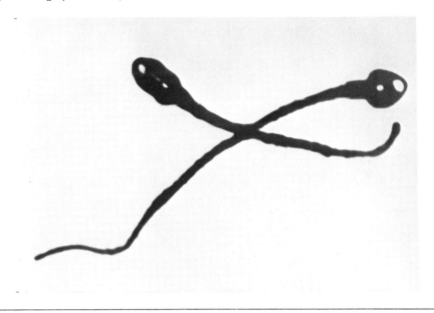

About the age of 16, full spermatogenesis is usually attained. Spermatids grow, develop, and rearrange their component parts, then finally mature into *spermatozoa*, the fully formed male sperm. For complete spermatogenesis to occur, the testes must be maintained at a temperature not exceeding 38° to 39°C (Weaver). The total process of spermatogenesis, from spermatogonium to mature spermatozoa, takes about 10 days; it is a continuing and constant process in the normal healthy adult male.

In very recent years noticeable differences between the X (female) and the Y (male) sperm have been discovered. The Y sperm has a small round-headed body with a long tail, while the X sperm has a large oval-shaped body and a short tail. Landrum B. Shettles of Columbia University—a leading scientist in this important area of research—believes that, by use of this and other information, the sex of a child can be removed from the realm of mere chance and can be predetermined by controlling the time of sexual intercourse (Shettles a, b, c). (Shettles supports his theory by research findings, although it should be noted that there is hesitancy on the part of some scientists to accept the reported differences between X and Y sperm.)

Ordinarily each ejaculation contains millions of both X and Y sperm, although the sperm count per ejaculate tends to diminish as frequency of intercourse increases. The higher the sperm count is, the greater the proportion of the male sperm; conversely, the lower the sperm count, the greater the proportion of female sperm.

It is reasonable to assume that the smaller-headed, longer-tailed Y sperm would move from vagina to ovum at a faster rate than X sperm do. It is also reasonable to assume that the larger-headed, heavier female sperm is stronger and will live longer—or will at least maintain its vigor longer—than the male sperm. The first healthy sperm penetrating the ovum (usually in the fallopian tube) fertilizes it and fixes the sex of the child.

For a couple wishing a boy, Shettles suggests that a preliminary alkaline douche be taken by the wife (two tablespoons of baking soda in a quart of water), that there be as deep penetration as possible at the time of ejaculation, that the woman experience an orgasm during the sex act, and that the couple abstain from intercourse until just *after* the time the wife expects to ovulate. The alkaline douche neutralizes the acid environment of the vagina, thus lessening the threat to the sperm. The deep penetration shortens the vaginal journey, which is hazardous to the male sperm. The woman's mucous secretion at the time of her orgasm is alkaline and therefore more favorable for male-producing sperm migration than for female-producing sperm. Abstinence appears to increase the proportion of male sperm, for one reason or another; also, timing intercourse to follow ovulation allows the lighter, faster-moving male-producing sperm a better chance to reach the waiting egg first.

For a couple wishing a girl, Shettles suggests that a preliminary acid douche be taken (two tablespoons of vinegar to a quart of water), that there should be shallow penetration at the time of ejaculation, and that the woman should not experience orgasm at the time of the sex act. There should be no abstinence from intercourse; however, intercourse should take place two or three days before ovulation is expected *and then cease*, so that the weaker male sperm will die off before the egg arrives on the scene (Shettles c).

For some reason that is not clear, artificial insemination results in a marked preponderance of males. When the semen to be used in the artificial insemination is allowed to stand in a container for a time before being injected into the uterus, the heavier (by about 4%) X (female) sperm settle to the bottom of the container, whereas the lighter Y (male) sperm rise to the top. Samples of the top third of such a collection of semen reveal an approximate 80% Y content, whereas the lower third contains about 80% X sperm. The middle third contains roughly equal amounts of male and female sperm (Kleegman b).

Since X and Y sperm are produced in equal numbers, there is speculation as to why the conception ratio of males to females is, curiously, about 160 to 100 (Shettles b). The implantation ratio of male to female zygotes (newly fertilized ova) has been estimated at about 120 to 100, and the birth rate of boy to girl infants is approximately 105 to 100.

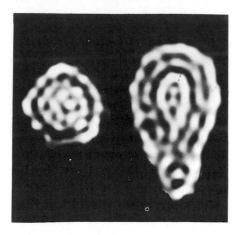

FIGURE 6.9 Microscopic view of sperm, showing chromosomal arrangements of Y (male) sperm, left; and of X (female) sperm, right. (Original magnification X 1000). Photograph courtesy Dr. Landrum B. Shettles.

There is substantial evidence that human sperm may live under ideal conditions for as long as 14 days after ejaculation. It is questionable how long they can live in the female genital tract, however. Researchers generally agree that the fertilizing capability of sperm lasts for only one or two days (Steen and Montagu).

Erection

Although the penis is ordinarily erect at the time of ejaculation, it is not necessary for it to be so. However, the penis must be at least partially erect if it is to penetrate the vagina and thus be capable of impregnating. Of course, a woman can become pregnant without penetration—e.g., through artificial insemination—but in the present discussion only the usual method of impregnation is implied.

Erection of the penis, which is controlled by nerves in the spinal cord at the lower end of the central nervous system, involves the synchronization of several reactions. These reactions are activated by several forces working separately or together: friction at the surface of the penis and/or surrounding areas, which sends impulses to a special (*sacral*) area of the spinal cord; sexual thoughts, dreams, erotic odors, etc., causing impulses to be sent to the spinal area from the brain; stimulation of the sexual system by sex hormones in the bloodstream; and impulses from full ejaculatory ducts.

Dilation of the arteries that feed blood to the penis results in engorgement of the spongy tissue (corpora cavernosa). This dilation is followed or accompanied by a simultaneous tonic (contractile) spasm of the muscles at

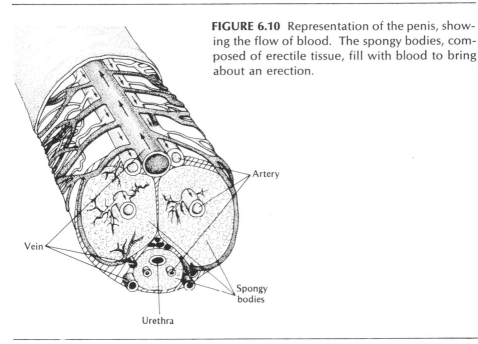

FIGURE 6.10 Representation of the penis, showing the flow of blood. The spongy bodies, composed of erectile tissue, fill with blood to bring about an erection.

the base of the penis near the anus, the spasm preventing the blood from escaping from the spongy tissue through the veins. These reactions are brought into play by inhibition of the vasoconstrictor centers of the sympathetic nervous system (located at lumbar spinal nerves 1-2), and by the excitement of the vasodilator centers of the parasympathetic system (located in sacral spinal nerves portion 1-3). The spinal centers just mentioned, although operating primarily on a reflex arc system, are in communication with the cortical, subcortical, and medulla oblongata portions of the brain.

Some men who have had the connection severed between the erection centers of the lower spine and the brain nevertheless continue to experience the erection and/or ejaculatory reflex. (Current research; Money a). The action of the brain would consequently appear to serve as a modification or control of the spinal reflex center, rather than as the most essential factor in producing erections. For example, when mild electrical stimulation was applied to experimental animals at the lower spinal cord and/or to the nerves passing between the lower spinal cord and the arteries of the penis, penile erections and ejaculations were produced (Stiller *b*).

So long as there is proper and sufficient stimulation from the nerve endings of the penis, and proper and sufficient impulses from the brain, a man will maintain his erection. It should be recognized that inappropriate impulses—e.g., such severe stimulation of the penis that excessive pain results, or a disturbed emotional state, such as fear, anger, guilt, anxiety, or shame—can cause an erection to collapse or can prevent its occurring in the first place.

Emotional difficulties are the most frequent cause of loss of erection, and of impotence as well. It is understandable that a man who fails to have a satisfying erection, then worries over his "failure" and about his abilities the next time he attempts intercourse, may be establishing a vicious circle of failure in his sexual behavior. (Methods of dealing with these problems will be discussed in Chapter 18, Sexual Inadequacies.)

Ejaculation

Ordinarily, erection sets the stage for ejaculation. The stimulation of the glans of the penis, the presence of sex hormones in the blood, impulses from taut seminal vesicles and ejaculatory ducts, nerve responses from erotic odors, sexual thoughts: all these messages stimulate the brain to bring about and maintain an erection, as well as to build up impulses in the ejaculatory center of the lower spinal cord. Nerve impulses from the male genitals are carried by the dorsal nerves of the penis to the pudendal nerves and enter the ejaculatory center via posterior penile roots (involving sacral spinal nerves 3-4). These impulses then travel to the section of the lower spine (lumbar spinal nerves 1-2) where, along with stimulation from the other areas mentioned, they build up to a threshold at which there is a sudden triggering of the process called ejaculation.

There is, first, a peristalsis of the ampulla of the vas deferens, the seminal vesicles, and the ejaculatory ducts, which moves the ejaculatory fluid containing the sperm to the membranaceous part of the urethral tract. Secondly, there is an accompanying clonic (alternation of contraction and relaxation) spasm in the urogenital floor muscles, which discharges the semen by spurting it through and out the penis. This physical reaction is accompanied by a distinct and highly pleasurable sensation known as *orgasm*, to which a later chapter of this book is devoted.

The strength of the ejaculatory force varies from man to man. Some men ejaculate with such force that the discharged semen may travel three feet or more beyond the penile meatus, while the semen of others may travel only a few inches, or simply ooze out the urethra. The strength of the force usually depends upon such factors as general health, age, degree of sexual stimulation, and the condition of the prostate. Most men report that semen is ejaculated with little force, although they sometimes tend to correlate the subjective pleasures of orgasm with the force of ejaculation.

It is perhaps coincidental that ejaculation and orgasm occur together. Ejaculation can occur in paraplegics, for example, if the spinal lesion is high enough not to have damaged the nerve area directly responsible for emission. But the paraplegic's ejaculation is unaccompanied by the subjective sensation of orgasm. Studies show that about 65% of paraplegics are capable of complete erections and another 20%, of partial erections; about 30% of the latter are able to have successful intercourse. Despite ejaculation, however, the fertility rate of these men is extremely low, because the spinal lesion in some manner impairs or destroys spermatogenic function. Paraplegic men may have dreams of vivid orgasmic imagery despite their total inability to experience the sensation of orgasm while awake (Money *a, i*).

The neuromuscular sensation of orgasm is the result of impulses from the triggered area of the lower spinal cord reaching the brain. Both erection and ejaculation may occur without any physical stimulation. The prime example is nocturnal emissions, which are the result primarily, if not exclusively, of erotic dreams. The dreams may have been preceded by prolonged abstinence, but in many instances they occur to sexually active people who, despite orgasmic recency, may become so aroused by some new erotic stimuli that they seek another orgasm through coitus or masturbation, or experience one during sleep. Such nocturnal response can occur night after night, especially among better educated young men, who appear more responsive than others to erotic stimuli of psychological etiology (Answers to questions). Furthermore, both men and women have been known to have orgasms from erotic thoughts alone or from stimulation of nongenital areas, such as the lips and breasts (Masters and Johnson *n*).

Stimulation of the nerves of the ejaculatory center to the threshold of response does more than initiate ejaculation. Ejaculation itself causes the previously dilated arteries to narrow, so that less blood flows to the penis than is drained off through the veins. The penis is thus returned to its flaccid state shortly after ejaculation.

7 THE FEMALE SEXUAL SYSTEM

THE FEMALE GENITALIA

The internal female genital organs consist of two ovaries, two uterine or fallopian tubes, the uterus (or womb), and the vagina.

The *ovaries*, which produce *ova* or eggs, are homologous to the testes of the male. They manufacture hormones that activate a woman's sexual desire, and that prepare and maintain the uterus for implantation of the fertilized ovum. Located on either side of the uterus in a recessed area of the lateral pelvic wall (*ovarian fossa*), the ovaries are held in a somewhat vertical position in an erect woman by the mesovarium and ovarian ligaments, which connect the ovaries to the uterus, and a suspensory ligament connecting to the abdominal wall. A pinkish grey body, each ovary is roughly the size, shape, and weight of an unshelled almond.

In each ovary of a newborn girl are some 200,000 to 400,000 follicles (Lloyd), each housing an *oocyte* (an ovum in an early stage of development). This number decreases possibly to 10,000 by puberty. In the physically mature female, one follicle ordinarily ripens into an ovum each month, usually midway through the menstrual cycle, although the time element varies. Since the average woman is fertile for approximately 35 years and ovulates about 13 times every year, it can be seen that only

400 to 500 of the many thousands of undeveloped ova are discharged. At birth, each immature follicle of the ovaries consists of an oocyte surrounded by epithelial cells. With the body's growth, development, and subsequent hormonal secretions, some of the oocytes commence to ripen into mature ova, marking the beginning of puberty.

If one were to examine the internal structure of a typical ovary, there would be found a number of round vesicles called *follicles,* each containing an ovum in one of several stages of development. Lying just beneath the ovary's cortex (outer layer), the follicles may be either *primordial* (not yet growing) or *graafian* (approaching the time when a mature ovum will erupt and be discharged). During the period when the follicles are very immature until the time that they reach full development, they sink deeply toward the center (medulla) of the ovary, where they grow and mature. The medulla consists of layers of soft tissue (stroma), which is abundantly supplied with blood vessels.

As the follicles grow, several layers separated by clear membrane

FIGURE 7.1 Schematic representation of the female pelvic region, showing organs of reproduction.

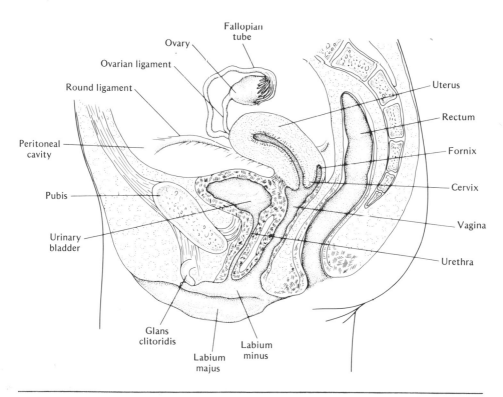

form around the ovum, creating tiny spaces between follicular cells. These tiny spaces eventually coalesce to form one larger space (*antrum*). The graafian follicle reaches a diameter of 12 to 15 mm and often occupies at least one-fourth of the entire volume of the ovary. The rapid increase in follicular fluid and size exerts pressure, which ruptures the wall of the ovary, discharging the ovum from the follicular cavity in a wave of fluid.

In most cases, and in a manner that is still not clearly understood, the liberated ovum is deposited in the uterine tube on the same side of the woman's body. There are exceptions to this process, as there are with most biological phenomena, in that ova have been known to enter the uterine tube on the opposite side. Just how these journeys through the peritoneal cavity come about is something of a mystery.

After the ovum is discharged from the ovary, the lining of the empty follicle grows inward and the vacated space is filled with *corpus luteum*. This new cell growth produces *progesterone*, the hormone that inhibits ovulation during pregnancy, aids in the implantation and maintenance of the embryo, and stimulates the mammary glands. Ovulation is generally assumed to occur alternately in each ovary, but one ovary may in fact discharge several times in succession. A single egg is usually released at the time of ovulation, but two or more ova from one or more follicles may be discharged.

In recent years the use of fertility drugs has enabled many women who were previously unable to ovulate to become fertile and have babies. Some of the drugs, however, cause several ova to mature and be discharged

---

FIGURE 7.2. Schematic representation of the ovary, showing developing follicles, a mature follicle, and the corpus luteum.

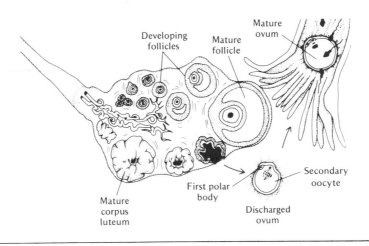

during the same ovulation period, resulting in a marked rise in the incidence of multiple births in many nations. In recent months there have been verified reports of exceptionally large multiple births, ranging in number from 7 children on several occasions, one delivery of 8, one of 9, and one record delivery of 15 babies (*Houston Post*; Nonatuplets in Pakistan; Sex in the news c). In very large multiple births, the death rate is exceptionally high.

Women not taking fertility drugs may ovulate more than once a month under normal circumstances. An additional egg is especially likely to be discharged during a peak of sexual excitation, even during menstruation, perhaps explaining the high incidence of impregnation during the so-called "safe" period—the time of the menstrual month at which conception is considered least likely to occur (Neubardt).

One of the *uterine* or *fallopian tubes* (after Gabriello Fallopius, 1523–1562) conveys the egg from the ovary to the uterus, and is also the place where fertilization of the ovum normally occurs. Each of the uterine tubes is about 4 inches long and is suspended by a ligament, allowing each tube to extend from the upper and outer part of its side of the uterus to the ovary. The flanged part of the tube connects to the ovary and slightly cups over it.

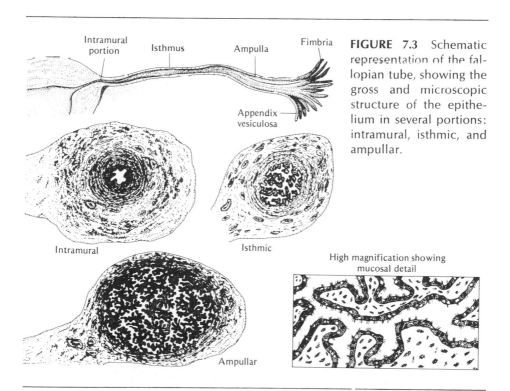

FIGURE 7.3 Schematic representation of the fallopian tube, showing the gross and microscopic structure of the epithelium in several portions: intramural, isthmic, and ampullar.

The fallopian or uterine tubes are musculomembranous structures that are usually divided into three sections: the intramural portion, the isthmus, and the ampulla. The *intramural portion* is included within the wall of the uterus. The *isthmus* is the narrow portion of the tube adjoining the uterus. It broadens into the *ampulla* just before it opens into the uterine cavity. The end (*infundibulum*) of the tube has small fingerlike extensions (*fimbria*), one of which extends to the ovary.

The uterine tubes are well supplied with blood from the vessels of the ovaries and the uterus, and have many miniscule hairlike protrusions (cilia) extending inward from the tubal walls. These cilia act in an undulating manner to sweep an ovum from the ampulla, where fertilization generally occurs, toward the uterus.

The *uterus* or *womb* is a hollow, thick-walled muscular organ shaped somewhat like a pear. In a mature woman, its size at the top measures approximately 2.5 by 2 inches. It narrows to a diameter of about 1 inch at the *cervix* (neck) and is about 3 inches long. Situated in the pelvic cavity between the bladder and rectum, it hangs slightly below and between the fallopian tubes, as if suspended from them like a garment on a clothesline.

The uterus is held in position by six ligaments: two broad ones extending from the uterus to the floor and wall of the pelvis; two round ones connecting the uterus near the openings of the fallopian tubes laterally to the pelvic walls; and the last two, the uterosacral ligaments, extending from the upper part of the cervix to the sacrum (the bone at the base of the vertebral column). When a woman stands erect with bladder and rectum empty, the uterus lies almost horizontal, with its *fundus* (upper end) forward, at a right angle to the vagina.

The uterus is divided into two parts by its *isthmus*, a slight constriction near the center (to be distinguished from the isthmus of the fallopian tubes). The larger portion—the *corpus* (body)—of the uterus lies above the second part, the *cervix*, which opens into the rear of the vagina. The opening of the cervix into the vagina is known as the *external os*, and its opening into the corpus is known as the *internal os*.

The walls of the uterus are particularly thick at the fundus, where the measurement may be 1.5 cm or more. The uterine walls are made up of three layers: the *perimetrium* (the outer layer or serosa), which consists of elastic fibrous tissue; the *myometrium* (the middle or muscular layer), which makes up most of the uterine wall, and which consists of bundles and layers of very strong smooth muscle cells; and the *endometrium* (the inner or mucosa layer), consisting of tissue that thickens as the uterus prepares for implantation of a fertilized ovum, but that sloughs off, if no pregnancy occurs, at the time of menstruation.

Uterine musculature is complex and highly efficient. The muscle bundles combine the uterus and its tubes and ligaments into an interlacing system that produces certain contractions during the period just before

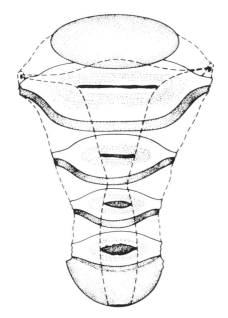

FIGURE 7.4 Representation of the uterus, showing the shape of its cavity and the cervical canal.

ovulation when estrogen production is at its peak. It is thought that these coordinated contractions in some way move the flanged openings of the fallopian tubes into the proper position to receive the ovum when it is discharged.

The uterine walls contain longitudinal and circular muscle fibers that spiral and run through the walls in both clockwise and counterclockwise directions. The basketlike interweaving of the muscles allows the uterus both to stretch to gigantic proportions during pregnancy, and to exert tremendous pressure by contracting in a downward manner at the time of labor. Contraction of these muscles also takes place at the time of a woman's orgasmic phase in her sexual response cycle (Masters and Johnson d).

The premise is an old one that the uterus acts in such a manner during orgasm as to "suck up" seminal fluid from the vagina through the cervix into its cavity, thus aiding in the migration of sperm. Masters and Johnson (n) have cast serious doubt on this theory because of certain reactions of the uterus, clinically recorded by them, during orgasm. They established that the uterus does indeed contract several times in orgasm, the number of contractions depending upon the intensity of the response. They observed, however, that the flow of the contractions is from the top of the uterus toward the cervix. The contractions would therefore be quite similar

FIGURE 7.5 Schematic representation of the normal uterus (front view) and append-ages, showing the comparative size of infantile, adult nonparous, and multiparous uteri. A side view of the multiparous uterus is also shown.

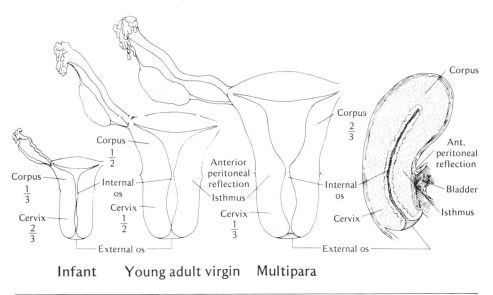

Infant   Young adult virgin   Multipara

to those of the first stage of labor and would therefore tend to expel, rather than to draw up, any matter at the uterine opening.

The cavity of the uterus is a flattened space that is little more than a slit, its total length being about 2.5 inches. The flattened cavity narrows to a minute opening at the internal os, and continues through the cervix as an opening smaller than a soda straw.

The cervix is smaller than the body of the uterus; the size ratio in mature women is about one to two. In the newborn the ratio is reversed, the cervix being about twice as large as the corpus. In young children, the ratio is about one to one. Physicians often describe women as having an infantile uterus when the corpus and the cervix are nearly the same size; such women are frequently incapable of bearing children. The body of the uterus grows proportionately larger because of hormonal secretions that commence at puberty, while the growth of the cervix merely keeps pace with the growth rate of the rest of the body.

The cervix is more fibrous than the corpus of the uterus, and its pal-mate (foldlike) lining contains glands that produce a mucous secretion, once erroneously thought to attract sperm cells (Masters and Johnson *n*). About 0.3 to 0.5 inch of the cervix extends into the vagina, thus producing a connection for the passage of sperm into the place where they may meet the ovum. During pregnancy, the cervix is often closed by a mucous plug that serves to separate the uterus from the vagina, keeping bacteria and other undesirable matter from entering the uterus and thereby reducing the possibility of infection.

The *vagina* is a muscular tube, capable of considerable dilation, which extends from just behind the cervix to an external opening in the vestibule of the vulva. About 3 inches long on the anterior or front wall, and about 3.5 inches on the posterior or back wall, the vagina extends upwards in an approximately vertical manner in a standing woman, roughly at right angles to the uterus. It is the organ that receives the penis during the act of sexual intercourse.

The walls of the vagina are in contact with each other under ordinary conditions, and are made up of three layers: (1) the *fibrous coat*, a thin layer of elastic fibrous tissue, which serves not only as an aid to contraction but also as a connective tissue to other bodily tissues; (2) the *muscular coat*, a layer of smooth muscles that run primarily in a longitudinal direction, although there are also bundles of circular muscular fibers in the vaginal canal (e.g., the sphincter muscle of striated fiber surrounding the external vaginal opening); and (3) the *mucosa*, which houses mucous crypts and many blood vessels. The mucosa's large folds give the vagina its wrinkled appearance. The entire area contains an intricate network of erectile tissue that serves to help dilate and close the vaginal canal (see Chapter 13).

The mucosal coat of the vagina contains no glands, as such, although mucous secretions of the uterine tissue sometimes aid in moistening the vagina. Vaginal lubrication, present during sexual excitement, is brought about by the vagina itself. It secretes a fluid through a process similar to sweating that remains something of a puzzle (Masters and Johnson *n*).

As sexual excitement builds and continues, small beads of "sweat" appear on the vaginal surface. Often the vaginal muscles contract suddenly, bringing the walls of the vagina together in such a way as to force the secretion out of the vagina in a spurting fashion. This secretion, along with the orgasmic platform contractions (see Chapter 13), is the foundation of the mistaken notion that women ejaculate as men do. However, the "sweat" merely serves as a lubricant to aid in penile penetration, making coitus easier to perform.

With the birth of children and the natural relaxation of muscles as a woman gets older, the vaginal muscles, no longer firm or strong, often sag. The result may be a vagina that is too large to allow for the partners' fullest coital satisfaction. This condition is especially bothersome for a man who depends largely upon friction of the vaginal wall against the glans of his penis to stimulate his erogenous nerve endings and to supply the sexual impulses that culminate in an orgasm. Similarly, the condition can also be annoying to a woman who receives little or no physiological pleasure from penile penetration—the vagina contains very few nerve endings that give

sexual pleasure—but who gains some psychological pleasure from penetration.

(Many women claim a sex act is incomplete and unsatisfying to them
without penetration. Empirical findings nevertheless indicate that, physically
speaking, an orgasm is an orgasm, whether attained by penetration, manual
manipulation of the genital area, or by some other technique [Ellis *b, j;*
Masters and Johnson *n*]. Any increase in pleasure from penetration would
therefore appear to be the result of psychological or emotional factors.)

A woman with overly relaxed vaginal muscles can strengthen them
by proper exercise (Clark *f*). She is advised to contract the vaginal muscles
as she would the urethral sphincter to halt urination midway. A series of
20 or so alternating contractions and relaxations should be repeated about
10 times a day. After a month of these exercises, a difference in the size
of the vagina will probably be noticeable. The exercises are not necessarily
time-consuming and can be done while the woman is busy with her daily
activities.

Scientific investigations of hundreds of women who performed such
exercises revealed that many of them subsequently experienced heightened
sexual responsiveness and satisfaction. These observations have caused
some researchers to conclude that the proprioceptive nerve endings in the
vaginal muscles, which are stimulated by the penis during coitus, possibly
account for the concept of "vaginal orgasm" (Clark *a;* Kegel).

Formerly, relaxed vaginas were made smaller or tighter by surgical
means. Such surgery is still performed, but only in extreme cases in which
muscle damage is severe or other physiological difficulties exist.

The *hymen* or maidenhead is the fold of connective tissue that partially closes the external orifice of the vagina. This tissue, if still intact, is
usually ruptured by the first act of sexual intercourse. More often, however,
the tissue is broken by accidents to the pubic area or by experimentation.
A ruptured hymen is certainly not *prima facie* evidence that a girl is not a
virgin. On the other hand, rare cases exist in which the hymen is so flexible
or pliable that coitus can take place repeatedly without rupturing the tissue.
The importance of an intact hymen to some women at the time of marriage
is attested to by the fact that a Japanese gynecologist not long ago performed for the ten-thousandth time a surgical operation creating an artificial hymen for a prospective bride (Sex in the news *a*).

If a woman approaches marriage with the hymen still intact, it is common practice for her physician to cut the tissue after applying a mild
anesthetic to the area. In the case of a ring-shaped (annular) hymen, the
doctor may suggest inserting and rotating the fingertips or using a small
dilator, either of which will stretch the tissue and permit penile penetration
without pain or difficulty. Obviously, the hymenal tissue usually does not
seal or close off the vagina completely, since the menstrual flow is dis-

charged as easily from virgins as from nonvirgins. The tissue is usually annular or perforated, or in some other way only partially obstructs the opening.

Pain accompanying first sexual intercourse—frequently assumed to be a cause of frigidity—is typically the result of the hymen's being ruptured. If the hymen has not been previously ruptured, it is foolish to allow the tissue to be torn by forceful penile penetration when a physician can cut or remove it beforehand.

In addition to the pain of tearing the hymenal tissue, there is often pain during early, and especially first, sexual intercourse because of powerful contractions of the vaginal muscles—usually the result of fear and ignorance of the facts of coitus. If a woman is relaxed and unafraid, there is little reason why she cannot comfortably and pleasurably accommodate a very large penis, even though she has never before had sexual intercourse. Women under emotional stress, however, even though they might be highly experienced sexually, can experience these vaginal muscle spasms (a condition known as *vaginismus,* discussed in Chapter 20), making forced penetration extremely painful or even impossible.

The Vulva

The external genital apparatus of a woman, known as the *vulva,* consists of the following visible parts or areas: the mons veneris (also called mons pubis), the labia majora (major or large outer lips), the labia minora (small inner lips), the clitoris, and the vestibule.

The *mons veneris* or *mons pubis* is composed of pads of fatty tissue lying below the skin over the pubic bone (*symphysis pubis*). It is covered with springy, curly hair. This area houses certain nerve endings that when stimulated by weight, pressure, or similar conditions can produce sexual excitement. From this prominent mound, two longitudinal folds of skin bearing pubic hair serve laterally to form the outer borders of the vulva.

The *labia majora* are the two folds of skin described above that enclose the vulval cleft. The lips are quite fatty; their inner sides contain sebaceous follicles and sweat glands but no hair.

The *labia minora* are also two longitudinal folds and are located within the major lips. Rich in blood vessels, nerve endings, and small sebaceous glands, they contain no hair or fat cells. These small lips form the lateral and lower borders of the vestibule; they fuse at the top to form the prepuce and to enclose the clitoris.

The labia minora are highly erogenous and are markedly sensitive to stimulation. Although they contain no erectile tissue of the usual type, the area does change its structure somewhat during sexual excitement, apparently through some manner of trapping blood. Under the influence

FIGURE 7.6 External female genitalia with four types of hymens. © Copyright 1954 and 1965 CIBA Pharmaceutical Company, Division of CIBA–GEIGY Corporation. Reproduced with permission from THE CIBA COLLECTION OF MEDICAL ILLUSTRATIONS by Frank H. Netter, M.D. All rights reserved.

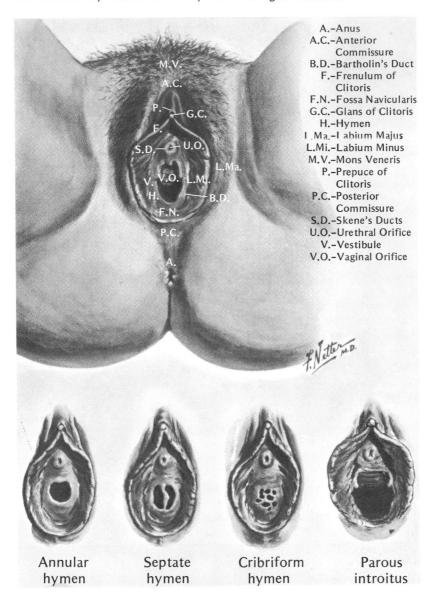

A.–Anus
A.C.–Anterior
   Commissure
B.D.–Bartholin's Duct
F.–Frenulum of
   Clitoris
F.N.–Fossa Navicularis
G.C.–Glans of Clitoris
H.–Hymen
L.Ma.–Labium Majus
L.Mi.–Labium Minus
M.V.–Mons Veneris
P.–Prepuce of
   Clitoris
P.C.–Posterior
   Commissure
S.D.–Skene's Ducts
U.O.–Urethral Orifice
V.–Vestibule
V.O.–Vaginal Orifice

Annular hymen   Septate hymen   Cribriform hymen   Parous introitus of such stimulation they flare out, exposing the vestibule, whereas under ordinary circumstances the lips are together, more or less sealing off the inner region.

The *clitoris* is a small cylindrical erectile structure situated at the top of the vestibule and at the lower border of the symphysis pubis. It consists of two *crura* (leglike stalks) arising at the pubic bone and fusing together to form the body or shaft, terminating in the *glans*, which projects between the bifurcated branches of the labia minora. The entire clitoris, except the glans, is underneath the upper part of the labia minora where its two lips join to form the clitoral prepuce or *frenulum clitoridis*.

The body of the clitoris can be felt just beneath the prepuce that covers it. Unlike the penis, the clitoris does not hang free; only its glans is exposed. It contains two corpora cavernosa (spongy erectile structures), which are enclosed by a dense fibrous tissue. With stimulation, these bodies may engorge with blood and become erect. The clitoris is ordinarily less than 1 inch in length (although striking variations in its measurements are on record). When sexually stimulated it may enlarge considerably—to twice its flaccid size or more—especially the diameter of its shaft.

The glans of the clitoris has a diameter of about 4 to 5 mm (Dickinson). Like the glans of the penis, it contains an abundance of nerve endings and is the most sexually excitable area of a woman's body. Direct contact with the glans—such as the man's pubic bone rubbing against it—and indirect stimulation through pulling and tugging of the area as the minor lips move in and out of the vagina, are coital methods of bringing a woman to orgasm. Masters and Johnson (*n*) have pointed out that, in self-manipulation of the clitoris, women stimulate to the side of it—usually the right side if they are right-handed, and conversely—rather than stimulating it directly.

It is possible to remove the clitoris completely without destroying a woman's erotic sensations, pleasure, or, even, her orgasmic capability. The nerve supply to the vulval area is so great that large amounts of erogenous tissue may be removed without significantly decreasing sexual gratification. It appears, therefore, that frequency and intensity of sexual activity, including orgasm, are related less to anatomical size or the amount of tissue than to other factors, including psychological ones (Money *h*).

Smegma, an accumulation of genital secretions, can collect under the prepuce covering the clitoris, resulting in abrasions and adhesions between it and the glans. This causes severe pain in many cases when the clitoris enlarges during sexual excitement. Circumcision was a former remedy, but in present-day practice a probe is frequently used in order to separate the prepuce from the glans and to rid the area of the smelly ragged lumps that produce the pain. Obviously it is difficult to enjoy sexual activity if this sort of pain accompanies it.

The *vestibule* is the cleft region enclosed by the labia minora. It houses the openings of the vagina and the urethra. This area also is rich in nerve endings and blood vessels, and is highly responsive to proper stimulation. The urethral opening or meatus is located about halfway between the clitoris and the vagina and is, of course, the opening of the tube through which urine passes from the bladder to outside the body. The greater vestibular glands, the *Bartholin's glands*, are situated on each side of the vaginal orifice. Each secretes a drop or so of lubricating fluid during sexual excitement. Although this fluid was once thought to aid in penile penetration, recent research has shown that the secretion is too slight to be of significant benefit in vaginal lubrication (Masters and Johnson *n*).

OOGENESIS

Oogenesis, the development of ova, corresponds to the male function of spermatogenesis. (A full discussion of other female sexual functions, including menstruation and the climacteric, fertilization, prenatal development, and birth, follows in Chapters 8 and 9.)

Although smaller than the period at the end of this sentence, the human ovum is a relatively large cell. It averages 0.13 mm in diameter and 0.000004 gm in weight, and is one of the largest of mammalian eggs (Eastman and Hellman). The development of ova has already been partially described in this chapter. The position taken in that discussion is the most widely accepted theory concerning the origin of human ova, namely (1) that ova grow within follicles which are present in the very early development of the ovaries' germinal epithelium; and (2) that they are present at the time of a girl's birth, but lie dormant until her sexual maturity, at which time they develop and become mature in a limited number, usually one by one. A second theory concerning the origin of ova is that they are not present at birth, but that they arise, fully developed, from the cells of the germinal epithelium as they are needed in the sexually mature female.

Oogenesis consists of four developmental stages: *oogonium, primary oocyte, secondary oocyte,* and *mature ovum.* In the first phase of development, the *oogonium,* or basic cell of the ovum, is enclosed in an ovarian follicle. It then develops into a *primary oocyte,* which is somewhat larger than the original cell. Just prior to ovulation, the primary oocyte undergoes a process known as *reduction division,* or *meiosis.* The paired chromosomes within the oocyte divide, with one of each pair going to each of the two daughter cells created by the division. The number of chromosomes in each daughter cell is therefore 23 rather than the usual 46.

Although each daughter cell contains half the chromosomes of the primary oocyte, only one of them contributes chromosomes to the union with the male sperm. This daughter cell, called the *secondary oocyte* (the third stage of oogenesis), is much larger than the other because it retains practically all the *cytoplasm* (the material that maintains the life of the cell's nucleus) of the original cell. The second daughter cell, which is referred to as a *polar body,* has little function and ultimately degenerates. The secondary oocyte moves in the process of ovulation from the follicle into the uterine tube where fertilization usually occurs, if it is to take place. In the fourth stage of oogenesis the ovum reaches full maturity and is capable of fertilization by a sperm.

8 MENSTRUATION AND THE CLIMACTERIC

Two dramatic changes take place in a woman's reproductive life: *menstruation* (the *menarche*), which usually commences in the early teens, and *menopause*, also called the *climacteric* or "change of life," which occurs some 35 years or so later.

MENSTRUATION

We have noted that most girls between the ages of 11 and 15 begin developing the physiological characteristics of puberty. Accompanying the development of breasts, reproductive organs, and secondary sexual characteristics is the *menarche*, which is that point during puberty when a monthly uterine "bleeding" called *menstruation* begins.

Although the menstrual cycle (the lapse of time from the onset of one menstrual flow to the day before the next one) can vary from 21 to 90 days and still be physiologically normal, the average length is from 28 to 30 days. Young women, especially teen-agers, tend to have longer menstrual cycles than older women do. A recent study of 30,655 menstrual cycles of 2316 women showed that the average number of days in the cycles of 15- to 19-year-old girls is 30.8 days, while for women 40 to 44 years of age, the average cycle is 28.3 days. Furthermore, the duration of the menstrual cycle appears to vary more among teen-agers and pre-menopausal women than it does among women in their twenties and thirties (Chiazze *et al.*). During the 30 to 35 years that a woman is capable of conception, she menstruates about 300 to 500 times.

Although menstruation can occur without ovulation's having taken place, the general purpose of the menstrual cycle is the preparation and maintenance of the uterus for the implantation of the fertilized egg. The menstrual cycle can be divided into three phases: the *destructive phase*, the *follicular phase*, and the *luteal phase*. So that these phases may proceed normally, there must be a well-balanced relationship between the central nervous system and the endocrine system.

DESTRUCTIVE PHASE   Progesterone, which has prepared and maintained the walls of the uterus for implantation of the fertilized ovum, is withdrawn when the corpus luteum regresses. This withdrawal, or even a lowered concentration of the hormone, causes the lining of the uterus to break down, slough off, and be discharged from the body in a form of bleeding. The monthly cycle is considered to begin with the first day of the destructive phase; this usually last from 3 to 7 days, the average being 4 or 5. The discharge consists not only of blood but also of other fluids and debris from the uterine wall in the form of mucus and fragments of *endometrium* (the cavity's lining), as well as dried epithelial cells from the vagina.

The amount of discharge during the destructive phase varies widely from woman to woman, and sometimes within the cycles of the same individual. On the average, however, the discharge amounts to approximately one cupful (6 to 8 ounces), with the amount of *actual* blood loss on even the heaviest day of flow being only about one tablespoonful. Menstrual blood is entirely venous in origin, and there is usually no clotting because the essential elements for clotting—e.g., fibrinogen and prothrombin—are missing.

A number of organic and psychic alterations can accompany the onset of the destructive phase. There may be an increase in frequency of urination, in the size and firmness of the breasts, in abdominal distension, and in skin disorders such as pimples. Fatigue, headaches, and irritability are sometimes involved. The latter changes, it should be noted, may be due to psychological factors related to certain unfortunate attitudes toward sex in general and menstruation ("the Curse") specifically, as well as to organic factors.

The toxic condition of the body increases as the uterine tissue dies and sloughs off. The bloodstream then picks up some of this toxic material and circulates it throughout the body. It will also be remembered that there is a marked decrease in the amount of progesterone in the body

FIGURE 8.1 The Menstrual Cycle: (1) During the early part of the cycle, an egg matures in the ovary; the endometrium begins to thicken. (2) About 14 days after the onset of the last menstruation, a mature ovum is released; the endometrium is thick and spongy. (3) The ovum travels through the fallopian tube; the ruptured follicle becomes the corpus luteum; fluids and blood engorge the uterine lining. (4) If the ovum is not fertilized, the endometrium breaks down and sloughs off in the form of bleeding (menstruation).

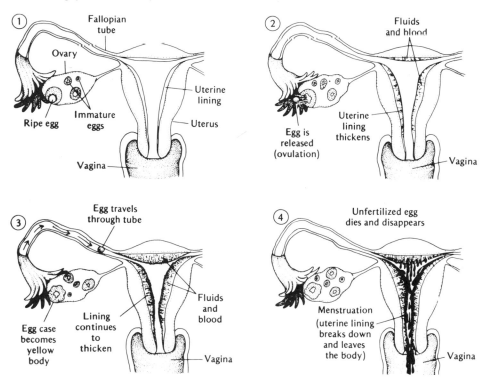

just before menstruation, producing an imbalance between it and estrogen. In some women this hormonal imbalance can elicit the unfortunate physical and emotional reactions described above.

Premenstrual changes in mood and body have been reported by the vast majority of women studied in this country. The degree of premenstrual tension that a woman experiences correlates well with her general response to stress—the better she handles stress, the less upset she becomes just before menstruation, and the easier she recovers from whatever stress she does experience.

A recent investigation revealed that during menstruation or the four days prior to it, girls scored 3% to 5% lower on high-school and college-level examinations than did girls in other stages of their menstrual cycle (Dalton; Science notes *i*).

FOLLICULAR PHASE   After the menstrual flow stops, the uterine wall is very thin. Under the stimulation of estrogen, which is secreted by the follicles located in the ovaries, the uterus begins a process of growth that lasts about 9 days. During this period many follicles (hence the name of this phase) contain developing ova, most of which cease to grow; only one usually reaches maturity in a single cycle. This graafian follicle at its full growth can occupy as much as one-fourth of the ovary. Approaching the fourteenth day of the menstrual cycle, the follicle ruptures and a mature ovum is discharged; this event is called *ovulation*. After the release of the ovum, the follicle (which is now called the *corpus luteum*, or yellow body) seals itself off with the aid of the luteinizing and luteotropic hormones that are secreted by the pituitary gland in the process described in Chapter 5.

LUTEAL PHASE   During the follicular phase the secretion of estrogen increases gradually. Estrogen concentration in the blood is at its maximum at the moment of ovulation. Following ovulation and the development of the corpus luteum, this yellow body begins actively to secrete progesterone. The concentration of estrogen decreases as progesterone begins preparing the uterus for the fertilized egg. The mucous membrane of the uterus becomes thicker and more vascular as small "lakes" of blood, called *lacunae*, are formed within the endometrium (wall) of the uterus. The lacunae provide nourishment for the ovum if it becomes fertilized and implants itself in the endometrium.

During the luteal phase, luteotropin, as well as the ovarian hormones, cause the amount of extracellular and intracellular fluid in the breasts to increase, resulting in greater size and sensitivity. Premenstrual congestion and swelling of mucous membranes sometimes cause a retention of fluid and a consequent temporary gain in weight of as much as 5 pounds.

It is interesting that about 20% of the women in one study reported a marked increase in their sex drive during the period just before menstruation (Shader and Ohly). Some authorities believe that the heightened sex drive is caused by the hormonal shift occurring at this time. Others think that the intensification is only another manifestation of a general rise in premenstrual tension. Some women, to be sure, experience a sharp decrease in sex drive premenstrually, although the number thus affected is somewhat less than those reporting a heightened desire. Of 28 separate studies conducted over a great number of years and involving many subjects, the results of 13 revealed that the peak of a woman's sexual desire occurs just after the menstrual flow begins. Nine showed the peak to be just before the flow, and 6 midway in the cycle (Cavanagh).

Heightened premenstrual sex drive appears also to be correlated with nonphysiological factors. For example, one study of highly anxious women who experience premenstrual tension revealed that 40% of those whose fathers' educational and occupational achievement was high also experienced heightened sex drive at this time, compared with only 20% of those women whose fathers were not high achievers (Shader and Ohly).

Recent biochemical research has shown that certain intracellular metabolic regulators in a woman's body, called *prostaglandins* (PGs), stimulate or inhibit many hormones, some of which act on the uterus. These substances seem to work in pairs. One inhibits and relaxes, the other stimulates and constricts. They not only work to produce abortion or to induce labor, but also are active during the early part of the normal menstrual cycle when one of the substances inhibits contractions of the smooth muscles of the uterus. Later in the cycle, the smooth muscles lose their sensitivity to the relaxing substance and some muscular cramping may occur.

If conception does not occur during the menstrual cycle, the corpus luteum degenerates and the concentration both of estrogen and progesterone decreases immensely. This sudden decrease in the amounts of both hormones is believed to bring about the destructive phase of menstruation, and the entire cyclic process then starts all over again.

There are rare instances in which extragenital bleeding occurs during the menstrual flow. Called "vicarious menstruation," such bleeding is usually from the nose, although it has been known to occur from the lungs, the retina of the eye, and so forth. This phenomenon is evoked by a sudden decrease in the size of the blood vessels (vasospasm) of the endometrium approximately 48 hours before the menstrual flow begins.

There is disagreement over the cause of this phenomenon. Some authorities relate it to *endometriosis*, an ectopic (misplaced) growth of the tissue that makes up the lining of the uterus; others relegate its causality solely to psychological factors. In 30% of the instances of vicarious menstruation, uterine bleeding is totally displaced, while in the remaining cases the two flows occur simultaneously (Dalven).

Since the part of the body most frequently involved in vicarious menstruation is the lining of the nose, it might be relevant here to note that an indirect relationship appears to exist between nasal functions and sexual activity. The mucous membrane of the nose, for instance, frequently swells during sexual excitation and may secrete more than its usual amount of mucus (Kinsey *et al. c*). Moreover, oral or nasal decongestants appear to have some effect on the endometrium of the uterus during the menstrual period, reducing discomfort and the flow as well (Alexander a). The Kinsey group pointed out the interesting similarity between a sneeze and an orgasm in physiologic buildup and explosive discharge of tensions (Kinsey et al. c).

Blindness appears to be related to the menarche, for studies show that blind girls generally begin menstruating six months earlier than other girls. This phenomenon is most apparent in those girls who are totally unable to distinguish light from dark (Sullivan, W.). Another phenomenon is that in paraplegic women—those with paralysis of the lower half of the body, affecting both motion and sensation in the pelvic region and the legs—menstruation usually continues unchanged following paralysis, and some cases of pregnancy have been reported (Money i).

There is general agreement among physicians that women should not coddle themselves during the menstrual period, but should carry on their activities in the usual manner. Participating in sports, taking a bath or shower, or shampooing the hair at this time, for example, will cause no undue stress and will not harm the reproductive organs.

Nor is there any physiological reason for refraining from sexual intercourse during the menstrual flow—although most present-day cultures impose restrictions against the practice (or at least express distaste for it), and some medical authorities in the recent past have gone so far as to suggest that coitus during menstruation will lead to physical distress. The research of Masters and Johnson (n), however, has shown clearly that the fear of distress is unfounded and that, indeed, sexual activity at that time may have just the opposite effect on the woman: i.e., it may provide relief from pain or discomfort. Of the 331 women who took part in an "orgasm during menstruation" study, only 33 objected to sexual activity on religious or esthetic grounds; 173 expressed desire for coitus, especially during the last half of the flow; and the remaining 125 had no special feelings in the matter one way or the other.

To test the effect of intercourse on menstruating women, all the subjects in a special Masters and Johnson investigation achieved orgasm in a laboratory situation through automanipulative means. During the last part of the orgasmic phase, the observers noted via a speculum (an instrument used for looking into a body opening, such as the vagina) that menstrual fluid frequently spurted from the external cervical os under contractile pressure that was powerful enough to expel the fluid through the vagina without touching either the speculum or the vaginal walls. The explosive force can be accounted for by a sudden contraction of the uterine muscles, starting at the fundus and moving toward the cervix. Perhaps the sudden clearing of menstrual fluid from the uterus and the relaxation of uterine muscles after the series of orgasmic contractions account for the reports of reduced pelvic cramping and backache from women who experience orgasm shortly after the onset of menstruatior..

THE CLIMACTERIC OR MENOPAUSE

When the average woman reaches the age of 45 to 50, her ovaries cease to produce and liberate ova, and the uterus gradually abandons the monthly process of shedding and regenerating its lining. This cessation of the menstrual cycle is called the *climacteric* or *menopause,* and its duration does not usually exceed two years. But as long as any menstrual periods occur at all, however erratically, the possibility of ovulation and hence of pregnancy remains. If a woman has not had a menstrual period for a year, on the other hand, she can be reasonably sure that ovulation has finally ceased and that conception is impossible.

The biblical account of Sarah's conceiving a child at the age of 90 notwithstanding, childbirth after 50 is an extreme rarity. During the last 100 years, only 26 authenticated cases of women past 50 having given birth to normal babies have been reported in the medical literature (From the editor's scrapbook *i*). The record for being the oldest woman to give birth to a child was set by a 57-year-old California woman in 1970 (Personality mailbag).

The climacteric can be quite disturbing and is sometimes beset with considerable emotional disquiet, even to the point of psychotic illness. Because of vastly improved techniques of hormonal therapy and other medication, however, most if not all of these distressing reactions can now be avoided or alleviated. Furthermore, tranquilizers and short-term psychotherapy are presently made use of in the treatment of climacteric symptoms, so that these menopausal difficulties are not nearly so troublesome as they have been in the past.

The glandular imbalance that occurs at the change of life is the source of an instability in the vasomotor system which, in turn, causes an irregularity in the diameter of the blood vessels. This fluctuation permits more blood to flow at one time—inducing "hot flashes"—and less blood at another. Hot flashes last from a second or so to several minutes, and can occur several times a day. The cause of the phenomenon is unknown, but it is interesting—and perhaps encouraging—that the more hot flashes a woman experiences during menopause, the less likelihood there usually is that other troublesome conditions will develop (Riedman).

Other symptoms associated with menopause are fatigue, dizziness, migraine headaches, chest and neck pains, insomnia, excessive desire for sleep, and depression. The chance that the climacteric will produce any mental disturbance is about one in 50,000, and only about 25% of all menopausal women have any sort of distressful symptomatology (Riedman). Generally speaking, the better the mental health of the woman before the climacteric, the fewer unpleasant symptoms she will have when it occurs (Coleman).

The median age for the onset of menopause advanced from 46.6 years in 1853 to 50.1 years in 1965 (Growing older—later). It has been observed that women who start menstruation earlier in life than average will continue menstruating longer. These findings seem to hold in other spheres of individual sexual life as well (Kinsey *et al. a, c*). For instance, people who begin erotic activity at an earlier age than average appear to maintain their sexual vigor longer. Furthermore, men and women who engage in frequent sexual activity are able to continue the activity later in life than the average person.

Some men undergo a climacteric, but usually not until they are about 55 years old. When it does occur in men, the climacteric is largely psychological in its impact, possibly resulting in some reduction in sexual vigor and interest because of the depressive or other negative emotional conditions it can induce.

As a man grows older he, too, undergoes certain physical changes that are somewhat analogous to those observed in the aging woman. The testes shrivel a bit and are less firm. Sperm production slackens, because the testicular tubules begin a degenerative process. The prostate gland becomes enlarged, and the ejaculatory fluid thinner and less copious. The production of male sex hormones slackens, and certain physical responses at the time of orgasm are weaker. Symptoms of depression or paranoia sometimes accompany the physical changes of the climacteric, and can affect men and women alike.

It is widely assumed that sexual activity ceases for both men and women during the later years of their lives. The truth of the matter is that sexual interest and capacity frequently extend into very old age. Despite the fact that a man's sex drive peaks in very young manhood and steadily declines thereafter, the average coital frequency of most men over 75 is approximately four times a month (Tarail). And the Kinsey researchers have demonstrated that a woman's sex drive reaches a peak in her thirties and remains the same until she is 60 or even older (Kinsey *et al. c*).

Following menopause, most women continue their premenopausal sexual pattern if they are in reasonably good health and if there is an available, compatible sexual partner. It is rare for symptoms of frigidity to appear suddenly with the onset of menopause. The postmenopausal woman is unlikely to lose her desire for and enjoyment of coitus. Rather, she is likely to enjoy coitus more, and more often. The reason, quite probably, is that the sexual inhibitions generated by fear of pregnancy are now removed (Goldfarb *et al.*).

If men and women refrain from continuing sexual activity in the later years of their life, the reasons are almost always psychological rather than physical. They may regard sexual activity at their age as being a little ridiculous, or be frightened that they might be unable to please their partner (Rubin *d*). Because she is no longer fertile, a woman may erroneously assume that her sexual drive must perforce disappear as well—and her assumption may become a self-fulfilling prophecy (Platt).

Despite a positive attitude toward continuing sexual activity in the later years, some men, because of reduced physiological functioning, are frightened into believing that their capacity for successful sexual performance is slipping irrevocably away. But leisurely erections, less vigorous prostatic contractions, and a diminished ejaculate or ejaculatory force do not affect the ultimate aim of fulfilling sexual activity—intercourse that brings orgasmic gratification to the man and his partner.

9 FERTILIZATION, PRENATAL DEVELOPMENT, AND BIRTH

FERTILIZATION AND PREGNANCY (GESTATION)

When a sperm penetrates an ovum, an immediate change occurs in the peripheral layer of the egg that prevents other sperm from penetrating it. Upon entering the egg, the fertilizing sperm loses its tail, while its head and the connecting piece (neck) expand, growing into the male *pronucleus* (head of the spermatozoon) and *centrosome* (an important protoplasmic body in subsequent cell division). At this point, the female pronucleus (nucleus of the secondary oocyte) and the male pronucleus approach each other; the nuclear membranes disappear and the gene-carrying portions (*chromatin*) of the two nuclei join, then re-form into two groups of equal number. Fertilization is now complete. The result is a fertilized egg containing the full component of 46 chromosomes common to all human cells.

Three general terms are used to describe the *conceptus* (product of conception) as it develops into the infant we know at birth. From the time of fertilization until the second week, the developing cell mass is referred to as a *zygote*; from the second to the eighth week, it is called an *embryo*; and from the eighth week until birth, a *fetus*. The appearance and initial development of all the rudimentary systems of the body mark

FIGURE 9.1   Ovulation, fertilization, and implantation.

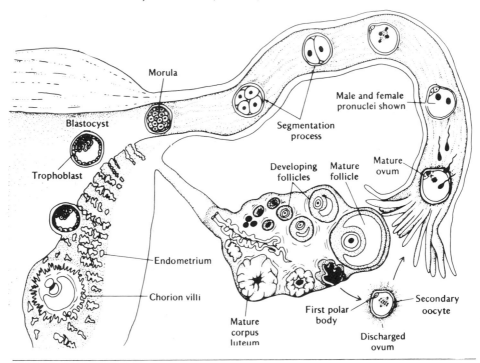

the end of the embryonic period. The last period, the fetal stage, consists of the further growth and elaboration of existing rudimentary systems.

The zygote undergoes the process of *segmentation*, or mitotic cell division, in which each daughter cell receives chromosomes identical in composition and number to those of the parent cell. The spherical zygote forms first 2 cells, then 4 by a cleavage at right angles to the first, then 8 by yet another cleavage in a third plane. These divisions create 4 cells above the original cleavage and 4 below. The 8 cells are further divided by a similar process into 16, then into 32, and so on. The increasing number of cells develops within the fixed outer bounds of the zygote, the outer dimensions remaining the same until implantation in the uterine wall.

The spherical cell mass into which the zygote develops, called a *morula,* moves slowly through the uterine tube and into the uterus. A cavity develops within it, which enlarges until there is an outer hollow sphere of cells, the *trophoblast,* from which the inner cell layer projects toward the center. At this stage the fertilized egg is referred to as a *blastocyst* (Steen and Montagu).

The inner ball of cells now forms two layers, the *ectoderm* and the

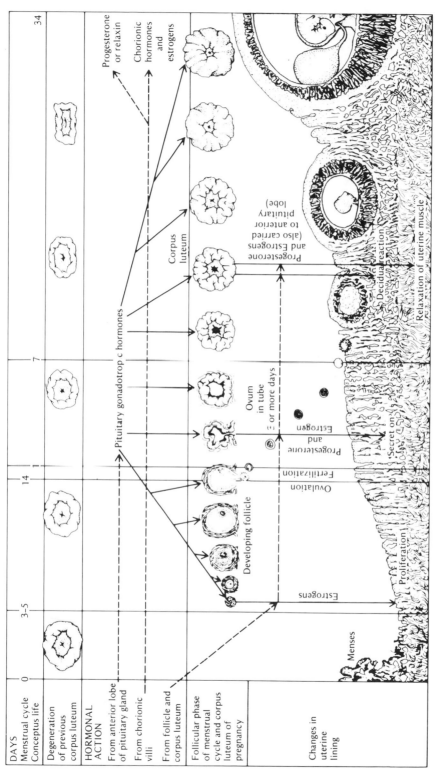

FIGURE 9.2 The ovarian cycle, the endometrial cycle, decidual development, and related hormonal action in a cycle during which conception has occurred.

endoderm, in such a manner that two cavities take shape simultaneously. Later a third cellular layer, the *mesoderm*, makes its appearance between the ecotoderm and the endoderm. These three layers of primitive germ cells, which are situated between the two cavities, constitute the *embryonic disc*, from which the embryo proper develops.

After the implantation of the embryo in the wall of the uterus, the ectoderm, endoderm, and mesoderm become differentiated. Eventually the developing infant's nervous system, sense organs, mouth cavity, and skin will evolve from the ectoderm. From the endoderm will come the digestive and respiratory systems. From the mesoderm develop the muscular, skeletal, circulatory, excretory, and sexual or reproductive systems (Arey; Steen and Montagu).

At about the seventh or eighth day after fertilization, the blastocyst comes into direct contact with the prepared wall of the uterus, the endometrium, and adheres to it. The cells of the trophoblast apparently produce enzymes that dissolve the maternal tissue to permit entry of the blastocyst, and by the twelfth day after fertilization the embryo has buried itself completely within the endometrium. Small fingerlike protrusions, the *chorionic villi*, grow from the *chorion* (the protective envelope surrounding and nourishing the embryo) outward into the maternal tissue. Eventually these villi limit themselves to the ultimate point of junction between embryo and uterus.

During embryonic life, peripheral membranes form and then extend beyond the region in which the embryo itself develops. They serve as a means of obtaining food and oxygen, and as an avenue for the elimination of wastes from the embryo. During the first 14 days of gestation, the embryo has not yet developed a functioning circulatory system, so that

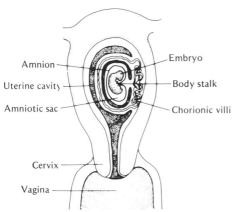

FIGURE 9.3 Schematic representation of an implanted embryo.

Amnion

Uterine cavity

Amniotic sac

Embryo

Body stalk

Chorionic villi

Cervix

Vagina

food must be obtained primarily by osmosis. Since the peripheral membranes are not incorporated within the body of the embryo and are discarded at the time of birth, they are called *extraembryonic* or *fetal membranes*. These membranes—including the yolk sac, chorion, amnion, body stalk, and allantois—begin developing about the second or third week of embryonic life.

Although virtually no yolk accumulates in the human ovum, a *yolk sac* is formed just as if a yolk existed. Lined with endodermal cells, this sac is the primary material from which the primitive digestive tract is made. As the embryo develops, there is a progressive constriction of the yolk sac until it is connected to the embryo only by a threadlike structure called the *body stalk*, which ultimately becomes incorporated into the umbilical cord.

The *amnion* is a thin, transparent, tough membrane composed of a layer of ectodermal cells with an external covering of mesodermal cells. The cavity formed by this membrane appears before the body of the embryo has taken a definite shape. It is filled with a clear watery fluid called the *amniotic fluid*. The developing embryo is suspended in this fluid by its umbilical cord.

Amniotic fluid has several important functions. It equalizes the pressure around the embryo, thus protecting it from jolts and mechanical injuries. It prevents the embryo from forming adhesions to the amnion, which could result in malformations. It permits changes in fetal posture and acts as a hydrostatic wedge to facilitate childbirth by helping to dilate the neck of the uterus. At about the fifth month of pregnancy, the fetus usually begins to swallow some of the amniotic fluid. The infant's first bowel movements, consequently, are a discharge of this liquid. The baby's respiratory passages may have to be cleared of some of the fluid after birth in order for normal respiration to begin.

The *allantois*, which ultimately constitutes part of the umbilical cord, is a tubular division of the posterior part of the yolk sac. During the embryo's later development, additionally, it fuses with the chorion in the formation of the placenta. Functionally, the allantois has no great importance in its own right, except that it acts as a rudimentary umbilical cord in the early weeks of gestation.

The *chorion*, the outermost extraembryonic membrane, completely surrounds the embryo. It is composed of two layers of epithelial cells: an outer ectoderm and an inner mesoderm. The most important role played by the chorion is in the formation of the placenta.

The *placenta* is formed by the interlocking of the *decidua basalis* (the portion of the uterine mucosa or endometrium directly underlying the chorionic vesicle) with the *chorion frondosum*, the external surface of the chorion, which is covered with villi. Comprised of uterine tissue and its interwoven villi, the placenta serves as a special organ of interchange between embryo and mother. The growth of the placenta is fairly rapid until about the fifth month of pregnancy. It has then reached its greatest relative size, approximately 50% of the internal surface of the uterus. The villi of the placenta are kept steeped in fresh maternal blood, which enters the placental spaces about the villi by means of small blood vessels. As the blood drains back into the veins of the uterus, it is replaced by fresh blood from the uterine arteries.

From the beginning of its development, the fetal blood circulation is a closed circuit. At no time during any stage of normal pregnancy do maternal and fetal blood intermingle. Commingling of the two systems can occur only in the case of injury to some portion of the placenta. Both maternal and fetal blood circulate within the placenta, but are kept separated by the walls of the umbilical blood vessels. All interchange between the two systems is by diffusion and absorption. A red blood cell, which is only about 0.00003 of an inch in size, is too large to pass through the openings of the walls. Yet chemicals and food bodies are small enough to penetrate the walls with no difficulty.

The fetal blood absorbs food and oxygen; it also eliminates carbon dioxide and other metabolic waste products, which are taken into the mother's blood and eventually expelled by her along with her own waste products. Although the cellular barrier between the two blood systems

---

FIGURE 9.4 Schematic representation of the placenta's attachment to the uterine wall, showing the interchange between the maternal blood vessels and the fetal blood vessels through the walls of the tiny villi.

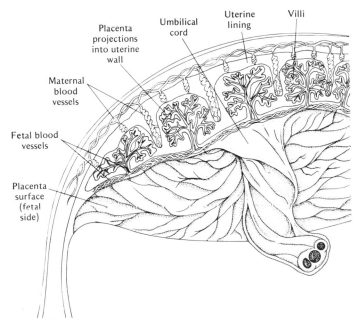

generally prevents the passage of bacteria and other disease germs, some substances are capable of crossing the barrier—e.g., antibiotics, certain viruses, and some disease germs, such as *Treponema pallidum,* which causes syphilis.

During the fifth week of pregnancy, the *umbilical cord* is formed. It is composed of the body stalk and its vitelline blood vessels, the allantois, and the umbilical blood vessels. The fully developed cord is about 20 inches long, which is also the average length of a full-term fetus.

Unusual Fertilization and Implantation

Although the union of ovum and spermatazoon usually occurs in the fallopian tube and the zygote then becomes implanted in the uterine wall, there are several exceptions—fertilization may be achieved by other means and implantation can occur in other sites. Some of these exceptions result in a full-term pregnancy and delivery of a healthy, normal baby. Others present difficulties which prevent the pregnancy from continuing to term.

Artificial Insemination

An increasingly popular method of treating infertility is artificial insemination (A. I.). In this process, sperm of the husband (A. I. H.) are mechanically introduced into the vagina or uterus of his wife at the time when conception is calculated as being the most likely to occur—or the sperm of a donor (A. I. D.), rather than those of the husband, are inserted.

Artificial insemination has been practiced in animal husbandry for years. As early as the fourteenth century, Arabic tribes are said to have secretly used semen from an inferior breed of stallions to inseminate the thoroughbred mares of their enemies (Lehfeldt a). Today, A. I. is regularly employed to build up the bloodlines of various species of animals. One thoroughbred bull can sire calves by many cows with a single ejaculate, and the semen can easily be refrigerated and shipped.

Artificial insemination of humans has been performed in this country with some regularity since the turn of this century, especially after the appearance of the early works of the famous American physician and sexologist R. L. Dickinson. Donor sperm produce pregnancy 80% of the time, whereas the husband's sperm artificially introduced are only 5% successful. The disparity in these percentages is understandable when one considers that the husband's sperm, for whatever reason, were incapable of effecting pregnancy by coition in the first place (Lehfeldt a).

In 1955, the Society for the Study of Sterility passed almost unanimously a resolution approving A. I. D., with the stipulation that the procedure must be in harmony with the medical opinion of the physician and the ethics of both husband and wife. Undoubtedly this resolution contributed significantly to the subsequent increase in all A. I. pregnancies (about 66% of them A. I. H.) in the United States from an estimated 50,000 in 1955 to 100,000 in 1958 and 250,000 in 1970 (Lehfeldt a; Smith, G. P.).

In 1956, Pope Pius XII stated unequivocally that the Roman Catholic Church opposed both A. I. D. and A. I. H. The Roman Catholic Church will, however, permit "assisted insemination" whereby an instrument is used to push the sperm toward and into the cervix after the semen has been deposited during marital intercourse.

Because of wars, atomic radiation, injuries, and illnesses, many couples are finding it expedient to take advantage of recent scientific advances in artificial insemination. These make it possible to store semen for a considerable period of time by freezing it, along with protective chemicals, in liquid nitrogen. Healthy babies have been born from both A. I. H. and A. I. D. conceptions in which the sperm used came from a sperm bank where they had been frozen and stored for as long as two years (Kleegman *et al.*; Sherman).

Incidental to A. I. D. are some interesting experiments presently being conducted with females of lower-animal species. Scientists have found that it is a simple matter to flush fertilized ova from the body of a genetic mother, store them for a reasonable period of time, and then implant them in the uterus of a "host" mother. For example, normal pure-blooded white rabbits have been produced with eggs flushed from pure-white female rabbits that, after refrigerated storage, were implanted and allowed to develop in the uterus of a pure-black foster mother. In some instances viable ova have been successfully stored for as long as 168 hours. But it has been found that the longer the eggs are stored, the greater is the loss of viability (Rosengard a).

A human egg has been fertilized outside the body of the woman producing it, then placed in the uterus of a "host" mother. The fertilized ovum implanted itself in the uterine wall and began normal development before the experiment was terminated for other reasons. In similar experiments, human ova have been fertilized in a test tube, remaining in it through several stages of development until they were destroyed (Rorvik b). Lambs born so prematurely that they would surely have died otherwise have been sustained with an artificial placenta until birth and have survived (Panagoras).

Parthenogenesis

Also called "virgin birth," *parthenogenesis* (Herrick, b) refers to the "fertilization" and development of the female's egg without any possible previous contact with a spermatozoon. A common occurrence in lower animals, this phenomenon is the sole method of reproduction among certain insects such as the honeybee.

Experimentation in parthenogenesis with various animals has shown that many stimuli will induce the process of development just as if the egg had been fertilized in the usual manner. For example, cooling the fallopian tubes of rabbits, heating the eggs of certain moths, and even applying saliva of human males to carp eggs have sufficiently stimulated the eggs to prompt their development (Herrick *b*; Steen and Montagu). A very high percentage of the eggs of virgin turkey hens undergo partheno-genesis in experimental circumstances, although the early death rate among the hatched birds is very high.

An obvious question arises: Is this phenomenon possible in human beings? There is no definite answer at present, and there is considerable disagreement among investigators, past and present. One thing is certain, however. If parthenogenesis were to occur, the offspring must invariably be female because of the way chromosomes are arranged in men and women. Since women have only one type of sex-determining chromosome (X), only the X chromosome could be passed on. Furthermore, a child born of parthenogenesis would inevitably be a replication of her mother, since her heredity would be based solely on the mother's genes (From the editor's scrapbook *h*).

A prominent researcher in the field of fertilization, Dr. Landrum B. Shettles, observed in a study of 400 human ova that the first stages of developmental processes had begun in 3 of these eggs, even though there could have been no contact with sperm. The logical conclusion would seem to be that if developmental processes in the human ovum can begin spontaneously, they should be able to continue to term (Herrick *b*). Only further research can uncover the answer.

The phrase "virgin birth" ordinarily conveys the idea of human pregnancy and subsequent birth without a previous act of sexual intercourse followed by union of ovum and sperm. In this context, the possibility of a true virgin birth has never been scientifically established. Impregnation without penile penetration, however, is a real possibility, and it is a phenomenon that happens more often than many realize. If, for instance, a man were to have his penis near or on a woman's vulva and ejaculate during sex play, semen could enter the vaginal opening and make its way through the vagina into the uterus. Or if a man were to ejaculate, get semen on his hands, and soon thereafter manually manipulate the woman's genitals (especially if he inserted a finger into the vagina), he could introduce sperm into the vaginal canal. If impregnation were to result in either of these instances, and if the woman's hymen were still intact, the subsequent parturition might accurately be called a "virgin birth."

Fertilization Outside the Fallopian Tube

Physicians have recorded a large number of cases in which women reporting for surgery shortly after they had engaged in coitus were found to have sperm in the fluid of the peritoneum (the membranous lining of the abdominal wall). This fact casts considerable doubt on the assumption that an ovum must be in the fallopian tube for fertilization to take place. Ova fertilized in these circumstances (*i.e.*, outside the fallopian tube) occasionally implant themselves in the abdominal wall or elsewhere, a phenomenon discussed in the next section of this chapter.

Ectopic Pregnancy

This phenomenon refers to the implantation of a fertilized ovum in any place other than the lining of the uterus. Ectopic pregnancy is, therefore, a misplaced pregnancy. There are several sites where these pregnancies commonly develop, the most usual being the fallopian tube. This is the *tubal pregnancy* that one sometimes hears of; and its incidence, according to various investigations made into the subject, is once in every 200 pregnancies (Eastman and Hellman).

Tubal pregnancies usually terminate themselves in one of two ways. There may be an abortion of the embryo or fetus from the natural opening of the ampulla of the fallopian tube into the abdominal cavity, an event known as an *abdominal abortion*, which usually occurs within the second or third month of implantation. Or there may be a *rupture* in the tubular wall, through which the embryo is expelled into the abdominal cavity. The rupture poses a more serious threat to the mother than the abdominal abortion does in terms of acute shock and extensive hemorrhaging, and is an important cause of maternal deaths (Eastman and Hellman; Netter).

If the embryo is young enough at the time of its discharge into the abdominal cavity, it is possible that it will be absorbed by the mother's system. Otherwise, surgery will be required to remove the product of the abortion and to repair or, more commonly, to remove the injured fallopian tube and stop the hemorrhaging. A tubal pregnancy is difficult to diagnose. But if a woman has missed a menstrual period and experiences any unusual vaginal bleeding or pain (especially if the pain is on one side only of the abdomen), she should see her obstetrician immediately. Given these symptoms, it is possible that the doctor can diagnose the condition before a rupture or abortion occurs.

A far less common form of ectopic pregnancy is an *abdominal pregnancy*, which occurs only once in 15,000 gestations (Eastman and Hellman). In these cases the placenta becomes attached to some structure within the abdominal cavity and, wherever attached, provides nourishment for the embryo as if it were in the uterus.

Some abdominal pregnancies continue to term, in which case the delivery must be by caesarean section. The danger of hemorrhaging in the mother is grave; furthermore, there is a high incidence of malformation among these infants and rarely does one survive (Eastman and Hellman). However, medical history cites a few cases in which a healthy child was delivered.

A follow-up study was recently made on a healthy mother and child 11 years after a successful abdominal pregnancy (Boyd). The fetus developed outside the womb in the abdominal cavity, the placenta being attached to the left ovary and to the abdominal wall. The pregnancy was of eight months' duration, and the baby weighed 5 pounds, 4 ounces at the time of its caesarean delivery.

When an abdominal pregnancy is not recognized and the fetus dies, it causes an irritation that accelerates the production of calcium by the mother. The consequence is a large deposit of calcium salts (bone-building material) around the dead fetus, which acts more or less to encase the "foreign" object and to protect the woman's body from being poisoned by it. The whole mass becomes calcified and results in what is called a "stone baby" (*lithopedion*), which may not be discovered and removed for several years, if ever.

How long such phenomena have been recognized in medical history is unclear, but the first authentic case (the famous Sens, France, Stone Baby) was reported in a sixteenth-century medical book. There is also a recorded case of one woman who carried such a baby for 35 years without being aware of its presence (Mozes c). Recently a 48-year-old Arizona woman delivered a seven-month stone baby that she had unknowingly carried for 14 years (Medical science notes c).

Even more rare forms of ectopic pregnancy are *ovarian* and *cervical pregnancies,* in which the embryo becomes implanted in an ovary or the cervix. Ovarian pregnancy typically ends with early rupture of the ovary and the absorption of the conceptus by the maternal system. Or a tumor composed of the degenerated conceptus may form in the ovary. Cervical pregnancy is typically identified because of bleeding, and must be terminated surgically (Eastman and Hellman).

There are recorded in medical history a few instances of pregnancies that occurred after a hysterectomy (surgical removal of the uterus), all involving some misplaced endometrial tissue wherein the fertilized ovum implanted itself; none of the fetuses survived. In a recent case a fetus developed in the cul-de-sac of the vagina. The woman's ovaries and fallopian tubes had been left untouched at the time of her hysterectomy and, in some inexplicable manner, an egg became fertilized and implanted itself in the vagina (Hanes).

Signs of and Tests for Pregnancy

The signs of pregnancy may be divided into three classes: the *presumptive signs*, which are largely subjective and are the individual experiences of each pregnant woman; the *probable signs*; and the *positive signs*. The last two classes are more objective than the first, and lie within the interpretive province of the physician and laboratory technician (Eastman and Hellman).

The *presumptive signs* are the first to be noticed—cessation of the menses; morning sickness; changes in the size and fullness of the breasts, as well as the development of a dark coloration of the areolae, or pigmented areas, around the nipples; fatigue; frequency of urination; and discoloration of cervical mucous membranes.

The *probable signs* consist of an increase in the size of the uterus; considerable softening of the cervix, commencing with the second month of pregnancy; enlargement of the abdomen at about the third month, when the distended uterus can be felt through the abdominal wall; and intermittent contractions of the uterus.

The *positive signs* are three in number, any one of which confirms pregnancy: the fetal heartbeats, which the examining physician can hear and count; active fetal movements, noticeable at the fifth month (although some fibrillating movement may be detected earlier); and the fetal skeleton, observable in X-ray films.

The vast majority of women quite understandably do not wish to wait several months to determine if they are pregnant. Nor is it advisable for them to do so, in the best interest of their own health and that of their babies. Most women, therefore, undergo endocrine tests which can give accurate proof of pregnancy approximately 3 weeks after implantation, or about 6 weeks after the last menstrual period. (Test results any earlier are unreliable because the hormonal secretion is too slight.) The endocrine substance that yields laboratory proof of pregnancy is the chorionic gonadotropic hormone secreted from the earliest days of implantation by chorionic villi protruding from the implanted fertilized ovum.

This hormone is found in the urine of a pregnant woman, a sample of which is used in the recently developed test for pregnancy known as the *agglutination* (clumping) *test*. A sample of the patient's urine is mixed with certain chemicals; if agglutination occurs, she is not pregnant. The test results can be determined in from 3 minutes to 2 hours, depending upon the pharmaceutical house that prepared the testing apparatus. The test has about 97% accuracy when performed at least 2 weeks after a menstrual period is missed. It has rapidly become the most popular pregnancy test used by laboratory technicians, replacing the earlier frog and rabbit tests.

Still another test for pregnancy, after a menstrual period has been missed, is the oral administration of the hormone progesterone. If the patient is not pregnant, the heightened progesterone level will cause menstruation to begin 4 or 5 days after the last dose of the hormone. If menstruation does not begin, then the patient is assumed to be pregnant. Some scientists regard this pregnancy test as being almost 100% accurate (Eastman and Hellman); others consider the evidence of its accuracy unconvincing (Crawley *et al.*).

Activities During Pregnancy

Much has been written about the dangers of travel, exercise, sexual intercourse, and driving during pregnancy. These activities are not dangerous for the healthy woman, however, when pursued moderately and sensibly; on the contrary, they are often beneficial to the expectant mother (Javert; Rutledge). During certain wars, pregnant women traveled by all modes of transportation, much of it uncomfortable, for hundreds of miles in order to be with their husbands. Yet they had a lower miscarriage rate than those women who stayed home. The emotional satisfaction of joining their husbands, even though it entailed considerable traveling, probably contributed to the good health of these young women.

FIGURE 9.5 Diagram showing the practicality of intercourse even in an advanced stage of pregnancy. The dotted line demonstrates the angle at which the penis may be introduced into the vagina.

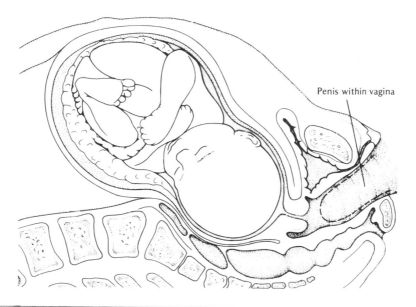

Penis within vagina

Sexual intercourse during gestation is ordinarily sanctioned and even encouraged until approximately the final six weeks (Javert). After this time, when sexual intercourse may become impossible for the wife because of abdominal size, sexual relief for her and her husband through such means as mutual masturbation is now recognized as valuable to each partner and to the marriage. As a matter of fact, if no sexual release is otherwise available for the husband during his wife's pregnancy and shortly thereafter, this is the time he is most likely to seek extramarital outlets for his sexual needs (Masters and Johnson n). Sensible precautions, of course, must be taken in regard to sexual, as well as other, activity during pregnancy. The obstetrician directing the pregnancy can offer guidance in these matters.

The adverse effects of smoking on the human organism have been well documented and widely publicized, to the extent that the federal government now requires a warning about the health hazards involved to be printed on each cigarette package. The deleterious effects of smoking on a fetus during pregnancy have not been so carefully investigated, but current research indicates some danger (Montagu b).

Tobacco smoke contains over 250 chemical compounds and substances, many of which, such as nicotine and tars, are noxious. Furthermore, smoke can be absorbed through the membranes of the mouth as well as by inhalation. And when the mother smokes, the heartbeat rate of the fetus is affected. These facts should be enough to deter any pregnant woman from smoking.

Research has indicated that the infant of a smoking mother is likely to be born weighing somewhat less than the baby of a nonsmoker, and that the possibility of a premature birth is doubled. The death rate and the incidence of malformation of infants whose mothers smoked during pregnancy also appears higher than those of nonsmokers' babies (Montagu b).

A very recent investigation, however, which was conducted under the aegis of the National Institutes of Health, offers conflicting evidence. Studying a total of 18,000 women, biostatistician Jacob Yerushalmy found that, although many women smokers do indeed bear low-weight babies, they also bore low-weight babies before they began smoking. The factor of low weight, he concluded, may therefore be related to the smoker, not the smoking, suggesting that biological and behavioral differences between smokers and nonsmokers should be investigated.

Yerushalmy also found that the mortality rate among babies of both normal and low birth weight is the same whether or not the mothers smoked. Most surprising of all was his finding that perinatal mortality (stillbirth or death within the first month) is substantially lower for babies of smokers—a finding for which he has "no reasonable explanation" (Goodall a).

Incidental to the subject of smoking, women who smoke cigarettes have been found less likely to become pregnant than nonsmokers are (Smoking deters pregnancy). Women who smoke have seven times more menstrual difficulties than those who do not. Only 4% of nonsmokers age prematurely, compared with 66% of smokers. Only 2% of nonsmokers experience a premature menopause, whereas 20% of smokers do so.

Age of Mothers and Family Size

Most women have their first babies between the ages of 20 and 24, although there have been substantiated reports of births to a girl as young as 5 and to a woman as old as 57 years (Clark *i*; Personality mailbag). Deliveries by still older women have been reported, but almost all investigations have failed to support their claims.

Recent scientific studies offer encouragement to women past 40 who wish to have children. The evidence is that they have as good a chance as younger wives of giving birth to a live infant (Posner *et al.*). But a woman past 35 or 40 wishing to have a baby is well advised to consult a geneticist or obstetrician before deliberately conceiving. For the evidence is that older women stand in greater danger than younger ones of producing a defective infant—for example, the incidence of mongolianism and chromosomal abnormalities is higher.

There is also a greater incidence of caesarean sections among older women (8% as compared with a general average of 3%). And the Metropolitan Life Insurance Company has reported from their study of 27.7 million births between 1951 and 1957 that multiple births are most likely to occur in women between the ages of 35 and 39.

There are, as anyone can testify, enormous variations in family size. Childless marriages are rather commonplace. But there is also a Russian couple whose marriage was "blessed" with 69 children born in 27 confinements—16 sets of twins, 7 sets of triplets, and 4 sets of quadruplets (News of the month c). The average number of children in white American families at any given time is 1.25, according to the 1970 census, and in black American families, 1.77 children (U.S. Bureau of the Census). (A family, according to the Census Bureau, consists of a household head plus one or more persons who are related to that head.)

Infertility (Sterility)

One-third of all United States couples experience difficulty in having a child, either because they are unable to conceive or, if conception does occur, because the wife is unable to continue the pregnancy to the point of producing a live birth (Westoff and Westoff). Approximately one couple out of every 10 is never able to have children, while pregnancy in some marriages would seem to occur with distressing frequency. When couples are purposely attempting to conceive a child, about 30% will succeed the first month, about 60% will have succeeded by the end of six months, and about 75% by the end of the first year.

The age of the woman has a significant bearing on her ability to conceive, the natural fertility of a woman progressively decreasing from her early twenties onward. If women aged 20 to 24 years are given a fertility rating of 100, women aged 25 to 29 years have a rating of 93 (or 93% of that of the younger women). Women aged 30 to 34 years have a rating of 85; those between 35 and 39 years, a rating of 69; those between 40 and 44 years, a rating of 35; and those between 45 and 49 years, a rating of 5 (Henry).

There are manifold reasons why a couple are, or seem to be, unable to conceive a child. The responsibility in 30% of the cases, it has been established, lies with the male. And the man is responsible in an important contributory way in another 20% (Amelar; Clark c). Many men, however, do not wish to accept the fact that they might be the source of their marriage's barrenness, believing it to be a reflection on their manliness.

The causes of male infertility are as varied and complex as those involved in female sterility and demand equally close study (Franklin et al.). Men often possess a low sperm count and in some cases have no active sperm at all, even though they are quite capable of having frequent and pleasurable sexual intercourse. Physicians consider a sperm count of less than 200 million per ejaculation as being so small that conception would be rendered difficult (Clark l).

When husbands are fertile but cannot impregnate their wives because of low sperm count, a procedure can be used whereby the sperm from many ejaculates are collected, pooled, frozen, and stored for a period of months. The semen is then thawed and concentrated by centrifugation, resulting in a much greater sperm concentration than normal. At the expected time of ovulation, semen is introduced into the uterus on several consecutive days in the attempt to impregnate (Kleegman et al.).

The effect that frequency of ejaculation has on sperm count and fertility is obviously a matter of individual variation, but, generally speaking, the optimal time interval between ejaculations to insure maximum fertility is about 48 hours. Too much or too little sexual activity can negatively affect a man's fertility (Charny; Masters and Johnson o). Recent experience indicates that, following the use of antidepressant drugs, sperm production is accelerated and fertility heightened. There is, as well, a concomitant increase in sex drive, energy, and interest (Kiev and Hackett).

Women may have any of several anomalies that interfere with the ability to conceive. There are, for example, congenital anatomical defects, such as imperfect fallopian tubes or uterus. In certain cases, all or any one of these organs, as well as the vagina, may be missing altogether. Sometimes organs of reproduction become nonfunctional because of acquired obstructions. For example, douching with water under pressure can force harmful bacteria into the fallopian tubes, producing an infection and subsequent scar tissue that permanently closes the tubes. In some women, ova simply do not develop properly. In others (very rarely) ova cannot be released from the ovary because its covering is too tough to rupture, even though the ova are capable of fertilization and proper development.

(It should be recognized also that women may be able to conceive yet have glandular difficulties, an abnormal endometrium, uterine tumors, or the like that will not allow them to carry a fetus to term.)

Women sometimes develop antibodies that eventually appear in the vagina and produce an immunity to sperm, making conception impossible (Masters and Johnson *b, c, n*). This immunity may be built up against the sperm of any man, but in some cases the immunity may exist against one man's sperm but not another's (Antibody's role). It is not unusual for a couple to be unable to have children together but, after remarriage, for each to produce children with another partner.

Male-Female Conception and Birth Ratios

It is an established fact that many more males than females are conceived, whatever the reason may be. But following conception the female survival ratio is higher than that of the male. The conception ratio is about 160 males to 100 females; the zygote implantation ratio is about 120 males to 100 females; and the birth ratio is 105 males to 100 females.

After the shattering experiences of recent wars, man finds some comfort in the notion that nature compensates for the combatants killed during hostilities by increasing, in some mystical way, the ratio of male to female births. Indeed, at first sight, it seems that just such a miracle occurred after World Wars I and II when there was, in fact, an increase in male births.

The noted biologist and anthropologist Ashley Montagu (c) offers this explanation. During wartime, he points out, people marry at a younger age. The younger mothers, being strong and healthy, provide fertilized ova a greater chance for survival and implantation, so that they tend to give birth to a higher percentage of males than older mothers do. Furthermore, since these young mothers are separated from their husbands, the enforced spacing between births is longer than usual, leaving the wives in a stronger physical condition to carry the next child to term and thereby increasing the likelihood of a male birth. Following Montagu's reasoning, what actually happens is that more male zygotes are implanted in the uterus and fewer male embryos die, producing a greater male to female ratio of births.

Can an Unborn Child Be "Marked"?

Because of the close connection between fetus and mother, it is understandable why many people assume that such experiences as sudden shocks or fright to the mother would cause her baby to be born with some physical or emotional "mark," most commonly a birthmark. The notion of a child's being prenatally "marked" in this manner is, however, completely false, since there is no direct connection between the nervous systems or blood systems of mother and fetus.

What usually happens is that, when a child is born with an unusual birthmark—for example, a skin discoloration in the general shape of a bird—the parents' faulty memory processes cause them to "remember" an incident while the mother was pregnant wherein she was attacked or in some way frightened by something of that shape.

Misinformed scientists have also been a party to perpetuating the "marking" myth. In 1836, for example, eight physicians signed a report, which appeared in an American medical journal, that a man had a face like a snake and could coil and uncoil his arm in a snakelike fashion because a rattlesnake had frightened his mother during her sixth month of pregnancy (Montagu a).

It is true, of course, that the mother supplies nourishment for the fetus; her diet and chemical intake can have a direct effect on certain physiological reactions of the child, both before and after birth. For example, if the mother grossly overeats certain foods, it is sometimes possible to cause in the child an allergic condition that continues after birth. Also, we have remarked that the physical condition of infants whose mothers smoked tobacco during their pregnancies will be affected by the smoking. However, these reactions are not what is usually meant by the "marking" of a baby; the latter theory is a physiological impossibility, so far as scientific investigation has been able to determine.

The Theory of Telegony

The influence of a "previous sire" on a later conception is a theory known as *telegony*. Despite its rather widespread acceptance among breeders of animals, and regardless of the writings of such scientists as the great Charles Darwin, there is no scientific basis for the theory, whether one is discussing humans or animals. Inadequate knowledge of the laws of heredity and unscientific methods of observation and control in animal breeding have led some people to the conclusion that, among humans, the offspring of a second husband might be affected by the wife's having been impregnated by her first husband or simply having had sexual intercourse with him.

A common occurrence that appears to give credence to the telegony theory concerns female dogs. Bitches remain in heat for several days, during which time they may mate with several males. Because female dogs have a maddening capacity for escaping the watchful eye of their owners and mating with almost any male that happens along, it is quite possible for them to have a litter of puppies of which none resembles the intended sire. There is in this instance no "carry-over" from the bitch's previous matings; it is simply that the puppies of the same litter have been sired by different dogs (Herrick a).

Can Humans and Infrahuman Animals Crossbreed?

This myth continues to have some adherents. However, not only is it impossible for humans to crossbreed with infrahuman animals, but interbreeding among the various genera of lower animals is equally impossible, although members of different species of the same genus may produce crossbred offspring. For example, a man and an ape cannot interbreed, nor can an ape and a tiger; but two members of different species—in the cat family, for example—can crossbreed.

Undoubtedly our knowledge of the wondrous creatures of Greek and Roman mythology—the centaurs, sphinxes, mermaids, and satyrs has lent credence over the centuries to the myth that humans and lower animals can interbreed.

Pseudocyesis and Couvade

An interesting phenomenon known to occur in both humans and lower animals is *pseudocyesis* or false pregnancy. A woman, for example, will develop symptoms that are remarkably similar to those of true pregnancy. She may cease menstruating, be consistently nauseated, and gain an inordinate amount of weight. In some instances the condition lingers for months before the symptoms disappear or are dispelled by psychotherapy. In extreme cases she will also develop a protruding abdomen and actually go into labor, only to find that the condition exists entirely because of emotional factors. All that she "delivers" is an accumulation of air and fluids.

A related phenomenon is the practice of *couvade* among some primitive cultures, wherein the husband retires to bed during his wife's parturition and suffers in much the same manner as she does during delivery. In more sophisticated societies the husband will sometimes (in approximately 11% of the cases) show some symptoms related to his wife's pregnancy (Husband's pregnancy symptoms). Less frequently, expectant fathers become severely nauseated, vomit, and suffer abdominal pains, all such symptoms disappearing after the wife has delivered their infant.

PRENATAL DEVELOPMENT OF THE CHILD

The development of the child during the 9 months before birth is more rapid than at any subsequent time during his entire life span. In the 20 years from an individual's birth to maturity, his body weight will increase approximately 20 times. By comparison, in the 9 months between fertilization of the ovum and delivery of a fully developed baby, the increase in weight is about 6 billionfold. The most rapid period of growth for the human organism, then, is the early phase of gestation. From the time of fertilization to the end of the first month, the egg increases in weight by about a million percent (from 0.000004 gm to 0.04 gm). During the second month, the weight increase is 7400%, dropping to an 1100% increase during the third month, and to a comparatively insignificant increase of 30% during the final month. The increase in rate of weight gain drops even more after birth. If this were not so, the infant would weigh from 160 to 170 pounds by the end of the first year of postnatal life (Eastman and Heilman).

The following general outline (Arey; Eastman and Hellman; Fisher, I.) of prenatal events, from the beginning of the mother's last menstrual flow preceding pregnancy through birth, is useful in obtaining a sequential view of the many aspects of fetal development.

First Month
First Week

The destructive phase of menstruation occurs.

An ovum is being prepared for ovulation.

Second Week

The follicular phase of menstruation occurs.

Ovulation occurs on approximately the thirteenth day of the menstrual cycle.

The ovum is fertilized by a sperm in the ampulla of the fallopian tube.

At the instant of fertilization, all hereditary characteristics are determined through the pairing of chromosomes from ovum and sperm.

Third Week

The fertilized ovum passes along the fallopian tube toward the uterus for a period of 3 or 4 days.

Cell divisions take place in the ovum during this journey.

Fourth Week

As the blastocyst comes into contact with the wall of the uterus, implantation commences.

Upon completion of implantation, the fetal membranes start developing.

Second Month

Fifth Week

The embryo now appears as a small bit of greyish flesh.

The development of the backbone begins.

The spinal canal commences to form.

The embryo is about $\frac{1}{12}$th of an inch in length and about $\frac{1}{6}$th of an inch in width.

Sixth Week

The head begins to form.

Construction of the backbone is completed.

The spinal canal is closed over.

Indentations in the skin appear where the eyes will form.

The tail of the embryo becomes distinct.

Rudimentary arms and legs are now visible.

The embryo has grown to about $\frac{1}{4}$ inch in length.

FIGURE 9.6 Human embryos, magnified 2½ times. Ages (left to right): 28 days, 31 days, 38 days, 39 days. The vertical line indicates actual size. From Eastman and Hellman. *Williams Obstetrics*, 13th ed., 1966. Courtesy of Appleton–Century–Crofts, Educational Division, Meredith Corporation.

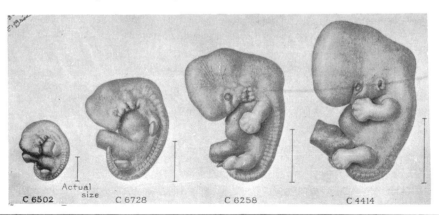

Actual size

C 6502   C 6728   C 6258   C 4414

FIGURE 9.7 Human embryos, magnified 1.9 times. Ages: 8 to 8½ weeks. The vertical line indicates actual size. From Eastman and Hellman. *Williams Obstetrics,* 13th ed., 19-66. Courtesy of Appleton–Century–Crofts, Educational Division, Meredith Corporation.

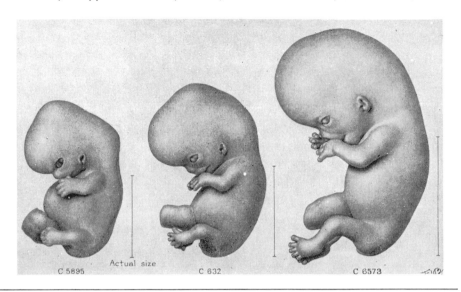

Seventh Week

Formation of the chest and abdomen is completed.

The eyes are more clearly differentiated.

The fingers and toes are beginning to take shape.

The embryo is now about ½ inch in length.

Eighth Week

The primary facial features are forming.

The ears begin to develop.

The embryo is almost an inch long, and weighs about ⅟₃₀th of an ounce.

Third Month

Ninth Week

The sympathetic ganglia and nerves have begun to form.

Stubby toes and fingers are identifiable.

The appendages are partially formed.

The formation of the gross facial characteristics becomes complete.

The liver, lungs, pancreas, kidneys, and intestines take on shape and begin to function to a limited degree.

The embryo is a bit over 1 inch in length and weighs about $\frac{1}{15}$th of an ounce.

Tenth through Twelfth Week

The following external bodily parts are completely formed by the end of this period: ears, arms, hands, fingers, legs, feet, and toes.

The fingernails begin to form.

The head remains proportionately much larger than the rest of the body.

The external genitalia begin developing their characteristic structure, and an expert may be able to determine the sex of a fetus born at this time. If the fetus is still in the amniotic sac, or is placed in a warm saline solution, spontaneous movements may occur.

The fetus is about 3 inches long and weighs about 1 ounce.

The fetus looks like a miniature infant from this point on.

Fourth Month
Thirteenth through Fourteenth Week

The sex of the fetus is easily distinguishable.

Fine downlike hair covers the skin.

Eyebrows and eyelashes make their first appearance.

Fifteenth through Sixteenth Week

Near the end of this period, fetal movements are felt and the heartbeat can be detected.

The fetus is about 8.5 inches long and about 6 ounces in weight.

Fifth Month
Seventeenth through Eighteenth Week

Fat begins to accumulate under the skin.

Hair on the head first appears.

Nineteenth through Twentieth Week

The fetus is now approximately 12 inches long and weighs 1 pound.

Should it be born at this time, it might live for a few minutes but cannot survive.

Sixth Month
Twenty-First through Twenty-Second Week

The fetus first opens its eyes.

FIGURE 9.8 Human embryos aged 25 days to 4 months. Actual size. From Arey. *Developmental Anatomy*, 3rd ed. Philadelphia: W.B. Saunders Co., 1934.

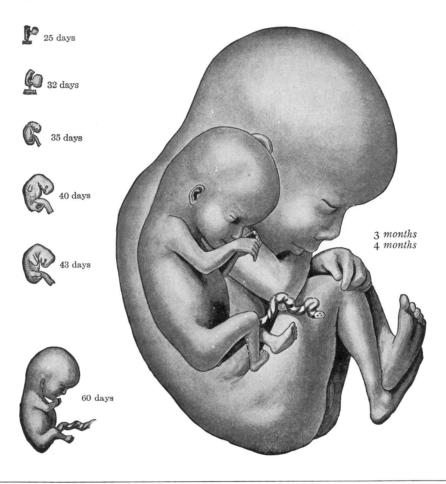

It is now covered with a cheeselike secretion called the *vernix caseosa.*

The head is fairly well developed.

The skin is wrinkled.

Twenty-Third through Twenty-Fifth Week

The fetus if born at this time can live several hours or even days. In one out of 10 instances, it will survive if given expert care.

It is now approximately 14 inches long and weighs 2 pounds.

Seventh Month
Twenty-Sixth through Twenty-Seventh Week

The testicles descend into the scrotum of the male fetus.

If the infant is born at this time, it has a 50% chance of survival.

Twenty-Eighth through Twenty-Ninth Week

The fetus is about 16 inches long and weighs just under 4 pounds.

It is an old wives' tale that a 7-month fetus has a better chance to survive than an 8-month fetus. The notion stems from the fact that most allegedly 7-month infants are in reality full-term. The older the fetus is at birth, the better its chance for survival.

Eighth Month
Thirtieth through Thirty-First Week

The development of almost all the organic systems is virtually complete.

The downlike hair that has covered the fetus commences to disappear.

Thirty-Second through Thirty-Third Week

If the baby is born during this time, its chance for survival is about 90%.

The length is now about 18 inches and the weight a little over 5 pounds.

Ninth Month
Thirty-Fourth through Thirty-Fifth Week

The fetus has attained full development.

The skin, still covered with vernix caseosa, has a smooth and polished look.

It has lost all the downlike hair that previously covered its body, except perhaps across the shoulders. The length of the hair on the head is about 1 inch.

The eyes are a slate color, and will not assume their final coloring until some weeks after birth.

Thirty-Sixth Week until Birth

The fetus's final development is rapid, and its weight gain is about a pound a week.

Of infants born at this time, over 99% will survive.

At birth, the baby's length is usually 20 inches and his weight approximately 7 pounds.

The prospective birth date of a child can be computed with a fair degree of accuracy by adding 280 days to the date on which the woman's last menstruation started. To be more precise, one would have to know the exact date of conception. Several investigations have demonstrated that conception can take place on any day of a woman's monthly cycle, even during the menstrual flow, despite the generally accepted theory that women can become pregnant only during the thirteenth to fifteenth day of the cycle.

The period of gestation varies from birth to birth, even with the same woman, and according to the sex of the child. Women who engage in strenuous physical exercise usually have their babies 20 days earlier than less athletic women do; brunette women deliver slightly sooner than

---

FIGURE 9.9   Lateral representation of the fetus in the mother's pelvis.

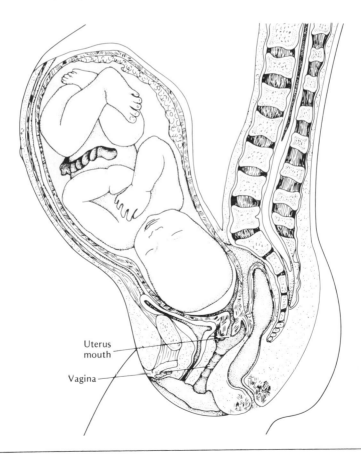

Uterus
mouth

Vagina

blondes do; girls are often born from 5 to 9 days earlier than boys are; and about 3% of pregnancies last 300 days or more (Clark *k*). The death rate among babies born after an overlong period of gestation is about three times that of babies delivered at normal term, probably because of the aging and withering of the placenta in the former instance (Alexander *b*). Most obstetricians will induce labor if they suspect placental shrinkage.

The size of babies at birth also varies considerably. The largest on record, born in Iran in February 1972, weighed 26.5 pounds, while the smallest surviving infant on record weighed only 1.5 pounds. Very large infants usually must be delivered by caesarean section.

The time of day at which a baby elects to be born seems to be a matter of random choice, although about 10% more are born at night than during the daylight hours. The most popular time of arrival is between 3 a.m. and 4 a.m.; the least popular, 3 p.m. More babies are born in August and fewer in April than in other months of the year. The mortality rate and the incidence of congenital defects are considerably higher among babies born during the first six months of the year than among those born during the last six months (Van Dellen).

It might be mentioned that the maternal and infant mortality rate for whites in this country is still lower than for blacks. In 1967, about three times more black women than white died in childbirth, and almost twice as many black babies under one month of age died as white babies of the same age (Westoff and Westoff). The differences, as one might expect, reflect the lower socioeconomic status and consequent poorer nutritional care of black mothers rather than racial differences (Westoff and Westoff).

About two dozen prenatal diseases and disorders can now be identified with almost 100% accuracy. In about 25% of the cases of severely defective unborn children, identification of the defect can be made early enough to permit therapeutic abortion (Sex in the news *e*). In recent months a center for the prenatal detection of birth defects has been established at the Johns Hopkins Hospital in Baltimore.

Birth Positions

The manner and incidence of birth positions and presentations are as follows:

Longitudinal, accounting for over 99% of birth positions.
1. *Cephalic* or head presentations, which constitute 96% of all longitudinal births.
   a. Head bent downward with baby's chin on breastbone.
   b. Head extended, face presenting.
   c. Head only slightly extended, brow presenting first.

2. *Breech* or buttocks presentations, accounting for 4% of all longitudinal births.
   a. *Frank,* the most common form; legs bent over abdomen with toes and shoulders touching and buttocks presenting over pelvis.
   b. *Footling,* with the legs, held straight in a standing position, presenting first.
   c. *Full,* the rarest of the breech presentations; baby sitting cross-legged in mother's pelvis.

Transverse, occurring once in 200 births. The fetus lies crosswise with a shoulder, arm, or hand entering the birth canal first. Either the fetus must be turned during labor, or a caesarean section is indicated.

Great pressure is, of course, exerted on a baby during delivery. In longitudinal cephalic presentations, the infant's head may be oddly molded in the birth process, or the facial features may be bruised and swollen. The buttocks and genital area of an infant born in a breech presentation often become swollen and discolored during delivery. These conditions are understandably quite distressing to the new parents, but the irregularities correct themselves within a few days of birth and there is very rarely any permanent damage.

Although a breech presentation is rather unusual, almost 50% of infants assume this position prior to the seventh month of fetal life. Most

FIGURE 9.10 Breech presentation (left) and transverse presentation (right).

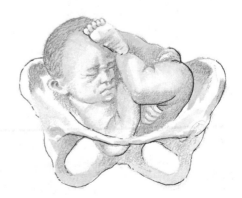

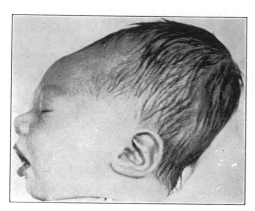

FIGURE 9.11 Molding of an infant's head at birth. From Eastman and Hellman. *Williams Obstetrics,* 13th ed., 1966. Courtesy of Appleton-Century-Crofts, Educational Division, Meredith Corporation.

infants in the breech position then make a 180° turn to the cephalic position before the ninth month. A fetus that does not make the turn can often be manipulated by the obstetrician into the proper cephalic position during the later stages of pregnancy.

BIRTH (PARTURITION)

Parturition, the process of childbirth, takes place in three stages. The *first stage* can be recognized by any one of three signs.

Powerful muscle contractions, which are called *labor pains,* will start to occur, usually at intervals of 15 to 20 minutes, each contraction lasting about 30 seconds. The first contractions are relatively mild and rhythmic, but increase steadily in frequency, intensity, and duration. They finally occur every 3 to 4 minutes, at which time the fetus is well on its way. Toward the end of labor, each contraction lasts a minute or more.

Labor contractions often feel as if they commence in the back and then move forward to the abdomen, primarily because the fetus is being pressed toward the back, as it has not yet made the turn into the vagina. Between contractions there is complete relaxation, a condition not found in most instances of muscle cramping. The first stage of labor should produce a dilation of the cervix from its normal size (about ⅛th inch) to approximately 4 inches, in order to permit the emergence of the baby into and through the 4- to 5-inch-long vagina. Each contraction pushes the baby downward, eventually with a force equal to 25 or 30 pounds of pressure. When the cervix is completely dilated, the first stage of labor has ended. This stage lasts about 16 hours for first babies, sometimes less, and about 8 hours in subsequent deliveries.

A second sign of the first stage of labor is the expulsion of the mucous plug from the base of the uterus. The mucus will be flecked with bright red blood. The purpose of the plug, as was pointed out previously, is to act as a barrier between the vagina and the uterus against the invasion of undesirable matter.

A third indication that parturition is imminent is the rupture of the amniotic membrane, which causes a flow of clear waterlike fluid to issue from the vagina.

When any one of the three signs of parturition is present, it is time to notify the obstetrician and to proceed to the hospital with reasonable haste. The expectant mother should refrain from eating after the appearance of any of these initial signs of labor. After the patient checks in at the hospital, she may spend a few hours in her room before it is time for the actual birth of the baby, unless there is some sort of emergency.

The *second stage* in the process of childbirth—from the time the cervix is completely dilated until the fetus is expelled—lasts approximately two hours in the instance of first babies and about one hour in subsequent deliveries. In some confinements, the amniotic membrane or sac will not have ruptured despite other initial signs of labor. The obstetrician will then surgically rupture the membrane. The head of the fetus at this phase presses on the mother's lower vagina and bowel, the pressure producing a reflexive action of the muscles in that area that helps to expel the fetus. The infant is pushed along the birth canal with each contraction until its head appears at the external opening of the vagina.

The mother is now placed on the delivery table in such a position that her knees are bent and her thighs are kept wide apart by leg holders. Wrist straps secure the wrists only for the purpose of preventing movement of the hands while the patient is anesthetized. The genital area, abdomen, and inner thighs are thoroughly cleansed, and the region is covered with a sterile sheet containing an 18-inch opening. The patient is catheterized (*i.e.,* urine is withdrawn from the bladder by means of a tube passed through the urethra) to be sure there will be no accidental voiding while the baby passes through the vagina. Severe pressure on a full bladder, furthermore, could be injurious to the mother.

As the head of the fetus pushes forward in the progress of labor, the tissue between vagina and rectum must stretch to an extreme degree. Frequently the opening to the vagina is not sufficiently elastic and the emergence of the baby's head forces a tear. To prevent this, the obstetrician often performs an *episiotomy,* which is a cutting of the tissue with scissors. The straight cut is simple to repair and heals rapidly.

The mother is now made aware that her help is needed to force the baby into the world by contracting her abdominal muscles to create additional pressure. The obstetrician, meanwhile, may apply pressure on her abdomen; it is sometimes helpful in speeding up the birth process if

FIGURE 9.12 Scissors in position for an episiotomy.

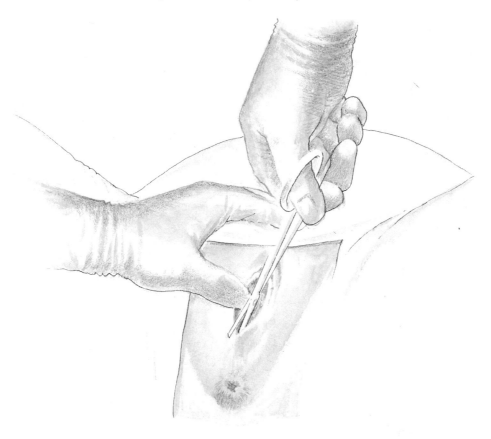

he applies pressure on the chin of the infant through the thin tissue of the perineum.

When the infant's head emerges from the vagina, it turns spontaneously either to the right or left, depending upon the way the shoulders are turned. The physician holds its head with both hands and gently guides it downward—never pulling, only guiding—while one shoulder and then the other emerges. After the expulsion of the head and shoulders, the rest is a simple matter because the trunk and limbs are quite small in comparison with the head and shoulders.

The baby sometimes emerges with too much skin for his face and head, giving him a wrinkled appearance. This is because the bones of the head, which have not yet grown together, overlap and decrease the size of

FIGURE 9.13 Principal movements in the procedure of labor and delivery.

1. Head floating, before engagement

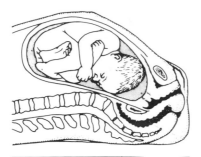

2. Engagement, flexion, descent

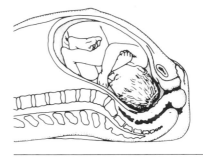

3. Further descent, internal rotation

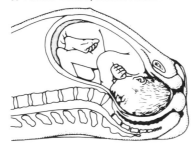

4. Complete rotation, beginning extension

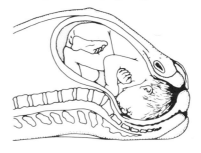

5. Complete extension

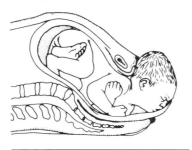

6. Restitution, (external rotation)

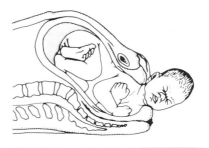

7. Delivery of anterior shoulder

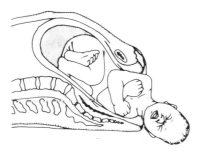

8. Delivery of posterior shoulder

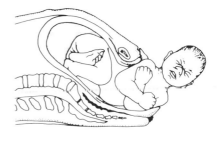

the skull in order to facilitate the birth. The head will quickly return to its normal shape and the wrinkles will fill out.

As the baby's head emerges, the obstetrician, using a rubber bulb-type syringe, removes any blood, amniotic fluid, or watery mucus that may have accumulated in the infant's nose and mouth. To facilitate his first breath, some doctors still hold the infant upside down by his heels and slap his bottom. But most physicians do not consider this necessary, since the change in temperature and atmospheric pressure is sufficient to cause breathing to start.

With an infant's first breath, a drastic change occurs in his circulatory and respiratory processes. Nourishment and oxygen had previously been supplied through the placenta by way of the umbilical cord. The same pressure and temperature changes that force the baby to breathe also create a vacuum in the chest cavity, and this vacuum causes blood from the ductus arteriosis to be directed into the baby's pulmonary artery and lungs. The sphincter muscle of the ductus arteriosis contracts, but never relaxes. Blood circulates to the heart through the pulmonary veins and fills the left auricle.

There is now no further need for an opening between the auricles, and a flap of tissue therefore closes the opening. It takes a few minutes for the process to be activated and to become effective. During this time the baby is bluish in color, but as circulation is directed into his pulmonary system he becomes pink. This process seldom fails, but if it does, the result is a "blue baby." Fortunately, modern surgery can correct this abnormality.

Now that the infant is breathing the oxygen of the outside world, he no longer needs the placenta or the umbilical cord. Once the cord stops pulsating and the baby is breathing regularly, the cord is clamped and cut about three inches from the abdomen. The clamp is left in place until the stub dries up and drops off.

To eliminate any possibility of a gonorrheal or other eye infection, a weak silver nitrate solution or an ophthalmic ointment of penicillin is used in the newborn's eyes.

In the *third stage* the placenta is delivered, about 15 minutes after the baby. Muscular contractions shrink the uterus and the area of placental attachment. This systolic action detaches the placenta from the uterine wall and expels it into the vagina within a short period—3 to 10 minutes. The obstetrician sometimes presses the uterus downward to facilitate expulsion. Occasionally his efforts are unavailing, and the physician must then follow the umbilical cord with gloved fingers and peel the placenta from the uterus.

If an episiotomy was necessary, the obstetrician repairs it with absorbable catgut. The tissue heals rapidly and without discomfort.

The baby's birth is now accomplished. All that remains to be done is

FIGURE 9.14 Inspection of the placenta immediately after its delivery.

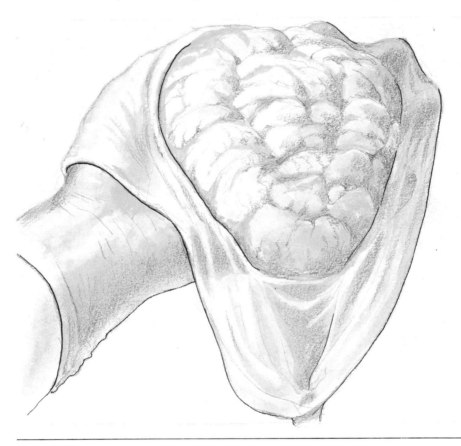

to wheel the mother to the recovery room and the baby to the nursery, while the nervous father is reassured and congratulated!

Caesarean Section

A caesarean section is a surgical procedure whereby the baby is born through a low transverse incision in the abdominal wall and in the anterior wall of the uterus. The popular but erroneous legend that Julius Caesar was delivered surgically gives the operation its name. Probably the term "caesarean" originated from an ancient Roman law, which was later incorporated into a legal code called Lex Caesarea. This statute was enacted to save children's lives by making it mandatory that an operation be performed on a woman who died in the advanced stages of pregnancy.

In the past, the death rate among women undergoing this surgery was exceptionally high because of hemorrhage and infection. Today, however, death following a caesarean section is extremely rare, and a woman may have 2 or 3 babies this way. Indeed, caesarean delivery of 5 or 6 infants to the same mother is no longer highly unusual. The scar tissue left by a ceasarean operation, however, is not as strong as normal tissue, which suggests a limitation on future pregnancies that must be terminated by a section. Physicians often suggest the tying of the woman's fallopian tubes after her third such delivery.

Anesthetics in Childbirth

For generations, girls have been indoctrinated in the belief that childbirth is an event burdened with suffering and threat to life. As an unfortunate consequence, the entire sex life of many women falls under the pall of their fears of pregnancy and childbirth. Coitus therefore develops overtones of unpleasantness and pain and becomes something to be avoided.

Anthropologists have demonstrated that suffering during childbirth is related to the individual woman's past experiences, her expectations regarding the nature and severity of childbirth pains, and the culture in which she lives (Melzack). There is, to be sure, some pain to be expected from the uterine contractions and vaginal expansion involved in parturition, but extreme suffering is likely to be an outgrowth of the cultural and emotional agents mentioned above. Understanding the birth process, having confidence in the obstetrician, and feeling secure within the marriage are important factors in an easy delivery. The art of relaxation and the ability to free oneself from fear are also directly pertinent. An interesting illustration of childbirth unencumbered by anxiety was the recent account of a Michigan woman who delivered a healthy infant weighing just under 8 pounds while she took an afternoon nap (Sex in the news *d*).

A strikingly valuable contribution to maternal peace of mind and comfort has been the introduction of anesthetics in the conduct of parturition. The art and science of anesthesia have become so refined that there is now rarely an excuse for any of the anguish traditionally ascribed to childbirth. It is curious to remember, however, that the initial reaction to the use of anesthetics in childbirth was distinct opposition from the clergy, who quoted the biblical pronouncement against women from Genesis 3:16, "In sorrow thou shalt bring forth children." Some physicians, as well, judged the use of anesthetics in this connection as being in opposition to nature. Most of these objections were dispelled in the popular mind, however, when Queen Victoria was delivered of her seventh child with the aid of anesthetics (Beigel *d*).

It is surprising that many people, physicians as well as laymen, still argue that a woman will not love her child unless she experiences pain during delivery. Such nonsensical thinking is rapidly disappearing. The indications actually are that if any difference in mother love exists, it is in an increase in love for the child during whose birth the mother did *not* experience any severe pain which she might later consciously or unconsciously associate with the child.

The "New" Childbirth

An approach to childbirth has developed in recent years that seeks to reduce a woman's pain during labor through prior physical and psychological conditioning, rather than through reliance solely on drugs and chemical means. Termed "natural childbirth" by its originator, Dr. Grantly Dick-Read, it is now more commonly called "prepared," "cooperative," or "controlled" childbirth, since these terms, unlike "natural childbirth," do not suggest a labor completely without help or medication. While opposed to the routine use of heavy sedation, the new approach to childbirth in no way insists on a woman's doing without light medication during labor or without some form of anesthesia during the actual birth if she or her doctor feels it is necessary.

Several methods of such childbirth preparation, ranging from physical training to hypnosis, are now prevalent. The approach most favored in this country is the psychophysical one, typified by the Lamaze method of psychoprophylactic childbirth. This method, which originated in Russia and was introduced to the Western world in 1951 by Dr. Fernand Lamaze, consists of a series of classes for the expectant parents. In them are outlined the physical and emotional changes occurring during pregnancy, labor, and delivery. They provide, as well, training in the muscle-control exercises and breathing techniques to be used during labor. The husband learns how to assist his wife in her practice sessions at home and during her confinement. The primary goal is to help the woman participate actively in the birth of her baby with a minimum of fear and pain.

Advocates of childbirth education feel that childbirth should be a rewarding experience for both parents. Consequently they are critical of the use of amnesia-producing drugs, as well as of the depersonalized obstetrical care and arbitrary separation of mother, husband, and baby practiced in many hospitals. They favor the presence of the husband in the labor room (and in the delivery room, too, if the doctor and hospital permit and the husband so desires); rooming-in privileges for the mother who wants her baby with her during her hospital stay; and breast-feeding.

Those wishing further information on this new approach to childbirth should read *Childbirth Without Fear* by Grantly Dick-Read, *Thank You, Dr. Lamaze* by Majorie Karmel, *Awake and Aware* by Irwin Chabon, or *Childbirth with Hypnosis* by William S. Kroger.

Multiple Births

Multiple births occur about once per 80 to 89 births (Carbary; Eastman and Hellman; Trainer). Twins occur once in 80 births, triplets once in 80 × 80 cases (6400), and quadruplets once in 80 × 80 × 80 cases (512,000). Heredity, the age of the mother, and racial factors appear to be of significance in that multiple births apparently occur more frequently in one family than in another, and to more women in their 30s than in their 20s. Blacks have more twins than do whites, who in turn have more twins than do Oriental women. Triplets are born to whites at a 1 to 10,200 ratio and to nonwhites at a 1 to 6200 ratio, this difference holding in both northern and southern states (Eastman and Hellman).

Identical twins develop from a single fertilized ovum that first divides and then separates, after which each part continues the process of cell division independently. Identical twins, consequently, possess identical sets of chromosomes and are therefore always of the same sex. They have a single placenta and chorion, but each twin is ordinarily contained in its own amniotic sac and is nurtured through its own umbilical cord. There are a few rare cases in which twins share an amnion; the latest occurred in February 1972 in Amarillo, Texas, and is only the forty-fourth such occurrence on record (*Houston Chronicle b*).

If the developing cell mass does not make a complete separation in the identical-twinning process, the result is *Siamese* (or joined) *twins*.

Fraternal twins develop from two separate ova, both of which are usually fertilized at relatively the same time. A single follicle may expel

---

FIGURE 9.15 Double-ovum or "fraternal" twins with separate placentas (left). Single-ovum or "identical" twins with a common placenta (right).

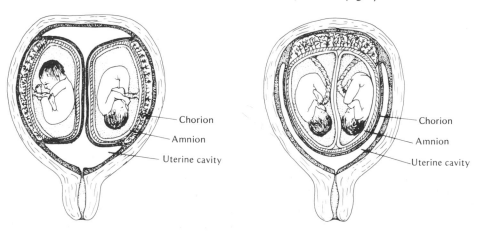

Chorion
Amnion
Uterine cavity

Chorion
Amnion
Uterine cavity

FIGURE 9.16   Various positions of twins in the uterus.

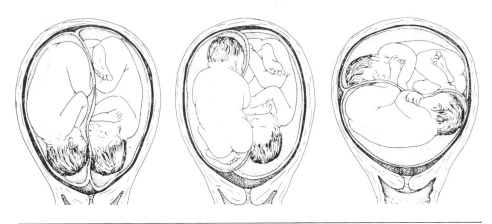

two or more mature ova, or ova in two or more follicles may develop to maturity simultaneously (Eastman and Hellman). Fraternal twins can be of the same or different sex, and have separate umbilical cords, chorions, and placentas. They bear no more resemblance to one another than siblings born separately.

The birth of most twins follows the usual pattern of parturition, although some interesting variations in the conception and birth process have occasionally occurred. For example, most twins arrive within a few minutes to an hour of each other; however, in some (infrequent) cases considerable time elapses between their births. In one instance, the twin babies arrived 48 days apart; in another, 30, with one infant being born in December and the other in January. Mothers have given birth to twins of two different races—fathered, it follows, by two men, the conceptions having taken place within a short time of each other. At least one birth of twins has been recorded in which the babies, clearly fathered by different men, had different blood types (Carbary).

Triplets may result from the fertilization of three different ova. More commonly, only two eggs are involved, one of which separates and then develops into identical twins. *Quadruplets* are for the most part the product of the fertilization of two ova, each of which separates and develops into a set of identical twins.

In multiple births, the percentage of males decreases with the number of children born. Among single births in one large sample, the percentage of males was 51.59%; among twins, 50.85%; among triplets, 49.54%; and among quadruplets, 46.48%. The explanation very likely is that from conception on, survival favors the female, so that in multiple births the biological tendency observed in single births is presumably increased (Eastman and Hellman).

Viable twin pregnancies will terminate about 22 days earlier than viable single pregnancies, the average gestation period for twins being 37 weeks.

Despite old wives' tales to the contrary, the future fertility of human twins, whether or not of the same sex, is no different from that of the singly born. Among lower animals, it might be noted, twins are in fact less fertile than animals born singly (Eastman and Hellman).

LACTATION

Lactation is the process of milk secretion from the mother's breasts following childbirth. The placenta not only provides for the development of the fetus through its linkage with the mother, but also produces the hormones that prepare the mammary glands for secreting milk. During pregnancy, these same hormones inhibit the pituitary gland from producing the milk-forming chemical until such time as it is needed.

Oddly enough, milk is not needed by the baby immediately after birth. The need usually arises from two to five days later. The first secretion the baby receives from the breast is *colostrum*, a substance present in the breast immediately after birth. The effect of colostrum upon the newborn is not positively known, but the substance is of high protein content and is believed to aid in giving the child immunity to many infectious diseases during the early months of his life (Steen and Montagu). Some obstetricians believe that it functions primarily as a laxative, helping to rid the infant's intestines of a substance called *meconium* (fecal matter consisting of mucus, bile, and epithelial threads). Colostrum disappears from the mother's breasts two or three days after delivery, and true milk replaces it.

After the placenta has been expelled and its inhibiting hormones are no longer produced, the mother's pituitary gland begins to produce *prolactin*, a lactogenic hormone that induces the lactation process. When lactation first begins, the breasts become swollen and congested. The ducts leading from within the breasts to the nipples fill with milk, and the mother usually experiences an uncomfortable sensation, or even pain, for a period of a day or so.

Lactation is often accompanied by such psychological and physiological symptoms as fatigue, headache, hot and painful breasts, and low-grade fever, for which the infant's sucking provides relief. In addition, it is the opinion of many doctors that the sucking also prompts certain uterine contractions that help reduce the uterus to its normal size.

Certain substances consumed by the lactating mother, such as alcohol, strong sedatives, and vegetable cathartics, may adversely affect the nursing infant. Alcohol concentration in the mother's milk, for example, is the same as in her blood. A nursing mother should therefore consume none of these substances unless they are approved by her physician.

Occasionally certain physiological difficulties are encountered in nursing a baby, in which case the physician can usually offer a solution. One of the most recurrent problems is an *inverted nipple*, a congenital anomaly resulting from fibrous bands holding the nipple in rather than allowing it to protrude in the normal manner. At the time of lactation, the mother may experience severe pain if the condition is not corrected. Sometimes a small suction cup may be used successfully to draw out the nipple; in other instances nursing will serve to correct the inversion.

Breast-feeding tends to delay subsequent conception by prolonging postpartum amenorrhea (absence of menstruation). However, a woman may ovulate before her first postpartum menstrual flow. Indeed, about one in 20 women starts another pregnancy without having menstruated after the preceding one (Tietze c).

Medical Economics noted in 1956 that only 12% of babies then leaving the hospital were breast-fed, whereas in 1946, the figure had been 33%, and, in the not too distant past, as many as 90% of all babies were breast-fed. The percentage appears to have risen only slightly since then, for in 1966—the last year for which valid statistics are available—only 20% of mothers breast-fed their babies (Mayer). One reason for this decline in breast-feeding is the fear of mothers that nursing will cause their breasts to sag, making their figures less attractive. Such a consequence is by no means inevitable—and the advantages of breast-feeding over bottle-feeding for both mother and infant are several.

Yet the apprehension remains. Women reveal anxiety over the shape and size of their breasts and often feel inferior in their role as a woman and sexual being if they consider their breasts too small. Indeed, sweater and brassiere-padding enterprises have benefited from this excessive concern over breast size (if, indeed, they have not deliberately encouraged it). At least one shop advertises, "We fix flats!" It is little wonder that people consider breasts a symbol of ultimate sexuality in view of the emphasis placed on them in advertisements and clothing styles. Even toy stores pander to this mammary preoccupation by keeping their shelves well stocked with the high-bosomed dolls for which little girls clamor.

Plastic surgeons have devised ingenious methods for remolding breasts into desired shapes and sizes through the use of surgery, plastics, and silicone, although this means of increasing a woman's narcissistic image is ill-advised in most cases because of certain physiological complications that sometimes develop. However, such cosmetic operations have now been fairly well perfected and many women—especially if some breast defect seriously impairs their attractiveness or self-image—reap considerable benefit from the surgery (Zarem).

Apparently neither men nor women realize that the appeal of the breast varies widely from culture to culture and from era to era, and that breast size and shape have nothing to do with sexuality, except insofar as psychological factors are concerned. It cannot be denied, of course, that both male and female breasts have many nerve endings which, when properly stimulated, often afford sexual excitement and pleasure. But there are an equal number of these endings in small breasts and in large ones. Since the supply of nerve endings is the same, regardless of breast size, it is a simple matter to make the calculation that small breasts are per square inch by far more erogenous than larger ones, and may in fact be a distinctly pleasurable advantage for both man and woman during sex play. Furthermore, very large breasts are not necessarily an advantage in lactation, because they often contain an excessive amount of fat tissue that can interfere with the function of the milk glands.

Breast development in a hormonally normal woman is largely a matter of heredity; exercise, injection of hormones, or applications of creams and salves are of little use in altering nature's design. Nevertheless, many persons of questionable ethics continue to bilk the small-breasted female public with various worthless and often expensive preparations and mechanical devices, as the National Better Business Bureau can testify. Sagging of the breasts can to some degree be prevented by well-designed and properly fitted brassieres. However, a good posture, sensible nutrition, and proper hygiene remain the biggest assets to an attractive figure. A physician can offer the best advice for preventing breast-tissue breakdown during pregnancy, lactation, and weaning. If a woman finds the dimensions of her breasts unsatisfactory, the use of a padded and properly supportive brassiere is the most sensible solution. And, as was mentioned, plastic surgery may be indicated in certain instances.

Women who are caught up in narcissistic breast symbolism too often avoid proper physical examinations for fear that some previously undetected abnormality of the breast will be discovered that will necessitate surgery, thus destroying their femininity. This refusal to face the possibility of a breast malignancy needlessly endangers the lives of many women, and a reassessment of their system of values is certainly indicated.

It is a normal phenomenon for many of the lower mammals to have multiple breasts and a milk-line that the mammary glands follow. About 1% of human females have more than the normal two, making the condition less uncommon than many would believe (Netter). There is usually only one extra breast in these cases; it is ordinarily nonfunctional, but it can be quite normally developed and functional. Men occasionally have breast development nearly identical to that of a normal woman. Surgery will usually remedy the anomalies of extra and abnormally oversized breasts (Netter), thereby reducing or removing altogether the stress that "being different" creates.

PART THREE

THE SEXUAL ACT

10 TECHNIQUES IN SEXUAL AROUSAL

Many authorities have made much of the fact that sexual stimuli affect men and women in different ways, but the point requires clarification. For the differences are less extensive than one is often led to believe, as the Kinsey investigators have demonstrated (Kinsey et al. a, c). For example, in a province one takes to be strictly male—burlesque shows and stag films—the Kinsey researchers found that 33% of the women in their sample had as strong a sexual response as men to such stimuli, while a small percentage had an even stronger one (Kronhausen and Kronhausen).

Although some fundamental male–female differences certainly exist with regard to sexual stimuli–response patterns, there is probably considerably less such dissimilarity between the sexes than there is individual variation among members of the same sex (Kronhausen and Kronhausen). Indeed, strange and interesting sexual excitants have been recorded in the erotic histories of both men and women. The Kinsey investigators report, as examples, that some women have been brought to orgasm simply by having their eyebrows stroked, by having their body or hair gently blown upon, or by having pressure applied to their teeth (Kinsey et al. c).

Basically, as has been noted, the sex drive of women is as powerful as that of men. But men and women in the main respond to different types of both psychological and physiological stimulation, and they respond to the same stimuli in a slightly different manner. Women have been conditioned for generations by a society muddled in its thinking on sexual matters to inhibit their sexuality, if not deny it altogether, and to stifle their normal response to sexual stimuli. These culturally imposed inhibitions no doubt account for the popular misconception that women are erotically less responsive than men.

Sexual arousal in humans, both male and female, springs from psychological as well as from physiological sources (Eichenlaub *a*; Ellis *b*; Maslow *a*). Such arousal usually begins with verbalization and indirect gestures (Eichenlaub *a*; Ellis *j*).

In time, a couple usually build up their own private store of verbal endearments, which are then used advantageously to set the stage for satisfying sexual interplay. A man can, and should, express to his partner his feelings that she is loved, exciting, and sexually desirable by calling her a pet name. A woman can, and should, convey her pleasure in her partner by responding readily with similar endearments (Eichenlaub *a*). Making the sexual partner aware that one enjoys his or her appearance, abilities, intellect, strengths, and the like is only half of a successful preliminary sexual interaction. The partner must also be made to know that he is enjoyed and appreciated as a lover.

To abandon oneself in an uninhibited expression of love and excitement, to have these manifestations eagerly accepted, to receive in turn spontaneous and equally unrestrained expressions of love and desire: these are the ingredients intrinsic to a sexual relationship in its deepest and fullest measure. Any person who confines his lovemaking activities merely to the search for orgasmic release soon learns that sex can become quite boring. The degree of pleasure and fulfillment derived from sex is great or small in direct proportion to what has been given. Anyone participating in sexual activity in a restricted, inhibited way, or simply to achieve the goal of orgasm, is cheating both himself and his partner.

The more reckless and uninhibited the response, short of causing severe physical pain, that a woman makes at the peak of sexual excitement, the more pleased most men are (Mozes *a*). This is not to say that a man expects his partner to be physically violent and uncontrolled, or verbally loud and offensive. Most men want a woman to express her excitement and involvement in somewhat more subtle ways, but nevertheless to leave little doubt that she has let herself go completely and has responded—authentically—exactly as she felt. This sort of open communication is not as difficult to achieve as it might sound. It can be assisted by actions such as smooth, silky, rhythmical body movements accompanied by low moans and gasps, all building to an expressive crescendo at the moment of orgasm. But whatever form the communication takes, freedom of response and expression is the key.

OVERCOMING SEXUAL INEXPERIENCE

On the man's shoulders, whether he likes it or not, commonly rests the burden of directing a couple's sexual activity. Furthermore, most women seem to expect their partners to proceed through all aspects of their sexual life with an air of confidence. One finds it difficult to fathom just how a young man is to acquire confidence if he is inexperienced, especially if he has been indoctrinated with fearsome warnings against "failure in bed," as most men are in their formative years. Nevertheless, even though the woman herself may be inexperienced, knowing very little about sex, its techniques, and its stimuli–response patterns, she is likely to expect her partner to be experienced and expert in the art of lovemaking—and she often will be dismayed if he is not (Caprio a, c; Ellis j).

Sexual adjustment in marriage, particularly when either or both partners are sexually inexperienced, may be made more difficult by unrealistic expectations. The new wife's expectation of expertise and confidence on the part of her young husband in the marriage bed frequently ignores the very real possibility that he, too, may be lacking in proper experience. Furthermore, it is also quite likely that he, as much as his bride, is a victim of society's sexual prohibitions and unsound training in sexual matters. It is indeed unfortunate that custom decrees fixed roles in male–female relationships. Most particularly is it so in the sexual relationship, in which the husband is expected to be dominant and, above all, confident. The disparity between expectations on the one hand and experience on the other, together with the faulty sex education that both husband and wife may have received, frequently paves the way for emotional stress that may eventually manifest itself in any of a variety of sexual problems.

One reason, perhaps, that newlyweds expect immediate lovemaking skill of their partner stems from the emphasis placed by the popular culture—Hollywood films, stories in women's magazines, and paperback novels—on romantic unrealities, which are presented as being basic to enduring marital relationships. Any sensible person recognizes that the absorbed, hypnotic state of romantic love cannot continue indefinitely. It must be replaced by realistic, committed, workable love. Unfortunately, celluloid productions and other fiction would have one think otherwise. They consequently exert an insidious effect on many marital relationships, in that they create expectations of oneself and one's marital partner that are almost impossible to fulfill.

Sexually inexperienced young men and women, therefore, are well advised to acquire as much dispassionate information about sexual techniques as they can from authoritative books, lectures, teachers, and the like—and it might be pointed out that one's peer group seldom falls into this category. It is certainly true that entering marriage with *only* academic information in the matter of human sexuality tends to make a couple's initial sexual experiences more mechanical than spontaneous, but their confidence will be greater than if they had no knowledge, or knowledge based chiefly on hearsay.

Confidence, together with an effort on the man's part at taking charge in initial sexual encounters, will enhance a couple's chances for sexual success in early marriage to a considerable degree. Even if the man does not feel as confident as he might like, he should conduct himself as if he knows what he is doing and as if he is in control of the relationship. His assumption of confidence will go a long way to instilling confidence in his wife. Once frank communication regarding their sex life is firmly established between husband and wife, helping one another toward greater sexual fulfillment becomes much easier.

MAINTAINING A GOOD SEXUAL RELATIONSHIP

In *The Sensuous Woman* ("J"), one of the most popular "how-to-do-it" sex manuals ever written, the author sets forth what in her opinion are the three greatest allies of a woman bent on keeping her man from wandering: imagination; sensitivity to his moods and desires; and the courage to experiment with new sexual techniques, as well as with exciting situations and places in which sexual encounters might take place.

The same allies, of course, will also serve a man well. One leading sexologist, investigating the primary criticisms that a group of American and Canadian women offered of men's lovemaking abilities and techniques, tabulated these results: men are too selfish; they do not properly prepare a woman for coitus, chiefly because there is insufficient sexual foreplay; men are in too much of a hurry; they want to "have sex," which of course differs significantly from making love (DeMartino *b*).

The critics continue: men are not sufficiently concerned that the woman be sexually satisfied; if they do express concern, it reflects more their own ego need to be recognized as "a great lover" than their genuine regard for the woman's needs. Men are not gentle in their approach; they are too crude, forceful, unromantic, or even violent during coitus. Men are unimaginative; their lovemaking techniques are far too mechanical and ritualistic. Men are much too inhibited in their sexual expression; their response is not free and spontaneous. They apparently feel that "letting themselves go" during coitus, especially at the time of orgasm, is an indication of weakness or unmanliness, that a "real man" should be stoic and eminently in control of his responses (DeMartino *b*).

For a man to become a good sex partner, or a better one, he must first be willing to admit that he does not know all there is to know about human sexuality. Many men, unfortunately, are unwilling to make this admission because it threatens their ego and masculine self-image. Thus entrenched in their sexual ignorance, they stumble along ineptly in their sexual relationships, lending much credence to the French maxim that "there are no frigid women, just clumsy men."

A woman, for her part, often has the romantic yet dangerously mistaken notion that her lover should anticipate her sexual needs and the unfolding of them with unerring accuracy. She therefore feels that she has no need to verbalize to him what pleases her sexually. Almost every man wants to please his partner. But in his attempt to outguess her, he frequently makes the wrong move and is mutely condemned as an inept lover. And when he does succeed in pleasing her, he is, unfortunately, frequently rewarded only by her silence (Hamilton, E.).

As superfluous as it may appear, it is nonetheless important to emphasize the fundamental significance of a clean and attractive body in successful sexual interaction. Sex appeal is most certainly not confined to the marriage bed; it exists between the partners at all times and should be carefully nurtured. Attractiveness should not be construed to mean facial and bodily handsomeness but, rather, scrupulous cleanliness of body and clothing, as well as taking the greatest possible advantage of all the physical endowments that nature has seen fit to bestow on each of us. Not everyone can be beautiful, but there is no excuse for anyone's not being attractively neat and clean at all times.

A man who is overweight, chronically unshaven, and slovenly dressed, and whose breath reeks of tobacco or alcohol, can hardly expect to be considered a desirable bed partner. Even if he has a session with shower, toothbrush, and razor later in the evening, his partner's memories of his earlier unattractiveness will detract from her pleasure in the sexual encounter. Similarly, a woman who looks better with cosmetics but neglects to make up her face, sits around home in bathrobe and curlers, allows herself to become significantly overweight or underweight, permits even faint urine, vaginal, or underarm odors to emanate, or does not often shave her legs and underarms is setting the stage for a loss of respect, admiration, and even love. Sexual failure cannot then be far behind.

Why, for example, should not a woman put makeup *on* before going to bed rather than taking it off? The apparition in bed of a woman in hair curlers, the absence of lipstick and eye makeup rendering her face pallid and uninteresting, is less than esthetically and sexually arousing. Perhaps one reason that premarital sex sometimes seems more interesting than sex after a few years of marriage is the effort that a single woman is apt to make to render herself exciting by careful attention to her general appearance.

It is, of course, expecting too much of a wife who has worked at a tiring job or who has had the sole responsibility for contentious, demanding children all day to be consistently rested, seductive, and glamorous at bedtime, just as it is unreasonable to expect a tense, harassed husband to act, or look, the role in bed of a cinematic idol. But, unfortunately, too many people after marriage stop making reasonable or even minimal efforts to keep themselves attractive and interesting in the eyes of their partner. Disenchanted with one another early in marriage, they find their sex life growing stale—or, worse, one or both begin to look elsewhere for the glamour that they feel is missing in the marital relationship.

Certainly before joining each other in bed, whether or not sexual activities are anticipated, each partner should see to it that he has at least a clean body, fresh breath, and neat, attractive nightclothes. To do otherwise is to neglect some of the most basic ingredients of a happy sex life.

This is not to say that some women do not become sexually aroused by the musty smell of a man who has recently perspired or that some men are not excited by the smell or taste of a woman's body that has not been scrubbed clean of its secretions, vaginal or otherwise. Generally speaking, however, most people are far more stimulated by a partner whose body is immaculately clean, the smell of cleanliness perhaps enhanced by the subtle fragrance of perfume or shaving lotion.

The sense of smell is almost as important in sexual stimulation as the sense of sight is (Eichenlaub a). There is, in fact, a physiological relationship between the tissues of the nose and of the sex organs, as was mentioned earlier. Frequently, also, conditioning plays a role in the relationship between the sense of smell and sexuality. During early courtship, for example, the faint scent of a woman's perfume or a man's after-shave lotion may become associated with their developing love and subsequent sexual arousal. Later in the relationship, the same pleasant scent may well serve to reestablish the excitement that developed during courtship. Conditioning quite naturally involves many sensory elements other than smell. Almost any occurrence that forms an association with love and passion during the period of courtship can later be woven advantageously into the fabric of the couple's sexual interaction.

On another level, the qualities of courtesy, kindness, and sensitivity to the needs and desires of others, which are so fundamental to all successful human interaction, are particularly vital to sexual relationships. Bearing in mind the widespread differences in individual needs and desires, it is incumbent upon each person to discover what, precisely, offers the greatest pleasure to his partner in the sexual relationship and to make a genuine effort to incorporate these discoveries into his technique of sexual approach.

For example, to most women a particularly meaningful part of lovemaking is being talked to during the act. Men frequently do not appreciate this need, or fail to meet it, despite the woman's asking her lover to "talk to me." Depending on the particular woman or the stage of lovemaking, the talk should vary from tender and whispered utterances of love to quite earthy, unrestrained expressions that under other circumstances might be considered vulgar (Hamilton, E.).

Pace as well as style is also a matter of individual taste. However, it is ordinarily wisest to proceed slowly and gently, with the goal in mind of bringing gratification to one's lover rather than hurrying to satisfy one's own needs. One should not hesitate, furthermore, even to sacrifice one's own present fulfillment altogether if it means giving greater pleasure to the lover. Not only is it a generous and loving thing to do, but also it will assuredly pay handsome dividends later. The best and certainly the least stressful way for each partner to determine the specific erotic desires of the other is to open wide the doors of candid communication. Neither partner is clairvoyant, and an inadvertently offensive gesture or clumsiness will tend to impede the present response and to inhibit response in similar circumstances at a future time.

Investigation of marital orgasm has revealed that when only 1 to 10 minutes of sexual foreplay is involved, 40% of wives report that they "nearly always" reach orgasm; 50% do so when foreplay is extended to 15 or 20 minutes; and 60% achieve orgasm if an even longer period of foreplay precedes coitus. Furthermore, there is a higher rate of orgasm among those women whose husbands can prolong intromission. When intromission lasts less than a minute before ejaculation occurs, only about 25% of wives achieve orgasm "always" or "nearly always"; about 50% do so if intromission lasts 1 to 11 minutes; and about 65% do so if intromission lasts longer than 11 minutes. Virtually all women are brought to the full extent of their orgasmic capacity if intromission lasts for 16 minutes or longer. The same investigation also revealed the incidental information that many marriages broken by separation or divorce had a history of short rather than long periods of coital intromission (Gebhard a).

Variations in sexual approach and setting can add considerable spice to marriage. Too often sexual acts become ritualized, stale, and unimaginative, engaged in only to provide relief of physical urgency. Couples who wish to preserve delight and vigor in their sexual interaction will work as consistently on this aspect of their marriage as on any other. A husband who impulsively sweeps his wife into his arms in the middle of a happy afternoon and carries her off to the bedroom for a wild lovemaking interlude—or the couple who occasionally have intercourse while showering or visiting some isolated beach—or who engage in an impromptu act of coitus in the backseat of the car when revisiting a "lover's lane" of their courtship years—or who pay an impulsive visit to a motel en route home from a concert—or the wife who surprises her husband by appearing in his study carrying two cold, very dry Martinis and wearing nothing but a smile—these couples are not likely to find sex dull, even after years of marriage.

Couples wishing to maintain sexual interest over a long period of time should also be aware of the negative effect that "too much too soon" can have on love play. A woman, for example, should know the charm and excitement of seminudity, especially in the early part of their sexual encounter (Neiger a). It has been observed that pictures of partly clad females—especially where a portion of the anatomy is "accidentally" exposed—are more exciting to men than many of the more frankly sexual poses.

A woman can put this information to good use. She can become more seductive as an evening wears on through progressive undressing that does not become complete nudity. This "teasing" frequently will not only put her partner in a state of sexual readiness that evening but will also serve his fantasies in the future when personal contact between the couple may not be possible (Levitt and Brady). (Once the appropriate point in lovemaking has been reached, however, the woman must abandon the pretense of holding herself back from her partner. Her teasing abandoned, she should then enter into the sexual act as freely, openly, intently, and intensely as possible.)

Playing soft music, using mirrors to observe closely the intimacies of the sex act, and perusing sensuous literature and art are other devices that help keep boredom out of the bedroom (Ellis b). Both men and women want variety in their sexual lives. If this ideal is reached within their marriage, there is considerably less likelihood that either will seek it elsewhere. Imagination and a willingness to experiment, coupled with an air of confidence and consideration, will serve most marriages very well.

It must be stressed, however, that a certain degree of monotony will inevitably enter a sexual relationship of some duration, no matter how much the man and woman love each other or how much novelty they attempt to introduce into their sex life. Psychic stimulation of the sort that heretofore caused almost immediate erotic arousal becomes increasingly ineffective, and the man becomes more and more dependent on his partner's direct stimulation of his penis to help achieve an erection. Since men typically feel a threat to their masculinity when penile erections are sluggish, couples are well advised to use this very effective means of attaining sexual arousal (Lief et al.).

It is for these very reasons that many marriage counselors recommend *planned romance*—setting aside a specific time for coitus, such as a Saturday afternoon when the children will be away visiting their grandparents. Other counselors disagree, saying that planning coitus ruins spontaneity. But total spontaneity in sexual activity disappears from most marriages after a few weeks in any event, even under the most ideal of circumstances. It would therefore seem that planned coitus, at least some of the time, promises more relaxed enjoyment and is more cementing to the marriage than spontaneous sexual experiences in which either or both partners are not at their best, emotionally or physically.

THE EROGENOUS ZONES

Erogenous zones are those parts of the body possessing a large concentration of nerve endings (sometimes termed "sexual nerves") that, when stimulated, cause sexual arousal. These areas are numerous, and they are basically the same in man and woman—although there are, of course, individual variations in the areas producing excitement and in the degree of arousal.

The French physician Ernest Chambard became in 1881 the first person to make a thorough scientific investigation into the erogenous areas of the human body, subsequently issuing a report of his findings. Since Chambard's time, various studies have demonstrated that the surfaces of mucous membranes are important erogenous zones, and that many of these are capable of erection and tumescence (Sentnor and Hult).

The most sensitive erogenous areas are the genitals and the areas surrounding them: the inner and outer regions of the thighs, the buttocks, and the abdomen. The nongenital erogenous zones extend over a large portion of the body, some areas being more sensitive than others. The breasts (particularly the nipples), armpits, small of the back, shoulders, neck, earlobes, scalp, eyelids, and especially the mouth, tongue, eyes, and nose are all areas rich in nerve endings (Eichenlaub a; Ellis a, j; Kinsey et al. a, c; Masters and Johnson n).

Sexual arousal takes place when messages are sent by the stimulated sexual nerve endings to the brain, which in turn transmits them to the centers of the lower spinal column controlling sexual impulses. These centers can also receive messages directly from the genital area without the intermediary transmission and relay of impulses by the brain (Coleman).

A psychological or physical block at some point can deter or even prevent sexual excitement. For example, messages of disapproval, unpleasantness, fear, pain, or injury can and often do delay or obstruct altogether the channel to sexual centers, thus preventing arousal. On the other hand, as has been mentioned, pleasant messages, such as a lovely sight, a gentle word, a soft touch, an exotic scent, or a harmonious sound can easily evoke sexual feelings. Pleasing sensory stimuli may produce erotic thoughts, which in turn may cause penile erection. Women, however, are apparently less responsive to this type of psychological stimulus than men are (Kinsey et al. c).

Although the erogenous zones appear to be a matter of heredity and, in general, are common to all people, individual differences, largely the result of conditioning, are wide. Present scientific data indicate that there are no abnormal erogenous regions, and those that are uncommon are so simply as the result of individual background and experience. For example, if a man were to tickle the sole of his partner's foot preceding each pleasant act of coitus, sooner or later foot-tickling would come to be associated with pleasurable intercourse, and the sole of the foot would become a conditioned erogenous zone for that particular woman. Should she later marry another person, however, the conditioned erogenous zone on the sole of the foot might well appear to be abnormal to her new husband (Williamson).

As with psychological factors that serve as potent erotic stimuli, mutual experimentation and frank discussion are the best ways to discover which physiological areas of stimulation are the most effective for individual sexual arousal (Caprio *d*; Ellis *j*). This is important precisely because of the marked degree of difference among members of the same sex, as well as between the sexes, in the preferred method of sexual arousal and the time required to become aroused. A man frequently becomes sexually excited with minimal tactile stimulation, while a woman often needs loving foreplay prior to the caressing of the erogenous areas of her body.

The genitals, the part of the body most responsive to stimulative techniques, contain millions of nerve endings concentrated in small regions of erectile-type tissue. For a man the most sensitive part of the genitalia is the glans or head of the penis, particularly the lower surface at the corona (ring) and frenum. Probably the most meaningful sexual response that a woman can show a man is her obvious enjoyment of his penis, and her willingness—or, better, her desire—to fondle, play with, kiss, look at, and take it in her mouth as well as in her vagina. Such acts denote acceptance of the man, and indicate to him that she enjoys and considers valuable a part of his anatomy that is highly meaningful to him (Hamilton, E.).

In a woman the clitoris and its glans (which contain a delicate network of nerve endings in erectile-type tissue covered with mucous membrane) are the catalyst for sexual excitation and orgasm. However, her entire vulval region, especially the vestibule and labia minora, are rich in nerve endings and are highly responsive to stimulation. The walls of the vagina, with the exception of the upper front area where the roots of the clitoris are located, are somewhat insensitive because they contain only a few nerve endings. The cervix is so insensitive that it can be cauterized or surgically cut without the aid of anesthesia (Sentnor and Hult). Nevertheless, some women apparently do experience heightened sexual pleasure from penile pressure against the cervix as it, in turn, moves the uterus and its supporting broad ligaments. Both of the latter are encased in the peritoneal membrane, which has great sensitivity (Clark *n*).

Some physiologists (Kegel) believe that penile stimulation of the highly sensitive nerve endings in the muscles encircling the vaginal opening generates great erotic pleasure. Women with weak vaginal muscles, according to these theorists, are perhaps unable to receive sexual satisfaction from coitus until these muscles are strengthened through the exercises described in Chapter 7. This knowledge of the female anatomy, along with clinical observation, has led some of the nation's outstanding sexologists to the conclusion that many women experience both clitoral and vaginal orgasms.

It is well known that the lower side of the penis is particularly sensitive because of the network of nerves surrounding the urethra. The female urethra, the meatus of which is slightly above or forward of the vaginal opening, is supplied with similarly sensitive nerve endings. When the area of the vagina nearest the urethra is gently stimulated—for example, by the in-and-out penile movements of coitus—the woman may experience erotic sensations that can add immensely to her sexual pleasure (Clark o).

The perineum of both man and woman is sensitive to manipulation. This area includes the anus and inner portion of the thighs, and extends from the anus to the lower region of the sexual organs. About half of all men and women, in fact, report that they experience erotic reactions to some form of anal stimulation (Kinsey *et al.* c). While the mouth, lips, and nose are widely recognized as highly erogenous areas, there is nonetheless considerable variation in the degree of their sensitivity, because of personal differences resulting, primarily, from conditioning and, secondarily, from differences in supplies of nerve endings, the latter condition being a matter of individual heredity. The breasts are another important erogenous zone common to both men and women. The nipples and areolae are especially responsive to several stimuli.

Developing One's Own Sexuality

Today more than ever before, the attitude is becoming accepted that both men and women have the right to seek as complete and satisfying sexual fulfillment as possible. It is reflected in many current books and articles, which discuss freely the importance of sexual completeness both in and out of marriage. No longer are the sexual needs of women considered subordinate to those of men. Men and women are encouraged to unloosen their inhibitions and permit themselves complete sexual responsiveness, despite lingering remnants of the sexual puritanism that has traditionally obstructed freedom of sexual expression (Comfort).

Sexual responsiveness (or the lack of it) is largely learned. The basic biological inclinations toward sexual responsiveness exist, of course, in both men and women. But beyond these physiological basics, the peaks, nuances, and joy of sexuality are learned and refined through experience and experimentation. How better can one understand the fine points of sexual sensitivity and responsiveness than by experimenting with his own body? All of us have done so throughout our lives. Unfortunately, however, guilt, shame, and fear, learned from outside forces, as well as ignorance, have prevented many of us from experimenting as fully with our own bodies as is required to develop our sensuousness to its greatest extent. (And it seems only reasonable that one cannot fully appreciate, enjoy, and fulfill the sexuality of another person until one can enjoy and fulfill his own.) However, certain techniques exist that are widely recognized as capable of leading almost anyone to new heights of sexual enjoyment and responsiveness.

Masturbation

Probably the most successful way of learning to respond to one's full sexual capacity is through self-stimulation. Masturbation is a perfectly normal, healthy act in boys and girls and in men and women, young and old. Nevertheless, it has long been a subject of great contention, and discussions of it are often rife with ignorance, misinformation, superstition, and shame. It is hence scarcely surprising that many people, especially the naive, come to believe that masturbation is an evil, abnormal, or, at best, infantile practice.

Only under extremely rare circumstances can masturbation be considered a sexual abnormality, especially since well over 95% of men and about 70% of women practice it at one time or another (Kinsey *et al. a, c*). It should be viewed as a sexual problem only when it becomes, as it occasionally does, part of the behavior pattern of psychotic patients, or is utilized as the sole method of sexual outlet when other outlets are readily available. Indeed, those who do not practice masturbation, or have never done so, are far more likely to be suffering from an emotional or sexual problem than those who have masturbatory experience. Suppression of the tendency to masturbate usually occurs when the individual's thinking regarding sexual matters is beclouded with guilt, fear, and perplexity (Ellis *a, b*).

Long prior to the birth of Hippocrates, the "Father of Medicine," down through the ages to 1900, the medical world remained largely ignorant of cause and effect in sexual behavior. Objectivity and a scientific approach were notoriously lacking in those paltry investigations that were made. Occasionally some brave scientific soul would reach out for enlightenment, but such men were few. Struggles through these dark ages toward an understanding of human sexuality were dealt a near deathblow in the mid-eighteenth century when S.A.D. Tissot of France wrote his *Onana, a Treatise on the Diseases Produced by Onanism*. Projecting his personal problems, to say nothing of his superabundance of ignorance, into his writings, Tissot wrote of the viciousness of "self-abuse," attributing most of the known medical disorders—including consumption, epileptic seizures, gonorrhea, and insanity—to the loss of semen through masturbation. It was Tissot who introduced the fatuous and totally unscientific idea that the loss of one drop of seminal fluid causes more bodily damage and weakness than the loss of 40 drops of blood (Dearborn).

Tissot's theories captured the attention of many, influencing medical men and laymen alike. Other "authorities" added their views to his until even today there still persist irrational social prohibitions against the perfectly normal, and probably beneficial, act of masturbation (Ellis *b*). Fortunately, the vast majority of people seem almost ready to accept masturbation for what it is—a not immoral and certainly harmless act of sexual stimulation and relief. The tide of ignorance concerning masturbation began turning in 1891 when Dr. E. T. Brady became one of the first authorities to challenge the concept of masturbation as a pernicious act, but even Brady considered self-stimulation somewhat dangerous (Dearborn).

The hysteria over masturbation reached such a pitch in the late nineteenth century that "depraved" women who resorted to it were frequently forced by their families to submit to a clitoridectomy (the surgical removal of the clitoris) as a method of control. French medical men, furthermore, expressed their dismay at an occupational hazard peculiar to seamstresses: the masturbatory up-and-down movements of their legs as they treadled their sewing machines were wont to cause orgasms. In at least one establishment, a matron was appointed to circulate among the seamstresses to detect runaway machines as the women became caught up in this "horrible" by-product of their profession (Duffy *a, b*).

Only where abnormality already exists, as in the instance of severely disturbed schizophrenic patients, does the possibility exist that masturbation could be carried to extremes. Nature carefully regulates each individual's sexual activity, and any form of it becomes unpleasant to him when it is overdone. Even in the case of, say, acute schizophrenia, any sexually excessive activity may just as easily involve coitus as masturbation. In either case, the excessive behavior is a symptom of the mental disorder, not the cause of it (Ellis *m*).

Problems that people tend to consider outgrowths of masturbation in fact existed before masturbation ever occurred. The only conflicts that masturbation generates stem from poor sex education and guilt on the part of parents, teachers, peers, and others who pass on their own disturbed attitudes toward a perfectly normal act (Ellis *a, m*).

The arguments against masturbation are legion, time-worn—and invalid. These are some of the more hackneyed ones:

Only the immature person masturbates. Refutation: Masturbation provides about 50% of the total sexual outlet of unmarried college-educated men between the ages of 26 and 30. Among women, the incidence of masturbation to orgasm increases until middle age, after which time it remains about the same (Kinsey *et al. a, c*). The act of masturbation, therefore, can hardly be called immature.

Masturbation is unsocial or antisocial. Refutation: It is true, of course, that masturbation usually takes place when the person is alone. But other forms of sexual behavior, including coitus, likewise are rarely carried out in public view. If a shy or withdrawn person masturbates, he does not become introverted *because* of masturbation any more than an outgoing, popular person who masturbates becomes extroverted because of it.

Masturbating too frequently causes fatigue and physical debilitation. Refutation: The human body exerts excellent control over the amount of sexual activity that the individual engages in. When he has reached the point of satiation, further sexual activity becomes physically unpleasant, so that it is virtually impossible for him to indulge in "too much sex." In any case, there is no logic in the premise that one form of sexual functioning more than another generates debility and fatigue. An orgasm is an orgasm, whether it is the result of coitus, heavy petting, or masturbation. When the body is orgasmically surfeited from any sexual activity, further sexual functioning is most unlikely to occur, if not altogether impossible.

Sexual fantasies associated with masturbation are emotionally unhealthy. Refutation: Fantasy is inescapably a part of human existence; few today would argue with the postulate that what is universal in human nature is also normal and acceptable. Our conscious mental state involves a continuous flow of fantasy, sexual and otherwise, whether of fleeting images or protracted, volitional daydreams.

Daydreams that are not purely fanciful play, in fact, an extremely important role in planning for the future, as we imagine ourselves in a series of life situations. We reject some prospects and accept others, according to our reactions to the imagined conditions. Erotic fantasies are no less important in planning for a satisfying future sexual life. Indeed, they can help the individual to formulate his code of behavior by providing him some advance perception of the negative consequences of certain actions— *e.g.,* the guilt feelings or pregnancy that might result from premarital coitus.

Sexual fantasy does not occur only during masturbation. It can take place in the absence of any sexual activity whatever, in the course of coition, and in homosexual contact, as well as during masturbation (Sullivan, P. R.). Its effects can be beneficial, indifferent, or detrimental, regardless of what form of sexual activity (or inactivity) it accompanies. Thus the married couple who have been titillated by sexual fantasies during the day will quite likely find coitus more exciting than usual that night. But when a shy, inhibited young person allows his endless romantic or sexual fantasy to impede him from facing actual encounters with members of the opposite sex, the daydreaming cannot be called healthy.

A woman may fantasize, quite normally, of being wooed and seduced by her church's choir director while she is, in fact, masturbating (or having sexual intercourse with her husband). To allow herself actually to be seduced by the choir director might well be a self-defeating, unhealthy act—and even a dangerous one should the husband learn of it. While it is quite normal, and actually rather common, for a woman to fantasy being made love to simultaneously by several men, and perhaps by a woman or two, it may well be a sign of maladjustment if she permits such an act to actually occur, for she then must contend not merely with her psyche, but with the law and her reputation as well.

As a further example, a young soldier separated from his wife may fantasy sex relations with a voluptuous bar-girl while masturbating, thereby preserving his ideal of marital fidelity. Yet another young husband separated from his wife may indulge in the same fantasies, but not masturbate, because masturbation violates his religious principles. Since his sexual tensions heighten his irascibility and interfere with his attending to his duties, sexual fantasy in his case cannot be considered beneficial.

All in all, it would seem more healthy than unhealthy that fantasy accompany masturbation; otherwise, masturbation becomes a mechanical, somewhat dehumanized form of sexual release. On the other side of the coin, fantasy—with or without masturbation—would appear detrimental to a young person (particularly) if so much time is invested in its pursuit that schoolwork is left undone and grades drop.

Another negative aspect of sexual fantasy lies in the person's attitude toward it. If he regards it as the equivalent of "dirty thoughts," it can only produce guilt feelings and anxiety. Rather than give up fantasy, however, it would seem more appropriate for the individual to attempt to break down his inhibitions against it.

As already suggested, a further danger—although, statistically, a remote one—is that the fantasy could become harmful or even dangerous if the individual were to attempt to translate daydreams of unacceptable behavior into actuality. But the chicken-or-egg controversy immediately arises: do the unacceptable desires arise from the subject matter of the fantasy, or the reverse? In any case, the content of daydreams no less than nocturnal dreams may give the therapist a key in unraveling some psychological difficulties that the individual may be experiencing.

Masturbation is sexually frustrating and not as satisfactory as sex relations with a partner. Refutation: Masturbation is frustrating only when the person feels guilt or shame about it, or when he expects more from it than is reasonable. It is certainly true that heterosexual relations are usually preferable to solitary masturbation. But if coitus is for some reason not possible or advisable, masturbation offers a satisfactory substitute in the release of sexual tension. In the case of women, furthermore, masturbation may be the only means of achieving orgasm (Ellis *a;* "M"; Sullivan, P. R.). One additional note: women observed during various sexual acts in a laboratory setting reported that orgasms resulting from such direct but noncoital methods as masturbation were physiologically more satisfying than those produced coitally, although the latter were more satisfying emotionally (Masters and Johnson *n*).

Certainly it is advisable, if an individual has anxieties concerning masturbation, and if self-stimulation causes him extreme guilt, that he avoid it until the underlying psychological problem is corrected. Similarly, if one has extreme and severe guilt about head-scratching, one should also avoid head-scratching until the underlying psychological difficulty in that instance is rectified.

The technique of masturbation customarily used by men is to grip the penis and move the hand back and forth at the desired pressure and tempo along the length of the penile shaft. The glans is stimulated somewhat as it is by in-and-out body movements during penile penetration of the vagina. The degree of pressure, the speed of stroking, and the use or nonuse of lubrication naturally vary from man to man.

About 67% of women who masturbate prefer to stimulate the clitoris by manual or digital friction of the vulval region (Ford and Beach *b*), although Masters and Johnson's research indicates that arousal is best accomplished when the stimulation is to the side of the clitoris rather than on the clitoris directly (Masters and Johnson *n*). About 20% of women prefer vaginal stimulation to other methods, and insert foreign objects into the vagina during masturbation; about 11% prefer stimulation of the urethral meatus; and 2% attain orgasm by pressing their thighs together in a rhythmical manner (Ford and Beach *b*). Some women achieve self-arousal and orgasm through directing a stream of water onto the genitals while bathing—either from the faucet of a tub or from the peppery spray of a shower (Kronhausen and Kronhausen). The running water provides a continuous pressure, with just enough variation in constancy to satisfy the physiological requirements involved in producing an orgasm. Women describe the sensation received from this method of self-arousal as being somewhat similar to that created by an electric vibrator, although less intense. Perhaps the use of water in self-stimulation has some psychological advantage in that an unconscious need to "cleanse away the guilt" engendered by masturbation is satisfied along with the sexual need.

Further information on frequency and incidence of masturbation is given in Chapter 17.

Learning About One's Own Sensuality

As described vividly in the best seller *The Sensuous Woman* ("J"), women can learn to heighten their sexual responsiveness through certain exercises. The woman who, because of a lifetime of sexual taboos and restrictions, is not freely responsive to sexual stimulation is advised to explore and experiment with her body to uncover its full sensitivity. She can begin by exercising her tactile senses while blindfolded. She can slowly and gently feel objects of different textures, allowing the resulting tactile sensations to become firmly fixed in her memory. She can then lightly stimulate various parts of her nude body with furry or fluffy material.

She is advised to relax by lingering in a hot bath while all stresses of the day float away. After delicately drying her body, she should stretch, roll, curl up, and otherwise maneuver herself in her bed, mist-sprayed with cologne, as she listens to music, with a flickering candle as the only source of illumination. She should follow this bit of self-indulgence by delicately rubbing and massaging her breasts, abdomen, and other curves of her body with her favorite lotion, all the while making herself as acutely aware as possible of the various tactile sensations that she is experiencing.

Since the mouth and tongue are highly important in lovemaking, the woman who wishes to develop her sensuousness should practice various flicking, stretching, clockwise, and counterclockwise movements of the tongue. These maneuvers can be practiced by running her tongue over her palms, between her fingers, and on her wrists and arms. She can also use an ice-cream cone, directing her tongue in various swirling patterns on the ice cream. This exercise not only enhances the finesse of tongue movement but also allows a woman to fantasy her own body's being thus caressed and stimulated by her lover.

The woman who wants to give and gain the greatest pleasure from lovemaking must practice muscle control. She must learn techniques of strengthening, tightening, and controlling muscles of the vagina, abdomen, back, and gluteal area. She is also advised to learn to coordinate her body movements with those of her lover; one of the best ways that this can be accomplished is through dancing. She should close her eyes and allow her body to melt into his and be led by him throughout the steps. She should concentrate on the feel of his body next to hers as they become attuned in rhythm, movement, and style. The feeling of sensuousness is also heightened if a woman permits herself the luxury of beautiful, delicate, and high-quality lingerie; a sensitive and responsive body deserves such pampering ("J").

Learning to masturbate successfully is probably the most important step for the woman in learning to come to orgasm easily and quickly: she learns what is required of herself and of her lover to give her the fullest sexual response. In addition, learning to breathe in a manner to reduce muscular tension is a valuable lesson in training oneself to reach orgasm. Tension begins to build with inhalation but is released with exhalation. Proper breathing can remove muscular tension from the groin, the pelvis, and buttocks, producing a warm and tingling sense of aliveness in the genital area that can add significantly to sexual pleasure and orgasmic response. Freedom from muscular tension, coupled with free, uninhibited fantasy of an erotic subject that her sexual imaginativeness can conjure up, are essential "keys to sexual heaven" (Hamilton, E.).

Although men commonly achieve orgasm more easily than women, they can benefit no less than women from practice in the art of becoming more sensuous, as the best seller *The Sensuous Man* ("M") points out. The first step, again, is a positive attitude toward sex, sensuality, and sex knowledge. The second step is a realization that the hands and mouth are of primary importance in making love to a woman and that penile size is of little importance. A man must develop the muscle control important to the maintenance of lengthy acts of coitus. He should also master the techniques of cunnilingus (application of tongue or mouth to a woman's vulval area), in much the same manner as is prescribed for the aspiring sensuous woman; however, the man's tongue in cunnilingus requires more strength and durability than a woman's does in fellatio.

Because the burden of the physical strain in coitus is chiefly the man's, he should keep himself in prime condition, perhaps by jogging or running a certain distance each day if his physician approves such a regimen. A man wishing to heighten his sensual awareness is also urged to develop his tactile sensitivity, in much the same manner as that suggested for women. Men are sometimes slow to realize that tenderness, sensitivity, and delicacy, when coupled with firmness, bring far greater erotic pleasure to a woman than a rough, forceful approach ("M").

FORMS OF HETEROSEXUAL AROUSAL

One should be reminded occasionally that any act that enhances sexual pleasure, that hurts no one, and that is out of sight and sound of an unwilling observer is permissible and should be engaged in freely (Ellis a; Stone and Stone). This reminder is especially timely in view of the persistent presence in bookstores of erroneous and misleading writings on human sexuality. Such books state outright or at least imply that petting, for instance (which includes any form of sexual foreplay and afterplay), more particularly petting to orgasm, may be harmful at the time or may interfere with future pleasure and fulfillment in coitus. To the contrary, the evidence is that those people who enjoy petting and are capable of responding freely to it are those most capable of responding freely to sexual intercourse and of deriving much pleasure from it (Beigel a; Ellis a, b, j; Kinsey et al. c). The only problems liable to arise from petting are unjustified feelings of guilt and congestion of the tissue in the sexual region, resulting in physical distress, when the petting is protracted but does not culminate in orgasmic relief (Ellis a, b, j; Kinsey et al. c).

Persons who are reluctant to involve themselves in sex play are often simply fearful that their partner will consider them too bold in their manner of sexual stimulation or response. The less inhibited member of a couple should start the coital foreplay, and then at the appropriate time should gently but firmly put the partner's hand and lips at the spots where they are most desired (Ellis *j*).

Sexual excitement is most easily heightened when a maneuver of advance and retreat is adopted (Eichenlaub a). Stimulation is instigated and then, after a brief buildup, withdrawn in a slightly teasing, tantalizing manner. Stimulation is begun again, carried to a more advanced point of excitement, and once more withdrawn. Quite naturally, timing is of the essence. Knowing just how long to continue advancing and retreating, recognizing when these efforts have produced an optimal level of sexual excitement, and then ceasing the teasing are the keys to success in this lovemaking strategy. To continue beyond this point may very well be interpreted as rejection by the recipient, so that what started out to be a promising adventure ends in stress and unhappiness (Eichenlaub a).

In Masters and Johnson's training sessions to help sexually inadequate husbands and wives overcome their difficulties, great emphasis is placed on the couple's establishing a "sensate focus," which means that they learn to think and feel sensually. Each partner is taught to use, with varying degrees of finesse, his hands and fingers to touch, stroke, massage, and fondle all parts of his mate's body. The purpose is not only to give the most meaningful and exciting erotic sensations possible to the partner, but also to enjoy oneself the matchless erotic pleasures growing out of an uninhibited tactile exploration of the total skin surface and body contours of a member of the opposite sex (Lehrman; Masters and Johnson *p*).

With proper use of the hands, not only can sexual excitement be built up in one's partner, but one's own excitement can be brought to and maintained at the response level of the other person. As an example, the man's light stroking and caressing of his partner's body with his fingertips will build her sexual excitement faster than his own. But when he uses the palms of his hands, as well as his fingertips (along with other excitants such as darting tongue-kissing), his own excitement usually develops at about the same tempo as hers (Eichenlaub a; Ellis *j*; Van de Velde). With this in mind, a man may pace the development of mutual excitement to achieve a synchronized crescendo.

Initial sexual excitement is brought about by light touch—not pressure—and the more intense and prolonged the sexual buildup, the greater the orgasmic response (Eichenlaub a; Masters and Johnson *n*). While at first the bodies of both the man and woman are stimulated with gentle, slow, generalized stroking, the caressing should gradually become more specific as sex play progresses. The general orientation of the stroking should be toward the erogenous zones, particularly the genitalia, the caressing being done in the teasing advance–retreat–advance manner already described. It is of special importance that the genitals be stimulated lightly at first because of the sensitivity and tenderness of the area; as excitement increases, the woman may wish the pressure to be heavier.

A woman's skin is considerably more sensitive to the touch than a man's is, and care should be taken, especially with a sexually inexperienced woman, to avoid overstimulation (Eichenlaub a).

Exceptionally gentle caressing will gradually "awaken" the nerve endings of the genital region, and will condition the woman to welcome this manner of lovemaking as something pleasant and exciting. Fingertip stroking of the abdomen and inner thighs with general movement in the direction of the genitals—will usually prepare a woman for more direct stimulation of the genitalia.

Breast manipulation is usually regarded as one of the most effective sexual stimulants for a woman. Indeed, a small percentage of women can be brought to orgasm by breast manipulation alone (Kinsey et al. c; Masters and Johnson n). Surprising to many is the fact that men can become as sexually excited from having their breasts stimulated as women become (Kinsey et al. c; McCary a). That men enjoy this stimulation is a normal response, and the pleasure has a sound physiological basis.

In lovemaking, a man should gently massage his partner's breasts, interspersing the manipulation with a light brushing of the nipple and an occasional tweak of its sensitive tip. Caressing with the hands can very pleasurably be alternated with soft moist kisses and an exploring tongue. The tempo of the tongue's movements can be changed occasionally, to erotic advantage, allowing it to dart back and forth across the nipple in a tense, rapid-fire, impertinent manner, before resuming once more the soft moist stimulation (Caprio d; Eichenlaub a; Ellis a, b, j).

The erogenous nerve endings in a man's breasts are limited to the nipples and areas immediately surrounding them. When a man's breast is stimulated by gently rolling the nipple betwen the thumb and finger, or by the sort of oral contact described in the previous paragraph, he is likely to experience the same sort of sexual desire and excitement that women do from the same techniques.

Kissing, like hand–fingertip caressing, should be varied in a teasing manner: open mouth, closed mouth; light lip pressure, heavy lip pressure; moist lips, dry lips, soft lips, nibbling teeth and lips; a darting, teasing tongue, a soft sensuous tongue. The lover's face and body should be covered with kisses as the point of action varies quickly, then slowly, from the lips to the eyes, hairline, earlobes, to the mouth again, to the breast, to the neck, to the abdomen, back to the lips. All the while, the tongue should also be participating in this exploration of the lover's body.

The kissing maneuver should be repeated again and again with increasing passion and delicate timing (Eichenlaub a; Ellis j; Van de Velde;

Vatsyayana). Ordinarily, kissing of the mouth should precede kissing of other parts of the body, except perhaps the hands. In the latter instance, it should be noted that having the palms of her hands kissed is a particularly exciting and stimulating experience for a woman (Eichenlaub a). There is also the psychological element of its being a rather courtly and tender gesture on the part of the man.

No matter what approach the man takes, his hands should seldom be motionless during the entire period of sex play. They should dart and slide over his partner's body—stroking, holding, caressing boldly and lightly, squeezing, and massaging—alternating strong palmar movements with light, silky stroking of the fingertips. As he brings his partner to successive levels of arousal, he must take heed of the very thin and delicate tissue of the vulva and vagina. These areas should not be manually stimulated unless the man's fingernails are clipped and smooth, and the vulval region well moistened with either bodily secretions or with a commercial product, such as K-Y Sterile Lubricant. The clitoris, furthermore, is often too sensitive to accommodate direct and uninterrupted manipulation comfortably (Eichenlaub a). Knowing that the regions to the side and around the clitoris are the sites of stimulation preferred by most women who masturbate can be helpful to a man in his love play (Masters and Johnson n).

As mentioned earlier, sex play should be a gradual, slowly unfolding experience, especially for the woman. It has been suggested that kissing and manual stimulation of erogenous areas should be carried on for at least 15 minutes before intercourse itself commences, although some couples prefer longer, others shorter, periods of stimulation (Stone and Stone). Couples should be warned, however, that an overly protracted period of sex play can actually interfere with maximum pleasure (Eichenlaub a). Kinsey and his associates report that many couples prefer sexual intercourse itself as a method of stimulation (Kinsey et al. a, c). Communication and good timing are once more essential; when both lovers are ready to proceed with coitus, they should let one another know.

Sexual stimulation is not a one-way street. The woman should reciprocate with the same sort of fervor that the man extends to her, not only because she wishes to excite and please him, but also because the act of exciting one's lover should be a highly pleasurable and fulfilling experience. When a woman is developing her erotic techniques, as Betty Cox has suggested in *Sexual Techniques During Prescribed Continence*, her partner should "tell her what pleases him and suggest what she should try to do that might be more interesting and more stimulating to him and her. However, a man should be very careful to make these suggestions gently. He should never, any time, show any sign of disapproval at her trials and errors."

There are many things a woman can do by way of lovemaking that will bring delight to her lover. She should initiate kissing or return his kisses passionately, stimulate his nipples orally and by fingertip and palmar manipulation, lightly rake her fingertips over his bare back, gently stimulate the scrotum and perineal area, and manipulate the penis with alternating light and heavy stroking (particularly at the glans and frenum). The woman, too, should remember the importance of the teasing game of advance and retreat in the art of building up sexual excitement.

In her efforts to determine what sort of lovemaking brings the greatest pleasure to her partner, the woman should bear in mind individual differences. For example, while some men prefer a gentle stroking of the penis, others may desire heavy pressure and squeezing in such a manner that there is tugging at the scrotum and perineal area. The woman should not hesitate to use her hands, mouth, thighs, legs, toes (even eyelashes, if it comes to that) to stimulate her partner. She should employ a variety of methods of arousal, and by all means she should let it be known that she thoroughly enjoys giving, as well as receiving, such pleasurable stimulation (Eichenlaub a).

In attempting to discover a pleasurable means of stimulating her partner's genitalia, a woman can often obtain a helpful guideline from any masturbatory techniques he may have used. If, for instance, a man stimulates himself with light, slow stroking of his penis, it is quite likely that he will welcome the same sort of caressing from his partner (Kronhausen and Kronhausen).

Women who masturbate will frequently insert their fingers into the vagina to aid their fantasy during self-stimulation. Since they are so conditioned, these women will probably find it pleasurable if their partners arouse them in the same manner during sex play.

A *vibrator* can be of value in heightening the pleasure of a couple's sexual interaction. Some women apparently cannot achieve orgasm with penile penetration, nor indeed can some reach it through any of the techniques of stimulation already discussed. But direct clitoral and vulval arousal through the man's application of a vibrator as he fondles and kisses her seldom fails to bring a woman to orgasm (Clark b; Ellis j).

A few women prefer the type of vibrator that the man attaches to the back of his hand. It allows him free movement of his fingers, to be sure, but most of the vibration is absorbed by his hand. Most women, therefore, find greater stimulation and gratification from the application of a rubber-knobbed vibrator directly on or to the side of the clitoris. Or a battery-driven penis-shaped vibrator can be applied directly to the clitoral area or inserted into the vagina, if such stimulation is desired.

Use of this vibrator meets with great success in producing single or multiple orgasms in women who might otherwise be incapable of reaching such an intense sexual response level. Furthermore, using a vibrator is much less tiring to men who otherwise must attempt arousal of their partners' genitals for prolonged periods of time before bringing about an orgasm, if it occurs at all. The man also remains free to kiss, caress, and stimulate his partner in any other way he chooses. Marriage counselors frequently recommend vibrator stimulation for women who are "frigid" or who experience difficulty in reaching orgasm, and to women without lovers who need sexual release (Masters and Johnson *n*; Rubin *c*). Few women fail to achieve an orgasm when they are properly stimulated by a vibrator, no matter what their previous history of sexual response has been. However, some couples find the vibrator too "mechanical" for their tastes. Others are afraid that their orgasmic response to this sort of stimulation will be so intense that other methods will be pleasurable only to a lesser degree (Rubin *c*).

Another form of sexual activity that is far more popular than many know is *oral-genital stimulation*. Kinsey's research showed that oral-genital contact had been experienced by at last 60% of those married couples who had gone to college, by about 20% of those who had gone through high school, and by about 10% of those who had gone only through grade school (Kinsey *et al. a, c*). That the first figure is so high may surprise some people, because of the traditional taboo that society has placed on this sort of sexual behavior. Many marriage counselors believe that considerably more than 60% of the higher educational-level group indulge in oral-genital sexual expression, but that they are reluctant to admit it because they fear disapproval.

The prevailing negative attitude toward genital kissing is primarily an outgrowth of the fact that many people regard the genital region as "dirty." The proximity in the woman of the anus and the urethra to the genitals, and the fact that the male penis is both a seminal and a urinary outlet are the physiological factors that have given rise to the "dirtiness" concept, but these do not constitute a logical objection to the act (Ellis *b*). Certainly if one allows his body to become unclean and malodorous, especially in the anal-genital region, any type of sexual contact is likely to become objectionable. However, with the great supply of cosmetic and hygienic products currently on the market, there is really no excuse for an offensive odor emanating from any part of the body—including the anal-genital area.

People seldom enjoy even kissing someone when his or her breath is reeking, to say nothing of entering into more intimate physical contact with someone who needs a bath. If one has recently eaten, or suspects that the mouth might otherwise be offensive, then one is well advised to tackle the problem with toothbrush and mouthwash. The same sensible precautions should be taken with the genitals. Because the folds of skin that partially cover the surface of the genitals are natural receptacles for a collection of smegma and secretions, the region should be cleansed in such a way that there is no chance of any offensive material or odor lingering. In the same fashion used in cleaning the ear, a finger should move in and around the folds of the genitalia to cleanse them. If a couple give this sort of attention to keeping themselves clean and pleasant-smelling, making whatever use is indicated of "personal hygiene" and cosmetic products, the objection to oral-genital contact on the grounds of "dirtiness" is less than valid.

It is generally agreed by couples who engage in oral-genital contact that it is an act to be enjoyed by both man and woman, whether giving or receiving. It is an accepted fact that the mouth and lips are erogenous zones common to nearly all people; and there is, in addition, an abundance of nerve endings in the tip of the nose. That these two areas of sensitivity universally exist no doubt accounts for mouth contact and nose-rubbing being the chief methods of "kissing" in our world, and for the fact that oral stimulation of the genitals is so pleasurable for many people (Sentnor and Hult; Williamson). Furthermore, recent neurophysiological studies (MacLean) have shown that there is a close relationship between the parts of the brain concerned with oral functions (amygdala) and those concerned with sexual functions (septum and rostral diencephalon). Stimulation of an area of the brain affecting oral activity will readily produce a "spillover" into areas governing genital function.

A couple may engage in mutual oral-genital contact during the early part of stimulation, but to continue the mutual act for any length of time or to the point of climax usually requires more acrobatic agility than most couples possess. Furthermore, simultaneous orgasms resulting from oral-genital stimulation—or even prolonged simultaneous oral-genital contact—present some of the same problems discussed under simultaneous coital orgasm (to be discussed in Chapter 13). That is, neither partner can properly concentrate at the same time on himself and the spouse to the fullest satisfaction of either while receiving such intense stimulation.

The clitoris usually receives the greatest measure of the man's attention during *cunnilingus* (from the Latin: *cunnus*, vulva; and *lingere*, to lick). Its sensitive glans can be stimulated in much the same manner as the nipples of the breasts are stimulated in mouth-tongue-breast contact. The tongue-stroking begins in a light, teasing manner with intermittent heavy, moist, bold tongue-stroking; then the technique is varied to keep pace with the heightening sexual excitement. As the woman's climax nears, and if the couple wish to bring it about in this manner, the man should put into action the findings of Masters and Johnson (n), which demonstrate that orgasm is best produced by a steady, constant stroking of the clitoral *area*. (At the height of sexual tension the clitoris withdraws under its prepuce, and direct contact can no longer be maintained in any case.) Other parts of the vulva, particularly the labia minora, are also sensitive to oral stimulation. Women who have experienced oral-genital stimulation report that the method is overwhelmingly pleasurable and effective, both as sex foreplay and as the primary avenue to achieving orgasm (Kronhausen and Kronhausen).

Kinsey has shown that wives are less inclined to engage in *fellatio* (Latin: *fellare*, to suck) with their husbands than their husbands are to engage in cunnilingus with them (Kinsey *et al. a, c*). Any such reluctance is almost always based on psychological blocks. If a wife will talk over carefully the matter of fellatio with her husband, she can usually overcome this reticence and eventually may find that the act is quite pleasurable.

The glans of the penis, especially at the frenum and contiguous areas, is highly sensitive to a woman's kisses and sucking, and to her warm, moist, now darting, now soft tongue. At the same time, she should also stroke the corpus of the penis with an up-and-down movement, occasionally fondling the testicles and scrotum. This technique of lovemaking can quickly bring the man to sexual heights that can easily terminate in orgasm. Van de Velde, who has written one of the classics among marriage manuals, gives unqualified endorsement to mouth-genital stimulation as a vastly pleasurable form of sexual behavior. So also have many other authorities in the field of sex and marriage (Clark *f*; Ellis *a, b, j*; Kronhausen and Kronhausen; McCary *a*).

Whether climax occurs as a result of manual stimulation, oral activity, or sexual intercourse is a matter each couple must decide individually. The method best suited to the particular coital occasion should readily be adopted, with each participant expending his best efforts to bring about maximum satisfaction for his partner (Eichenlaub *a*).

Many variations of the sex act, together with special techniques for heightening pleasure during the various phases of increasing sexual response, have been proposed in marriage manuals and other writings on sexual matters (Eichenlaub *a*; Ellis *a, b, j*; Ellis and Abarbanel *a, b*; Kinsey *et al. a, c*; Kronhausen and Kronhausen; Maslow *a*; Masters and Johnson *f, n*; Sentnor and Hult; Stone and Stone; Trainer; Van de Velde; Vatsyayana). However, because of their individual and combined personalities and preferences, each couple need to discover—through open discussion and uninhibited experimentation—just what brings them the greatest erotic pleasure.

What one couple find exciting, another might find dull or even repulsive (Eichenlaub *a*). One person, for instance, might find highly pleasurable the application to the perineal area of crushed ice wrapped in a cloth at the time the paroxysms of orgasm commence, whereas another might find it a rather ludicrous (if not chilling) experience (Eichenlaub *a*). Some couples have found that the application of certain mild chemicals, such as Mentholatum, to the glans of the penis or to the vulval region (or even the use of the salve as a lubricant during coitus) enhances sexual pleasure, while others would find such a practice physically painful. Some desire anal stimulation or the insertion of fingers or small objects into the rectum during certain phases of the sexual response cycle. Others consider anal techniques unnecessary, repugnant, even barbaric. Whatever the sexual variation, it should be introduced spontaneously and with obvious desire by one participant, and received happily by the other.

Successful sexual relations, in short, are *caring* relations, in which each partner is sensitive to the desires of the other. This caring, indeed, can continue well beyond the experiences of sexual arousal and release. For sex relations do not—or, rather, should not—end with orgasm (Eichenlaub *a*; Ellis *j*; Van de Velde). Many couples find the interval after the sex act to be as pleasant and emotionally fulfilling as any other part of it. To hold each other in a close and lingering embrace, to discuss softly the delights of the experience they have just shared, to caress the lover's body with tender, sweeping movements of the hands, to doze and relax with intertwined bodies, all serve to aid in the emotional fulfillment. Other couples are completely overcome by the release of physical and emotional tension and are ready to drop off into a deep and restful sleep after a brief expression of love and appreciation. Lovers must give as careful attention to the partner's wishes concerning the period of resolution of sexual tensions as they do to each other's preferences in the matter of sexual foreplay.

The implications of this discussion for marriage today are manifold. Sex is a pleasurable, significant part of marriage, and both the husband and wife should do everything in their power to make it as joyous and satisfying as possible. Lovemaking can fulfill both the psychological and physiological needs of human beings in a way that nothing else in marriage is capable of doing. It can be approached in a variety of ways, any one of which may be highly pleasurable to one couple, undesirable to a second, simply dull to a third. Sex can be a rather grim business in a marriage when it is unsatisfactory. But it can also be fun. A well-known and respected psychologist, A. H. Maslow *(a)*, summarized a healthy love relationship perceptively when he wrote:

> It is quite characteristic of self-actualizing people that they can enjoy themselves in love and in sex. Sex very frequently becomes a kind of game in which laughter is quite as common as panting. It is not the welfare of the species, or the task of reproduction, or the future development of mankind that attracts people to each other. The sex life of healthy people, in spite of the fact that it frequently reaches great peaks of ecstasy, is nevertheless also easily compared to the games of children and puppies. It is cheerful, humorous, and playful.

11 APHRODISIACS
AND
ANAPHRODISIACS

Almost since the beginning of civilization, man has been interested in methods of controlling sexual appetite. Most often he seems to seek means of increasing sexual desire (*aphrodisiacs*), but there are also times when he wishes means of diminishing it (*anaphrodisiacs*). He has sought to achieve these ends through a variety of foods, drugs, mechanical devices, and physical activities.

APHRODISIACS

Certain foods have long been thought to have sexually stimulating properties. Ideas concerning the erotic value of various foods seem to spring from two sources. First, the rarity or newness of a food (such as the potato when it was first brought to England) has given hope to some that at last a great sexual stimulant has been discovered. Second, the "doctrine of signatures" is applied, wherein it is assumed that sexual strength can be gained by eating foods that have external characteristics resembling a sex organ—bananas and oysters, for instance, with their superficial resemblance, respectively, to the penis and testicles (MacDougald).

The oyster has long been thought to contain sexually arousing properties, but chemical analysis shows that it consists of water (75%), protein (10%), and carbohydrates (10%), plus small amounts of fat, sugar, and minerals—none of which can in any way affect sex drive or performance (Neiger *b*). In one of the most obvious applications of the "doctrine of signatures," many Chinese place unshakable belief in the potency of powdered rhinoceros horn. (It is not difficult to see how the succinct word "horny" came to have the meaning of "strong sexual desire" in the vernacular.)

A story was recently circulated in the press of the alleged aphrodisiac qualities of peanuts. Just how the lowly and seemingly innocent peanut gained such a reputation is cloudy. Perhaps it is simply an example of the "doctrine of signatures" in miniature. One result, however, was that the headmistress of a South African high school promptly banned peanut-butter sandwiches from her girl students' lunch boxes (Houdek)!

The notion that a food's shape has a bearing on its aphrodisiac properties should be patently absurd. Why, then, do people continue to place unwarranted value on some foods as aphrodisiacs? First of all, it is often difficult to distinguish between fact and folklore; few people are experts on the properties of various foods, fewer still on the physiology of sexual desire. The psychological impact, therefore, of *believing* that raw bull's testicles ("prairie oysters," as they are sometimes called), or clams, or celery, or tomatoes are an aphrodisiac is sometimes strong enough to produce, at least for a while, an elevation in sexual desire and performance. What was only a temporary triumph—and a psychological one at that—is considered to be a direct result of consuming a "wonder" food, and the discovery is passed on to the next person wishing to be transported to new heights of sexual capacity.

A further psychological influence is the strong association between hunger and sex as the most powerful of physiological drives. To be sure, highly nutritive foods are essential to optimum physical well-being and functioning. For certain sensuous people there is, in fact, a distinct aphrodisiac effect in a gourmet meal that is served leisurely and elegantly in an atmosphere of candlelight and lovely music. The sex drive of most men and women, however, decreases significantly after a meal, especially a heavy one. Furthermore, it has been demonstrated time and again that those who are overweight and who consistently overeat suffer from decreased sexual drive and ability.

The only persons for whom food can act as a true aphrodisiac in a sense are the nutritionally deprived and those whose hunger is severe and threatening. Studies made during World War II, for instance, showed that sexual drive decreased in direct proportion to the degree of hunger that the individual was experiencing. As hunger became more and more a relentless companion, food became almost an obsession, crowding out sexual thoughts entirely (Frankl; Keys). (It has also been suggested that the reason so many Americans think of sex as the most important thing in the world is that they have never been hungry [Udry *b*].)

The most famous of the alleged sexual stimulants is alcohol. It is presumed that alcoholic consumption propels sexual drive to new heights of capability and desire. The truth is that alcohol, when taken in considerable quantity, is a depressant. It narcotizes the brain, thus retarding its reflexes, and dilates the blood vessels, thus interfering with the capacity for erection. Physically, alcohol decreases sexual abilities. On the other hand, it also tends to remove, temporarily, feelings of guilt and fear in the area of sexuality from the minds of some people, making them less inhibited than they normally would be.

Study of the effects of alcohol on the sexual activity of dogs, whose behavior (in contrast to human behavior) is not significantly complicated by psychological and emotional factors, has provided some interesting insights on the action of this depressant. After administering varying amounts of alcohol to dogs, H. Horsley Gantt found that, in general, even a very small amount of alcohol made it more difficult for the animals to achieve erection and to ejaculate. The larger the amount, the greater the difficulty, and very large doses destroyed the capability altogether. In some animals, temporary sterility was induced, with the sperm count dropping as much as 92%. Like humans, however, each dog in the experiment reacted differently to the alcohol. Normal dogs were the least affected sexually, while one very neurotic dog that was totally impotent attained strong erections after imbibing a large amount of alcohol (Stiller *e*).

A study of 20,000 well-educated, liberal men and women of high socioeconomic status revealed that for almost 60% of them alcohol heightened the enjoyment of sex. The women were more of this opinion than the men, probably because alcohol can remove sexual inhibitions, women tending to be more sexually inhibited than men (Athanasiou et *al.*).

The removal of inhibitions through consumption of alcohol often more than counterbalances loss in physical ability. There can therefore be an actual increase in sexual functioning despite depressed physical reactions. In a study conducted in Great Britain, for example, 40% of both men and women reported that alcohol increased their sexual drive (Alcohol and sex).

It can generally be accepted, however, that if a person's sexual drive and ability increase after the use of alcohol, one of two forces (perhaps both) is at work: the stresses of daily living—possibly quite unrelated to sex—have acted as temporary inhibitors to sexual impulses, or some real emotional block exists in the area of sex (McCary *d*). Getting past the strains or crises of the moment or ridding oneself of emotional conflicts concerning sexuality would probably do more for sexual functioning than alcohol.

The most popularly known drug used to reinforce sexual drive is *cantharides* (Spanish fly), derived from the *Cantharis vesicatoria*, a beautiful beetle found in southern Europe. The insects are dried and heated until they disintegrate into a fine powder, which is then taken internally, causing acute irritation of the genitourinary tract, specifically the mucous membrane of the urethra (MacDougald). Accompanying this inflammation is a dilation of associated blood vessels, all of which produce a certain stimulation of the genitals. The drug can thus indeed produce penile erection, but usually without an increase in sexual desire. Furthermore, if cantharides is taken in excessive doses, it can cause violent illness or even death. The drug is not an effective sexual stimulant and is seldom used in modern medical practice.

Another drug to which aphrodisiac qualities are attributed is *yohimbine*, taken from the yohimbé tree native to Africa. Its primary use in most nations has been as a diuretic and in the treatment of such disorders as neuritis and meningitis. But yohimbine also stimulates the lower-spine nerve centers controlling erection and has long been used by African natives for sexual arousal.

Any present-day use of yohimbine should be under the direction of a physician, and even then there is some doubt about its real effectiveness. Effective or not, yohimbine is generally conceded to be the most widely used drug for increasing sexual drive.

One also hears of the aphrodisiac qualities of both arsenic and strychnine, which, when given in the proper (very small) doses, are said to heighten sensitivity to several stimuli. A drop too much and the problem obviously ceases to be one of mere sexual sluggishness. There are, of course, claims made for the aphrodisiac effects of various addicting or habituating drugs—hashish, opium, morphine, cocaine, marijuana, and LSD. Like alcohol, these drugs release inhibitions, which are at the root of many problems of impaired sexual functioning. But, like alcohol, drugs taken in large enough quantities usually have the opposite effect of an aphrodisiac.

Marijuana has gained many devotees as a sexual stimulant. In reality, however, its effect on the sex drive is at best only indirect. The drug distorts time perception and may produce the illusion that a sexual climax is somewhat prolonged. Also, it tends to make the user extremely suggestible. Thus if he believes firmly that the drug is a sexual stimulant, it may well have that effect on him. As a true aphrodisiac, however, it is a failure (Churchill). An additional, sobering, consideration comes from recent evidence presented by the American Medical Association that marijuana smokers have a higher incidence of impotence than nonusers (United Press International a).

About 25% of the sampling of 20,000 well-educated young adults mentioned earlier reported that they had experienced coitus while under the influence of marijuana; about 80% of this number claimed intensified sexual pleasure (Athanasiou *et al.*).

Timothy Leary, erstwhile leader of the LSD cult, has declared: "There is no question that LSD is the most powerful aphrodisiac ever discovered by man" (Playboy interview). Yet there is no biochemical or pharmacological evidence to support the contention that LSD, marijuana, or similar drugs contain any sexually stimulating properties (Freedman). Not only are they not aphrodisiacs, but also, according to results of a recent six-year study in England, women users of amphetamines, marijuana, and LSD have a higher than average rate of congenitally malformed babies and more stillbirths than nonusers (Sex in the news g).

It should be emphasized that use of marijuana or the other drugs mentioned above, as an aphrodisiac or for any other purpose, is illegal except upon medical prescription. Also, it is illegal throughout the United States to administer any alleged aphrodisiac for the purpose of seducing another person.

Recently there have been intriguing reports of the accidentally discovered aphrodisiac effects of two drugs used for quite different purposes. One, called *PCPA*, has been used experimentally to treat schizophrenia and certain types of tumors. The other, *L-dopa*, is being prescribed, no longer experimentally, for patients suffering from Parkinson's disease (called "the shaking palsy"). Many L-dopa patients have shown dramatic remission of their disease symptoms, with the side effect in some 2% of them being hypersexuality. For example, some elderly male patients who had not had coitus in five years began engaging in it daily after administration of L-dopa. Similar results have been reported in the use of PCPA (Has a real aphrodisiac been found?; Tagliamonte *et al.*).

Unfortunately, optimism about the aphrodisiac qualities of both PCPA and L-dopa must be tempered with several notes of caution. Both are powerful drugs, and all their effects and side effects have not yet been fully measured. The large-scale experimentation needed to determine their specific aphrodisiac potentials has been conducted only with animals, and extrapolation of these experimental results to humans is not warranted. Nevertheless, human experimentation appears justified in the case of these two drugs, although one is wary of the usual excitement attending anything new that is allegedly aphrodisiac.

A drug that is reputed not so much to increase sex drive as to intensify orgasmic pleasure is *amyl nitrite*. Some individuals report that inhaling amyl nitrite at the instant of orgasm enhances the pleasure of the experience. Apparently the drug relaxes the smooth muscles and consequently produces vasodilation of the genitourinary tract. Some of its side effects are arresting, however—dizziness, headaches, fainting, and, in rare cases, death. Clearly its use is most ill advised unless prescribed and directed by a physician (Louria).

Erotic pictures; songs; literature; recordings of squeaking bedsprings accompanied by heavy breathing, moans, and gasps: all titillate the sexual interest and drive of some people. Marriage counselors frequently prescribe pornographic films or books for couples whose sex life has become lackluster and apathetic. When experience with erotic stimuli has been limited and infrequent, new sexual excitement and interest almost certainly will occur from increased exposure. But immunity to such stimulation develops rapidly if the exposure is overdone. Some external erotic stimuli are more successful with one sex than the other and their effectiveness varies from person to person of the same sex.

Aphrodisiacs are not likely to increase sex drive unless a psychological component of suggestion is present that might whet the sexual appetite and increase the drive momentarily; or unless the individual is physically debilitated, in which case such treatment as hormonal therapy might be of benefit.

All in all, good health, plenty of rest and sleep, an adequate amount of exercise, and freedom from emotional tension remain the most effective aphrodisiacs for man (Kelly, G. L. a; Rubin j).

ANAPHRODISIACS

Techniques used in an attempt to decrease sexual interest and drive have varied through the ages—from cold baths and going barefoot, as suggested by Plato and Aristotle (MacDougald) (one can well imagine what happens to amatory desire when a bare foot steps on a sharp stone); to wearing chastity belts and penis cages, as suggested by the Romans and British at one time; to the use of chemicals and tranquilizers.

The best known method for decreasing sexual appetite is the use of the chemical *potassium nitrate*, or saltpeter. Actually, this is an almost completely neutral chemical, except that it is a fairly effective diuretic, which perhaps accounts for its far-flung but undeserved reputation as a sex deterrent. It is a failure as an anaphrodisiac.

Recently, experimentation with the drug Ismelin (*guanethidine sulphate*), used for the treatment of high blood pressure, showed that erectile potency, ability to ejaculate, and intensity of climax were all reduced significantly by intake of the drug. Side effects of stomach cramps, diarrhea, and general loss of physical energy were reported by one-half the subjects (Money and Yankowitz).

Physicians occasionally prescribe certain tranquilizers and other drugs in an attempt to decrease sexual desire. Limited success has been reported. Some doctors shy away from their use, however, fearing that these drugs might have the same effect as alcohol: that is, removal or reduction of emotional blocks might produce results opposite to the desired ones by releasing even stronger sexual yearnings or unusual sexual behavior.

Male patients who are being treated with the female hormone estrogen for various maladies almost always experience a decrease or cessation in sexual drive and interest. By contrast, male hormones prescribed for women frequently have the opposite effect, causing an increase in sexual interest and enjoyment. Unfortunately, estrogen has an undesirable feminizing effect on men and male hormones, a masculinizing effect on women (Neiger *b*).

In England recently, an antipotency drug (*cyproterone acetate*) was administered to a group of violent sex offenders in an attempt to decrease their aggressive sexual impulses. Success was reported in the experiment, but it is far too early in the investigation to determine if the drug is truly effective in this regard and whether it produces harmful side effects (Intelligence report). The drug has also been used by a total of 111 physicians to reduce sex offense in Germany and Switzerland, with reported success (Associated Press *d*).

In summary, it can be stated that most information regarding aphrodisiacs is based more on folklore than on scientific evidence. In those instances where there seems to be some change in desire and ability, the drugs are probably affecting bodily functions only remotely related to sexual function. Sexual ability is affected indirectly, if at all. Any changes, therefore, would be based on psychological, not physiological, factors. Every drug is potentially dangerous if used without medical advice.

12 POSITIONS IN SEXUAL INTERCOURSE

No single position of partners in sexual intercourse is more "normal" or more "acceptable" than another. There are many positions, variations of them, and variations upon the variations. All are at least of academic interest. Many of them are challenging, and some simply cannot be assumed unless the partners possess acrobatic aptitude in addition to a singular ability to defy gravity. There are valid reasons for knowing about and experimenting with different coital positions. Sexual instinct is a drive requiring direction, both for its pleasurable and its procreative aspects. This chapter is presented as an aid in that drive's adaptation and fulfillment.

This discussion will not focus on the number of coital positions possible to sexual partners. Coital variation is, of course, almost limitless. It has been estimated that there are as many as 14,288,400 positions for cunnilingus alone (Legman). Rather, we shall aim at a broader understanding of the reasons for experimentation and the benefits accruing from it. The four most common and basic positions in sexual intercourse (and the advantages and disadvantages of each) will be described, but variations of the four will not be. With a little imagination, a sensible attitude toward sex, and an uninhibited approach to experimentation, the individual should be able to work out his own adaptations—and that is the way it should be.

Rare is the person who has observed another's sexual behavior; hence one's empirical knowledge is likely to be extremely limited. A certain amount of sound scientific information on sexual techniques exists, however, and has been available in literature for centuries (Vatsyayana). Moreover, people are increasingly willing to respect and examine mores different from those by which they were reared and to recognize that sex education is often regrettably inaccurate, and that a process of reeducation may be needed.

The sexual act involves two persons, both of whose needs must always be considered. Not only a couple's immediate situational success but also their future harmonious adjustment are often directly correlated to their skill in using pleasurable amatory techniques. Most of the "shoulds" and "should-nots" of sexual behavior are contingent on the mutual pleasure, comfort, and satisfaction of the two people involved—and upon those alone (Ellis a; McCary a). Before coition can be truly successful, each person must be just as aware of the needs of his partner as of his own. Experimentation and variation in coital positions therefore assume major importance as part of the effort to achieve optimal fulfillment for each partner. Any and all positions of sexual intercourse that both partners find satisfactory and pleasurable should be used by them without guilt, shame, or reservation (Greenhill).

Unlike lower animals, human beings must be taught, in one way or another, how to conduct the act of sexual intercourse. Extensive research into sexual behavior has disproved the popular notion that the art of love comes naturally (Harlow and Harlow a). Even the elementary facts of coitus must be learned.

Aside from the intellectual benefits of such knowledge, distinct emotional gains accrue from broad sexual experimentation. One's self-concept is often enhanced by a certain amount of successful coital testing. Feelings of self-confidence and security must exist before one is free to give and take—without fear or guilt—in any human association, including coitus. Only with an understanding and appreciation of the mechanics of sexual intercourse, which must be learned, can a high level of mutual harmony be attained. The higher one's level of comprehension of human sexuality is, the more meaningful his relationships and the greater his pleasure will be.

Experience and confidence, combined with thoughtfulness, can make sex far more pleasurable than it would be otherwise. Stephen Vizinczey, in his book *In Praise of Older Women*, makes this succinct observation:

Trying to make love with someone who is as unskilled as you are seems to me about as sensible as learning to drive with a person who doesn't know the first thing about cars either.... Whenever I see a man reaching out for a woman with painful uncertainty—as if he had something to apologize for, as if he expected her to suffer his desire instead of sharing it—I wonder....

But the benefits of sexual experimentation extend beyond those of an emotional or intellectual nature. Sexual experimentation yields very practical benefits as well. Variety in coital positions makes sexual activity more interesting and can prevent its becoming humdrum (Greenblat). Equally important, some positions are more pleasurable to one partner than to the other, and it is vital that the preferences of each be served. Masters and Johnson (n) have found that the most intense and pleasurable sexual responses of both men and women occur when there is freedom from muscular tension and cramping during the coital act. Some sexual positions provide this freedom to a much greater degree than others.

In addition, the desirability of certain positions may alter from time to time, depending upon such conditions as health, weight, and pregnancy (Eastman and Hellman; McCary a). Furthermore, some coital attitudes are more conducive to conception than others. Positions also vary according to whether coition is spontaneous or anticipated, whether it takes place in cramped or adequate space, and whether it occurs in absolute privacy or with some danger of discovery. The experience and genital size of each spouse are also important determinants in choosing a position. In fact, there are about as many reasons for varying coital activity as there are coital positions.

Most couples do their sexual experimentation during the earlier years of their marriage and then settle down to the use of the one or two positions that best suit them (Eichenlaub a). If one partner has particular difficulty in becoming aroused or in reaching orgasm, it is usually helpful if the couple assume one of their preferred positions after having first experimented with other ones. Often the position fixed upon by a couple can be more easily assumed by their first taking a quite different one and then shifting or rolling into the desired one (Ellis b). For example, intromission can first be made in a face-to-face position; after penetration has taken place, the couple can then shift to a side-by-side position before orgasm is reached.

The "traditional" European and American sexual position of man atop woman is, of course, by far the most common one in our culture. Many Americans are surprised, however, to learn that this position, which they regard as being the "normal" one, has not been so considered in other cultures. As a matter of fact, man atop is called the "missionary position" in certain primitive cultures. And the Kinsey group discovered drawings dating back as early as 3200 B.C. that depict the woman-atop sexual position as being the most common one.

The second most common position—man supine, woman atop—is used occasionally by 35% of the college-educated males, 28% of high-school-educated males, and 17% of grade-school-educated males. Thirty-five percent of women born before 1900 and 52% of women born after

1900 have used the woman-atop position frequently. The side position, face-to-face, is used by 26%, 23%, and 16% of men in high, middle, or low educational groups, respectively. Thirty-one percent of all women have experienced coition in this position. The rear-entry position has been used by 11% of the college- and high-school-educated male groups, and by 8% of the grade-school-educated men. About 15% of all females have experienced rear-entry coition (Kinsey *et al. a, c*).

Face-to-Face, Man-Above Position

It was pointed out above that this is probably the most common position for sexual intercourse in our society, so commonplace that it is often termed the "normal" one. Most women express a preference for this position, and about 70% of American males have never copulated in any other

FIGURE 12.1   Face-to-face coital position, man above.

manner (DeMartino *a*; Kinsey *et al*. *a*). Indeed, laws exist in some states making it illegal and punishable for husbands and wives to try sexual positions other than "normal" ones (Zehv *b*).

Ordinarily, vaginal-penile contact is quite easily achieved when the woman reclines on her back with legs apart and knees bent. She can shift her pelvis or perhaps place a small pillow under her buttocks to help adjust the slant of the vagina for easy and deep penetration. In this, as in all coital positions and positioning, it is usually advantageous for the woman to use her hands to guide the penis into the vagina. She is the best judge of the exact location of the vaginal opening and the angle of the vaginal canal. Her role in guiding the penis is important not only for ease of penetration but also because of the psychological value of her indicating by this action a full and zestful participation in the sexual act (O'Conner).

It is sometimes desirable for the woman to close her legs after entry, thus constricting the vaginal opening and walls, in order to provide more friction against her partner's penis. This pressure against the base of the penis at full penetration helps him maintain erection.

The man partially supports himself on his elbows and knees to avoid putting his full weight on his partner. He is largely in control of the bodily rhythms, as his weight and size limit her to circular, up and down, and rocking pelvic movements. The man should try to keep contact with the clitoris by putting pressure on the upper part of his partner's vulva. Pressure on her pubic bone is helpful in that it sandwiches the clitoris between it and the point of the man's bodily contact, which is usually at his pubic bone. There are numerous variations on the man-astride position, such as the woman's pulling her knees to her shoulders, or locking her legs around her partner's body.

Advantages of the face-to-face, man-above position are many. In this posture, the woman is usually relaxed, and the man has the primary initiative; in our culture, this male-superior position appears to carry certain psychological advantages. Entry is simple, and any adaptations that bring pleasure to the couple can be made easily. It is convenient for couples who enjoy the man's pelvic thrust. In addition, the man can often maintain penetration after he has had an orgasm, and the position facilitates caressing, kissing, and affectionate intimacy between the two. It is an excellent position for impregnation, as the woman can keep her knees raised after the ejaculation, improving chances of the sperm's entering the uterus (Ellis *b*; Greenblat).

The disadvantages of the face-to-face, man-above position are the obverse of its advantages. The woman's movements and active participation may be too restricted; penetration may be too deep for her comfort. It may also be uncomfortable for a woman with an obese or awkward partner, and it may be too acrobatic for older or stouter couples. Some

FIGURE 12.2 Face-to-face coital position, woman above.

men have difficulty in maintaining contact with their partner's clitoris in this position, and manual stimulation of that organ is difficult during coitus. The position is often too exciting for the man, causing him to reach climax too quickly. Furthermore, it is uncomfortable and inadvisable for women in the last stages of pregnancy (Ellis *b*; Greenblat).

Face-to-Face, Woman-Above Position

The woman-atop position is often assumed to give the woman a chance to express herself (by way of a departure from her usual "passive" position). She can govern contact with her clitoris, and can, as well, control the tempo of movement and depth of penetration. The position can also be modified so that the man rests on his elbows and draws up his knees for the woman to lean back on. His arms and hands are thereby left free to clasp and caress her. Intromission is accomplished by the woman's lowering her body, usually in a sitting position with knees bent, over her supine partner and guiding his penis into her vagina. Couples may find it more pleasurable to achieve penetration in some other position, and then to turn or roll over gently, so that the penis does not slip from the vagina nor orgasm occur in the process.

The Dutch physician Van de Velde has declared that coitus with the woman astride "affords the summit in excitement and response, the acme of specific physical sexual pleasure, to both man and woman." It is also his contention (although there is little supporting evidence) that this position, because it is so stimulating and vigorous, might be too exhausting for older couples and should be attempted by them only occasionally.

The advantages of the face-to-face, woman-above position are numerous and are also uniquely individual. A woman possesses maximum control and freedom to express herself sexually when she is astride her partner. The position permits fullest penetration, yet she can avoid any discomfort or pain to herself because she regulates the depth of penile entry. Clitoral contact is easier in many cases, and the friction of erotic stimulation more intense. Furthermore, the woman does not have to contend with the man's weight. Consequently she can control such pleasurable movements as pelvic thrusts, which both she and her partner may find most exciting. A man may be able to delay orgasm more successfully because little physical exertion or strain is imposed on him in this position. These facts may be of significance to him if his partner is slow to reach climax, or if he tends to ejaculate prematurely or is in poor health. Masters and Johnson (p) frequently have a couple use one of the variations of the face-to-face position—the woman in a squatting position above the man—in their training sessions to overcome sexual inadequacies (see Fig. 18.3). Their reason is that this position allows the man complete relaxation in coital activity and permits the woman to control the timing and movements required in certain phases of the treatment.

There are further advantages. The man's hands are free to caress his partner's breasts or any other part of her body. The woman can rest full-length upon the man; this complete bodily contact often affords pleasure and excitement to both partners. The position is therefore especially useful when the woman is much smaller than the man. It also allows for such interaction as conversation and the observation of each other's facial expressions. Furthermore, a man frequently welcomes this position because the burden of coital movement is primarily the woman's, thereby permitting him to relax and abandon himself to the pleasures of erotic fantasy.

There are disadvantages, however, to the face-to-face, woman-astride position. The man's freedom of movement and pelvic thrust may be too restricted for his tastes, or the sacrifice of his "male-superior" position may cause him to lose his erection, sexual drive, or even interest. Since he is not controlling the coital movements, his penis may persistently slip out of the vagina. The woman may find that penetration is too deep in this position, causing her pain. It is not a good position for impregnation, as the sperm are likely to seep out of the vagina after ejaculation. Neither is it a comfortable position during pregnancy (Eichenlaub a; Ellis b; Greenblat; Van de Velde; Vatsyayana).

Many women are not so athletically inclined that they enjoy such vigorous sexual participation. They may feel uncomfortable in such an "aggressive" role, and some men are of the persuasion that their masculinity is threatened if they assume a lower or "passive" position. Both these objections are faulty, for any position that gives pleasure to both partners should be freely assumed.

Face-to-Face Side Position

Coitus can often be achieved more restfully when the partners are lying on their sides facing one another. Both have an ease of motion, and either can withdraw or otherwise control the movements of intercourse. The side position has many variations. Often one partner is largely on his back with his mate resting on him (Hirsch). The woman raises her upper leg and crosses it over the man in order to permit entry. Sometimes the side-to-side position is assumed after the partners have begun in another position and have rolled onto their sides. There is complete freedom to maneuver arms, hands, and legs in this position. The partners are under little physical strain since neither is supporting the weight of the other. The couple can often go to sleep with contact maintained after completion of the act (Eichenlaub a; Greenblat; Vatsyayana).

In addition to its relatively comfortable and restful nature, the side-by-side position carries further advantages. Its interlocking attitude allows maximum contact between the man's body and the woman's clitoris. The man can cradle his partner between his legs and hold her in close and continued contact. This position is especially helpful when conditions of fatigue, ill health, or obesity exist, or if one partner is considerably taller than the other. It is often a satisfactory position for coitus during the last months of pregnancy. Both partners—especially the man—can regulate their pelvic thrusts and can often thereby prolong sexual activity before orgasm. Penile withdrawal and reinsertion are possible without very much change of position or adjustment, and a steady coital rhythm can easily be sustained (Ellis b).

An important variation of the face-to-face side position is what has been described by Masters and Johnson as the *lateral coital position* (see Fig. 18.4). They state that this position is reported to be "the most effective coital position available to man and woman, presuming there is an estab-

FIGURE 12.3 Side coital position, face–to–face.

lished marital-unit interest in mutual effectiveness of sexual performance"
(Masters and Johnson *p*). It provides, they declare, the greatest flexibility
for free sexual expression by both sexes because neither partner is pinioned.
Its mutual freedom permits easy pelvic movement in any direction. The
muscle cramping and tiring common to other positions is circumvented
because the partners do not have to support each other's or their own
body weight. The position is especially effective for a woman, since she is
free to engage in slow or rapid pelvic thrusting, according to the level of
her sexual tensions. It is also the position in which a man can best develop
and maintain his ejaculatory control. Masters and Johnson maintain that
this position is chosen for coitus 75% of the time by couples once they
have tried it.

The primary disadvantages to the side position are the inconstancy
of contact and the fact that some couples find it less comfortable than most
other positions. It is not easy for some persons to achieve entry or to

maintain sufficiently stimulating pressure on the vulval area in this position. Other couples, preferring more vigorous coition, find the position inadequately stimulating, since it offers little possibility for deep pelvic thrusts and penetration. Movements may be difficult in the interlocking position because of restrictions placed on certain parts of the body.

Rear-Entry Position

Facing his partner's back, the man can accomplish intromission in any of several manners. Both partners can be on their sides, the man entering the woman from the rear. The woman can kneel, or lie on her stomach, as her partner enters her. Or the man can sit (on bed or chair) while the

FIGURE 12.4 Representation of the erect penis inserted into the vagina.

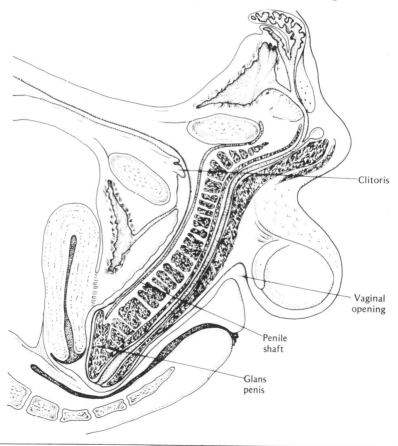

Clitoris

Vaginal opening

Penile shaft

Glans penis

woman sits on his lap with her back to him. And there are numerous other variations to rear-entry intromission (Eichenlaub a; Ellis b; Vatsyayana).

Entry from the rear when both partners are on their sides exacts less exertion from the woman and places less pressure on her than other coital attitudes do. For this reason it is a position often recommended for coition in the advanced months of pregnancy. Rear entry is also restful for a man, as he can be more relaxed than when he is astride a woman. This posture shortens a woman's vagina, which may be advantageous since less of the penile shaft is required to effect deep penetration. Because the woman's buttocks are in the way, not much of the penis can be introduced into the vagina in this position, but whatever degree of penetration is possible can be easily regulated by the man. Often the man finds the pressure of his partner's gluteal (buttocks) area against his body to be quite exciting. Furthermore, his hands are left free to encircle her body and to caress her breasts, clitoris, legs, or whatever other area pleases them both (Ellis b). Some women find the position painful, however, because penetration is deep in the foreshortened vagina. Others object to it because it seems unnatural and animalistic to them.

Side-by-side rear entry is particularly relaxing to a couple when either or both are tired, debilitated, old, or convalescent, although the entry is not always easy to make or maintain. Contact is usually lost after the man's orgasm. The position, furthermore, offers little assistance toward conception. For very stout persons, or for a man with a small penis, the side-rear position presents special difficulties (Eichenlaub a).

The knee-chest attitude is a more active form of rear-entry coitus, in which both partners assume a kneeling position. The woman can rest her arms and head on pillow or bed, and her partner presses his body against her buttocks to effect entry. Sexual activity is usually quite vigorous in this position, especially for the man. Knee-chest rear entry is recommended as a favorable position for conception, because the semen remains in the vagina for a longer time and closer to the opening of the uterus than in other coital positions (Eichenlaub a; Greenblat).

Although the rear-kneeling position is psychologically and physiologically exciting for some persons, it is objectionable to others, and for the same reasons—namely, its novel and vigorous nature. One or both partners may object to rear entry because it lacks face-to-face intimacy, or because the nature of its approach becomes associated in their minds with anal intercourse, thereby carrying with it (as it does for some people) homosexual or other repugnant overtones.

Another rear-entry coital posture is one in which the woman lies on her stomach and her partner attempts penetration while lying on top of her. It is awkward and not sufficiently pleasurable to be used by many couples (Ellis b).

Rear-entry sitting coition involves the man's seating himself on the

FIGURE 12.5 Rear-entry coital position.

edge of a bed or chair and his partner's sitting down on his penis with her back to him. This variation of the face-to-face sitting position is much enjoyed by many couples because of the closeness of contact and freedom of movement it allows them both (Ellis *b*).

Sitting positions offer singular coital variety and novel enjoyment to some couples. However, the deep penetration often resulting from these postures can also prove uncomfortable or even harmful to the woman, and in such instances should be avoided—or at least controlled.

As already noted, there are an infinite number of variations on the coital positions that have been discussed—e.g., standing, sitting face-to-face, man standing between the legs of the woman whose torso is on a bed—but a detailed examination of them will not serve present purposes.

FIGURE 12.6 Variations of the basic coital positions.

Face-to-face, man-above (man kneeling)

Face-to-face, man-above (woman's legs fully elevated)

Face-to-face (both partners standing)

Face-to-face, woman-above (both partners sitting)

Rear entry, side-by-side

As with other forms of spontaneous sexual activity, coital postures are various, and all are acceptable. Coital position should be governed only by the tastes of the individual couple, their imagination and dexterity, and the occasion at hand.

The forms of sex relationships that individuals establish, whether in or out of marriage, are a result of social learning, acceptance or rejection of social standards, and personality dynamics. Emotionally secure persons who are free of sexual guilt and shame are capable of experimentation along the entire spectrum of human sexual expression, including coital positions. As a result they are much more likely to enjoy their sex life than those people who are more inhibited and sexually hobbled (Zehv *b*). A couple should take care, however, to avoid an exaggerated concern for the "how" of sexual intercourse while they are engaging in it. Coitus may otherwise assume artificial or mechanical overtones that can detract from the freedom and spontaneity of the relationship.

Coitus is not a gymnastic feat, an endurance contest, or an event of constant laboratorylike experimentation. It is, rather, a mutual act involving a wide range of techniques and postures. Whatever techniques of love play, sexual intercourse, and postcoital caressing found by a couple to bring mutual pleasure should be freely enjoyed by them.

13 ORGASM

We have emphasized that the methods and techniques of sexual activity of individual people are many and that they produce varying degrees of pleasure. A method or technique is the "right" one only insofar as it is satisfactory and serves its purpose; what is "right" for one person may not be "right" for another. But no matter what techniques are employed or how intense the enjoyment is, the *ultimate* goal is an orgasm.

An orgasm is a highly pleasurable, tension-relieving, seizurelike response that is the summit of physical and emotional gratification in sexual activity. The neurological and physiological structures and responses that give rise to orgasmic reactions have been discussed in Chapters 6 and 7. In this chapter we shall examine the particular arousal that leads to an orgasm, which involves a marked rise in blood pressure and pulse rate, faster and deeper breathing, engorgement of special tissues with blood, and, finally, an explosive release of muscular and nervous tension. This release is followed by a rather quick return to the normal or nonstimulated state. The subjective sensation of orgasm is centered in the pelvic region of both men and women: in the penis, prostate, and seminal vesicles of men; and the clitoris, vagina, and uterus of women (Masters and Johnson *n*).

Orgasm is a short-lived experience (lasting usually about 3 to 10 seconds) that has an intensity many find difficult to understand. However, if another body need—for example, hunger—were to be satisfied in an equally short period of time, perhaps a similar intensity of reaction would be experienced.

The works of the two best known and most influential sex research teams—the late Alfred Kinsey and his co-workers, and William H. Masters and Virginia Johnson—have emphasized the similarities, not the differences, between male and female human sexual behavior and response (Kinsey *et al. c*; Masters and Johnson *n*). Both research groups conclude that there are few dissimilarities between male and female orgasm, the most noticeable difference being, of course, that male orgasm is accompanied by ejaculation.

It perhaps should be mentioned here that a few men do, in fact, experience orgasm without ejaculation, but that it is a rare and special occurrence. Some men have *retrograde ejaculations,* which means that the semen is discharged into the bladder rather than through the penis. Since external evidence is lacking, it appears that the man does not ejaculate, although in reality he does. This condition is caused by some anomaly at the junction of the ejaculatory ducts and urethra within the prostate, either as a result of prostatic surgery, an accident, or some caprice of nature. About 80% of men who have undergone prostate surgery will experience retrograde ejaculation, although the sensation of orgasm remains quite normal (Hotchkiss).

FIGURE 13.1 Schematic representation of a normal ejaculation and a retrograde ejaculation.

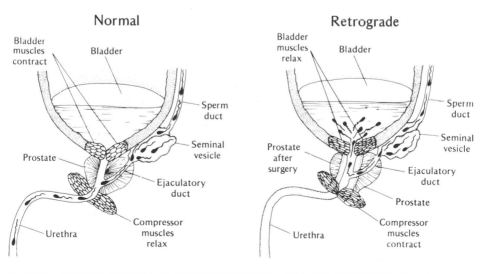

Sometimes drugs, especially certain tranquilizers (From the editor's scrapbook *b*), may inhibit the ejaculatory centers, yet not affect the erection centers of the neural network involved in orgasm. (The possible value of these drugs in treating premature ejaculation is apparent.) In other instances, diabetes will inhibit ejaculation at the time of orgasm.

Fewer women than men experience orgasmic response, although women are considerably more capable than men of having multiple orgasms. There are exceptions, of course, but it is safe to state that nearly all healthy men almost always achieve orgasm once sexual stimulation progresses to a certain point. About 95% of women are capable of reaching orgasm at some point during their lifetime. Only 70%, however, are able to achieve it during their first year of marriage, owing, no doubt, to the stringent sexual controls to which they have been subjected from early girlhood (Kinsey *et al. c*).

Because of the abundance of nerve endings in the region of the clitoris and vulva and the almost negligible number of nerve endings in the vagina, many women find that masturbation (as well as other forms of similar direct stimulation), rather than coitus, brings them more orgasms, in faster succession, and with a more intense physical response. In support of this point, women who have taken part in various sexual acts in a laboratory setting report that orgasms produced by direct noncoital methods, such as masturbation, are more satisfying and fulfilling physiologically than coitally produced orgasms, although the latter are more psychologically and emotionally satisfying (Masters and Johnson *n*). Most men, on the other hand, find it easier and more satisfying to achieve orgasm through coitus than through other methods.

A man usually achieves orgasm within about 4 minutes of intromission, while a woman requires from 10 to 20 minutes of sexual intercourse before she attains an orgasmic response. However, with manual, electric vibrator, or oral-genital stimulation, a woman can usually reach orgasm in less than 4 minutes (Kinsey *et al. c*).

The debate has long raged over women's capacity for experiencing multiple orgasms, despite the abundance of clinical evidence attesting to their capability for this sexual response. Even after publication of their research data and clinical findings, the Kinsey researchers found themselves criticized for their "fantastic tale" of multiple orgasms in women (Pomeroy *c*). Perhaps the findings of Masters and Johnson (*n*) will convince skeptics of the validity of the Kinsey group's conclusions. It has now been established through empirical and clinical evidence that women are capable by natural endowment of multi-orgasm. Many, in fact, are able to have six or more orgasms during a single period of sexual activity (Masters and Johnson *o*). Kinsey and his co-workers (*c*) report that 14% of women regularly have multiple orgasms, and Masters and Johnson (*n*) show that, if the sexual stimulation producing a woman's first orgasm is continued, a second and a third orgasm—perhaps more—will follow. Furthermore, the women in the Masters and Johnson sampling report that, subjectively, they found the second and third orgasmic responses to be more intense and more pleasurable than the first.

Although men supposedly possess a stronger sex drive, they are not nearly so capable as women of multiple orgasms. Only about 6% to 8% of men are able to have more than one orgasm during each sexual experience, and when the capacity for multiple orgasm exists it is usually found only in very young men (Kinsey *et al.* a). Kinsey and his co-workers reported that the highest frequency of orgasms among men discovered by them was 26 in a 24-hour period—the experience of a 13-year old boy. One adult male in their study reported averaging 33 orgasms per week for over 30 years (Kinsey *et al.* a). Those men who have a second orgasm shortly after the first relate that the pleasure of the first is superior to that of the second, in direct contrast to women's subjective reports (Masters and Johnson n).

Despite women's capacity for orgasm, the unfortunate fact remains that they do not, as has been pointed out earlier, reach orgasm as easily as men. Psychological blocks would seem to make the difference. This explanation is understandable in the light of society's many archaic if not downright fallacious attitudes—e.g., the double standard, and the alleged shame and sin that many moralists impute to human sexuality, all of which set the stage for sexual conflicts in both partners, but especially in the woman. Another powerful inhibitor to a woman's orgasm is her fear of becoming pregnant.

The quality of an orgasm—that is, the intensity, length, and overall pleasure—may vary from person to person and within the same person from one act of coition to another. Recency and frequency of occurrence can influence the quality of the next sexual experience, as can such factors as anxiety, guilt, depression, anger, indifference toward one's partner, and distaste for one's surroundings. These factors not only can affect the quality of the orgasm, but also, if strong enough, can block the response altogether. As would be expected, women, because of their being subjected to the double standard, report a greater variability in the subjective quality of their orgasms than men do (Marmor *et al.*).

When men experience little pleasure or sensation in climax, the basis is rarely physiological, although such organic pathology as neuropathy or diabetes can cause it, as can certain drugs. Diminished pleasure at the time of orgasm is usually psychological and reflects dissatisfaction with the sexual relationship, or emotional barriers such as fear, anxiety, aggression, hostility, fatigue, or, perhaps, boredom. Appropriate physical or psychological treatment can usually be of considerable aid in alleviating the problem (Lear).

In recent years there has been increasing concern on the part of both men and women over the woman's ability to achieve orgasm. They see orgasm as not only a goal for the woman but also her due. When she fails to achieve orgasm, therefore, both partners tend to experience a feeling of inadequacy and failure (Gebhard a). On the other hand, some women still cling to the idea that enjoyment of their sexuality is immodest, animalistic, or unwomanly. With such emotional shackles it is not difficult to understand why these women have difficulties with sexual responsiveness on any level—in contrast to men, who typically derive much pleasure from their sexual life and achieve orgasm with great ease. The answer must lie in the fact that men are less encumbered by the psychological barriers that hinder women. These unhealthy conditions will not be alleviated immediately. But once people can arrive at a code of ethical sexual behavior based on rationality rather than on shame and guilt, many of the sexual problems facing society today will be corrected.

In their exacting and highly significant research program on the human sexual response cycle, Masters and Johnson have described with scientific precision the physiological reactions that men and women experience during the various phases of sexual stimulation (Masters, W. H. a, b; Masters and Johnson a, d, e, g, h, i, j, l, m, n). They found it convenient to divide the sexual response of both sexes into four phases: the *excitement phase*, the *plateau phase*, the *orgasmic phase*, and the *resolution phase*. In their laboratory demonstration of what had been surmised before by some scientists, clinicians, and laymen, Masters and Johnson established that a variety of physical and psychological stimuli can produce sexual excitement, whereas adverse stimuli, or a variation of stimulative techniques, can shorten, prolong, or interrupt erotic arousal.

When effective sexual stimulation is employed, the recipient enters the *excitement phase,* which varies in length of time from a few minutes to hours, depending upon the effectiveness, intensity, and continuance of the techniques used, and upon the degree of freedom from adverse stimuli, whether physical or psychological. Generally speaking, the longer the excitement phase, the longer the resolution phase; these are the two most protracted phases of the sexual response cycle.

The second phase, the *plateau phase,* is intense but of short duration. And the third or *orgasmic phase* is extremely short, lasting from 3 to 10 seconds (sometimes longer in women). When the stimulation that was effective in evoking the excitement phase is continued, the plateau phase is reached. From this point, continuation of the same arousal techniques will culminate in the peak of the sexual cycle, the orgasmic phase. During the last or *resolution phase,* the sexual system retrogresses to its normal nonexcited state, the length of this phase being directly proportionate to that of the excitement phase.

There is little individual diversity in the pattern of men's response during the orgasmic phase. On the other hand, women—as a group (especially) and individually—display wide diversity in their orgasmic response, both in duration and intensity. For some women orgasm is a short-lived experience; for others, an extended one. Some experience mild orgasms, while others have such intense ones that they become unaware of their surroundings, occasionally even to the point of losing consciousness momentarily. Sexually inadequate women (who seldom or never experience orgasm) are far more likely to control their spontaneous movements toward the end of coitus than are sexually adequate women (who usually or always respond with orgasm) (Adams).

There is a significant variation in the response of men and women following coitus. After orgasm, the man enters the *refractory period* (a state of temporary resistance to sexual stimulation) of the resolution phase. Sexual stimulation that was previously effective and pleasurable now becomes unavailing and distasteful. Women, on the other hand, usually do not enter a refractory period. They generally remain capable of returning to earlier phases of the sexual response cycle, and, if the same sexual stimulation that produced the first orgasm is continued or reapplied, they may experience one or several more orgasms.

The duration of the orgasm itself within a given individual is about the same whether it occurs as a result of sexual intercourse, manual or oral stimulation, or use of mechanical devices. There is also great personal variation in the pleasure and intensity of orgasm, depending upon the individual's preferences in the matter of sexual stimulation.

Following is a summary of identifiable human physiological responses as they occur in the excitement, plateau, orgasmic, and resolution phases of sexual expression. Those persons interested in studying and understanding the human sexual response cycle in greater detail should read the basic two-volume work on sexual behavior by Kinsey *et al.* (a, c) and, especially, Masters and Johnson's *Human Sexual Response* (n). The following material is primarily a summary of the latter authors' extensive investigation into the physiology of both men's and women's sexual responses.

THE FEMALE SEXUAL RESPONSE CYCLE

The Excitement Phase in Women

The Breasts

The most noticeable response observed in the breasts is the erection of the nipples. During the excitement phase, an increase in nipple length of 0.5 to 1.5 cm and in nipple base diameter of 0.25 to 1.0 cm may be expected, although excessively large or extremely small nipples do not enlarge as much as normal-sized ones. This erection is maintained throughout the entire cycle. There are exceptions to the erection response, notably among women with inverted nipples, which are incapable of erection. Factors other than sexual arousal can also cause nipple erection—e.g., cold weather, cold baths, and removal of an excessively binding brassiere.

As sexual tension continues and increases, the pigmented area of the breast surrounding the nipple (areola) becomes engorged and swollen, giving the false impression that the nipple-erection response has been lost, at least partially. Venous blood is trapped in the breasts during the excitement phase, and they enlarge about 20% to 25% by the end of this phase. The veins of the breast become more noticeable during the early part of this phase, because they become engorged with slow-flowing venous blood, forming the familiar "vascular tree" of the breasts.

The Sex Flush
The vascular-flush phenomenon, called the *maculopapular sex flush* by Masters and Johnson, is one of the most singular reactions to erotic stimulation. A flush of the skin, beginning at the stomach region and at the throat and neck, then spreading quickly to the breasts, appears with varying individual intensity during the excitement phase. As a rule, the intensity of the flush is in direct proportion to the intensity of the stimulation received. About 70% to 75% of sexually stimulated women exhibit the sex flush on occasion, as compared with about 25% of sexually responding men.

Myotonia
Generalized reactions during the excitement phase (and others) demonstrate that a woman responds sexually with her whole body; her reactions are not limited specifically to the pelvic zone. Increased tension (*myotonia*) of voluntary muscles—and, to a limited extent, of some involuntary muscles—is observable during the excitement phase, especially the latter part. As the phase progresses and tension increases, the woman's movements become more restless, forceful, and swift, and there is involuntary tensing of the muscles in the abdominal region.

The Rectum, Urethra, and Bladder
There is sometimes a voluntary contraction of the rectal muscles, along with those of the buttocks, during the excitement phase, the contraction being an attempt to push sexual tension toward ultimate orgasmic response. No other reactions in these areas have been noted during this phase.

Cardio-Respiratory-Perspiratory Responses
Increase in heart rate and elevation of blood pressure parallel the buildup of sexual tension during the excitement phase. There are no noticeable respiratory or perspiratory reactions.

The Clitoris

The clitoris, when viewed under magnification, undergoes a sustained tumescent reaction during the excitement phase, although tumescence can be detected by the naked eye in less than 50% of the cases. During this phase the loose, wrinkled external skin that surrounds or covers the clitoris fills out as the glans tissue beneath it expands through venous congestion. As sexual tension mounts, the diameter of the clitoris increases and there is a congestive elongation of its shaft, although the latter occurrence can be visually detected in less than 10% of the cases. Clitoral tumescence persists throughout the period of sexual stimulation.

Fewer than 50% of women show clinically obvious tumescence of the clitoral glans; it becomes observable only after sexual tension has progressed into the late part of the excitement phase. Direct manipulation of the clitoral region will produce more rapid and greater enlargement of the clitoral glans than will less direct stimulation (such as fantasy, breast manipulation, or sexual intercourse).

The Vagina

The vagina reveals its first evidence of anatomic response during the excitement phase. Within 10 to 30 seconds after psychological or physiological stimulation has begun, the vagina begins to lubricate itself through the "sweating" phenomenon discussed earlier. Small droplets of clear fluid appear on the walls of the vagina; as sexual tension increases, the droplets coalesce to form a moist coating of

FIGURE 13.2 The female pelvic region, showing the enlargement of the vaginal blood vessels and the "sweating" of the vaginal walls during sexual arousal and climax.

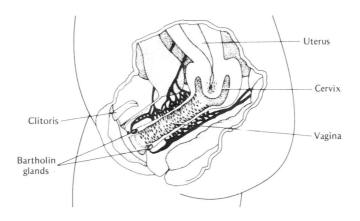

the entire vaginal wall, completely lubricating the vaginal barrel. Since there is practically no glandular tissue in the vagina, it must be assumed that the lubricant is produced by vasocongestive activity in the vaginal barrel.

As the excitement phase continues, both the width and the length of the inner two-thirds of the vaginal passage increase by about 25% over their nonexcited dimensions. The entire vagina becomes dilated, but expansion is limited to its inner two-thirds. (Under nonexcited conditions the walls of the vagina—especially in women who have never borne a child—are in a state of apposition; that is, the walls are touching.) The wrinkled surface of the vagina stretches and flattens, and the vaginal mucosa thins with the expansion.

The vagina also undergoes a color change during the excitement phase—from its usual purple-red color to a rather patchy deep purple. The entire vaginal barrel becomes consistently darker in the subsequent phases.

The Uterus

During the early part of the excitement phase, a rapid, irregular contraction phenomenon (*fibrillation*) begins in the body of the uterus. There is evidence of a developing vasocongestive reaction in the uterus during this phase. The longer the phase lasts, the greater the increase in the dimensions of the uterus over its unstimulated size. If a woman is sustained for an excessively prolonged period in the excitement or plateau phase, the uterus may show a twofold or threefold increase over its normal size.

In the latter part of the excitement phase as the plateau phase nears, the entire uterus is pulled upward into the lower abdomen. This lifting of the cervix, along with the involuntary expansion of the vaginal walls, produces a ballooning or tenting effect in the innermost two-thirds of the vagina. (A retroverted uterus, incidentally, prevents this particular response.) Contrary to earlier theories, the cervix is in no way responsible for vaginal lubrication.

The Labia Majora

The labia majora (major lips) respond during the excitement phase in different ways, depending upon whether the woman has borne children (*multipara*) or not (*nullipara*). In the nullipara, the major lips thin out and become somewhat flattened. There is a slight elevation of the lips upward and outward, and they flare away from the vagina. The flattening process is not usually complete until late in the excitement phase, or until the beginning of the plateau phase.

In the multipara, the major lips become greatly engorged, often increasing in size by two or three times. There is usually a marked gaping of the lips at the meatus of the vagina so that the "anticipated mount-

FIGURE 13.3 The female pelvic region, showing organs and tissue in a normal, un-excited state.

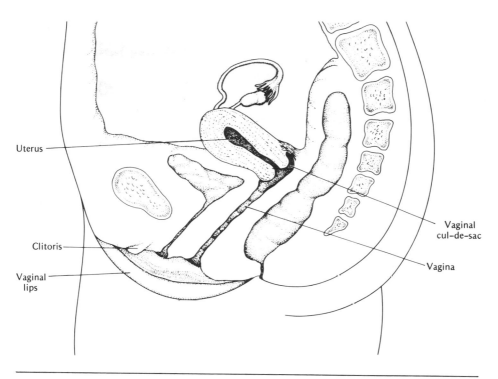

Uterus

Clitoris

Vaginal lips

Vaginal cul-de-sac

Vagina

ing process" will not be impeded, even though the major lips hang in a rather loose and pendulous manner.

The Labia Minora

The labia minora (also referred to as the minor lips, inner lips, or sex-skin) begin enlarging in the excitement phase. By the end of the phase, or perhaps early in the plateau phase, they demonstrate a two- to threefold increase over their normal thickness. This thickening of the inner lips adds a centimeter to the length of the vaginal barrel, perhaps more.

The Bartholin's Glands

During the excitement phase the Bartholin's glands produce very little mucoid secretion, and then usually not until the very end of the phase or in the plateau phase. The amount secreted is insignificant (very seldom more than one drop for the nulliparous woman, and rarely more than two or three drops for the multiparous woman), and the discharge occurs too late in the sexual response cycle for it to be of value as a lubricant. The presumed roles, therefore, of the Bartholin's glands as a source of vaginal lubrication for easeful penetration by the penis, and as an anti-acidity agent to assist the sperm to survive longer in the vagina, can be discounted. These functions appear, rather, to be carried out by the fluid secreted in vaginal "sweating."

The Plateau Phase in Women

The Breasts

In a continuing response pattern that might more accurately be considered an extension of the excitement phase, the breasts reach their peak of expansion during the plateau phase. The areolae become so enlarged during this phase that they partially cover the erect nipples, giving the illusion that there is a loss of nipple erection. Breasts that have never fed a baby usually show more expansive ability that those that have been suckled. Because of changes wrought by previous glandular distention and venous drainage, suckled breasts, in comparison with unsuckled breasts, apparently have a somewhat reduced tumescence capacity.

The Sex Flush

Of those subjects who evidence a vascular reaction to sexual stimulation by a skin flush, most of the body surface will now be involved. The rose-colored mottling spreads over the top and sides and then the undersides of the breasts. The flush may also become visible on the lower abdomen and shoulders and, as tension increases and orgasm nears, may appear on the back, buttocks, and thighs. Late in this period, the intensity of the color and the expanse of the flush reach their peak.

Myotonia

Muscular tension in the sexually stimulated woman is observable from head to toe during this phase. She frequently reacts with facial grimaces, flaring of nostrils, and marked strain of the mouth. The cords of the neck become rigid and stand erect (especially with the approach of orgasm), the back arches, and the long muscles of the thighs become very tense.

The muscles of the buttocks are often purposefully made more tense in the striving for orgasm. Late in the plateau phase, involuntary spastic contractions of hand and foot muscles develop into grasping, clawing movements (*carpopedal spasm*). Involuntary muscle contractions lengthen the vaginal barrel.

The Rectum, Urethra, and Bladder

The same voluntary contractions of rectal muscles noted in some women during the excitement phase frequently continue during the plateau phase.

Cardio-Respiratory-Perspiratory Responses

As the plateau phase continues, an elevation of heart rate from the usual 80 to a rate of 110 to 175 beats per minute may be expected.

During the latter part of this phase, there is also an elevation of blood pressure, with a rise in systolic pressure of 20 to 60 mm Hg over the normal 120, and a rise in diastolic pressure of 10 to 20 mm Hg over the normal 80. Hyperventilation (increase in respiratory rate) is first noticed during the plateau phase. No perspiratory responses are detectable in this phase.

The Clitoris

The clitoris exhibits its most singular response to sexual stimulation during the plateau phase. With almost perfect consistency among all women, the body and glans of the clitoris withdraw from their normal pudendal overhang position and pull back deeply beneath the foreskin or hood. At the very end of the plateau phase, just before the orgasm, the retraction is so pronounced that there is at least a 50% reduction in the total length of the clitoris. If sexual stimulation is removed during the plateau phase, the clitoris will resume its normal overhanging position; if stimulation is reapplied, the clitoris will withdraw again.

The Vagina

There is particular activity of the outer third of the vagina during the plateau phase, following a certain degree of dilation in this area during the excitement phase. During this second phase, marked vasocongestion within the vaginal canal occurs: the entire outer third, including

---

FIGURE 13.4 Representation of the clitoris during sexual activity, showing (A) its normal unstimulated state; (B) its response during the excitement and plateau phases; and (C) its response at the end of the plateau phase and during the orgasmic phase.

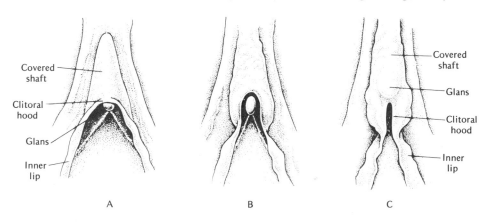

the encircling muscles (bulbocavernosus), becomes distended with venous blood. The central space of the outer third of the canal is reduced by about 33%. The distended muscles involuntarily contract, causing the vagina to tighten around the shaft of the inserted penis during coition as the woman nears orgasm. The congested outer third of the vagina and the engorged labia minora have been given the name *orgasmic platform* by Masters and Johnson.

The depth and width of the vagina increase only very slightly during the plateau phase.

The Uterus

During this phase, the uterus elevates as fully into the lower abdomen as its supportive tissue and ligaments allow, producing an increased tenting effect in the inner portion of the vagina.

Fibrillation of the corpus of the uterus intensifies as the response cycle progresses from early excitement to late plateau phase. Further vaso-congestion of the uterus during this period produces a temporary increase in its size.

The Labia Majora

The labia majora show no further changes during the plateau phase other than an elaboration of the changes that began in the excitement phase.

Nulliparous women may develop thick, heavily engorged major lips if stimulation is prolonged.

The Labia Minora

The color of the sex-skin (labia minora) of nulliparous women changes from ashen pink to bright rose, and toward the end of the excitement phase deepens further to a scarlet hue. A multiparous woman experiences greater dilation of the veins in the minor lips than the nulliparous woman does, so that the sex-skin coloration of the former can be expected to be deeper, ultimately darkening to a wine color during the plateau phase. There is a definite correlation between the intensity of these color changes and degree of sexual excitation. In those women who progress satisfactorily through the excitement phase but who are unable to achieve orgasm, the labia minora become bright pink but never a deeper color. Marked color changes are evidence of an impending orgasm.

The Bartholin's Glands

If the Bartholin's glands have not previously secreted their fluid, and if they are to produce such a secretion, they do so now. Prolonged penile thrusts during coitus may stimulate the Bartholin's glands to secrete, but frequently they do not.

The Orgasmic Phase in Women
The Breasts
There are no noticeable changes in the breasts at the time of orgasm, although they may appear to be heavy and pendulous because of the spasmlike reaction of the entire body when the climax occurs.

The Sex Flush
The intensity of the flush is proportionate to the intensity of the orgasm.

Myotonia
The myotonic reactions observed in the latter part of the plateau phase usually continue and intensify in the orgasmic phase. During orgasm, muscular strain may be so severe as to cause aching and soreness the following day. The woman is so extensively caught up in her orgasmic response that there is a loss of voluntary control, and she is unaware of her muscular reactions.

Orgasm produces muscular changes in the body far beyond the contractions of the orgasmic platform and uterus. There are also involuntary contractions of the perineal area, the rectum, and the lower abdomen. Both superficial and deep muscles are involved, and the entire pelvic region is irregularly and spasmodically elevated in deviation from its usual flat positioning. Other parts of the body, such as the neck, hands, arms, feet, and legs, exhibit individual responses at the time of orgasm. Corded neck muscles are an easily observable reaction just before and during orgasm, indicating the marked and generalized muscular strain that the body undergoes at this time.

Further changes during this phase may include flushing and slight swelling of the face and expansion of the rib cage. The more effective the stimulation has been, the more completely the woman's whole body becomes involved in the release of physiological and psychological tensions.

The Rectum, Urethra, and Bladder
Involuntary contraction of the sphincter muscles of the rectum may occur during the orgasmic phase, especially if the orgasm is intense. As with the contractions in the outer third of the vagina, the rectal contractions occur at 0.8-second intervals. The rectal muscles may contract in strong orgasmic responses as many as five times. These systolic rectal reactions have been observed more frequently during automanipulation than during sexual intercourse.

Women sometimes experience an involuntary distention of the external meatus of the urethra during orgasm. When this occurs, the distention disappears and the meatus returns to its normal state before the orgasmic phase is over. A woman occasionally feels an urge to urinate during or immediately after orgasm, and there is possibly a loss of urine as sexual tension mounts. More multiparous than nulliparous women have a tendency to urinate involuntarily at this time, because their sphincter muscles are more flaccid (Clark g).

Cardio-Respiratory-Perspiratory Responses

There is a further slight elevation in the heart rate beyond that reached in the plateau phase, usually higher when a woman masturbates than when she engages in coition. Although the blood pressure in women continues to climb, the rise is not as great as that in men during this phase. A woman's blood pressure shows an elevation of 30 to 80 mm Hg above the normal 120, and an elevation in diastolic pressure of 20 to 40 mm Hg above the normal 80. Respiration may increase to a rate of 40 breaths a minute (20 a minute is normal) during this phase. The increase in intensity and duration of any respiratory changes is directly correlated with the intensity and duration of sexual tension. If the orgasm is mild or of short duration, there may be no increase in the respiratory rate. There are still no perspiratory reactions at this stage of the response cycle.

The Clitoris

The clitoris shows no specific reaction at the time of orgasm. That is to say, under present laboratory conditions it is not possible to observe the clitoris during this phase, since it is retracted beneath the hood of the labia minora.

The Vagina

The vagina shows a unique response during the orgasmic phase. The orgasmic platform, which is first noticeable during the plateau phase, contracts strongly in intervals of about 0.8 second. There are at least

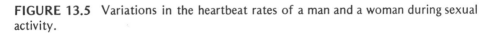

FIGURE 13.5 Variations in the heartbeat rates of a man and a woman during sexual activity.

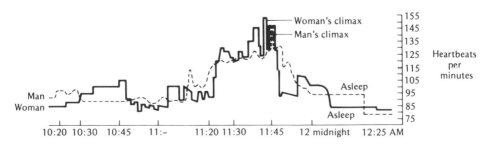

3 or 4 such contractions, and there may be as many as 15. The interval between contractions lengthens after the first few responses, and the intensity also diminishes. The strength of the contractions varies from person to person, and individual contractile experiences also vary.

The Uterus
The rapid but irregular contractions noted in the corpus of the uterus during the earlier phases move into an identifiable pattern during the orgasmic phase. The contractions are somewhat similar to those of the uterus during the first stage of labor. Typically, they begin at the top of the uterus (fundus) and work their way downward through the middle portion, terminating in the lower section of the cervix. It is noteworthy that the contractile reactions do not begin until 2 to 4 seconds after a woman first experiences orgasm. Current research findings indicate that uterine contractions are more severe when orgasm has been brought about by masturbatory techniques than by coition.

FIGURE 13.6 The female pelvic region, showing the changes in the size and position of organs and tissue during increasing sexual excitement and orgasmic response. Note the ballooning and tenting effect of the inner portion of the vagina. The dotted lines show the organ positions during orgasm.

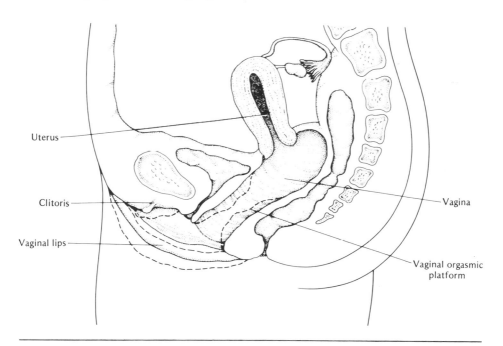

The Labia Majora
There are no observable changes in the labia majora of either the nulliparous or multiparous woman during this phase.

The Labia Minora
No reactions of the labia minora have been observed during the orgasmic phase.

The Bartholin's Glands
No reactions of the Bartholin's glands have been observed during the orgasmic phase.

The Resolution Phase in Women

The Breasts
There is an almost immediate loss of the measleslike rash that has covered the breasts. Detumescence of the areolae occurs, giving the false impression that the nipples are again becoming erect. What actually happens is that the nipples, which have been partly obscured by the engorged areolae, remain erect longer than the areolae do; the "new" nipple erection is in fact only the "old" nipple erection once again becoming observable. The erect nipple usually undergoes *involution* (return to normal size) before the breast loses its vasocongestive reaction. The breasts are slow to return to normal size; in a nulliparous woman, they often remain enlarged for 5 to 10 minutes after orgasm.

The Sex Flush
The maculopapular rash disappears during this phase in the reverse order of its development during the excitement and plateau phases. It quickly fades from the buttocks, arms, thighs, abdomen, and back, but is much slower to disappear from the neck, chest, breasts, face, and finally, the upper abdomen or stomach area.

Myotonia
Muscular tension declines rapidly during the resolution phase. If sexual stimulation is not reinstated, the tension usually disappears completely within five minutes of orgasm.

The Rectum, Urethra, and Bladder
No responses have been observed during the resolution phase.

Cardio-Respiratory-Perspiratory Responses
Heart rate, blood pressure, and respiratory rate show an early return to normal during the resolution phase. About 33% of all women develop a widespread film of perspiration during this phase as the skin flush resolves. Almost immediately after orgasm a thin coating of perspiration may appear over the chest, back, and thighs. Heavy perspiration may appear on the forehead, upper lip, and the axillae

(underarms) of a woman—especially if her face became mottled by a flush reaction during the earlier phases. Sometimes the entire body is coated with perspiration.

Although some women quite naturally perspire from the physical exertion of coitus, the perspiratory reaction described above is apparently not related to this exertion, since the response occurs regardless of the degree of physical activity of the first three phases. The copiousness of the perspiratory response parallels the strength of the orgasm.

The Clitoris
The clitoris returns to its normal pudendal overhang position within 10 seconds after the vaginal contractions cease. The time required for the return of the clitoris to its pre-excitement-phase state is roughly the same as that required for the primary loss of penile erection after a man ejaculates. However, vasocongestion of the clitoral glans and shaft may remain for 5 to 10 minutes after orgasm and occasionally may persist for as long as 30 minutes.

The Vagina
The vagina's first retrogressive change occurs in the outer third portion of the vault. The vasocongestion that produced the vaginal orgasmic platform during the plateau phase now quickly disappears, causing the diameter of the outer third of the vaginal passage to increase as the area returns to normal size.

The inner two-thirds of the vagina reverts to its normal collapsed state, although this process is rather slow and irregular: first one zone, then another, relaxes. The vaginal walls regain their rough, wrinkled surface, and the deep color of the vagina fades, this retrogressive process frequently lasting for as long as 10 to 15 minutes.

The Uterus
Early in the resolution phase, the elevated uterus rapidly returns to its normal position in the abdominal cavity. The contractile pattern that the uterus displayed during the earlier response phases ceases, vasocongestion disappears, and the organ returns to normal size. Multiparous and nulliparous experimental subjects who were sustained in an excessively prolonged plateau phase of sexual tension developed vasocongestion, together with a 50% to 100% increase in uterine size.

After orgasm the uterus remained enlarged for 10 minutes in nulliparous women, often 20 minutes in multiparous women. When orgasm did not occur, the increased uterine size persisted for as long as 60 minutes.

Immediately after orgasmic response there is a slight spreading apart of the external os (opening) of the cervix, which continues for the first 5 to 10 minutes of the resolution phase. Earlier scientific opinion was that this reaction aids in the passage of sperm into the uterus, and that a sucking effect is produced at the cervix at the time of orgasm. Recent investigations demonstrate that the slight widening of the external os does not aid sperm transportation and that there is no sucking process in the uterus at the time of orgasm.

The Labia Majora

The labia majora return to normal size faster in nulliparous women than in the multiparous. The labia majora of the former resume their normal thickness and flaring of the edges, and return quickly to a midline positioning that partially covers the vaginal outlet. In the multiparous, engorgement of the major lips may persist for 2 to 3 hours before complete detumescence.

The Labia Minora

The labia minora quickly return (usually in 10 to 15 seconds) to the light pink color of their preexcitement state. Even when the lips had become scarlet or burgundy during the plateau phase, the color fades to light pink within 2 minutes or less. There is an unevenness of hue during the process of returning to normal, but resolution of the sex-skin color is usually total within 5 minutes after orgasm.

The physiological return to normalcy during the resolution phase occurs in the reverse order of the changes that took place in the excitement and plateau phases. In this final phase, the minor lips first lose their discoloration and then their vascular tension, the latter effecting a reduction to normal size and a resumption of midline positioning.

The Bartholin's Glands

There are no observable changes of the Bartholin's glands during this phase.

It will be noted that the description of the female sexual response cycle contains no mention of any reactions by the ovaries and fallopian tubes. No direct observations have been made of these organs during the cycle, so their reactions are not known. Some response may occur, but until more satisfactory techniques of investigation are developed, little can be said about the activity of these organs throughout the cycle.

THE MALE SEXUAL RESPONSE CYCLE

The Excitement Phase in Men

The Breasts

About 60% of all men experience nipple erection during the sexual response cycle. When this erection occurs, it usually takes place late in the excitement phase and continues throughout the other phases. Nipple erection may be brought about by direct stimulation, although it ordinarily occurs spontaneously.

The Sex Flush
The measleslike maculopapular sex flush appears on about 25% of sexually responding men (as compared with 75% of sexually responding women), and develops in much the same fashion as it does in women. The flush may appear late in the excitement phase, but it does not usually make an observable appearance until well after the plateau phase is under way. When it occurs, the flush customarily begins over the stomach region, then spreads to the chest and later to the neck and face. In a few cases the rash extends to the shoulders, arms, and thighs of a man.

Myotonia
Muscular tension or myotonia becomes clinically observable in the latter part of the excitement phase, although the reaction is more pronounced during the plateau phase. Muscular contractions at this point, involving primarily the voluntary muscles, are evidenced by both restless and purposeful movements. Involuntary muscular movements are more likely to occur during the late part of this phase, at which time some elevation of both testes toward the perineum takes place, along with tension in the long muscles of both legs and arms and in the abdominal musculature.

The Rectum
There are no noticeable rectal reactions during the excitement phase. However, *direct* stimulation of the region at this time may produce irregular contractions of the external rectal sphincter.

Cardio-Respiratory-Perspiratory Reactions
As sexual tension increases, there is a corresponding increase in heart rate and blood pressure. There are no observable changes in breathing rate or in perspiratory reaction.

The Penis
Effective sexual stimulation will produce erection of the penis, as its three spongy cylindrical bodies of erectile tissue become engorged with blood. Depending upon the type and intensity of sexual stimulation, the excitement phase may continue for a long period, during which erection may be partially lost and regained many times. Penile erection may be impaired in the excitement phase by adverse stimuli, such as sudden loud noises, noticeable changes in lighting or temperature, fear, and anxiety. With penile erection, the urethra, of course, also lengthens. As the excitement phase progresses, the penile

urethral passage increases twofold in diameter, and the urethral opening (meatus) widens. Only minor penile changes occur during the next two phases (plateau and orgasmic).

The Scrotum
Sexual tension causes contraction of the smooth muscles and vasocongestion of the tissue of the scrotum. Because the tissue thickens, and because there is a constriction and elevation of the scrotal sac, testicular movement is now restricted primarily to a perpendicular plane.

The Testes
With excitement-phase tension comes a shortening of the spermatic cord (contraction of cremasteric musculature), which causes both testes to elevate. There is also a slight rotation of the axis of the testes. A prolonged excitement phase (lasting more than 5 to 10 minutes) may make the scrotal sac and cremasteric musculature relax, returning the testes to their original suspended position.

The Secondary Organs
There are no noticeable changes in the prostate, vas deferens, or seminal vesicles during the excitement phase other than a shortening of the vas deferens as the testes are pulled toward the body.

FIGURE 13.7 The male genitalia in the preexcitement phase. The dotted lines represent the organ positions in the excitement and plateau phases. Note that the testis and the scrotum move up, toward the body cavity.

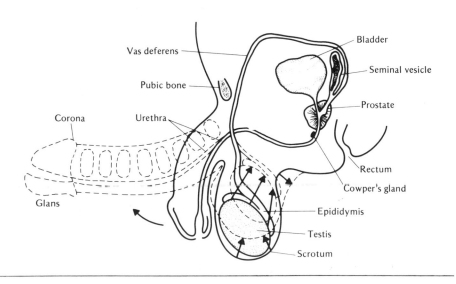

The Cowper's Glands
These glands evidence no noticeable reactions during this phase.

The Plateau Phase in Men
The Breasts
Nipple erection, if it is to occur and did not take place in the previous phase, will take place now and will be maintained through the plateau phase.

The Sex Flush
If the flush is to occur and has not made its appearance during the earlier phase, it will become noticeable during the plateau phase, especially in the latter part. A man is less likely than a woman to exhibit this response. If it ever happens at all, it is a sporadic occurrence in men, appearing prominently during one sexual experience, yet totally absent during another. Psychological factors (such as intense anticipation) and temperature factors (such as a heated rather than a cool room) may influence the appearance of the sex flush.

Myotonia
Both voluntary and involuntary muscular tensions increase during the plateau phase. There may be strong contraction in the muscles of the neck, face (especially around the mouth), and abdomen. If a man is in the supine position during coition, he may also show carpopedal spasm (marked contraction of the striated muscles of the hands and feet), indicating a high level of sexual excitement. As tension mounts and orgasm nears, clutching, clawing, and grasping contractions of the hands, if they are not otherwise occupied, may take place. The human male is more likely to display carpopedal reactions during masturbation than during sexual intercourse.

The Rectum
Rectal response in this phase is similar to that of the excitement phase.

Cardio-Respiratory-Perspiratory Reactions
Increased sexual tension produces hyperventilation, commonly during the latter part of the plateau phase. Heart rate increases from the usual 70 beats per minute to a range of 100 to 175 beats per minute. Blood pressure elevates; systolic pressure may increase above normal by 20 to 80 mm Hg, and diastolic pressure by 10 to 40 mm Hg. The elevation in some instances may be even higher. There are no noticeable changes in perspiratory reactions during this phase.

The Penis
Only minor changes are noted in the penis during the plateau phase. Late in this phase the corona of the glans becomes more tumescent,

and there may be a deepening of the mottled reddish-purple color of the glans and the area just below the corona.

The base of the urethra (the urethral bulb) increases to three times its normal size. Late in the phase there is additional distension of the urethral bulb, indicative of impending orgasm, although the amount of distention varies considerably from person to person.

The Scrotum
There are no noticeable reactions or changes in the scrotum during the plateau phase.

The Testes
The testes must undergo at least partial elevation before the human male can experience a full ejaculatory sequence. Once the testes become positioned next to the perineum, the orgasmic phase will inevitably follow if effective sexual stimulation is maintained. In nearly all men, one testicle hangs slightly lower than the other does. The lower testicle, which in about 85% of all men is the left one, may move up and down in the scrotum by means of muscular contractions throughout the first two sexual phases. In many instances, the testicle of shorter suspension becomes elevated early in the plateau phase.

There is also a vasocongestive reaction in the testes that increases their size over the unstimulated, noncongested state by approximately 50%; the increase may be as much as 100% in some men. Generally speaking, the more protracted the plateau phase of sexual tension is, the more severe the vasocongestion and the more marked the increase in testicular size.

The Secondary Organs
There are no observable changes in the prostate, vas deferens, or seminal vesicles during this phase other than the inevitable movement of the vas deferens following the movements of the testicles.

The Cowper's Glands
These two glands secrete two or three drops of preejaculatory mucoid fluid during this phase.

The Orgasmic Phase in Men
The Breasts
No reactions of the breasts are noticeable during this phase.

The Sex Flush
When present, the flush persists during this phase. The degree of flush usually parallels the intensity of the orgasm.

Myotonia
During the orgasmic phase, there is loss of voluntary control plus severe involuntary-muscle tension throughout the body. The male or-

gasmic response is one that, to a large degree, is based on vasocongestion and myotonia involving the total body. The involuntary reactions that cause a man's ejaculation have been described in some detail in Chapter 6.

The Rectum

The sphincter muscles of the rectum commence involuntary contractions at approximately 0.8-second intervals, although the number of such contractions is usually only 2 to 4.

Cardio-Respiratory-Perspiratory Reactions

Hyperventilation continues into the orgasmic phase, the respiratory rate frequently rising to 40 breaths per minute. The recorded rates of heart beat range from 110 to 180 beats (or more) per minute. The lower the number of heart beats per minute during a resting, non-stimulated state, the smaller the rise in heart rate is in a sexually active and sexually stimulated state. Blood pressure during this phase goes even higher than it does during the plateau phase. Systolic pressure rises from 40 to 100 mm Hg, and diastolic pressure from 20 to 50 mm Hg above normal.

Only occasionally does a man experience a perspiratory response during this phase. If it is to occur it usually takes place early in the resolution phase. If there is a perspiratory reaction during this period, it occurs with the final ejaculatory contractions.

The Penis

A rapid distention of the urethral bulb is a signal of an imminent orgasmic response. This distention occurs simultaneously with the collection of seminal fluid in the urethra at the prostate gland, at about the time the response cycle advances from the plateau to the orgasmic phase. The bulb's distention is so great that it can be seen with the naked eye.

Regularly recurring contractions of the urethra and of the muscles at the base of the penis and around the anus produce the penile ejaculatory reaction during the orgasmic phase. The intervals between contractions are roughly the same as those between orgasmic vaginal contractions—0.8 second between the first 3 or 4 major responses, followed by a lengthening of intervals between contractions. (Contractile force also diminishes after the first few contractions.) The urethra continues to contract slightly and irregularly for several seconds after the initial expulsive responses, the interval between the final contractions lasting perhaps several seconds.

The Scrotum

There are no observable reactions of the scrotum during the orgasmic phase.

FIGURE 13.8 The male genitalia in the orgasmic phase. The dotted lines represent the positions in the completed resolution phase. Note that the testis and the scrotum move down, away from the body cavity during the resolution phase.

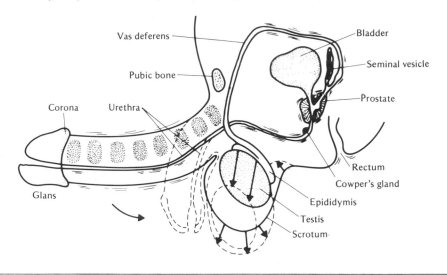

The Testes
No reactions of the testes are observable during this phase. Many researchers believe, however, that there may well be some response for which adequate observation and recording techniques have not yet been developed.

The Secondary Organs
The entire ejaculatory process involves the prostate, vas deferens, and seminal vesicles. Their contractions produce the sensation that ejaculation is imminent and then trigger ejaculation. Apparently, contractions of the secondary organs begin in the vasa efferentia (the tubes leading from testicle to epididymis), continue through the epididymis, the vas deferens, and, finally, the seminal vesicles. The systolic action of the prostate, which forces the seminal fluid through and out the urethra, is easily observable and measurable.

The Cowper's Glands
These glands respond in no observable fashion during this phase.

The Resolution Phase in Men
The Breasts
If erection of the nipples occurred during the excitement phase, up to

an hour is needed after ejaculation before they resume their normal size.

The Sex Flush
As in a woman, the man's maculopapular sex flush disappears rapidly during the resolution phase. Fading of the flush is in the reverse order of its appearance in the excitement phase.

Myotonia
In the absence of further sexual stimulation, the muscular tension that built up during the first three sexual response phases almost always dissipates during the first 5 minutes of the resolution phase.

The Rectum
The contracted sphincter muscles of the orgasmic phase relax by the time that the expulsive contractions of the urethra terminate. No other reactions are noticeable.

Cardio-Respiratory-Perspiratory Reactions
Hyperventilation, which reaches its peak during the orgasmic phase, resolves in the refractory period of the resolution phase, immediately after orgasm. Heart beat rate and blood pressure return to normal.
About 33% of all men show a perspiratory reaction immediately after ejaculation. As in women, the perspiration may appear over the entire body, but it is usually confined in men to the soles of the feet and palms of the hands. This response may occur whether or not there was strong physical exertion or an accompanying sex flush during coition.

The Penis
Detumescence occurs in two stages. The primary loss of erection occurs in the early refractory period, at which time the penis reduces from the dimensions of full erection to a size 50% **larger** than its usual flaccid state. This early loss in size is rapid. The secondary stage of detumescence persists for a much longer time, especially when there is residual sexual stimulation.

After orgasm, the time involved in the return of the penis to its normal unstimulated size depends upon the form and duration of stimulation received during the excitement and plateau phases. For example, a prolonged period of vaginal penetration may produce marked penile vasocongestion, which often prolongs the primary stage of penile detumescence and hence delays the secondary stage of erection loss. On the other hand, penile involution may be speeded up by sufficiently intense external asexual stimuli. If a man removes his penis from the vagina shortly after orgasm, and, more particularly, if he does something unrelated to sexual activity, such as walking about, urinating, reading, or smoking, detumescence will occur rapidly in both its primary and secondary stages.

The urethra, as well as the broadened urethral meatus, revert to their customary dimensions shortly after ejaculation.

The Scrotum

Involution of the scrotal skin occurs in either of two quite different patterns during the resolution phase, a given pattern appearing fairly consistently in each individual. About 25% of all men experience a slow return of the scrotum to its normal nonstimulated state. The remaining 75% experience a rapid loss of congestion accompanied by an equally rapid retrogression of the scrotum to its relaxed, loosely wrinkled prearousal appearance.

The Testes

In the resolution phase, the testes undergo a loss of vasocongestion and a reduction in size. The involutional pattern is about the same as that for the scrotal sac, and similarly can be a swift or a protracted process. Generally speaking, the longer the plateau phase persists, the longer it takes for the testicles to decrease in size during the resolution phase.

The Secondary Organs

No changes have been observed in the prostate, vas deferens, or seminal vesicles during the resolution phase.

The Cowper's Glands

These glands have given no evidence of change during this phase.

Despite the foregoing physiologic detailing of human orgasmic response, the conclusion must not be drawn that sexual competency or a happy marriage depends on orgasm accompanying each sexual experience. This simply does not hold true for either men or women. Sexual response to the point of orgasm is highly desirable because of the great physical and emotional pleasure and release involved. It is, however, by no means crucial to a happy and fulfilled life. And overemphasizing orgasm can lead to conflicts that are damaging to the enjoyment of coition and the emotional relationship between husband and wife (Beigel c).

The desirability of simultaneous orgasms for the man and the woman has long been the subject of speculation (Ellis b). Naturally, if both partners prefer orgasms at the same time—and many couples do, claiming that it affords them the greatest enjoyment and satisfaction—then they should strive for this goal. However, some aspects of sexual response should be considered prior to embarking upon the uneven struggle toward simultaneous orgasm, or before accepting the premise that it offers the ultimate in amatory achievement.

Essential to rewarding sexual activity is the effort to give one's partner the fullest measure of concern and satisfaction. If either person is primarily concerned with gratifying himself, or is caught up in his own impending orgasm, he cannot give full attention to his partner. Similarly, if overmuch attention is being devoted to the partner's sexual gratification, appropriate concentration on one's own response and pleasure is impossible.

Furthermore, men and women react quite differently in bodily movements at the time of orgasm. The man's tendency is to plunge into the vagina as deeply as possible at the moment of orgasm and to hold this position for a length of time, to be followed perhaps by one or two deep, deliberate thrusts. The woman's tendency, on the other hand, is to have the same stroking, plunging movements of the excitement and plateau phases continued during the orgasmic reaction, with perhaps an acceleration of the thrusts and an increase of pressure in the vulval area. These two highly pleasurable patterns of movement are obviously incompatible. Since both cannot be executed at the same time, whichever pattern is carried out during simultaneous orgasm must perforce detract from the full pleasure of one of the partners.

The arguments, therefore, would appear to be stronger against than for simultaneous orgasm. It is easier for a man to have an orgasm, but he is usually capable of only one. The sensible conduct of coition would seem to be that the man delay his own pleasure until his partner is fully satisfied: the couple can thereby devote full attention to giving the woman as many orgasmic responses as she wishes, and both can then concentrate wholly on providing the man with as satisfying an orgasm as possible.

The desire to please is frequently the cause of women's "faking" orgasms. Realizing that many men place great value on their ability to bring their partners to orgasm on practically every coital occasion, some women pretend to have an orgasm when in fact they may not be even close to having one. Other women may pretend to have an orgasm simply to end that particular sex act or in an effort to hide their own orgasmic deficiency (Rosenbaum). Whatever the motivation, women who usually experience orgasm are considerably more likely to pretend to have one when they actually did not than women who seldom or never experience orgasm (Shope b).

Whether or not a woman should ever pretend to have an orgasm is a topic of much debate (Ottenheimer et al.). It is fairly clear, however, that she should not do so on a regular basis, for pretense accomplishes nothing more than a perpetuation of her inability, which might cause an eventual rift in the couple's relationship. A more sensible approach is to search for the cause and to correct the problem through psychotherapy if necessary.

Women may claim that they achieve sexual satisfaction in a sex act even though they fail to reach a climax. Investigation has shown, however, that on such occasions they are much more aware of sexual tension than on those occasions when they reach orgasm. This finding tends to support the argument that, although sexual satisfaction from coitus can be gained without climax, relief from sexual tension cannot. Such residual tension can spill over into other areas of a woman's life and cause problems without discernible etiology (Shope a).

As has been pointed out, orgasmic responses vary for the same woman, and the variation is even greater among women as a group (Beigel c). Sensible efforts should be expended by the man to give his partner as strong and pleasurable a sexual response as possible—just as a woman, it might be mentioned once more, should strive to gratify her partner sexually. There should be no great anxiety, however, if the woman does not respond as intensely as either partner had hoped.

Considerable sexual satisfaction may be derived by the woman from petting, coitus, or other methods of stimulation, even when these activities do not culminate in orgasm of either great or mild intensity. If feelings of desperation are kept out of the sexual relationship, it will tend to retain the areas of satisfaction already achieved, allowing the couple to aspire to more intense levels of fulfillment.

Because of premarital or extramarital involvement with women of profound sexual desire and response, some husbands are led to believe that their wives should respond to them with the same frequency and intensity. What these men fail to realize is that the very strength of the sexual drive in some women impels them into nonmarital involvements, whereas their wives may simply not possess such strong sexual needs. The inference cannot be drawn that one partner, because of his or her less intense sexual drive, is any the less loving or concerned for the welfare of the marriage.

It cannot be overstressed that, although the material in this chapter has focused on the physiological considerations of human sexuality, it must not be inferred that the emotional aspects of sexuality are of less importance. A close human relationship and deep emotional involvement—love, if you wish—are of paramount importance to a complete and fulfilling sexual experience. Physiological sexual needs can be relieved without love, closeness, or even understanding. But no one can really attain complete emotional, physical, and sexual satisfaction, in all its beauty, without the intermingling of those elements. Ask any person who has had sexual intercourse in both circumstances.

14 BIRTH CONTROL

Human beings "have always longed for both fertility and sterility, each at its appointed time and its chosen circumstances" (Himes). Yet only in very recent years have serious efforts been made to teach people about birth-control techniques and to make contraceptives easily available to them.

A conservative estimate is that about 20% of all children born in this country (over 1 million annually) are unwanted by at least one parent. The number of unwanted children born to poor parents is proportionately more than double the number born to the more affluent. Furthermore, the percentage of unwanted children advances sharply according to the child's birth position in the family: *viz.*, 66% of all sixth (and subsequent) children born are unwanted (Westoff and Westoff). It should be pointed out that an *unwanted* pregnancy is not necessarily the same as an *unplanned* pregnancy. The evidence is that perhaps as many as 50% of all pregnancies are unplanned (The sex scene).

This country's birth rate has steadily declined, to be sure, between the year 1800 and the present time (7.0 births per woman in 1800 vs. 2.3 in 1971) (Rosenthal). Despite this decline, however, the vast majority of population experts express great concern that, at the present rate of growth, the world's peoples will double in number during the next 35 years, and that the world's resources will be inadequate to sustain the needs of this burgeoning population. The birth rate per couple needed to maintain the world's population is 2.1.

Birth control is obviously the only plausible solution to the problems posed to both the individual and the human race by uncontrolled, hazardous, or injudicious pregnancies. The primary purposes of birth control might be thus tabulated:

1. *To curb further population expansion.* The most important factor in solving the dilemma of overpopulation is, without a doubt, responsible family planning.
2. *To aid early sexual adjustment in marriage.* During the inevitable period of marital adjustment, sexual compatibility may be reached earlier and in a more satisfactory manner if fear of pregnancy is removed. It has also been shown that a wife's sexual responsiveness is directly related to the degree that both she and her husband are satisfied with their present method of contraception (Adams).
3. *To space pregnancies.* Spacing the arrival of children allows a couple to give full consideration to the mother's health and to the family's economics. It has been claimed that when births are only one year apart, the death rate for babies is about 50% higher than when births are two years apart (Guttmacher a).
4. *To limit family size.* Most couples prefer for many and various reasons to limit the size of their families. A primary consideration is that excessive childbearing can leave the mother with certain undesirable physical conditions, such as high blood pressure, varicose veins, and relaxed vaginal tissue. Furthermore, after the birth of the second child, the chance of infant mortality increases with each additional child borne by the same mother.

   Social factors also influence the number of children that individual couples want (only 10% want more than four). Women are often reluctant to spend all their young and energetic adult lives being a mother to a baby or child. By limiting the number of children and properly spacing them, they can frequently have their children during the first few years of marriage, leaving the later years for a more leisurely life and, hopefully, a more meaningful one with regard to their commitment to a profession or to the community.

   A child's success in later life, incidentally, appears to be related to the size of its family. Of the adult men in this country, two times as many "only" children complete high school as those who have three or more siblings. Economic considerations also play a role. Yet impoverished adults of working age have twice as many children to provide for as do adults with adequate incomes. In other words, those who can least afford children seem to have the most (Chilman).

5. *To prevent pregnancy among the unmarried.* The sociological problems and personal distress to all concerned in a nonmarital pregnancy are legion—a subject discussed in Chapter 21.

6. *To avoid aggravation of existing illnesses or diseases.* Many illnesses and diseases—tuberculosis, heart and kidney disease, an advanced stage of diabetes (especially when complicated by damaged blood vessels), emotional disorders, nervous afflictions, recent surgery for cancer—raise questions about the advisability of pregnancy.

7. *To prevent the perpetuation of inherited diseases.* Spread of inherited diseases, e.g., Huntington's chorea, can, obviously, be best controlled by preventing the pregnancy of an afflicted woman or a woman married to an afflicted man.

The probability of conception resulting from a single act of sexual intercourse in which no protection against pregnancy is employed is only 2% to 4% (Tietze a). It has been established, however, that if coitus occurs two days before ovulation, the probability for pregnancy is 5%; one day before ovulation, the probability rises to 30%; on the day of ovulation, 50%; one day after ovulation, the probability drops to 5% (Lachenbruch).

Birth control and contraception are often discussed as if they were synonymous terms, but they are not. *Contraception* may be defined as any means or device permitting coitus between fertile partners that prevents conception. Contraception is, however, only one form of birth control. Methods of birth control fall into four major categories: abstinence, sterilization, abortion, and contraception.

ABSTINENCE

The dictionary definition of abstinence is "self-denial; an abstaining from the gratification of appetite." Clearly, sexual abstinence in marriage should be mutually agreeable; otherwise, it becomes merely "spouse-denial." Since human beings are equipped with intricate and complex mechanisms for both experiencing and gratifying sexual appetites, abstinence would seem to be in opposition to human nature. Indeed, the practice of abstinence in marriage as a method of birth control might very well cause people to question the advisability of marriage itself.

There are those advocates of abstinence who base their arguments on Freud's theory of sublimation. They go only so far as to point out that sexual urges may be sublimated and expressed in socially acceptable and beneficial ways. They do not explain that sublimation is an unconscious process, and that, even then, total sublimation can never be achieved. No empirical evidence has been uncovered to indicate that sublimation of biological drives can really be accomplished. As a matter of fact, a conscious attempt to sublimate sexual urges can result in such psychological malfunctions as frigidity, impotence, inability to concentrate, irritability, and insomnia, or in such physical problems as premature ejaculation, difficulty in achieving erection, prostatitis, ovarian and vulval congestion, and decreased sex drive.

Voluntary abstinence is less damaging to the normal functioning of the organism than is involuntary abstinence. In any event, normal sexual urges can find relatively harmless outlets, such as through dreaming to orgasm, which both men and women do.

There are, of course, occasions when abstinence becomes a matter of consideration for one's spouse or oneself—for example, during an illness, during late pregnancy, immediately after childbirth, and to avoid contracting or spreading venereal disease. Even in these cases, the partner not physically involved may wish to have some sexual outlet, whether by engaging in such acts as oral or manual stimulation with the spouse, or by self-stimulation.

Abstinence before marriage is, in general, still highly esteemed by our society. This sanction is founded in biblical proscriptions against premarital sexual relations, and on the romantic notion that it is good for marriage partners to have their first sexual experience together. Some sociological studies would seem to indicate that sexual adjustment in marriage may actually be more successful when husband or wife, or both, have had previous sexual experience, although other studies do not support these findings.

STERILIZATION

Sterilization is a surgical procedure whereby a person is rendered sterile—i.e., incapable of reproduction. The incidence of sterilization as a birth-control technique is higher among women than among men.

In 1960 an estimated 5.6% of white women in the U.S. between the ages of 18 and 39, or their husbands, had undergone a sterilization operation. By 1965 this percentage had risen to 8% (5% of the women and 3% of the men in this age group). Today it is estimated that a sterilization operation has been performed in one marriage out of every 10, and the percentage continues to rise each year (Westoff and Westoff).

The reasons for sterilization typically fall into three categories:

1. *Eugenic sterilization* is performed as a means of protecting the physical or mental well-being of the next generation. Three types

of persons have commonly been objects of eugenic consideration.

The habitual criminal. The rationale for sterilizing a habitual criminal is based on the theory that "the criminal mind" is inherited. A recent decision by the Supreme Court has ruled against such a measure as being cruel and unusual punishment. Furthermore, there is little scientific evidence that inheritance plays any part in criminal behavior.

The moral pervert. In most cases involving perversion, legal enforcement of sterilization would be tantamount to punishment. In one instance, an exhibitionist submitted to castration in preference to serving a prison sentence for his deviate actions. This method of treatment is unlikely to benefit either exhibitionists or society, inasmuch as these and many other sexual deviates are

FIGURE 14.1 Schematic representation of the female reproductive system, showing the effects of a tubal ligation. Note that in sterilization, the surgical procedure is followed on both sides of the body.

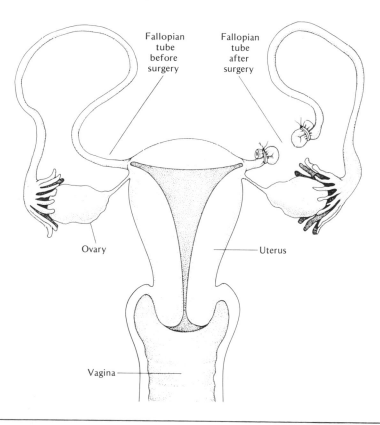

Fallopian tube before surgery

Fallopian tube after surgery

Ovary

Uterus

Vagina

often driven to their behavior because of self-doubt regarding their masculinity. Only a vengeful public or the offender's unconscious desire for punishment is served by such punitive measures.

The person with an inheritable mental disease or deficiency. In 1927 a Supreme Court decision decreed that a third-generation imbecile may be sterilized. California law makes it mandatory that an imbecile be sterilized before he can be released from an institution. In other states, similar legislation has been expanded to include persons suffering from schizophrenic and manic–depressive psychoses, which are interpreted as inheritable mental diseases a highly questionable assumption.

2. *Therapeutic sterilization* is sometimes performed when certain pathological conditions are present in either husband or wife: tuberculosis, cancer, cardio-renal-vascular diseases, hypertension and high blood pressure, and kidney disorders; or when certain Rh blood incompatibilities exist (Russell).

3. *Socioeconomic considerations* form the basis for the majority of sterilization operations performed. The range of motivations for requesting the operation is extensive. From a legal standpoint, the surgeon is often on uncertain ground. However good his intention to help his patients, he must be careful to guard himself against later lawsuits brought by the persons upon whom he performs the operation. Many who seek sterilization seem to have neurotic reasons for doing so in the first place; these same neuroses or sociopathic attitudes may therefore prompt them to bring suit against the physician who was merely trying to help them (see Chapter 22, Sex and the Law).

Methods of Sterilization in Women

Female sterilization, a more complicated procedure than male sterilization, is of five types. *Tubal ligation,* or *salpingectomy,* is a major surgical procedure in which the fallopian tubes are cut, resectioned, and tied so that the two ends are prevented from meeting, thus keeping sperm and ova from contacting one another. The operation takes about 15 minutes to perform but requires a five-day hospitalization. Furthermore, the woman feels the effects of the surgery for three to four weeks. Surgeons' fees vary, of course, but they average about $300. The effects are thought to be reversible in about 50% of the cases (Westoff and Westoff).

Laparoscopic sterilization, also called *laparoscopy,* has recently captured considerable attention in this country. The patient is given a general anesthetic and two small incisions are made in her abdomen. The laparoscope (from the Greek: looking into the abdomen) is inserted in one opening. Through the second is passed an electrical instrument that severs the fallopian tubes and cauterizes their ends. Only Band-Aids are needed to cover the incisions.

This procedure is inexpensive and leaves no scars, and the patient remains in the hospital just until she is fully awake. Only one fallopian tube in 1000 has spontaneously rejoined in this country's experience with the operation. Attempts at purposeful rejoining have been only 20% successful (Carolina Population Center; Westoff and Westoff).

Oophorectomy, the surgical removal of the ovaries, brings the process of ovulation permanently to a halt. *Hysterectomy* is the surgical removal of the uterus (a process that may or may not include removal of the uterine tubes and ovaries). *Total salpingectomy* involves the removal of the fallopian tubes. Any of these three operative procedures quite obviously renders a woman permanently sterile, but they are not resorted to for the purpose of sterilization alone, but to remove certain abnormalities, such as a fibroid tumor.

A form of *reversible sterilization* for women has very recently been developed. It appears to be safe and effective, with minimal complications. The technique involves placing small clips around the fallopian tubes, thereby blocking the union of sperm and egg. The extent of surgery required to emplace the clips, or to remove them if the woman later wishes to become pregnant, is minor. The operation at present is performed in a hospital, but it is expected that the technique may soon be offered on an outpatient basis (Associated Press *f*).

One investigation of 35,000 tubal ligations found that about 1 in 200 of the sterilization operations failed to prevent subsequent pregnancies (Eastman and Hellman). Women's sex drive is not likely to be impaired following sterilization; on the contrary, there may well be an increase in drive because of the sense of freedom engendered by removing the fear of pregnancy.

Methods of Sterilization in Men

Of the two types of sterilization available to men, *vasectomy* is by far the most desirable. Vasectomy is the surgical procedure of cutting and tying the semen-carrying ducts, the vas deferens. A small incision is made in the scrotum, and the vas deferens is lifted out so that about an inch of the tiny tube can be cut away. The tube, or duct, is then tied at each end where the section was removed, preventing the sperm's passage from the testicles to the ejaculatory ducts. This procedure must be followed on each side of the body. The site of the incision is well above the testicles and in no way disturbs them or their functioning. The man remains potent but sterile; the sperm he now produces are absorbed by his body.

A vasectomy is a simple operation that can be performed in a hospital or in a doctor's office, with either a local or general anesthetic. After-

FIGURE 14.2. Schematic representation of the male reproductive system, showing the effects of a vasectomy. Note that in sterilization, the surgical procedure is followed on both sides of the body.

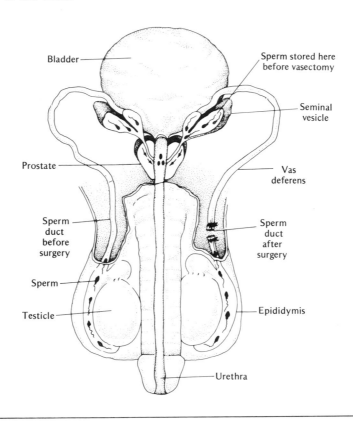

wards, the patient should remain relatively inactive for about 48 hours; at least he should do no heavy work for that period of time, or longer. The doctor usually advises the use of a suspensory for several weeks to prevent any pulling of the testicles, and to minimize soreness during the healing process.

The patient remains in a state of fecundity (fertility) for several days following the vasectomy, because his first ejaculations thereafter will contain sperm stored in the seminal vesicles and ejaculatory ducts prior to the surgery. After 6 to 10 ejaculations, the vasectomized man's seminal fluid will almost certainly be sperm-free. But the wisest procedure is to rely upon a microscopic examination of the ejaculate to establish beyond doubt that it contains no sperm cells. Following a vasectomy, sperm occasionally accumulate in a small sac at the site of the incision, causing a granuloma (or nodule) to form in the scrotum. This accumulation is typically harmless and will dissipate in time.

The effects of a vasectomy can be undone surgically by rejoining the severed ends of the vas deferens. Statistics indicate that there is a 60% to 90% chance that the effects of vasectomy can be reversed so that some sperm will be ejaculated; there is then a 30% to 40% chance of impregnation after reversal (Russell; Westoff and Westoff). However, few men ever seek the corrective surgery. Out of approximately 11.5 million vasectomies performed in India, as an example, there have been fewer than 10 requests for reversal surgery (Chase).

Sperm banks offer another solution for the man who might change his mind after a vasectomy, but only if he anticipates the possibility. Before surgery he need only store a sample of his ejaculate, to be used later in the artificial insemination of his wife if they decide to have a child. At least four such centers for the freezing and storage of semen presently exist in the United States, offering a form of "fatherhood insurance."

The "tying of tubes" in men is much simpler, quicker, cheaper, and less dangerous than its counterpart operation performed on women, the tubal ligation. Yet many men steadfastly refuse to have the operation performed on themselves, though they willingly consent to a tubal ligation for their wives. This selfishness probably can be accounted for, in the first place, by the fact that it is women who conceive and bear children, and hence suffer any pain or difficulty associated with the birth process. Women, therefore, should be "willing to pay the price" for the operation.

Secondly, men frequently associate any cutting near the testicles with castration and are fearful of such an operation, despite the fact that they know rationally that vasectomy does not decrease the sex drive or their ability to satisfy that drive. In one investigation into the impact of vasectomy on 151 men who underwent the operation, 17.9% reported an increase in sexual appetite, 74.2% showed no change, and only 7.9% reported a slight diminishing of sexual desire; these results are fairly typical of such investigations (Russell). The increase in sexual drive is probably a consequence of psychological factors, such as a reduction of anxiety because the fear of impregnating the wife has been removed.

Other factors also appear implicated in the reticence to undergo vasectomy, as revealed by an investigation of a group of vasectomized men and their wives by means of personal interviews and psychological testing (Ziegler et al. a). In the personal interviews—in which, of course, only conscious beliefs were expressed—the parties voiced unanimous satisfaction with the operation. In the psychological testing, however, in which unconscious feelings were revealed, both husbands *and* wives showed more anxiety, greater vulnerability to actual or imagined physical ailments, and a greater degree of overall sex maladjustment than the control subjects did. The husbands also manifested more concern about masculinity than a control group did.

The researchers concluded that, despite the statements of the couple to the contrary, both husband and wife disclosed unconscious and unfounded concern about the man's possible loss of sexual ability or masculinity, suggesting that the couple equated vasectomy and castration. Four years later a follow-up study revealed that differences in the anxiety levels between the vasectomized and control couples had largely disappeared. The one exception was that the vasectomized men continued to display more unconscious concern about their masculinity, which they attempted to compensate for by increased coital frequency (Ziegler *et al. b*).

Despite the skill and care of the surgeon, a few vasectomies prove unsuccessful and pregnancy results. There may have been a spontaneous rejoining or recanalization of the severed vas deferens. Or a freak of nature may exist in the form of an unsuspected, supernumerary third or even fourth vas. Whatever the cause, pregnancy following a vasectomy can be the source of severe marital misunderstanding and discord. It is therefore well, when vasectomy is the birth-control measure of choice, to understand beforehand that the surgical procedure is not always successful. In response to questionnaires sent to 1721 physicians, 96 reported that spontaneous recanalization had occurred among their patients (Belt). The percentage of recanalization after vasectomies is not known, but is thought to be exceedingly low.

Voluntary sterilization operations are becoming increasingly common among men in the United States. Some 750,000 were performed in 1970 alone, 90% of them in a doctor's office (In the news *d;* Edey). The number will doubtless rise in the future unless some other absolutely safe birth-control method for use by men is developed, for continence, *coitus interruptus*, and the condom are at present the only other alternatives. Vasectomy clinics are being established in ever-growing numbers throughout the country, primarily under the aegis of local Planned Parenthood Centers.

Castration is a method of sterilization, known and used since ancient times, in which both testicles are surgically removed. If the man is an adult, castration does not necessarily mean impotence, although there is a gradual loss of sexual desire with the passage of time because of loss of male hormones produced by the testicles. This hormonal deficit may also cause such physiological changes as an increase in voice pitch, decrease in beard growth, and excess fat. However, the undesirable changes in secondary sexual characteristics following castration can often be corrected with proper hormone therapy.

ABORTION

Abortion is the spontaneous or induced expulsion from the uterus of an embryo before it has reached a point of development sufficient for its survival, generally considered to be the twenty-eighth week of gestation (Neumann).

Spontaneous abortion is medical terminology for a miscarriage that occurs prior to the third month of fetal life. It is not a form of birth control. *Induced abortion* is a term used for expulsion of the embryo in consequence of an intentional effort to terminate a pregnancy. Because it involves a purposeful act, it is a form of birth control and is therefore germane to this discussion.

Spontaneous Abortion

Spontaneous abortions, also called *miscarriages*, occur at a much higher rate than many people realize. It has been estimated that about 33% of all fertilized eggs abort before the next menstrual period is overdue. In these cases most women never realize that they are—or were— pregnant. An additional 25% of all pregnancies miscarry between the time of fertilization and labor, meaning that almost 60% of all pregnancies end before a viable birth occurs. These abortions and miscarriages occur, of course, without any human intervention (James).

Some of the factors related to a high incidence of spontaneous abortion are of interest. For example, white women have only half the number of miscarriages that black women do. Fetal death rate is lower when the mothers are 20 to 24 years old than when they are under 20. Among women older than 24, fetal mortality rises rapidly with advancing age. There are 97 fetal deaths per 1000 pregnancies among mothers in the 20 to 24 age group, in comparison with 219 deaths per 1000 pregnancies among mothers 35 and older (Kiser *et al.*).

Controlling for age factor, the miscarriage risk in a first pregnancy is lower than it is in subsequent pregnancies. And the risk rises in each additional conception: e.g., the risk is about twice as high in a fourth pregnancy as in a first. Furthermore, if a woman has already had one miscarriage, she runs twice the risk of other women that she will miscarry a second time. In multiple births the fetal death risk rises in direct proportion to the number of babies conceived. There are 15 fetal deaths per 1000 pregnancies in single births, 42 per 1000 in twin births, and 61 per 1000 in triplet births (Westoff and Westoff).

Induced Abortion

The subject of purposeful abortion appears throughout history in social, economic, political, and—particularly—religious contexts. The Chinese are said to possess the oldest method of abortion, the procedure having been described in a manuscript over 4000 years ago.

It is true that, in their early history, Jews were an aggressive people who were desirous of increasing, rather than decreasing, their tribal numbers as a means of protecting themselves against their foes more effectively. The notion is mistaken, however, that the ancient Hebrews were so opposed to abortion that they applied the biblical mandate "a life for a life" and assessed the death penalty against anyone implicated in an abortion. The truth of the matter is that neither the Talmud nor related Judaic historical documents contain any such proscription against abortion. Jews have traditionally held perhaps the most liberal views of the world's peoples toward all forms of birth control. Judaism, like Japanese Shintoism, holds that the fetus becomes human only when it is born (The desperate dilemma of abortion).

Abortion's strongest opponent (at least its most vocal one) is probably the Roman Catholic Church. Yet the Church's position in the matter has shifted several times over the centuries. The earliest Christians called abortion infanticide. Later theologians debated the issue of animation of the fetus: at which point of development might it be considered murderable? By the twelfth century the penalty of excommunication was generally withdrawn in cases of abortion—provided that the fetus, if male, was less than 40 days old (80 days for females!).

This position remained largely unchanged until 1588, when Pope Sixtus V declared that all abortions were a form of murder. Three years later his successor, Pope Gregory XIV, withdrew all penalties against those involved in an abortion, except when it was performed after 40 days of pregnancy. This decree held until 1869, at which time Pope Pius XI condemned all abortion, regardless of circumstance and length of pregnancy. The Church's present attitude toward abortion was thus established only 100 years ago (Westoff and Westoff).

Opinion was divided on abortion in ancient Greece. Hippocrates, the father of medicine, rejected the concept of abortion as a means of population control. He included in his oath, the Hippocratic Oath still taken by physicians today, a pledge not to give a woman an abortive remedy, which he considered an interference with nature. But his opinion was actually a minority one. (It is interesting to speculate on what present-day attitudes toward abortion would be if someone from the majority group had written the physicians' oath.) Aristotle considered birth control the best method of population control through which an orderly community might best be developed, and he regarded abortion as an acceptable alternative if other methods of birth control failed (Neumann).

To the Romans, abortion was simply the removal of a portion of the body, like an arm or leg. The idea that abortion is akin to murder did not occur to them. Here again, considerations of population control predominated, although abortion came to be practiced so extensively among the ruling classes that the ratio of citizens to slaves became a matter of grave political concern. As a result, efforts were made to outlaw abortion, but they met with only partial success.

Abortion remains today the principal method of population control in some countries and among certain primitive tribes. Among the world's most advanced nations, on the other hand, war and famine have paradoxically been accepted by many as "nature's method" of reducing burgeoning populations. We live in an era in which man possesses almost inconceivable control over natural forces. Surely, then, he does not have to wait passively for a tragic war or the literal starvation of large masses of people to remedy the problem of overpopulation. Indeed, many physicians, medical societies, government officials, and certain religious groups are increasingly demanding that laws regarding abortion and other methods of population control be restudied and revamped in the light of today's conditions. A June 1972 Gallup poll revealed that 64% of the American public (including a majority of Roman Catholics) favored liberalization of abortion laws. This figure stands in stark contrast to the scant 15% who were in favor in 1968 (40% in 1969) (*Houston Chronicle*).

Generally speaking, the higher a woman's education, the more receptive she is to the idea of abortion. White women tend to be more in favor of abortion than black women at all levels of education. The group most favorable to abortion appears to be white non-Catholic college graduates; the group least favorable, white Catholic college graduates, 30% of whom reject all grounds for abortion as invalid (Westoff and Westoff).

The Incidence of Induced Abortion

Authorities differ in their views on the incidence of abortion (Neumann). Some state that there are as many as 1 million induced abortions per annum in the United States, while others set the figure at half that number. Of these induced abortions, the vast majority are criminal by legal definition. However, in the first 6 months following the liberalization of abortion laws in New York State, 75,000 legal abortions were performed in New York City alone (Westoff and Westoff). While married women seeking abortions were once said to outnumber single women 4 to 1, the ratio between married and single women is now about 50–50, most experts agree (*Newsweek*). Of pregnancies among single women, 89% are terminated by induced abortion, as compared with 17% of married women's pregnancies (Gebhard *et al. b*).

There is a greater incidence of abortion in urban communities—reportedly as high as 1 for every 5 births—than in rural areas, where 1 abortion is performed for every 9 births.

In certain Middle European countries the incidence of legal abortion appears to be greater than that of live births. In Hungary, as an example, there are about 150 abortions per 100 births. In Belgrade alone, there are 4 abortions for every child born. In Yugoslavia, Czechoslovakia, and Poland, the ratio is about 130 to 100. Abortion is, in effect, probably the most common form of birth control in these countries. Why? Largely because legal abortion is easy to obtain and cheap—in some instances as low as $5 or $10. Furthermore, contraceptives are in short supply and women are distrustful of their use (Walker, C).

California's liberal abortion law is credited with lowering that state's birth rate, both legitimate and illegitimate, between 1970 and 1971. Legitimate births dropped 11½%, while illegitimate births dropped 16%. The national birth rate dropped only 6% during the same period (Abortion law shows results).

Reports on maternal deaths resulting from both therapeutic and illegal abortions seem to indicate that they constitute a high percentage (about a third, some say) of the total maternal deaths in the United States. These figures are often used by those who oppose legalizing abortion. But the totals are not strictly valid because they lump together all abortions, legal and illegal. Most authorities will readily agree that, if abortions are performed under the proper and sterile conditions of an operating room, the maternal death rate is somewhat lower than in full-term deliveries.

In 1971 the World Health Organization reported that throughout the world there occur from 3 to 4 maternal deaths per 100,000 abortions, compared with 20 maternal deaths per 100,000 births in countries with good obstetric services (Associated Press b). Since abortion was legalized in New York State, pregnancy-related deaths have declined by 56% (United Press International b). One report, in fact, reveals only 3 deaths in 30,000 abortions performed by capable persons (Eichenlaub b). Unfortunately, too many abortions are performed under nonsterile conditions and by unskilled persons, and the death rate in these circumstances is understandably high.

Methods of Inducing Abortion

A private New York foundation dealing with population research, the Population Council, concluded recently that the optimum time to perform an abortion is between the eighth and tenth week of pregnancy. Earlier than that the uterus is somewhat susceptible to damage because of its rigidity. Abortions taking place after the thirteenth week of pregnancy are three or four times more risky than those performed earlier, the greatest risk of all apparently being to women who wait until the fifteenth or sixteenth week (Safest abortion time calculated).

The following discussion of abortion methods includes those most often used in situations in which the pregnant woman does not have access to a legal abortion. Where induced abortion is legal, physicians most often use one of the methods described in the section on therapeutic abortion which follows.

Abortion has been attempted through a wide range of techniques. There are primitive methods, such as jumping on the abdomen; using sticks as uterine probes; using potions made from animal secretions, dung, herbs, and seawater; and having recourse to magic and mystical incantations. There are attempts at self-induced abortion through medications and violent physical exercise. And there are visits to illegal abortionists. Some of them are competent physicians; many are dangerous amateurs.

Pills advertised to correct menstrual irregularities are frequently taken in the hope of inducing an abortion. These pills are usually extremely strong laxatives containing one or more such herbs as tansy, ergot of rye, aloes, or quinine. Strong medication of this type has been known to produce severe poisoning, leading to blindness and other permanent disabilities. Strenuous physical exertion—lifting of unusually heavy objects, jumping from high places, or violent exercise—is as ineffective in inducing an abortion as the pills just described.

Abortions induced by others may involve drugs or spraying the uterus with chemicals. But the most common procedure is a form of dilation and curettage of the womb, which is most often done by the woman's husband or an abortionist, who inserts some sort of instrument into the uterus and scrapes away the embryo.

Abortionists' fees vary according to the socioeconomic status of the patient and, supposedly, of the abortionist as well: the higher the status, the higher the cost. Single women pay a higher fee than married women, but the highest price of all is paid by widows and divorcées. Age and race are additional factors in the cost of abortion: women under 31 pay about 20% more than older women; black women pay less than white women. As would be expected, the cost of abortion increases with the cost of living; present-day fees range from $150 to $1000 or more. A staggering $350 million is spent annually in the United States on abortions.

Recent investigation demonstrates clearly that the woman who sought an abortion and was granted one is better adjusted mentally after the event than the woman whose request for abortion was denied. For example, 24% of women denied an abortion revealed lingering psychiatric disabilities from 7 to 11 years afterwards, in contrast to only 0% to 2% of those women who were granted an abortion. Furthermore, children born to mothers whose application for a therapeutic abortion was denied have greater social and emotional handicaps than their peers do (Levene and Rigney).

Investigations into the medical and legal problems related to abortion reveal that "abortion in itself is a safe, simple procedure without clinically significant psychiatric sequelae, but it becomes an emotionally traumatic experience because of medico-legal obstacles." (Fleck). There are, to be sure, more legal abortions performed now than in the recent past, at least in New York, California, Hawaii, and Alaska. Even so, far too many women are still denied the right to have a legal abortion when they want one. (For a more complete examination of the legal aspects of abortion, the reader is referred to Chapter 22.)

In New York, 80% to 90% of the legal abortions now performed are done on an outpatient basis, under local anesthetic, and through the vacuum-suction technique. The Blue Cross Insurance Company of New York will cover abortions for single women and dependent children and Medicaid covers abortion for both single and married women. City hospitals perform the operation on minors without parental consent if the patient is at least 17 years old and is married, or is self-supporting and living away from home. Fees for abortion at city hospitals in a pregnancy of less than 12 weeks range from $200 upwards on an outpatient basis (Westoff and Westoff).

In those states still clinging to stringent abortion laws, the woman—single or married—who can afford to pay is in a favored position. She can go to a hospital and have a "perfectly legal" curettement performed by a physician. A woman from the slums, on the other hand, often must turn to a practical nurse or to a poorly trained abortionist who might use a knitting needle or coat hanger in an attempt to induce the abortion. The more likely result is death for the mother (A need for reform; Beigel f; Caprio c).

Therapeutic Abortion

Therapeutic abortions are usually recommended when certain pathologic conditions exist. The most common are serious cardiac conditions, tuberculosis, certain malignancies, diabetes, some kidney diseases, certain mental diseases, German measles during the first three months of pregnancy, and an Rh factor (an agglutinating property of human red blood cells) in certain cases.

Therapeutic abortions are performed in several ways (Neumann), some of the most frequently used of which are these:

The procedure of *dilation and curettage* ("D and C," as it is called in medical circles) is frequently performed if pregnancy has not progressed beyond the twelfth week. This procedure should be performed in a hospital with the patient under anesthesia. The cervix is dilated by inserting graduated sizes of instruments to stretch the opening, the largest dilator being about the size and shape of a small cigar. Once dilation is accom-

FIGURE 14.3 Lateral view of the female reproductive system, showing a dilation and curettement. The dilator opens the cervix through which the curette is inserted to scrape the lining of the uterus.

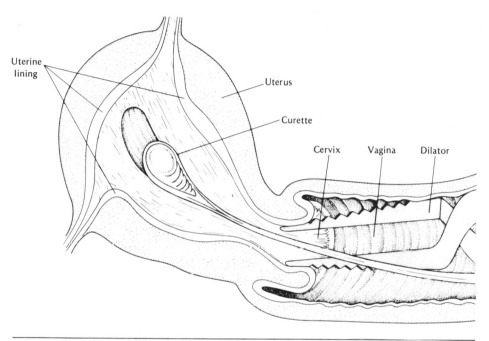

plished, a spoonlike instrument, a curette, is used to scrape the implanted embryo or early fetus from the uterus. The embryo or fetus is usually broken up into small pieces in the process of raking out the uterine material. Care must be taken not to perforate the wall of the uterus.

A new method of abortion, called *vacuum curettage,* has recently come into rather prominent usage in Europe and America. In this procedure, the cervical canal is stretched, a tube inserted into the uterus, and a vacuum pump used to suck out the embryo and other uterine content. The technique is easier and faster to perform than the more common D and C and causes the patient less trauma (Westoff and Westoff).

A new and valuable use of the vacuum (suction) technique has recently been developed to correct delayed menstruation. Called *menstrual regulation,* the process requires no medication, takes about two minutes to perform, can be done on an outpatient basis at a relatively low cost, and ends a delayed menstruation without pain or bothersome side effects (Abortion in two minutes). The process involves inserting a thin, flexible plastic tube into the uterus without the necessity of cervical dilation; then the month's menstrual lining (including a fertilized egg, if one happens to be present) is sucked out with a specially designed suction syringe.

The procedure is performed within the first two weeks of the woman's missed period. Because this is too soon after ovulation for existing laboratory tests to make an accurate diagnosis of pregnancy, there is no way for the woman—or legal authorities—to know whether she was pregnant when the procedure was performed. This procedure not only precludes prosecution for abortion, it permits the woman who might be bothered by having an abortion to free herself of the possibility of the burden of an unwanted pregnancy without having the guilt of a known abortion.

A new method developed in Sweden for abortion after the third month of pregnancy is now used with some frequency in this country. A needle is used to withdraw a certain amount (usually 200 cc) of amniotic fluid through the wall of the abdomen. The fluid is then replaced with an identical amount of salt solution of a specified strength. Abortion occurs spontaneously, usually within 24 hours.

Laminaria is a procedure wherein a pencil-shaped object made of seaweed is inserted into the cervix. The pluglike insert swells when it becomes moist and gradually dilates the mouth of the womb. At the same time the upper end of the plug acts as a foreign body in the corpus of the uterus, and after two or three days the uterus contracts and expels both plug and fetus. Although this method is not used in America, it is employed extensively in Europe, reportedly with success.

Hysterotomy is a method used after pregnancy has reached 12 weeks. One hysterotomic technique is actually a minor caesarean section, a procedure resorted to because the fetus is too large for usual vaginal methods of removal. Another technique entails a vaginal incision near the cervix, with a slit then being made in the lower part of the uterus through which the fetus is removed.

Less popular techniques include the following:

X-ray radiation is administered, halting the development of the embryo. Spontaneous expulsion then follows within a week or two. Because the extent of damage to the reproductive organs by radiation cannot be predicted, this method is seldom resorted to. X-ray used on a pregnant woman in an unsuccessful attempt at abortion, or for any other reason, is a grave hazard to the child. Research evidence indicates that there is a 50% higher death rate from cancer among children who had been X-rayed *in utero* than among those who had not (Ubell).

Antagonists and *antimetabolites* are used to affect or interfere with cell growth and folic acid metabolism, ultimately killing the fetus. Undesirable consequences may occur, however, such as the development of anomalies in the fetus rather than its destruction. Use of these drugs may also affect the mother's bone marrow or cause other physical difficulties.

CONTRACEPTION

In mankind's long search for effective forms of birth control other than abortion and infanticide, primitive people evolved some curious contraceptive techniques, some of them effective, most of them ineffective, and many quite dangerous. As would be expected from those who are attempting to cope with the unknown or the imperfectly understood, primitive people often involved their religious beliefs, superstition, and magic in efforts to control fertility.

An ancient Chinese belief, for example, held that a woman would not become pregnant if she remained completely passive during coitus. The philosophy underlying this belief was that a woman's enjoyment of intercourse was evil and merited punishment, of which pregnancy apparently was one form (Finch and Green). Even today some women persist in the belief that if they urinate after coitus, or have intercourse while standing, they will not become pregnant. The truth is, of course, that urine does not pass through the vaginal canal. However, if immediately after coitus one assumes the position typically taken in urination, some of the sperm might be kept from entering the uterus.

The oldest medical prescription for a contraceptive, dating back to about 1850 B.C., is found in the Egyptian Petri Papyrus. Women were advised to use a vaginal suppository concocted of crocodile dung and honey. The pastelike substance was apparently expected to prevent the sperm from entering the cervix (Allen, C. d). Over the centuries some incredible birth-preventive substances and techniques have been tried—mouse dung, amulets, and induced sneezing, as examples. Some methods were at least partially effective; and when they were, a refinement of them occasionally led to a reasonably efficient contraceptive. The ancient Greeks, for instance, wrote that certain materials permeated with oil might constitute a workable contraceptive because oil impedes the movement of sperm. Thereafter, oil-saturated papers were inserted in the vagina to cover the cervix—a crude forerunner, perhaps, of today's diaphragm.

The eighteenth-century Italian adventurer Casanova is alleged to have used a gold ball as a contraceptive, placing it in the vagina to block the sperm's passage. He is also credited with using half a hollowed-out lemon as a diaphragm to cover the cervix. Perhaps the lemon shell did serve as an effective contraceptive, for citric acid can immobilize sperm. But if Casanova's reputation for prodigious sexual activity was deserved, and if in fact he managed not to impregnate any of his ladies (as he claimed), the most logical explanation is that his frequent ejaculations maintained his sperm count at so low a level that he was sterile in effect if not in actuality.

Just when the *condom* or penile sheath was first used is unclear. Some writers say that it has been used for many centuries, perhaps even by the ancient Romans. (It is possible that the word comes from the Latin word *condus,* meaning a *collector.*) Others claim that the famous sixteenth-century anatomist Fallopius, who identified the female uterine tubes bearing his name, invented the condom. Still others give credit to a Dr. Conton or Condom, a physician in the court of England's Charles II (1660-1685), suggesting that the sheath was named for him. Whatever its early history, the sheath was originally used more as a protection against venereal disease than as a contraceptive (Tietze *b*).

The German scientist Graefenburg is generally credited with having introduced, in 1920, the use of foreign objects in the uterus to prevent pregnancy. This method is the forerunner of the *intrauterine contraceptive device* (IUD), which is one of the most popular methods of present-day birth control. Instead of the plastic coil used today, Graefenburg used a coiled silver ring. Unfortunately, however, the metal often caused an infection. But Graefenburg was not the first to use this technique. Centuries ago the Arabs put pebbles into the vagina or the uterus of their female camels to keep them from becoming pregnant on long caravan treks across the desert (Westoff and Westoff).

The efficacy of a specific modern method of contraception is determined by comparing its incidence of success with the incidence of pregnancy in couples who use no means of contraception—the latter assessed at 60 to 100 pregnancies in 100 years of coital experience (Lehfeldt *b*). For example, if couples using condoms as a contraceptive device show a pregnancy rate of 11 per 100 years (1200 months) of exposure, and if nonusers of any contraceptive methods show 100 pregnancies per 100 years of exposure, it is calculated that 89 out of 100 pregnancies were prevented by the use of the condom, and that its use as a contraceptive device is 89% effective. The following equation demonstrates the usual method of calculating the effectiveness of a particular contraceptive method.

$$\text{Pregnancy rate} = \frac{\text{number of pregnancies} \times 1200 \text{ months (100 years)}}{\text{patients observed} \times \text{months of exposure}}$$

If, say, 100 couples have used a particular contraceptive method for five years and if 50 pregnancies have occurred despite the use of the method, the equation would be as follows:

$$\text{Pregnancy rate} = \frac{50 \times 1200}{100 \times 60} = \frac{60{,}000}{6{,}000} = 10$$

When the pregnancy rating of a contraceptive method is below 10, its effectiveness is rated as high; if the rating is between 10 and 20, the effectiveness is considered to be medium; and if the rating is above 20, the effectiveness is ranked as low (Eastman and Hellman).

In 1955 it was estimated that 7 in 10 couples used some form of contraception. By 1960 the number had risen to 8 in 10. In 1965 the National Fertility Study showed that, of white women 18 to 39 years of age,

84% had at some time used a form of contraception. When the number of those who planned to do so in the future was added (most of whom had been married only a short time), the figure rose to 90%. When women who cannot conceive were excluded from the sample, the percentage who had used contraception (or expected to do so) rose to 97% (Westoff and Westoff).

The educational level of the couples was directly related to whether or not they used contraceptives: the higher the education, the more likely the couples were to use contraception (Freedman *et al.*).

Contraceptives Available Only With A Doctor's Prescription

With the exception of the condom, the more reliable forms of contraception now available must be prescribed by a physician and should be used only with medical supervision.

The Diaphragm

A *diaphragm* is a thin, rubber, dome-shaped cup stretched over a collapsible metal ring, designed to cover the mouth of the womb (the cervix). Properly fitted and used with a contraceptive cream or jelly, the diaphragm seals off the cervix and prevents sperm from entering the womb. The cream or jelly is toxic to sperm and provides lubrication as well. This device in no manner interferes with the conduct or pleasure of intercourse.

The diaphragm can be obtained only by prescription from a physician and must be fitted by him the first time, because of individual physiological differences in women. Being fitted with a diaphragm of the correct size and shape is of vital importance, both for the wearer's comfort and for its effectiveness as a contraceptive. After the initial examination and insertion of the diaphragm, the physician will instruct his patient how to insert it properly herself, and how to remove it.

A woman must usually be refitted with a new diaphragm every two years and after each pregnancy. A virgin cannot be fitted with one until her hymen has been broken. Some physicians are therefore reluctant to prescribe a diaphragm for a woman until after her honeymoon.

A diaphragm may be inserted several hours before coitus or immediately preceding it. It must not be removed until 4 to 6 hours after intercourse, and it may be left in place for as long as 24 hours. Douching (discussed more fully hereafter) is unnecessary, since the natural processes of a healthy woman keep her vaginal tract clean. If she prefers to douche, however, she must wait at least six hours following coitus in order for the spermicide cream or jelly, or the naturally acid condition of the vagina, to destroy the sperm. Diaphragms are considered by many to be inconvenient, uncomfortable, and rather difficult to use (Rodgers *et al.*). For other couples, the advance preparation implies a loss of spontaneity that detracts from sexual pleasure.

When the diaphragm is used together with contraceptive foam, its effectiveness improves significantly, making it one of the safest of all birth-control techniques (Sikes). Used together, the two have a pregnancy rate of 4 to 10.

Oral Contraceptives

It was demonstrated in 1937 that the administration of the ovarian hormone progesterone would inhibit ovulation in rabbits. Since that time endocrinologists, biologists, chemists, and physicians, working together and separately, have developed a method of contraception for human beings that is apparently superior to any method previously employed (Searle).

In 1954 an *oral contraceptive* in the form of a pill was used in laboratory studies; two years later well-controlled studies were made in Puerto Rico and Haiti to determine its safety and effectiveness. The experiments were tremendously successful. Since that time, pharmaceutical houses have been working overtime to supply the public with oral contraceptives and to produce even better ones.

The birth-control pill (popularly called "the Pill") is a combination of synthetic hormones (progesterone and estrogen) that, when taken in adequate dosage, prevents ovulation by mimicking the hormones produced naturally by the body during pregnancy. If no ovum is released, pregnancy obviously cannot occur. The Pill actually does several things to prevent pregnancy or to make it extremely unlikely to occur (Trainer). First, pituitary gonadotropin production is inhibited, interfering with the growth and development of the ovarian follicles. In addition, the uterine mucosa is affected in such a manner as to make implantation more difficult and early spontaneous abortion more likely if an egg were to be fertilized. The mucous plug of the cervix is thickened and made more formidable by the hormonal agents, thereby helping to prevent sperm from entering the uterus. In the early 1970s about 30 different brands of contraceptive pills were available, most of them to be taken as follows:

Counting from the first day of her monthly menstrual period, a woman starts taking the pills on the fifth day. She must swallow one pill daily, and preferably at the same hour, for 20 days. Menstruation will start two to five days after the last pill is taken, although in about 3% of the cases it fails altogether to commence. In the latter event, a physician

FIGURE 14.4   The major contraceptive measures in use today.

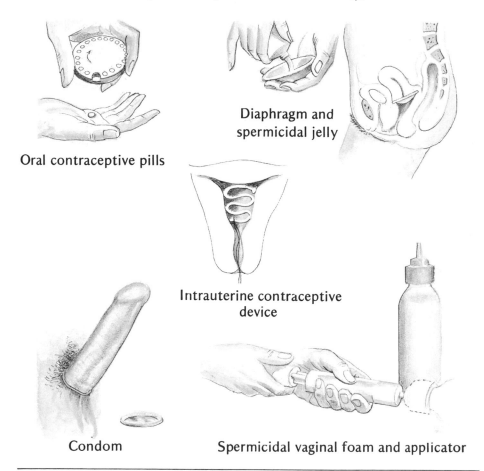

Oral contraceptive pills

Diaphragm and
spermicidal jelly

Intrauterine contraceptive
device

Condom   Spermicidal vaginal foam and applicator

usually advises his patient to commence a new round of 20 pills seven days after the last pill was taken, or he will offer alternative suggestions.

If one pill is missed there is a chance of pregnancy, but it is rather remote. If taken as prescribed, contraceptive pills are virtually 100% effective—and their success is unequaled by any other means of contraception.

During the early months of taking contraceptive pills, women seem to experience little reduction in sexual desire. The knowledge of being well protected against an unwanted conception often removes anxiety from both husband and wife, thereby increasing sexual desire in both partners. A comparison of women of similar ages, education, and religious background showed that those using the Pill engage in coitus with an 18% to

45% higher frequency than nonusers do, depending upon their socio-economic background (Westoff et al.). Even when coital frequency remains unchanged, women taking the Pill report consistently that they derive greater satisfaction in sexual relations than they did when using other methods of birth control or none at all (Rosengard b). From 1965 to 1970 the percentage of married couples using the birth-control pill rose from 15.3% to 22.3% (Associated Press e). Countless single women use the Pill as their preferred contraceptive method.

Authorities have warned women, however, to expect some loss of sex drive after protracted use of the Pill because of its interference with normal hormonal production (Trainer). Masters and Johnson report that a reduction in women's sex drive occurs after their taking the Pill for 18 to 36 months, and they suggest that other contraceptive methods be substituted for the Pill from time to time, according to the advice of the individual woman's physician, so that the original hormonal balance can be restored (Masters and Johnson o). The Pill is also used to treat certain discomforts and disorders of the menstrual cycle, such as irregularity, too copious flow of blood, and discomfort before or during menstruation.

As contraceptive pills have been used, studied, modified, and improved upon since their initial introduction, the negative side effects have largely been removed. Occasional discomfort or unpleasantness may still be experienced by some women who take them, especially in the first months. The most common symptoms reported are mild gastrointestinal disturbance, nausea and a bloated feeling, increase in weight, and spotting and irregular bleeding. Other occasional negative side effects are persistent menstruallike cramping and painful swelling of the breasts (Trainer).

From time to time one hears frightening accounts (often from reputable sources) of the inherent dangers of taking the Pill. However, these reports have usually been greatly exaggerated and are rarely balanced by the hazards of unwanted or dangerous pregnancies that the Pill might have prevented. The following paragraphs set out the threats of Pill usage—and of the failure to do so.

The most serious side effect associated with the Pill is that its estrogen content increases the coagulatory action of the blood, thereby increasing the risk of thromboembolic (clotting) disorders. Studies done in England and the United States have shown that women on the Pill are seven times more likely to die from blood-clotting than women not taking it. This means that, of every 100,000 women on the Pill, about three will die of thromboembolism caused by the Pill. These findings would discourage many birth-control-pill users if they did not probe more deeply into the matter (Westoff and Westoff).

Among the 8.5 million women using the Pill in the course of a year, whether strictly according to prescription or in a more casual way, 340,000 pregnancies can be expected to occur. If they used other methods of birth control, these same 8.5 million women would have almost 2.5 million pregnancies. Statistically, it can be expected that, of the women who use the Pill, 324 will die of thromboembolic disease. However, there would be 1179 deaths if these same women used other, less effective contraceptive methods, because of illicit abortions or the complications arising from pregnancy, childbirth, and the postpartum period. It is obvious that the risk of dying is 3.5 times greater without the Pill than with it, thromboembolic disorders notwithstanding (Westoff and Westoff). Among women using no method of birth control, incidentally, the risk of maternal death is 7.5 times greater than it is among women taking the Pill (Hardin). Furthermore, there is no evidence that such a serious complication as cancer arises from using the Pill, even in women who have taken it for as long as 10 years (Associated Press a).

Following the alarmist U.S. Senate hearings in 1970 concerning the Pill and the subsequent publication of a Food and Drug Administration leaflet describing the disorders and dangers associated with its use, the ranks of women taking the Pill thinned somewhat. Since that time, however, voices of reason have prevailed, as endocrinologists and gynecologists alike have joined forces to proclaim the Pill as eminently safe for most women, especially when its advantages are weighed against its risks.

Since the Pill suppresses milk production, its use is not recommended during the period just after childbirth when a mother is nursing her baby. Furthermore, there is evidence that if a mother takes the Pill while she is nursing a male child, the unusually combined hormones in her body can work their way into the baby's bloodstream through her milk and have a feminizing effect on him (Curtis).

This means of contraception, as has been pointed out, is considered 100% successful when used as directed. Even when a woman occasionally misses taking one, the Pill still has the excellent pregnancy rate of 3 to 7, equaling the best mechanical device.

A pharmaceutical house has recently produced an effective oral contraceptive for dogs. Administered each day for 30 days before the female's estrus period, the Pill suppresses that period without affecting the animal's capacity for producing healthy litters in the future (News of the month b).

Intrauterine Contraceptive Devices (IUDs)

IUDs are small plastic or metal devices of various sizes and shapes that are designed to fit into the womb. Plastic is preferred over metal because of its flexibility and the greater chance of its not being rejected by the subject's body tissue. In some way the IUD acts as an irritant to prevent implantation of the fertilized ovum in the uterine wall. Technically, this method is more correctly called *contraimplantation* than contraception.

The device must be selected and fitted in the uterus by a physician.

It remains permanently in place until the user wishes to become pregnant, at which time the doctor removes it. After the birth of a child, it may be repositioned in the uterus until another pregnancy is desired. The device in no way affects the health of any children borne by the woman or her ability to conceive.

There are certain disadvantages to using IUDs: expulsion by the uterus without the wearer's knowledge (although this can be avoided simply by checking it regularly), and, in some instances, bleeding and pain. About 10% of all IUDs are expelled during the first year after insertion, although about 40% of women who do expel the device manage to retain it once it is reinserted (Westoff and Westoff). About 2% to 3% of women develop an infection when the IUD is inserted, but perforation of the uterus is extremely rare (Segal and Tietze).

Since the device is a foreign body, the uterus resists it for a while; but once the initial discomfort is past, the user is no longer aware of its presence. Two threads hang from the device down through the cervix into the vagina, so that a frequent check can be made there to determine that it has not been expelled.

Of the variety of shapes and sizes in which IUDs are available, the best known are the spiral, loop, bow, and ring. The National Committee on Maternal Health, which recently conducted a large-scale study of IUDs, gathered the individual case histories of almost 25,000 women who had used variously shaped IUDs for at least a year (Tietze b). Of these, the loop was found generally to be the most effective and comfortable, as well as having a low rate of spontaneous expulsion. About 20% of women using IUDs abandon their use after one year, and the rate rises to about 50% after five years (Westoff and Westoff).

A remarkable new IUD has recently been introduced, offering great promise in terms of effectiveness, retention, and comfort. The T-shaped device is much smaller and easier to insert than the more conventional loop. Furthermore, the incidence of spontaneous ejection, bleeding, and cramping is considerably less than with the loop. Wrapped with copper—which appears to be an additional deterrent to embryo implantation—the polyethylene T has proved, in the initial stages of its use, to be virtually 100% effective. Its cost is minimal, and its effectiveness lasts several years. And there is nothing in the medical literature to suggest that the minute amount of copper released by the T is in any way harmful to the body. The device is not in popular use in America at the time of this writing, but it is likely in the near future to be judged as one of the most effective, simple, and economcial contraceptive devices on the market (Rorvik a).

Since 1949, IUDs have been submitted to clinical examination of their effectiveness, and the test results have been watched with interest by various planned parenthood groups. Studies indicate that IUDs are not yet 100% effective, but that they rank among the most adequate means of contraception available. As the devices continue to be perfected, more and more United States doctors are prescribing them for their patients. In 1965, by way of illustration, IUDs were the method of choice of only 1% of women practicing contraception. In 1970, by contrast, IUDs were being used by an estimated 2 million women (Westoff and Westoff). The most successful of the IUDs have a pregnancy rating of about 2 to 3.

Pap smears (clinical tests made to detect cervical cancer) have been taken from thousands of IUD users. They reveal neither occurrence of cancer beyond its normal incidence in the female population nor evidence of other adverse effects that could be attributed to the devices.

It is interesting to observe the readiness with which the large population of India has accepted this particular means of birth control—not only for themselves, but for their sacred cows as well (Science notes *d*)! The government, aware of the many problems caused by the unrestrained productivity of the sacred animals, yet unable to destroy them even for use as food, decided to take unusual steps toward control. A special IUD has been devised for the cows, and it is hoped that their birth rate can be thereby controlled without public outcry. Furthermore, ingenious veterinarians have developed workable IUDs for cats and dogs—much to the delight of pet owners.

Contraceptives Available Without A Doctor's Prescription

The Condom

The most widely used contraceptive device in the United States, the *condom* is made of strong thin rubber or of sheep's intestine. At its open end, which is about an inch and a half in diameter, is a rubber ring. The closed end is usually plain, but it may have a pocket to provide space for ejaculated semen, thus lessening the possibility of its bursting. The condom usually measures seven and a half inches in length.

Since the U.S. Food and Drug Administration placed condoms under its control, the product has been improved. The only drawback to its being totally effective is the possibility of breakage during use, or of its slipping off after ejaculation, with the result in either event that semen may be spilled into the vagina. The second eventuality can be avoided if there is adequate vaginal lubrication and if the condom is held onto while the penis is being withdrawn from the vagina after ejaculation.

Condoms should always be inspected before use by blowing air into them, and it is advisable afterwards to fill them with water to be sure that no breakage has occurred. If a condom breaks in use, a contraceptive cream or jelly should be applied vaginally at once. If none is available, a water douche should be used, since water is highly spermatoxic.

The efficiency in design and manufacture of the present-day rubber condom dates from about 1920, although the discovery of vulcanized rubber in the 1840s made large-scale production of the condom possible more than a 100 years ago. Condoms made of linen or silk were used by the Italians and Chinese before the seventeenth century, principally as a prophylactic measure against venereal disease (Tietze *b*).

Prior to the development of the vulcanization process, the French and English used sheep gut or the amniotic membrane of newborn lambs (Trainer) to fashion fairly satisfactory condoms. In recent years, manufacturers are again producing gut condoms, which, while more expensive than rubber condoms, appear to be as safe as the rubber one. They are, furthermore, aesthetically preferable because they interfere less with body warmth and other pleasurable sensations experienced during coitus.

With the exception of withdrawal (discussed in subsequent paragraphs), the condom is probably the most frequently employed birth-prevention technique, although it is used more in nonmarital than in marital coitus. About 750 million condoms are produced each year in the United States. They are cheap, available in most pharmacies, simple to use, and easily disposable.

Some men object to the condom because it dulls somewhat the pleasurable sensations of coitus. Also, its use may interfere with the natural progress of mounting sexual tension, because sex play must be interrupted to put it on. The pregnancy rate of the condom can be judged to be about 10 or 11, since estimates in individual studies range from 6 to 19. The condom is certainly the best method, after total abstinence, of preventing the spread of venereal diseases.

Chemical Methods

The most effective of the chemical methods of preventing conception are *creams, jellies,* and *vaginal foams.* They are used for two reasons: they serve to block the entrance to the uterus, and they contain an ingredient that is toxic to sperm. They must be introduced at least 5 to 15 minutes before ejaculation occurs; if intercourse is repeated, more cream or jelly must be used.

Another chemical method involves the use of a *vaginal suppository,* a small solid cone that melts at about 95°F. It is toxic to sperm, but a disadvantage in its use is that it must be inserted at least 15 minutes before ejaculation if it is to be effective. Suppositories usually have one of three bases—cocoa butter, glycerin gelatin, or soap. Pregnancy rates vary from 5 to 27.

Vaginal tablets have the same drawbacks as suppositories. The moisture needed to dissolve them may not be present in sufficient quantity.

The tablets, moreover, are very unstable in damp climates. They are given a pregnancy rate of 8 to 27.

Douches

The purpose of douching is to flush seminal fluid from the vagina before it has a chance to enter the mouth of the womb. Actually, however, sperm move so quickly that the douche often fails to reach them. Although water makes a satisfactory douching solution, strong soapsuds, three table-spoonfuls of vinegar, or a teaspoonful of alum per quart of water is probably better. Douching is not medically approved as an effective method of birth control; it has the unsatisfactory pregnancy rate of 36. It serves better to cleanse the vagina than to prevent pregnancy.

Other Contraceptives

A *sponge and foam combination* is a contraceptive that is inexpensive but relatively ineffectual. The sponge is dipped in water and squeezed; the contraceptive ingredient is then added and worked into a foam. The sponge, which is inserted deep into the vagina before intercourse, will remain effective for several hours. Another sponge can be added to the first one if intercourse is repeated. The sponge must remain in place for six hours following the last act of coitus. No douche is necessary.

Another contraceptive means is a *tampon containing a spermatoxic chemical*, which is inserted into the vagina as close to the cervix as possible. The chemical is a contraceptive jelly that begins a foaming action upon contact with sperm. This method and the one described in the preceding paragraph have the poor pregnancy rate of 27 to 42.

A recent innovation in contraception consists of *foam preparations* inserted into the vagina by way of an aerosol spray can. These products contain effective spermicidal powders; they are easy to apply and have a pregnancy rate of from 3 to 10.

As part of their extensive research on human sexual response, Masters and Johnson investigated the effectiveness of eight commercial contraceptive products (Johnson and Masters). None of the methods tested—two creams and one each of a vaginal jelly, liquid, gel, tablet, foam, and suppository—was given perfect scores in the various tests performed. Each of the women taking part in the tests had her cervix capped, used the contraceptive according to the manufacturer's instructions, and engaged in artificial coition by means of a plastic penis until she had an orgasm. At this point, fertile semen was introduced into the vagina, and samples of vaginal content were taken from various parts of the vagina. The first sample was taken within 1 to 5 seconds after semen injection, followed by samples taken after 15 seconds, 30 seconds, 60 seconds, 2 minutes, and 5 minutes. In another series of artificial coitions, which involved the same contraceptives and which was similarly conducted to the point of orgasm, the same sampling procedure was instigated 1 hour after injection of semen, then 3 and 5 hours later.

Findings of the study were that the diaphragm failed in a large percentage of the cases investigated (8 of 30) because of vaginal and uterine enlargement during the sexual response cycle, and because reinsertion of the penis after the initial insertion and withdrawal tended to dislodge the diaphragm from its snug and properly fitted position. There was evidence, furthermore, that even a highly spermatocidal chemical may not be effective if the substance containing it does not dissolve or spread properly within the vagina. A chemical may be very effective in a suitable foam, but ineffective in a jelly, cream, or foaming tablet.

Other Methods of Birth Prevention

Within the definition of contraception—which includes any agent or voluntary means of preventing conception—the following methods of birth control are also commonly considered forms of contraception. However, since they do not involve mechanical or chemical methods, they are discussed separately.

Coitus Interruptus or Withdrawal

This technique requires the man to withdraw his penis from the woman's vagina before he reaches a climax. Many couples rely upon this technique of birth prevention for years with both success and satisfaction and without experiencing any of its alleged dangers to health. Certainly it is the oldest known form of contraception. It is mentioned in the Old Testament (Genesis), and anthropologists report that it has been widely used throughout the world for centuries.

The popular misconception that prolonged reliance on this method will inevitably cause premature ejaculation is not supported by evidence. But there are certain disadvantages to it. Sexual intercourse cannot be enjoyed in a relaxed mood by either partner if the uppermost thought is withdrawal in the nick of time. For a woman slow to reach orgasm, pre-ejacualtory withdrawal by her partner may not allow sufficient time for her to reach orgasm. In such cases the result may be congestion of blood in her genital organs and, possibly, chronic pelvic pain and other gynecological complaints. This reaction may of course follow any sexually stimulating experience that is prolonged yet does not result in orgasm.

The first few drops of the ejaculate contain the great bulk of the male spermatozoa. Should the man be slow to withdraw, and should any of this first ejaculate enter the vagina, *coitus interruptus* can very easily be a failure as a means of birth prevention. Furthermore, the secretion in the Cowper's glands of many men contains sperm cells that frequently ooze into the vagina even if no ejaculation follows (McCary a).

Probably the most distressing aspect of *coitus interruptus* is the onus on the man to withdraw at the crucial moment. When ejaculation is imminent, the typical male impulse is to drive the penis as deeply into the vagina as possible and to hold it there. This impulse is quite inimical to the movements of withdrawal. The man should also time coital activity so that his withdrawal and ejaculation occur after his partner's climax. In addition, he would be most unwise to reenter the vagina for a considerable period of time after ejaculation, because of the presence of residual sperm in his urethra.

Generally speaking, those couples who use *coitus interruptus* extensively do not find it particularly undesirable, while other couples despise the technique. Depending upon the care and timing of the man, the pregnancy rate is from 8 to 40.

The Rhythm Method

This technique relies upon timing coitus so that it occurs only when the woman is supposedly infertile. Authorities differ on the subject, but it is a generally accepted biological postulate that an ovum lives approximately only 24 hours after ovulation unless it is fertilized (Landis and Landis; Lehfeldt b). Sperm released into the uterus remain alive and capable of fertilizing the egg for about 48 hours. This means that only during 3 days per month can a woman become pregnant. The difficulty, of course, is pinpointing the exact 3 days.

As a general rule, the average woman releases an ovum 14 to 16 days before her next menstrual period is due. If she menstruates every 28 days, she should ovulate midway between the two periods—about the thirteenth to fifteenth day after the first day of her period. In a 25-day cycle, ovulation should occur between the tenth and twelfth days; if it is 35 days, between the twentieth and twenty-second days. About 70% of women ovulate between the eleventh and fifteenth days of the cycle (Lachenbruch).

Because different women menstruate on different schedules, a written menstrual record should be kept for 12 consecutive months to determine the fertile ("unsafe") and infertile ("safe") days. The following formula for calculation is suggested (Trainer): Subtract 19 from the number of days in the shortest menstrual cycle observed during the preceding year to get the number of "safe" days during the first half of the cycle (beginning with Day 1 of the cycle). Next, subtract 11 from the number of days in the longest cycle of the preceding year to get the number of "safe" days during the last half of the cycle.

For example, if the shortest cycle for the preceding year was 24 days and the longest cycle was 28 days, the first calculation is made this way: $24 - 19 = 5$. This means that the 5 days beginning with Day 1 of the menstrual flow are considered "safe." The second calculation is made this way: $28 - 11 = 17$. This means that the time from the 17th day of the cycle to the beginning of the next menstruation is considered "safe." This leaves 11 days of the menstrual cycle—the sixth through the sixteenth during which conception is considered possible.

Only about a third of women are regular enough in menstruation so that they can safely use the calendar rhythm method to avoid conception (Brayer *et al.*). Women who vary as much as 10 days or more in the length of their cycles should have medical advice to determine their "safe" period. After childbirth the first few menstrual cycles may be very irregular, making the rhythm method particularly unreliable at that time.

A refinement of the rhythm system, based on the same biological postulation concerning the time of monthly ovulation, is the *temperature method* of birth control. This technique goes further than a mere series of calendar observations of the date on which menstruation begins. It is founded on the additional premise that there is a distinct correlation between changes in body temperature and the process of ovulation. A woman's temperature is usually relatively low during menstruation itself and for 8 days thereafter—13 days in all. At the time of ovulation, midway in the cycle, there is a dip in temperature and then a sharp rise of $\frac{1}{2}°$ to $\frac{7}{10}°$. The elevation persists for the remainder of the cycle, then drops one or two days before the onset of the next period.

To achieve any sort of accuracy in predicting her "safe" period according to this method, a woman should record her temperature, preferably upon awakening, every morning for 6 to 12 months. The primary difficulty in so determining a "safe" period for intercourse is that in some women the changes in temperature are not so pronounced or so consistent, although a doctor is much more skilled in interpreting temperature charts than the layman. Another difficulty is that more than one ovum can mature during any one cycle. Furthermore, current research (Buxton and Engle) indicates that the time interval between ovulation and the temperature rise can vary up to 4 days. Whichever the approach, rhythm or temperature, the technique has a pregnancy rate of 14.

According to the latest estimates, the failure rates of the most commonly used birth-control techniques are as follows: the Pill, 5%; IUD, 8%; diaphragm, 18%; condom, 19%; withdrawal, 23%; rhythm, 30%; and foam, 32% (Westoff and Westoff). At first blush these figures seem exceptionally high, but one must remember that carelessness in the proper use of a particular technique increases its incidence of failure.

Some of the techniques with a particularly poor record of effectiveness prove, when used properly and consistently, to have a more impressive safety record than the most effective methods used haphazardly. One survey of persons with low income revealed that less than half possessed sufficient knowledge to use a contraceptive effectively. This ignorance was particularly apparent among young people aged 15 to 18 years (Speidel).

BIRTH CONTROL TECHNIQUES OF THE FUTURE

There is considerable evidence that people need a much better method of fertility control than is now available. The side effects of the Pill, and fear of it, have caused many women to abandon its use. Other facts pointing to the need for more effective methods of birth control include the discomfort, expulsion rate, and occasional failure of the loop; the high failure rate of most other contraceptives; and the great number of abortions and unwanted children. About 75% of all American women are sterile, pregnant, or trying to become pregnant; or they are using a birth-control technique that is relatively ineffective, inconvenient, messy, or incompatible with the natural, spontaneous enjoyment of intercourse. Realizing these facts, scientists are turning their attention to new techniques and methods of birth control. In their excellent book *From Now to Zero*, Westoff and Westoff have summarized the most promising of the new methods presently in an experimental stage.

The *Mini-pill* is a new contraceptive containing no estrogen, the suspected cause of most of the dangerous and unpleasant side effects of the present Pill, and little progestin (synthetic progesterone). The Mini-pill does not exert control over vaginal bleeding and menstrual irregularity, as the Pill does. But it virtually eliminates the danger of thrombogenic complications and most other unpleasant side effects. The Mini-pill does not interfere with the woman's ovulatory process or menstrual flow and, since it is taken every day of the month, the irksome chore of counting pills and of stopping and restarting a series is obviated. The Mini-pill is probably successful because its progestin content makes the cervical mucosa thick and sticky rather than thin and watery, as it becomes during ovulation, thus preventing sperm from passing through to the uterus.

Another technique involving a low dosage of progestin is currently being developed. An inch-long spaghettilike capsule containing progestin is inserted into the woman's leg, arm, or groin by means of a hypodermic needle. The capsule releases just enough progestin at a constant rate to keep her from becoming pregnant. If she then decides to have a baby, it is necessary only to remove the capsule. Capsules capable of releasing progestin for as long as a year, three years, ten years, or a lifetime may be used. This method of birth control is safe and convenient; there is nothing to remember and nothing to buy, and the implant in no way interferes with sexual pleasure. The cost will probably be less than a dollar, plus the doctor's fee for injecting the device.

Still another device making use of a low progestin dosage as a means of contraception is the *vaginal ring.* The hormone is homogenized with plastic and formed into a ring somewhat like the diaphragm. Inserted into the vagina, the ring remains for a month releasing enough progestin throughout to keep the woman infertile for the entire month.

Ovariotexy is another new and unique form of contraception. Through an incision in the lower abdomen, a silastic bag is placed around each ovary. Discharged ova are trapped in these sacks, thus blocking their union with sperm. If the woman later decides to have a child, another incision is made and the sacks are removed (Science notes *j*).

A *"morning after"* pill containing a large dose of estrogen has also been developed. It prevents implantation of the fertilized ovum in the uterine wall, and is effective even if taken as long as three to five days after coitus. The primary value of this pill lies in its use as an emergency procedure in cases of rape, since the high estrogen content usually makes the woman quite ill. Other possibly detrimental side effects have not yet been determined (Westoff and Westoff).

An after-the-fact birth-control method holding great promise involves the use of *prostaglandins*, fatty-acid derivatives produced by many tissues of the body. Among other functions, prostaglandins normally act on the uterus to cause the contractions of childbirth (or spontaneous abortion). Tablets containing prostaglandins are inserted into the vagina of a pregnant woman every 2.5 hours until menstrual bleeding begins. Abortion results in almost every case, even for those women who are as much as 22 weeks pregnant. The abortion, furthermore, is a complete one, seldom requiring a curettage to remove any remnant of the conceptus (Bardin).

A woman who accepts other birth-control methods but rejects the idea of abortion can simply insert the tablet into the vagina a day or so before her menses is due. In this way she will never know whether the ensuing bleeding is a normal menstrual flow or the result of an abortion. If a woman has no objection to using prostaglandins as an abortifacient, the law of averages suggests that she will probably need to take them only once or twice a year. A fertile woman engaging in an average amount of intercourse without any protection against impregnation will, statistically speaking, become pregnant about three times a year. If she makes some use of the "safe-period" technique of birth control, she can reduce her pregnancies to perhaps one a year.

The use of prostaglandins is still too new for an accurate assessment of any serious side effects, although none have manifested themselves as yet. Scientists are at present greatly encouraged by what they know of prostaglandins. The substances abound naturally in the body, and the amounts needed to effect uterine contractions appear to be too small to affect other organs (Rorvik a).

It has also been predicted that vaccines will be developed to immunize a woman against her husband's sperm, much as one is now vaccinated against smallpox, and to immunize a man with substances inhibitory to sperm production.

Scientists at the University of Georgia have identified a substance called *DF (decapacitation factor)* in the fluid surrounding human sperm cells. This substance, which protects the surface layer of sperm, must be removed if a sperm is to penetrate an ovum. The Georgia scientists believe that female enzymes act to destroy DF, thus making the sperm's penetration of the ovum possible. Fertilization might be prevented, they theorize, if destruction of the DF by these enzymes could be blocked, or if DF could be biosynthesized and introduced into the fallopian tubes (Westoff and Westoff).

Biochemists continue to work on a pill for men that will induce temporary sterility. To date, however, there are unfortunate side effects when men use a pill of this nature, in that sex drive is reduced and the intake of alcohol causes some abnormal reactions. Much further experimentation on a contraceptive pill for men is therefore indicated (Rubin a; Westoff and Westoff).

Another possibility is a hormone implant for men similar to the one devised as a birth preventive for women. It is theorized that a high level of testosterone in a man's body inhibits spermatogenesis. Therefore, a capsule containing testosterone, implanted beneath the skin, would release the hormone steadily and thereby block sperm production. Scientists are not optimistic about the prospects of this procedure, however, since testosterone and the other androgens are critically linked with prostatic cancer. To arrive at a hormonal dosage low enough not to seriously affect metabolic processes, yet effective enough to block spermatogenesis, is a goal that now appears remote (Rorvik a). A pill that acts to prevent sperm from maturing may be more of a possibility (Westoff and Westoff).

Work is also going forward on a silicone rubber plug to be inserted in the vas deferens to block the passage of sperm. A plug of this sort could later be removed with comparative ease if the man wished to father a child (Westoff and Westoff).

15 SEX
IN THE
LATER
YEARS

In past generations, society's failure to recognize the sexual needs of its older members was always a serious matter. Today that failure has become critical. For in the early 1970s there are more than 35 million Americans 65 years of age or older. That figure is expected to approach the 50-million mark by the year 2000. Many of these older men and women have living spouses; still others contract new marriages. (In the 1960s, for example, there were 35,000 marriages a year involving people 65 years old or older [Rubin g].) With or without partners, all these "senior citizens" have sexual needs, and these needs are perfectly normal ones, as we shall demonstrate. It is unrealistic and unfair to countenance any longer the mythology that such a large segment of the American (or any other) population is incapable of sexual activity or is uninterested in it—or, what is the more insidious fallacy, that it is "unseemly" for erotic yearnings to persist into venerable old age.

PSYCHOSEXUAL ASPECTS OF AGING

At the base of the pyramid of misconceptions about sex among the aged is the essentially Victorian philosophy regarding human sexuality:

that sexual activity is primarily a procreative function, and that those beyond their reproductive years should practice sexual self-denial. It is therefore "not quite nice" for older people to have sexual yearnings. Another attitude prevalent in our society that works against sexual expression in the older person is the idealistic concept linking sex, love, and romance—with the implicit corollary that all three are provinces belonging solely to the young.

Opinions revealed in one study of youth (Brandeis University students, aged 17 to 23 years) are probably typical of most young people's attitudes on the subject of sex and aging. Almost all the students expressed the belief that sexual activity does not exist in the lives of most old people, or is unimportant to them (Golde and Kogan).

Small wonder, then, that the older person is frequently perplexed by his or her sex drive and ashamed of it! The prevailing American attitude suggests that he should live in a sexual vacuum. His children very likely say (voicelessly), "Sex is for the young. Act your age." He may be further confounded if he seeks advice from a physician on a sexual problem, whether physical or psychological in nature, for the doctor may, unfortunately, have his own sexual hangups or be no better informed on sexual matters than his patients are. In such a case the doctor may only intensify the older person's feelings of guilt and bewilderment by answering any sex-related questions with: "Well, what do you expect at your age?"

Even Freud was a victim of this faulty thinking. At the age of 41 he wrote to a friend complaining about his moods, adding: "Also, sexual excitation is of no more use to a person like me" (Fromm, E.). Unless a physician understands the psychological importance of sexual expression in the elderly, he can do irreparable damage to his geriatric patients' sexuality, to say nothing of their general mental and physical health.

Older people typically enter the stage of life euphemistically called "senior citizenry" with trepidation and fear about new roles for which they have had very little preparation. Their children are gone from home, leading lives quite independent of their parents. The husband has often been forced to retire from his job before he was physically or mentally ready to do so. Quite likely both he and his wife have been shoved aside by the young in social and community affairs. From this enforced inactivity and society's indifference (if not prejudice) toward older people, there quite understandably develops the equation "Young is good; old is bad." And the aging person, along with everyone else, tends to internalize the concept that *old* is a dirty word.

Just how old is old? It is unjust—and unscientific—to establish that a man is old solely according to the number of years that he has lived, a criterion that Harry Benjamin has called "the tyrannical rule of the calendar" (Benjamin a). In terms of optimism, flexibility, and contribution, there are many people who can be called old at 25; conversely, a Picasso, Casals, Russell, or Shaw would be judged young at 90.

When does the aging process actually begin? It may be said with some justification that the science of geriatrics begins where the science of pediatrics leaves off. Aging is a gradual process: a person is not young one day and old the next. Aging is a sequence extending over a lifetime of subtle, often imperceptible change—just as daybreak blends into daylight, daylight into twilight, and twilight into darkness without a discernible shift (Weinberg, J.).

We have seen that sexual performance is not simply a biological function centered in the genitalia. Its complexities involve the entire personality, past experiences, and attitudes, as well as the brain and central nervous system, which control the physiological aspects of sexual behavior. By the time a person's sexual apparatus is mature, his behavior, sexual and otherwise, is largely under the control of the psychological, social, and cultural influences of his environment—both good and bad (Rubin g). These influences are so powerful that they prepare the self for many of the otherwise alarming changes in body and mind commonly associated with advancing age.

The aging person's lessened physical vigor and the diminution in his social and professional status often damage his previously healthy self-concept. He begins to *feel* old, sometimes long before, physiologically, he has begun to age significantly. A good sexual relationship at this critical time of life can provide much-needed warmth and comfort, and can be a highly effective source of self-reassurance. For both the older man and the postmenopausal woman, the feeling of being needed and loved at this time of life is of great importance to mental well-being. Of equal importance is the realization that he or she possesses the capacity for giving needed love and affection.

Since there is so much to be gained from continued sexual activity in the later years, and since coitus (although not the only feasible source of sexual outlet) is almost always physiologically possible, why do so many older people shrink from it? For some, of course, sex has never been very important. The aging process therefore provides a convenient excuse for giving up an activity that has always been, very likely, a source of anxiety. For many more, however, the popular belief that people past 50 years of age have little interest in sex (or, if they *have* an interest, are sadly lacking in capability) becomes a self-fulfilling prophecy. Sensing disapproval or ridicule from younger segments of the population, the older person develops guilt over his sexual desires and seeks to deny or to extinguish his sexuality altogether.

PHYSIOSEXUAL CHANGES IN THE AGING WOMAN

In contrast to men, women demonstrate few changes in the pattern of their sexual response as they grow older. Kinsey and other researchers

have shown that a woman's sexual desire ordinarily continues undimin-
ished until she is 60 years of age or older, after which its decline is very
slow, if a suitable outlet is available (Kinsey *et al. c;* Masters and Johnson
n; Rubin *j;* Sex behavior of older women).

There are certain physiological changes concomitant with the menopause, to be sure, and some of them can make coitus unpleasant—e.g.,
thinning vaginal walls; diminshed vaginal lubrication during sexual excitation, making the vaginal vault less distensible and more liable to injury
or pain; and, in some women, severe pain caused by uterine contractions
during orgasm. But these problems are merely signals of postmenopausal
hormone deficiency and can be circumvented by hormonal replacement,
administered either orally or by suppository. Hormones otherwise have
almost nothing to do with an older woman's libido or coital performance
(Belliveau and Richter; Kaplan and Sager; Kinsey *et al. c;* Lief *et al*).

After the age of 40, women may begin to experience a sharp decrease
in the secretion of estrogen, a decrease that continues gradually for the
remainder of their lives (LeWitter and Abarbanel; Rubin *j*). In the relatively
unenlightened medical world of the 1800s, physicians understandably
reasoned that, since the ovaries dwindle in their production of estrogen
at and after the menopause, a woman's sex drive would accordingly decrease. It is now known that a woman's sex drive often does not diminish
even when the ovaries are surgically removed. In fact, removal of a woman's
adrenal glands (which, in the female, produce the male sex hormone
androgen) has a far greater negative effect on her libido than ovariectomy
does (Rubin *g*).

A hysterectomy, like menopause, does not normally end a woman's
sex drive. By definition, *total hysterectomy* involves the removal of the
uterus only, whereas *panhysterectomy* involves the removal of the uterus,
fallopian tubes, and ovaries. In the first instance, there would not even
be the reason of hormonal imbalance to account for loss of sex drive.
If any change occurs, in fact, it might be in the direction of increased drive,
since fear of pregnancy is removed. Some hormonal changes will occur
following a panhysterectomy but, again, the deficiency can be rectified
therapeutically.

Women are taught to equate menopause with the end of youth,
vitality, vibrance, attractiveness—and usefulness. Even more ominous are
the rumors that the menopausal woman is likely to go mad, or develop
cancer, or be forever afflicted with the erratic (although minor) physical
symptoms that accompany menopause. It is small wonder, then, that for
many women the "change of life" means something more like the end
of life (Rubin *g*).

Given a sexually interested, active partner, the sex drive of a woman
following menopause or hysterectomy will quite likely remain unimpaired
(Daly). Reduced sexual activity in the aging woman (assuming that any
hormonal deficiency has been corrected) suggests that her husband has

little interest in sex; that she has no sex partner; that she is seeking a reason to terminate her sex life; or that she has fallen victim to some unfortunate folklore.

All women should take heart from Masters and Johnson's summary comment on sex and the older woman. Despite a reduction in both intensity of physiologic sexual response and the rapidity of it, they state that "the aging human female is fully capable of sexual performance at orgasmic response levels, particularly if she is exposed to regularity of effective sexual stimulation. . . . There seems to be no physiologic reason why the frequency of sexual expression found satisfactory for the younger woman should not be carried over into the postmenopausal years. . . . In short, there is no time limit drawn by the advancing years to female sexuality" (Masters and Johnson n).

PHYSIOSEXUAL CHANGES IN THE AGING MAN

As a man grows older, certain physical–sexual changes become evident. The size and firmness of the testicles diminish, and they do not elevate to the same degree during the sexual response cycle that they did when he was younger. The seminiferous tubules thicken and commence a degenerative process that, to an ever-increasing degree, inhibits the production of sperm. The prostate gland often enlarges, and its contractions during orgasm are weaker. The force of ejaculation weakens, and the seminal fluid is thinner and more scant. Orgasm is slower in coming and may not last as long as it once did. The intensity and duration of the sex flush during sexual excitation abate, and the involuntary muscular spasms accompanying orgasm decrease (Belliveau and Richter; Masters and Johnson n). Whereas a man may have required only a few seconds of stimulation to achieve erection when he was young, as an older man he may require several minutes. His erections are less vigorous and frequent, although the potential remains the same.

Despite these changes, the older man has, in fact, certain advantages over the younger one because his ejaculatory control is much greater. He is able to maintain an erection for a considerably longer time without feeling the ejaculatory urgency that plagues the younger man.

The aging man may lose his erection rather rapidly after ejaculation and be unable to attain another for several hours or, even, days. If he or his partner desires coitus more frequently than his erectile ability permits, there is a way around the problem. During coitus, the man should withdraw before he reaches orgasm. With minimal sexual stimulation he can easily attain another erection and then begin coitus anew. Although his ejaculatory capacity does not keep pace with his erectile ability, he now possesses the enviable faculty of prolonging intercourse indefinitely.

The sex drive of older men generally follows their overall pattern of health and physical performance. Secretion of the male sex hormone androgen in a man of 30 is 55 units per 24 hours. It dwindles to about 8 units a day by the age of 60; the secretion remains fairly constant thereafter.

Masters and Johnson emphasize the importance of the older man's accepting two physiological facts: (1) at no time in a man's life does he lose the capability of erection, except in extremely rare instances involving injury to or pathology of the CNS; and (2) loss of erectile ability, therefore, is not a natural part of the aging process (Masters and Johnson *p*).

The physical change causing the greatest difficulty in older men (although younger men can be similarly afflicted) involves the prostate gland. It is a wonder that an organ as small as the prostate, whose functions are not spectacular, should cause men so much trouble, to say nothing of anxiety. Yet the prostate is destined to become enlarged in from 20% to 50% of all men in their middle years and thereafter, although only 35% of the cases will require surgery. Why such a large proportion of men are so afflicted is not completely clear, except that prostatic enlargement is part of the general aging process and is in some way related to the amount of male hormones produced by the testes (for we know that eunuchs do not suffer from this problem) (Rubin *g*).

Although *prostatitis*—inflammation of the prostate—is not uncommon among young men, *prostatectomy*, the surgical removal of all or part of the prostate, is far more common among men past 50. Even when surgery is required, however, the vast majority of men who were potent beforehand retain their potency afterward. (A full discussion of the several operative procedures is contained in Chapter 20.) The conclusion drawn in a study reported in the *Journal of the American Medical Association* was that a willing sexual partner is the most important factor in a man's retaining his sexual ability after prostate surgery (Finkle *et al.*).

If a man ceases to function sexually after prostatic surgery, the reason may well be that he was looking for an excuse to end his sexual life. He may want to be free of the marital obligation of intercourse or he may fear that intercourse will aggravate cardiac or other physical disabilities, even minor ones. Or in past attempts to find a sexual outlet he may have met with disapproval from his wife—or his children or neighbors may have expressed disapproval of sexuality in older people.

Once a man's prostatic dysfunction is properly treated, his general health, well-being, and sexual performance will almost certainly improve as well. The attack on physical problems in middle age, however, should not end with treatment of the prostate. Anything that improves general health will also have a beneficial effect on sexual functioning. Hormonal or thyroid treatment may be indicated; perhaps the thyroid gland, the body's regulator, can be made to function more efficiently by medication.

If the older man's physical problems are complicated by a defeatist attitude toward the future of his sex life, then consultation with a psychotherapist might be greatly helpful. Especially after the age of 50, a man should consult a urologist regularly. He should be careful, however, to choose one who understands the need in a man for regular and frequent sexual outlet and who will do whatever is possible to ensure it.

Coital Capacity in Aging Men

Men's capacity for sexual intercourse is, of course, limited by their potency—their ability to achieve and maintain an erection. Statistics on the subject of potency are revealing. The Kinsey researchers have shown that, among men aged 35 years, only 2% are impotent; of those aged 55, only 10%; and of those aged 75, 50%. Despite the last figure, the average frequency of coitus among all men over 65 is approximately four times a month (Kinsey et al. a). Other researchers also emphasize that there is no specific point in the aging process at which sexual activity dwindles and disappears, but rather that it decreases in advancing age at about the same rate that it has been doing since young manhood (Bowers et al.; Finkle et al.; Freeman; Masters and Johnson n, p; Newman and Nichols; Rubin g; Tarail).

One study of older men ranging in age from 55 to 86 years revealed that, despite a gradual decline in sexual desire, 65% of those under 70 were still potent, and 33% of those over 70 were (Finkle et al.). More than 75% of the men in another study, whose average age was 71 years, reported that they still felt sexual desire, and 55% reported that they were still capable sexually. The frequency of coital activity ranged from three or more times a week to once every two months (or less). About 40% of these men reported that they noticed a definite reduction in sexual desire by the age of 60, about 70% by the age of 70, and about 80% by the age of 80. Consistent with the findings of similar investigations, this study revealed that the sex drive of the older individual is directly related to the intensity of his sex drive in youth. Men in whom the onset of sexual desire was early and strong in youth maintained the strongest desire and greatest capability in the advanced years of life (Freeman; Newman and Nichols; Rubin g).

That an older man experiences erection during sleep and upon first awakening in the morning offers irrefutable evidence of his sexual capacity in later life, even though he may not actually be sexually active. Obviously the man capable of nocturnal or early-morning erections has no physiological barrier to erection. If he is incapable of penile erection in a sexual encounter, then the barrier is emotional and psychological. Of men 75 years and older, 60% report that they still have involuntary morning erections, although the average declines from 4.9 times a week in youth to 1.8 times a week by the age of 65, and 0.9 at 75 (Kinsey *et al.*, *a*, *c*; Rubin *b*).

One study of men aged 70 to 96 years (average age, 80.5 years) revealed that they continued to have erotic dreams productive of erection. Some 30% of these men, furthermore, whose average age was 75.6 years, demonstrated an erectile capability no different from that of much younger males (Kahn; Rubin *o*).

Since the vast majority of older men—over 90% in one study—do not cite physical disability as a deterrent to sexual frequency (Tarail), only one conclusion can be drawn. The agents militating against their continuing to perform sexually are primarily psychological ones.

Having had a venereal disease, however, does appear to affect a man's sexual capacity in his later years. One study of sexually potent men, aged 60 to 74, showed that those with a history of VD engaged in coitus on an average of 14.1 times a year, while those who had never had VD averaged 24 times a year (Bowers *et al.*).

COITAL INCIDENCE IN LATER YEARS

One of the best known and most detailed investigations on the subject of sex and older people compared the sexual activities, interests, and attitudes of 250 persons living in Durham, North Carolina. The subject population included married, single, divorced, and widowed men and women between the ages of 60 and 93 years (average age, 70). Both black and white subjects of various socioeconomic levels were included. The 149 married subjects were grouped into four classes according to age: 60 to 64 years, 65 to 69 years, 70 to 74 years, and 75 years and over (Newman and Nichols).

The first three groups contained about the same percentage of sexually active subjects—60%. Of the group older than 75 years, about 30% remained as sexually active as subjects in the other three. But the investigators were careful to point out that many of the subjects in the oldest group or their spouses were afflicted with chronic illnesses—such as arthritis, arteriosclerotic heart disease, and diabetes—that militated against sexual activity (Newman and Nichols).

The married women in this study reported less sexual activity than the married men did, possibly because they were more reluctant to disclose details of their sex life. The more likely explanation, however, rests on the fact that women usually marry men older than they. The average age of the married women in this study was 70, and that of their husbands, 75. At this advanced age the husbands possibly lacked the interest or capacity for maintaining an active sex life with their younger wives (Newman and Nichols).

Of the 101 subjects in this study without a marital partner, only 7%

were sexually active, whereas of the 149 subjects still married and living with their spouses, 54% were sexually active to some degree. These findings are supported by the results of other studies, especially those of Masters and Johnson, which point clearly to the fact that an essential factor in a continued and active sex life is a willing and cooperative sex partner (Friedfeld; Masters and Johnson *n, p*).

The black subjects in the North Carolina study were significantly more active sexually than the whites (70% compared with 50%). But this observation is probably more indicative of socioeconomic differences than racial ones (Newman and Nichols), for similar differences in degree of sexual activity exist when persons—no matter what their age—of the lowest socioeconomic stratum (in which blacks unfortunately predominate) are compared with those of the higher strata.

The North Carolina investigators concluded, in company with other researchers, that despite a gradual decline in sexual interest, capacity, and activity, older persons in reasonably good health with sexual partners whose health is also good can continue to be sexually active into their 70s, 80s, or even 90s.

A study of some 800 men listed in *Who's Who in America*—educators, business leaders, attorneys, engineers, physicians, clergymen, and writers—all of whom were past 65 years of age—yielded similar results. Of the total sample, 70% engaged in sexual intercourse with some regularity, averaging one to four acts of coitus a month. Almost 50% of the 104 men between the ages of 75 and 92 reported that they still engaged in satisfactory coitus, six of them more than eight times a month (Rubin *b*).

These findings are particularly interesting in light of the results of studies suggesting that men of low socioeconomic status engage in coitus more often than men of higher status. The discrepancy may be due, however, to the fact that the men listed in *Who's Who* were high achievers who, generally, had always experienced good physical and mental health (Rubin *b, g*).

Another interesting finding in this study of prominent men was that the oldest subject still engaging in satisfactory coitus was a 92-year-old clergyman. Of the various professionals in the study, furthermore, the clergy as a group reported a higher percentage rate of satisfactory coitus than any other group. The highest rate of impotence was found among editors, publishers, and journalists, followed closely by physicians. Of 40 married physicians, 17 were impotent (Rubin *b, g*).

The question quite naturally arises why one elderly man should function satisfactorily within his marriage while another does not. On the basis of their investigation into the sexual behavior of older males, Masters and Johnson (*n*) describe six factors responsible for loss of sexual responsiveness in later life: (1) the monotony of a repetitious sexual relationship (usually translated into boredom with the partner, which the Kinsey group described as "psychologic fatigue"); (2) preoccupation with career or economic pursuits; (3) physical or mental fatigue; (4) overindulgence in food or drink; (5) the physical or mental infirmity of either spouse; and (6) fear of failure associated with or resulting from any of the former categories.

Fear of failure is especially devastating to a man's potency. As Masters and Johnson point out, "Once impotent under any circumstance, many males withdraw voluntarily from any coital activity rather than face the ego-shattering experience of repeated episodes of sexual inadequacy" (Masters and Johnson *n*).

Effects of Monotony on a Sexual Relationship

Coital monotony usually results from a long-married couple's allowing sex to become a mechanical activity, an event now totally lacking in imagination. A study of 100 consecutive cases of older men seeking treatment for impotence revealed that many were impotent only with their wives, undoubtedly a result of sexual monotony (Wolbarst).

Even when the excitement and stimulus of a new sexual partner provide a fillip to flagging virility, however, a man typically reverts to his previous level of potency in a relatively short time. This is especially so if the couple fail to expend strong effort to keep the new relationship exciting and novel (Rubin *o*). One research project demonstrated that sexual adequacy in aging white rats increased when the animals had a chance to copulate with a number of females. As soon as the males had reached a certain age, however, the stimulating effect of variety became weaker and weaker, until copulation eventually ceased altogether (Botwinick; Rubin *g*). It should be borne in mind, however, that lower animals are not as capable of introducing stimulative innovations into their sexual acts as humans are.

The sexual relationship in most upper-middle-class marriages can be accurately described as devitalized, despite the fact that the couple's financial affluence gives them much innovative latitude in their marital routine. Although many of these couples are still in their 40s, sex is typically a predictable, brief encounter following a Saturday night social gathering at which both partners probably drank intemperately. Some of the wives in such marriages describe their sex life as "legal prostitution, not much better than masturbation," while many husbands refer to their wives as "legal, inexpensive, clean mechanisms for physical gratification" (Cuber with Harroff; Rubin *g*).

Despite this gloomy generalization, there are nonetheless many advantages to a long-standing marital relationship. Each partner knows what to expect from the other; each has adjusted, at least to a degree, to the other's foibles and peculiarities; and many of the rough edges that caused friction in the early years of marriage have now worn smooth (Rubin *g*).

With concerted effort from the outset of marriage, a couple can learn to circumvent those pitfalls of a close relationship that may lead to boredom and monotony. As they grow older they can reap the rewards of enjoying one another and the warmth generated by a long, close relationship.

Sexual Outlets Other Than Coitus

A major challenge to older men and women is finding the means to satisfy their sexual needs when their spouse has died or is no longer interested in sexual activity. Many have been counseled by experts in the field of marriage to use self-stimulative methods to gain relief from erotic tensions, and those following this advice frequently find that maintaining some form of sexual expression helps to prevent depression, frustration, and hostility.

After coitus, the most important form of sexual outlet for both sexes in later life is masturbation. It is an established fact that about 25% of men above 60—even those still enjoying coitus—masturbate regularly (Kinsey et al. a; Rubin b). Among older women, the actual or potential value of masturbation as a sexual outlet is particularly understandable. About 45% of all women between the ages of 65 and 74 are widows; among women past 75, the figure jumps to about 70%. Furthermore, the number of widows in our society increases at the rate of 100,000 each year—twice the annual increase in the year 1900 (Rubin g).

About 59% of unmarried women between 50 and 70 years of age admit to masturbating. Approximately 30% of older women supplement marital coitus with masturbation (Kinsey et al. c). Older women remain capable of multiple orgasms, and indeed many frequently resort to various means, such as masturbation, to fulfill their multiorgasmic needs and to keep their sex lives active and satisfying.

Laura Hutton of England contends that the health record of women who have masturbated regularly through the years is better than those who, because of guilt feelings, have not done so. Dr. Hutton recommends that a woman needing release of sexual tension seek it through this easiest and most satisfying of means (Hutton).

In sum, masturbation is certainly not a practice limited to the young and immature, despite public opinion to the contrary. It is a valid means of sexual release for those of maturity and advanced years as well.

Heterosexual coitus and masturbation are not, of course, the only forms of sexual outlet available to the older person. There is also homosexuality. From a study done of 1700 men whose average age was 64, it emerged that over 6% had engaged in homosexual acts after they had reached the age of 60. Surprisingly, homosexual behavior had not been an important sexual outlet for them since they were teen-agers—in fact, the vast majority were either married or widowed. For most of their adult lives, then, they had lived an entirely heterosexual married life (Calleja).

Although this group included men from diverse backgrounds, ranging from agriculture to the professions, the researchers did not consider them strictly typical. Even so, that the homosexual pattern emerged after the age of 60 is most interesting. Why did these men turn to homosexuality? The men themselves, all in good physical and mental health, placed great emphasis on the empathy they felt for their male sexual companions. In fact, they felt that the sexual activity was perhaps of less importance than the warmth and sensitivity they found in their partners.

These men considered themselves quite masculine (and so did the researchers), and they likewise considered their partners to be very virile. In fact, they expressed a certain revulsion for effeminate men. Some stated that they had become practically impotent with women by this time of their lives, but found themselves fully potent with some of their homosexual partners. The overriding need, then, was for affection, something the subjects felt they were not getting in sufficient degree (for whatever reason) from their families. As people grow older, sometimes their need for affection also grows, and the need for sexual satisfaction may increase accordingly (Whiskin).

It is true that some of these men felt guilty about their homosexual behavior because of religious and social disapproval. But they confessed that, guilty or not, they did not have inner resources strong enough to renounce the relationships. However, if the percentage revealed by this research is reasonably accurate, one can see that homosexuality constitutes a relatively minor mode of sexual expression among elderly men (Calleja).

The late Isadore Rubin, a pioneering authority on the sexuality of the older person, wrote with much cause of "the need for our entire society to recognize the normality of sex in the older years, to establish the right of older persons to express their sexuality freely and without guilt, and to clear away the obstacles in people's minds which prevent the fullest and most creative expression of that sexuality" (Rubin *g*).

It cannot be emphasized strongly enough that a man's loss of sexual potency with advancing age is in almost all cases the outgrowth of psychological inhibitions rather than of physical incapacity (Rubin *d*). Indeed, loss of sexual vigor with age should be no greater than the loss of other physical capabilities. A man or woman of 60 is hardly capable of running 100 yards as quickly as he or she might have at 20. But the chances are excellent that the feat can still be accomplished by proceeding at a leisurely pace and feeling no anxiety about running less swiftly, or less often, than in the hayday of youth.

For all mature couples, be they 21 or 90—but especially for the older ones—sexual interaction should be an expression of the total personality of each individual and of the deep commitment each has made to the other. In addition to coitus, the sexual drive may find expression "in the need for continued closeness, affection, and intimacy, and in a continued cultural and intellectual interest in eroticism, or in the need for some romance in life" (Rubin g).

A word should be addressed to the heart patient (young as well as old) who, understandably, may be most hesitant about resuming his or her sex life after a coronary attack. Indeed, death has been known to occur because of the violent coronary response to sexual activity. Furthermore, heightened blood pressure can lead to rupture of blood vessels, particularly in older persons. These severe reactions are rare, however, and the admonition to observe total (or near total) sexual abstinence is not applicable to most heart patients; it is reserved for those with very serious coronary involvement.

The heart patient and his partner must first of all understand that heart beat and blood pressure will unquestionably rise to very high peaks during sexual activity, even if he plays a physically inactive role during coitus. This is not to say that he cannot engage in sensible sexual behavior and draw considerable benefit from it. He *is* warned, however, against prolonged coition, fatiguing sexual positions, and extended sex play. Controlling these circumstances will permit him the fulfillment of coitus without undue threat to his health. As in other medical matters, the prescription (or proscription) of his physician must be rigidly observed.

Whether a coronary patient should continue sexual activity is aptly summed up in a story of a recovering patient who questioned his physician in the matter. "By all means, have sexual intercourse," replied the doctor, "but only with your wife. I don't want you to become too excited." There is probably too much truth in that account for it to be humorous. A recent study of men with heart disease who died as a result of coitus revealed that 27 of the 34 deaths occurred during or after extramarital intercourse (Ueno).

PART FOUR

TODAY'S SEXUAL ATTITUDES AND BEHAVIOR

16 ATTITUDES TOWARD SEX

Psychologist Allen Fromme, in his book *Sex and Marriage*, has observed, "Our sexual behavior is essentially the result of our attitudes towards sex; and these attitudes, in turn, are a product of how we have been brought up." We have already noted in this text that sex education begins with the first intimate mother-infant contacts (Calderone e). But instruction in sexual matters involves infinitely more than the interrelations between parents and child; significant roles are played by many other influences. Not only the demands and expectations of the culture in which one lives, but also special differences in sexual ethics within that culture work to shape sexual attitudes—and, in consequence, sexual behavior.

Cultural differences produce as wide a variety of attitudes toward sexual matters as they do in other areas of human interaction. It comes as a surprise to many Americans to learn, for instance, that their condemnatory views on premarital and postmarital sexual activity are not shared by the majority of the world's cultures (Bell a; Murdock a). Of 158 societies investigated in one study, 70% are tolerant of premarital sexual intercourse, although this permissiveness does not extend to include sanction of adulterous relationships (Ehrmann b).

Anthropological investigations have consistently revealed that cultures

271

encouraging women to be completely free in their sexual expression produce women whose amatory reactions are as uninhibited and as vigorous
as those of their men. Cultures in which there is approval of women's
having orgasms produce women who have orgasms. Cultures withholding
such approval produce women who are incapable of orgasm (Kronhausen
and Kronhausen).

With regrettable ease, sexual attitudes often fall under the pall of
such cultural maladies as misinformation and prudery. For example, women
of emancipated modern societies are frequently troubled with menstrual
difficulties of one sort or another. Yet Margaret Mead's anthropological
studies of the women of Samoa uncovered only one woman in the entire
population who even understood what was meant by pain or emotional
upset during menstruation. That particular girl was in the employ of the
island's white missionary family!

All people are to a degree inclined to cling to their traditional ways
of thinking and conducting themselves, whether in political, religious, sexual, or other matters. A reluctance to accept change or to be swayed by
outside influences, however rational or beneficial, is found not only in
major cultures, but within specific subcultures as well.

All cultures place specific restriction on the expression of sexuality.
Yet hardly any group fails to recognize that, if sexual needs are not expressed in one way, they *will* be in another. Thus by denying healthy
manifestations of sexual impulses, a culture or subculture encourages their
vicarious expression in the guise of psychoses, neuroses, personality maladjustments, guilt, inadequacy feelings, and true sexual perversion. (In
the last part of the nineteenth century, a physician wrote in a medical
journal that he did not believe that one bride in 100 married with the
expectation of sexual gratification [Brown, D. G. b]. What direction the
expression of these women's suppressed sexual desires took is a question
that the physician failed to answer.)

Much of a normal person's behavior is influenced by the inhibition
and consequent displacement of sexual needs into other channels. For
example, we are consciously disturbed by the thought of premarital or
extramarital sexual relationships, yet are excessively interested in them.
Consider how many of us laugh at or express horror over the less than
conventional behavior of certain luminaries in the entertainment world,
yet voraciously consume every account of it, however exaggerated.

We satisfy our own desires, conscious or unconscious, by identifying
with these people. At the same time, by pointing an accusing finger at
them, we avoid self-guilt. Tensions accruing from the denial of our own
desires are thus drained off through great interest, joking, and laughter
(Ellis a). Certainly no sensible person suggests that control and appropriate
expression of our sexual needs according to time and place are unnecessary. But to set up unrealistic and unreasonable prohibitions, whether

directly or through the mechanism of guilt, is setting the stage for trouble now or later.

A CLIMATE OF ATTITUDINAL CONFLICT AND CHANGE

Much has been said and written in recent years about the sexual revolution that is allegedly taking place. Research findings and clinical judgments are, however, inconsistent in their conclusions as to whether such a revolution is indeed occurring today. (The evidence is unmistakable that a significant sexual revolution did occur in the 1920s, when women born around the turn of the century came of age and set new sexual standards [Ellis *n;* Kinsey *et al. c;* Rubin *f*].) A true sexual revolution, by definition, means a dramatic change in the attitudes and ethics governing sexual behavior as well as in the behavior itself. Conclusive evidence of such a change does not as yet exist (Davis, K. E.), but there are signs that revolt looms on the horizon.

The evidence seems clear from recent research that the incidence of sexual *activity* among young adults has indeed increased, primarily in the areas of heavy petting and coitus within relationships of deep involvement. Yet the most significant change by far has been a growing liberalization of sexual *attitudes*.

The group in whom these changes are the most pronounced is young adult women, whose liberalized premarital sexual behavior and sexual attitudes are approaching those of young adult men, although they still lag somewhat behind. "For women," one investigator has remarked, "a clear consciousness of sexual urges exists and a majority of college women will have experiences of heavy petting, will approve of premarital coitus when in love or a meaningful relationship exists between partners, and a substantial minority (perhaps majority by senior year) will have engaged in premarital coitus. College women thus are having more sexual experiences, earlier and probably with more partners than was true of the pre-1960 students" (Davis, K. F.).

As we have suggested earlier, significant changes in human mores, behavior, laws, and social institutions occur only gradually. Changes in what a culture considers acceptable sexual behavior are especially slow because the orientation and experiences of childhood impose such strong limitations on freedom of erotic behavior in adulthood (British Council of Churches; Ellis *n;* Rubin *f*). And yet one can hardly have escaped noticing a change in sexual attitudes in recent years. Witness the growing freedom with which sexual topics are discussed in the various communication media, schools, churches, and governmental circles—as well as at cocktail parties and by the man on the street.

But many persons unaccustomed to casual conversation on sexual topics fail to understand that talk and actions are not necessarily one and the same. Attitudes (and the ease of discussing them) are not to be confused with behavior (Coombs a). And inconsistency between sexual attitudes and behavior is still a characteristic of the American culture. Even those for whom a decision in the matter of a sexual ethic is most pertinent—today's young people—are bewildered and bedeviled by the dichotomy between prevailing sexual attitudes and sexual behavior. For example, although 75% of the college girls in one study expressed the belief (attitude) that their classmates were "sleeping around," surveys at the time consistently pointed out that only 20% of all college girls were in fact experiencing premarital intercourse (behavior) (Sex in the news b). Another inconsistency, within a different population, was pointed up by a study involving sexually active lower-class delinquent girls, whose average age was 15.8 years. It revealed that 91% of the girls, despite their behavior, believed premarital coitus to be wrong (Ball and Logan).

Ira L. Reiss (b) has examined in some detail various conflicting American premarital sexual standards. Among them he lists *abstinence* (premarital intercourse is wrong for both men and women, regardless of circumstances); the *double standard* (premarital intercourse is acceptable for men, but unacceptable for women); *sexual permissiveness when affection exists* (premarital intercourse is right for both men and women under certain conditions—in a stable relationship involving engagement, love, or strong affection); and *permissiveness without affection* (physical attraction alone justifies premarital intercourse for both men and women). Tabulating the attitudes of high-school and college students, as well as of older adults, toward certain forms of sexual behavior in males and females, Reiss emerged with the results shown in Table 16.1. The fact that in both groups petting and coitus were more consistently approved of for males than for females is evidence that vestiges of the traditional double standard still

TABLE 16.1   Approval of Petting and Full Sexual Relations by Stage of Relationship

| | ADULTS | | STUDENTS | |
	For Males	For Females	For Males	For Females
Petting:				
When engaged	60.8	56.1	85.0	81.8
In love	59.4	52.6	80.4	75.2
Strong affection	54.3	45.6	67.0	56.7
No affection	28.6	20.3	34.3	18.0
Full Sex Relations:				
When engaged	19.5	16.9	52.2	44.0
In love	17.6	14.2	47.6	38.7
Strong affection	16.3	12.5	36.9	27.2
No affection	11.9	7.4	20.8	10.8
N	(1390)	(1411)	(811)	(806)

persist. That approval of sexual involvement decreased as the level of emotional commitment in the relationship decreased is evidence of permissiveness when affection exists, for both sexes. Even so, "a small (5% to 15%) but not insignificant number of college women find full sexual intercourse acceptable even if there is no particular affection between the partners. For them, physical attraction, momentary impulse, or curiosity are enough to justify coitus" (Davis, K. E.).

Kinsey found that women were less likely to demand virginity of their husbands at the time of marriage than men were to expect their brides to be virgins (23% vs. 40%) (Kinsey *et al*. c). However, the double standard seems to be collapsing in the matter of virginity. A recent Gallup poll, conducted on 55 separate college campuses, revealed that men and women now think very much alike on the subject; 75% of these students expressed the view that virginity in the person whom they marry is unimportant (In the news c). The results of another study, however, indicate that the double standard, interestingly enough, continues to plague American college men (Christensen and Gregg). Although 55% of the sampling expressed approval of premarital coitus, 75% of them nevertheless stated that they would prefer to marry a girl without coital experience. Because both men and women tend to regard sexual conquests and experience as indications (however stereotyped) of masculinity in a man, many women prefer that the man be nonvirginal at marriage (Burgess and Wallin).

Lester Kirkendall (a) has developed an ethical approach to the rightness or wrongness of premarital intercourse. This ethic is based on the premise that premarital sex is all right if it increases the capacity to trust, brings greater integrity to personal relationships, dissolves barriers separating people, enhances self-respect, engenders attitudes of faith and confidence in other people, fulfills individual potentials, and fosters a zest for living. In a study involving the presence of these factors in the sexual relationships of 200 male students, it was concluded that a "sexual relationship is an interpersonal relationship, and as such is subject to the same principles of interaction as are other relationships" (Kirkendall and Libby a).

Generally speaking, then, it seems fair to say that the sexual attitudes and behavior of men and those of women are converging today. Women expect the same sexual freedom that has traditionally been accorded men only. Men, on the other hand, rather than moving in the direction of greater promiscuity, are slowly drifting toward the traditional female norm (Rubin p).

Several studies made in the late 1960s and early 1970s revealed that from 50% to 85% of college males considered premarital coitus acceptable (although only about 65% actually had premarital intercourse). Factors affecting this permissive attitude were race, age, semester in college, strength of religious belief, and region of the country. Thus, older youths who had little religious conviction and who were attending eastern, western, or southern colleges were more permissive than younger, religiously inclined midwesterners (Davis, K. E.).

As many as 70% of the college women sampled approved of premarital coitus for themselves if they were "in love," although only about 35% to 50% actually engaged in coitus before marriage. Only 40% or less found it acceptable under the less involved conditions of strong affection, if no exploitation existed. For college women, permissive sexual attitudes were related to having been in love two or more times and to being emotionally involved in a dating relationship (going steady, being pinned, or being engaged). Women's view of themselves as sexual beings appears still strongly related to feelings of romance, affection, and love (Davis, K. E.).

In recent years, attitudes appear to be much more predictive of behavior than they have been in the past. In 1958, 41% of the females and 65% of the males with premarital sexual experience held permissive sexual attitudes as compared to 78% of the females and 82% of the males in 1968. It is interesting to note that, as attitudes and behavior become less disparate, fewer males and females report negative reactions to first nonmarital coital experience (Christensen and Johnson).

Despite all the information about human sexuality being dispensed nowadays, and despite the new freedom with which sex is being at least discussed, the attitudes that many young people are absorbing about sex appear to be much the same as those of previous generations. That is, boys are sexier than girls; one marries "good girls" and has sex with "bad girls"; masturbation is "not quite nice," an activity one tries to avoid or at least does not voluntarily admit to; girls have no need to masturbate; reproduction and VD are permissible sexual topics for discussion, but the pleasures of sex are not, because the pleasures will automatically follow falling in love and getting married (Gagnon and Simon). Little wonder the sexual attitudes of young people today are often confused, contradictory, and self-defeating!

One of the most significant social changes to occur in recent years has been the emergence of women toward a position of equality in American society. The freedom and parity that women are demanding—and, to some extent, enjoying—in the United States have had a profound effect upon prevailing sexual attitudes. Most women today are unwilling to accept the notion that they and men are subject to different sexual standards. They expect the pleasures received from sexual activities as well as the restraints on them to be equally applicable to both sexes (Bell a; Poffenberger b). Despite recent liberalizing tendencies in the realm of women's rights, however, certain differences between the sexual attitudes of the two sexes continue to be forged by such factors as childhood rearing, societal expectations, and certain physiological forces.

An interesting side effect of this struggle for equality is that the sexual attitudes of present-day American women are often considerably healthier than those of American men. Chroniclers of sexual histories, whether researchers or clinicians, have found that women are far more open and honest in supplying personal data than men are. Frequently becoming entrapped in questions of self-esteem, men may attempt through boasting to compensate for what they feel is a threat to their self-image. As a consequence, the data they provide are often unreliable (Maslow *b*).

Is There Growing Moral Decadence Among Today's Youth?

Since the beginning of recorded history, older generations have been in a state of shock over the supposed immorality of the younger generation. About 2400 years ago Socrates wrote:

> Children now love luxury. They have bad manners, contempt for authority. They show disrespect for elders and love chatter in place of exercise. Children are now tyrants, not the servants of their household.

And in the eighth century B.C., the Greek poet Hesiod wrote:

> I see no hope for the future of our people if they are dependent on the frivolous youth of today, for certainly all youth are reckless beyond words. . . . When I was a boy, we were taught to be discreet and respectful of elders, but the present youth are exceedingly wise and impatient of restraint.

It is not surprising, then, that newspaper and magazine articles, organized groups, and individuals are crying out that America is on the brink of ruin because of the sexual misconduct of its young people. There are, to be sure, those incidents that incite public outrage, and these, one suspects, constitute the "evidence" of the alleged general moral degeneration among the young. But there have always been such occurrences, and there are no more now—if as many—than in the past. Despite some popular hue and cry, there is considerable evidence that young people today are behaving responsibly, demonstrating moral strength in an active concern for the welfare and rights of others. Young men of today do not seem to lie, cheat, or otherwise trick girls into bed as their fathers might have done. And girls entering into sexual relationships with young men before marriage appear to do so because they want to, and because they expect to enjoy the experience—an experience, it might be added, that women today are more likely to enjoy than ever before, because of the gradual dissipation of Victorian and puritanical inhibitions that have traditionally hampered women's sexual enjoyment (Masterson).

The new sexual climate has many advantages. The elimination (or at least reduction) of sex-related guilt, hypocrisy, dehumanization, secrecy, and morbid fascination, which clouded physical relationships in the past, is a healthy development (Farnsworth).

When young people do rebel against the values of older segments of the population, the older generations have to look at their own behavior for at least part of the answer. As long as those of us who are older continue in some of our own neurotic and self-defeating behavior patterns, we are not likely to get very far in persuading young people to listen to what we have to say.

Why should a youngster believe an adult about the dangers of, say, smoking marijuana when that same adult smokes cigarettes from a package clearly labeled, "Warning: The Surgeon General Has Determined That Cigarette Smoking Is Dangerous to Your Health"? The argument that smoking marijuana is illegal, while smoking tobacco is not, will quite likely be ignored. Young people of today are not thoroughly convinced of the value of laws, mainly because their parents frequently act in defiance of them—for instance, by driving 50 miles an hour in a 40-mile-per-hour zone. The fact that there is little traffic does not change the existence of the law, or the requirement to obey it, any more than does the fact that many authorities question the dangers of marijuana justify smoking it. Because of the Vietnam war, business and political corruption, widespread dishonesty, and the older generation's poor record of marital stability, youth is no longer convinced of the wrongness of premarital sex or that marriage is an ultimately desirable goal (Teen-age sex).

It might be mentioned that those youngsters who take drugs are apparently more likely to have premarital coitus than nonusers. However, rather than drugs leading to greater or earlier sexual activity, it would appear that if a youth breaks one cardinal rule of society (in this case, taking drugs) it is easier for him to break other ones—specifically, the proscriptions against premarital sex (Teen-age sex). This same premise is, of course, equally applicable to the behavior of adults.

In every society there will be a cadre of rebellious youth, whose behavior will outrage certain segments of its citizenry. Unfortunately such outrage has a tendency to radiate in the public mind to include all youth. Given our present-day climate of unrest, the only surprise is that there are not more acts of rebellion. In actuality, group rebellion has often forced some of our most needed social reforms, although such insurgence is interpreted by many simply as further evidence of the failure of adults to maintain proper control of their charges.

As an aside on notions about today's alleged moral decay, John Gagnon, a noted sociologist and sexologist, offers an interesting insight into the formulation of rumors and opinions and how they become assimilated into individual attitudes (Gagnon b). One person relates to another, as an example, that he has the flu. The other responds by saying that he also has a touch of flu, and that several members of his family have likewise been unwell. He then comments to a co-worker later in the day to the effect that there is "certainly a lot of flu going around," although in reality its incidence at that time might be quite low. The only infection here is the infusion of one person's attitude into another's through verbal interchange.

This sort of "infection" is even more likely to occur in discussions of the supersensitive topic of premarital sexual intercourse. Because the subject is a "hot" one, rumors about prevailing sexual behavior spread far more rapidly than rumors about such pedestrian subjects as a flu epidemic. Furthermore, there is far less possibility of checking out the accuracy of sex-related rumors (Gagnon *b*). By this process of attitudinal infection, certain segments of the public come to believe that there is a general moral decay among today's young adults.

RELIGIOUS, RACIAL, AND CULTURAL INFLUENCES ON SEXUAL ATTITUDES

Almost all studies of the subject have shown that the intensity of religious belief greatly influences people's attitude toward and involvement in sexual behavior. "When age, marital status, size of hometown, fraternity membership, father's political inclination, and religious affiliation are each held constant, the relationship between sex attitudes and religiosity remains significant. These tests lead one to conclude that there is a relationship between the importance one attaches to religious matters and one's attitude toward premarital sexual relations, a relationship which cannot be accounted for by any of the background factors tested" (Dedman).

Among whites, the more devout and frequent a churchgoer an individual is, the less liberal his sexual attitudes and behavior are likely to be. This finding holds for both white males and females, but is considerably stronger among women than among men. However, these findings do not hold for black subjects to a significant degree. Recent studies have found that three to four times more black girls than white girls experience premarital coitus in their teens. Furthermore, more grammar-school- and high-school-educated black girls have experienced coitus than have white boys of the same educational level (Rainwater *a*). Blacks, both male and female, are much more likely to view premarital coitus as acceptable behavior than are whites, a finding that holds true even when socioeconomic and education factors, as well as the incomes and occupations of the fathers, are matched between the two racial groups (Reiss *g*).

Another contrast between the sexual attitudes of blacks and those of whites is interesting. Upper- and middle-class blacks are much less accepting of premarital coitus than are those of the lower class, but among whites this disparity is not found. Indeed, since the 1940s the upper- and middle-class white groups have become increasingly accepting of premarital sexual relations (Reiss *j*; Sutker and Kilpatrick).

In the light of the data contained in Table 16.2, attitudinal permissiveness toward premarital sexual behavior appears to be most liberal among black males, followed by white males, black females, and, finally, white females (Reiss e).

TABLE 16.2 Sexual Permissiveness in Relation to Race, Sex, & Church Attendance

	FREQUENT CHURCH ATTENDANCE		INFREQUENT CHURCH ATTENDANCE	
	Male	*Female*	*Male*	*Female*
White	40%	5%	77%	53%
Black	83%	44%	91%	58%

Attitudes toward first coitus and other sexual experiences and the significance of them to the individual vary considerably, as well, according to social class and educational group. Members of one group frequently view the behavior of another with fascination, contempt, disbelief, or horror.

A study of three groups of impoverished urban boys (whites from Appalachia, blacks, and Puerto Ricans) showed that all felt abusive and exploitative toward girls and would use them as things, not people (Rosenberg and Bensman). About 85% of Americans never go to college. Yet the 15% who do so make the country's laws, serve as its judges, run its prisons, write its textbooks, edit its newspapers, and generally set the ideal or expected standards of behavior. It is this educated 15% who have declared that "sex is a beautiful and sacred thing." But such a concept is absolutely meaningless to the vast majority of the population (Lowry).

ATTITUDINAL FORMATION IN YOUNG PEOPLE

Many changes in sexual attitudes have their basis in the protracted period of adolescence imposed on present-day American youth. Our society requires longer periods of scholastic and vocational training than ever before, thus extending societal adolescence. Yet today's young people become physically mature at a considerably earlier age than previous generations did. Thus the period of social adolescence is now approximately twice as long as it was 100 years ago (Bell a; Jones).

During this prolonged preparation for adulthood, the two sexes begin to develop divergent attitudes toward premarital sexual activity. The natural feelings of insecurity bred by adolescence and heightened physical drives (especially in boys) make the adolescent particularly susceptible to the hawkings of Madison Avenue extolling the supreme value of sex appeal in attaining popularity, success, admiration, security, and the like. Boys are propagandized through the various mass communication media to believe that their masculinity (*i.e.*, success as a *man*) depends upon their success in seduction. The further they go with girls sexually, the more masculine they are in their own and their peer group's eyes.

Young girls, on the other hand, are indoctrinated by the communication media in the importance of being "sexy." They are lured to purchase an often ludicrous and useless conglomerate of products that, according to the hawkers, are guaranteed to increase sexual attractiveness. A girl is indeed in a delicate position. She must appear and act "sexy" in order to attract as many boys and to have as many dates as possible—the symbols in her all-important peer group of popularity and social success. But at the same time she must hold the line of propriety, because otherwise she risks losing her "good girl" status and, consequently, prestige. Girls—at least in their younger dating years—too often are favorably evaluated by their peer group only in terms of their popularity in dating (and the number of boys whom they cause to make open affectionate commitments), coupled with their ability to remain free of sexual involvements (Bell a; Waller and Hill).

The female sexual tease is also a logical outcome of such attitudes. She may become what Albert Ellis terms a Donna Juanita, a female Don Juan: able to satisfy her needs only when she knows she has captured a man's attention and has made him desire her sexually. If she can accomplish this goal without coition, so much the better, for underlying this syndrome are pervading doubts about her sexual desirability and capability. Frequently she sees herself as being in competition with all women, so that the only male who can fulfill her needs is one already committed to another woman (Mathis c).

The dynamics behind such a girl's need to be appreciated for her physical attractiveness are easy to understand. When as a young child she wore a pretty dress and smiled sweetly, she gained considerable attention simply because of her comeliness. A small boy, however, does not win attention similarly. He must "do something" to prove his worth—flex his muscles, show how fast he can run, or boast that he can whip other boys in fights. Thus, an attractive physical appearance often becomes a woman's key to recognition, whereas physical power or success is the indicator of a male's desirability. Indeed, 82% of men report that sexual attraction was a distinct factor in their selection of a partner, whereas it figures in the choice of only 50% of women (Greene, B. L.).

Younger teen-agers tend to accept uncritically the traditional sexual standards of their parents. But as they grow older and begin to think increasingly independently of their parents, they come to a progressively greater extent under the influence of outside values, particularly those of their peer group. They begin to adopt a more permissive sexual code of behavior (Bell a; Reiss c). Gradually learning from older adolescents that the preachments of their conscientious parents are not so fearsome as they had once believed, they begin to reject them. Old sanctions of eternal damnation in punishment for transgression cease to be threatening. Teen-agers also learn from their peers how to keep from being "found out" and thus to avoid parental or societal wrath.

Young people today challenge more and more openly the legitimacy of religious and social institutions that for centuries have been regarded as sacred (Shiloh). They no longer readily accept theological doctrine or traditional codes of ethics as guidelines for their sexual behavior (Blaine).

Many youths lead well-behaved, orderly, moral lives simply because they fear the consequences of doing otherwise. Therefore, when they reject their old patterns of behavior they have no standard by which to conduct their lives, and are left to their impulses and strong sexual feelings (Frank). Sensible parents should anticipate these possibilities and take proper steps to instill in their children a realistic code of ethical behavior, a code that will retain its validity after the children have left the home and its direct influence. The edict "don't do it because you will be punished" simply will not hold over the years.

A close, accepting, and loving family relationship is far more effective in controlling the sexual behavior of teen-agers than are threats of dire punishment, eternal or temporal. Research shows that girls who get along well with their fathers and mothers are far less likely to be sexually experienced than those who do not. The same holds true for boys who get along well with their mothers (Kirkendall and Libby *b*).

Self-Defeating Teen-Age Behavior

Girls in their mid-teens begin to recognize that, in our society, the male is supposed to be strong and confident, and to offer security to his female. Not having the insight, tutelage, or experience to evaluate what constitutes genuine strength on the part of boy or man and, furthermore, feeling inadequate themselves, many girls actually do not know what to look for by way of indicators of masculine strength, and may come to accept certain warped manifestations as qualities of manliness.

These are the girls who are often impressed by the antiestablishment youth who is defiant of rules and of the society that makes them; the school drop-out committed to drugs, tobacco, alcohol, and profanity, and to little else in life; the motorcyclist or dragster who is as reckless of human life as he is of human sensibilities. These girls have no way of assessing such behavioral patterns as being attempts by the boys to mask the marked feelings of inferiority that threaten to overwhelm them.

The very things, therefore, that a young girl wishes to avoid—inadequacy and weakness in a man—are what she is unwittingly courting when she looks to the "tough guy" as an ideal. An unfortunate by-product of this twisted set of values is that the "nice" boy, who displays kindness and honesty in his dealing with others and has no need to prove his adequacy by unacceptable acting-out behavior, is often ignored or regarded with downright contempt by such a girl.

Other factors enter into the emotional complexities of such girls. They are crossing the threshold into physical maturity and feel inadequate to cope with the accompanying social and sexual problems. Since such girls evaluate themselves as rather worthless and insufficient beings, the boys who behave decently and compassionately toward them cannot, they reason, have very good judgment. Or if the boys offer their friendship so unselfishly, they must not be of much value themselves.

It follows, according to these girls' rationale, that the boys who callously ignore or mistreat them are exhibiting good judgment, and are therefore the obviously strong masculine ones, the social or sexual worthies. Furthermore, these girls have normal sexual desires and wishes, but frequently feel guilty about them; and it ensues in their thinking that, in our society, guilt demands punishment. Therefore, by selecting one of the "tough guys," such a girl is able not only to satisfy her sexual desires but at the same time to assure her punishment because, unconsciously or otherwise, she realizes that, sooner or later, she will be mistreated or rejected by this unsavory boy. It is, incidentally, a widely recognized phenomenon among psychotherapists and marriage counselors that many women marry "problem" men—for example, alcoholics—because they have an unconscious need to be punished.

Drug abuse is possibly the most dangerous of the pseudo solutions used by insecure, discomfited teen-agers. Boys and girls who feel alienated from their families and the society in which they live are prime targets for drug abuse. There are also those who, feeling insecure, attempt to assure the approval of their peer group by experimenting with drugs to show that they are not "chicken"—that they are worthy of being a part of "in-group."

Parents, Children, and Sexuality

Clinical observations and the results of empirical research have frequently underlined the marked discrepancy between what parents have themselves experienced (or are experiencing) by way of sexual activity, and the code of sexual ethics they profess to their children. It is also interesting that the parent's own attitude of sexual permissiveness is unrelated to the attitude of permissiveness held by the student son or daughter. However, how the student *perceives* or *interprets* his parents' sexual permissiveness is related to his own permissiveness (Walsh).

Psychotherapists have long observed more regret among women who remained virgins till marriage than among those women who did not. These clinical observations have been upheld by the results of several investigations (Bell a; Burgess and Wallin; Kinsey et al. c), which show that those women who have had premarital coition are not sorry. They maintain that they would repeat their behavior if they had it to do over again; *however*, they expect their daughters to conform to a more conservative ethic (Burgess and Wallin; Kinsey et al. c). Essentially the same findings have been reported by Cuber and Harroff, whose sampling was from the highly educated influential upper-middle-class stratum of society.

In a recent study, 30% of the mothers interviewed admitted that they had experienced premarital coitus. But only 3% of them had a permissive attitude toward like behavior in their daughters, and 9% toward their sons. Slightly over 50% of the fathers in this study reported that they had experienced premarital coition. But less than 10% expressed a permissive attitude toward their daughters' experiencing premarital coitus, and less than 20% toward their sons' doing so (Wake).

The question naturally arises: why have mothers behaved in one way and felt no regret, yet expected their daughters to behave in a contrary manner? The explanation lies primarily in the significant differences between men and women in their perception of the relationship between sexual attraction and emotional commitment (Ehrmann a).

For a man, love typically follows sexual attraction, whereas, for a woman, sexual involvement follows romantic attachment (Calderone d; Ehrmann a, b; Kronhausen and Kronhausen). Usually, a woman must have a strong emotional attachment before she allows herself to become sexually involved. She must be convinced that it is she, the person, who is important to the relationship, not simply her sexual potential (Vincent b). A recent investigation, for instance, demonstrated that women enter a university with conservative sexual attitudes, then shift later in their academic life to more liberal ones, but *only* if they develop a deep emotional attachment or become engaged (Bell and Buerkle). The liberalizing of their attitudes appears to be an outgrowth of their emotional commitment.

A mother, then, in her own premarital sexual experiences may have had strong feelings regarding the significance of emotional involvement as a precedent to sexual contact, but cannot accept the fact that her daughter also recognizes the importance of this sequence. Furthermore, because she defied the sexual prohibitions of her own rearing by engaging in premarital coitus, the mother may now carry a residual guilt. This guilt can break through and be projected onto her maturing daughter in the form of disapproval of any premarital sexual experience on the part of the girl. In addition, the mother cannot identify sufficiently with the daughter to appreciate the strength of the girl's feelings when she becomes emotionally attached to a young man. Neither can she accept the fact that her daughter has perhaps, after careful thought, evolved a liberal sexual ethic of her own.

The sexually restrictive admonishments through which a mother attempts to indoctrinate her daughter quite likely will be no more effective than they were in her generation. But the unfortunate consequence will be the same—generation after generation of women who tend to follow their emotional and sexual inclinations, but with concomitant guilt and shame, because they have violated the sexual ethic with which they were reared.

Parents stress to their daughters (and, to a lesser extent, to their sons) that love is an important aspect of happiness in boy-girl relationships. They thereby increase the likelihood that their children will engage in premarital sexual intercourse, for research clearly indicates that love is a key motivator in girls' premarital coitus (Ehrmann a, b; Reiss f). The indications are that those girls who start dating, kissing, and other inceptive behavior at an early age are the ones most likely to have early sexual intercourse (Kirkendall and Libby b).

Through a national survey, Reiss appears to have uncovered the answer to the disparity in attitudes between older and younger people regarding premarital intercourse (Reiss j). When he merely compared the two groups as a whole, he found only an 8 or 9 percentage-point difference in attitudes between them (the older group being the more conservative, needless to say). However, when he divided all those in the older group of, say, 45 years of age into subgroups according to whether they were single, married without children, married with young children, or married with teen-age children, he found some radical differences. Acceptance of premarital intercourse spiraled significantly downward within the same age group from the single person to the married, to the married person with young children, to the one with teen-age children. Reiss concluded that these differences in attitude were based not upon age, but upon the individual's feelings of responsibility for the behavior of others, especially his dependents.

This study also showed that, as siblings become older and assume a surrogate-parent role for younger children in the family, their permissiveness toward premarital intercourse declines. Between the ages of 10 and 20, the individual's acceptance of premarital sexual behavior increases markedly. Following marriage, however, it slowly decreases until the children born of the marriage reach the age of 20. A parent aged 40 and his 20-year-old daughter are crossing the opposite ends of the acceptance cycle, one at the low point, the other at the high. Despite these differences, however, almost 66% of the young people surveyed in one broad study expressed the belief that their sexual standards and those of their parents were similar (Reiss a).

THE ROLE OF GUILT IN SEXUAL ATTITUDES AND BEHAVIOR

The more guilt that a youth feels about his sexual behavior the more restricted is his level of intimacy in premarital sexual experiences (Mosher and Cross). However, guilt itself is not necessarily an inhibitor of sexual behavior. Interestingly enough, most young people gradually increase their sexual involvement to minimize whatever guilt they feel about their premarital sexual activity. About 90% of women and 60% of men report that they eventually come to accept the sexual behavior that once made them feel guilty (Reiss a, j).

For example, a couple might begin with kissing only, but feel some guilt about it. They then involve themselves in the kissing behavior again, but this time they do not feel the same degree of guilt. They continue the kissing episodes until the guilt disappears altogether. Next they move to a level of greater sexual intimacy—say, to petting. Again they feel guilty, but they overcome it by repeating the same behavior over and over again until the guilt disappears. They then move to another level of intimacy, and so on.

Ten steps may be involved in the progress from kissing to coitus. Although there is considerable distance between Steps 1 and 10, there is likely to be no more distance between Steps 9 and 10 than there was between Steps 1 and 2. In new dating situations, furthermore, women quickly progress to the level of sexual activity that they had reached in earlier relationships (Ehrmann a). Only the speed with which women move through the various levels of intimacy and the age at which they marry distinguish one from another. Thus a woman who marries early—say, at the age of 18—may not have moved through all 10 levels of sexual intimacy by the time she marries. But the woman who finishes college and does not marry until she is 22 or 23 has had more time in which to progress through the various levels of intimacy. She is therefore less likely to be a virgin at the time of her marriage than the woman who marries at 18.

Slightly over 50% of teen-age girls admit to guilt feelings if they go "too far" in petting with their dates, while only 25% of the boys express similar guilt. These views stand in curious contrast to statements made by the other teen-agers in these samplings (33% of the girls and 75% of the boys) who are more conservative in their sexual conduct, yet indicate that they desire greater sexual intimacy on dates. Boys appear interested in petting and sexual intercourse on dates, while their girl friends are willing to neck (mild embracing and kissing limited to face and lips), but wish to hold the line there (Bell and Blumberg). As the relationship becomes more serious, however—from dating, to going steady, to engagement—sexual behavior becomes more intimate, and guilt over sexual endearments becomes less for both sexes (Bell and Blumberg; Christensen and Carpenter).

Patterns in guilt feelings undergo a change over a period of time in both sexes, especially among older unmarried groups. Clinicians have presented convincing arguments that many men are beset with considerably more guilt over sexual matters than women are. Their premise is that women, in nonmarital sex relationships especially, usually and understandably want reassurance that they are desired and respected for more than their sexual performance. Women also want assurance that their men will not "kiss and tell," and that they will maintain the same level of regard for them after coitus as before.

A man, on the other hand, feels that, as the instigator of the sex act, he is the "seducer," and that the responsibility for the woman's participation rests squarely upon his shoulders. To placate his own guilt or anxiety, therefore, he must feel either that there is love in the relationship, or that the woman is "bad." Furthermore, since he feels guilty about his "seduction" of the woman, he comes to regard her as the instigator of his guilt. He is then impelled to express his hostility and anger by quarreling or fighting with her, speaking to her in a degrading manner, or otherwise manifesting his rejection of her—the very woman who thought enough of him to share with him the most intimate of human experiences.

It is important to human sexual enjoyment, most especially for women, that sex-oriented guilt be reduced to a minimum. Studies have shown that the more guilt over sex that an individual feels, the less is his desire for sex, the fewer orgasms he experiences, and the less sexually responsive he is (Kutner; Leiman and Epstein).

Because of unrealistic romantic ideals, many men and women are unprepared to accept the probability that there are thousands of persons whom they could love and to whom they could be satisfactorily married. If a married man is attracted to another woman, he may interpret it as meaning that he no longer loves his wife. Because he thinks he can love only one woman at a time, he begins, consciously or unconsciously, to concentrate on the negative aspects of his wife and the positive ones of the other woman in order to make the new attraction acceptable to him (Vincent *f*). Or perhaps the husband falls in love with another woman and develops guilt feelings. If he were not married he would feel no guilt; therefore, he reasons unconsciously, his wife is the instigator of his guilt and deserves his hostility. He thereby directs his negative feelings toward his wife, the only innocent party in the triangle.

ATTITUDES TOWARD NONMARITAL SEX

The evidence gathered from questionnaires completed by 20,000 politically liberal men and women—well educated, of high socioeconomic status, and predominantly under 30—revealed that only 1 of 10 advocated chastity until marriage. Over 50% felt that premarital sex equips people for more stable and happier marriages; about 75% had themselves experienced premarital coitus. About 80% of the total sample believed that extramarital sex might be acceptable under certain circumstances, although only about 40% of the men and 36% of the women had actually engaged in it (Athanasiou et al.).

Adultery (nonmarital sexual intercourse between a man and woman, at least one of whom is married at the time to someone else) has been condemned in practically all Western cultures because of the threat it poses to the family unit. Furthermore, it is unequivocally condemned in Judaic–Christian moral theology. In the history of no culture, however, has men's extramarital coition been consistently controlled or severely punished, whereas women have universally been subjected to a much more stringent code of sexual ethics. These differences in attitude are primarily a result of the fact that, if women were to engage in extramarital coitus, it would threaten the economic stability of the entire society, would reflect on the masculinity and social prestige of their husbands, and, in the case of pregnancy, could raise the question of paternal responsibility (Harper a).

Extramarital coitus causes more complications for the middle classes than for either the higher or lower social classes. Wives of low social status appear rather to expect their husbands to form outside attachments; and they seem not to object to these affairs so long as they are not conducted flagrantly. At the upper social levels, persons involved in an extramarital affair exert sufficient and intelligent care so that no one learns of it (Kinsey et al. a).

Wives at every social level are more condoning of their husbands' extramarital affairs than husbands are of adultery on the part of their wives. Only 27% of the women in Kinsey's sample said that they would consider their husband's adultery sufficient grounds for seeking a divorce, while 51% of the men indicated they would regard infidelity on the part of their wives as being totally destructive of the marriage (Kinsey et al. a, c).

Perhaps husbands would be less upset by their wives' infidelity if they realized with what detachment and dispassion some women can manage an extramarital affair, sexual or otherwise. A certain type of woman can "love and leave," or have coitus with a man, and then attend to her obligations at home without remaining emotionally involved or carrying residuals of guilt. Neither does she necessarily compare her husband's sexual skills unfavorably with those of her lover, which an adulterous husband sometimes does. Tradition would have us believe that the man is the emotionally controlled and dispassionate one in a marriage. Yet in the majority of cases it is he who, upon the discovery of infidelity, rants, threatens, retaliates, divorces, or even kills one or both lovers (English b).

Among lower social groups, Kinsey's study found a considerable amount of extramarital coitus of which the partner was aware. Yet this knowledge did not appear to interfere with the affection between husband

and wife or the stability of the marriage, since the adultery was kept on a more or less physical basis. Nevertheless, extramarital intercourse actually caused less difficulty in the marriages within higher social groups because persons other than the two people involved very seldom knew about it (Kinsey *et al. c*).

Although extramarital affairs incur moral, legal, and social condemnation, and often create unique difficulties for one or both partners, the participants nonetheless frequently view their attachment as an opportunity for love, excitement, adventure, romance, renewed vigor, enhanced ego, and return to youth—all the dreams that marriage was supposed to fulfill but did not, or no longer does. The partners, however, are frequently disappointed in their expectations.

In his book *Extra-marital Relationships*, Gerhard Neubeck has made a perceptive study of the motivation in adultery. The reasons most frequently given by men for sexual infidelity are these: desire for variety in sexual experience, retaliation, rebellion, new emotional satisfaction, the unexpected evolution of sexual involvement from friendship, the wife's encouragement, and the aging factor. The research cited by Neubeck suggests that marital infidelity (sexual or emotional) is not *necessarily* related to either unsatisfactory or weak marital relationships nor to neurotic inclinations or personalities.

The constellation of motives surrounding extramarital sexual relations is coming to be better understood. A young man proves his worth by various accomplishments, the first of which is winning the "right" woman. As he grows older, he strives to maintain that image by succeeding in educational, business, and community pursuits. His wife, who has never been able to separate her sense of worth from the ability to attract men by her physical appearance and charm, finds that she now plays a secondary role in his upward migration. In his absorption in his work, he may ignore her, causing her to begin questioning her self-worth.

Compounding a woman's self-doubts at this point is the dwindling importance of her maternal role as, one by one, her children leave home. She now develops a growing awareness that she is nearing or has passed what most consider to be the apex of physical attractiveness. At this point she may begin to look outside her marriage—often to a man 10 to 15 years her junior or senior—to gain reassurance that she is still physically attractive and sexually desirable (Vincent *i*).

Thus it appears that in prolonged extramarital affairs, sexual fulfillment is not the overriding motivation. Most of these relationships endure primarily for reasons that fall somewhere between intellectual and sexual fulfillment. The relationships may last for 10, 15, even 20 years. Mistresses of middle-aged men are not the young voluptuous women that the stereotype would have us believe. They are, rather, near the age of the men involved, and they work to support themselves (Cuber).

Men and women maintain prolonged extramarital relationships for several reasons. Either they cannot have the relationship on any other basis, or they wish to escape the "entrapments" of marriage—caring for children, maintaining a "public image," and other obligations—or they are disenchanted with the institution of marriage. The last group sums up its position with "romance, yes—marriage, no" (Cuber).

SEXUAL ATTITUDES AND MARITAL ADJUSTMENT

Finally, there must be an appreciation of the role that personality plays in the creation of sexual attitudes. In a particularly meaningful study by A. H. Maslow (*d*), the importance of emotions and of personality factors in marital happiness and sexual adjustment is clearly indicated. Following are some of his related findings.

Women who rate high in dominance feelings (or high self-esteem) are considered to be self-confident and self-assured, and to possess a high evaluation of the self. They display feelings of superiority while showing a lack of shyness, self-consciousness, and embarrassment. Women who empirically rate low in dominance feelings (low self-esteem) show the opposite personality characteristics, while middle-dominance subjects fall about midway between the two extremes. Because dominance traits affect behavior as well as feelings, high-dominance women are much more likely than low-dominance subjects to masturbate, to have premarital sexual intercourse, to volunteer for sex research studies, not to shun pelvic examinations, and the like (Maslow *d*).

However, despite the fact that Jewish women are generally found to be higher in both dominance feelings and dominance behavior than Catholic and Protestant women, they show a higher percentage of virginity than either of the other two religious groups. Women who are *strongly* religious—whether Jewish, Catholic, or Protestant—are more likely to be virgins, not to masturbate, and to have lower ratings for "sex attitude" (a term used by Maslow to describe personal reactions to sexuality) than women with less pronounced religious feelings.

Women of low dominance feelings avoid the upper position during sexual intercourse while those with very high dominance feelings frequently prefer that position. The low-dominance man or woman often dislikes or is afraid of sex. The most satisfactory marriages are those in which the husband equals or is somewhat (but not markedly) superior to his wife in dominance feelings. On the other hand, if the wife has higher dominance feelings than the husband, or if the husband is markedly more dominant than the wife, social and sexual maladjustments are likely to be found, unless both are very secure persons. Moderately sexed women are more likely to reach orgasm during sexual activity if they feel loved and secure than if these components are weak or lacking entirely. In the matter of sheer sexual satisfaction, a monogamous state is preferable to a promiscuous choice of sexual partners, but monogamy does not satisfy the emotional needs of ego-insecure people.

A high-dominance woman is attracted only to a high-dominance man and wants him to be straightforward, passionate, and somewhat violent or animalistic in their lovemaking. She wishes him to proceed quickly without prolonged wooing. The middle-dominance woman prefers gentle, prolonged wooing where sex, as such, is woven into a pattern of loving words, tenderness, soft music, and low lights. As Maslow puts it, "The high-dominance woman unconsciously wants to be raped; the middle-dominance woman wants to be seduced" (c). He might have added that the low-dominance woman wishes to be left alone.

People who are rated high in "sex attitude" appreciate sex for its own sake and wholeheartedly approve of it, while people who are rated very low are highly puritanical and inhibited in their sexual attitudes, and reject sex as something disgusting. A large portion of the high-dominance subjects like and engage in oral-genital activity; and generally speaking, the higher the dominance rating (with ego-security held constant), the more attractive they find the external genitalia of the sexual partner. In marriages of high-dominance people, the couples very frequently have experimented with almost every form of sexual activity known to sexologists. While these sexual acts would likely be considered pathological by low-dominance subjects, they contain no pathological connotation for high-dominance subjects. Maslow is thus led to conclude: "It would appear that no single sexual act can *per se* be called abnormal or perverted. It is only abnormal or perverted individuals who can commit abnormal or perverted acts. That is, the dynamic meaning of the act is far more important than the act itself" (c).

Although marital happiness depends to an important degree upon sexual adjustment, the consistent observation of clinicians is that sexual adjustment in marriage is possible even when sexual responsiveness is nominal. Furthermore, if most other areas of the marital interrelationship are satisfactory, a wife may consider herself happy in marriage even though she is unresponsive sexually. Conversely, when any significant nonsexual aspect of the marriage is unsatisfactory, a wife may be unhappy in marriage even though she may be highly responsive sexually (Adams).

In his 1929 book *Research in Marriage*, G. V. Hamilton, a prominent early researcher in the field of marriage, reported that almost 75% of the divorced women interviewed did not experience orgasms during their first year of marriage. Some 20 years later, another renowned researcher in this field, H. J. Locke, reported that 90% of happily married women found pleasure in sex while only about 50% of divorced women had done so.

P. H. Gebhard discovered in his research that wives who reach orgasm

90% to 100% of the time in marital coitus are more often found in "very happy" marriages than in any others. Only 4% of women in "very happy" marriages never reach orgasm in coitus. This percentage gradually increases in the other marital-happiness categories, reaching 19% in marriages classified as "very unhappy." Researchers have concluded that marital happiness and female orgasm do correlate, but only in marriages at both extremes of the continuum (Gebhard *a*).

Most of the scientifically sound research into the effects of a woman's premarital sexual experiences on her marital adjustment show that there is only a slight correlation between happiness in marriage and premarital experience (Anderson, W. J.; Burgess and Wallin; Reiss *h*). However small the correlation, the indications are slightly in favor of premarital chastity.

The relationships between sexual satisfaction and marital satisfaction are complexly intertwined. A wife's sex interest and responsiveness are directly related to her husband's sexual satisfaction, which in turn contributes to his marital satisfaction, which increases her sex interest and responsiveness . . . *ad infinitum* (Udry *b*).

A word about affection. Many people in our culture, especially men, have difficulty entering into a warm, close, loving interchange with others. Little boys are often taught that to be tender and compassionate is to show characteristics of being a "sissy"; little girls are admonished that it is "forward" to be warmly responsive. Growing up in an environment that restricts positive emotional responses makes it likely that the individual will learn to express only negative emotions, such as anger and hostility. Nonetheless, these people grow into adulthood with the abstract knowledge that some warm emotional exchanges are vital and expected in successful sexual interaction. But because they learned in their formative years to express only negative emotional responses, such people will actually instigate quarrels or fights with their sexual partner in order to express the only type of emotionality they understand. Men who have never learned how to express tenderness, or who are afraid to do so, will often ignore the woman with whom they are sexually involved, or make belittling remarks to her. These men *want* to demonstrate their commitment but, not knowing how to use the appropriate positive emotions, they use the only emotional expressions that they are familiar with—the negative ones.

Wives often accuse their husbands of showing affection toward them only when they have intercourse in mind; husbands deny this. What often happens is that the husband commences simply to show affection to his wife with no ulterior motive in mind; but in the process of expressing affection, especially if his wife responds warmly, he becomes sexually excited. The wife then judges only in terms of the final outcome.

Fortunately, both men and women can be taught to allow themselves the joy of experiencing close, warm, and loving relationships. If they have not acquired this knowledge through normal maturational processes, or through experience and observation, psychotherapy can help them gain insight into the immense value of manifestations of affection. When men and women recognize that free expression of affection is certainly nothing to fear, nor a barometer of weakness or effeminacy, all their human relationships, including the sexual one, will be much fuller and happier.

Much is heard today about the role of love in all aspects of human behavior, most especially human sexual behavior. The arguments range from "sex is empty and animalistic without love" to "sex can be fun and enjoyable without love and those who insist upon imposing love into a sexual relation are simply guilty about sex and trying to convince themselves that the act can somehow be made acceptable."

Points are often made concerning the difference between "loving someone" and "being in love with someone," the first usually interpreted to mean a deep concern over the welfare of a person, the second a romantic or sexual feeling for him or her. The two types of love are not, of course, necessarily exclusive. Indeed, in courtship days, in the early part of most marriages, and in those fortunate marriages of long and happy duration, the two coexist. It is when the romance, excitement, and "magic" disappear or significantly decrease in a marriage that the marriage counselor most often hears "I still love my husband [or wife] but I am just not 'in love' with him anymore." Such a state can be dangerous in any marriage; it can be disastrous when either or both spouses are immature or hold unreasonable expectations for their marriage. Married partners frequently use the excuse of no longer being "in love" with their mates as a license to seek romance with another person.

From earliest recorded history the word *love* has carried thousands of definitions and meanings. Probably the description of perfect love that best fits the concept embodied in the world's great religions—Christianity, Judaism, Islamism, Hinduism, and Buddhism—is stated in the thirteenth chapter of First Corinthians (Lederer and Jackson): "Love is patient, kind, non-envious, never boastful, not conceited, not rude, never selfish, not quick to take offense. Love holds no grudges and delights not in sin, but in truth. It believes, hopes, and endures all things. . . . There are three lasting values: faith, hope, and love. The greatest of these is love" (McCary and McElhaney).

The great American psychiatrist Harry Stack Sullivan offers perhaps a more practical definition of love in *Conceptions of Modern Psychiatry:* "When the satisfaction or the security of another person becomes as significant to one as is one's own satisfaction or security, then the state of love exists."

In the First Isadore Rubin Memorial Lecture, Mary S. Calderone pointed out how the word *love* has been made to "cover such a multitude of trivial as well as important emotions that . . . it has been downgraded from 18 to 6 carats" (*f*)! For example, because one of the almost constant aspects of love is longing, the unwanted, unloved child silently wishes each morning that "my mother [or father] will love me today." That person is likely to carry this longing into adulthood, translating it to mean "I wish that he [or she] will *desire* me today," thus erroneously equating sexual desire with love.

For Dr. Calderone, a condition much more realistic than love in meaningful human relationship is *intimacy*, which is fundamental to love. Two basic requirements for the evolution of intimacy are time and privacy, because they provide the opportunity for development of its five primary components. In order of development, these components are: *choice, mutuality, reciprocity, trust,* and *delight.* One chooses, on a conscious basis, those few with whom he or she can or shall be intimate. The choice must be a mutual one, since a unilateral choice would obviously exclude intimacy. In true intimacy one cannot be more intimate than the other, thus the third component, reciprocity. But none of the foregoing will prevail and thrive without mutual trust, a step involving multiple small revealments as each individual opens his innermost self to the other. Small revelations about himself allow the individual to test the safety of revealment. As trust is built on these successive, successful experiences, intimacy develops to its ultimate expression—delight in one another.

The delight of two people in one another "in an atmosphere of security based on mutuality, reciprocity, and trust . . . whatever their age or sex, this surely is what we all seek in human relationships yet do not all achieve, certainly never in quality, in our lives. . . ." If this sort of intimacy develops and persists over the years, Dr. Calderone suggests, neither major physical infirmities, nor aging, nor fading physical handsomeness, nor reduced sexual potency, nor even infidelity will destroy the relationship. "In intimacy two people are constantly saying to each other without words, 'I delight in you as a whole person and you delight me, and I can, I want to, I *may,* express this delight in such and such ways' " (Calderone f). One of the most meaningful ways—because it is one of the most delightful—is through sexual expression. Perhaps intimacy is the force that binds "loving" someone and being "in love" with someone.

17 SEXUAL BEHAVIOR IN REVIEW

In earlier chapters key physiological, psychological, and social factors in the sexuality of men and women have been examined, at different stages of development and in many contexts. In this chapter the most common forms of human sexual behavior are reviewed, enabling the reader to place insights gained from earlier chapters into better focus.

THE SEX DRIVE

Of interest are certain shifts in the sexual patterns of both men and women as they grow older. A lad in his teens ordinarily has a very strong sex drive and is capable of almost instant erection; four to eight orgasms a day are not unusual. The refractory period after his first orgasm may last only seconds. He usually wants sexual release whether or not he has any emotional attachment to the sex object, and whether or not he is occupied with other matters, such as school or sports. If no sexual partner is available, he will achieve sexual release through masturbation and nocturnal emission.

As a man approaches his 30s he remains highly interested in sex, but

295

the urgency is less acute and he is satisfied with fewer orgasms. Erections still occur quickly and detumescence is slow to take place, but by his late 30s the refractory period has lengthened to 30 minutes or more. Sexual slackening continues through the 40s. By the age of 50, the average man is satisfied with two orgasms a week and the refractory period is commonly 8 to 24 hours. At this age, the focus of sexual pleasure has usually shifted from an intense genitally centered sensation to a more generalized sensuously diffused experience (Kaplan and Sager).

The development of sexuality reveals far more individual variation among women than among men. Typically, women's sexual awakening is a slower process, not reaching its peak until the late 30s or early 40s. Women do not appear to experience the same sexual urgency during their lives that men do. In their teens and 20s their orgasmic response is slower and less consistent than it is in their 40s. In their 30s, and frequently after childbirth, women begin to respond more intensely to sexual stimulation. They also initiate the sex act more frequently than they did in the past. The incidence of extramarital sex is greatest among women in their late 30s. Vaginal lubrication (the measure of female sexual response equivalent to male erection) occurs almost instantly for women in this age group, and many experience multiple orgasms.

Women in their 50s and 60s may experience a slight decline in sex drive and are usually less preoccupied with sex than in their earlier years. But they still seek out and respond to sexual situations, and masturbation either to supplement coitus or as the sole method of satisfying sexual needs is quite common. Although a woman's sexual response moderates as she ages, she remains quite capable of multiple orgasms—even until her late years. She apparently maintains the same physical potential for orgasm at age 80 that she had at age 20. Learning is an extremely important determinant in female sexuality, whereas it is of relatively less importance in the male (Kaplan and Sager).

Human sexuality ordinarily expresses itself in six ways: masturbation, nocturnal orgasm, heterosexual petting, homosexual relations, sexual contact with animals, and heterosexual intercourse (Kinsey *et al. a, c*)—the order in which they will be discussed in this chapter.

It should be noted that, for the purposes of this discussion, the levels of educational achievement referred to should read as follows:

grade-school (low educational group)—8 years of schooling or less;
high-school (middle educational group)—9 to 12 years of schooling;
college (high educational group)—13 years of schooling or more.

Reference is also made in this chapter to the incidence and frequency of the various patterns of sexual behavior. *Incidence* refers to the number of individuals in a sample population who have experienced a particular form of behavior, whether one time only or 1000 times. *Frequency* refers to the number of times that the particular form of behavior has been engaged in by the same person (or by a percentage of the population).

MASTURBATION

The term *masturbation* is applied to any type of self-stimulation that produces erotic arousal (Kinsey *et al. a*). It is a common sexual practice among both males and females in premarital, marital, and postmarital states. Boys and girls begin the practice at an early age, 13% of both sexes in Kinsey's sample having masturbated by their tenth birthday (Kinsey *et al. c*; Reevy).

Males

The incidence of masturbation to the point of orgasm among men is generally fixed at about 95% of the total male population. The college group in Kinsey's study had the highest incidence (96%); those who had attended only high school, second highest (95%); and those who had attended only grade school, the lowest (89%) (Bell *a*; Kinsey *et al. a*). Slightly over 67% of all boys experience their first ejaculation through masturbation; about 75% learn how to masturbate from verbal or printed sources (Kinsey *et al. a*; Rubin *b*).

On the average, adolescent boys masturbate about 2.5 times a week, although 17% masturbate from 4 to 7 (or more) times a week. The incidence of masturbation in men declines progressively in postadolescent years, although some men frequently continue to masturbate on a sporadic basis throughout adult life (Ford and Beach *b*). About 70% of married American men who have graduated from college will masturbate occasionally (for 9% of their total sexual outlet). The incidence is considerably lower in the married male grade-school group (29%) and in the married high-school group (42%). Approximately 25% of all married men above the age of 60 who are capable of satisfactory coitus also masturbate (Kinsey *et al. a*; Rubin *b*).

Kinsey's study showed that genital manipulation was by far the most common technique of masturbation among men (95%). In 72% of the cases, fantasy always accompanied masturbation; in another 17%, fantasy was present only occasionally (Kinsey *et al. a*).

Masturbation among the men in the Kinsey sample occurred most frequently among religiously inactive Protestants, and least among orthodox Jews and devout Roman Catholics (Kinsey *et al. a*).

Females

According to Kinsey's findings, masturbation ranks second only to heterosexual petting among the erotic activities of unmarried young women (comprising 37% to 85% of their total sexual outlet, depending upon the subcultural group), and second after coition among married women (about 10% of their total sexual outlet). From the late teens to the age of 45 and after, the incidence of masturbation increased for all groups of women in the Kinsey sample (*Kinsey et al.* c).

Of all types of sexual activity among women, masturbation ranks first as the most successful method of reaching orgasm—in 95% of its incidence, a climax is reached. Furthermore, women reach orgasm more quickly through masturbation than through any other sexual technique (75% in under four minutes) (Kinsey *et al.* c).

From 50% to 80% of all women masturbate at one time or another in their lives, whether or not they are aware of it (the variance in figures resulting from differences among the results of several investigations into the subject). Many women do not recognize that indirect, pleasurable stimulation of the genitals, as in squeezing the thighs together or riding horseback, can be considered a form of masturbation.

The Kinsey group reported that 34% of the women who had never gone past grade school, 59% of the women who had attended high school but not college, and 63% of the female college graduates had masturbated (Kinsey *et al.* c). Recent studies indicate that these percentages are little different today from what they were in the 1953 Kinsey study (Davis, K. E.).

The range of masturbatory frequency among the women in Kinsey's sample was from once or twice in a lifetime to 100 orgasms an hour. Of those women who masturbated to the point of orgasm, however, there was a striking similarity in frequency, regardless of age or marital status: once every two to four weeks (Kinsey *et al.* c).

Most (57%) of the women in the Kinsey study accidentally discovered how to masturbate by exploring their own genitals. Another 40% learned techniques of autoeroticism through verbal or printed sources (Kinsey *et al.* c).

In contrast to men, among whom there is a decline in the frequency of masturbation after the teen-age years, the active incidence of self-stimulation to orgasm among women increases up to middle age, after which time it remains fairly constant (Kinsey *et al.* c). Of the unmarried women between 50 and 70 years of age in one study, 59% admitted to autoeroticism, as compared with 30% of the married women in the same age group (Sex behavior of older women).

The large majority of women (84%) in Kinsey's sample who stimulated themselves used genital manipulation, while a few others employed thigh pressure (10%), muscular tension (5%), or simply fantasy unattended by physical stimulation (2%). Fantasy was an invariable accompaniment to masturbation for 50% of the women who stimulated themselves, but only an occasional one for a few others (14%) (Kinsey *et al. c*).

Among those women who had never masturbated to orgasm before marriage, 31% to 37% failed to reach orgasm during coitus the first year of marriage, while of those who had previously masturbated to orgasm, only 13% to 16% failed to have coital orgasm the first year (Kinsey *et al. c*).

Religious background is related to the frequency of masturbation. The more devout the religious commitment, the lower the incidence of auto-eroticism (Kinsey *et al. c*).

NOCTURNAL ORGASM

It has long been recognized that men experience nocturnal emissions or "wet dreams." Although women obviously cannot have nocturnal emissions, it is nonetheless true that they too have erotic dreams, which frequently culminate in orgasm. Curiously, however, this type of sexual outlet is persistently ignored in studies of female sexuality (Kinsey *et al. c*). (For both men and women, sexual dreams often have a distressing way of stopping just short of orgasm.)

Today, guilt is rarely associated with nocturnal emission, but in 1930 a well-known sex educator had the following to say on the subject:

> [It is] nothing to be alarmed about. It is perfectly natural; even the saints had to suffer it. The only thing to remember is that you are not allowed to cause the emission intentionally; and, secondly, although you cannot help feeling the pleasure if you awake, you must not surrender yourself to the pleasure accompanying the emission. You are not bound to stop the emission; you probably could not do so anyway. The best procedure is: try to think of something else, forget about the emission, say a Hail Mary, and turn over and go to sleep.... Any intentional causing of the emission is serious, especially because of the frightful habit it starts so easily. This sin is called self-abuse (Kirsch).

Whether the above passage offered adolescent boys much insight into nocturnal emission is problematical, but it certainly revealed quite a bit about its author.

Males

Almost 100% of the men in Kinsey's sample had experienced erotic dreams, and almost 85% had had dreams that culminated in orgasm. Erotic dreams occurred most frequently among young men in their teens and 20s, but approximately 50% of all the married men continued to have nocturnal emissions. This form of sexual expression constituted 5% to 12%

of the total sexual outlet for the single men, 3% to 5% of the total outlet for the married men, and from 4% to 6% for previously married men. Because married men of all ages have a much greater opportunity for release of sexual tension than single men do, the frequency of nocturnal emission among them was only about 66% that of the single men (Kinsey et al. a, c).

The incidence of nocturnal emission was found to be considerably higher among college youths than among the less well educated, probably because college men do more petting that is not followed by orgasm, so that their sexual tensions are therefore more often at a high pitch at bedtime. Over 99% of the college men had had sexual dreams to orgasm at some time during their lives; but only 85% of those who had attended only high school, and 75% whose education had ended at grade school had had nocturnal emissions (Kinsey et al. a).

This form of sexual outlet is unique in that it is beyond the individual's conscious control. The incidence of nocturnal emission, therefore, bears little relationship to religious affiliation or strength of religious conviction.

Females

As many as 70% of all the women in Kinsey's sample had had dreams of sexual content, although only about half had had dreams culminating in orgasm (Kinsey et al. c). Because a woman, unlike a man, reveals no physical evidence that an orgasm did occur, there is some question concerning the accuracy of data showing that 37% of the women actually did dream to orgasm. However, there was no doubt in the minds of the women having the dreams that orgasm had occurred.

The incidence of sexual dreams to orgasm reaches a peak among the women in their 40s. Kinsey's research showed that women in all age groups, married or single, had an average of 3 or 4 such dreams a year. Over one-fourth of the married women (28%) and more than one-third of those previously married (38%) had had dreams to orgasm. These dreams constituted 2% to 4% of the total release from sexual tension for the single girls, 1% to 3% for the married women, and among the previously married, 4% to 14% (Kinsey et al. c).

There was no correlation between frequency of nocturnal dreams to orgasm and a woman's religious or educational background, although fewer women of devout religious convictions than those of less serious commitment ever had such dreams (Kinsey et al. c).

HETEROSEXUAL PETTING

The sexual outlet termed *heterosexual petting* involves conscious, sexually oriented physical contact between persons of opposite sex that does not involve actual coitus (Kinsey *et al. c*). In the context of this discussion, the significance of petting as a means of sexual expression will be limited to premarital petting, inasmuch as petting in marriage is assumed to be a foreplay to sexual intercourse or an outlet chosen by the partners in preference to coition as a means of achieving orgasm.

Petting is by no means limited to human beings; many lower animals employ varying forms of it both before and after copulation. The significance of petting for both man and lower animals as an arousal technique in relation to coitus is widely recognized. Petting is also useful to human beings as a means of achieving orgasm, especially during the years before marriage.

Males

There was a somewhat higher incidence of petting in Kinsey's sample among the men born after 1910 than among those born earlier, but the difference was slight in comparison to the sharp difference in incidence among women of the two age groups.

By the age of 15, 57% of all the males sampled had done some petting; by 18, 84% had petted, and by 25, 89%. Almost all the occurrences had involved erotic arousal, but only about 33% of these males had ever become involved in petting to orgasm (Kinsey *et al. a, c*).

The often significant differences in the percentages of boys and men who had engaged in a particular petting practice were directly related to their social, economic, and educational backgrounds. A distinct correlation existed between frequency of petting and educational attainments. Those men with the lowest education had petted the least; men of the middle group were next; and the men of the high educational group had petted most of all. The frequency with which the men had petted to orgasm was as high as 7 times (or more) a week, but the average incidence was 3 to 5 times a year. About 25% of all the men had had 5 or fewer petting partners during their lifetime, while 37% had had 21 or more partners (Bell *a*; Kinsey *et al. a, c*).

The range of petting practices is wide. Of the total male population in Kinsey's sample, almost 100% had engaged in simple kissing; 55% to 87% had engaged in deep kissing; 78% to 99% in manual manipulation of a woman's breasts; 36% to 93% in mouth-breast contact; 79% to 92% in manual manipulation of a woman's genitalia; and 9% to 18% of unmarried youth (4% of the less educated to 60% of the educated married men) in oral stimulation of their partner's genitalia. The two percentages cited in each instance refer to men at the two extremes of educational achievement (Kinsey *et al. a, c*).

Educational achievement also correlated significantly with the occurrence of men's petting to orgasm. According to the levels of schooling reached, the lowest educational group had achieved a climax through petting only 16% of the time, while the second group had done so 32% of the time; 61% of the petting in the college-level group had culminated in orgasm (Bell a; Kinsey *et al. a, c*).

Females

Almost 100% of all married women have had some sort of petting experience prior to their marriage, and 90% of the entire female population, whether or not they ever marry, engage in petting at one time or another. By the age of 35, 80% of those women in Kinsey's sample born before 1900 had had petting experience; of those born between 1900 and 1909, 91% had petted; and of those born between 1910 and 1919, 98% had petted. The increase in percentages would seem to be the result of the "sexual revolution" of the 1920s; women born after the turn of the century gradually, but steadily, became less sexually inhibited (Kinsey *et al. a, c*).

Simple kissing is engaged in at one time or another by nearly all women at all educational levels. More sophisticated methods of petting, however, are directly related to educational achievement, decade of birth, and incidence and frequency of coitus. The more advanced the level of education, the more liberal the woman is in the types of petting she engages in. In Kinsey's study, those women born in 1910 or after were more liberal in their petting practices than those born before 1910. As would be expected, frequency of premarital coitus was directly related to freedom in petting. As one would also expect, the more sophisticated and liberal the method of petting is, the fewer were the women (at all educational levels) who had tried it (Kinsey, *et al. c*).

Heavy petting, usually defined as genital stimulation of one or both partners in an unclothed state, was participated in by 52% of the Kinsey college female sample (Kinsey *et al. c*). This figure is 8% to 40% lower than comparable figures obtained in more recent studies. Samplings made in the late 1960s show that a substantial majority of college women (60% to 90%) find intimate petting an acceptable form of sexual behavior. Approximately 28% of college women have experienced heavy petting with three or more partners, and over 50% have engaged in heavy petting with someone they did not love. Almost 60% of the college women in one sample had experienced heavy petting while still in high school (Davis, K. E.).

The type of petting more slowly accepted than others, because of social taboos, is oral-genital contact. This form of sexual stimulation, however, is apparently now rather widely accepted as an erotic outlet—and a normal, healthy one—by the majority in the higher socioeducational groups. About 65% of the younger women at the upper educational levels in Kinsey's sample who had had premarital coital experience more than 25 times had had their genitals stimulated orally prior to marriage; 62% of these women had orally stimulated the genitals of their partners (Kinsey *et al. a, c*).

Between the ages of 21 and 25, 31% of all the women sampled had established a pattern of regular participation in premarital petting to orgasm. The average occurrence among women aged 15 to 55 was 4 to 6 orgasmic responses through petting a year, although the frequency was as high as 7 to 10 times a week. In the 16- to 25-year-old age group, petting afforded as much as 18% of the women's total sexual outlet before marriage. It consistently provided a higher percentage of the total sexual outlet for women of all ages than it did for men in comparable age groups. More than 50% of the women had indulged in premarital petting over a period of 6 years or more. The number of partners with whom they had engaged in petting varied from 1 only (10%) to 21 or more (19%). Over 33% of all the women had experienced premarital petting with more than 10 men (Bell *a;* Kinsey *et al. a, c*).

Like most other forms of sexual behavior for women, petting was significantly related to religious background. The more pronounced the commitment to a religion, the more restricted the sexual behavior. Interestingly, however, religion ultimately had little influence, one way or the other, on frequency of petting to orgasm, even among the most religiously devout. Once these devout women achieved orgasm through petting, they engaged in such activity as often as less devout women did (Bell *a;* Kinsey *et al. c*). The rationale quite often is that petting allows a woman sexual gratification without depriving her of her virginity, a condition highly prized by many women.

HOMOSEXUAL RELATIONS

The term *homosexual relations* refers to the use of a partner of the same sex for sexual gratification. In our society it is usually deplored as a mode of sexual behavior, although sanctions against it are considerably more stringent for men than for women. In New York City, for example, in a particular 10-year period of time, only one woman was convicted of "homosexual sodomy," while over 700 men were found guilty on the same charge (Kinsey *et al. c*).

Homosexual contact among infrahuman mammals is found among both males and females. Animal homosexuality is considerably more common than is popularly believed (Ford and Beach *a*). A pattern of exclusive homosexual behavior in a particular animal is rare, however, and is found chiefly in immature animals and those that are sexually deprived (Pomeroy *f*).

A recent study of 20,000 well-educated, liberal men and women of high socioeconomic status confirmed Kinsey's earlier conclusions that more than one-third of all men and nearly one-fifth of all women have had at least one homosexual experience involving orgasm. (A substantial number of other women [22%] have considered engaging in homosexuality.) Both homosexual men and homosexual women have their first *heterosexual* intercourse at an earlier age than heterosexuals do. About 17% of the homosexual women and 18% of the homosexual men sampled had their first coitus before the age of 15, as compared with only 6% of the heterosexual women and 9% of the heterosexual men (Athanasiou et al.; Kinsey et al. a, c).

Lesbians (female homosexuals) are more likely to reach orgasm than heterosexual women are, and are twice as likely to be multiorgasmic on each sexual occasion as the latter. This finding confirms the conclusions of Masters and Johnson that orgasm, multiple orgasm, and greater intensity of response in a woman are all more likely through masturbation or digital manipulation than through sexual intercourse (Athanasiou et al.; Masters and Johnson n).

Males

It is generally accepted by sexologists that about 4% of all white men in the United States are exclusively homosexual all their sexual lives, 8% are exclusively homosexual for at least 3 years between the ages of 16 and 55, and 37% have experienced at least some form of overt homosexuality to the point of orgasm in their lifetime. Furthermore, 10% of all men have some homosexual experience after marriage (Kinsey et al. a). (See Table 17.1.) Although these data apply to white males, it has been estimated that the percentages are equally pertinent to the black American male population (Cory).

TABLE 17.1 Homosexual Experience Among Men to Point of Orgasm

Educational level	Single, to 35 years of age	Total male population
Grade school	50%	27%
High school	58%	39%
College	47%	34%

In the Kinsey study, educational levels bore a different relationship to the incidence of homosexuality than to most other means of sexual expression. While the incidence of homosexuality among single men in the three educational groups was not significantly different, there was a great difference among the groups in the percentage of their total sexual outlet that homosexual practices constituted (Kinsey et al. a). (See Table 17.2.)

TABLE 17.2   Homosexuality Among Single Men Constituting Total Sexual Outlet

Educational level	Ages 16-20	Ages 21-25	Ages 26-30
Grade school	6.85%	8.06%	14.04%
High school	10.81%	16.31%	25.95%
College	2.43%	3.72%	8.82%

For all single men there was a gradual increase (from 5% to 22%) before the age of 40 in the percentage of total sexual outlet that homosexuality afforded. For married men, homosexuality represented less than 1% of the total outlet. For the previously married in this age group, there was also a gradual increase in total outlet, from 9% to 26% (Kinsey *et al. a*).

Some men who engage in homosexual practices are rather promiscuous. Although 51% of them have only one or two sexual partners, 22% have over 10 partners. Homosexual men do not ordinarily concern themselves with finding a steady or permanent partner until they reach the age of about 30. Prior to that, they seem intent upon seeking the satisfactions of the moment rather than establishing a lasting relationship (Sonenschein).

Generally speaking, the Kinsey study indicated that religious factors had a bearing on both the incidence and frequency of homosexual contacts. The more intense an individual's commitment to religion, the less often he participated in homosexual activity. The incidence of homosexual contacts was slightly higher among Catholic men than among the other two religious groups, the incidence among Jewish men falling behind that of Protestants (Kinsey *et al. a*).

Females

Homosexuality appears to be somewhat less common among women than among men. The occurrence of both exclusive and partial homosexuality among women is only two-thirds of that among men (Cory). It is generally found, additionally, that most female homosexuals are bisexual. Either they have had heterosexual experiences, or they will have them in the future, or they will shift back and forth between homosexuality and heterosexuality. Only 33% are exclusively homosexual (Bieber, T.) In a recent study of lesbians, 67% of those who declared themselves to be exclusively homosexual at the time of questioning reported earlier heterosexual relationships (Kaye).

The findings of some investigations indicate that as many as 50% of all women have harbored "intense feelings" for another woman or women at some point during their sexual life. Most sexologists, however, agree with the more conservative conclusions of the Kinsey investigation that only 28% of women (compared with 50% of men) have experienced some sort of homosexual response (Davis, K. B.; Kinsey *et al. a, c*). Only about 1% to 3% of the female population between the ages of 20 and 35 in Kinsey's sample were exclusively homosexual, although an additional 2% to 6% in this age bracket were "more or less exclusively homosexual" (meaning that, rarely, there might have been a heterosexual contact).

In homosexual relationships, twice as many men as women experienced a sexual response short of orgasm, while three times as many men as women experienced orgasm (Kinsey *et al. c*.).

In contrast to other types of sexual outlet, there was apparently no more female homosexuality among those women born after 1900 than among those born earlier. The incidence of lesbianism at various educational levels differed, to be sure, but the figures did not correlate with those pertaining to male homosexuality. The percentages of women who, by the age of 30, had experienced homosexual contact to the point of orgasm were these: those educated to the level of grade school, 6%; high school, 5%; and college, 10% (14% for women having attended graduate school). The percentages of those who by the same age had had overt homosexual contacts short of orgasm were: 9% (grade-school level), 10% (high school), 17% (college), and 24% (graduate school) (Kinsey *et al. c*).

In the early years of active homosexuality, women in the two lower educational groups had a higher frequency of orgasm than college women did. But these differences subsequently disappeared, so that frequency of orgasm averaged once every 2 or 3 weeks for women of all three educational levels (Kinsey *et al. c*).

Kinsey's study showed that female homosexuality is largely confined to single women and, to a lesser extent, to the previously married. Although 19% of his total female sampling had had active homosexual contact by the age of 40, when the factor of marital status was introduced the pattern of active homosexual incidence for the same age group shifted to: 24% of the women who had never been married, 9% of the previously married, and only 3% of the married women (Kinsey *et al. c*).

By the age of 20, a mere 4% of the Kinsey female sample had had orgasmic response through lesbian contacts. By age 35, however, 11% had experienced orgasmic response through homosexual outlet; among women in their mid-40s, the figure was 13%. Of those women who had homosexual associations, from 50% to 66% had experienced orgasm at least occasionally (Kinsey *et al. c*).

The sexual expression of greatest importance and most cherished by the lesbian, in company with many heterosexual women, is embracing and close total body contact. Genital activity and orgasm are frequently of secondary importance (Kaye).

Of all women who have engaged in any form of homosexual activity, Kinsey's study has indicated that about 33% have fewer than 10 experiences, and that many have only 1 or 2. The homosexual experiences of 50% last for a period of 1 year or less, while the activity of another 25% is spread over 2 to 3 years. Half the women (51%) engaging in homosexual activity in Kinsey's sample limited their experience to a single partner, another 20% had had 2 partners, and only 4% had 10 or more partners (compared with 22% of the men who had 10 or more partners) (Kinsey *et al. a, c*).

The duration of established lesbian partnerships is comparable to that of heterosexual relationships. About 65% of the lesbians in one study had remained 1 to 9 years in a single partnership and 17% for 10 years or more. By comparison, 48% of the heterosexual women in the study had stayed for 1 to 9 years with one male partner, and 40%, for 10 years or more (Rubin *l*).

Official records identify about 20% of the female prison population as being homosexual, although prison staff members estimate that between 30% and 70% of the inmates have lesbian affairs while in prison. Female inmates themselves estimate the incidence of affairs to be between 60% and 75% (Ward and Kassebaum).

Of those women surveyed by Kinsey who had the most extensive homosexual experience, only 20% expressed definite regret. Almost 90% of all the women with homosexual experience themselves declared that they would keep as a friend any woman with a history of lesbianism. They were less accepting (74%) of male friends with a history of homosexuality (Kinsey *et al. c*). The lesbian ordinarily professes many rigid and moralistic attitudes, and adheres to the code of conduct established by her circle of lesbian friends. She is not likely to "take up" with just anyone, and avoids "one-night stands" because her reputation might otherwise suffer (Bass-Hass).

According to Kinsey's findings, the more devout adherents in all three religious groups had less homosexual contact to the point of orgasm than the nondevout. Among women (as well as among men) only nominally affiliated with the Catholic Church, 25% had experienced homosexual contact to orgasm, while 5% of devout Catholic women had had this experience. Among Protestants and Jews, a similar correlation existed between degree of religious involvement and homosexual experience (Kinsey *et al. c*).

SEXUAL CONTACT WITH ANIMALS

A taboo against sexual relations with animals is well established in the Old Testament and in the Talmud. Sexual contact between humans and infrahumans (also called *bestiality*) has occurred since early civilization, but is highly abhorrent to most people who have not had a similar experience. The extent of such sexual activity among either men or women is extremely small. Its significance in a study of sexuality lies in its social impact rather than in its importance as a sexual outlet (Kinsey *et al. c*).

Males

As would be expected, male contact with animals, whenever it exists, is found primarily among boys reared on farms. Between 40% and 50% of all farm boys in Kinsey's study had had some sexual contact with animals, but only 17% had experienced orgasm as a result of animal contact. About twice as many men (32%) as women (16%) were erotically aroused by seeing animals in copulation. About 15% of the rural males of only grade-school achievement had had some sexual experience with animals to the point of orgasm, but the figure increased to 20% for the rural high-school group, and to about 27% for rural males who were college-educated (Kinsey *et al. a, c*).

Sexual contacts with animals varied in frequency from once or twice in a lifetime to as high as 8 times a week for some adolescent rural boys; the average for those involved was about twice a week. The period of time over which these contacts occurred was ordinarily limited to 2 or 3 years; most sexual contact with animals occurred in preadolescence before the boy was capable of orgasm. Sexual contact with animals represented considerably less than 1% of the total sexual outlet for the men in both urban and rural communities (Kinsey *et al. a*).

City boys had limited sexual experience with animals. Their contacts were customarily with household pets, and with animals on a farm that they might visit during vacations (Kinsey *et al. a*).

Females

An extremely low percentage of the total female population have ever had any sexual contact with animals. About 1.5% of the women in Kinsey's study had had sexual contact with animals during preadolescence (usually as a result of accidental physical contact with a household pet), and only 3.6% of the female sample had had sexual contact with animals after their adolescent years. Of those sexually precocious women who were able to have orgasms prior to adolescence, 1.7% had experienced their first orgasm in animal contact (Kinsey *et al. c*).

Only about 16% of Kinsey's total female sample had ever been erotically aroused by witnessing coitus between animals. Out of the entire 5940 women in Kinsey's study, 29 had caused dogs or cats to stimulate their vulval area orally, and 2 had had coitus with dogs. Only 25 of these histories contained instances in which women had been brought to orgasm by sexual contact with animals, and the method was primarily oral stimulation of their genitals. Of those women who had engaged in bestiality, half had had only a single experience, and a fourth had had 6 or more contacts (Kinsey *et al.* c).

HETEROSEXUAL INTERCOURSE

The average man or woman is more interested in coitus with a member of the opposite sex than in any other type of sexual outlet, although other methods of outlet are significant in the sexual lives of both men and women. Ordinarily, heterosexual intercourse is thought of in relationship to marriage, but premarital, extramarital, and postmarital heterosexual coition must also be considered in analyzing this sexual outlet.

Premarital Heterosexual Intercourse

The term *premarital heterosexual intercourse* commonly refers to coition between two single persons, although one of the partners may be married (Ehrmann *b*).

Males

As discussed earlier, the American culture generally accords considerably more latitude in sexual expression to men than to women. Premarital sexual intercourse is the most controversial of these sexual outlets—the one most often considered in discussions concerning the double standard of morality.

Kinsey's study indicated that, at some time or another before they were married, 98% of the men who had attended only grade school, 84% of men who had attended high school only, and 67% of men with college education had had sexual intercourse. The decade in which men were born appeared to have little or no correlation with the frequency of premarital coitus, in contrast to rather sharp differences in the correlations between birthdate and frequency among women (Kinsey *et al.* a, c).

Studies conducted in the 1960s and early 1970s indicate that the rate of premarital coitus for college men runs from 58% to 65%, approximating the early Kinsey figures. A 1970 study of 200 newlyweds, conducted in Pennsylvania, revealed that 75% of the couples had had coitus with each other before marriage (and 30% of the women were pregnant when they married) (Otto).

Although the incidence of premarital sexual intercourse among college men has not changed appreciably, its psychological and sociological aspects have altered considerably. These men tend to have coition with a woman whom they love or care for deeply, rather than with a prostitute or casual pickup as their fathers would have done. College men are now faced at a somewhat earlier time of life with the necessity for integrating their sexual attitudes and behavior, their emotional feelings, and their standards of appropriate conduct (Davis, K. E.).

Between the ages of 16 and 20, the grade-school group of men in Kinsey's sampling had had seven times greater frequency of sexual intercourse than the college group had had. This disparity in coital frequency lessened only slightly between the groups of older single men of the same educational levels. Depending upon age level, the college group had obtained from 4% to 21% of its total premarital sexual outlet from coitus; the high-school group, from 26% to 54%; and the grade-school group, from 40% to 68%. Also, the unmarried college men had commonly engaged in coitus for the first time at an age 5 or 6 years older than that of the unmarried men at lower educational levels when *they* had first experienced coition (Kinsey *et al.* a).

The correlation between premarital intercourse with prostitutes and educational level followed the same trend. According to the Kinsey study of single men aged 25, 74% of the grade-school group, 54% of the high-school group, and 28% of the college group had had coitus with prostitutes. The total sexual outlet sought from prostitutes by single men rose, between the ages of 16 and 40, from 6% to 23% for the grade-school group, from 3% to 11% for the high-school group, and from less than 1% to 3% for the college group. Furthermore, sexual intercourse with any woman, prostitute or otherwise, never accounted for more than 21% of the total sexual outlet of single college men, whereas coitus could constitute as much as 68% of the total sexual outlet for single men in the lower educational groups (Kinsey *et al.* a).

Recent studies put the percentage of college men having coitus with prostitutes at 4.2% to 14%, most figures being lower than that of the 1948 Kinsey report (Davis, K. E.). At least two studies suggest a much higher incidence, however. One investigation, of male students at a large southwestern state university, revealed that 42% of the subjects had had coitus with prostitutes (Frede). A similar investigation revealed that 43% of a college-student sampling had had sexual relations with a prostitute, 50% of that number having visited the prostitute in company with a group of other young males. As a matter of fact, 29% of the total sample of men in this study had participated in a form of "group sex" in which one woman (not necessarily a prostitute) and two or more men were involved (Benson).

The point should be made that the incidence of premarital sexual intercourse among men may range from a single contact to 35 or more coitions a week (the latter pattern sometimes persisting for as long as 5 years or more). Many men, particularly those at the upper end of the social–educational scale, limit their premarital coition to one woman—often the woman they eventually marry. Other men, particularly at the lower end of the social–educational scale, may copulate with as many as several hundred women (Kinsey *et al. a*).

Among the unmarried men in Kinsey's sample who had coitus regularly, frequency was at its maximum during early adolescence, averaging about 2 contacts a week. Among males in their teens and 20s, the average was about 1.4 times a week, dropping to a lesser frequency among older groups of unmarried men. The lowest education group maintained a level of 2 to 4 coitions a week—which, incidentally, equaled the average incidence of coition among married men in the same age bracket (Kinsey *et al. a*).

A few single men had sexual intercourse with older women—single, married, or divorced. However, almost all the coital experiences of single men were with single women, usually of their own age or slightly younger (Kinsey *et al. a*). Studies have shown that boys of a higher social stratum often sexually exploit girls of a lower social stratum, but that, in college populations, young men and women customarily have their sexual experiences with persons of an equal social class (Ehrmann *b;* Hollingshead). Four percent of college men have engaged in coitus for such ulterior motives as money or to earn a favor (Davis, K. E.).

In Kinsey's study of men, religion, at all social-educational levels, bore a direct relationship to the incidence and frequency of premarital sexual intercourse. Devout Catholics and Protestants experienced less premarital coitus than did the less devout. Interestingly, religiously inactive Jews had less premarital coitus than did the orthodox Jews (although the incidence of experience did not differ greatly except among early pubescents up to the age of 15). Kinsey speculated that this discrepancy possibly resulted from the strong condemnation with which the Jewish faith views masturbation (Kinsey *et al. a*).

In one study of the effect that premarital coitus has on the relationship between engaged couples, 92.6% of the men and 90.6% of the women felt that it had been a strengthening force; 1.2% of the men and 5.4% of the women felt that it had had a weakening effect; and the remainder were undecided (Burgess and Wallin).

Females

It should be noted that Kinsey drew his conclusions about premarital coition among women from data concerned only with sexual activity after early pubescence (about 10 years of age). This is probably not a serious drawback, inasmuch as most sexual behavior by prepubescent girls is merely experimentation and sex play—although, of course, there are exceptions.

It was pointed out earlier that a rather noticeable change occurred in women's sexual behavior about 1920, affecting almost every aspect of their sexual lives. Of the women in Kinsey's study, over twice as many of those born between 1900 and 1910 had had sexual intercourse before marriage as those born before 1900 (36% as compared with 14%). Since that time the increase has leveled off onto a fairly consistent plateau. It is of interest to note that, despite the increase in premarital coital *incidence* among women born after 1900, the percentage of women who attained orgasm coitally before marriage remained about the same—50% at the age of 20, 75% by the age of 35—no matter which generation was under consideration. The *frequency* of premarital coital experience also remained remarkably consistent for women of all generations (Kinsey *et al. c*).

Prior to marriage, almost 50% of all women in Kinsey's sample had experienced coitus and 67% had experienced orgasm. But only about 17% of the orgasms had resulted from coition, which lagged far behind masturbation as the unmarried women's primary source of sexual outlet. Girls under 16 had had only 6% of their total orgasmic experience from premarital coitus; girls between 16 and 20, 15%; and those still unmarried in their early 20s, 26%. After the early 20s, coition became more important than petting to single women as a source of orgasm, lagging not far behind masturbation (Kinsey *et al. c*).

The high percentage of women in Kinsey's study who had engaged in premarital coitus surprised and disturbed many people. It should be pointed out, however, that about half the single women who were coitally active had sexual intercourse only with the men whom they eventually married. Furthermore, most of the women's premarital coition took place only during the year or two preceding marriage.

About 50% of the women who married by age 20 had had premarital sexual intercourse. The same percentage held for those who married between 21 and 25. Of those women who married between the ages of 26 and 30, however, between 40% and 66% had experienced coition. Except for girls who married quite young, premarital coitus during the early teens was relatively rare; only 3% of all girls had experienced it by age 15.

As held true in other types of premarital sexual activity in the Kinsey study, the frequency of premarital coitus did not reach its peak until the women involved were in their late 20s, after which it remained remarkably regular. Of those single girls under the age of 20 who engaged in coition, sexual intercourse occurred on an average of once every 5 or 10 weeks, while the frequency was about once every 3 weeks among older single women. The frequency of premarital coitus among women as a group and individually often varied considerably. About 20% of the group who experienced premarital coition had coitus as often as 7 times a week (7% having it 14 times in the same period), but there were usually intervals of complete (or relatively complete) sexual inactivity between the sexually actives times (Kinsey *et al. c*). Interestingly, some girls who have premarital intercourse are capable of multiple orgasms from the very beginning of their coital experience (Kinsey *et al.* c; Masters and Johnson *n, o*; Terman a).

Of all the women in Kinsey's study who engaged in premarital coitus (whether or not they eventually married), 53% had a single partner, 34% had 2 to 5 partners, and only 13% had 6 or more partners. Of married women who had premarital coitus, 87% had at least some of their coital experience with the men they eventually married, and 46% had intercourse only with their future husbands. Only 13% of these women had premarital coitus with men other than their future husbands but not with the latter (Kinsey *et al.* c).

An inverse relationship has been found to exist between a woman's social class and premarital coitus with her husband. Only 31% of the upper-class women in one study had experienced premarital coitus with their husbands, whereas 82.5% of the lower-class women had done so (Kanin).

Attractive girls have greater opportunity for exposure to the sustained and convincing romantic blandishments of young men than less attractive girls do. They therefore have greater opportunity to engage in coitus with men who care for them and are more likely (56%) to have premarital coitus than are women of moderate (31%) or little attractiveness (37%). Attractive girls also have the largest average number of sex partners (Kaats and Davis).

The age at which marriage occurs has a significant impact on the incidence of premarital coition at the various education levels. At first glance, Kinsey's 1953 findings would lead one to believe that single college girls are much more coitally active than girls of the two lower educational groups: the data showed that 60% of the girls who had gone to college, 47% of the girls who had finished high school only, and 30% of those girls who had not gone beyond grade school had had premarital coitus (Kinsey *et al.* c). (These statistics, incidentally, stand in striking contrast to those concerning men, wherein 67% of men with college education and 98% of those with only grade-school education were found to have had sexual intercourse prior to marriage [Kinsey *et al.* a].)

Despite the seemingly high incidence of premarital coition among college girls, certain facts should be borne in mind. Because girls who are schooled only to grade-school or high-school level tend to marry at a considerably earlier age than college girls do, they have fewer prenuptial years in which to form attachments that might lead to sexual intercourse. As Kinsey pointed out, among women within a given age group *after* the age of 20, no matter what their educational background, coital experience before marriage was about equal.

A larger proportion of girls with little education begin their coital experience at an earlier age than girls with more education do. Between the ages of 16 and 20, 38% of the grade-school group, 32% of the high-school group, and about 18% of the college group in Kinsey's sample had premarital coitus. The relationship between the *frequency* with which girls have coitus and their educational level is not as consistent as the relationship between the incidence of premarital coitus in the female population and educational level (Kinsey et al. c), although lower-class women tend to engage in more premarital coitus than middle-class women (Peretti).

Investigations since the Kinsey group's have found that the incidence of premarital intercourse among college girls is increasing. Various studies between the years 1945 and 1965 showed that about 25% to 30% of co-eds of all ages and class standings had premarital coitus, whereas studies conducted In the late 1960s and early 1970s showed the rate to be about 35% to 50% (Bell a; Kaats and Davis). As expected, however, the percentage of premarital sexual experience was highest (55%) among co-eds in certain liberal eastern colleges; the lows ranged from 19% in a southern university to 12% in a church-affiliated college (Packard).

Other investigations support the contention that there has been a recent liberalization in both the sexual attitudes and behavior of college women. A carefully controlled comparison of 1958 and 1968 co-eds in the same large urban university revealed that the number of girls having premarital coitus while in a dating relationship rose from 10% in 1958 to 23% in 1968; the rate while going steady, from 15% to 28%; and during engagement, from 31% to 39% (Bell and Chaskes).

In 1958 most co-eds having premarital coitus were engaged to their partners. In 1968, however, the greatest number were merely dating or going steady with their partners. The rate of coitus among co-eds in both decades is lowest among Catholics and highest among Protestants, with Jews in between. But in this 10-year span, the rates went up proportionately in all three groups (Bell and Chaskes).

A second (independent) study, comparing the same 10-year span, 1958 and 1968, found that the incidence of premarital coitus had increased significantly among women but not among men. On a Mormon campus, the percent of premarital coital experience among women rose from 10% in 1958 to 32% in 1968 (among men it remained the same: 37%). On a midwestern campus the rate of premarital coitus for women rose from 21% in 1958 to 37% in 1968, while for men it was about 50% in both years (Christensen and Gregg).

In a 1967 study of freshman women at a state university, it was found that 7% were nonvirgins. A study of the same group in their senior year revealed that 39% had engaged in premarital coitus. Furthermore, data on freshman women entering the same university in 1970 showed that 15% had already engaged in premarital sexual intercourse, more than double the 1967 figure (Walsh).

In 1953, Kinsey found that 3% of his white women subjects were nonvirgins at age 15, and 23% had had premarital coitus by age 21. In a similar survey made in 1971, 11% of the 15-year-olds were nonvirgins, and 40% of the single women had lost their virginity by age 20 (Teen-age sex).

The evidence is clear that there was considerably less guilt about premarital coitus among the 1968 co-eds than among those questioned in 1958. If they had experienced premarital coitus in a dating relationship, 65% of the 1958 vs. 36% of the 1968 co-eds thought they "had gone too far"; while going steady, 61% in 1958 vs. 30% in 1968; while engaged, 41% in 1958 vs. 20% in 1968 (Bell and Chaskes).

With regard to the setting chosen for their premarital coition, 58% of the women in Kinsey's sample so involved had coitus at least some of the time in their parents' home. Furthermore, while a small percentage of women attending college and living away from home had coition in the college town, by far the greater number had it in their hometowns during visits and vacations. Almost half (48%) had some part of their coital experiences in their partner's home, 40% had some part in a hotel or in similar accommodations, and 41% had a portion of their total experiences in an automobile (Kinsey *et al. c*).

Kinsey found a correlation between date of birth and site of premarital coition. Automobiles, for instance, doubled in popularity as a site over the 35-year period covered by his 1953 sampling (Kinsey *et al. c*). In a recent study of delinquent girls, all of whose first coitus occurred between the ages of 12 and 15, over 60% stated that they were in automobiles at the time (Ball and Logan). However, moralists who worry that the automobile is the downfall of modern-day girls will be interested to know that many of Kinsey's older subjects had sex relations in a horse-drawn buggy! The first coital experience of both men and women is usually with someone near their own age whom they have known for some time. Coitus quite probably occurs in the woman's home, as was said, and is remembered without regret (Lowry).

Premarital coital experience for the women in Kinsey's sample was directly related to their degree of religious involvement, whatever the faith. Women who were least religiously active engaged most frequently in premarital sexual intercourse, the moderately devout the next most, and the devout the least of all. By the age of 35, slightly over 60% of the single Protestant and Jewish women who were inactive in their churches or synagogues had had premarital coitus, as compared with 55% of religiously inactive Catholic women. Among single devout Protestant women of the same age, about 30% had had premarital coitus, while 25% of devout Catholic and nonorthodox Jewish women (no figures on orthodox Jewish women were available) had had the experience (Kinsey *et al. c*). Of couples who attended church regularly, 28% had engaged in premarital coitus. The percentage increased to 48% when only one of the couple was a regular churchgoer, and to 61% when neither attended church regularly (Kanin and Howard).

Marital Heterosexual Intercourse

According to legal and moral codes of our Anglo-American culture, coitus between husband and wife is the one totally approved type of sexual activity (excepting, of course, erotic dreams) (Kinsey *et al. a*). It is the sexual outlet most frequently utilized by married couples. Yet, as a conservative estimate, sexual relationships in about 33% of all marriages are somewhat inadequate (Bell *a;* Burgess and Wallin; English *a*). (Masters and Johnson [*p*] set the figure at 50%.) An unsatisfactory sexual relationship in marriage usually generates other problems, partially because much is expected of sex. Almost everyone enters into marriage having heard countless tales of both the glories and the pitfalls of sexual intercourse. The negative aspects of sex (such as feelings of guilt and fear of inadequacy or rejection) are expected to be dispelled as the groom carries his bride across the threshold of the bedroom. About 90% of husbands and 74% of wives cross that threshold with attitudes of eager anticipation; the remaining husbands and wives enter their marital chambers with attitudes of disgust, aversion, or indifference toward sexual relations (Burgess and Wallin).

Of all married couples who stated that sex has been about as important in marriage as they had anticipated, 66% rated their marriage "very happy," whereas 33% rated their marriage as "average" or "less than average" in happiness (Bell *a*). After 20 years of marriage, however, most couples report that they are less satisfied with every aspect of the marital state—including sex—than they were during the earlier years (Pineo). Furthermore, sexual closeness tends to lessen with the birth of each child unless the couple take conscious steps to maintain it (Feldman).

The sex drive is usually somewhat greater in men than in women, especially during the early years of marriage, although each sex curiously tends to misjudge the drive of the other (Burgess and Wallin). A serious problem arises from this misjudgment. If their sex needs differ sharply, a husband and wife may work out some sort of compromise in the frequency of their sexual activity that, unfortunately, meets the needs of neither (Bell *a*).

As a group, husbands desire (or at least report that they desire) sexual intercourse more frequently than their wives. A recent study of middle-class couples, all parents in their late 30s whose marriages averaged 13.5 years in length, has supported this theory. The average husband *desired* intercourse 9.28 times per month compared to the average wife's desire of 7.78 times. The husbands reported that the *actual* frequency was 6.98 times per month (25% below preference), whereas the wives reported that the *actual* frequency was 7.78 times per month, the same as their preference. Husbands underestimated (by 16%) their wives' desire for coitus, reckoning it to be 6.50 times per month, whereas, by contrast, wives overestimated (by 23%) their husbands' desire, believing it to be 11.40 times per month (Levinger).

Only 6% of the respondents reported that the wife's desire for intercourse exceeded that of her husband, but in actual fact the coital desire of 15% of the wives exceeded that of their husbands. No husband in the study admitted that he desired coitus less frequently than it actually occurred. Of those wives who wished to have intercourse less often, 60% reported a higher actual frequency than their husbands did. Of those who wanted coitus more often, a mere 15% reported greater actual frequency than their husbands did. Only 20% of those wives who preferred less frequent coitus reported a lower actual frequency than did their husbands, whereas 53% of those wives who wanted more coitus reported a lower actual frequency than their husbands did (Levinger).

The effects of the revolution in women's sexual behavior that occurred 50 years ago can be seen in the following statistical sequence. In a study made in the 1920s, two out of three married women reported that their sex drive was less strong than that of their husbands; very few women claimed to have a stronger drive (Davis, K. B.). In another study, conducted in the 1940s, 64% of the women reported satisfaction with the frequency of marital intercourse, while 16% said it occurred too frequently and 20%, too infrequently (Burgess and Wallin). A third study, recently completed, showed that 66% of the wives considered the frequency of marital coitus to be "about right," 2% said it was "too frequent," and 32% "too infrequent" (Bell c).

It is important to remember that a woman's sex drive and needs, unlike a man's, tend to be periodic and to vary according to particular moods and situations. Even women who have had a very good sexual adjustment are able to accept long periods of sexual deprivation without undue stress (Zehv a).

Males

Only an exceedingly small number of married men do not participate, at least occasionally, in marital coitus. Even among husbands in their late 50s, only 6% in Kinsey's sample refrained from marital intercourse. These statements, of course, do not mean that marital sexual activity is confined to marital coitus. Actually, Kinsey found that marital intercourse provided only 85% of the total sexual outlet for married men, the remaining 15% being derived from masturbation, nocturnal emissions, petting, homosexual activity, extramarital coitus, and, in some rural areas, animal contact (Kinsey et al. a).

Many may be surprised to learn that about half the sexual outlets of the entire male population are socially disapproved and, to a large extent, are illegal and punishable by law. Only 60% of the American male population are married at any one time, yet between adolescence and old age each 100 men average 231 orgasms a week. Correcting for the increased incidence of coition and total sexual outlet in marriage, one is led to conclude that only 106 orgasms a week per 100 men are from marital coitus (45.9% of their total sexual outlet). If 5% of the total outlet is accounted for in nocturnal emissions, then approximately 50% of men's total sexual outlet is obtained through illegal or disapproved sources (Kinsey et al. a).

That differences exist between various subgroups in frequency of sexual intercourse has long been recognized. Early Jews stipulated in the Talmud the conjugal obligations of men, whereby each man was advised to perform according to his strength and occupation. Those who have constant leisure could copulate nightly; workers employed in the city, twice a week; workers employed out of the city, once a week; donkey drivers, once a week; camel drivers, once every 30 days; sailors, once every 6 months; scholars, once a week (and it is customary for a scholar to be intimate with his wife on Friday night).

A recent study that included 2655 married males revealed new information concerning the "normal" frequency of sexual intercourse (Pearlman).

TABLE 17.3   Frequency of Intercourse Among Married Men

Age	3-4 times per week	1-2 times per week	1 time per week	3 times per month	2 times per month	1 time or less per month	None
20-29	45.2%	29.6%	18.3%	0.9%	4.0%	0.3%	2.3%
30-39	26.5%	29.5%	25.6%	3.7%	8.4%	4.9%	1.2%
40-49	13.6%	28.1%	28.3%	5.0%	11.8%	8.9%	4.2%
50-59	5.2%	16.2%	27.1%	4.1%	17.4%	19.0%	11.0%
60-69	0.9%	6.0%	19.0%	2.2%	13.7%	25.0%	33.2%
70-79	0.4%	3.6%	6.7%	1.2%	8.8%	21.8%	57.0%

An interesting contrast in incidence of marital intercourse in relation to total outlet for men at the various educational levels was revealed in Kinsey's findings. Among lower educational groups, about 80% of the total outlet in the early years of marriage was provided by marital coitus, the incidence for this group increasing to 90% as the marriages continued.

For the college-educated man, marital coitus provided 85% of the total outlet during the early part of marriage, but by the time he had reached the age of 55, only 62% of his total sexual outlet was provided by marital coitus (Kinsey et al. a). The assumption is that these college-educated men had reevaluated the moral restraints placed on them during their early life, finding them less constrictive and threatening than they formerly were. They had come to the conclusion that they should have the sexual experiences missed earlier in their lives. However, it should be emphasized that half the remaining 38% of their total sexual activity aside from marital coitus was not with another woman (or man), but consisted of the solitary act of masturbation or nocturnal emissions (Kinsey *et al. a*).

Petting in marriage is usually considered to be only an introduction to sexual intercourse, although every method of arousal known to man has become a part of the marital erotic repertory. As we have seen, educational achievement exerts considerable influence on attitudes toward precoital stimulation. About half the total population, especially those with less education, are uninterested in prolonging the sexual act. They want to proceed with coition as quickly as possible to achieve orgasm in the shortest period of time. The man with only a low level of education may limit his precoital activity to a simple kiss without causing any upset to his wife. Similar perfunctory behavior on the part of the college-educated husband, however, would be interpreted by his wife as rejection or a lack of interest.

The average college-educated husband will spend from 5 to 15 minutes—sometimes an hour or more—in precoital petting. Once coitus is under way, he will attempt, more often than a man of lower education, to delay orgasm (although 75% of Kinsey's total male sample reached orgasm within 2 minutes). About 90% of college-educated men prefer to have intercourse in the nude, but only half as many of the grade-school group have ever had intercourse without being clothed. Because college-educated men are capable of a higher level of abstraction than men with only grade-school and high-school educations, they can be more excited by external erotic stimulation. Consequently, they prefer to have intercourse in a lighted room where they can observe the nude body of the partner and the act of coition itself (Kinsey *et al. a*).

Precoital techniques of petting in marriage are similar to premarital ones. Since marital coition is readily available, however, the length of time devoted to petting is usually not as protracted within marriage as before. Among Kinsey's sample population, precoital marital petting was limited to less than 3 minutes in 11% of marriages, 4 to 10 minutes in a third of them, and 11 to 20 minutes in another third. About 22% of couples—primarily in the groups with higher education—extended petting beyond 20 minutes (occasionally for as long as an hour or more).

Decade of birth also affected marital petting techniques. Eighty percent of those women born before 1900 had manually manipulated and 29% had had oral contact with their husband's genitalia. Among those women born between 1920 and 1929, 95% had manually manipulated and 57% had had oral contact with the male genitalia. About 33% of the married women born before 1900 remained clothed during coitus, while only 8% of those born during the 1920s kept clothes on during coition (Kinsey *et al. c*).

It might be mentioned also that, for many women, the need for cuddling and closeness is of considerably greater importance than the need for coitus itself. In fact, some wives lure their husbands into sexual intercourse just to satisfy this very real need to be held or cuddled. They are willing to barter coitus for close body contact, which tends to reduce their anxieties and to promote relaxation and feelings of security (Hollender).

The belief exists among the lower, less well-educated social classes that men are much more highly sexed than women are and that a woman's sexual gratification is of less importance than a man's. College-educated women and increasing numbers of others today hold that they have as much right to sexual fulfillment as their husbands do. These women are consequently more satisfied with their sex lives than their less-educated sisters are. In contrast to men with less education, highly educated men are sensitive to the sexual needs of their wives. For example, the research of Masters and Johnson (*n*) showed that 82% of men with some college education expressed concern for their partner's satisfaction, in contrast to a mere 14% of men with no college education. Lower-class males feel less total involvement in sex at any given time than higher-class males do, and their interest in sex decreases more rapidly with the passage of time than that of higher-class men (Bell *b, c*; Rainwater *b*).

Because marital coitus (again, excepting nocturnal emission) is the only sexual outlet totally sanctioned by all religious groups, one would expect the frequency of marital coition to be greater among the religiously devout than among the religiously inactive—or that, at the very least, there should be no differences in frequency between the two groups. The frequency of marital intercourse, however, was lower among the religiously active Protestants in Kinsey's sampling than among the inactive Protestants. (Insufficient data on Catholic and Jewish groups prevented similar comparisons.) It is difficult to escape the conclusion that the puritanical early religious training of devout Protestants carries over into marriage and continues to inhibit sexual expression, despite the couples' conscious acceptance of the "rightness" of marital coitus (Kinsey *et al. a*).

Females

Practically all married women participate in sexual intercourse, although there is a gradual decline in frequency after the first two years of marriage. Men, too, it will be remembered, experience marital coitus less frequently in later years of life, but the decline among women is somewhat steeper. Kinsey found that at the age of 50, the incidence in his sampling of those still engaging in coitus was 97% of the men and 93% of the women; at the age of 60, the percentages were 94% and 84%, respectively. Curiously, marital coition is the only form of sexual outlet among women that undergoes such a decline with advancing age (Kinsey *et al. a, c*).

For women who married in their late teens, the average (median) frequency of marital coitus was 2.8 times a week in the early years of marriage, 2.2 times a week at the age of 30, 1.5 times a week at the age of 40, once a week at the age of 50, and once every 12 days (0.6) at the age of 60. About 14% of all the married women had marital intercourse 7 or more times a week, although the percentage of wives experiencing this frequency dropped to 5% at the age of 30, and to 3% by the age of 40.

This decline in frequency is rather puzzling in light of Kinsey's findings that women reach their peak of sexual desire between the ages of 31 and 40. However, since men's sexual drive peaks between the late teens and the age of 25, and thereafter shows a decline, it is probably the aging of men that causes the decrease in women's marital coital frequency (Armstrong; Kinsey *et al.* c). During the first year of marriage, 75% of all women studied attained orgasm at least once during coitus. The percentage gradually increased to 90% after 20 years of marriage (Kinsey *et al.* c).

It should be remembered that the decline in frequency of marital coitus after the first two years of marriage does not necessarily imply declining interest in other forms of sexual activity. Kinsey showed that the incidence of female masturbation and nocturnal dreams involving orgasm increases after marriage, then remains fairly steady at its maximum level until wives become 60 years of age or even older. Between the ages of 21 and 25, 89% of a married woman's total sexual outlet is derived from marital coition. After the age of 25 there is a gradual but consistent decline, so that by the time a woman reaches the age of 70, only 72% of her total sexual outlet is provided by marital coitus (Kinsey *et al.* c).

A recent study (Bell and Bell) of 2372 married women in all educational levels, whose average length of marriage was 13.2 years, revealed that the average number of acts of coitus per month was 9.4 for those aged 26 to 31; 7.4 times for those aged 31 to 41; 6.1 times for those aged 41 to 50; and 4.1 times for those aged over 50. The study showed further that those women who reported that their sex life was "very good" had coitus on an average of 10 times per month; those with a "good" sex life, 8.6 times per month; "fair," 6.3 times; "poor," 5.1 times; and "very poor," 2.3 times per month. Of all aspects of sexual activity, married women claim to find greatest satisfaction from the following: closeness or feeling of oneness with partner, 22%; orgasm, 21%; coitus, 20%; foreplay (petting), 19%; "everything," 9%; oral-genital contact, 7%; other responses, 2%. The aspects of their sex life liked the least were: anal or oral sex, 21%; "messiness" after coitus, 17%; no orgasm, 16%; routine or ritual nature of sex, 12%; excessive or rough foreplay, 12%; "nothing," 9%; coitus, 6%; "not enough sex," 4%; other responses 3%.

The Kinsey study found few differences in frequency of marital coitus among women at different educational levels. However, for every age group there was an increase in coition to orgasm as the educational level rose. During the first year of marriage, for example, 34% of the grade-school group, 28% of the high-school group, about 25% of the college-educated group, and only 22% of the graduate-school women failed to reach orgasm during marital coition. Of those women capable of reaching climax in marital coitus, orgasm was achieved in about 75% of their coital experiences. During the later years of marriage, the incidence of female orgasm in coition increased for all education levels, although the incidence was consistently greater among the higher education groups.

No changes in frequency of female coital experience in marriage according to decade of birth were observed. But there were significant differences between decade-of-birth groups in the incidence of response to orgasm in marital coitus—the women born during the 1919–1929 decade showing about a 25% increase in the incidence of orgasmic response over those women born before 1900 (Kinsey et al. c).

As previously noted, the incidence of masturbation, premarital petting, and premarital coitus was inversely related to a woman's religious devoutness. It has also been noted, however, that once a woman had had these experiences, the frequency of her sexual activity continued, bearing little or no relationship to her religious background. The same pattern applies to marital coitus. A pattern of frequent coition was somewhat slower to develop among the more devout women, but once the frequency was established, no further relationship to the degree of religious involvement existed (in contrast to the findings concerning Protestant males).

A correlation did exist, however, between the percentage of total sexual outlet provided by marital coitus and a woman's devotion to her religion. The more devout women experienced from 4% to 12% more of their total outlet in marital coition than did the women who were religiously inactive. There were no differences in the incidence of sexual intercourse leading to orgasm, except that devout Catholic women were less likely to have orgasms during marital coitus than women of the other religious groups (Kinsey et al. c). This tendency probably stems from a fear of pregnancy that would affect Catholic women more than others, because of their church's proscriptions against certain birth-control measures.

Kinsey (c) and Terman (a) found that almost 15% of all the women in their samples regularly responded with multiple orgasms. Masters and Johnson (n) conclude from their investigations that the percentage is somewhat higher, saying further that "woman is naturally multiple-orgasmic in capacity" (Masters and Johnson o).

Extramarital Sexual Activity

The phrase *extramarital sexual behavior* customarily means *adultery* in most people's thinking. However, many sexual outlets other than coition are technically implied in the total scope of extramarital behavior. In this discussion, unless otherwise indicated, extramarital sex relations will refer to extramarital coition only—that is, nonmarital sexual intercourse between a man and woman, at least one of whom is married at the time to someone else.

For men, the frequency of extramarital coitus, as with other types of sexual activity, decreases with age. For women, in keeping with certain other forms of sexual activity, both the frequency of extramarital coitus and the percent of total outlet that it represents increase with age (Harper a). Because of society's attitude toward extramarital affairs, the participants will usually go to rather extreme lengths to hide or deny their adultery. As a result, only the most careful, detailed, and sophisticated investigations can uncover even an approximation of the actual incidence and frequency of extramarital coition. The experience of psychotherapists confirms this secretiveness; they find their patients reluctant to admit to adulterous conduct, despite an extended time in therapy and the confidential nature of the therapeutic relationship.

Although changing ethical values are producing a shift in attitudes toward both premarital and extramarital sexual activity, the censorious judgments of religious and social groups are still powerful enough to make adultery a relationship that is sometimes destructive to marriage (Harper a). In Kinsey's sampling of 415 divorced couples during whose marriages extramarital coitus had occurred, over 33% of the subjects admitted that the adultery had been a prime factor in the disruption of their marriages (Kinsey et al. c).

A recent sampling of 20,000 politically liberal, well-educated young men and women of high socioeconomic status revealed that the men having extramarital coitus usually began their affairs sooner after marriage than the women did. Of the men, 73% had had their first affair within five years of marrying, compared with 57% of the women. But once the women began to have affairs, they experienced extramarital intercourse with about the same frequency as the men did (Athanasiou et al.).

Males

Most married men admit to at least an occasional desire to have an extramarital affair, and a conservative estimate is that from 50% to 75% of them actually do experience extramarital coitus at some point during their marriage (Ellis o; Kinsey et al. a; Terman a).

Men of the lowest educational group in Kinsey's sample had had more extramarital coitus during the early years of marriage (as well as more premarital coition) than men of the other educational levels. College men had had less premarital coitus and less extramarital coitus during the early years of marriage than other educational groups. As marriages continued, the involvement in extramarital intercourse decreased for the less educated group from 45% during the late teens to 27% by age 40, and 19% by age 50. Among the college-educated married group, in contrast, only 15% to 20% had had extramarital intercourse in their late teens, but the incidence increased to 27% by the time this group reached the age of 50 (Kinsey et al. a).

Frequency of extramarital coitus among men of lower education dropped from once (1.2) a week between the ages of 16 to 20, to once in 2 weeks (0.6) by the age of 55. Extramaritally involved men who had attended college averaged one extramarital coital contact every 2 or 3 weeks between the ages of 16 to 20, the average increasing to almost once a week by the age of 50 (Kinsey et al. a). Between the ages of 16 and 20, men of lower education had over 10 times (10.6) as much extramarital coitus as college men of the same age did. Laborers and semiskilled workmen aged 16 to 20 had almost 17 times (16.7) more extramarital intercourse than did young men of the same age who later entered the professions (Kinsey et al. a).

Men frequently become promiscuous in their nonmarital sexual behavior once they begin it, no matter whether it involves premarital coition, extramarital coition, or homosexual contacts. The married men in Kinsey's sample derived between 5% and 10% of all their orgasms from extramarital coition, intercourse with prostitutes comprising from 8% to 15% of their extramarital coitus (Kinsey et al. a).

Females

Kinsey's study showed that, among white American married women, 26% will have extramarital sexual intercourse by the age of 40. During the 14 years between the ages of 26 and 40, the incidence of extramarital coition among women rose from 7% to 26% (Kinsey et al. c).

For most age groups, the incidence of response to orgasm in extramarital affairs was about the same as its occurrence in marital coition— from 78% to 100%, depending upon the group studied. For those having extramarital intercourse, the lowest frequency—once in 10 weeks—was among married teen-age girls. From that point on, the figure rose to one contact every two or three weeks for married women in their 40s.

The notion is almost universal that men customarily prefer sexual intercourse with somewhat younger partners. Sexological investigations, however, have shown that men frequently prefer coition with middle-aged or older women. The reason appears to be that, since the sex drive in women reaches its peak between the ages of 35 and 40, a woman of that age or older is ordinarily more responsive than a younger woman. Furthermore, she is more experienced sexually and has a better knowledge of sexual techniques. She has also thrown off many of the taboos and inhibitions that plague most younger women, making her a freer and more responsive partner (Kinsey et al. c).

Education, decade of birth, and religious factors had a direct bearing on extramarital coitus among the women of Kinsey's study. Nearly a third (31%) of the college-level women had had extramarital intercourse by the age of 40, as compared with about 24% of those in the same age group who had had only grade-school or high-school education. Of those women born before 1900, 22% had had extramarital coition by the age of 40; of those born after 1900, 30% had had the experience.

At every age level, the lowest incidence of extramarital intercourse was among the religiously devout. By the age of 30, for example, 7% of religiously active Protestant women had had extramarital intercourse, as compared with 28% of religiously inactive Protestant women (Kinsey *et al.* c).

About 41% of the women who had had extramarital affairs had limited their activity to a single partner; another 40% had had 2 to 5 partners in their total extramarital experience; 16% had had between 5 and 20 partners; and 3% had had more than 20. Up to the date that their histories were taken, about 33% of these women had had extramarital coitus 10 times or less. About 42% had limited their extramarital affairs to 1 year or less; about 25% had had affairs over a 2- to 3-year period; and about 33% had continued extramarital sexual experiences over a period of 4 years or longer (Kinsey *et al.* c).

In the Kinsey study, 40% of the women who had had extramarital coitus believed that their husbands knew of it, and an additional 9% thought that they suspected it. When these figures are added to the percentage of wives whose husbands had no suspicion whatever of their wives' affairs, it indicates that for 71% of these adulterous wives no marital difficulty had yet developed on this ground (Kinsey *et al.* c).

The frequency of extramarital petting has risen in recent years, and such petting takes diverse forms. In fact, light petting under certain circumstances—for instance, at a cocktail party or dance—has become rather widely accepted in many groups. Almost 15% of the married women in Kinsey's sample reached orgasm when they engaged in extramarital petting, including 2% who did not allow extramarital coitus but did pet (Kinsey *et al.* c).

Kinsey's findings showed that, of those women who experienced extramarital coitus, 68% had also had premarital intercourse (in contrast to 50% of his total female sample who had experienced premarital coition). Of those women who had not experienced extramarital coitus, 83% stated that they had no expectations of doing so, while only 44% of those who had had extramarital intercourse stated that they did not expect to renew their activity (Kinsey *et al.* c).

PART FIVE

SEXUAL COMPLICATIONS

18 SEXUAL INADEQUACIES

The declaration by the nation's leading authorities in human sexual functioning, Masters and Johnson, that at least 50% of all marriages in this country are plagued with some form of sexual inadequacy or dysfunctioning is a depressing commentary on mankind's most important institution (Masters and Johnson p; Lehrman). The entire structure of a marriage is affected by sexual inadequacy, because the distress experienced by one partner directly affects the other and, indeed, the relationships with other family members as well. In documenting the course of treatment prescribed in various forms of sexual inadequacy, Masters and Johnson have repeatedly emphasized that there is "no such entity as an uninvolved partner contending with any form of sexual inadequacy" (Masters and Johnson p).

A recent survey revealed that the average physician encounters professionally about three cases a week in which problems of sexual maladjustment exist (Mace b). The actual number of patients with sexual problems is undoubtedly considerably higher than this survey indicates. Many physicians do not routinely enquire into the sexual aspect of their patients' lives for the obvious reason that their medical specialty precludes it. A more compelling reason is that they are beset with sexual problems themselves and are discomfited by discussing sex with their patients.

Studies have consistently shown that the physician who asks his patients specifically about their sexual adjustment will uncover far more sexual problems than the physician who waits for his patient to volunteer such information (Pauly and Goldstein). Psychiatrists, psychologists, social workers, and other specialists in human behavior report that as many as 75% of their patients have sexual problems that require help (Wiener).

The overwhelming majority of complaints to physicians about sexual problems come from wives. These women express dissatisfaction with their inability to achieve orgasm easily and their lack of sexual desire. They lament also that they do not feel affectionate toward their husbands, or complain that they find sex too overwhelming or physically uncomfortable.

The sexual problems most frequently discussed in doctors' offices by men concern impotence or premature ejaculation, the infidelity of their wives, and how often intercourse should normally be expected to occur (Mace *b*).

Sexual dysfunctioning may, of course, be caused by deep-seated and serious mental problems. In very rare cases, it may result from some physical disorder. However, the vast majority of sexual inadequacies are the emotional by-products of early conditioning—in or outside the home— or the result of simple ignorance in sexual matters and about human relationships. In practically all instances, psychogenic sexual dysfunctioning could have been circumvented had the individual received an adequate and well-timed sex education (Blazer; Masters and Johnson *p*).

Studies done in the area of human sexual inadequacy have been limited primarily to middle-class men and women of better-than-average education. This choice of subject population has been determined by several circumstances. First of all, those of poorer education and, hence, of lower income cannot afford the financial burden of professional assistance with their emotional problems. They are consequently seldom seen at clinics where sex problems are dealt with. Second, even when lower-income patients do seek psychological help, the attending physician seldom refers them to specialists in the field of sexual dysfunctioning.

Third, the double standard is more entrenched among the less well-educated than among those with a better education. Lower-class women therefore do not expect to experience orgasm in the marital relationship. And their husbands tend to deny any contributory sexual inadequacy on their own part, for such an admission would constitute an unfavorable reflection on their masculine self-image. Less well-educated men, for example, do not ordinarily regard premature ejaculation as a problem. Rather, it is the expected standard of performance, because neither they nor their wives recognize the importance of female orgasm.

Lastly, people of low socioeconomic status do not appear to be afflicted with the variety or severity of sexual inadequacies that frequently beset those of higher status. Perhaps the ability of the better educated to do abstract thinking enables them to experience a wider range of sexual pleasures but, at the same time, makes them more vulnerable to sexual hang-ups. Why this disparity exists between the two socioeconomic groups can only be guessed at, however, pending considerably more research on the subject (Lehrman).

Cooperative interaction between sexual partners is essential to continuing adequate sexual performance, just as it is essential, on a mental and emotional level, to the maintenance of a good overall marital relationship. When conditions exist that prevent easy synchronization of mental signals with bodily movements, sexual difficulties will inevitably ensue. And the condition underlying most instances of sexual failure or malfunction is fear.

In explaining Masters and Johnson's work (which the authors purposely wrote in technical, oblique language so that its primary audience would be the interested professional rather than the sexually curious layman), Nat Lehrman draws an excellent analogy between the effect of fear on a man's sexual functioning and on a professional golfer's game. The golfer has a short, relatively easy putt to make, but suddenly becomes acutely aware that he is under the scrutiny of a large gallery and that a great amount of money is at stake. He becomes overly self-conscious of what he is doing and fearful that he may be unable to do it properly. The smooth interaction between body and mind that had previously resulted in a well-coordinated game disappears as fear numbs him and disrupts his normal bodily rhythm. Result: he swings awkwardly and misses the putt.

The golfer's disappointment over missing the putt is natural and understandable. But, what is worse, the failure undermines his self-confidence. And, unfortunately, the memory of the one failure can lay the foundation for the next one. Thus fear of failure and failure itself pyramid: our golfer soon evaluates himself as being inadequate and performs accordingly. So it is with sexual performance. The more self-conscious we become about our physiological functioning, the less likely it is that we can function as we should wish (Lehrman).

Another major causative factor in almost all sexual inadequacies, as said earlier, is rigid religious conformity. "Unequivocally, absolutely, religious orthodoxy is responsible for a significant degree of sexual dysfunction. And it doesn't matter which of the three major religions is involved" (Lehrman).

Men and women with sexual inadequacies are almost invariably the victims of negative sexual conditioning during their formative years. Therapy should therefore be directed, in part, toward assisting the patient to (1) abandon or alter the negative aspects of his sexual value system; (2) retain and elaborate upon the positive ones; and (3) add new, positive experiences and develop new values that will aid in the success of the ongoing relationship.

Masters and Johnson's primary therapeutic approach in treating sexual inadequacy is "to restore sex to its natural context, so that it functions, as it should, like breathing—spontaneously and without conscious effort" (Lehrman). This goal is most easily achieved, in their experience, by a therapy team consisting of a man and a woman, because no man can thoroughly understand female sexuality—and conversely.

This team approach often offers each partner—especially the woman—the unique opportunity of having a sympathetic therapist of the same sex who will interpret his or her feelings and symptoms to the partner. An additional asset in this approach is that patients do not feel they must somehow win the approval and confidence of the counselor of the opposite sex. It is also desirable that one member of the therapy team be from the biological sciences and the other from the behavioral sciences. (Dr. Masters is a gynecologist and Mrs. Johnson a psychologist, as an example.) (Lehrman; Masters and Johnson p).

It is undoubtedly true that every three-year-old has pleasurable, positive sensations and attitudes relating to sex. Before he reaches his teens, however, these normal reactions will have been distorted by society's prevailing attitude that sex is dirty and evil. Added to this negativism are the fears, ignorance, and misinformation concerning sex that young people so easily absorb from their environment. It is understandable that the positive sexual attitudes of early childhood can be destroyed, to be replaced, perhaps permanently, by negative ones.

Part of the program designed by Masters and Johnson for the sexually inadequate person is to reestablish the positive, pleasurable sensations and attitudes naturally present in early childhood through the use of a therapeutic tool that they call *sensate focus*. The keystone of sensate focus is the sense of touch, through which the patient is brought back into contact with his sensory reactions. He learns to touch, feel, caress, and explore all the skin surfaces and mounds of his sexual partner's body with his fingers and palms. He can thus be taught to revert to the uninhibited sensual responses of early childhood. He is removed, furthermore, from the role of mere spectator in sexual activity and is placed in a position from which he can effectively communicate with his sexual partner—a position of giving and receiving pleasure.

As part of the training in touching and feeling, special consideration must often be given to the inhibitions that many people have concerning the coital fluids—the man's seminal fluid and the woman's vaginal secretions. Masters and Johnson have had a special lotion concocted by chemists and cosmeticians, which has a texture somewhat like that of these bodily secretions and which also softens the hands. By using this lotion the patient being taught to touch and feel not only can apply a smoother, softer, more sensitive touch to his partner, but also begin to lose his inhibitions about sexual fluids in the process.

Also prominent in Masters and Johnson's therapeutic armory is a reeducation program designed to dispel many of the misconceptions about human sexuality that interfere with satisfactory sexual performance. Additionally, the patients are taught specific techniques to be used in dealing with specific problems.

IMPOTENCE

In the context of sexual dysfunction, *impotence* (from the Latin: without power) can be defined as a man's inability to attain or maintain an erection of sufficient strength to enable him to perform the act of intercourse. Three types of impotence are recognized: *organic, functional,* and *psychogenic* (Kelly *b*).

The first of these, *organic impotence,* is relatively rare and is caused by some anatomical defect in the reproductive or central nervous system. *Functional impotence* may be caused by a nervous disorder, excessive use of alcohol or certain drugs, deficient hormonal functioning, circulatory problems, the aging process, or physical exhaustion—any of which can interfere with the functions of the various sex organs. *Psychogenic impotence* is by far the most frequently encountered type of impotence (Harper *b*). This malfunctioning is usually caused by the emotional inhibitions or blocking of certain impulses from the brain that act upon the neural centers of the spinal cord controlling erection.

There are, of course, no absolutes in judging male erotic drive and capacity. The strength of the individual man's sexual impetus can, in fact, fall anywhere along what has been likened to an 11-point continuum (Ciociola). At one end of the scale is (1) a total absence of both desire and capacity for erection; followed by (2) the presence of erotic desires unaccompanied by a physical capability for erection; then (3) ability to attain partial erections through special types of stimulation; (4) strong erections and ability to have sexual intercourse if tumescence can be instigated and maintained through special methods of stimulation; (5) spontaneous morning erections, but none at other times of the day, no matter which stimulative technique is employed; (6) weak erections under almost any circumstance, but firm erections and vaginal penetration possible only after extensive caressing of the penis; (7) erections occurring from caresses of the body and other erotic stimuli; (8) spontaneous erections if the nontactile erotic stimulus is strong; (9) spontaneous, immediate erections even though the erotic stimulus is very mild; (10) strong, vigorous, spontaneous erections, accompanied by a strong sex drive; and, at the far end of the scale, (11) very strong and vigorous erections and a powerful sex drive; a man with this degree of potency can have many and prolonged acts of intercourse during one sexual contact, with or without ejaculation, and he may have two or more climaxes without loss of erection.

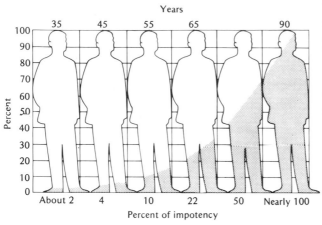

FIGURE 18.1 Schematic representation of the incidence of impotence in men. The shaded areas indicate the average percentage of men who usually suffer from impotence at various ages.

Masters and Johnson have classified psychogenic impotence as being either *primary* or *secondary*.

Primary impotence implies that the man has *never* been able to achieve or maintain an erection of sufficient firmness to engage in coitus. Research and clinical observation have consistently revealed that the causes most frequently underlying primary impotence are these: the family, especially untoward maternal influences; severe religious orthodoxy, which hampered the individual's psychosocial development; homosexual involvement; or an emotionally scarring experience with a prostitute.

The specific maternal influence productive of primary impotence is often difficult to identify, although in some cases there is evidence of overt mother–son sexual encounters that stopped just short of intercourse. Rigid religious environments can also have a sexually crippling effect, as has been stated.

Despite a relatively stable religious, family, and personal background, if a man's first sexual encounter is with a prostitute and the experience is singularly squalid and dehumanizing, he may be unable to function sexually then or thereafter with anyone else. In some cases a man's first attempt at coitus, even when not with a prostitute, proves to be so emotionally traumatic that primary impotence results.

Early indoctrination into homosexual practices, especially when the homophile alliance lasted a year or more, can also produce primary impotence even though the man now has a conscious desire to function heterosexually.

In other men the psychodynamics of the dysfunction lie in a complex interaction of many factors in their background. But, regardless of the specific cause, Masters and Johnson consistently observed two character-istics in all the cases of primary impotence treated by them: fear, and an unusual sensitivity to unknown psychological influences that apparently would not have caused primary impotence in the impotent man's peer group.

Secondary impotence is defined as a sexual dysfunction in which the man has had at least one successful coital experience, but is now incapable of it. This man is typically successful in his first attempt at coition, and continues to be effective in dozens or perhaps thousands of coital en-counters thereafter. But the day arrives when, for one of many reasons, he fails to achieve erection. A single failure, of course, in no way means impotence. Virtually all men at one time or another, particularly when upset or very tired, are unable to attain an erection or maintain it long enough for penetration (Ellis *j*).

A first-time failure in achieving an erection, however, or several failures occurring within a short period of time generate such fear and apprehension in some men that they can no longer function sexually. Fear of failure becomes a self-fulfilling prophecy, and a pattern of erectile failure is established. When a man fails to achieve penile erection in 25% of his sexual attempts, the condition may be correctly diagnosed as sec-ondary impotence (Masters and Johnson *p*).

As has been stated, men are often led to believe that they have grown too old to function sexually. They have so effectively convinced themselves of this fallacy that they do indeed become impotent, despite the fact that they continue to have morning erections and erections during sleep. The one fact which emerges clearly is that a man with a morning erection *is* capable of having an erection; any failure at other times has psychological rather than physical causality (Harper *b*). Almost all men have erections every 60 to 80 minutes during sleep (and sleeping women develop vaginal lubrications at about the same time intervals), whether or not they are capable of erections during the waking state (Fisher *et al.;* Masters and Johnson *q*).

Masters and Johnson have listed these causes of secondary impotence, in descending order of frequency: a history of premature ejaculation, in-temperate alcoholic consumption, excessive maternal or paternal domina-tion in childhood, inhibitory religious orthodoxy, homosexual conflict, inadequate sexual counseling, and certain physiological inhibitors (Lehr-man).

An adequate masculine self-image, usually acquired by a boy through identification with his father, is quite obviously linked to successful sexual functioning. But either parent can undermine a young man's confidence in his masculinity and, hence, in his potency—the mother, by mercilessly domineering her husband or otherwise trying to destroy him; the father, by establishing unattainable goals for his son.

In those cases, in which premature ejaculation is the herald of impotence, the evolution of the problem typically follows this course: the man regularly ejaculates prematurely, and at first his wife is tolerant. But as the years pass she complains more and more. She feels that the condition is solely her husband's "fault" and demands that he do something to correct it—immediately! The husband, who perhaps has been insensitive to the severity of his wife's sexual frustration, finally internalizes her accusations. He now views himself as a grossly inadequate lover and decides that at all costs he must learn to delay ejaculation.

He tries all manner of techniques to take his mind off the pleasurable sensations of coitus. But he succeeds only in blocking his full emotional involvement in coition. In his anxiety and overconcern about satisfying his wife, he typically cannot control his ejaculation any more successfully than he did in the past. Not wishing to risk additional failure, he begins to avoid coition altogether, using any excuse possible. Sooner or later, however, his wife approaches him sexually and he discovers to his horror that he does not respond with an erection. He is now struck with the thought that he has a problem of considerably greater magnitude than premature ejaculation—that he is now totally incapable of coitus. Thus failure generates fear, and fear generates further failure (Masters and Johnson p).

The evolution of impotence caused by immoderate use of alcohol follows much the same pattern. In the life of the man so affected, alcohol figures prominently—martinis at business luncheons, highballs for relaxation before dinner, and a procession of evening business functions and social gatherings at which spirits flow freely. Despite the man's greater-than-average consumption of alcohol over a period of years, his sexual functioning has always been satisfactory. Then some incident occurs that alters everything. Perhaps he somehow angers his wife in the course of an evening during which he has had many drinks. He decides to make amends by making love to her. To his dismay he cannot achieve an erection, partly because of the alcohol and partly because of his reaction—fear, anger, shame—to his wife's anger. His wife, because she is still irritated with him, does nothing to stimulate him sexually, either physically or psychologically.

A day or so later the man finds himself pondering this sexual failure. He firmly determines to accomplish that night what he had failed to do two nights before. Evening comes; there are several drinks "to relax" and a heavy meal with wine. But, unfortunately, determination is the only firm thing in the picture as erection once again fails to occur. This failure is almost inevitable because the burden of anxiety and fear bred by the first failure has been physiologically complicated by a heavy intake of alcohol and food. In attempting to "will an erection," the man has effectively ensured a second failure. Fear and failure reinforce one another, and a vicious circle is thus welded.

Secondary impotence may also have its foundations in unhealthy maternal relationships, which may have bred unconscious incestuous desires or association of all women with the mother image. Some men become sexually incapable because of conscious or unconscious disgust, anger, or hostility toward their wives.

Enough has probably been said of the role of religious orthodoxy in sexual dysfunctioning. Masters and Johnson only summed up what many have long suspected when they observed: "Severe religious orthodoxy may indoctrinate the teen-ager with the concept that any form of overt sexual activity prior to marriage not only is totally unacceptable but is personally destructive, demoralizing, degrading, dehumanizing and injurious to one's physical and/or mental health" (Masters and Johnson p).

Homosexual conflict can contribute to secondary impotence in two ways. The individual may be caught in an unconscious tug-of-war between homosexual and heterosexual desires. Or he may have had an episode or perhaps sporadic experiences of homosexuality. Although he is basically heterosexual, these experiences have confused his sexual self-image and render him now heterosexually impotent.

The ills resulting from inadequate sexual counseling have already been firmly established in this text. Suffice it to say here that guilt and shame, usually relating to some childhood experience or stemming from faulty sex education, are common contributors to sexual inadequacies.

The Treatment of Impotence

Of primary importance in the initial treatment of impotence is resisting the temptation to make a direct attack on the problem of inadequate erection. The impotent man must instead be convinced that he does not have to be *taught* to have an erection. He must learn to relax and enjoy the physical pleasures of body contact and the emotional interaction with his sexual partner without feeling a compulsion to achieve a firm erection. The husband and wife must become attuned to one another's needs and learn to fulfill those needs. For it is only through giving pleasure to the other that either partner can receive it (Masters and Johnson p).

The main therapeutic goals in the treatment of impotence are: (1) to remove the husband's fear of failure; (2) to divest him of a spectator's role in sexual activity by reorienting his emotions and sensations toward active, involved participation; and (3) to remove the wife's fear of her husband's being sexually ineffective (Masters and Johnson p). All concerned must recognize that fear is causing the problem and that, in a very real sense, there is "nothing to fear but fear itself."

The importance of the wife's role in aiding the husband in combating his (actually, their) sexual difficulties cannot be overemphasized. If a wife allows herself to betray disappointment over her husband's failure, she will increase his anxiety and guilt feelings, which will only intensify his inhibitions. She should offer not only compassion and reassurance, but also any physical stimulation that he needs to attain and maintain an erection.

After a couple learn the art of giving pleasure in order to receive pleasure, the method of overcoming the specific problem of impotence is relatively simple. They are instructed to fondle and caress one another's genitals and breasts. Erection is still not the specific goal at this point. The couple are told merely to relax and do what is sexually pleasurable; erection will occur in time because neither feels compelled to produce it. Once the man does have an erection, the couple are encouraged to let the penis become flaccid again, then to stimulate it once more into another erection, and to repeat this cycle several times. This procedure allows both partners to observe for themselves that if the husband has one erection, he can have another one, and that the loss of penile firmness is not necessarily a permanent one (Lehrman).

At no time are the couple encouraged by the therapist to attempt intercourse. The old pervasive fears of many couples have been rearoused by a therapist who tells them, "You are ready, so tonight's the night!" Masters and Johnson insist that the couple refrain from attempting intercourse during the early days of therapy, no matter how ready or confident the man feels. After about 10 days, the wife is instructed to initiate the first coital attempt.

The husband lies on his back and the wife assumes the female-superior position (see Fig. 18.3). She manipulates his penis into an erection and at the appropriate time guides the penis (still manipulating it) into her vagina as she very slowly moves her hips. If the penis becomes soft after insertion, it is withdrawn; she again manipulates it into an erection and reinserts it. But if it again becomes flaccid the couple are instructed to desist from further sex play at that particular time. Once the penis can remain firm after intromission, the wife is to remain still to allow the husband to do the pelvic thrusting. In the final days of treatment, both share the pelvic movements. Ejaculation and orgasm will follow if the couple do not attempt to force the response (Masters and Johnson *p;* Lehrman).

In treating cases of primary impotence, Masters and Johnson report a success rate of 59.4%, and in cases of secondary impotence, 73.8%. It should be remembered that, if the success achieved through the prescribed treatment is not maintained for at least five years, the therapy is considered a failure (Masters and Johnson *p).*

A recently developed surgical procedure offers some additional hope to men suffering from physiologically induced impotence. The procedure consists of implanting a rod of silicone in the penis to prevent its collapse during coitus. Because the procedure is still in the experimental stage, its lasting effectiveness and possible negative side effects cannot yet be evaluated (Lash). The willingness to undergo this surgery, however, is a clear demonstration of the lengths to which some men will go to combat impotence.

EJACULATORY DYSFUNCTION

Premature Ejaculation

Many people assume that premature ejaculation is primarily the result of a physical condition, such as a penis made abnormally sensitive by circumcision. One assumption is that the glans of the circumcised penis is more sensitive to the frictions of masturbation or coitus than is the uncircumcised penis. The circumcised man cannot therefore delay ejaculation as long as the man whose foreskin is still intact.

Neurological and clinical testing of tactile discrimination (sensitivity to touch) has failed, however, to reveal any difference in the sensitivity of a circumcised and an uncircumcised penis. In most instances of the latter, the prepuce or foreskin retracts from over the glans during a state of penile erection, especially during coition, exposing the glans during the sex act to the same degree of stimulation experienced by the circumcised glans. But even in those cases in which the prepuce does not fully retract, the response to stimulation of the penis, circumcised or uncircumcised, is the same.

Control of ejaculation, or lack of it, is related far more to self-training and to emotional factors than to such physical conditions as an overly sensitive penis (Mozes b). From the outset of such a discussion, however, it is judicious to settle the question of what premature ejaculation is—and is not. To be sure, it is a condition causing anxiety and stress for many men and women; it frequently bedevils a marriage or seriously impairs a sexual relationship.

Some authorities declare arbitrarily that ejaculation is premature if it occurs before penetration or within 10 seconds thereafter. They say further that ejaculation occurring anytime after 10 seconds of intromission, but not within the man's conscious control, must be considered "early ejaculation." Other authorities state that the man who cannot control his ejaculation for at least one full minute after penetration should be described as a premature ejaculator (Kinsey et al. a; Mozes b).

Another group of sex researchers define premature ejaculation in terms of the sexual requirements of the individual partners, and are not concerned about specific periods of time. Prominent in this group are Masters and Johnson, who designate a man as being a premature ejaculator if he cannot delay ejaculation long enough after penetration to satisfy his sexual partner in at least half of their acts of sexual intercourse together. Because of the prestige of these two sexologists, their definition will probably become the one accepted by scientists in the field of human sexuality (Masters and Johnson *p*).

Many men expect too much of themselves as lovers, and hence feel shamed and sexually inadequate if their "staying power" after penile penetration is minimal. Yet the Kinsey group found that perhaps 75% of all men ejaculate within two minutes after intromission (Kinsey *et al. a;* Mozes *b*). This is not to say that, because they are in the large majority, these men should not work at learning techniques for delaying ejaculation. Sexually aroused bed partners will both feel cheated if orgasm occurs within mere seconds of penile insertion. Not only is the man's confidence in himself as a lover weakened, but also he has been denied the intense pleasure of prolonged penile plunging. As for the woman, if the couple depend upon intercourse to bring her to orgasm, she is left almost completely unfulfilled and most assuredly will feel frustrated. Repetition of this sort of bad timing can understandably spell quick death to what might otherwise have been a thoroughly satisfactory sexual relationship.

The penis does not control ejaculation, premature or otherwise. The brain does, and usually unconsciously, via the spinal cord. The best evidence of this fact is that ejaculations can occur during sleep or while a man is unconscious. The psychological forces in premature ejaculation are legion, as we have seen. An element of revenge is often present in it—toward the particular woman or toward women in general. Or the man may be unduly tense, tired, or lacking in self-confidence in his sexual abilities. Intercourse may have been preceded by an overlong period of sexual abstinence; or the man may have been under a prolonged period of sexual excitement, because of foreplay, before intromission was attempted (Thorne).

Only rarely does premature ejaculation have a physical basis, as has been pointed out. The glans may be abnormally sensitive because of, say, a chemical irritation. Or the prostate or the verumontanum (a part of the urethra) may be infected. But beyond these rare incidents, premature ejaculation is usually caused by emotional or psychological factors. Given the cooperation of his wife, a man can train himself (except when the cause is purely physical) to withhold orgasm until both want it to happen. The main enemy is the fear and anxiety engendered in the man by previous failures. Once he gains confidence in his "staying power" and accepts the fact that all men face the problem at one time or another, the battle is half won. To assist him toward confidence in his abilities, several routes can be taken.

Some counselors (Aycock; Kelly *b*) recommend that a local anesthetic (*e.g.,* Nupercainal) be applied to the penile glans—care being taken not to smear any on the woman's vulva—a few minutes before intercourse. The assumption is that the deadening effect of the anesthetic will decrease the sensitivity of the penis, thus delaying ejaculation. Others prescribe the wearing of one or more condoms to reduce the stimulation generated by the friction, warmth, and moisture within the vagina. Since muscular tension is a notorious catalyst in ejaculation, the man's lying beneath the woman and thus taking a more passive role in coitus is believed by many to be helpful in controlling premature ejaculation. Muscular tension that terminates in early response for the man is one of the reasons (along with fear of detection) why sexual intercourse in the cramped confines of an automobile is unsatisfactory.

Some men also find that taking a drink or two before coitus helps, since alcohol is a deterrent in all physiological functioning. Other men claim similar success through concentrating on singularly unsexy thoughts, such as their income tax payments. (It is suggested, however, that the man take care not to let his partner know of his diversionary thoughts, lest he be dumped from the bed before ejaculation, premature or otherwise.) Despite some writers' rather naive, out-of-hand condemnation of these methods, most psychotherapists who work with problems of ejaculation control find them useful when patients are undergoing a period of reconditioning during which they strive toward greater confidence in themselves.

Having an orgasm and, after a short rest, attaining another erection often permit a man to experience a more prolonged act of coitus the second time. Some men masturbate shortly before they expect to have sexual intercourse. Because their sex drive will thereby be decreased, they can then prolong intercourse later.

The technique of delaying orgasm *can* be learned, and probably the best method is one requiring the cooperation of both husband and wife. Variations have appeared in several publications, most recently in the Masters and Johnson book *Human Sexual Inadequacy*. Self-treatment is possible, but since the problem is a shared one, the best chance of success lies in both partners' consulting a psychotherapist. They will, first of all, be assured that premature or early ejaculation is a reversible phenomenon; they will also be instructed in the somewhat complicated technique of bringing about its reversal.

The technique requires that the wife manually stimulate her husband's genitals until the point that he feels the very earliest signs of "ejaculatory inevitability." (This is the stage of a man's orgasmic experience at which he feels ejaculation of seminal fluid coming, and can no longer control it.) At that moment the female partner immediately ceases her massage of the penis. She then squeezes its glans or head by placing her thumb on the frenulum (lower surface of the glans) and two fingers on top of the glans, applying rather strong pressure for three or four seconds. The pressure is uncomfortable enough to cause the man to lose the urge to ejaculate. Such

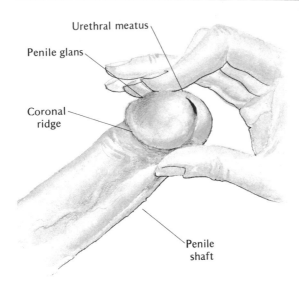

Urethral meatus

Penile glans

Coronal ridge

Penile shaft

FIGURE 18.2   Demonstration of the "squeeze technique."

"training sessions" should continue for 15 to 20 minutes, with alternating periods of sexual stimulation and squeezing.

In later sessions, the husband inserts his penis in his wife's vagina as she sits astride him until he senses impending orgasm, at which point he withdraws and his wife once more squeezes the penis to stop ejaculation. Use of these techniques is continued in further sexual encounters until, progressively, the man is capable of prolonged sexual intercourse, in any position, without ejaculating sooner than he wishes.

Masters and Johnson sound two notes of caution to those using this technique. First, the technique will be unavailing if the man himself applies the pressure to his penis; and, second, the couple must not treat this new-found sexual skill as a game and overdo it. If the technique is used immoderately, the man may eventually find that he has become insensitive to the stimulation and will be unable to respond to it. He may then very easily develop new fears, this time about his potency, thus running the risk of developing secondary impotence.

Masters and Johnson (p) report a 97.8% success rate in the treatment of premature ejaculation.

In the many sexual histories taken by Masters and Johnson, as well as by other researchers, in the study of premature ejaculation, a consistent causal pattern for the disorder has unfolded. When the man so troubled is over 40, his first experiences in sexual intercourse were typically with prostitutes. A generation or so ago, the prostitute attempted to hurry her client along to orgasm as quickly as possible, perhaps to relieve his sexual tensions but primarily to make room for the next paying customer. After only two or three such experiences, the prostitute's client could easily become conditioned to a pattern of quick ejaculation. To his dismay, he later found that this response pattern had carried over into his adult, mature sexual encounters.

Younger men have not frequented houses of prostitution nearly so frequently as their fathers did. Rather, their first sexual encounters were typically with girls of their peer group. These experiences usually took place in a parked car, in the imminent danger of being spotlighted by the police; or on a couch in the living room of the girl's parents, where at any moment her father was liable to bound into the room, shotgun in his hand and blood in his eye. The anxiety engendered by these settings served to condition many younger men to the pattern of quick ejaculation.

Another form of teen-age sexual behavior can also help to condition the man to premature ejaculation. After extensive petting, the youth, possibly fully clothed, lies atop the girl, rubbing his penis over her vulval region by moving his body back and forth, as is done in intercourse, until he ejaculates. (Aside from the unfortunate conditioning of the male, the girl's unrelieved sexual tensions, and additional cleaning bills, about all one can say of this technique is that it prevents unwanted pregnancies, preserves the girl's virginity, and affords the lad some sexual release.)

There is also the man who has had wide sexual experience as a teen-ager, in the process of which he has developed a near-total lack of regard for women. The female exists, in his thinking, solely for his gratification, an instrument for his sexual release. Her needs and welfare are of no concern. Intercourse, in his selfishness, is truly a mounting process, in which delay of orgasm is neither necessary nor desirable. In fact, the most consistent and significant characteristic uncovered by Masters and Johnson in their study of the early sexual histories of premature ejaculators is that these men were concerned only with their own sexual gratification, to the utter disregard of whether or not their partners achieved any sexual release.

Lastly, the practice of *coitus interruptus* (withdrawal) as a birth-control technique sometimes conditions premature ejaculation. The man finds himself unable to control ejaculation because he has never had to do so (Masters and Johnson p).

In any discussion of premature ejaculation, a word of caution must be injected. It is important to understand that at any one time or another almost every man has experienced ejaculation more swiftly than he or his partner would have liked. The essential thing is that the man not become anxious over possible future failures. Otherwise, what is a normal, situational occurrence may become a chronic problem.

Ejaculatory Incompetence

Ejaculatory incompetence is a relatively rare form of sexual inadequacy in which a man cannot ejaculate while his penis is in a woman's vagina. He may, however, be able to ejaculate by masturbating, or during a homosexual encounter, or, in the case of some married men, with a woman to whom he is not married (Masters and Johnson *p*). Or he may not be able to ejaculate at all (Ovesey and Meyers).

Sometimes a man with a quite satisfactory, normal ejaculatory ability loses it because of a psychologically traumatic experience. In other cases, the dysfunction is rooted in his distaste for his wife. The failure to ejaculate is merely a means of rejecting her. In other instances, fear of impregnating, the wife's known adultery, and the danger of children's walking in on the couple during coitus can cause a husband, consciously or unconsciously, to withhold his ejaculate.

Non-ejaculators clearly possess sexual "staying power," thus providing their wives with such prolonged sexual intercourse that multiple orgasms frequently result. Nevertheless, it is often the wife who seeks help in correcting her husband's ejaculatory incompetence—because she wants a child, or feels that her husband is not sexually normal, or suspects that she, herself, is not an adequate sexual partner.

Because ejaculatory incompetence is the direct opposite of premature ejaculation, the methods of treating the two are quite different, as might be expected. The wife is instructed to use manual or oral manipulative techniques or artificial aids (e.g., a cream or lotion having the consistency of vaginal secretions) to stimulate her husband to orgasm extravaginally. Once he does ejaculate, no matter how long it takes, the couple have overcome a major psychological hurdle. "When she has brought him pleasure, he identifies with her [*sic*] (not infrequently for the first time in the marriage) as a pleasure symbol rather than as an objectionable, perhaps contaminated, sexual image" (Masters and Johnson *p*).

The orgasm brought about by the wife's efforts not only gives the man pleasure and constitutes the first step in overcoming his ejaculatory dysfunction, but also allows the wife to demonstrate to her husband the happiness that she feels in pleasing him. This is invaluable in recementing a crumbling sexual relationship.

In the second step of this training program, the wife assumes the female-superior coital position (see Fig. 18.3) and stimulates her husband with the techniques that she has already proven will trigger an ejaculation. She should proceed just to the point of "orgasmic inevitability," at which time she should hurriedly insert his penis into her vagina so that at least a part of his ejaculation occurs intravaginally. Once the couple have had several successful episodes of this sort, less and less precoital play will be necessary before orgasm occurs normally during intromission.

Masters and Johnson report a success rate of 82.4% in treating ejaculatory incompetence in this manner.

FEMALE ORGASMIC DYSFUNCTION

Traditionally, the word *frigidity* has been used in association with a woman who has a total or partial lack of sex drive. But because the word has different meanings for different people, it is more confusing than useful in a discussion of sexual dysfunctioning or inadequacy. For example, a husband may desire coitus seven times a week while his wife desires it, or is orgasmic, only three times a week. This husband may consider his wife "frigid," whereas the husband who desires coitus three times a week would consider her sex drive perfectly normal. (The third husband who desires sex only once a week might well call her a nymphomaniac!)

Masters and Johnson have therefore discarded the rather meaningless word "frigidity" in favor of the more descriptive phrase, *female orgasmic dysfunction.* According to their concept, a woman suffers from orgasmic dysfunction when she does not go beyond the plateau phase in sexual response (Masters and Johnson *p*).

Masters and Johnson place nonorgasmic women into two major categories: those with *primary orgasmic dysfunction* and those with *situational orgasmic dysfunction.* The woman belonging to the first category has never achieved an orgasm in her life through any method of sexual stimulation. The woman in the situational category has managed to achieve at least one orgasm in her life, whether by coitus, masturbation, or some other form of stimulation, but no longer does so (Masters and Johnson *p*).

The causative factors in female orgasmic dysfunction are *organic, relational,* or *psychological* (Ellis *d*). Organic causes include injuries to or constitutional deficiencies in the sexual apparatus, hormonal imbalance, disorders of the nervous system, inflammation or lesions of the internal or external genitalia and surrounding areas, excessive use of drugs or alcohol, and the aging process.

Relational factors suggest that the husband may be a "marital moron" whose selfishness, overeagerness, or stupidity throttles romance and fills his wife with revulsion toward sex (Coleman). Resentment on the part of either marital partner (usually the wife), for whatever reason, can inhibit or destroy sexual functioning. So also can any of a number of other forces, realistic or unrealistic, that militate against a good overall relationship between husband and wife (Ellis *d*).

A common relational cause of orgasmic inadequacy in a woman is her inability to accept her mate. She may find him sexually unattractive or undesirable; he may be a poor provider; or he may not be the man she wanted to marry. For whatever reason, he does not fit her concept of "the right man" (Masters and Johnson p). Because a woman is typically aware that sexual capability is highly important to her husband, she can, by withholding her sexual response, express her conscious or unconscious hostility toward him and produce havoc in his self-esteem (McGuire and Steinhilber).

The most common and by far the most important causes of orgasmic dysfunctioning are psychological (Coleman; Ellis a, b, d), typically such emotional problems as shame, guilt, and fear. Many women in our culture are indoctrinated from an early age, either directly or by implication, into a warped sexual attitude (Ellis d). They are taught to suppress sexual feelings, thereby formulating a negative sexual value system based on the implication that sex is bad, wrong, and dirty (Masters and Johnson p).

A woman thus indoctrinated comes to judge all sexual relations, whether in or out of marriage, as rather evil and to be avoided. Even if she cannot avoid sexual activity on the physical plane, she can minimize her participation by refusing to become involved in the interaction of sexual response. The inhibitory forces interfering with sexual warmth and responsiveness are legion. A girl may expect physical pain at coitus and therefore dread it. She may fear rejection or condemnation by her husband if she lets herself go sexually or be frightened of becoming pregnant. She may have homosexual tendencies, be too emotionally tied to her father, or bear a repressed hostility toward men in general. All these circumstances can inhibit her from responding warmly to her husband (Ellis b, d).

One other notable and rather sad cause of many women's inability to respond sexually is their overconcern with orgasmic response. Such women approach sexual activity with a grim determination, which is usually self-defeating, to reach a climax (Ellis d). What is quite obviously needed is a more relaxed attitude. These women should cease criticizing and condemning themselves because they do not experience rapid or multiple orgasms or because their climaxes are not as monumental as they fancy "modern" women's should be. Once they begin to enjoy coition for the pleasure it *does* give them (and their husbands), their chances eventually to have orgasmic responses will increase significantly.

The Treatment of Female Orgasmic Dysfunction

Most barriers to warm sexual interaction can be toppled if treated with patience by both husband and wife. Albert Ellis recommends coping with frigidity through self-therapy in conjunction with any medical or psychological treatment that seems advisable (Ellis b, d). These are some of his suggestions for arousing an unresponsive woman:

Select a suitable time for sexual activity, e.g., when the woman is rested and as free from immediate troubles as possible.

There should be a minimum of disharmony between the partners at the time chosen.

Kindness, consideration, and expressions of love usually prove more effective than rough treatment.

The husband should acquaint himself with the parts of his wife's body that are especially responsive to stimulation, and they should be caressed.

It is often effective to take brief periods of rest between efforts at arousal.

Genital, particularly clitoral, stimulation should precede intromission.

Mild stimulants are sometimes useful.

The wife's focusing on sexually stimulating fantasy is helpful, while the husband can offer encouragement through using terms of endearment and emphasizing his distinct interest and pleasure in her. Sexually arousing conversation often is of benefit.

If arousal is attainable but the woman is to an extent sexually insensitive, then one or more of the following procedures are recommended: steady and rhythmic pressure, intermittent or forceful strokings, and verbal encouragements. A woman's stimulating herself is often a valuable aid to her husband in his attempts at arousing her.

The use of deep, forceful penile-vaginal penetration is often helpful, although it may call for special coital positions together with prior or simultaneous noncoital stimulation. Orgasm, whenever and however possible, is the goal; simultaneous climax is not important.

Stimulative methods, such as oral-genital contact and especially the use of hand vibrators, are frequently successful in producing orgasmic response in a woman. Whatever technique promises success should be used. It bears repeating that orgasm, whenever and however achieved, is the objective. Once orgasm is attained and the woman gains confidence in her ability, subsequent orgasms are usually more easily and more frequently reached.

In 1973, Seymour Fischer published the results of a five-year study of factors involved in women's sexual responsiveness. Conducted among 300 middle-class married women in Syracuse, New York, this investigation failed to confirm many previously held beliefs about female sexuality. For example, no relationship was found between a woman's orgasmic responsiveness and her husband's sexual technique, her source of sex education, her parents' attitudes toward sex, or her religiosity, femininity, general mental health, traumatic sexual experiences (or lack of them), sensitivity to stimulation, or premarital and marital experience. The women who experience orgasm through vaginal penetration were no more emotionally mature than those who achieve it through direct clitoral stimulation.

In fact, about 66% of the women stated that, of the two, they prefer clitoral stimulation. Probably the most interesting of Fischer's findings is that highly orgasmic women are more likely than others to have been reared by fathers who were dependable, caring, demanding men who were "insistent that their daughters meet certain moral standards and expectations" (Fischer, S.).

It should be understood that many of Fischer's conclusions stand in opposition to many well-designed research investigations of the recent past. Most authorities in the field of human sexuality are firm in their belief that a woman's sexual responsiveness is contingent upon many circumstances and that to offer an explanation based upon a single factor is a far too simplistic approach that does not take into consideration known facts.

Masters and Johnson assert that the key to successful treatment of female orgasmic dysfunction is understanding the patient's sexual value system, always bearing in mind that woman, far more than man, must feel that she has society's permission to express her sexuality. The therapists' first task, then, is to determine what the woman's sexual attitudes are. She may simply be unrealistic in what she expects from the sexual relationship or from her husband, thus committing herself to a state of constant disappointment, which blocks her sexual response. In a round-table discussion with both husband and wife, the therapists determine what pleases her sexually and what repels her. They then explain that the female partner must be taught to respond to sexual stimulation within the framework of her particular attitudes and sexual desires (Calderone *a;* Masters and Johnson *p*).

Following this clinical discussion, the couple put the sensate-focus theory into practice, nude, in the privacy of their bedroom. The man sits on the bed with his back against the headboard and his legs spread apart. His wife sits between his legs, her back against his chest and her legs over his. In this position she can guide his hands to indicate which tactile sensations are the most pleasing to her.

The couple have been advised that stimulation should be directed toward the inner thighs, the vaginal lips, and the clitoral area. Because of its great sensitivity, and the possibility of pain or unpleasantness, direct contact with the glans of the clitoris is to be avoided at this point. Furthermore, the woman may well be striving to overcome her resistance to emerging as a sexual being. She might therefore be overwhelmed by—and retreat from—sexual sensations that come too rapidly or are too intense. If vaginal secretions are insufficient to keep the vulval area moist, liberal use of a commercial lubricant (e.g., K-Y ointment) is recommended. Through the teasing technique of advance and retreat, first one and then another erogenous zone is stimulated, care always being taken not to stimulate the genital region too long at a time.

As in the treatment of all sexual inadequacies, the partners are discouraged from attempting to reach orgasm; they are told simply to seek and sustain sensual pleasure. Once they can successfully reach one level of pleasure, they move to the next, and then to the next. On each day of the treatment, they repeat the cycle from the beginning, working through each plateau of erotic pleasure that they have previously attained.

As the next major step, the woman is advised to mount her husband in a comfortable, relaxed position, usually the female-superior position. Once his penis has been inserted, she remains quite still so that she can feel and enjoy the penile containment.

After full penetration she may begin slow, controlled pelvic movements to heighten her pleasurable sensations. The husband remains motionless, allowing her to direct her movements to her full satisfaction. When she feels the urge to do so, she may increase the speed and force

FIGURE 18.3   Female–superior coital position.

of her pelvic thrusts. She may then indicate to her partner to begin cooperative hip movements.

During any coital activity, it is recommended that the couple take several "breaks" and lie in each other's arms, quietly caressing one another. This quietude gives the woman an opportunity to think and feel sexually, something that is not often possible during actual coition. A key to ultimately achieving an orgasm is to enjoy quiet, unhurried sensate pleasure and to guard against the attempt to force or *will* an orgasm.

Having successfully progressed thus far, the couple may now enter the final phase of their self-training program—intercourse in the lateral coital or the side-by-side position. This position gives the man better control over his ejaculation, and allows the woman more freedom to regulate her hip movements. Coital mobility is very important, but move-

FIGURE 18.4 Lateral coital position.

ment uninhibited by any conscious thought processes is probably of greater importance. It has been found that women who can consciously control their coital movements at the height of intercourse are not so likely to reach orgasm as are those who lose control of their movements (Shope *b*).

Masters and Johnson (*p*) describe in detail the steps to be taken in shifting from the female-superior position to the lateral coital position. (Compare Fig. 18.3 with Fig. 18.4.) The husband elevates his wife's right leg and moves his left leg outside hers, extended at approximately a 45° angle. The wife now extends her right leg and rests it on the bed in such a way that she supports her weight primarily on her left knee. As these changes occur, the wife leans forward to make her trunk parallel to her husband's. While the husband holds his wife's body close to him with his encircling arms to maintain penile insertion, the couple roll to his left. Once they are settled into the lateral position, their trunks are to be separated at about a 30° angle. The man then rolls from his left side and rests on his back. The wife should now be resting largely on her stomach and chest, facing her husband, with her left side slightly elevated. Sometimes it is advantageous to use pillows to help support and maintain this attitude. This position frees the woman's left and the man's right arm for body caressing. Her left knee and right leg, meanwhile, provide comfortable and easy support for her free pelvic thrusting, as the couple's sex tensions require.

Masters and Johnson report 83.4% success in their treatment of primary orgasmic dysfunction and 77.2% in situational cases—an 80.7% overall rate of success.

The Unconsummated Marriage

It should be mentioned here that emotional barriers are sometimes so overwhelming that a woman altogether refuses to attempt sexual intercourse even though she is married. Several scientific investigations have been made into the causes and nature of unconsummated marriages. One of the most extensive and revealing of these studies concerned 1000 American Caucasian females ranging in age from 17 to 47 years (average age, 29 years) (Blazer). The length of marriage—and period of nonconsummation—ranged from 1 to 21 years (average length of marriage, 8 years), with 98% of the women having been married for more than 3 years. Of the sample, 76% had married between the ages of 20 and 29.

All of the 1000 were deemed physically capable of sexual intercourse. A gynecologist examined each of the subjects and if there was any doubt about a woman's being virginal, she was excluded from the sample. Although none of the women had engaged in coitus, about 25% of them did participate in mutual masturbation with their husbands.

The reasons given by these 1000 wives for their sexual abstinence fell into the following categories:

Fear of pain in the initial intercourse—203 (20.3%).

Opinion that the sex act is nasty or wicked—178 (17.8%).

Impotent husband—117 (11.7%).

Fear of pregnancy or childbirth—102 (10.2%).

Small size of the vagina—82 (8.2%). (Physical examinations revealed that neither husbands' nor wives' genitals were beyond the range of normalcy.)

The couple's ignorance regarding the exact location of the wife's sex organs—52 (5.2%).

Preference for a female partner—52 (5.2%).

Extreme dislike of the penis—46 (4.6%).

Deep objection to intercourse unless impregnation is intended—39 (3.9%).

Dislike of contraceptives—33 (3.3%).

Belief that submission of woman to man implies inferiority—31 (3.1%). (Reasons given by these women for entering marriage included "the thing to do," "fear of being an 'old maid'," and "security.")

General dislike of men—30 (3.0%).

Desire only to "mother" their husbands—14 (1.4%).

Fear of damaging husband's penis—12 (1.2%).

Fear of semen—9 (0.9%).

The conclusion drawn by the researchers in this study was that, if these psychosexually disturbed women had been given appropriate sex education at an early age, the sexual problems of at least 80% to 85% of them very likely would not have existed—or persisted. Even in the absence of proper sex education, psychotherapeutic treatment of married virgins is reported to be about 70% successful.

DYSPAREUNIA

Dyspareunia is painful coitus. It can happen to both men and women, although women are affected far more frequently than men are. Men sometimes experience acute pain at the time of erection, but that is not actually dyspareunia. It can be said to occur in men only when orgasm causes severe, jabbing pain. The pain is commonly the result of congestion of the prostate, seminal vesicles, or ejaculatory ducts, or an inflamed verumontanum. In other cases, the pain may be caused by an irritation of the glans penis in the uncircumcised male arising from poor hygienic habits. Peyronie's disease (see Chapter 20) can also make coitus painful for a man. Otherwise, dyspareunia in men is extremely rare.

Dyspareunia in women frequently has its inception in tension, fear, or anxiety over initial sexual intercourse, and the pain can involve vagina, cervix, uterus, or bladder. The vaginal muscles become taut and coitus can be painful, especially if the husband is clumsy or insensitive. Furthermore, depending upon the type and thickness of the hymen, pain may be experienced when the tissue is ruptured by penile penetration (Ellis *b*; Kelly *a*; Netter).

Coitus may be painful because of lesions or scar tissue formed in the vaginal opening as a result of an episiotomy, a crude nonprofessional abortion, or rape, especially gang rape (the last quite predictably capable of causing as much emotional as physical trauma productive of dyspareunia). An accumulation of smegma under the clitoral foreskin may harden and cause a painful burning sensation when the clitoris enlarges during sexual excitation. (Women who counterfeit pain as a way of avoiding coitus seldom complain of the symptoms described above; instead, they typically complain of "deep pain," which they claim is especially severe with pelvic thrusting [Lehrman].) Some women suffer considerable pain when the cervix is touched and moved by the penis during sexual intercourse; coitus, in fact, becomes impossible at times.

Dyspareunia in postmenopausal women frequently occurs because the mucous membrane of the vagina has become fragile and thin, sometimes shrinking in thickness to a fraction of its size in younger women. It therefore does not secrete sufficient lubrication for easy penile intromission. Vaginal creams containing female hormones are frequently prescribed in such cases to act as a lubricant and to stimulate the mucous membrane (Clark *h*; Rubin *j*).

A displaced or prolapsed uterus is another persistent cause of painful coitus in women. So also are polyps, cysts, and tumors of the reproductive system. Some women suffer pain during sexual intercourse because the vaginal barrel is irritated by the chemicals contained in contraceptive creams, foams, jellies, or suppositories. Other women react painfully to the rubber or plastic that condoms and diaphragms are made of, and to excessive douching.

Still other women produce insufficient vaginal lubrication during coition, so that coital movements produce a painful or burning sensation. (In this last case, coital discomfort can be avoided by using a commercial lubricant.)

Medical opinion is that if dyspareunia persists over a period of time, small undetected lesions in the vagina (which cause 85% of the cases) are to be suspected (Kleegman *a*). Furthermore, any infections of the vagina, uterus, bladder, or surrounding areas can obviously make intercourse painful for a woman. Surgically severing particular nerves leading to the uterus has given complete relief from dyspareunia in some cases. The surgery does not diminish the sexual enjoyment of 80% of the women so treated (Wright).

Medical and surgical approaches are clearly of great value in attacking many of the causes of dyspareunia. Nevertheless, the benefits of psychotherapy should not be overlooked when the foundations of the disorder appear to lie in emotional blocks and fears.

Vaginismus

Vaginismus is an extremely powerful and often severely painful contraction of the muscles surrounding the vaginal tract. Anticipated pain of first penile penetration, or fear or guilt concerning sexual intercourse, can cause these muscular spasms, which may persist for long periods of time. In severe cases an attempt even to introduce the penis into the vagina will often produce agonizing pain making penile penetration impossible. In less severe cases, the vaginal spasms merely delay intromission or make it more difficult.

Masters and Johnson assert that the chief cause of vaginismus is an impotent husband whose repeated attempts at sexual intercourse followed by an equal number of failures have so greatly frustrated his wife that she protects herself subconsciously by closing the vaginal doors. Other im-

---

FIGURE 18.5 Schematic representation of the vagina, showing the vaginal muscles, relaxed (left) and contracted (right).

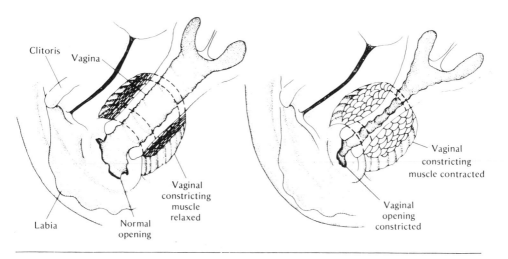

portant causes of vaginismus are the inhibitions formed by emotionally traumatic experiences, such as rape; inner conflict growing out of homosexual tendencies; and physical anomalies that make intercourse extremely painful (Masters and Johnson p).

The noted marriage counselor David Mace has suggested an additional dimension in the problem of vaginismus. He theorizes that in some instances the woman is saying to her partner, in effect, "I am afraid to let you come fully into my life by opening myself freely and trustfully to you" (Mace c).

Husbands as well as wives must understand the dynamics behind vaginismus and must avoid any behavior that will produce discomfort for either partner. A selfish, inconsiderate, and brutal husband can do irreparable damage to the marriage by forging ahead like a battering ram in his attempts at sexual intercourse when his wife is suffering these muscular spasms.

Vaginismus, strangely, seldom occurs in women of the lower socioeconomic-educational strata. It is an affliction almost exclusively of women in the upper levels of these groups (Kelly a).

Sometimes local anesthetics applied to the vulva, vagina, and hymenal area before intromission is attempted are successful in reducing the pain. But professional assistance is often required. The therapist can explain the causes of vaginismus and perhaps demonstrate to the husband that the insertion of even a finger into the constricted vagina will produce great distress.

In treatment, the wife is given several dilators of graduated sizes to use in stretching the vaginal muscles so that she can comfortably accommodate her husband's penis (Shaw). After the largest dilator can be inserted without stress or pain, she is encouraged to retain it for several hours each night—perhaps to sleep with it in place throughout the night. Use of dilators for a three- to five-day period is usually highly successful in helping to relieve the involuntary spasms of vaginismus (Masters and Johnson p). Because the dysfunction frequently has its roots in the psychological quagmire of fear, guilt, and shame, however, physical efforts at overcoming it may be unsuccessful and psychotherapy may therefore be indicated.

All 29 of the patients treated by Masters and Johnson for vaginismus found relief from their symptoms. Of these, 20 experienced orgasm for the first time and 6 regained their ability to achieve orgasm. Only 3 remained nonorgasmic (Masters and Johnson p).

19 SEXUAL VARIANCE

One of the major problems in the field of sexology today—and, indeed, in the whole realm of mental health—centers around the question of what is normal sexual behavior and what is abnormal.

Too many people are ready to stigmatize any sexual activity that deviates from their own method of sexual behavior as being aberrant or perverted (Ellis a). Yet in the course of human history, sexual practices and ethics have varied widely within and among different cultures. What is usual in one culture may be unusual in another, and thus may become branded as abnormal, although unusual sexual behavior is not tantamount to perversion simply because it is out of the ordinary for a given culture. Indeed, as Judd Marmor (a) points out, "our attitudes concerning nudity, virginity, fidelity, love, marriage, and proper sexual behavior are meaningful only within the context of our own cultural and religious mores." In discussing the differences between healthy and unhealthy sexual behavior, he says further:

> In our culture, a key distinguishing factor between what is regarded as healthy or unhealthy sexual behavior is whether such behavior is motivated by feelings of love or whether it becomes a vehicle for the discharge of anxiety, hostility, or guilt. Healthy sexuality seeks erotic pleasure in the

context of tenderness and affection; pathologic sexuality is motivated by needs for reassurance or relief from nonsexual sources of tension. Healthy sexuality seeks both to give and receive pleasure; neurotic forms are unbalanced toward excessive giving or taking. Healthy sexuality is discriminating as to partner; neurotic patterns often tend to be nondiscriminating. The periodicity of healthy sexuality is determined primarily by recurrent erotic tensions in the context of affection. Neurotic sexual drives, on the other hand, are triggered less by erotic needs than by nonerotic tensions and are therefore more apt to be compulsive in their patterns of occurrence.

Many terms are used by the public and professionals to describe sexual behavior that, in their view, differs from the normal: *sexual abnormality, deviation, aberration, perversion, variance.* But as the subject is studied more objectively, it becomes increasingly apparent that true sexual abnormality is very difficult to define and pinpoint. The term *variance* is therefore gaining increasingly broad acceptance as the fairest word to use— the one least emotionally charged or connotative of disapproval.

The present discussion is not intended to add fuel to the fire of this controversy, but, rather, to allow the reader to view different forms of sexual expression in an objective light, and perhaps thereby to attain a better understanding of certain of his fellowmen.

Men reveal a far greater tendency toward variant sexual behavior than women do. The dynamics behind this gender difference are related perhaps to the fact that boys develop a stronger sex drive earlier in life than girls do. They are therefore exposed to a greater number of sexual experiences that could possibly lead to variance. Furthermore, men are much more interested in injecting variety in their sex life than women are, which also might result in a conditioned preference for one form of variance or another.

It is possible for an individual to label himself as a pervert simply because he lacks basic knowledge of what normal sexual behavior really is. He consequently believes that his fantasies and behavior, or the frequency of either, deviates markedly from the public norm (Everett). When humans do engage in truly abnormal sexual behavior on a continuing, compulsive basis, the behavior is typically unrelated to sexual needs. Rather, it is a symbolic, ongoing attempt to solve deep-seated personal problems (Auerback b).

The only way that individuals can really know what constitutes acceptable sexual behavior within their society, and therefore function sexually without guilt or fear of discovery, is for that society to establish liberal but definitive outer limits of sexual normalcy. The boundaries of acceptability must be set by those acts that society judges as being *true* sexual aberration, not mere variation. Within these boundaries a society can then develop an orderly pattern of acceptable expressions of sexuality (Erikson).

Sociologists and other behavioral scientists have recently begun to view sexual variance as a social process rather than as a social disease (Denfield and Gordon). Howard Becker in his book *Outsiders* sums up this new position thus:

> We ought not to view it [variant behavior] as something special, as depraved or in some magical way better than other kinds of behavior. We ought to see it simply as a kind of behavior some disapprove of and others value, studying the process by which either or both perspectives are built up and maintained.

Society seems, then, to be progressing toward a more liberal definition of what constitutes normal sexual activity. Generally speaking, if sexual behavior is not harmful to the participants, if it is carried out by consenting adults (adults who are willing to assume all responsibility for their acts) without any sort of coercion, and if it is out of sight and sound of unwilling observers—it should be considered acceptable, whether or not others would care to participate in similar acts. These criteria, then, would probably serve as a valid basis on which to judge what is and is not variant behavior (Ellis a).

Sexual variance may be considered as falling into three categories: (1) variance in the method of functioning and quality of the sexual striving; (2) variance in the choice of the sexual partner or object; and (3) variance in the degree and strength of the sexual drive (Thorpe *et al.*).

VARIANCE IN METHODS OF FUNCTIONING AND QUALITY OF SEXUAL STRIVINGS

Sadism

Sadism is a sexual abnormality wherein the disturbed person gains sexual gratification, or at least an increase in sexual pleasure, by inflicting either physical or psychological pain upon his partner in the sexual relationship. The aggressive act has no purpose other than that the pain thus caused is the source of sexual gratification.

The term *sadism* derives from the name of the French author, the Marquis de Sade (1740–1814). This man wrote extensively of his erotic exploits, which included several marriages, being arrested for cruel acts in houses of prostitution, luring a shopkeeper's wife into a house where he horsewhipped her at gunpoint, eloping with his wife's sister, administering poisonous "aphrodisiac" drugs to guests, and severing the veins of a woman whom he confined to a house, in addition to inflicting hundreds of scalpel wounds upon her.

The causes of sadism are as varied as the means of expressing it. The disturbed person may have been taught, consciously or unconsciously, to have disgust for anything sexual. Because normal sexuality is unacceptable to him, his acts of cruelty are a punishment of his partner for engaging in something so shameful.

Another source of sadism is a fear of castration (feelings of inferiority), wherein the sadistic acts reassure the sadist that he is more powerful than his partner, and therefore need have no fear. Until the sadist convinces himself that he plays the superior role in the sexual relationship, his partner remains overwhelmingly threatening to him. In other cases, the sadist's behavior is merely a method of acting out repressed hostility towards his parents (Coleman; Moore; Thorpe *et al.*).

Whipping, biting, pinching, and slapping are typical of the acts of physical pain inflicted by the sadist. If sadism is expressed verbally, it is in the form of sarcastic remarks, belittling, threatening, teasing, or bullying. As with nearly all forms of sexual variance, sadism is found more frequently among men than women, probably because of its aggressive nature. It should be remembered, however, that this aggressiveness may be unconscious and expressed indirectly or deviously, as well as through the conscious and direct actions mentioned above.

Lust murder is the extreme of sadistic sexual abnormality, as the victim must be murdered and mutilated in order to provide the perpetrator with sexual gratification. In true lust murders, no coitus occurs; orgasm is the outcome of the act of murder and mutilation. At least at the time of the act, such a person's mental illness is at the psychotic level. The underlying cause of such violence often relates to a fear of possible rejection by a mature woman, and an accompanying hostility and aggression.

Masochism

Masochism is the mirror image of sadism. The disturbed person receives sexual pleasure or gratification from being hurt, physically or mentally, by his sexual partner. This disorder also derives its name from a historical figure, the Austrian novelist Leopold von Sacher-Masoch (1836–1895). A Doctor of Law at the age of 19, he experienced a long career of masochistic involvements. His first love, an older woman who insulted and victimized him at every turn, finally left him for a Russian adventurer. He then met a princess who compelled him to serve as her valet and secretary until she tired of him. After affairs with two baronesses, the second a lesbian, he married an extremely ugly woman who satisfied his craving for punishment but who eventually deserted him.

Masochism, like sadism, develops from an attitude of shame and disgust toward normal heterosexual relationships. The masochist uses the pain and punishment inflicted on him to wash away the guilt he associates with his sexual desires. In other cases, he dominates his partner with his ability to endure punishment, which to his way of thinking proclaims to the world his strength and superiority, and which also serves to muke him the center of attention. Often, the sexual partner is identified with a parent-figure who dominated him as a child. For example, the masochist may remember experiencing sexual excitement in childhood while being beaten, a sensation centered in the erogenous zones of the skin about the buttocks and the muscles below the skin.

Many sexologists believe that the masochist does not actually wish to be beaten or otherwise to undergo physical pain, but merely wants to signify his acquiescence to his partner by his willingness to submit to physical or mental maltreatment. In all events, it appears that the masochist is so fearful of rejection that he is willing to be subjected to almost any humiliation or punishment that will please his partner and win for him, as he sees it, affection and acceptance (Coleman; Moore).

According to certain psychoanalytic interpretations, the masochist considers suffering a prerequisite to pleasure, since pain and sexual pleasure are somehow connected in his past experiences. In addition, stressing one's own helplessness is an appeal to the threatening or protecting power that now rests in his partner. In men, masochism is often a symbol of self-castration which, in their view, robs others of the power to castrate them.

This aberration may also take the form of mental masochism wherein the individual seeks out mental rather than physical suffering. Anthropologists and psychologists view sadomasochistic behavior as an essential part of the mating relationship of many lower primates and other animals. And in primitive societies, forms of sexual violence, such as deep scratch and bite wounds, are commonplace. However, when individuals deliberately conjure up fantasies of ill-treatment that are sexually exciting, or when they actively seek physical and psychological pain, such as from chaining, beating, switching, kicking, and verbal abuse, as means of enhancing their sexual powers and pleasure, there is cause for concern and psychological treatment is definitely indicated (Coleman; Thorpe et al.).

Exhibitionism

Exhibitionism is a variance wherein sexual gratification is derived from exhibiting the genitals to unwitting (and typically unwilling) sexual prey. Its pathology lies in the fact that satisfaction is gained in a vicarious manner rather than through a straightforward sexual experience. A relatively common sexual problem, it is involved in 35% of all arrests for sexual violations (Allen, C. a). Far more men than women are exhibitionists, although just how many women do actually exhibit themselves is impossible to determine. The public has a more tolerant attitude toward the exposed bodies of women than it does toward those of men, and women found exposing themselves would probably not be reported by the beholder.

The inception of this behavior is, classically, the exhibitionist's feeling of insignificance or inadequacy: he hopes to gain the attention he craves through exhibition. Some psychoanalysts believe that this deviancy stems from a fear of castration, the exposure of self being explained as an attempt to disprove castration. Others claim that exhibitionism is an extreme form of autoeroticism based on narcissistic (self-love) impulses.

Typically, the male exhibitionist is a quiet, timid, submissive person who lacks normal aggressiveness and who is beset with feelings of inadequacy and insecurity. He is usually described as being "nice" but immature. He characteristically was reared in a cultural atmosphere of overstrict and puritanical attitudes toward sex, and his formative years were dominated by a powerful, engulfing mother. Despite the fact that most of these men are married, the sexual relationship with their wives is quite likely a poor one. All these influences work to create in exhibitionists pervading doubts and fears concerning their masculinity (Coleman). Indeed, when one applies such criteria as frequency of coitus with spouse or lover, degree of impotence, number of coital partners, and age at which first coital experience occurred, the typical exhibitionist must be judged as undersexed (Mathis *b*).

Since the exhibitionist obviously hopes his actions will have a profound shock effect on the viewer, the woman who responds hysterically to his behavior merely feeds his illness. Confronted by an exhibitionist, a woman's most sensible approach is calmly to ignore the act and to suggest that he stands in need of psychological help and can benefit from it.

Pseudoexhibitionism is often confused with true exhibitionism. In this syndrome, a person is under stress because heterosexual relations are not available, and he exhibits himself only as a poor substitute for the sexual intercourse that he prefers.

It should be remembered that the exhibitionist is more of a nuisance than a menace. He rarely becomes involved in more serious crimes; and when he does, his criminality is classically of a nonsexual nature. The exhibitionist seldom exposes himself while he is close to his victim. He chooses, rather, to remain at a safe distance—usually from 6 to 60 feet away (Gebhard *et al. a*).

Exhibitionism frequently is linked with a compulsive pattern of behavior wherein the display occurs in the same place and usually at the same time of day, indicating the exhibitionist's desire or need to be apprehended. In these linkage cases, the prognosis is fairly good. The factors involved in their exhibitionistic tendencies are more easily made clear and intelligible to the majority of these patients than they are to most nonlinkage ones. Understanding the etiology of their difficulties, they appear to feel that a serious effort on their part will lead to a more healthy sexual adjustment.

Scoptophilia and Voyeurism

Scoptophilia and voyeurism are disturbances in which the viewer of sexual acts and erotic things derives unusual sensual pleasure and gratification. There is a difference between the two: *scoptophilia* refers to pleasure gained from observing sexual acts and genitalia, while *voyeurism* involves only the scrutinizing of nudes (Karpman). The terms are frequently used interchangeably, however, with voyeurism being the more popular.

In the case of the voyeur (commonly called a "Peeping Tom"), the viewing is usually done secretly. In his efforts to observe the sexual activity of others, he often peers hopefully through windows, or he may go to such lengths as to bore peepholes through walls and doors of toilets, dressing rooms, and guest rooms. Only a small number of women are known to be voyeurs or scoptophiliacs. According to FBI reports, nine men to one woman are arrested on charges of "peeping."

Like other sexually variant behavior, these two deviant phenomena are believed to develop as defense mechanisms against what the individual feels is a threat to his self-evaluation. By engaging merely in surreptitious examination of sexual details, he guards against any personal failure in coitus, at the same time enjoying a feeling of superiority over those whom he secretly observes. According to psychoanalytic interpretation, fixations relating to certain events witnessed as a child, e.g., seeing parents in the act of sexual intercourse, underlie voyeurism.

As in the case of exhibitionism, many of the milder incidents of voyeurism may in fact be classified as *pseudovoyeurism*, since they are merely substitutes for preferred but unattainable coitus. Furthermore, the desire to view the naked body of one's sexual partner is certainly normal; so also is the pleasure a couple experience in viewing themselves by way of mirrors in the act of coitus itself. Viewing becomes abnormal only when it is consistently preferred to petting or sexual intercourse.

Nudism

Nudism is regarded by some as an aberration because they erroneously equate it with exhibitionism. Social nudism, however, is not a sexual deviation. As a matter of fact the overall atmosphere in most nudist camps is, because of rigidly enforced rules of behavior, more suggestive of asexuality than of sexual permissiveness (Weinberg, M. S.).

To many people, clothing symbolizes restraints of personality and character structure. They reason that, once these artificial restraints are removed through nudity, they will become more relaxed psychologically and their interpersonal relationships will improve. The average nudist is also the average citizen, although he may have freed himself of certain taboos that the rest of us remain shackled with.

The male nudist, in company with almost all men, prefers watching a woman undress to finding her already nude. The vast majority of both male and female nudists report that their coital frequency remains unchanged as a result of practicing nudism, although over 33% of them express the opinion that nudism has contributed positively to their sexual happiness (Hartman *et al.*).

Troilism

Troilism (also *triolism*) is the sharing of a sexual partner with another person while the third person looks on. It also may involve two couples having sexual relations at the same time in the visual presence of each other. The traditional view of the troilist is of a sexual inadequate who cannot perform the sex act unless he is partaking in the "sharing" experience (Branson a).

Many sexologists are of the opinion that troilism encompasses elements of voyeurism and exhibitionism. Others believe that it is an expression of latent or disguised homosexuality, since the troilist may identify with his marital partner during these erotic activities. However, the premise that troilism is sexually variant must be reexamined in the light of recent preliminary research findings concerning mate-swappers (see pages 391-393). In any case, troilism is far more prevalent among men than among women, in that men usually instigate the behavior pattern and derive the greatest pleasure from it—at least initially.

Transvestism

Transvestism, or *cross-dressing*, refers to excitement or gratification, either emotional or sexual, derived from dressing in the clothes of the opposite sex (Brown, D. G. a). There is some doubt, because of the curious nature and ramifications of this behavior, whether it should be included in this or the second category of variance. However, since the disturbance seems more a matter of functioning than of deviant choice of sexual object, it is included here. Although most people think that transvestites are drawn primarily from the homosexual segment of the population, in actuality such behavior is found among the heterosexual, asexual, and bisexual population as well.

The practice usually begins in early childhood and is often evoked by parental rejection of the sex of the child. An unattractive woman will sometimes retaliate by dressing in a man's clothing. Whatever the cause, many transvestites engage only in normal and acceptable sexual activities,

their strange dressing habits on "special occasions" being their only deviation. Most of these people are able to make a satisfactory adjustment to
sex and marriage, especially when they receive understanding and cooperation from their marriage partner.

Authorities agree that the majority of transvestites are decidedly *not*
homosexual. In fact, 74% of the 272 transvestites surveyed in one study
were married, and 69% had fathered children; only 25% admitted having
any homosexual experience at all (Benjamin *d*). This last figure is especially
interesting, since the Kinsey researchers found that 37% of all men have
had at least one homosexual contact to the point of orgasm in their lives.

The differences between the homosexual and the transvestite have
probably been best established by an active transvestite, who writes and
lectures extensively on the subject under the name of Virginia "Charles"
Prince. Transvestism, Prince points out, is typically a secret pursuit involving
only one individual; homosexuality obviously must involve two people,
and, furthermore, to attract a partner, the homosexual must reveal himself
as being one. The transvestite might be said to possess two personalities,
one male and the other female, which alternately assert themselves. By
contrast, the homosexual is always a homosexual (Prince).

Transvestism is obviously not a phenomenon new to the twentieth
century. As a matter of fact, a pre-Revolutionary governor of New York,
Lord Cornbury, had sufficient temerity to appear in public in female garb.
Philippe, Duke of Orleans and brother of France's "Sun King," Louis XIV,
was also a celebrated transvestite.

Herodotus, the early Greek historian, wrote of a primitive group of
people living on the shore of the Black Sea in which the men not only
wore female clothes but engaged in traditionally female activities. He attributed their behavior to repeated horseback-riding accidents that led to
atrophy of the reproductive organs, and subsequent impotence and effeminacy! Similar organic theories concerning transvestism persist today, along
with theories placing the onus on hormonal imbalance. But these theories
are discredited by practically all specialists in the field of sexology (Brown,
D. G. *a*).

Estimates vary, but transvestism exists today in possibly less than 1%
of the population. The difficulty in making a more accurate estimate of its
prevalence lies in the secrecy with which perhaps 90% of transvestites
induge in their cross-dressing habits (Brown, D. G. *a*).

The pattern of cross-dressing varies among transvestites. In one instance, women's apparel is worn only periodically. In another, the man
has a fetishlike fondness for a particular article of women's clothing—e.g.,
panties or a brassiere—which he habitually wears under his own masculine
clothing. In yet another, the yearning to wear women's finery may be so
deeply ingrained that the transvestite discards men's clothing entirely
to embark upon a lifelong masquerade as a woman.

Transvestites typically attest to a sense of pleasure and relaxation when wearing the clothing of the opposite sex, expressing a relish for the feel of the cloth and for the view of themselves thus attired in the mirror. A man's cross-dressing allows him to express the gentle, graceful, sensuous side of his nature, a part of him that has somehow become identified with the feminine gender and that society does not permit him to express as a man.

There is nothing in the present-day understanding of genetics to support the contention that transvestism results from an inborn, instinctive predisposition toward it. As was said, the evidence is strong that transvestism is the direct result of a learning process, typically beginning in earliest childhood. The parents of transvestites (classically the mother) attempt to mask their great disappointment that their baby boy is not a girl by dressing him in feminine clothing, allowing his hair to grow long, and curling and beribboning it until he reaches school age. Sensing the beloved mother's approval of his feminine appearance, a boy can easily absorb the attitude that "girl is good." Another form of conditioning is a punishment whereby the boy is forced to wear some piece of little-girl apparel (the "pinafore punishment," as it has been called) (Brown, D. G. a).

Treatment of this variant behavior in the attempt to alter it includes psychotherapy (especially the use of aversive conditioning techniques) and the administration of hormones (although hormonal treatment is quite useless if the purpose is to bolster the man's masculine interests and behavior). Female-hormone injections are sometimes given, however, in those cases in which the man wishes to sacrifice some of his sex drive for a softer skin, less facial hair, and larger breasts. In some cases, the individual actually seeks surgery to change his genital structure to that of the opposite sex. These people, however, usually have deep-seated and serious psychiatric problems and should more correctly be called *transsexualists* rather than transvestites.

The transvestite, however, is seldom a transsexual as well. In fact, the majority of transvestites, being otherwise normal sexually—most establish normal heterosexual relationships, as stated earlier—would cringe at the suggestion of a sex-transformation operation. They merely wish to be left alone to indulge in their cross-dressing habits.

Transsexualism

Transsexualism, also called *sex-role inversion*, is a phenomenon in which an individual's anatomy and sex-role (or gender) identity are incompatible with one another (Green and Money). Although there are female transsexualists, the vast majority are male; that is, with rare exceptions, the transsexualist has the genetic and anatomical characteristics of a man. His chromosomes include the XY pair designating the male sex; he possesses normal male genitals, internally and externally; and he is capable of impregnating a woman. In no instance is the difference between the *sex* assigned by nature and the *gender identity* (Shainess) acquired through social conditioning more dramatically demonstrated than it is in the transsexual. The man knows that he is a male, yet he rejects his maleness totally. Not content with dressing as a female, as the transvestite is, he wishes to live the life of a woman—emotionally, physically, sexually. The male sex organs become such hated objects that attempts at self-castration or suicide are not uncommon among transsexuals. As Harry Benjamin—an endocrinologist and a recognized authority on transsexualism—puts it, the transsexual views his sex organs as a deformity (Buckley). Transsexualism is obviously a far more profound problem than transvestism.

The transsexual wishes to be loved as a woman by a "straight" man. He does not wish to be loved by a homosexual, whose love-sex object is another man. The transsexual is firmly convinced that some cruel caprice of nature has imposed upon him the body of a male while at the same time endowing him with the emotionality and mentality of a woman. It should be pointed out that transsexuals are not hermaphrodites—that is, they do not possess, even to a limited degree, the physical characteristics of both sexes. The problem is at the other end of the body. In his mind, the transsexual is convinced that he was given the wrong body.

The causative factors in transsexuality appear to be much the same as those in transvestism and homosexuality. The transsexualist's mother is typically an unhappy woman, who clutches her son to her bosom—literally and figuratively—entering into an intensely close relationship with him from which the father and the other children of the family are excluded (Green, R.).

The rejection of the sex assigned him by nature accounts for the dogged determination of many transsexuals to undergo a sex-change operation, despite the inherent legal and social difficulties attending such a procedure. (Imagine, for example, the passport problem when a transsexual goes abroad for such an operation as a man and returns as a woman.) It is logical to expect that most transsexuals would also be transvestites, and indeed they are, since they reject so completely the male role. Transsexuals wish to be responded to as women, not as men; hence their only hope to attract "straight" men is to present themselves to the world as female (Money and Brennan).

There are perhaps 2000 people in the United States who have undergone sex-reassignment operations, although, for obvious reasons, the identity of very few is known (Buckley; Goodall *b*). Until recently, American transsexuals had to go to Europe or Casablanca for a sex-change operation. However, fostered by the interest of Harry Benjamin (*c*), American medicine has in recent years given reluctant consideration to the dilemma of the transsexual.

Many doctors shrink from what is to them a mutilation of the human body. But, as Benjamin (d) has pointed out, all forms of psychotherapy have been singularly unsuccessful in helping these people who, in company with the transvestite and homosexual, are notoriously resistant to change. Since the transsexual's mind cannot be made to adjust to his body, Benjamin contends, the only sensible and humane course to follow is to make the body adjust to the mind.

Undergoing a sex-reassignment operation is almost a technicality for the transsexual, since he has so thoroughly rejected his sex already. Among the few hospitals and clinics in the United States that will consider his application for surgery are the Johns Hopkins Hospital, the Gender Identity Clinic at Harvard University, and the Stanford University Medical Center. These institutions perform a limited number of such operations after exhaustive consideration of each applicant. Primary requirements for consideration are that the individual has lived as a member of the opposite sex for a considerable time and has undergone female hormonal treatment. It is significant that persons approaching such operations—which involve, in a man, the removal of testicles and penis, leaving sufficient skin to form an artificial vagina—have not been known to get "cold feet" and back out. Their determination to shed the appendages of their hated genetic sex is that strong.

The Harvard Gender Identity Clinic has gathered data with respect to the postoperative lives of 13 patients on whom the operation had been performed, in addition to 4 already operated on elsewhere who underwent further reconstruction work at the clinic (Money and Brennan). Ten of these subjects had established a sexual association of some duration with a man (who will be referred to as the husband, although not all the couples had entered into a formal marriage). Of the 7 husbands on whom data were available, all had had heterosexual experience before establishing the relationship with the patient, and 2 had been previously married.

Concerning homosexual experience, one husband claimed to be bisexual and one admitted to a single homosexual contact at the age of 14. All the others maintained that they had had no homosexual contacts in their lives. Two authorities in the area of sexual disorders and abnormalities, John Money and John G. Brennan, state that "the transsexual male, though an incomplete and impersonating female, obviously projects at least the minimum of feminine cues needed to attract the erotic attention of a normal male" (Money and Brennan).

Sexual Oralism

Sexual oralism refers to pleasure obtained from the application of lips, tongue, and mouth to the sexual organs of one's partner. It is considered deviant, however, only when it is used to the exclusion of all other methods of sexual outlet. True deviation from traditional techniques in sexual activity is becoming more and more difficult to pinpoint; what is considered a deviation by one group may be perfectly normal behavior in another. For example, methods of extravaginal intercourse are frowned upon by some people, yet readily accepted by others.

Fellatio (oral stimulation of the penis) and cunnilingus (oral stimulation of the vulva) have gained reasonably wide acceptance as methods of sexual foreplay and outlet, especially in the higher educational groups. Many people will not readily admit to these practices, however, for fear of being denounced as abnormal (Eichenlaub a; Ellis b; MacLean; Van de Velde).

Sexual Analism

Sexual analism refers to the use of the anus for copulation. *Sodomy* is another term for this act, although its legal interpretation may encompass a much wider range of sexual variance. Sexual analism is seldom practiced in heterosexual contacts, except for occasional experimentation; but up to 50% of male homosexuals in the U.S. use this technique as a preferred method of sexual intercourse (Carrier; Kinsey *et al.* a).

When anal intercourse is preferred over vaginal coitus (except as a matter of simple experimentation), the explanation typically offered by psychotherapists is that it represents an extension of a childhood association between excretion and coitus, the orifices for both being near one another in a "forbidden" area of the body. Later, sexual excitation comes from experiencing erotic pleasure associated with something forbidden. There are, furthermore, those who regard sex as something "dirty" and feel the need to satisfy their sex drive in a way that is, to them, highly symbolic of this "dirtiness." Sodomy is not widely practiced, however; only about 3% of husbands engage in it with their wives (Gebhard *et al.* a; Storr).

Masters and Johnson state that the most persistent organism invading and infecting a woman's vaginal tract originates in the bowel. Following anal intercourse, if a man were to penetrate the vagina, he might thus infect it by his bacterially contaminated penis (Masters and Johnson p). A woman wishing to avoid certain vaginal infections should insist that her partner not penetrate both rectum and vagina during a single sexual encounter.

Homosexuals and, to a lesser extent, heterosexuals make use of other body parts in sexual relations—for example, using the space between the thighs, which is an act called *interfemoral sexual intercourse*. Scientific opinion is that there is nothing physically or psychologically wrong or abnormal with nonvaginal methods of coitus.

VARIANCE IN THE CHOICE OF SEXUAL PARTNER OR OBJECT

Homosexuality

Homosexuality, as noted, implies that an individual is sexually attracted to a member of the same sex, or has manifest sexual relations with him or her. In existence since the dawn of civilization, homosexuality was practiced openly and widely by the Romans. The ancient Greeks regarded homosexual love as being not only natural but also more exalted and tender than heterosexual love. Among the citizen class, heterosexual love often represented a practical situation—an ordered household, tax refuge, and the means of producing legitimate progeny. Homosexual love, on the other hand, was considered more properly entwined with the philosophical, intellectual, and spiritual pursuits so prized by the Greeks (Karlen). Public attitude toward homosexuality today, however, is quite different from what it was in the distant past.

Kinsey and his co-workers established that there are degrees of sexuality, and they devised a seven-point scale to categorize the heterosexual–homosexual balance (Kinsey *et al.* a). At one extreme is exclusive heterosexuality in which no homosexuality is involved. This is followed by predominant heterosexuality with only incidental homosexuality. Then follows predominant heterosexuality, but with more than incidental homosexuality.

FIGURE 19.1 Schematic representation of the Kinsey continuum of heterosexuality-homosexuality.

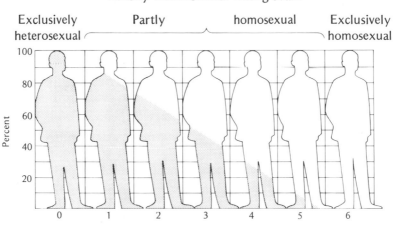

Kinsey homosexual rating scale

At midpoint, there is sexual functioning at equal heterosexual and homosexual levels. Still further along the continuum is predominant homosexuality, but with more than incidental heterosexuality; then predominant homosexuality with only incidental heterosexuality; and, finally, exclusive homosexuality with no heterosexual leanings at all.

True homosexuals experience their first orgasm with another person at an earlier age than heterosexuals do (Bieber, I.). To recapitulate the findings of the Kinsey researchers, 60% of all boys and 33% of girls have engaged in at least one act of overtly homosexual sex play with another person by the age of 15. They found also that 37% of the male and 13% of the female population engage at one time in their lives in some form of homosexual activity to the point of orgasm. Of men, 8% have been exclusively homosexual for a period of at least three years, and 4% have been homosexual all their lives (Kinsey *et al. a;* Reiss *d*). A study of 2200 college women showed that over 50% had experienced intense feelings for other women (Davis, K. B.).

The consensus among authorities, however, is that male homosexuals outnumber female homosexuals about two or three to one, although the cause for this imbalance is frequently debated (Kinsey *et al. a, c*). The average male homosexual has his first homosexual experience some time before his fourteenth birthday; the average lesbian, at about 19 or 20 years of age (Kaye).

Homosexual expression is usually thought to fall into three patterns: active, wherein the individual plays the male role regardless of his own sex; passive, in which the participant, whether man or woman, plays the female role; and mixed, in which the individual assumes an active role one time and a passive role the next. The mixed role is the pattern most frequently followed by homosexuals.

Principal homosexual practices include masturbation, sodomy, fellatio, cunnilingus, and interfemoral coitus. These activities may or may not also involve sadism, masochism, fetishism, voyeurism, and other behavior indicative of emotional problems. In view of these practices, the terms *passive* and *active* are not accurately descriptive of most homosexuals or most homosexual acts. A homosexual male may be active with one partner and passive with another, although he typically does not play the active and passive role with the same partner (Carrier). Evelyn Hooker, one of the best known researchers in the area of homosexuality, considers the terms *insertor* and *insertee* to be more definitive than active and passive (Hooker *b*).

It is interesting to note that homosexual practices vary from one culture to another. The results of most investigations carried out in the U.S. and England suggest, for example, that oral intercourse is preferred over anal coitus by most Anglo-American male homosexuals. In Mexico, however, 86% of the male homosexuals interviewed preferred anal intercourse and 90% practiced it. Furthermore, most of the Mexicans who engaged in oral-genital intercourse more than occasionally, had done so with men from the United States (Carrier).

Contrary to popular belief, there are no physical characteristics common to all homosexuals. Far too often, passive or frail men and aggressive or robust women are unfairly stigmatized as homosexuals. It is not unusual, on the other hand, to find men and women, quite masculine and feminine, respectively, in their appearance and behavior, who nonetheless lead homosexual lives. It has become almost a professional aphorism among therapists that a considerable number of the weight-lifting "muscle men" whom one commonly sees on the beaches are homosexual. Nevertheless, only about 15% of the males who have extensive homosexual experience and about 5% of such women can be identified by their appearance as being homosexual (Pomeroy *d*).

Suggested Causes of Homosexuality

Theories concerning the dynamics of homosexuality are various, emphasis typically falling on the roles of hereditary tendencies, environmental influences, or sex hormonal imbalance (Coleman; Pomeroy *e*).

"Nativistic" theorists argue that this variance is inborn. They point out that most homosexuals grow up in a culture that encourages heterosexuality and that they are usually ignorant of their homosexual tendencies until they reach pubescence and first encounter opportunities for homosexual attachments and expression. Therefore, these theorists reason, the homosexual propensities must have been inborn and not learned. At first glance, the data on assumed anatomical differences between confirmed homosexuals and heterosexuals of the same sex appear to be rather significant and to uphold the nativistic theory. Close examination, however, reveals that the alleged dissimilarities are actually far from supportable on the basis of current scientific evidence (Ellis *g*).

There is more convincing evidence that homosexuality is the outgrowth of environmental pressures and other conditioning factors (Coleman; Kinsey et al. *a*, *c*; Pomeroy *e*; Thorpe et al.). The individual may seek homosexual outlets, for instance, as the result of an accidental but pleasurable homosexual incident in childhood, or because of having been segregated with others of the same sex for long periods of time (e.g., in a boarding school or correctional institution). The most likely explanation, however, probably lies in the realm of parental influence.

Pathogenic patterns in the family life of homosexuals have been noted. Typically, the mother is unhappy in her marriage. She turns to her son, developing a close and intimate relationship with him that is tinged with romance and seductiveness but that stops short of physical contact. The relationship engenders guilt in the son because of his own incestuous desires toward his mother, causing him eventually to avoid all women. A serious involvement with another woman would be a gross disloyalty to his mother, he feels, or, worse, would be tantamount to incest.

Because of his wife's obvious preference, the father comes to resent the son and discourages his growth along masculine lines; furthermore, the father typically shows a favoritism toward his daughter, if he has one. Envious of the father-daughter relationship and fearful of his incestuous feelings toward his mother, the son rejects the masculine role and seeks to assume the role of a daughter (Bieber *et al.*).

Many other psychological pressures may act together or separately to veer a boy toward homosexuality (similar forces steer a girl toward it). The father may have been a weak, aloof, and ineffectual force in his son's life, leaving the boy to develop an excessive attachment to the mother that he never outgrows.

A more common father-son interaction that can culminate in the son's becoming a homosexual, however, is one in which the father is harsh, overly aggressive, and too much of a "tough guy" to allow his son to enter into a close relationship with him. The boy does not identify with his father and does not learn the masculine role in life. This sort of father frequently attempts to teach his son to be a real "he-man." But he prevents the very thing he wants for his son by not establishing a relationship rooted in the tenderness, acceptance, understanding, and love that are necessary to a healthy association between father and son. Thus, the son may become frightened of the "masculine" role epitomized by his father, or be otherwise unable to accept it, and he may go in the opposite direction. That is to say, he identifies with the feminine role, with its implications of warmth and understanding, as a defense against the unfortunate relationship he has with his father (Bieber *et al.*).

Other causative factors in homosexuality are to be found in the home. A boy's parents, wanting a daughter, may have rejected his sex from birth. Or the child's sex education may have been so faulty and larded with guilt, or the relationship between his parents so bad, that homosexuality provides an escape from the feared and contemptible example of heterosexuality that he or she witnessed in the home. In the case of a girl, there may be a deep-seated hatred of the father. Or, frozen out by a cold mother, she may seek in another, older woman the maternal love that she was denied as a youngster.

The dynamics behind homosexuality are not generated solely in the home, however. Other sociological forces upon particularly vulnerable adolescents can be equally powerful. For example, a boy's relationship with girls may have been so unsatisfactory and threatening that he seeks instead the companionship of his own sex in order to avoid a repetition of his failures. Similarly, a sensitive girl who has been callously rejected by a boy she loves may decide never again to run the risk of another rejection, and therefore may turn to women for warmth and acceptance. Experiences such as these have led some behavioral scientists to conjecture that homosexuality is always associated with an unconscious fear of heterosexuality (Marmor *b*).

If a parent or teacher discovers an adolescent sexually experimenting with another boy (such experimentation is quite common and normal) and calls him a "queer," the lad may come to the conclusion that he alone in the world is guilty of such a "crime," that he is "different," that he is a true homosexual. (The same sequence of events is, of course, equally applicable to a girl found experimenting sexually with another girl.) The power of suggestion is so strong that a boy may come to the conclusion that he is homosexual, even though he has never been sexually aroused by a male. In this age of emphasizing the importance of success on the sporting fields, furthermore, the physically small, attractive boy who is athletically disinclined may be labeled "sissy" and come to think of himself as a homosexual.

Psychoanalytical explanations of homosexuality are based on several environmental circumstances, usually involving in men a strong castration fear and an Oedipus complex, as we have noted. A strong infantile, yet sexual (Oedipal) attachment to the mother puts the child in competition with his powerful father who could, the child reasons, attack and destroy the pleasurable area of his body (fear of castration). To protect himself, the threatened boy child avoids all women (they being confused with the mother), and turns to men with the same fondness that his mother demonstrated toward him.

A similar triangular interaction among a girl child, her mother, and her father may engender a comparable syndrome in a daughter's sexual development. Heterosexual anxieties aroused during childhood can also inhibit a girl's heterosexual adaptation and encourage homosexuality. The evidence is strong that a heterosexual environment fraught with sexual taboos, threats, and fears favors the development of lesbianism (Kaye).

A third theory advanced regarding the cause of homosexuality concerns an imbalance of sex hormones. The urine of a normal man or normal woman reveals hormones of both sexes; however, one dominates the other. It is suggested that if the dominance is reversed, homosexuality will result. This theory has alternately gained and lost support over the years, and while it is not usually considered significant in a study of homosexuality, the sex research team of Masters and Johnson has recently renewed interest in such biological correlates in homosexuality. When the testosterone and sperm-count levels of a group of 18- to 35-year old male homosexuals were compared, endocrine variants in bisexual homosexuals did not differ from those in heterosexuals. But those subjects who were predominantly or exclusively homosexual displayed "diminished plasma testosterone concentrations and impaired spermatogenesis" (Kolodny *et al.*).

Researchers have been unable so far to determine whether the anomaly is testicular, pituitary, or hypothalamic in origin. They also warn that this endocrine dysfunctioning has yet to be found in a majority of homosexuals. Even if it were to exist, however, it might be the result primarily of homophile psychosocial orientation rather than the cause of homosexuality.

In a recent and comprehensive compilation of research into the psychodynamics of homosexuality, Warren Gadpaille reaffirmed that early childhood experiences are the major influence in the individual's ultimate sexual adaptation or maladaptation (Gadpaille b). He emphasizes that very little trauma may be required "to derail psychosexual development, especially in the male. . . ."

Because of the male's extreme vulnerability in the development of masculine characteristics and maleness in general, Gadpaille suggests that one should not view child-parent conflict as the only possible trauma productive of homosexuality. "The central importance of maternal (or, generally, parental) influence must be reconsidered, and greater significance must be accorded to peer relationships in childhood—particularly childhood sex play. . . ."

Much diversity of opinion obviously exists regarding the etiology of homosexuality. And as long as the causes remain undetermined, curative efforts cannot be expected to meet with much success. Homosexuals themselves cling tenaciously to their sexual practices. They attempt to adjust to two societies, seeking to belong to both; quite naturally they fall short of this goal. Those who do seek psychological help without outside pressure having been brought to bear are typically far more concerned over their anxiety and fear of discovery than they are about their homosexuality *per se.* Many authorities believe that those homosexuals who are turned from their variance by psychotherapy are not truly homosexual but are, rather, pseudohomosexuals—people who look to members of their own sex for love, affection, and sexual expression because, although they have an emotional preference for members of the opposite sex, they are distinctly afraid of the latter. Other authorities are firm in their conviction that true homosexuality exists, but can often be corrected if the patient has a desire to change (Bieber *et al.;* Ellis *k*). Still other authorities believe that psychotherapeutic efforts should be directed simply toward helping the patient accept his homosexuality and adapt to it (Coleman).

Attitudes Toward Homosexuality

The attitude of the average American toward homosexuality differs from that of many other cultures (Pomeroy *b, d, e*). A study of 193 different societies throughout the world showed that 28% of them accepted male homosexuality, at least to an extent, but only 11% accepted female homosexuality (Murdock a). Among 225 American Indian tribes, 53% accepted male homosexuality, again at least to a limited degree, but only 17% of the tribes accepted female homosexuality (Pomeroy b). In the typical American community, however, the reverse of these acceptance patterns is true. Male homosexuality is severely denounced, often to the point of violence, while female homosexuality receives only token disapproval, if any at all.

Within the American culture male homosexuality is more of a threat to men than female homosexuality is to women. It is widely recognized among psychotherapists that men who have an underlying fear of their own homosexual tendencies are frequently vociferously abusive in their attacks against homosexuality (A psychiatrist looks at the problem). Those who do not feel threatened by any homosexual leanings within themselves are more understanding and relaxed in their dealings with people of homosexual proclivities. It is believed that transsexualists, especially those who change sex by surgical means, are so afraid of homosexuality that they would rather give up their maleness altogether than face their homosexual tendencies (Pomeroy a).

Men frequently become sexually aroused by a display of female homosexuality even though they may find viewing any sexual activity between two men offensive. Women usually show little interest in witnessing any manifestations of either male or female homosexuality (Pomeroy b).

In the desire to rear their children to be free from homosexual tendencies, parents should pay close attention to Carlfred Broderick's summary of the basic conditions necessary for normal heterosexual development.

> First, the parent (or parent-surrogate) of the same sex must be neither so punishing nor so weak as to make it impossible for the child to identify with him. Second, the parent or surrogate of the opposite sex must not be so seductive, or so punishing, or so emotionally erratic as to make it impossible for the child to trust members of the opposite sex. Third, the parents or surrogates must not systematically reject the child's biological sex and attempt to teach him cross-sex role behavior (Broderick a).

It is an unfortunate experience for a youngster between the ages of 7 and 16 to be seduced by a homosexual, but the effects are seldom permanent. These boys are no more liable to become homosexuals than boys who have not been seduced, and the evidence is that they later marry and lead quite normal lives (From the editors scrapbook c).

It should be remembered that homosexuals—or people with almost any other sexual variance—can be as religious, moralistic, loyal to country or cause, inhibited, bigoted, or censorious of other types of sexual variance as anyone else can. They manifest no greater number of other serious personality problems than one would expect to find in the normal population (Hooker a, b).

When skilled clinicians compared the life histories and results of batteries of psychological tests of a carefully matched homosexual and heterosexual sampling, no distinction between the two groups could be found, refuting the concept that homosexuality is an illness (Hoffman a). Fortunately, Western societies are finally making some effort to evaluate homosexuality with compassion rather than with condemnation (Wolfenden).

Pedophilia

Pedophilia is a form of sexual variation wherein adults derive erotic pleasure from relationships of one form or another with children. Pedophilic practices include exposure of the genitals to the child, and manipulation and possible penetration of the child. Of all sex offenders, about 30% are classed as *pedophiles*, most of them being men (Ellis and Brancale). This group is usually less aggressive and forceful than rapists, although public outrage against them is often stronger.

Many child molesters are mentally dull, psychotic, alcoholic, and asocial. Most fall within the age range of 30 to 40 years, the average age being 37 (Coleman; McCaghy; Revitch and Weiss). Older offenders seek out very young children, while younger offenders appear to concentrate their attention on adolescent girls (Coleman; Revitch and Weiss).

The child molester is among the world's most feared and despised men. He is typically branded as a "sex fiend," "sex maniac," "dirty old man," or "pervert." Yet excessive physical violence occurs in probably no more than 3% of all cases of sexual molestation; and only about 15% of all adult–child sexual contacts involve any kind of coercion, including threats (McCaghy).

It is interesting that these offenders have a Victorian attitude toward sex in that they believe in the double standard, assess women as being either "good" or "bad," insist that their brides be virgins, and so forth (Gebhard *et al. a*; Rubin *i*). It is both curious and disquieting that imprisoned sex offenders in general exhibit strong religious convictions. They see themselves as very devout, practice religious rituals faithfully, respect the ministry, read the Bible regularly, and take part in long and self-centered prayers that they believe can cure their illnesses.

These same men, however, are overly concerned about sexual matters, feel guilty and doomed, think that life has been unfair to them, and are painfully pulled in the opposite directions of sex and rigid piety (Barr and Bertram). About 90% of sex offenders admit to having received religious training in childhood (Allen, G. H.), yet only from 0% to 33% (depending upon the type of sex offense) report that their sex education came from their fathers or mothers (Gebhard *et al. a*).

Typically, the child molester is not a stranger lurking in the shadows, as so many parents think. Studies consistently show that from 50% to 80% of all child molestation is committed by family friends, relatives, or acquaintances. Although the Kinsey statistics show that 80% of girls who had been molested were "emotionally upset or frightened," the upset was, generally speaking, about as great as if the child had been frightened by a spider or a snake (McCaghy). If the child had any lingering effects from the experience it was probably caused by the hysterical reaction of parents or teachers to the incident.

Most psychologists concur that sexual experiences at the hands of a pedophile are less traumatic to the child than to his parents. If parents can deal with such unfortunate occurrences in a controlled manner, the child will usually suffer no residual trauma.

Child molesting in one form or another is more common than most people realize. Kinsey and his co-workers found that 20% to 25% of their middle-class female sample had been directly approached between the ages of 4 and 13 by adult males (or males at least five years older than they were) who made or attempted to make sexual contacts. Such experiences are even more common among lower-class females. Among college students studied, 30% of the men and 35% of the women reported that they had had some form of experience during childhood with sexual variants. Among the women, 50% of these experiences involved exhibitionists, and among the men, almost 85% involved homosexual overtures. In many such cases the children are "collaborative" victims (McCaghy).

This deviation usually develops as an attempt on the part of the pedophile to cope with a fear of failure in normal interpersonal and heterosexual relationships, especially with a sexually experienced adult; or the attempt to satisfy a narcissistic love of himself as a child (Kopp). Efforts to rehabilitate pedophiles through psychotherapy have shown promising results, although some of them become recidivists (relapsed offenders or criminals). A prison sentence, however, does little if anything to alter the subsequent behavior of sexual deviates, although society is, of course, protected from them during their term of imprisonment (Coleman).

Not all men charged as sex offenders against children are disturbed or sick men; some have simply been trapped. It is a sad truth that our culture places an inordinate emphasis on physical beauty. Advertisements incessantly stress the advantages of being sexually attractive. As a consequence many girls in the 12- to 15-year-old age bracket, especially those who have been poorly guided by their parents in the matter of healthy self-evaluation, feel inadequate because of their youth. Many therefore turn to cosmetics and sophisticated clothing and conduct in an effort to give the appearance of being older than they really are. Unable to judge such a girl's true age, men frequently get caught in the legal trap of a statutory rape charge (Gebhard et al. a).

In their book *Sex Offenders,* the Kinsey group reported a not untypical case of a man snared in such a situation. The girl involved had appeared to him quite mature, even though somewhat heavily made up and provocatively dressed. She drank her liquor with ease and held her own in the sexual banter. She proved to be an experienced and satisfactory sexual partner. Unfortunately, she was under legal age of consent and the man was taken to court. "I knew I was done for," he stated, "when I saw they had braided her hair in pigtails and had given her a rag doll to hold" (Gebhard *et al. a*).

Bestiality

Bestiality is sexual gratification obtained by engaging in sexual relations with animals. Kinsey and his investigators reported that 17% of men reared on farms have reached orgasm through sexual relations with animals, and many others probably have had some sort of sexual contact with animals (Kinsey *et al. a*). It is thought that in some rural societies where there is an insufficient number of cooperative women, this behavior has no more significance than masturbation as a sexual release (Coleman).

If the pattern of behavior becomes fixed, however, bestiality might be considered a mechanism to avoid feared failure with the opposite sex. Or it may be a means of avoiding distress or threat because relations with any woman signifies incest with Mother. In many cases the individual shows his hostility or contempt toward women by identifying them with animals, or by choosing animals in preference to them.

Zoophilia

Zoophilia is an unnatural love for animals, although the term is usually used interchangeably with bestiality. The term *zoophilia erotica* was coined by Krafft-Ebing, one of the pioneers in the study of psychopathology of sexual behavior. This type of anomaly is fairly common among rural people and small children. As a sexual variation it can take several forms, such as deriving sexual pleasure from fondling animals, from observing the sexual activities of animals, or from a fetish built around animal skins or furs (Allen, C. *a*; Coleman; Thorpe *et al.*).

Necrophilia

Necrophilia is a rare sexual deviation emanating from profound emotional disturbance, almost always of psychotic proportions. It involves sexual gratification stemming from the sight of a corpse, or actually having sexual intercourse with it, sometimes followed, in either instance, by mutilation of the corpse (Thorpe *et al.*). The necrophile may kill to provide himself with a corpse, have sexual relations with it, mutilate it, and even descend to cannibalizing his victim. This rare but obviously severe form of sexual deviation may be explained as an attempt by the individual to dominate someone, even if it is a cadaver (Coleman).

Experts in the field of human behavior must always, of course, exercise caution before declaring any act the product of a grossly disordered mind. Even in the case of such grotesque behavior as necrophilia, the danger exists that the professional will allow personal feelings to warp his scientific judgment. This observation notwithstanding, most professionals view necrophilia as the most deviant of all sexual aberrations.

Pornography and Obscenity

Pornography is written or pictorial material deliberately designed to cause sexual excitement (Gebhard *et al. a*). Usually the material is obscene or immodest, but the responsibility of so labeling it lies with the courts. *Obscenity* consists of utterances, gestures, sketches, and the like that are judged repugnant according to the mores of our society. Most obscene behavior, such as crude writing on the walls, telephone calls (usually anonymous), or public remarks, is sexually assaulting in nature. The subject of sex is no doubt chosen because of its almost certain shock effect, or because the behavior is indicative of actual fantasy.

Coprolalia is an obscure term used to describe obscene language. Most people, of course, enjoy using and hearing earthy words at times, especially while engaging in sexual activity. However, when such words are spoken to a person who has neither directly nor indirectly invited them, or when such utterances are the main source of an individual's sexual pleasure, then coprolalia becomes offensive and unacceptable, probably constituting sexual variance.

By generating fright or shock in his victim, the person making an obscene telephone call, like the exhibitionist, is attempting to deny (at least unconsciously) a deep-seated, morbid fear of sexual inadequacy. The anonymity of the telephone protects him from being evaluated as he evaluates himself—as an uninspiring, physically laughable creature. Usually a poorly integrated, immature person who is severely deficient in self-esteem and meaningful interpersonal relationships, the offender attempts to satisfy his narcissistic needs through the responses of others (Nadler).

Both pornography and obscenity are illegal in all states, but there are widely varying interpretations of the offenses and their penalties. (For a discussion of the legal ramifications of these offenses, see Chapter 22, Sex and the Law.)

The attitude of American men and women toward pornography is varied indeed. Many consider it informative or entertaining; others believe that it leads to rape or moral breakdown, or that it improves the sexual relationship of married couples, or that it leads to innovation in a couple's coital techniques, or that it eventually becomes only boring, or that it causes men to lose respect for women, or that it serves to satisfy normal curiosity. More people than not report that the effects on themselves of erotica have been beneficial. Among those who feel that pornography has detrimental effects, the tendency is to see those bad effects as harming others—but not one's self or personal acquaintances.

Pornography (from the Greek: *harlot* and *writing*, assumed to mean advertisements made by prostitutes) is by current definition written or pictorial material purposefully designed to cause sexual stimulation. Those possessed with a passion for expurgation and a determination to control the moral behavior of others typically cite two reason why someone (usually themselves) should sit in judgment on what others may or may not read: (1) children's minds are corrupted by such material, and (2) it provokes sexual criminality or other sexual acting out.

The first question that immediately arises is just what constitutes pornography. No matter how many laws are passed, lechery, like beauty, remains in the eye of the beholder. A massive Rubens nude will evoke admiration for its artistic merit in one person, some degree of sexual arousal in another, and moral indignation in a third. The same nude might evoke in a fourth only thoughts of the local reducing salon. Is the Bible pornographic? Is Shakespeare? Chaucer? St. Augustine? John Donne? Benjamin Franklin? All have, amazingly, been subjected to censorship, which is an indispensable tool in the business of purification.

That prototype of the self-appointed guardian of public morals, Dr. Thomas Bowdler, was heard to say, "Shakespeare, Madam, is obscene, and thank God, *we* are sufficiently advanced to have found it out!" Lady Macbeth's famous cry, "Out, damned spot" was therefore rendered, "Out, crimson spot." The mention of Queequeg's underclothing in *Moby Dick* was deleted. Huckleberry Finn's being "in a sweat" became "in such a hurry" (Perrin). Ridiculous? Of course. But because censorship is almost always based on false premises and administered by the unenlightened or overzealous, it almost inevitably comes to a ridiculous or dangerous end.

Does Pornography Harm Children?

Young people, it is generally assumed, are particularly vulnerable to the arousal of strong sexual desires as a result of reading prurient material. But the contention that pornography has a degenerative effect upon them—or even upon children—is highly debatable. Certainly there is no research or clinical data to support the argument. In the most recent refutation, the President's Commission on Obscenity and Pornography—a 19-man team of experts conducting a two-year study—stated among its preliminary conclusions in August 1970, "There is no evidence to suggest that exposure of youngsters to pornography has a detrimental impact upon moral character, sexual orientation, or attitudes" (Commission on Obscenity and Pornography a).

The prominent sociologist and family-life educator Helen Branson (c) has pointed out that, although almost all moralistic laws are passed in the name of "protecting our youth," the real responsibility of protecting the young from any demoralizing or dehumanizing force in society belongs to the family. Inculcating proper attitudes toward life in general and sex in particular will prevent pornography from having a detrimental effect on youngsters.

Mrs. Branson considers it healthy to have pornography out in the open. She advocates discussing it in the classroom—and, more importantly, in the home—so that it will be stripped of its secrecy and will therefore lose much of its appeal. As a matter of interest, Mrs. Branson questioned her students about where they had come upon the pornography that they had read. The answer is intriguing: more than half claimed that they had found it among the personal effects of their fathers (Branson c)!

John Money, professor of medical psychiatry and pediatrics at Johns Hopkins, also finds pornography a useful tool in instructing the young (Branson c). Demonstrating, as it usually does, the positive and negative sides of sex, pornography can be used to illuminate the difference between the two. It does not cause the children to imitate, he says, any more than reading the Bible "sets them to playing Crucifixion games."

Sex-Related Criminality and Pornography

The consensus of such professionals as psychiatrists, psychologists, sex educators, social workers, and marriage counselors is that sexual materials cause neither adults nor adolescents any harm. Yet the argument persists that pornography stimulates people to commit criminal sex acts. And when making an arrest for a sex offense, law-enforcement officers may, true enough, find the back seat of the culprit's car sagging under a collection of "dirty" books and magazines. However, the age-old chicken-or-egg quandary immediately arises: which came first, interest in pornography or the sex crime?

As in the case of the harm that pornography is alleged to cause children, there is no scientific evidence supporting the linkage between pornography and sexual criminality. The preliminary report of the Presidential commission mentioned earlier contains this statement:

> Research indicates that erotic materials do not contribute to the development of character defects, nor operate as a significant factor in antisocial behavior or in crime. In sum, there is no evidence that exposure to pornography operates as a cause of misconduct in either youths or adults.

Rather, a careful examination of imprisoned sex offenders shows that they "have histories of sexual repression as youngsters growing up in strict families," suggesting that this repression, "not stimulation by pornography, is what leads them to sex crimes" (Commission on Obscenity and Pornography a).

The Kinsey group's 25-year study of sex offense shows that pornography has quite a different effect from what it is commonly believed to have. Of its entire sample of 2721 men, of which less than half were imprisoned sex offenders, only 14 had never been exposed to pornography. This almost universal exposure provides a valid basis for drawing certain conclusions about the effects of pornographic material on an adult (Gebhard *et al.* a).

For a man to respond strongly to pornography, two conditions are important: youthfulness and imagination, the latter characteristically lacking in sex offenders. As a group, they are not youthful, and, being poorly educated, their imaginativeness and ability to project, to "put themselves in somebody else's shoes," are limited. Their response to pornography is accordingly blunted. The Kinsey researchers suggest that a typical reaction of a sex offender might be, "Why get worked up about a picture? You can't do nothing with a picture."

Not only did the Kinsey group reject the premise that pornography is a spur to sexual criminality, but it went on to suggest that a man's *inability* to gain vicarious sexual pleasure through some form of erotica may possibly cause him to break out into a display of unacceptable overt sexual behavior. While this view was once judged as being simply the thoughtful speculation of researchers who have spent a great many years studying sex offenders, it has recently received empirical support from a much-publicized experiment in Denmark, a subject examined more fully in Chapter 22, Sex and the Law.

A 1966 survey of New Jersey psychologists and psychiatrists revealed that practically none had ever seen a normal patient with a history of delinquency whose delinquent behavior had been prompted by pornography. Two-thirds of these professionals thought, as a matter of fact, that such "literature" would reduce delinquent acts by providing substitute outlets (Katzman).

Some 3400 psychiatrists and psychologists were polled by the University of Chicago Department of Psychiatry as part of a research project to determine what relationship (if any) they had observed to exist between pornography and such asocial sexual behavior as rape. It is obviously difficult to measure the long-term effects of pornography experimentally; this research therefore focused on the clinical experience of professionals dealing with disordered human behavior. While a scant 7.4% of these therapists reported cases in which they were "somewhat convinced" of the linkage between pornography and sexual acting out, 80% said that they had never encountered such a case. An even larger number—83.7%—were convinced that the person exposed to pornography was no more likely than the unexposed person to commit an act of sexual aggression. Furthermore, 86.1% of these therapists thought that people intent on stamping out pornography are frequently bedeviled by their own unresolved sexual problems. Two-thirds of the clinicians polled in this study opposed censorship because of the climate of oppression that it creates, and because of the inhibitions it imposes on human creativity (Rubin *n*).

Pornography and Sexual Acting Out

The President's Commission concluded from its investigation, according to its preliminary report, that during the 24 hours following the viewing of highly erotic material there may be some sexual arousal and, in some cases, increased sexual activity. But, the commission observed, basic attitudes and sexual patterns do not change because of such sexual stimulation. In several experiments reported by the group, a large number of men and women watched pornographic films. It was found that 90% of the couples aged 20 to 25 years, and from 30% to 60% of those between 40 to 50 years of age, were aroused by what they saw (women as well as men, it should be pointed out). The commission's report contained the comment that "there are no recorded instances of sexual aggression, homosexuality, lesbianism, exhibitionism, or sexual abuse of children attributable to reading or receiving erotic stimuli among several hundred participants in the 12 experiments reviewed" (Commission on Obscenity and Pornography *a*).

As a result of exposure to erotica, the masturbatory or coital behavior of some individuals does, in fact, increase; for a few others, it decreases. The majority report no change in the form or frequency of their sexual activity. And if sexual activity does show an increase, it is short-lived, generally disappearing within 48 hours. If the increased activity is masturbatory, it typically occurs among those individuals with established masturbatory habits or among those who would prefer an established sexual partner who happens not to be available. An increase in coital frequency following exposure to erotica generally occurs among sexually experienced persons with an established and available sexual partner. In one study, middle-aged married couples reported that both frequency and variety of coital performance increased in the 24-hour period after they viewed erotic films. Furthermore, following erotic exposure people show greater tolerance toward others' sexual behavior than they did before, although their own standards do not change (Commission on Obscenity and Pornography *a*).

No one denies that the young are more vulnerable to what they read than are those who are older, more sophisticated, and more critical. However, by extrapolating from Mayor Jimmy Walker's observation that no girl was ever ruined by a book, one can safely say that pornography has a negative effect only on the mind that was disordered to begin with. As the Kinsey group summed it up, "Pornography collections follow the pre-existing interest of the collector. Men make the collections, collections do not make the men" (Gebhard *et al.* a).

Does Pornography Have Any Value?

A surprising detail revealed by the report of the President's Commission is the purely educational value of pornography. From the evidence it appears that pornography can enlighten the ignorant—assuming, of course, that the information contained in it is factual—and that it fosters less inhibited attitudes toward sex. Thus, when a healthy and informed attitude toward sexuality exists, pornography is not a significant source of information about sexual behavior. But when sexual ignorance prevails, pornographic material does have a positive value for both adolescents and adults. Over a half of the adult patrons of hard-core pornographic films surveyed in one study reported that a significant factor underlying their attendance was a search for information (Berger *et al.*; Winick).

Clifford Allen, an English psychiatrist and author of several books on sexual aberrations, has commented that he does not consider "girlie" magazines to be a corrupting force. The only danger he sees in pornography is that lonely young men, instead of seeking the reality of taking a "real, live girl" to the movies or to a dance, may instead seek the vicarious, distorted daydream world created by these books or magazines (Allen, C. c).

One might also argue, however, that pornography does add some spice to what would otherwise be the completely dull and lackluster sex life of these unfortunate men. It is highly doubtful that perusing pornographic material would psychologically hinder such a man when he eventually attempts to establish a normal social relationship with a girl. In the meantime it is possible that obscene material serves as a harmless sexual release and that it might psychologically help those who are sexually repressed. There is little clinical or empirical evidence, however, to prove either contention (Stokes *et al.*).

Who Are the Patrons of Pornography?

Approximately 85% of adult men and 70% of adult women in the United States have been exposed at some time during their lives to material of explicitly sexual content in either visual or textual form. Most of this experience apparently was volitional, and exposure to words and pictures was about equal. Individual exposure to erotica does not appear to be an ongoing phenomenon, however; that is to say, only about 40% of adult males and 26% of females report having seen graphic depictions of coitus during a given two-year period (Commission on Obscenity and Pornography b).

A variety of factors appears to relate to the incidence of individual exposure to erotica. Men are more likely to be exposed to it than women, young adults more likely than older ones, and people with more education more likely than the less well educated. People who read a broad assortment of books, magazines, and newspapers and who see a general range of films search out and come upon more erotica than those whose exposure to these media is more limited. The more socially and politically active have greater exposure than those who are less active. Those who attend religious services often are less likely to have contact with erotic material than those whose attendance is less regular (Commission on Obscenity and Pornography b).

Most Americans have their first taste of explicit sexual material during adolescence—about 75% before the age of 21. Adult males report retrospectively that their adolescent experience was not an isolated incident or two, but tended to be both extensive and intensive (Commission on Obscenity and Pornography b). Several recent studies of high-school- and college-age youths confirmed that minors today have considerable exposure to erotica, much of it in preadolescent and adolescent years. More than 50% of the boys were so exposed by the age of 15, and the girls, a year or two later. By the time they reach the age of 18, roughly 80% of boys and 70% of girls have seen pictures of coitus or have read descriptions of it. Substantial numbers of adolescents have had more than a casual exposure, although the incidence does not in the least indicate an obsession with erotica (Commission on Obscenity and Pornography b).

People's exposure to specific sexual material, either in pictorial or written form, has been studied, the depictions including nudes with sex organs showing, coitus, oral-genital contact, homosexual activity, and sadomasochistic behavior. More striking than the number of adults so exposed (85% of the men and 70% of the women) was the number of young people who had been. Between the ages of 15 and 20, 49% of the boys and 45% of the girls reported having seen at last five or more such depictions (Commission on Obscenity and Pornography b).

Persons younger than 21 rarely purchase pornography, and the mails are negligible sources of it. By far the most common source of erotica is friends, the exposure usually occurring in a social situation in which the material is freely passed around. There is some evidence that the less socially active young person is less likely to see erotica than his more social friends (Commission on Obscenity and Pornography b).

Exposure to erotica in adolescence, then, is widespread, and occurs primarily in a group of peers of the same sex (or several members of both sexes). These experiences seem to have more social overtones than sexual ones.

Patrons of so-called "adult" bookstores and cinemas are predominantly white, middle-class, middle-aged, married males. The men typically are dressed in business suits or neat casual attire; they usually attend the film alone, perhaps on an impulse while out shopping. Almost no one under 21 is observed in these establishments, even when it is legal for them to be there. The average patron appears to have had fewer than average sex-related experiences during adolescence, but to be more sexually oriented as an adult than the average male adult (Commission on Obscenity and Pornography b).

The vast majority of "for-adults-only" books are written expressly for heterosexual males; about 10% are directed toward the male homosexual market, and less than 5%, for males with fetishistic tastes. Virtually none of these books is intended for female consumption.

Cinematic hard-core pornography has apparently found a new audience of late. In the past, such films were typically shown at stag parties—meaning, of course, that the audience was solely male. The usual audience reaction was either open silent embarrassment or vulgar and raucous behavior by which they hoped to mask their discomfiture. Today, however, such films are shown in ordinary neighborhood theatres (or, perhaps, in special "minitheatres"), where 80% of the audience are couples. Most of them are in their 20s and 30s, and their behavior is that of any other cinema audience—well mannered and controlled (Shearer).

The college-educated, religiously inactive, and sexually experienced are more likely to be aroused by erotica than religiously active persons of less education and sexual experience. Not surprisingly, young persons are more likely to be aroused by erotica than older ones. In general, persons who are older, less well educated, and who have no great experience with erotica, and persons who are religiously active or who feel guilty about sex are most likely to judge a given erotic stimulus as obscene (Commission on Obscenity and Pornography b). In a 15-day experiment utilizing saturation exposure to erotica, it was demonstrated that repeated exposure to such material resulted in a marked decrease in its capacity to generate sexual arousal and interest (Commission on Obscenity and Pornography a).

Factors in Individual Judgments of Obscenity

One study, involving a large number of subjects, investigated the factors leading an individual to judge pictures or books as being obscene. These determinants appear more related to the individual's psychological makeup, occupation, and particular socioeconomic and educational milieu than to the sexual act seen or read about. The subjects of this study were asked to view two sets of photographs. One, of women in various poses, was of the type found in popular magazines; the other set had been confiscated by the police. The subjects were asked to rate the pictures according to their erotic properties and their obscenity. Persons of lower socioeconomic status rated nudity as obscene, even if no genitalia were shown. They were more likely than subjects of higher socioeconomic and educational strata to regard any nude photo as being sexually exciting (Higgins and Katzman).

Black and white photos were judged as being more obscene than color photos; pictures of poor photographic quality more obscene than those of higher quality; unattractive models more obscene than pretty ones, regardless of the pose; and erotic scenes in an indoor setting more obscene than those in an outdoor setting.

A study was conducted to assess the reaction of a group of college men to photographs depicting various sexual acts and women in several stages of undress. The young men found the pictures of women, which were typical of those adorning the pages of the "better" magazines for men, more exciting than stills of explicit sex acts. (The photographs depicted female masturbation, two women and one man in various coital and oral-genital activity, and heterosexual cunnilingus.) Pictures of partially clad women, like those found in daily newspapers and popular magazines, were considered more sexually arousing than pictures usually classified as hard-core pornography (e.g., homosexual acts and heterosexual sadomasochism) (Levitt and Brady).

The researcher's own attitude toward obscenity has been shown to exert a significant influence on the judgment of his subjects as to what is or is not obscene. The researcher with sexual conflicts involving obscenity will unconsciously inject his bias into any instructions that he gives his subject population. If he projects the view, consciously or unconsciously, that sex is odious, more of his subjects will rate the pictorial matter of the investigation as obscene than would if he projected the attitude that the material is erotically innocuous.

No one denies that genuine pornography and obscenity exist. However, apart from their presenting sex often unrealistically, and sometimes as something ugly and unhuman, the chief objection must lie in their literary, theatrical, or pictorial worthlessness, rather than in their power to corrupt.

Any legal curbs on pornography and obscenity imply the imposition of censorship—an eventuality that any thinking person would wish to avoid. As early as 1644, John Milton—a Puritan among Puritans—addressed Parliament in opposition to censorship, which he regarded as the handmaiden of tyranny. He argued that reading everything one wishes is the means of gaining knowledge of the good and evil, the ugly and beautiful that flourish indiscriminately in the world. Corrupting forces, he said, are everywhere present, and they can only be met by building up an inner discipline and *the ability of rational choice*. Censorship serves no such purpose, especially since its course, as history reveals, has led inevitably to the imposition on the masses of the prejudices, tyrannies, and, usually, the stupidity of the few.

"If the purpose of pornography is to excite sexual desire," says Malcolm Muggeridge (formerly editor of *Punch*), "it is unnecessary for the young, inconvenient for the middle-aged, and unseemly for the old" (New pornography). No one admires or wishes to encourage pornography (except, of course, the writers or purveyors thereof). But the alternative to it is censorship—which would mean that the Song of Solomon is in as much danger of oblivion as an eastern magazine called *Screw*.

Fetishism

Fetishism is defined as a psychosexual abnormality in which an individual's sexual impulses become fixated on a sexual symbol that substitutes for the basic love-object (Caprio c). Usually the articles are fondled, gazed upon, or made part of masturbatory activities. They may be articles of underclothing, hair, shoes (especially high-heel shoes), or gloves. (For some unexplained reason, rubber has very strong appeal to the fetishist.) Or the object of the fetishist's fixation may be a bodily part of the opposite sex, such as hair, hands, thighs, feet, ears, or eyes. The fetishist is almost always male, and in acquiring his sex symbols he often commits burglary or even assault (Karpman).

Fetishism is actually an intensification of the normal tendencies existing in all males. More erotically responsive to visual stimuli than women are, men find certain objects more sexually exciting than others—sweaters, hair, breasts, buttocks, or legs. Men often jokingly refer to themselves as being "breast men," or "leg men," or "fanny men." It is therefore understandable that the symbol of the basic love object can become the love object itself in certain personality structures (Moore).

Fetishists are typically aggressive and antisocial, and are beset with fears of impotency. Fetishism is a form of sexual regression; the individual obtains sexual gratification from a particular object or bodily part because of its unique relationship to some childhood conditioning. The particular fetish-object somehow became associated with sexual excitement, or with the love and acceptance the fetishist once received from his mother (Caprio c). Childhood experiences and habits, then, reinforced by later unsatisfactory interpersonal relationships, are the most frequent causes of the fetishist's seeking comfort and sexual pleasure in objects rather than in people (Dickes).

Two fetishistic patterns that deserve attention are *kleptomania* and *pyromania* (Coleman). Kleptomania is compulsive stealing, usually of an object that is of no value to the thief, except for its sexual symbolism or because of its association with sexual gratification. The kleptomaniac is typically an emotionally disturbed woman who is beset with feelings of being unloved and unwanted (Alexander c). Occasionally the thief is a boy or young man who takes women's undergarments (particularly panties) in order to achieve erotic stimulation through the symbolic nature of the clothing, and through the excitement and suspense of the act of stealing (Coleman). When apprehended, these individuals are reluctant to admit to the sexual implications of their behavior.

Pyromania is compulsive firesetting that often has sexual overtones. The relationship between fire and sex is apparent from such terms as "in heat" and "becoming hot" for someone. The pyromaniac typically experiences mounting tension, restlessness, and an urge for motion as the first symptoms of an oncoming act of pyromania. Sexual excitement and gratification in the form of tension release usually occur as the person—always a man and usually young—sets the fire, or as he watches the early stages of the conflagration (Robbins et al.).

Once orgasm occurs, the individual usually feels guilty and frequently steps forward to extinguish the fire (Coleman; Gold). Many pyromaniacs can give no reason for their impulse to set fires; others claim revenge as their motive. A large number of these fetishists are psychotic (Stiller d), and about half are mentally defective or of subnormal intelligence. The non-psychotic arsonist is usually acting in a framework of frustration, anger, loneliness, and desperation (Robbins et al.).

Frottage

Frottage is an act performed for the purpose of obtaining sexual pleasure from rubbing or pressing against the desired person, and the perpetrator is called a *frotteur*. Such conduct often passes unnoticed, as it may be performed in crowded public places, e.g., a subway or elevator. The dynamics behind this behavior are probably similar to those of exhibitionism. At worst, the frotteur is an unappealing, sexually inadequate man who would probably be frightened of the opportunity for sexual intercourse with an adequate, adult woman.

Saliromania

Saliromania is a sexual disorder, found primarily in men, that is characterized by the desire to damage or soil the body or clothes of a woman or a representation of a woman. These men frequently have marked feelings of sexual inadequacy, or have come to associate strong aggressive impulses with sex, the latter frequently being a consequence of unreasonable guilt feelings surrounding normal sexual desires. The hostility often is expressed symbolically by the throwing of acid, tar, ink, or the like on a strange woman or a statue; by cutting and tearing women's clothing; or by defacing or disfiguring a painting or statue. The beheading a few years ago of the famous mermaid statue in the harbor of Copenhagen was very likely the act of such a disordered man. Saliromaniacs usually become sexually excited to the point of erection and perhaps ejaculation during their acts of destruction.

Gerontosexuality

Gerontosexuality is a variance in which a young person has a distinct preference for an elderly person as the object of sexual interest. The economic considerations of a marriage between a person who is quite old and one who is very young may well be more important than the sexual aspects (Allen, C. a). However, when there is an actual sexual preference for a person of advanced years, there may be an indication of a sexual desire for a parent-substitute.

Incest

Incest is sexual intercourse between two persons, married or not, who are too closely related by blood or affinity to be legally married. Laws relating to incest bear little uniformity from state to state and are often highly confusing (Sherwin a). When marriage is involved, for instance, certain states have legislated separate penalties for the marriage itself and for the sex act.

Incest does not come before the courts often. Of those convicted of sex offenses, only 6% or 7% were charged with incest (Cutter). While the number of reported cases of incest in the United States is only about 2 per million population each year, the act of incest nonetheless probably occurs far more frequently than statistics reveal or the average citizen realizes. Since it is an intrafamilial experience, it is difficult for an outsider to detect; and the shame and guilt felt by the family members cause them to hide and deny it (Cavallin). The offense is more likely to occur in families of low socioeconomic levels than in others (Cutter).

The person who commits incest against children usually comes from a sordid home background, shows a preoccupation with sex, drinks heavily, and is often unemployed, giving him ample opportunity to be at home with the children. The incest offender against adults is typically "conservative, moralistic, restrained, religiously devout, traditional and uneducated" (Gebhard *et al. a;* Rubin *i*). In about 60% of the incidences of adult father-daughter incest, the daughter was a voluntary participant; in only 8% of the cases did she resist. Many studies of incestuous father-daughter relationships suggest that the father often has unconscious homosexual strivings and noticeable paranoid traits (Cavallin).

The most common form of incest is probably brother-sister, especially in poor families where children of both sexes must share a bedroom; the next most common is father-daughter incest (Coleman). Mother-son incest appears to be rare; its incidence may be somewhat higher than is suspected, however, because neither party is likely to report it.

Incest is not universally a taboo. Most cultures, however, both primitive and modern, are of the opinion that family and subculture survival depends upon expansion through marriage outside the immediate family. Only recently has the interest of the scientists been directed toward this ancient problem, although novelists, poets, and scholars have often probed the subject and have contributed much to our understanding of it (Masters, R. E. L.). Sexologists are presently attempting to determine the real and measurable effects of incest on the contemporary world, without regard to the biases of ancient societies.

Many psychotherapists believe that a child is less affected by actual incest than by seductive behavior on the part of a parent that never culminates in any manifest sexual activity. One theory is that the problem of unconscious incestuous desire may well underlie all cases of neuroses and psychoses, and that actual incest will not have such a deleterious effect upon the child because parental approval of the behavior is implicit. The child, therefore, will have little residual guilt—except later, perhaps, when he grows older and reads and listens to the opinions of others in the matter of incest (Masters, R. E. L.).

Mate-Swapping

Mate-swapping (also called *swinging*) has been defined as "the sexual exchange of partners among two or more married couples" (Bell *d*). The old term *wife-swapping* is now generally rejected by the participating parties, as it implies an inequality between the sexes wherein the wife is the property of the husband, to be traded off to another man.

The custom is an acceptable and normal one in certain of the world's cultures. In some Eskimo tribes, for example, offering one's wife to a guest is considered a matter of courtesy and hospitality (Stiller *a*). In the American culture, however, mate-swapping is generally viewed negatively and the participants, as strange, at least, if not downright neurotic or depraved. That the phenomenon is not as rare as most people believe can be judged by the estimate that in 1970 approximately one million Americans regularly engaged in mate-swapping (Bartell *b*).

Mate-swapping—as with so many sexual patterns that differ from what is considered usual and normal—has been condemned out of hand as a sexual aberration. Yet far too few scientific investigations have been made of the phenomenon, or of the motives and personality structures of the participants, to determine just how neurotic the behavior and its advocates might be. Only recently have behavioral scientists begun to study mate-swapping with proper objectivity and an appropriate scientific approach.

Because people (men especially) tend to become bored by routine sex with one partner, some social scientists think that an acceptable solution for the need for novelty must be found. Prostitution was once thought to fulfill the need for novelty without threat to the marriage, because the risk of romantic involvement with a prostitute was slim (Davis, K.). Later, pornography was regarded as serving the same purpose (Polsky). More recently, according to these behaviorists, mate-swapping has been adopted as the means of providing sexual variety, allegedly without damage to the marital relationship, the big difference being that the woman's sexual needs are taken into account as well as her husband's (Denfield and Gordon). And, indeed, with the development of essentially failure-proof contraceptive methods, women can now indulge their sexual desires with more freedom and pleasure than ever before (Rosen).

Mate-swappers, to the surprise of many, frown on an extramarital affair unless all of the marriage partners involved are fully aware of it. "Swingers" believe that the real danger to marriage in extramarital sex lies in the risk of romantic involvement with another person and the dishonesty inherent in a secret affair. Swappers maintain that they engage in swinging to improve and support their marriage (Rosen).

"Swingers" are a relatively mobile group of higher-than-average education. They are primarily Caucasian, affluent, and upper middle class. Despite the fact that they do not regularly attend church, they consider themselves neither atheistic nor agnostic. In the samplings studied, the proportion of Jews, Catholics, and Protestants match that of the general population. And there is apparently no difference between swingers and nonswingers in strength of either childhood or present religious interest. Mate-swappers, surprisingly, are more politically conservative than nonswingers are, although (not surprisingly) their sexual attitudes and behavior are more liberal. As examples, they do not condone the double standard, and are accepting of such sexual behavior among others as oral-genital contact and homosexuality (Bartell *b*; Rosen; Smith and Smith).

In contrast to nonswingers, mate-swappers prefer marriage partners who have had premarital sexual experience. In addition to their extramarital sexual activity, swingers have more sexual intercourse within the marriage than nonswingers do. And while mate-swappers scored significantly higher on a sex information test than nonswingers did, both groups reported the same history of unsatisfactory discussions of sexual matters with their parents. Also, there appears to be no difference between the two groups in attitudes toward pornography or in frequency of contact with it. Female swingers are orgasmically more responsive than their non-swinging sisters.

In most cases, the husband is the one who first suggests mate-swapping. But once the idea is proposed, the wife offers less resistance to the prospect than the husband does. Conclusions drawn from what little research has been done into the psychodynamics of mate-swapping suggest that swingers are not sexual perverts nor are they mentally or emotionally disturbed (Rosen). Rather, the ongoing and first academically accepted investigations into the phenomenon point to the fact that swingers are, in the main, "responsible middle-class people. In public places they conform to the norms of middle-class behavior" (From the editor's scrapbook *j*). It should be recognized, however, that to date no long-range study has been made of the effects of mate-swapping on the marriages or emotional health of the participants (Neiger *c*).

Group sex sometimes involves many people. Men and women may participate in equal or unequal numbers of whom none, some, or all may be married. Heterosexual or homosexual relations, or both, may occur at the same time within the same group. The significant aspect of group sex is that the experience is shared by all the participants, physically or visually.

Mysophilia, Coprophilia, and Urophilia

Mysophilia, coprophilia, and *urophilia* are descriptive words for several forms of obsessive interest in excretory processes (Allen, C. *a*). The words are easily definable from their etymology: *philia,* deriving from the Greek word meaning affinity for; *myso-,* meaning filth; *copro-,* meaning dung; and *uro-,* meaning urine. The causes of these forms of variance are usually related to repressed sexual yearnings and the association of anything sexual with "nastiness" and "dirtiness." Some psychoanalysts see them as defenses against castration anxiety by a symbolic equation such as "feces equals penis."

It has long been observed that children often associate urination and defecation with the sexual acts of their elders. The child may make the further association between the protruding (fat) abdomen in pregnancy (sexuality) and food and the gastrointestinal system, setting the stage for unconscious association of sex with the processes of elimination.

While extreme forms of coprophilia are found mostly in men, urophilia is more generally associated with women. Perhaps this tendency in women is due to the anatomical proximity of urethra, vulva, and clitoris, and a greater likelihood of genital stimulation during urination.

VARIANCE IN DEGREE AND STRENGTH OF SEXUAL DRIVE

Nymphomania

Nymphomania refers to the behavior of a woman whose abnormally voracious sexual hunger overshadows all her other activities. It is sometimes, although rarely, the outgrowth of certain physiological anomalies; more often, the disorder has a psychological basis (Auerback a).

Characteristically, true nymphomania involves an uncontrollable sexual desire that must be fulfilled when aroused, no matter what the consequences. The sexual craving is unquenchable regardless of the number of orgasms and the pleasure received from them. Nymphomania is compulsive sexual behavior in the true sense of the word, impelling the victim to irrational and self-defeating activities with all the stresses and problems that any compulsion causes. Typically, the nymphomaniac is consumed with feelings of self-contempt because of society's attitude toward excessive sexual behavior in any form (Ellis and Sagarin).

It must be stressed, however, that few words in our language are as misapplied as "nymphomania." It is bandied about by the man-on-the-street; it is a popular theme in Grade-B films, and a frequent topic of discussion in fraternity houses; and everyone from the minister to the mailman claims to know at least a half-dozen such women. Yet, as a sexual disorder, nymphomania is quite rare. Many people have little general knowledge about human sex drive, let alone an understanding of individual differences in sexual needs. An individual who encounters sexual conduct which does not conform to his own narrow range of expectations may, consequently, feel bewilderment and consternation.

Most men are sexually fulfilled after one orgasm and care very little about continuing sexual activity afterwards. Sexually mature women, however, are not usually satisfied with one climax only, most of them requiring two or more orgasms to reach sexual satiation, especially during episodes of clitoral manipulation. (Many women during masturbation may experience 5 to 20 orgasms, or more, during one episode [Masters and Johnson g, l].) Men who do not understand this normal sexual need of many women are likely to believe they are involved with a sensual freak who refuses to recognize the end of a good thing when she arrives there. Not understanding female sexuality, such men often stigmatize a perfectly normal woman as being a nymphomaniac simply because she happens to have a healthy sexual appetite.

There is yet another type of man who, through ignorance or, perhaps, cruelty, accuses his wife of nymphomania because her sexual desire exceeds his own. It is true that men on the whole want sexual activity more frequently than their wives do, especially during the earlier part of their marriages. But there are certainly exceptions to this generalization, and some men simply do not realize this fact or are unwilling to admit it. Because their own desires are satisfied by coitus two or three times a week, they are amazed that a woman might wish intercourse six or seven times a week, which is just as normal a level of sexual need as their own. If such a man has feelings of inferiority and uncertainty about his own masculinity, he is likely to be so threatened by such a woman that he must find some way to fight her. Hence he calls her a nymphomaniac; by branding her as "abnormal," he preserves his self-image of "normalcy" by implication.

The consensus of psychotherapists and marriage counselors is that most cases of alleged nymphomania that they see are actually not that at all. They are, rather, cases in which there is a pronounced and disturbing difference between husband and wife in strength of sex drive, both being quite likely within the realm of normalcy in their sexual needs. The gap in sexual desire between husband and wife can only be filled by the less sexually needful partner's finding some means other than coition to satisfy the other partner; or by the partner with greater drive using masturbation as a supplement to sexual intercourse. Compromise frequently leads to frustration of one or both partners, as has been said.

Psychological explanations for genuine nymphomania are that the woman may be attempting to compensate for sexual deprivation in adolescence and early adulthood, or that she is perhaps seeking a means for release of excessive emotional tensions. She may have fears of frigidity or latent homosexuality, which she seeks to disprove through her nymphomania, or she may be using the opposite sex as an unconscious means of revenge against her father (Thorpe *et al.*). Probably the most frequent cause is an inordinate need to be loved and accepted, involving a carryover of early-childhood emphasis on the value of the physical body as a tool to gain attention, recognition, and acceptance. A therapeutic program through which the patient can reevaluate herself is about the only successful method of treating nymphomania.

Satyriasis

Satyriasis is an exaggerated desire for sexual gratification on the part of a man. Causative factors in this condition parallel those in nymphomania. An additional etiological factor may be an unconscious attempt to deny castration, or to reinforce a faltering self-view regarding masculinity and adequacy (Auerback a).

The public does not show as much concern over men who are "oversexed" as it does over similarly "afflicted" women. As might be expected, this disparity in attitudes has its roots in the traditional sexual role designated to females. Women's deviation from their assigned erotically passive role is therefore likely to be more noticeable. The incidence of true satyriasis and nymphomania is about the same—both are very rare disorders—and each can be successfully treated with psychotherapy.

Promiscuity and Prostitution

Promiscuity is generally defined as the participation in sexual intercourse with many people on a more or less casual basis. Promiscuity is to an extent condoned—or at least tolerated—for men, but it is strenuously condemned for women.

Studies involving personality and family backgrounds of promiscuous women indicate that they have generally made an uneven and perhaps incomplete progression to physical, emotional, intellectual, and social maturity. The investigations show that these women, before they left home, participated minimally in such group interaction as sports and other extracurricular activities. They neither entered into organized group experiences nor accepted the responsibility for their own behavior. Characteristically they blamed parents, husbands, and friends for their own failures and shortcomings. Their promiscuity was not caused by a strong sex drive; rather, it resulted from their attempt to use sex to cope with other emotional problems (Lion *et al.*).

To a large extent, men follow the same behavioral patterns in their promiscuity (which has been called "Don Juanism") as women do. In the case histories of almost all of the men studied, promiscuous behavior proved to be the result of feelings of inadequacy, emotional conflicts, and other personality problems. There was no evidence that their sex drive, as such, was stronger than that of average men (Kirkendall *b*; Safier).

A charge of promiscuity practically never appears on court dockets, even though laws against it abound. *Fornication*—coitus between unmarried persons—has, for instance, been legislated against in several states, but indictments are rare. Prostitution, on the other hand, is illegal almost everywhere in the United States (Benjamin *b*) and is frequently prosecuted.

Prostitution, the participation in sexual activities for monetary rewards, has existed in one form or another throughout recorded history. It has been called, with much justification, the world's oldest profession. Through the ages it has been condemned, cursed, and attacked by people of nearly all societies and from all walks of life. Yet prostitution is with us today, and it is safe to predict that it will remain with us in the future. Nevertheless, as the standards of woman's sexual freedom more and more approximate those of man and as the sexual relationship within marriage improves, indications are that the role of these demimondes in society will be of less and less importance (Rubin *m*).

Kinsey and his associates (Kinsey *et al.* a) found that 69% of white males had had some experience with prostitutes. However, over the past several decades there apparently has been a steady decrease in the number of professional prostitutes in America, and in the frequency with which men consort with them (Benjamin *b*). For example, the 1948 Kinsey study revealed that about 20% of its college-educated sample had had their first coital experience with a prostitute. But in the 1967 companion study, this figure had fallen to an estimated 2% to 7% (Rubin *m*).

Men visit prostitutes for many reasons: they may want variety in their sex life; they may be too shy, too embarrassed, or too physically handicapped to find heterosexual outlets elsewhere; they may need to gratify their variant sex urges, such as sadomasochistic or fetishistic tendencies, and can pay to have them satisfied; they may wish to have sexual activity without the troublesome obligations so often associated with less anonymous sexual intercourse; or perhaps their wives are pregnant, or a child has been born and they feel in competition with it for the wife's affection. In associating with prostitutes, however, men often forget that, since prostitution is illegal, they run the risk of blackmail, arrest, and scandal, to say nothing of the dangers of contracting VD or of being robbed (Allen, C. *b*; Benjamin *b*; Masters and Johnson *n*).

In ancient times, the prostitute was held in high esteem in certain Mediterranean societies. Today, however, she is generally looked upon as the most derelict member of her sex. Many prostitutes enter the profession because of easy money, although most are disappointed in this respect, as they become victimized by pimps, corrupt city officials, or blackmailers. Some enter out of a sense of adventure, others to find romance. Far more often than many realize, the client develops a strong attachment to a prostitute and offers to marry her (Benjamin *b*; Winick and Kinsie).

Still other women become prostitutes because they are highly sexed and actually enjoy most of the sexual experiences prostitution affords them. Some become prostitutes because of a neurotic need to punish and degrade themselves, or as an act of rebellion against parents and society. Many prostitutes are simply mentally deficient, emotionally disturbed, lazy, or otherwise unable to engage in regular employment. A great many women enter the profession on a temporary basis. Once their financial difficulties are in better control, they return to their work as salesgirl, teacher, secretary, or housewife (Benjamin *b*).

Many people believe that women are often forced into prostitution through "white slavery" channels. However, only about 4% of prostitutes surveyed by the Indiana Institute for Sex Research had actually been forced into the profession (Gebhard *b*).

The same study revealed that the attitude of the prostitute toward her clients is similar to that of anyone providing a service to customers: she likes some, dislikes others, and feels indifferent toward still others. Over 66% of those surveyed professed having no regrets over having entered the profession. Prostitutes are, however, subjected to certain occupational hazards, in that about 66% of this sampling, as an example, had contracted syphilis or, more commonly, gonorrhea. On the other hand, only 11% of the women had been impregnated by their customers, although another 59% had become pregnant by a friend or husband. Most of the women in this survey (about 75%) had been married but were now divorced or separated (Gebhard *b*).

Contrary to what many think, the incidence of lesbianism among prostitutes is not high. Neither is there a high incidence of drug use or addiction among them, nor are they lacking in orgasmic response (at least according to the Indiana survey). Over 60% of the sample had had no homosexual experience whatever, and only 24% had had pleasurable lesbian contacts 10 times or more. A scant 9% of the sample had ever experimented with hard drugs or had been addicted to them (Gebhard *b*).

Younger prostitutes and call girls are more sexually responsive to their customers than "housegirls" and those who are older. Only 20% of the younger prostitutes and call girls said that they never reach orgasm with a client, while almost 25% reported that they almost always do. Of the "housegirls," 25% claimed never to have reached orgasm with a customer; only a few reported that they always do so. Prostitutes are more orgasmically responsive to their men friends and husbands than other women are, and from 27% to 45% experience multiple orgasms. Only 10% are anorgasmic (Gebhard *b*).

The commonly held view that the prostitute is the prototype of a "bad girl" becomes interwoven into the pattern of many men's sexual conflicts. One such pattern has been called the "prostitute vs. princess syndrome"—the concept that "bad girls do, good girls don't." Boys are taught that their mothers and sisters are pure and good, and would never have involved themselves in the heinous act of premarital intercourse, and that the only sort of girl who would do so is bad—that is to say, a whore. The princess of this syndrome is the "girl next door," who reminds the young man of all mothers and sisters and who is the type he should marry. The prostitute of the syndrome is not, of course, actually a prostitute. She is merely from the "wrong side of the tracks," and hence is adjudged a sexual libertine, or she was a princess who fell from grace by allowing herself to become erotically active. The prostitute type, then, is seen as being sinful and lustful, and is not considered marriageable.

Paradoxically, the prostitute-princess ethic accepts sexual contact with a "bad," lustful, sensual girl as being not only permissible, but also fun and enjoyable. But to become sexually involved with a princess would be to defile her—in effect, a defilement of all mothers and sisters. It easily follows that men caught up in the prostitute-princess dichotomy find to their dismay that a marriage ceremony does not eradicate the notion that coitus with the princess is tantamount to coitus with Mother; not only is the princess besmirched, but symbolic incest further distorts the picture. These men quite understandably find it impossible to function sexually with their princess-wives to any satisfactory degree, whereas they can perform most enjoyably with a prostitute, or with a girl whom they unconsciously identify as being a prostitute type because she enjoys her sexuality or because she is their social inferior. Fortunately, such men can usually be helped by psychotherapy.

The male prostitute generally serves a male clientele, although from time to time brothels have been established for the pleasure of women. The award-winning film *Midnight Cowboy* is an excellent characterization of a young man attempting to earn money specifically from his sexual services to women. (A man's failure in this profession is no doubt attributable to his physiological inability to function beyond the point of sexual satiation, whereas a woman can function endlessly despite the absence of any erotic desire.) The "gigolo" is often thought of as a male prostitute; but he is usually employed more as a companion or escort than for sexual services (Hoffman *b*).

Some male prostitutes ("hustlers") are, of course, homosexual. Most, however, are young men who think of themselves as being quite masculine in appearance and orientation. They allow themselves to be "picked up" by men, usually older ones, in order to make some easy money. The hustler allows his male client to perform fellatio on him, for which privilege he receives money; there is rarely more to the relationship. A homophile seeking a male prostitute wants a "straight" partner. A hustler therefore attempts to magnify his masculine image by wearing a leather jacket, boots, and skin-tight bluejeans (Hoffman *b*).

At first, many young hustlers think of themselves as heterosexuals who simply "sell themselves" to other men. But they are actually using homosexual prostitution to become self-professed homosexuals. Their early overt self-image of heterosexuality and their actual, but covert, homosexual self create too threatening a gap to bridge without the transitional period of prostitution (Hoffman *b*).

Rape

Rape is sexual intercourse forced on an unconsenting person, nearly always a woman. Legal penalties for rape are quite severe, most states assessing a death penalty or life imprisonment as the maximum sentence. The rape victim is usually between the ages of 18 and 25, although of course the person attacked is occasionally a very young child or an old woman.

Typically, the rapist is about 26, is from a low-income, culturally deprived background, and is mentally retarded or of dull-normal intelligence. He is likely to have had emotionally unstable parents and a weak, often alcoholic, father; the majority of rapists, however, come from broken homes. The rapist is usually emotionally immature, received little supervision from his parents in his youth, and is frequently physically unattractive (Gebhard et al. a; Rubin i).

Rape does not require full penile penetration of the vagina. The slightest attempt at penetration is sufficient to constitute rape by legal definition. Neither must ejaculation have occurred to satisfy this definition. Furthermore, tricking a woman into coitus by pretending to be her husband —for example, while she is under hypnosis—constitutes rape even though she gives her full consent (Czinner).

Statutory rape involves a girl under statutory age—usually 18 years. The legal definition of this felony revolves around the concept of "lawful consent." Many girls in these cases lied about their ages and purposely enticed the accused into coitus. They are nonetheless, because of their tender years, legally considered incapable of assessing and comprehending the nature of their actions. Most men convicted on charges of rape are accused on statutory grounds (Slovenko b). There is the occasional case wherein a woman is charged with raping a male; the charge is almost always statutory rape because the boy involved is underage (Oliver).

One fact should be noted: a woman who is emotionally disturbed may accuse a man of rape with whom no intercourse has taken place (he may even be a total stranger). Furthermore, an adult consenting woman may bring a charge of rape against a man with whom she has had intercourse. Her motive may be revenge; or she may be projecting her feelings of guilt, which her ego structure cannot handle, onto the man, who in reality participated in coitus no more freely than she did (Beigel f).

Seduction

Seduction is any technique of persuasion or bribery used to obtain consent for unlawful sexual intercourse, the implication being that the partner was not a totally willing one. Another definition of seduction is any behavior that initiates or encourages the sexual involvement of another person. Legally, the essence of its definition as a crime lies not in the sex act itself but in the fraud which the seducer practiced upon his "victim." Seduction in one form or another is considered a criminal act in 38 of the 50 states. Three states (Illinois, New Mexico, and New York) recently repealed their seduction statutes, while two (Alabama and Massachusetts) recently introduced them. Possible penalties range as high as 10 years in some southern states (20 in Georgia): 5-year terms of imprisonment are common (Mueller b).

Seduction has become a commonplace occurrence in our lives, however, in that its techniques are taught formally in charm schools and informally in a variety of ways—by parents and peers, and through the behavior and dress of film stars (Salzman *b*). Women are rather more subtle in their techniques than men, although both sexes employ the methods best suited to their roles and individual needs.

In those instances of seduction in which difficulties arise, a promise of marriage is typically involved, and breach-of-promise lawsuits often follow. Seduction is not, of course, an act of sexual variance as such, but the manner in which seduction is carried out may be indicative of emotional or sexual problems—e.g., "If you really love me, you'd prove it."

Many psychologists consider that seduction is motivated by an unconscious desire to avenge oneself against all members of the opposite sex, or the wish to buttress a sagging ego, or the desire to compensate oneself for sexual inadequacies, real or imagined. Others believe that seduction is merely part of a generally hedonistic pattern of behavior, which is not necessarily neurotic or destructive—a zestful pursuit of the pleasures of sex that is no more unhealthy than relishing the gratifications of food, drink, or frequent games of golf (Reiss *i*).

Adultery

Adultery is an act of sexual intercourse between a married person and someone other than the legal spouse. Where legislation against adultery exists, prosecution is rare and the penalties assessed are usually relatively light. In American society the traditional double-standard approach to sex has altered over the past few decades, so that both partners are now expected to restrict their sexual activities to the marriage. Earlier, husbands were accorded more sexual latitude (Bell *a*). The seriousness with which this violation of marital vows is held can be judged from the fact that in many states adultery is the only legal grounds for divorce.

Whether the husband or the wife is the offending party seems to determine how serious a threat adultery is to the marriage—a remnant, perhaps, of the double standard. A single transgression by the wife may very well do irreparable damage to the marital relationship, while a similar transgression by the husband is often forgiven if he has not become involved in a lengthy affair, which would suggest his having formed a love relationship with the other woman (Bell *a*). The explanation for these two divergent attitudes probably lies in the notion that a married man supposedly can have sexual relations with a woman other than his wife for physical pleasure only, conferring on the relationship no emotional commitment, but it is assumed (erroneously in some cases, as we have noted) that a woman must be in love with the other man before she wants a sexual relationship with him (Vincent *b*).

Adultery is more common than many realize. Kinsey and his co-workers (Kinsey *et al. c*) and others (Ellis *p;* Terman *a*) have found that, by the age of 40, 26% of married women and 50% to 75% of married men have had adulterous relationships. Of the women, 41% have restricted these affairs to one partner, 40% have had five or fewer partners, and 19% more than five partners. Most of those who have had an extramarital affair are not in restrospect distressed by the experience to the extent that they would not repeat the behavior in similar circumstances.

Approximately 50% of the adulterous wives in the Kinsey sampling believed their husbands knew about their affairs; in 42% of these instances the husbands took no retaliatory action nor posed any difficulty for the wives (*Kinsey et al. c*). In fact, more often than many would think, these husbands had encouraged their wives to have extramarital affairs. Some wished to provide themselves with an excuse for their own adulterous behavior, but, more commonly, the encouragement stemmed from a desire to allow the wives the "opportunity for additional sexual satisfaction" (Kinsey *et al. c*). Certainly this latter reasoning reflects a shift in attitude on the part of American husbands and offers interesting grounds for speculation on the future of sexual mores in our culture. Even with these changes in attitude, however, adulterous relationships often put at least an additional strain on the marriage and frequently cause greater unhappiness than the experiences are worth.

20 SEXUAL
DISEASES
AND
DISORDERS

It is a simple matter to see the relationship between the meaning of the word *venereal* (from the Latin *venus:* love or sexual desire) and the usual source of venereal disease (VD), which is sexual contact. The causative organisms of VD are ordinarily found only in human beings, and they cannot live long outside the human body. The diseases, therefore, are almost always acquired by direct sexual contact.

These diseases attack men, women, and children alike throughout the world, and are considered among the most serious afflictions of mankind. The discovery of penicillin and other antibiotic drugs has made it clear, however, that it is possible to control VD. It now seems that complete eradication of the diseases is a realizable goal, if public apathy does not again hamstring the efforts of responsible agencies, as it did in the United States in 1956 just at the point when syphilis was almost eliminated as a major threat to health. At that time, faulty economic reasoning caused government officials to withdraw funds that would possibly have enabled public health agencies to eradicate the remnants of the disease. Those relatively few persons still infected with syphilis caused the disease again to become widespread, and after a short time all progress—a near-victory over syphilis—was lost.

Since 1965 and persisting through 1969, the number of reported cases of infectious syphilis leveled off, at least, and perhaps even declined. But in 1970 the number of cases rose 8%—and the increase in 1971 was 16% (VD: the epidemic). The avowed goal of the United States Public Health Service—the complete eradication of syphilis—is an ambitious one, success depending upon early detection and treatment of all infected persons and their sexual contacts (From the editor's scrapbook e).

Controlling VD is difficult for many reasons. Physicians are reluctant to report new cases in private patients to public health officials, especially when the patients are adolescents, among whom the increase has been the greatest in recent years. As a result, persons who infected the adolescents—and those, in turn, whom the adolescents have infected—are not contacted and treated.

Adequate public funds necessary to assist medical authorities in searching out and treating infectious contacts are not now available. The legal problems in controlling VD are legion, for it is impossible to legislate effectively against human behavior leading to the spread of VD. Further, there is a natural reluctance on the part of both adults and teen-agers to divulge the source of their contacts (or even to seek treatment, in many cases). Then, too, most young people do not feel free to turn to their parents with a problem of this nature, nor do they often have ready access to physicians in whom they can confide. (Even when they do, teen-agers are more reticent than adults to divulge the full history of their sexual behavior.) The difficulties involved in accurately judging the number of cases of VD active at any one time are thus all too obvious. The American Social Health Association estimates that the incidence is perhaps four times greater than reported (Smartt and Lighter).

Although progress has been made toward the eradication of syphilis, it has been dwarfed by the rampant rise in the incidence of gonorrhea in the United States and many other parts of the world—a proliferation that has now reached epidemic proportions. The means used to bring syphilis under fairly successful control are not applicable to gonorrhea. In syphilis, which has an incubation period of about three weeks, the contacts can often be sought out and treated before they reach the infectious stage. Gonorrhea, by contrast, has an incubation period of a scant two to eight days. Public health officials therefore lack a sufficient period of grace to ferret out the sexual contacts of the newly diagnosed gonorrheal patient before the disease becomes manifest in those contacts and is perhaps being transmitted to still other persons (Quinn).

The incidence of gonorrhea reached a peak in 1947, after which it declined steadily, leveling off in the years 1957-1958. In 1959, however, the incidence began rising once more and continued to do so until 1970, when it approximated its 1947 level. Between 1963 and 1970 the number of reported cases of gonorrhea increased by 75%; the current rate of increase per annum is about 15%. And there is, unfortunately, no indication that this pestilence will abate in the next few years (Quinn; Smartt and Lighter).

The clinical picture is not wholly black, however. Past gonorrhea research has been singularly hampered by the resistance of laboratory animals to the gonococcus organism. But scientists have recently succeeded in infecting the chimpanzee with gonorrhea (alas, poor chimps!), a breakthrough that will doubtless permit more exhaustive studies of the disease than have been possible heretofore, leading, it may be hoped, to more successful means of detection and treatment (Brown et al.; Galton).

Prompted into action by the increasing number of adolescent cases of VD, public health agencies have made various studies to determine what sort of teen-ager becomes infected. Which stratum of society does he come from; to what extent are ethnic, religious, and similar factors involved; and what unique pressures, if any, impel a twentieth-century American adolescent toward premarital sexual experimentation, which too often ends with a venereal infection?

The studies reveal no "typical" teen-ager who is more likely than another to contract VD. The infected young people studied were of all personality types and represented the whole spectrum of American society. Of the cases treated at VD clinics, the majority, as might be expected, came from low-income minority-group families. The other infected youngsters were no doubt treated by their private physicians. Otherwise, the statistics showed that, although most of those infected had commenced high school, only about 15% had graduated. A few were attending college. About 25% attended religious services, while 50% of their parents did so (Deschin b).

No essential difference was found in the degree of promiscuity among ethnic groups, although there was a higher VD rate among nonwhites than among whites (Deschin b). In 1969, as an example, the number of reported cases of gonorrhea was 15 times greater among the ethnic group designated "other" (which in the United States means, primarily, blacks) than among whites. Twice as many white males as white females had gonorrhea. Of the "other" group, males had three times the incidence of gonorrhea that females did. The report of larger incidence among males of both ethnic groups is quite likely correct; but the figures are also likely to be biased upward because of inadequate reporting of infection in women (United States Department of Health, Education and Welfare). About 80% of women (and a few men) have no clinical signs or symptoms of gonorrheal infection and therefore do not suspect that they are diseased. These individuals constitute to a large extent the nucleus of ongoing gonorrheal infection, since they infect their sex partners unknowingly (Smartt and Lighter).

A Los Angeles study of 1000 gonorrheal patients, aged 15 to 60 years and of low socioeconomic status, revealed that 80% had a history of previous venereal infection, over 50% of them having been first infected between the ages of 15 and 19. Over 25% of those with a first-time infection became reinfected within the 6-month period of the study (Epidemic gonorrhea).

Another such study, conducted in social hygiene clinics in New York City, involved 600 adolescents between the ages of 12 and 19. All had had coital experience, and 63% (70% of the boys and 30% of the girls) had at least one venereal disease at the time of their appearance at the clinic. Among the 379 infected young people, 42% had had an earlier venereal infection, and 15%, two or more earlier infections (Deschin b).

Promiscuity and homosexuality are considerably more prevalent among boys than girls, with a correspondingly higher rate among boys of VD. Studies have revealed an extremely high rate of VD among male homosexuals, but an insignificant incidence among lesbians. Only 3% of men infected with gonorrhea name another man as the infectious contact, whereas from 12% to 18% of syphilitic males contract the disease from another male (Ketterer). Thus one of the segments of the population showing the greatest increase in venereal disorders in recent years has been the male homosexual group (Tarr and Lugar; Trice et al.).

The most significant fact uncovered in the public health agencies' studies was that teen-agers with VD come from families lacking wholesome interpersonal relations—families within which bonds of mutual understanding and confidence do not exist (APHA Western Branch Conference report). Only 21% of the group studied had obtained their knowledge of sexual matters from their parents, while 64% had obtained it from their peers. Those youngsters who had received sex education from adults who were meaningful to them showed less tendency toward promiscuity. All the teen-agers in the study lacked adequate information in the sphere of sex and VD. All were extremely ignorant of the elementary facts of biology and hygiene. And all lacked serious involvement in school and work. They were frank in revealing their sexual behavior and ignorance about VD, and they expressed feelings of religious conflict and guilt over their sexual activity (Deschin b).

It has been postulated that the improved contraceptive methods of recent years, such as the Pill, have led to an increase in promiscuity and, thus, to a rise in VD. As pointed out earlier, there is no evidence that the availability of effective contraception leads to greater promiscuity, even though fear of pregnancy is largely removed. It is true that the contraceptive use of the condom—which offers the best protection against VD during coitus—has declined since the advent of the Pill. But it should be remembered that the rise in the incidence of gonorrhea began at least seven to eight years before there was widespread use of the Pill (Quinn).

Strong sexual drive and lack of self-discipline are not of themselves breeders of promiscuous behavior. People are promiscuous because relationships encompassing mutual understanding and confidence have been absent from their lives. VD patients almost always see themselves as worthless, unlovable victims of some force over which they have no control. When seriously depressed by these feelings, they seek relief in irresponsible sexual relations. The traditional American attitude that associates security with love, and love with sex, exacerbates their misguided attempts to solve emotional problems through sexual acting-out behavior. If these people can be assisted toward a more satisfactory self-image, their general adjustment to life will improve as well (APHA Western Branch Conference report).

In the urbanized and mobile society of twentieth–century America, old cultural patterns have given way to an increasing degree to mass conformity. Scientific, religious, and social concepts have changed with often bewildering rapidity. Adolescents are frequently left with no clearly defined ethical values or rules of behavior. In a mobile society, their relationships are often of a transitory nature, encouraging amoral attitudes and casual sexual encounters. Venereal disease is often, unfortunately, the end result.

Sex education to combat this vicious circle should begin—as already pointed out—with family-life education emphasizing the importance of individual duty and responsibility. Helping young people to understand themselves and their place in society is critical, beginning in the family and continuing in school, in church, and throughout the life of the individual. Private physicians and public health agencies cannot eradicate VD without the cooperation of the individual, the family, the school, and the church.

Society must face the fact of VD when it appears. When there is even the slightest suspicion that one's partner or oneself may have VD, prophylactics should be used during sexual intercourse. The simplest and best prophylactic for men, if they suspect their sexual partner is infected, is the use of a condom during coition, followed by a thorough soap-and-water cleansing of the genitalia afterwards. Women with an infected sexual partner should use an antiseptic vaginal douche, also followed by a soap-and-water cleansing of the genitalia.

VENEREAL DISEASES

A discussion of most types of venereal diseases, both the well known and the little known, now follows. It is presented in the belief that sex instruction is dangerously incomplete without such information. It also rests on the belief, now supported by research, that knowledge can help to curb promiscuity as well as the spread of the diseases themselves.

Gonorrhea

Gonorrhea (from the Greek: flow of seed) is the most ancient, and most prevalent, of all venereal diseases. A recent report presented before the Pan American Health Organization estimated that the incidence of gonorrhea is second only to that of the common cold among communicable diseases in the United States. It is further estimated that, in the 1970s, 1.5 million Americans will annually become infected with gonorrhea (*Hospital Tribune*).

Chinese writings dating back as early as 2637 B.C., as well as the unmistakable references in the Bible to gonorrhea, attest to its existence for many centuries (Blau; Fiumara). The word *gonorrhea* was first used by the Greek physician Galen in 130 A.D. to describe the disease; however, the causative organism was not identified until 1839, at which time it was given the name *gonococcus*. Until the advent, in 1943, of the "miracle drugs" and their remarkable effect on the organisms of VD, gonorrhea was not easily cured, and complications often resulted in ailments requiring specialized treatment. Since that time the disease is usually considered to be relatively minor and is easily treated.

Primarily a disease of the young, gonorrhea's highest incidence today is among men 20 to 24 years old. Its second highest incidence is among 15- to 19-year-olds; 25% of those infected are under 20, and 65% are under 25. After 25 the incidence declines steadily. Among men 50 years and older, the incidence is about the same as it is among boys 14 years and younger (Brown, W. J.; United States Department of Health, Education and Welfare).

Gonorrhea is almost always contracted during sexual intercourse with an infected person. Curiously, however, a recent study of United States Navy personnel in the Philippines revealed that, even without the use of prophylaxis, the risk of acquiring gonorrhea by sexual contact with an infected female is only about 22% (Holmes *et al.*).

The gonococcus organism usually restricts its attack to the genitourinary area, although the rectum may be infected by extension from the genitals or from anal intercourse (Blau). Gonococcus has been known to involve the skin, joints, and, much more rarely, the brain and blood system.

Gonorrhea in a man usually manifests itself by acute *urethritis* (inflammation of the urethra). A thin watery discharge from the penis commences from 2 to 7 days following the date of infectious sexual contact, becoming thicker and greenish-yellow in color within another day or two. The patient typically feels an urgent and frequent need to urinate. The act of urination is accompanied by a burning sensation at the tip of the penis, which is now swollen and inflamed.

Painful complications, which are sometimes serious, commonly result from gonorrhea. One of the most agonizing is *epididymitis*, a condition characterized by a swelling of the structure leading to the testes, the latter sometimes becoming as large as an orange and extremely painful. Other complications are arthritis, iritis, conjunctivitis, skin infections, and, more rarely, endocarditis and meningitis. Gonorrheal infection of the prostate can become chronic, causing a man to remain infectious for a considerable length of time. Urethral stricture is another common and serious complication. The obstruction thus produced predisposes the patient to an attack of *pyelonephritis* (inflammation of the kidney) (Blau; *Dorland's illustrated medical dictionary*). These complications, which are typically accompanied by fever, malaise, and marked debility, repeatedly caused the death of gonorrheal victims prior to the introduction of antibiotic drugs in treating the disease.

As mentioned earlier, most women infected with gonorrhea are, in the absence of clinical symptomatology, unaware of it. When the disease does manifest itself, the first symptom is a vaginal discharge beginning 2 to 7 days after infectious contact. The vulva then becomes red, raw, and irritated. There is an urgent and frequent need to urinate, and urination is accompanied by pain and a scalding sensation.

Gonorrheal complications in women are considerably more common and severe than in men, primarily because women are so often unaware of the infection and, hence, delay in seeking medical attention, and because diagnosis and treatment are more difficult (Fletcher and Landes). The two major complications that women can develop from this disease are inflammation of the Bartholin's glands (*bartholinitis*), and inflammation of the fallopian tubes (*salpingitis*). In bartholinitis, the gland on one or both sides of the vulva swells and becomes tender and painful. An abscess or a cyst sometimes forms in the affected gland, requiring medical or, occasionally, surgical attention (Ball; Blau; TeLinde).

Acute salpingitis often produces severe lower abdominal pain on one or both sides of the body, accompanied by fever and malaise. A tubal abscess can form on either or both sides, depending on the extent of inflammation of the fallopian tubes. These conditions frequently cause severe colicky abdominal pain, menstrual irregularity, chronic invalidism, and sterility. Surgical treatment is often required if the conditions are to be properly corrected (TeLinde).

It has been observed that patients with gonorrhea-induced salpingitis and tubal or ovarian abscesses usually had been exposed to the disease during their menstrual flow, or soon thereafter. During those times the epithelial tissue of the internal genitalia is thin, providing an excellent medium for the flourishing of the gonococcus organism (Goss).

Children are sometimes accidentally infected with gonorrhea, although such an occurrence is uncommon, since the source of the infection is almost always sexual intercourse. However, children have been infected through mutual masturbation, sexual exploration and experimentation, and sexual assault. At one time, nearly 33% of all blindness in children was the result of gonococcal ophthalmia, which the newborn acquires in the birth process from its infected mother. This affliction has now been almost completely eradicated by treating all newborn babies with preventive medication: instillation in the eyes of a solution of silver nitrate or penicillin (the latter being the more modern technique) (Blau).

Gonorrhea is commonly diagnosed through microscopic examination of a smear of urethral or vaginal (cervical) discharge. A modern method of diagnosis know as the "fluorescent antibody technique" has been found effective in detecting the organism in patients who show no clinical signs of infection. Treatment of gonorrhea with antibiotics is simple and effective, but any complications stemming from the original infection will, of course, require specialized treatment.

The treatment of choice for men is a single intramuscular injection of 2.4 million units of penicillin. The recommended dosage for women is double that for men, or 4.8 million units; the dosage is divided into two injections, given during a single visit to a clinic. One of the tetracycline drugs may be successfully substituted when the patient is allergic to penicillin, or is penicillin-resistant (Brown *et al.*). There are recent reports of gonococcal strains that are highly resistant to treatment with penicillin and alternate antibiotics, making their cure less of a certainty than that of other strains (Brown, W. J.).

Syphilis

The physician Fracastoro in 1530 published a poem, which achieved wide popularity, about a shepherd named Syphilis who had been stricken with a disease that, until then, had been known as "the great pox." The disease has been known ever since as *syphilis*.

It is still debated whether Columbus and his crew brought syphilis to America from Europe, or whether they contracted the disease from West Indian women and then carried it to Europe. Indeed, study of the bones of American Indians has revealed evidence that syphilis existed in America at least 500 years before Columbus's voyages (News of the month a). But whichever the direction, syphilis spread in epidemic proportions across the known world within a few years after Columbus and his men returned to Europe from their historic journeys. Columbus himself probably died, in 1506, from *general paresis* (one of the neurological disorders resulting from syphilitic infection) (Coleman). It was about 400 years later, in 1905, that the causative organism of syphilis was discovered. A short time later, the relationship between syphilis and paresis was recognized.

The cause of syphilis was found to be a corkscrew-shaped spirochete known as *Treponema pallidum,* a cylindrical body with 8 to 14 rigid spirals that is best seen with the aid of a dark-field microscope. Subsequently, in 1913, the scientists Noguchi and Moore found this same spirochete in the cerebral cortex of patients dying of general paresis.

Once the villain spirochete had been identified, extensive studies were made of the disease, and effective methods of diagnosis were developed (the Wassermann test, for example). Until 1943, when penicillin was discovered to be a quick and easy cure for syphilis, the best known treatment had been a combination of bismuth and arsenic administered alternately and slowly over an extended period of time—up to 2 years, or longer— coupled with fever induced by typhoid germs or by extensive applications of heat. Today penicillin can cure practically any case caught in time; in many instances, only a single powerful injection is necessary.

Despite the fact that penicillin has been universally used in the treatment of a broad spectrum of infectious disease since 1943, *Treponema pallidum* has not become immune to it and remains fully vulnerable to its antibiotic action. The recommended dosage for men is 2.4 million units given intramuscularly during a single visit to a treatment center. A penicillin-sensitive patient can be treated with tetracycline or erythromycin (Brown *et al.*).

EARLY SYPHILIS   Early syphilis is subdivided into *primary* and *secondary* stages of infection. It is important to recognize the disease during its early phase (the 2 years following infection) because it can be most easily cured then; irreversible tissue damage has not yet occurred. This is also the period when the patient is most infectious and is the greatest menace to public health.

The *primary stage* of syphilis is easily identified by a lesion or a *chancre* (sore) that usually appears in the anal-genital area from 10 to 40 days after sexual contact with a diseased person. In about 10% of the cases, the chancre may appear in the mouth or on the tonsils or lips, and the infection may be extragenital in origin (Eagle).

The chancre begins as a small red papule (circumscribed elevation of the skin) that becomes eroded and moist. The only other sign of infection at this stage is a painlessly swollen lymph gland at the site of the regional lymph drainage: for example, if the chancre is on the penis or labia minora, the glandular swelling will be in the groin. During the early primary stage, the invading microorganisms leave the bloodstream and enter other tissues of the body, usually causing the lesions characteristic of the secondary stage of syphilis. If the disease is adequately treated in its primary stage, a cure is easily effected and the danger of transmission removed. Without treatment, the primary chancre heals in 4 to 10 weeks. The surface warning signal is thus removed, but the danger of internal damage remains.

The *secondary stage* is characterized by a non-itching eruption (giving rise to the name "great pox" to distinguish the disease from small pox) or rash of the skin, usually on the trunk of the body. The rash—which begins after 6 weeks and usually within 3 months—is sometimes so indistinct as to escape notice (Lewis). Other symptoms appear at this time, but their significance, as being possibly related to syphilis, is usually recognizable only by a competent physician: glandular enlargement, throat infection, headaches, malaise, and a low-grade fever. There may also be a loss of eyelashes and eyebrows, and alopecia of the scalp, giving it a "moth-eaten" appearance (Secondary syphilis). Secondary lesions then heal, without treatment and without leaving scar formation, within a few weeks or months—possibly a year.

Although coitus is by far the most common means of transmitting syphilis, it is not the only means. The progress of syphilitic infection in the secondary stage of infection may induce eruptions in the mucous membrane of the mouth, causing the saliva to swarm with spirochetes. It is obvious, therefore, that the contagion can be passed on to another person by kissing, especially if there is a break in the skin in or around the mouth (Clark *p*).

THE LATENT PERIOD   The *third stage* of untreated syphilis (also called the latent period) commences at least 2 years after the initial infection. The disease is termed *early latent* when the patient has been infected less than 4 years or is under 25 years of age (Lewis). Syphilis is considered to be *late latent* when infection has persisted longer than 4 years or when the patient is over 25 years old. The latent period is dangerously deceptive; all symptoms associated with syphilis disappear, and the latency may last for months or years. It was at this stage during the great syphilis epidemic of the fifteenth century that the disease was thought to be cured. During latency, syphilitics do not infect contacts, but the results of a blood serology test are always positive. Such a test is the only reliable method of diagnosis. Without treatment, the disease can now progress to the destructive stage of late syphilis.

LATE SYPHILIS   The *fourth stage*—called late syphilis—may manifest itself in any organ, in the central nervous system and cardiovascular system, and, particularly, on the skin. These symptoms can appear as late as 30 years after the initial infection. Late lesions may appear in the mouth and throat and on the tongue, usually accompanied by thickening of the tissue or destructive ulcers. These late lesions are responsible for the crippling, disabling, and disfiguring effects of syphilis. A chronic inflammatory process may develop in this late stage, involving bones, joints, eyes and other organs, and, especially, the cardiovascular system.

Although the disease still rages, modern methods of diagnosis and treatment have eliminated syphilis as "the great scourge." In 1970, for example, some 20,000 new cases were reported in the United States, although it is estimated that some 70,000 to 75,000 persons were actually infected—small figures, nonetheless, when they are compared with those of new gonorrheal infections. Deaths from syphilis numbered only 2381 in 1967 in contrast to 9377 in 1947. In 1947, as well, there were 6000 first admissions to hospitals for syphilis-induced psychoses; in 1967 there were a mere 162 (Brown, W. J.).

Nevertheless, syphilis still cannot be classified as a benign disease because of the deadly effects in some untreated cases. It has been shown, however, that about 50% of those persons who contract syphilis and receive no treatment will experience no disability or inconvenience. Another 25% will have some residual evidence of the disease, but will suffer no disability or shortening of life (Blau). The reason that such a high proportion of untreated syphilitics suffer few or no ill effects from the disease is not known, but some speculate that resistance to the disease is built up because of the administration of penicillin and other antibiotics to these people in the treatment of other, earlier illnesses.

The incidence of *congenital syphilis* (syphilis existing at birth) has greatly diminished in recent years because of improved routine prenatal care and treatment of mothers. In 1941 there were 13,600 cases of congenital syphilis diagnosed in children under 1 year of age. By 1970 that figure had dropped to 300.

Nevertheless, congenital syphilis has not been totally eradicated. A syphilitic mother usually transmits the disease to any unborn offspring during the first 2 years of her infection. If the mother is treated before her fourth month of pregnancy, the child is usually born nonsyphilitic. In these instances, only 1 infant in 11 is born with the disease (Pund and Von Haam).

Congenital syphilis usually manifests itself early in life by certain pathological symptoms, although the symptoms may not appear until the victim is 10 or 15 years of age, sometimes not even until he is as old as 30. The course of congenital syphilis is similar to that of the second and third stages in the contracted form of the disease.

Pupillary signs are frequently the only indication of congenital syphilis. More often, presence of the disease is manifested in various degrees of mental defects ranging from mild deficiency to imbecility and idiocy. There are sometimes developmental defects such as hydrocephalus or brain atrophies. Sclerosis and convulsions are also occasional developments from congenital syphilis.

Untreated syphilis may produce certain severely disabling disorders, the two most common being *neurosyphilis* and *general paresis*. In the past, about 5% of all untreated cases of syphilis developed into general paresis. Recently the figure has dropped to about 3%, although the reason for this decrease is not known (Coleman).

Neurosyphilis occurs in about 25% of untreated cases of syphilis (Pund and Von Haam). It can affect every part of the cerebrospinal system in one or any combination of the three forms of the disease: meningovascular neurosyphilis, paresis, and tabes dorsalis. Paresis and tabes dorsalis, especially, are often accompanied by vascular (pertaining to the blood vessels) or meningeal (pertaining to the membranous covering of the brain) complications.

Clinical signs of neurosyphilis are many. Whether they are mild or severe, acute or chronic, depends on such circumstances as onset, rate of progress, and extent of the affliction. There may be headache, dizziness, nausea, various subjective pains, numbness, attacks of unconsciousness, or epilepticlike convulsions. The list of personality disorders that may accompany neurosyphilis is also lengthy: restlessness, dullness, irritability, apathy, anxiety, depression, defective memory, mild or severe delirium, dementia, and so forth. On the other hand, the disease can exist without any clinical indices.

General paresis is a chronic progressive syphilitic disease with which certain physical symptoms are associated, as well as the better known psychological indications of psychosis and progressive mental deterioration (Coleman). The disease usually makes its appearance from 10 to 20 years (occasionally longer) after the primary syphilitic lesion. It is commonly observed between the ages of 30 and 50, more frequently in men than in women.

General paresis is often fatal; it may affect any and all areas of the nervous system, and is frequently confused with functional psychotic illnesses. Pupillary changes and a positive serology test are often the only factors calling attention to the actual nature of the disease. The symptoms, typically of psychotic proportions, may range from sudden manic or depressive reactions to a more complex syndrome—e.g., anxiety, insomnia, hypochondria, fatigue, irritability, loss of interest, and a loss of power to concentrate. Because its symptoms resemble those of various psychological illnesses, general paresis is sometimes referred to as "the great imitator."

Juvenile general paresis usually manifests itself at some time between the age of 10 and the time of adolescence. The symptoms typically involve delusional trends, depression or excitement, defective memory, general loss of interest, and disorderly conduct. These reactions are frequently masked by pronounced mental deficiency or convulsions. Juvenile paresis progresses more slowly and in a less clear-cut manner than the adult forms of the disease do, although the physical symptoms of the two are the same. The disease is rarely found today because of prophylactic measures taken with a syphilitic mother-to-be (Ball; Coleman).

Chancroid

Chancroid (caused by the streptobacillus of Ducrey) is a highly contagious disease typically spread through sexual intercourse. It is characterized by ulcerations, usually at the points of physical contact, and by local lymph-gland swelling. The first sign of chancroid appears about 12 to 16 hours after infectious sexual intercourse has taken place. It usually takes the form of an inflamed papule or pustule, which soon breaks down to become a ragged-edged ulcer that is filled with dead tissue. The ulcer varies in size, but may become extremely large and destructive of the skin affected (Ball; Blau).

Ordinarily the suppuration from the ulcer will infect the contiguous area on a man's prepuce, frenum, or penile shaft. In a woman, the ulcer usually forms on the labia majora, vestibule, or clitoris. Occasionally the lymph glands of the groin may swell, cause pain, and rupture. If not treated, chancroid ulcerations can drain for months. The adverse effects of this disease are considerably greater in women than in men (Pund and Von Haam).

Chancroid may be contracted in conjunction with other venereal diseases, such as lymphogranuloma venereum, granuloma inguinale (both discussed below), gonorrhea, and syphilis. Accurate diagnosis and treatment therefore require expert clinical and laboratory techniques. Sulfonamides, which are the drugs commonly chosen to combat chancroid infection, usually produce a cure in as short a time as 3 to 8 days. Certain other antibiotics are similarly effective (Blau).

Granuloma Inguinale

Granuloma inguinale, a chronic disease, is unique primarily because of its extensive ulceration and scarring of skin and subcutaneous tissues. The disease is more prevalent in temperate and tropical zones than in colder climates. The genitals are a special mark for attack, but extragenital sites can also be invaded. The disease is infectious, but it is not necessarily contracted through sexual intercourse. "Venereal" is not, therefore, a wholly appropriate label for the infection (Blau).

At the onset of granuloma inguinale, a small red papule appears, ordinarily on the penis or labia, but occasionally on other parts of the body, such as the face, neck, anus, rectum, or groin. Lesions enlarge and spread, and the ulcerations grow together to form a larger area of infection. The tissue degenerates into a red, moist, malodorous, granulated, and frequently bleeding mass. Spontaneous healing does not ordinarily occur; a slow extension of the ulceration is capable of destroying much of the tissue of the entire genital region, which then becomes replaced by thick scar tissue.

The absence of lymph-node involvement is a marked feature of the disease and is an excellent diagnostic aid. The organism itself is difficult to isolate, even in scrapings from active lesions. Identification must usually be made by microscopic examination of stained slides. The disease can be cured by careful treatment with antibiotic drugs of the mycin family (Ball; Blau; TeLinde).

Lymphogranuloma Venereum

Lymphogranuloma venereum, a systemic disease, is caused by a virus that invades tissues in the anal-genital and inguinal areas. The primary lesion manifests itself a few days after sexual contact, in the form of a small blister that soon ruptures to form a shallow ulcer with clear-cut edges surrounded by reddened skin. The blister is painless and heals rapidly without leaving a scar. The initial lesion may appear on the glans, prepuce, vulva, vaginal walls, or cervix, or in the urethra or anal region. If the virus is contracted during cunnilingus (oral-vulval contact), it can cause the tongue to blister and swell, a reaction often followed by swelling in the glands of the neck (Blau).

Approximately 2 weeks after the primary lesion, the invasion of the virus progresses to a secondary stage, characterized by pain in the groin followed by visible enlargement of the lymph nodes. These may be the only indications until the third stage, when symptoms become quite obvious: elephantiasis of the penis, scrotum, or vulva.

Diagnosis of lymphogranuloma venereum is rather difficult to make, even in the laboratory. The Frei skin test, however, has a high diagnostic accuracy and should be performed in every suspected case. Antibiotic drugs have not elicited the near-miraculous cures in the treatment of this disease that they have in many other venereal diseases, but prognosis is rendered more favorable through treatment (Blank and Rake; TeLinde).

NONVENEREAL DISEASES

Many diseases, infections, and inflammation affecting the male and female sexual systems may have no relationship to sexual activity. But in each instance some part of the internal or external genitalia is affected and may possibly be aggravated by sexual contact.

Nonvenereal Syphilis

Nonvenereal syphilis, an endemic infection acquired in infancy, is caused by an invasion of a parasitic organism closely related to the treponemal organism causing venereal syphilis (hence its inclusion here). Frequently referred to as "yaws" or "pinta," the disease affects many people in widely separated parts of the world, and typically thrives in warm, moist climates and in conditions of filth. Penicillin has been used successfully in many countries in mass eradication campaigns conducted by the World Health Organization (Blau).

Trichomoniasis

Trichomoniasis is the most common of the minor gynecological diseases. It afflicts approximately 25% of all women patients, yet is seldom written about or discussed. Many married women—and their husbands, as well—suffer from this annoying infection, although men seldom experience the copious discharge, itching, and burning that are symptomatic of the ailment in women. Until very recently the infection has been extremely resistant to treatment (Netter; Shafer a).

Trichomoniasis is caused by a minute one-celled animal, the *trichomonas vaginalis*. A flagellated parasite approximately the shape and size of a paramecium and moving in the same manner, the organism propels itself by a constant thrashing of small whips at one end of its body. Thousands of these organisms can be seen when a bit of infected vaginal secretion is examined under a microscope.

Trichomonads do not burrow into the tissues, but live on the surface of the membranes. They do not invade the womb or the fallopian tubes, but normally limit their attack to the membrane of the vagina and perhaps the cervix. The first indication of infection is usually a white or yellowish vaginal discharge, accompanied by itching and burning. In many women this discharge causes constant inflammation and soreness of the external area of the vulva. A separation of the inflamed labia commonly reveals a thick, smelly, bubbly discharge in the vestibule.

In other women, trichomoniasis tends to cause severe itching rather than soreness. Practically all women who have endured this infection report that their underclothing is quickly soiled by the discharge, which, together with the irritation or itching, seems to worsen immediately before and after menstruation. Some women experience severe symptoms, others, mild ones. Why some women more than others are susceptible to trichomoniasis remains a perplexing gynecological question. Whether the symptoms are mild or severe, a doctor should be consulted immediately if there is the slightest indication of infection.

Ordinarily an infected man has no symptoms except for a slight, thin, whitish discharge; occasionally urination causes an itching and burning in his urethral tract. If one marital partner is found to be infected with trichomoniasis, the other should be examined also. Nothing is accomplished by curing one partner, only to have him or her reinfected by the other. Careful examination reveals that husbands of infected wives also have the infection in 60% of the cases (Medical science notes *d*). It is possible for a couple to pass these infectious parasites back and forth for many years, especially as the husband frequently does not realize he is infected. Trichomonads house themselves under the foreskin of a man's uncircumcised penis; in severe cases they may also invade the prostate.

It is not known just where these microscopic animals come from, or precisely how one contracts the disease (other than from an infected sexual partner). Many gynecologists state that there is a similarity between the trichomonads of the vagina and those found in the bowels. However, parasitologists maintain that the two types are actually quite different. They further claim that trichomoniasis is a venereal infection in that it is transmitted only by sexual intercourse. Still other scientists believe that the infection is not necessarily a venereal one, because it can be contracted in a swimming pool or a bathtub, where the organism may rather easily gain entry into the vaginal tract.

A relatively new drug called Flagyl is reported to be almost 100% effective in the treatment of trichomoniasis (Shafer a). Obtainable by prescription only, the drug is administered orally and renders a cure within 10 to 14 days for both men and women. If, for one reason or another, the drug cannot be used, some other form of medication can be applied to the vaginal area, and antiseptic douches are recommended.

Trichomoniasis is usually complicated by monilia (discussed below) and perhaps by one or several other various associated pathogenic bacteria. Treatment of trichomoniasis and any accompanying bacterial infection should be rigorously pursued, for, while the disease is not considered serious, it can nonetheless be tormenting and sexually inhibiting.

Moniliasis

Moniliasis (commonly called "monilia") is a fungus infection of the genital region, affecting women primarily, that can cause acute discomfort. The monilia organism has the power to lie dormant for long periods of time—in a woman's vagina or under the foreskin of a man's penis—until circumstances become favorable for its activation. More frequently than not, monilia accompanies other infectious organisms, such as trichomonads (Netter; Shafer a).

Examination of a genital area afflicted with monilia reveals white cheesy spots on the vulva, in the vagina, and on the cervix. Minute ulcerations of the labia minora may also be present, accompanied in some instances by a thick or watery vaginal discharge. All these symptoms can eventually lead to a raw, bleeding surface if treatment is not prompt and careful.

Most organisms causing infection and irritation in the vagina thrive on menstrual blood. Therefore, women who are harboring such a fungus as monilia commonly complain of the greatest discomfort and distress just before and just after menstruation.

Monilia is sometimes found in children. It is quite likely to afflict women who have diabetes or who have been overtreated with antibiotic vaginal suppositories, which can kill off the native protective bacilli in the vaginal tract. A cure can be accomplished, however, with persistent and adequate treatment under the direction of a gynecologist.

Peyronie's Disease

Peyronie's disease is one in which a fibrous tissue develops in the space above and between the two large spongy bodies (corpora cavernosa) of the penis. In about 20% of the cases calcium deposits develop in the fibrous tissue, and occasionally there is a hardening of this tissue into cartilage and bone. As the disease progresses, the penis may be deviated to the left or right, or upwards, often making erections extremely painful and sexual intercourse impossible (Netter; Walker, K.). The only function disturbed by this disease is erection.

Treatment with drugs has been tried, but the results have been unimpressive. The advisability of surgery is equally questionable, since it entails a singular hazard: erectile capacity may be destroyed. X-ray treatment, however, has reportedly improved or cured the disorder entirely in 83% of patients treated (Duggan). The disease occurs primarily in middle or old age.

Venereal Warts

Venereal warts are actually benign tumors. They are probably a result of a filtrable (capable of passing through a filter that blocks ordinary bacteria) virus infection. In a man, they usually appear around the base of the glans and develop quickly in the moist environment of a tight prepuce. A woman may develop venereal warts at the site of the labia

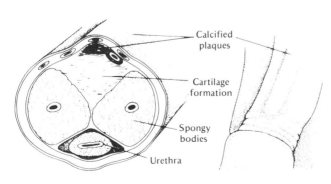

Calcified plaques

Cartilage formation

Spongy bodies

Urethra

FIGURE 20.1 Schematic representation of the penile shaft, showing the effects of Peyronie's disease. Note the abnormal formation of calcium along the top of the penis between the spongy bodies.

and perineum; the growths can spread to cover the entire area. They usually become manifest only after the menopause. Venereal warts may be transmitted to other persons or to other parts of one's own body. They should be examined microscopically so that the seriousness of the condition can be determined (Blank and Rake; Netter).

Tuberculosis

Tuberculosis of various genital areas sometimes occurs in both men and women. *Tuberculous prostatitis* is not a common disease, but it is found in about 12% of all terminal cases of tuberculosis. Although the normal glandular tissue of the prostate is replaced by a crumbly fibrous growth and calcification as the disease progresses, tuberculous prostatitis is almost always painless. The infection can also invade the epididymides and testicles. In all instances, these infections are secondary to a primary active tubercular infection outside the urogenital tract, especially in the lungs.

Among women, tuberculosis constitutes about 2% of all diseases of the upper genital tract. The fallopian tubes and uterus are typically affected. Only rarely are other reproductive organs involved (Ball; Netter; TeLinde).

Carcinoma

Carcinoma (cancer) can, of course, strike any part, or related part, of the sexual system. Its symptoms are diverse, and one should immediately consult a physician upon recognizing any suspicious signal, such as the seven outlined by the American Cancer Society:

Unusual bleeding or discharge

A lump or thickening in breast or elsewhere

A sore that does not heal

Change in bowel or bladder habits

Persistent hoarseness or cough

Persistent indigestion or difficulty in swallowing

Change in size or color of a wart or mole.

There appears to be more than a casual relationship between cancer in specific areas of the body and certain physical, social, and health factors. For example, both penile and cervical cancers have been thought to bear a definite relationship to a man's having been circumcised or not. The theory is that smegma and other impurities, which can so easily collect under the prepuce of an uncircumcised penis, predispose a man to penile cancer. Furthermore, the theory continues, the same impurities under a husband's prepuce predispose his wife to cervical cancer (Ball; Licklider; Netter).

Recent studies of Lebanese Christians and Moslems fail to support this theory, however. These studies revealed no relationship between cervical cancer in Lebanese wives and the fact that their husbands were circumcised (as Moslems are, early in life) or were not circumcised (Lebanese Christians rarely are). The low incidence of cervical cancer among Jewish women appears to be related to factors other than the circumcision of their husbands (Abou-David; Rosato and Kleger).

The age at which a woman first has sexual intercourse seems to bear some relationship to the risk of her later developing cervical cancer. Women who begin coitus early in life and continue to engage in it on a regular basis thereafter are more liable to develop cancer of the cervix than women who marry later in life (Christopherson and Parker; Rotkin).

The evidence further suggests that promiscuous sexual activity in women is positively correlated to the incidence of cervical cancer. Whether the explanation lies with the frequency of sexual intercourse, the strength of the sex drive, personality factors, or the increased possibility for contact with men whose genitalia are unclean or diseased is not known (Pereyra). Further support for observations concerning cervical cancer and the promiscuous woman comes, perhaps strangely, from the fact that nuns have a considerably lower incidence of cervical cancer than is found in the general population. However, nuns have cancer of the uterus, ovaries, and breasts as frequently as women in the general population do (Science notes *h*).

A common virus, called *type 2 herpes*, which is transmitted through sexual contact, has also been linked to cancer of the cervix by research teams at both Baylor College of Medicine in Houston, and Emory University in Atlanta. This virus is similar to the herpes virus responsible for cold sores (In the news *a*).

It bears repeating that all sensible precautions against cancer should be taken. The lives of thousands of women could be saved every year if they had regular—at least annual—gynecological examinations that include a Pap smear test. A simple and painless procedure, the Pap test involves taking a sample of cervical fluid by means of a cotton swab and examining the fluid for the presence of cancer cells. Cancer cells in deep tissue work their way to the surface and will appear in the smear taken from the surface of the cervix.

It might be mentioned that those women who for medical reasons (e.g., cancer) must undergo a clitoridectomy can take solace from present-day knowledge of the physiology of sexual response. The woman who was sexually responsive prior to having a vulvectomy—a much more radical surgical procedure than a clitoridectomy is—usually remains capable of orgasm once sexual intercourse is resumed (Melody).

Elephantiasis

Elephantiasis of the scrotum involves a marked growth of its subcutaneous tissues and epidermis, producing an enlargement varying from slight to monstrous. In extreme cases the scrotum may touch the ground and weigh as much as 200 pounds. In women, elephantiasis may manifest itself in excessive growth of the labia majora. Ordinarily indigenous to tropical regions, this disease is only rarely found in the United States.

Filarial elephantiasis is caused by a parasite carried by certain mosquitoes. Lymph glands invaded by the parasite typically swell, secondary infections develop, and scrotal enlargement occurs. *Nonfilarial elephantiasis* results from disorders of the lymph glands, usually an aftermath of chronic streptococcal infection. Elephantiasis is treated through medication and a proper support for the enlarged scrotum. Surgery is sometimes indicated (Blank and Rake; Netter).

Infectious Mononucleosis

Infectious mononucleosis is neither a nonvenereal disease nor a sexual disorder in the sense that the terms are used in this book. Its inclusion in this section rests with its popular name, "the kissing disease." It is an acute infectious disease of the lymph glands, characterized by the sudden onset of fever, marked fatigue, chills, sweating, headache, sore throat, and loss of appetite (Blank and Rake; *Dorland's illustrated medical dictionary*; Medical science notes c). Because severe and even fatal complications occasionally occur, all instructions of the attending physician must be rigidly followed.

How the disease (which is caused by a filtrable virus) is transmitted has not been definitely determined, although many authorities suspect deep kissing with an infected person. One study found that 71 of 73 "mono" patients had engaged in deep kissing at the exact time the incubation period for mononucleosis would have commenced for them (Medical science notes c). In the course of the disease, fever usually subsides after 5 days. Other acute symptoms abate within 3 weeks, although some symptoms may persist for months.

Dermatoses

Dermatoses (or skin diseases) of the genital region are fairly common, and the causative organisms and substances are legion. Chemicals—such as those contained in soap that is not rinsed off properly after a shower—can collect in the sensitive areas of the genitalia and produce irritation or burns (Corsini). The difficulty may be compounded by attempting a cure with medication too strong for the distressed area. Unfortunately, many people adopt the premise that if a little medicine is good, a lot will be even better.

—— *Tinea cruris,* or "jock itch," is another sort of dermatosis afflicting the genital region. A fungus infection, its initial symptoms are reddish, scaly patches that may develop into large, highly inflamed zones with stressful itching and considerable pain. The affliction has a striking similarity to athlete's foot. Such conditions as sweating, tight clothing, and inadequate drying of the genitalia after a bath provide a favorable environment for the development and flourishing of this infection (Netter).

Scabies and *pediculosis* (crabs) are two forms of dermatoses caused by parasites that can invade the genital area (Ellis *b;* Netter). Scabies is a highly contagious skin disorder in which a female mite (*Sarcoptes scabiei*) burrows between the layers of skin and deposits her eggs. Little vesicles housing the mite and her eggs appear on the skin surface and soon develop into papules, pustules, and a rash that itches formidably, especially at night. Appropriate medication, prescribed by a physician, can usually rid the victim of scabies in a short period of time.

In *pediculosis pubis* the pubic hair is infested with crab lice (*Phthirus pubis*), the bites of which cause an itchy skin irritation. Scratching produces further irritation and a brownish discoloration of the skin may develop. The crab louse usually buries its head in the follicles of the pubic hair and attaches its body to the hair itself. These parasites commonly pass from one person to another through sexual contact with an infected partner, although they may also be picked up from a toilet seat or bed (Ellis *b;* Netter).

Herpes genitalis is an acute skin disease affecting the external genitals. It is caused by the same herpes simplex virus that produces cold sores or fever blisters on the lips and nose. Little blisters develop that burst to form small ulcers, or that dry and harden into a crust (Blank and Rake; Netter).

Psoriasis is a disease of the skin characterized by scaly red patches. It may attack the genital region as well as other parts of the body. *Pruritus,* an excruciating itching, typically accompanies psoriasis and other skin diseases. Medication usually provides relief for the itching, and the condition clears up in a short period of time (Netter).

Folliculitis is an inflammation at the opening of the hair follicles that is precipitated by various sorts of infection, including staphylococci. The infection finds a suitable environment in which to flourish when the skin is not kept clean, clothing is too tight, and bodily resistance is generally low (Netter).

Inflammation of Internal and External Genitalia

The suffix -*itis* added to the name of an organ indicates inflammation of that organ. Many disorders of the internal and external genitalia of both men and women fall into this grouping.

Vaginitis is a fairly common vaginal irritation; the inflammation is caused by such conditions as bacterial invasion, the introduction of foreign objects into the canal, and the use of strong chemicals. Children, especially, inject small objects (coins, marbles, pins, sticks) into the vagina, possibly in a clumsy attempt at masturbation. Douching with too high a concentration of chemicals, overmedication, tampons that are inserted and then forgotten, and incorrectly placed pessaries can all cause chemical burns and inflammation of the vaginal tract. Furthermore, it is well known that a general impairment of health can reduce bodily resistance to contagion, making one more susceptible to low-grade infections such as vaginitis. "Nonspecific vaginitis" is an affliction that is considered gynecology's most perplexing unsolved problem. Sexual intercourse when such conditions exist may be the source of even further irritation in the vaginal tract (Netter; Shafer a).

Excessive douching or the use of overly strong solutions is the basic evil in many instances of vaginitis, because such douching destroys nature's protective organisms, *Doderlein's bacilli*, which normally inhabit the vagina. When this happens, the acid condition of the vagina is reduced and hostile bacteria find a suitable place for development; any of various vaginal maladies can be the consequence.

All too often, women—especially the young and newly married ones— are overly concerned about feminine hygiene. They apparently feel that if a little douching is good, more must be better. They therefore increase the strength of the solution and the frequency of its use; the results in the long run are often distressing. A study of prison women showed that daily douching with water, or with a mild vinegar or alkaline solution, did not produce the changes in the vaginal lining or any other ill effects claimed by some gynecologists (Science notes b). The real danger, then, would seem to come from douching with harsh chemicals.

During and following menopause, the lining of the vagina undergoes a marked change. Diminished hormonal production causes the membrane to become much thinner—perhaps 25% of its former thickness. While this change should in no way decrease a woman's sexual desire or ability, the tissue of her vagina does become more fragile, and she is more easily made uncomfortable, or even injured, by sexual activity. These difficulties are frequently corrected by inserting suppositories or creams containing estrogen into the vagina periodically to keep it soft, elastic, and thick. Similar results can be obtained through the administration of female sex hormones, orally or by injection. Such treatment should be prescribed and directed by a physician (Clark *h;* Rubin *j*).

Probably the best method of warding off vaginitis is to maintain good general physical health, coupled with wholesome attitudes toward sex and feminine hygiene. Every woman should have a checkup by a gynecologist at least once a year—preferably semiannually.

Cystitis refers to inflammation of the bladder, a disorder that may occur in a variety of ways (Netter; TeLinde). Symptoms usually include a severe burning sensation in the urethra during urination, a frequent need to urinate, and sharp pain in the lower abdomen. Women who have inflammation of the bladder often report that the pain is especially severe when they have sexual intercourse, and that they must often discontinue coition because of the pain (Ellis *b*).

The bladder may become infected when lowered bodily resistance facilitates the attack of existing internal bacteria on an already irritated bladder, or when germs enter the bladder via the urethra. Irritation of a woman's bladder may occur as a result of frequent sexual intercourse, because the bladder tends to become somewhat displaced by the pressure of the penis against both it and the urethra through the vaginal walls. This condition occurs not infrequently during honeymoons, giving it the rather graphic name of "honeymoon cystitis" (Rowan).

Obviously bladder inflammation can be better controlled when the body is otherwise healthy. Furthermore, good personal hygiene will do much to combat the problem once it occurs. Treatment should include thorough cleansing of the external genitalia as well as of the urethral opening with surgical soap. In addition, a woman will fare better if she will empty her bladder before sexual intercourse, and if she will use a lubricating jelly when nature appears not to supply a sufficient amount of vaginal secretion. Both these measures will decrease pressure on the abdominal organs through the vagina during coitus.

It should be pointed out that cystitis can have emotional as well as organic causes. Frequently it is related to conflict over sexual matters, in which case psychotherapy can be very helpful in bringing about a cure. As with all diseases and disorders discussed here, a physician should be consulted at the first signs of cystitis, for early investigation and treatment may enable the patient to avoid serious complications.

Epididymitis is a fairly common sexual disorder among men. It involves inflammation of the epididymis, that important structure closely attached to each testicle. The epididymis is in a rather vulnerable position to become infected from the testis below, or from above, by way of the vas deferens, should an infection spread from an affected prostate gland or seminal vesicle. Gonorrhea would appear to be a predisposing factor in epididymitis, for in one of five cases of the former, the victim becomes infected with epididymitis as well (Netter).

There are degrees of this infection, both in duration and in severity of symptoms. Mild cases involve only slight swelling and tenderness, which respond readily to treatment. In severe cases the entire testicular structure may be greatly swollen and painful. The disease can lead to growths and strictures, possibly resulting in sterility, that only surgery may be able to correct.

Some cases of chronic epididymitis persist for years. Nonsurgical treatment involves extensive use of certain drugs, a balanced and wholesome diet, rest, and a warm climate.

Prostatitis, an inflammation of the prostate gland, is a common problem among men (far more so among older ones). The condition may be either acute or chronic.

Since the discovery of antibiotics, however, acute prostatitis is rare. In the past it frequently accompanied gonorrhea but is now seen only occasionally, usually as the result of staphylococci infection following catheterization (Ellis b; Netter). Chronic prostatitis can lead to an eventual enlargement of the prostate, but not necessarily so. A clear relationship exists, however, between infrequent sexual activity and the temporary enlargement of the prostate that typically accompanies chronic prostatitis. It can also follow prolonged infection of other parts of the body. It is estimated that from 30% to 40% of American men in the 20- to 40-year-old age group suffer from chronic prostatitis (Finkle a; Stiller c).

In either acute or chronic prostatitis, symptoms may include a thin mucous discharge, especially in the morning. There may be pain in the lower back, testicles, perineum, posterior scrotum, and, perhaps, in the tip of the penis (Cawood). Prostatitis can also lead to painful or inadequate erection, premature and sometimes bloody ejaculation, impotence, and sterility. Additionally, many patients reveal collateral emotional stress and hypochondriacal complaints far out of proportion to the severity of the disease.

A urologist typically recommends prostatic massage, antibiotics, and prolonged warm baths to clear up prostatic infection and to bring about drainage of the congested gland. However, it is somewhat difficult to eradicate the infection completely because of the complexity of the ductwork of the sexual system.

The prostate tends to enlarge as a man grows older—about 20% of all men are so affected after middle age. (For further discussion of this subject, see Chapter 15.) It is not definitely known what causes this enlargement, although the most widely accepted theory is that an excess of the male hormone androgen is responsible. Since the prostate encircles the neck of the bladder, any enlargement (as well as inflammation or infection) can make urination difficult.

If the condition is not corrected, the man may experience difficulty or pain in urination or incomplete emptying of the bladder. In severe cases it can eventually cause total urinary retention. Such secondary complications as serious bladder infection, kidney stones, and uremic poisoning often follow. Hormone therapy is often successfully used to correct an enlarged prostate (Geller), but surgery to remove all or part of it (*prostatectomy*) is sometimes indicated.

The surgical approach in prostatectomy can be made via the abdomen, or through the penis (a process called transurethral prostatectomy), or from a point between the anus and scrotum (a perineal prostatectomy), the procedure being dictated by the seriousness or urgency of the condition. (Another procedure holding much promise is the cryogenic probe, which freezes the prostate or the offending enlargement in it, thus destroying it and leaving the dead tissue to be cast off by the body.)

But what of sexual potency after the removal of a noncancerous prostate? A recent study on the effects of the three major types of prostatic surgery in patients who had been potent before surgery revealed that 95% who had undergone transurethral surgery, 87% who had undergone abdominal surgery, and 71% who had undergone the perineal incision retained their potency. The reduced percentage in the third instance is attributed to the surgical approach having been made through sex-related nerve centers, involving greater risk to the nerves controlling erection. Selection of the operative procedure does not necessarily represent the free choice of the surgeon, however. It is dictated primarily by the seriousness of the case, as well as the age and physical condition of the patient (Finkle *b*).

When the prostrate is cancerous, the possibilities of a man's retaining his potency after prostatectomy are not so favorable. Surgery in this case is often of necessity a much more radical procedure, since tissues around the prostate must also be removed as a safety measure. Furthermore, advanced prostatic cancer, even when metastasized throughout the body (it typically spreads to the bones of the pelvis and spine before the patient is aware that anything is wrong), may be controlled dramatically when castration is performed or the patient is treated with female hormones. Both these treatments, of course, militate against the patient's retaining his potency.

But about 80% of prostatectomies are, fortunately, performed to correct nonmalignant growths, and these patients have every reason to expect to retain their sexual vigor. When one does hear of a case in which potency was lost following a prostate operation, one has to question whether the cause was truly physical, or whether negative psychological forces were at work. Did the man *expect* to lose his potency, thereby almost guaranteeing its loss? Did his surgeon fail to discuss the sex-functioning aspects of the operation with him? Or, worse, did he perhaps compound his patient's silent fears by having him sign a paper relieving the doctor of responsibility in the event impotency followed the surgery? Had the man's sexual relationship with his wife prior to the operation become so dreary and unsatisfying that he welcomed an excuse to abandon it? Had his wife not properly understood the effects of a prostatectomy and, expecting impotency, appeared to reject him, thus precipitating his impotency? Or was she afraid to resume intercourse because she feared it might in some way endanger her husband's health?

Another matter that concerns men facing a prostatectomy is whether they will continue to enjoy intercourse even If potency is preserved. Because the structures within the prostate, notably the ejaculatory ducts emptying into the urethra, are as a rule unavoidably damaged (although less frequently with the transurethral than with the open approaches), it is no longer possible for the man to ejaculate normally. Instead of being expelled through and out the penis, the ejaculate may flow backward into the bladder in what is termed a *retrograde* or *dry ejaculation*. (The semen is later discharged in the urine, and there is no harmful effect whatever on the man.)

Some men miss the pleasant sensation of the pulsation of ejaculation, which lessens or is missing altogether after the prostate operation. But this is a loss to which they quickly become adjusted (Trainer).

Prostatic cancer, typically a "silent" cancer, claims the lives of more men past 50 than any other form of cancer does. Many of these deaths could be avoided if men would take the simple precaution of undergoing an annual prostatic examination by a urologist. It is a brief and painless examination, performed per rectum, in which the physician seeks signs of cancer, such as hard lumps, in the prostate. He can also catch nonmalignant prostatic difficulties before they become serious ones (Shafer *b*).

Peritonitis is an infection of the peritoneum, the membrane lining the abdominal walls. In women it is frequently caused by purulent matter draining from the fallopian tubes into the peritoneal cavity. The infection may be generalized, or it may be localized in the specific area where the drainage collects. The type and area of infection, the resistance of the patient, and the timing and type of treatment—all affect the mildness or severity of peritonitis, as well as its potential danger. Even after the condition heals, adhesions result that cause organs in the cavity, such as the uterus and rectum, to change their fixed position. Backaches, pain during elimination, and distressful copulation are typical secondary symptoms. Diathermy, medication, and, occasionally, surgery are methods of treatment (Netter; TeLinde).

Balanitis causes the surfaces of the penile glans and prepuce to become swollen, tender, and itchy. The area may reveal ulcers, venereal warts, and fissures—and, in severe cases, gangrene. Chemicals, drugs, infection, fungi, and special irritants in the urine caused by metabolic disorders act together or singly to produce this problem. Early medical attention is essential (Netter).

Verumontanitis, inflammation of the verumontanum (an area located on the floor of the posterior urethra in the male), is often caused by diseases of the prostate or seminal vesicles. Various disorders of this area, such as congestion, inflammation, granulation, and hypertrophy, may require hormone or other medical treatment, or perhaps surgery. Premature ejaculation, frequency of urination, and obstructed ejaculatory ducts causing low back pain may be symptomatic of disorders of the verumontanum (Netter; Stiller g).

SEXUAL DISORDERS

Sexual disorders are customarily considered to be physical anomalies of the genitalia caused by hereditary, constitutional, or postnatal factors.

Priapism is a continual and pathological erection of the penis. There is usually an erection of the corpora cavernosa without an accompanying erection of the glans of the penis or the corpus spongiosum (the small lower spongy body). The onset of priapism is sudden, painful, and unaccompanied by sexual desire (Walker, K.).

The origins of this disorder range from leukemia to inflammation of the genitourinary system to tumors and inflammation of the central nervous system. If erection persists for 2 days or more, thrombosis of the large spongy bodies occurs, followed by the possibility of a gristlelike replacement of the spongy bodies, rendering future penile erection impossible (Netter).

Hypospadia, occurring once in every 500 births, is the second most common malformation (after club foot) in male babies at the time of delivery. It is a congenital defect although apparently no hereditary factor is involved. Because the genital fold fails to close completely during prenatal development, the urethral opening is on the underside of the penis rather than at its tip. In glandular hypospadia, the urethral meatus is slightly below and to the back of the normal site of the opening. In penile hypospadia the opening is somewhere along the lower part of the penile shaft.

Plastic surgery should be performed as soon as possible on any child with this anomaly to ensure that the urethra and corpora cavernosa will develop properly and in straight alignment. Men in whom this condition is never corrected usually remain capable of engaging in coitus. If the meatus is sufficiently recessed on the penile shaft, however, these men will obviously have difficulty in impregnating their wives (Netter; Stiller g). A similar anomaly (in which the urethra opens into the vagina) occurs in women but is rarely bothersome.

Epispadia is much more rare than hypospadia and is usually associated with a congenital malformation of the bladder. In this disorder, the urethral opening is on the dorsum (top) of the penis. The epispadiac penis typically curves upward, is deformed, and requires early plastic surgery (Netter; Stiller g).

Phimosis is an anomaly in which the prepuce is abnormally long and cannot be pulled back or retracted from over the glans of the penis (Levie). Fibrous growths sometimes attach the prepuce to the glans, making even the attempt to draw it back quite painful (Netter). Smegma may collect, leading to ulceration or inflammation of the penis. Surgery, usually in the form of circumcision, can correct this difficulty.

Strictures of the reproductive tracts are found in both men and women. In the male urethral system, *strictures* (abnormal narrowing) can evolve in the prostatic, penile, and bulbous portions of the urethra. The symptomatology frequently involves difficulty in passing urine, accompanied by a burning sensation and mild urethral discharge. Psychological factors can enter the picture as well, frequently causing the added complication of impotency. The origin of these strictures is an infection of the urethral tract precipitated by scarring, blows, or injuries, or by tears and punctures made in the inept application of catheters and similar instruments. The disorder varies in severity.

In women, strictures of the reproductive tract are found not only in the urethra, but also in the internal cervical os and the fallopian tubes. If the cervical os is blocked, conception becomes impossible and there will be a damming up of menstrual flow and other tissue debris. Dilation of the os or urethra gives some relief, although this procedure will not remove the scar tissue. A stretching process is necessary, but it must be done gradually and over a long period. Physicians believe that overzealous treatment merely aggravates the conditions (Netter; TeLinde).

Polyps are pedunculated (stemlike) growths that arise from the mucosa and extend into the lumen or opening of any body cavity. They are true tumors, the inception of which is a morbid enlargement of the mucous membrane. Polyps may be found in any bodily area where there is mucous tissue. In the male genitalia, the tumors are benign and are usually found within the penile meatus. Urinary disturbances, such as painful, difficult, and urgent urination, as well as difficulties in sexual functioning are the usual symptoms of this disorder. Minor surgery is ordinarily sufficient to correct the problem (Netter; Shaw; TeLinde).

Cysts are sacs, containing a liquid or semisolid substance, that develop abnormally in some part of the body. They may appear in the bladder or urinary tract, in the prostate, Cowper's glands, or scrotum, and in the vagina, uterus, vulva, or Bartholin's glands, causing inordinate retention of urine and various sexual malfunctionings. The size of cysts varies considerably. The method of treatment depends upon a number of factors, such as the cyst's location, size, and rate of growth (Ball; Netter; Shaw; TeLinde).

Edema (abnormal amount of fluid in intercellular tissue) of the scrotum results from inflammation or other disturbances in the vascular or lymphatic system. Such occurrences as physical trauma, allergic states, and insect bites may produce an edematous reaction, which, because of the loose and elastic nature of scrotal tissue, causes the scrotum to swell to near basketball-size proportions (Netter).

Hydrocele, a fairly common male birth malformation (ninth in frequency) involves a collection of fluid within the two layers of tissue making up the *tunica vaginalis* (membranes covering the testes). As the testes descend from their abdominal position (usually at the seventh month of prenatal life) they carry with them two layers of the peritoneum. Any abnormality in these layers of tissue can provide a natural environment for a variety of hydrocele conditions. Hydroceles can also follow physical trauma, operations, infection of the epididymis or other areas, gonorrhea, and tuberculosis. Suspending the scrotum and surgically removing the fluid and distressed portion of the tunica vaginalis are suggested methods of treatment. In some cases the fluid is drawn off with a hollow needle, although this procedure always introduces the possibility of infection (Clark *d*; Netter; Sex in the news *a*; Stiller *g*).

Spermatocele is a soft swelling on either side of the scrotum, the result of an intrascrotal cyst. The cyst obstructs the tubular structure between the testicles and epididymis, causing a blockage of sperm and a collection of fluid. The fluid has a milky coloration because of the millions of sperm and lipids trapped there. Surgery is the usual method of treatment (Clark *d*; Netter).

Varicocele is a swelling of the veins that lead to the testicles. In 99% of such cases, the varicocele develops on the left side of the testicles; only 1% develop bilaterally. Perhaps 1 man in 10 has some degree of spermatic vein dilation. There can be rather severe pain, accompanied by a sensation of pulling and tugging at the testicles, the symptoms tending to disappear when the patient lies down and allows the blood to flow out of the veins. A suspensory can relieve the discomfort of the excessive weight, and cold baths may temporarily alleviate swelling and pain, but a surgical procedure is usually required to correct the condition (Clark *d;* Netter).

Hematocele is an accumulation of blood in the tunica vaginalis, usually resulting from an injury. Spontaneous hematocele may be a result of syphilis, arteriosclerosis, diabetes, or an inflammatory condition within the scrotum. Surgery is the treatment of choice (Clark *d;* Netter).

Cystocele is a hernial protrusion of the bladder through the vaginal wall. It is especially common, though in varying degrees of severity, among women who have had children. The muscles supporting the vagina become torn or considerably weakened, allowing the bladder to push through. A sensation of dragging or tugging in the lower abdomen, frequent urination, incontinence, and infection are common symptoms. Sometimes pessaries may help correct the less severe of these conditions, but more often surgical repair is required. Rupture of the perineal area, or damage to it, may produce *rectoceles*, wherein the vagina becomes closed by a bulging rectum (Netter; TeLinde).

Torsion of the testicle is an abnormal rotation of the testicle causing a blockage of the blood supply to that organ. The rotation is precipitated by any of several physiological conditions. The amount of damage varies, depending upon the degree of torsion and how long the condition persists. If severe torsion is allowed to continue for as long as a few hours, necrosis of testicular tissue or even complete gangrene in the area can result. Survival of the testicle depends upon prompt diagnosis and appropriate corrective procedures, such as untwisting the spermatic cord. Manual efforts to correct the torsion without opening the scrotum are unsuccessful; the condition must be rectified by open surgery (Netter).

Undescended testes (cryptorchidism) are found in about 1 boy in 50 at the age of puberty, but this ratio dwindles to approximately 1 in 500 among adult men. The delay in the descent can be caused by an inadequate gonadotropic hormone secretion; a congenital defect in the gonadal germ cells, or the absence of them altogether; or physiological failure, such as a malformed inguinal ring, in the structure through which the testes pass from the abdomen to the scrotum (Ellis *b;* Netter).

Testes that remain undescended after puberty will progressively degenerate, and eunuchoidal (having only partial external genital structure) symptoms will develop, especially if both testicles are involved. Hormonal treatment will often effect a successful descent of the testicles. When physical defects block what would otherwise be a normal descent, or when some cosmetic repair is desirable, surgery is indicated. In other instances the descent of the testes is faulty in that they enter foreign areas and lodge there. These *ectopic testes* require surgery to effect proper placement in the scrotum (Garrett).

Monorchism is the condition of having only one testicle in the scrotum, an anomaly that only a physician can confirm after a thorough examination. Monorchism is of no clinical significance, inasmuch as the existing testicle produces sufficient quantities of both hormones and sperm for normal physiological and sexual functioning. The condition nevertheless causes feelings of sexual inadequacy in certain men (Wershub). In other men one testicle is significantly smaller than the other. This inequality is not monorchism, however, since two testicles are present and both are functional.

Anorchism is the congenital lack of both testicles. The condition is extremely rare, but when it does exist it is characterized, predictably, by the lack of sexual desire. The man is, furthermore, incapable of erection and emission. And he possesses such feminine characteristics as scanty facial hair, narrow shoulders, wide hips, and a high-pitched voice (Wershub).

Testicular failure may involve either the interstitial cells that produce male hormones, or the spermatic tubes where sperm develop, or both. In almost all instances, failure of the interstitial cells involves failure of the spermatic tubes, although the reverse is not necessarily true. *Hypogonadism* (insufficient secretion of the gonads) produces eunuchoidal characteristics, sometimes involving overmuch growth of the long bones. The afflicted boy, although shorter in stature than others his age, will have proportionately very long arms and legs. Approximately 75% of eunuchoidal boys are underweight because of poorly developed muscles and bones. But even so, these boys commonly develop excessive fat over the abdomen, around the mammary glands, above the pubis, and on the buttocks (Netter). External genitals are extraordinarily small and poorly developed, and the prostate and seminal vesicles may also be markedly underdeveloped. Secondary sexual characteristics are typically feminine in appearance.

Testicular failure may be intrinsic, or it may manifest itself at any of the different stages of a boy's development and growth. Treatment usually consists of endocrine therapy and meets with rather good success.

Ordinarily, the interstitial cells begin to produce the hormone androgen when a boy is about 12, as has been said (although the hormonal production can begin as early as 8 years of age, or be delayed until a man is, say, 22) (Netter). When the production is impeded, the youngster frequently becomes obese and his genital development is retarded. Diet sometimes hastens laggard pubescence. Hormonal treatment, however, is commonly used to accelerate the process and thus avoid any physical problems (which will very likely correct themselves in time when the development eventually commences). The treatment also serves to prevent psychological and emotional difficulties that are liable to develop from a feeling of "being different" and from the little cruelties inflicted by the boy's peer group.

Testicular failure can also manifest itself in sterility without the presence of any overt signs of changes in the external genitalia.

Sexual precocity may have its origins in a premature development of hypothalamic centers, in which event the disorder is said to be of the *cerebral* type. Certain dysfunctions of the adrenal cortex or the interstitial cells of the testes cause the *endocrine* type of the disorder. Primary and secondary sex characteristics are prematurely well developed in young boys so affected. They may have the appearance of a small adult (endocrine type); or their physique may be inordinately muscular and their bone structure mature, although they maintain other boyish characteristics, and development of the central nervous system is normal (cerebral type) (Netter). Similar manifestations in girls are discussed below.

Neoplasms of the ovaries are growths on or within the ovaries, sometimes so greatly affecting the hormonal output of these organs that marked changes in secondary sex characteristics take place. Some *feminizing neoplasms* develop in prepuberal girls, typically resulting in rapid and premature enlargement of the breasts, premature development of the genitalia, and early growth of pubic hair. In the sexually mature woman, there may be irregular uterine bleeding, endometrial growth, or breast enlargement.

Masculinizing neoplasms cause such changes in physical characteristics as hirsutism (abnormal hairiness), enlargement of the clitoris, overdevelopment of muscles, and a masculine lowering of the voice. The condition can also induce such defeminizing changes as sterility, amenorrhea, and decrease in breast size. Most incidences of masculinizing neoplasms occur in women between the ages of 25 and 45, although girls as young as 15 and women as old as 65 have been affected by the anomaly. Other endocrine changes may result from abnormal growths in hormone-producing glands, such as the adrenal or the pituitary (Netter; Shaw).

Chromosomal anomalies are of several kinds. Since early in this century, it had been thought that man's cellular structure contains 48 chomosomes (from the Latin, *chromo*: color; and *soma*: body; so called because they become visible if put in special dyes). Recently, however, careful research revealed that there are normally only 46, represented by 44 *autosomes* (nonsex chromosomes) and an additional pair of *sex chromosomes*, labeled XX in the female and XY in the male.

It was first observed in 1938 (and has since been studied in detail) that certain congenital sexual disorders are related to an abnormal *karyotype*, a term used to indicate an arrangement of chromosomes (Briggs; Turner).

Furthermore, it was discovered in 1949 that there is typically present in the cell nuclei of female mammals a substance called *chromatin* (the more readily stainable portion of the cell nucleus, shaped like a drumstick), which makes women chromatin-positive. Chromatin is absent in the cells of males; hence males are chromatin-negative. The substance is present in a week-old female embryo and will continue to be present throughout its pre- and postnatal life. The presence or absence of sex chromatin also plays a crucial role in some congenital human sexual disorders (Barr and Bertram; Shaffer).

Best known of the chromosomal abnormalities are *Turner's syndrome* and *Klinefelter's syndrome.* These conditions are believed to arise from the faulty splitting of the 23 pairs of chromosomes in the process of spermatogenesis and oogenesis. The result is a germ cell (ovum or sperm) that contains an extra sex-determining (X or Y) chromosome or that is lacking one (Gonads, disorders of).

If an atypical ovum containing 22 chromosomes is fertilized, an XO sex karyotype, or *Turner's syndrome,* is the result, rather than the normal XX or XY karyotype. The total number of chromosomes in this case is 45: 44 autosomes and only 1 X chromosome instead of the normal 2. The abnormality will produce a woman having the primary external sex structure of a female, although poorly developed and infantile in size, but having no ovaries. Besides the deficiencies in the primary and secondary sex characteristics, other typical indications of this disorder are a short stature, winglike folds of skin extending from the base of the skull to an area over the clavicle, and a broad, stocky chest. Deafness and mental deficiency are also fairly common (Netter; Shaffer).

In *Klinefelter's syndrome* a 24-chromosome ovum is fertilized, creating an XXY karyotype and making a total of 47 chromosomes. This additional female (X) sex chromosome and the presence of chromatin produce a man of incomplete virilization and distinctly feminine appearance. The testicles are small and incapable of producing mature sperm, and breast development is prominent. These men, furthermore, show a tendency toward mental impairment, and a large number can be characterized as having inadequate personalities. Predictably, their sex drive is low (Money f).

A third form of chromosomal anomaly discovered in certain men, which has attracted considerable attention of late, involves supernumerary Y chromosomes (e.g., XYY, XYYY, or even XYYYY karyotypes). Some investigators have speculated that the disorder creates a "supermale," one more prone than the average man to undisciplined, aggressive, criminal, or sociopathic behavior. Indeed, appeal against the death penalty of the convicted murderer of eight young nurses in Chicago was based on this premise. On the same ground the murderer of a prostitute in Paris was given a light sentence by the jury; the psychiatric and genetics experts could agree only that the syndrome brought on difficulties of "comportment and humor." In a similar case in Australia an accused murderer was acquitted on grounds of insanity (Chromosomes & crime; *Houston Chronicle a;* Money f).

In a few studies made of the effects of a man's possessing an extra

Y chromosome, consensus among the investigators has by no means been reached. They agree only that subnormal intelligence, tall stature, and severe acne appear to be associated with the XYY anomaly (Chromosomes & crime). Nevertheless, results of 11 studies of this phenomenon reveal a significantly higher proportion of XYY males in prison populations (1.8% to 12.0%) than in the general population (0.14% to 0.38%), suggesting some causal relationship between sociopathic behavior and this chromosomal abnormality (Gardner and Neu).

Geneticists also speculate that maternal age is associated with a child's having one too many chromosomes (called *trisomy*). As the mother's age advances beyond 30 years, the incidence of trisomy doubles for every 5 years of her age. Paternal age seems associated with the XO karyotype (Turner's syndrome) (Lenz *et al.*).

Similar abnormal karyotypes are created when normal ova are fertilized by sperm having 22 or 24 (or more) chromosomes.

As more precise scientific instruments are developed and techniques for investigation are refined, new discoveries in the field of chromosome structure continue to be made. For example, individuals with XXXY, XXXXY, and XXYY karyotypes have recently been identified (Briggs; Lloyd).

Atrophic conditions of the vulva involve loss of fatty tissue in the mons pubis and labia majora; reduction in size of the clitoris and labia minora; loss of elasticity of the skin; inflammation, abrasions, and fissures of the vulva; and development of a leatherlike condition of the vulval tissue. *Atrophic conditions of the vagina* include a reduction or loss of its wrinkled surface; shrinking of the mucous membrane; narrowing of the canal, especially at the apex; formation of adhesions; and an ill-smelling, irritating discharge. Causality may be related to aging, removal of ovaries, X-ray, or fungal invasion (Netter; Shafer a).

Varicose veins of the vulva usually arise during pregnancy when intrapelvic pressure retards venous flow. An aching, "dragging" sensation may be felt in the pelvic region. The symptoms may be more severe while the woman is standing, then tend to disappear when she is lying down. Surgery can correct this and other circulatory disorders of the vulval region (Netter).

Congenital anomalies of the vagina, uterus, and fallopian tubes are more common than many realize. For example, the vagina may be closed (*gynatresia*) or missing entirely. (In the latter case, an artificial vagina that is functional for sexual intercourse can be surgically constructed.) Double vaginas also occur; one is usually considerably larger than the other, or the vagina may be divided into two parts by a septum, as the nose is. Similar anomalies are also found occasionally in the uterus (rudimentary, double, divided) and in the tubes (rudimentary, extra ampullae, blocked opening). And the uterus or tubes may be missing altogether. If the organs exist even in a malformed state, they may or may not be functional, depending upon how extensively they are affected. Such congenital anomalies are usually a result of the mullerian ducts having failed to fuse completely or properly during prenatal development (Ball; Masters and Johnson *n*; Netter; TeLinde).

An *imperforate hymen* is a condition wherein the vagina is sealed off by a solid mass of hymenal tissue. The condition may go unnoticed until the onset of menstruation. Unless the hymen is punctured at the menarche, however, the menstrual fluid is necessarily retained in the vagina and the uterus must enlarge in order to contain the flow. Incision of the hymen corrects the condition easily and quickly.

A *fibrous hymen* is not a common occurrence, however often the condition is discussed in medical writings. The hymenal tissue in this instance is inordinately thick and tough. It must be surgically incised before penile penetration is possible (Netter; Shaw; TeLinde).

Vaginal fistulae are pipelike openings that may develop between the bladder and vagina, urethra and vagina, or rectum and vagina. The etiology may be congenital, as in hypospadia (in which the urethra empties into the vaginal tract); or traumatic, as from obstetrical or surgical injury. Malignant tumors can also produce these unwelcome fistulae.

Urinary incontinence and severe infection are only two of the possible consequences of such anomalies. Surgical treatment is difficult and complicated; however, recent advances in operative methods used in the investigation and correction of pelvic disorders make prognosis more favorable than it was in the recent past (Ball; Netter; Shaw; TeLinde).

Abnormal uterine bleeding is the most frequent gynecological complaint encountered by physicians. The term "functional uterine bleeding" refers to hemorrhages not precipitated by detectable anomalies. If ovulation should not occur, too little or no progesterone is secreted, yet the secretion of estrogen continues. The result in some instances—although not all—is that the proliferation or growth phase of the menstrual cycle persists, and with it comes a thickening of the uterine mucosa (endometrium).

In these circumstances there is no growth stimulation of the ovarian follicles because ovarian estrogen inhibits the release of FSH (the follicle-stimulating hormone) from the pituitary gland. The uterine lining therefore thrives under the continued flow of estrogen, and the nonstimulated and unruptured follicles gradually convert into cystic structures. This process reduces the level of estrogen, which causes some FSH production and hence the development of some new follicles. The growth process of the endometrium is repeated, eventually producing both gross and microscopic changes in the endometrium itself. The irregular hormonal interplay produces unnatural growth in the uterine tissue; abnormal bleeding (abnormal both in frequency and amount) from the uterus may result. In about 66% of the cases of functional uterine bleeding, *endometrial hyperplasia* (that is, excessive growth of the uterine lining) is present.

Endometrial hyperplasia may be induced simply by the presence of polyps, or by the more serious conditions of uterine carcinoma, pregnancy disorders, or psychogenic states. (Birth-control pills inhibit ovulation, but they do not cause a disturbance in hormone balance; they therefore act to prevent malfunctions of this nature.) Women should not delay in consulting a gynecologist when any unusual or abnormal complex of symptoms pertaining to the reproductive system manifests itself (Ball; Netter; Shaw; TeLinde).

Cervical erosion is in most cases due to congenital defects or childbirth injuries. The usual symptoms are red granular tissue in the area in and around the external cervical opening or os. Any break in the cervical tissue, such as unhealed lacerations caused by childbirth, or any unusual exposure of the cervical mucous glands to the bacteria inhabiting the vaginal tract makes the cervix susceptible to infection, which is usually chronic and low-grade. Infection of this area may lead to erosion and ulceration of the cervical tissue, correction of which may require a partial excision of the cervix (*Dorland's illustrated medical dictionary;* Netter; Shaw; TeLinde).

Displacement of the uterus is said to exist when the womb becomes fixed in an abnormal position. The usual uterine position in a woman standing erect is approximately at right angles to the axis of the vagina, putting the uterus in an almost horizontal plane above the bladder. For various reasons, the ligaments supporting the uterus may become too taut or too loose, and the organ shifts to an unusual position, exhibiting a slight to great degree of deviation. The shift frequently causes painful menstruation, backaches, and pelvic congestion and makes sexual intercourse uncomfortable. If there is no pain connected with uterine displacement, there is no necessity to correct the condition. The displacement does not seem to interfere with the possibility of a woman's becoming pregnant, and properly positioning the uterus apparently does not increase the chances for pregnancy (Netter; TeLinde).

Prolapse of the uterus means that the supportive uterine ligaments have relaxed to such an extent that the uterus protrudes into the vaginal canal. The degree of prolapse can be slight, wherein the supporting tissue relaxes minimally to permit only a small portion of the uterus to drop into the vagina; or second degree, wherein the cervix actually protrudes from the vagina; or complete, in which the entire uterus protrudes from the vaginal barrel.

Prolapse of the uterus usually pulls down the bladder as well, and there is often an accompanying cystocele. Functional bleeding, backaches, a "bearing-down" feeling, and difficulties in elimination are typical symptoms. Surgery is usually required to correct the condition, especially if the prolapse is second degree or complete (Ball; Netter; Shaw; TeLinde).

Uterine myomata or *fibroid tumors,* found in 4% to 11% of women, vary greatly in size and position. The description "fibroid" is something of a misnomer, in that these tumors form from muscle cells, not from fibrous tissue. Their incidence is greatest among women in their 50s, although women considerably younger may develop uterine tumors of prodigious size. It is thought that hormonal imbalance of some sort produces fibroid tumors, since it has been established that existing ones either shrink or remain static in their dimensions after menopause. In about 50% of the cases, excessive bleeding is a symptom, and eventual calcification in a fibroid tumor is not unusual. A gynecologist can easily determine in each case the most suitable method of treatment indicated (Ball; Netter; Shaw; TeLinde).

Endometriosis involves the ectopic or aberrant growth of the endometrium (lining of the uterus). Symptoms of the disorder may include sterility (32% to 53% of the time), dysmenorrhea, backaches, and painful sexual intercourse. While the condition can exist as long as the ovaries produce hormones, it is most often found in women in their 30s. The tissue can commence growth in any of various parts of the body—the cervix, abdominal walls, intestines, Bartholin's glands, vulva; even the umbilicus may be encroached upon by ectopic endometrium. But the tissue always retains the histologic and biologic characteristics of uterine mucosa. Treatment depends upon the severity of the symptoms and includes cervical dilation, surgery, or simply encouraging the patient to become pregnant. Surgery usually involves removal of the organs or areas invaded, together with the surrounding tissue (Ball; Netter; Shaw; TeLinde).

Menstrual cramps, if their origin is physical, are usually caused by a tilted or infantile uterus, inadequate dilation or blockage of the cervical os, endometrial disorders, and similar anomalies. Psychological factors are a more likely cause of menstrual cramps than physiological conditions are (Clark e; Mead; Melzack).

Hermaphroditism is the condition in which an individual has the gonads of both sexes; that is, both ovarian and testicular tissue is present (Netter). Cases of true hermaphroditism are extremely rare; perhaps fewer than 100 valid incidences appear in the medical literature of the entire world (Austerman and Beach; Money d). It would be possible, technically, for a hermaphrodite to impregnate as a male and also to conceive as a woman (Netter). Indeed, Brazilian doctors recently reported the case of a true hermaphrodite who had a developing fetus in the womb, and who also possessed testicles capable of producing sperm. Furthermore, the person claimed to be both the father and the mother of the child (Money d)! Even if the report of pregnancy were true, the validity of the claim to dual parenthood is open to considerable doubt, however, for the female

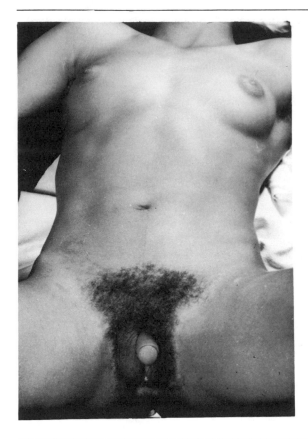

FIGURE 20.2 Photograph of a true hermaphrodite with a left ovary, a right testis and 44 + XX chromosome count. The subject always lived as a male and was married and a stepfather. From Money. *Sex Errors of the Body.* Baltimore: The Johns Hopkins University Press, 1968.

hormones produced by the ovary would undoubtedly sterilize the testis, making the person incapable of fertilizing ova and rendering self-impregnation impossible.

Pseudohermaphroditism is a much more common disorder than true hermaphroditism is; some form of it appears in about 1 infant of every 1000 born (Green and Green). The male pseudohermaphrodite has gonads that are testes, at least from a histological standpoint, but his external genitalia are either ambiguous or feminine in appearance. The gonads of a female pseudohermaphrodite are ovaries, but her external genitalia (and often other of her bodily characteristics) appear, to a greater or lesser degree, to be those of a male.

Because pseudohermaphrodites usually have both male and female sex organs in rudimentary form, their genetic sex is difficult to determine. Because accurate identification is so difficult, it is not uncommon for a pseudohermaphrodite to be brought up as a member of the wrong sex.

Childhood influences quite naturally predispose the individual to assume the interests, attitudes, and sexual behavior of one sex, however much his somatic characteristics may be those of the opposite one—another indication of the superiority of psychological over physiological factors in sexual matters (Money *b*).

In animals lower than primates, sexual behavior is primarily a process of biological stimulus and response. Cyclical release of hormones stimulates the female to copulate, and odorous vaginal secretions attract the male. Very little of these animals' behavior is under the control of the cortex of the brain. In general, the larger the brain cortex is, the greater the control that an animal has over its behavior and the smaller the role that mere instinct plays in its copulatory behavior.

Humans, of course, possess the largest and the most intricately structured cortex of any animal; man's cortex accounts for about 90% of his total brain volume. Sexual control and, indeed, sexual behavior in man are therefore based more on conscious effort, desire, and patterns learned from past experience than they are in lower animals. (Some female animals, as a matter of fact—*e.g.*, the rabbit, rat, cat, and dog—may copulate even though the entire cortex has been removed.)

The learning process (in which the cortex figures prominently) is therefore especially important in man's sexual functioning. That is why biological and psychic sex identity can be two different things in the same individual. Psychological sex, or gender-role identification, is not established until a child becomes verbal, usually between the ages of 18 and 36 months.

If the parents have made an error in correctly identifying the child's biological sex, but recognize this error before the thirtieth month and treat the child accordingly thereafter, little psychic damage will result. But if the parents attempt to assign a different gender role after this age, the child may never accomplish the psychological switchover—at least, not without severe emotional stress and conflict—and hormonal treatment will be of little or no avail. Thus training and the learning process, not mere blind biological instinct, govern man's sexual orientation and account for the great diversity of sexual expression found among humans (Barclay; Bing and Rudikoff).

When external somatic characteristics are in any way ambiguous regarding the sex of a newborn child, it is essential that the parents seek the advice of specialists at once. Sometimes surgery is indicated, not only to alter the sexual characteristics of the child, but also to alleviate or prevent the emotional problems that typically accompany such anomalies (Money *b*).

Congested ovaries or testicles may develop if a woman or man engages in prolonged, sexually stimulating petting for which there is no culminating release through orgasm. As it is a common occurrence during an engagement period, the term "engagement ovaries" is frequently used. Protracted but unrelieved sexual tensions cause blood to concentrate in the ovaries and other areas of the internal genitalia, producing a swelling and congestion of the tissues, which is the source of the pain. A woman's vulva may also become painfully congested for the same reason. In men, protracted sexual excitement without orgasmic relief gives rise to a concentration of blood in the testicles, which creates conditions of swelling, pain, and aching, popularly called "stone-ache" (Masters and Johnson n; Menaker).

Congenital and acquired anomalies of the breast are found in both men and women. The most frequent of these disorders among men is *gynecomastia,* in which there is a feminization and abnormal increase in breast size. Studies of armed services personnel have reported that from 7 to 13 cases of gynecomastia are discovered in every 100,000 men; other medical authorities consider these figures unrealistically high, however (Rector).

Gynecomastia may have its inception in adolescence when an endocrine change ordinarily takes place. It may also occur in adulthood as a result of endocrine disorders, or because estrogenic substances have been medically prescribed to combat certain ailments, such as prostatic carcinoma. Endocrine medication to shrink excessive tissue, or simply surgery to remove it, are the most popular methods of treatment.

Women may possess one or more extra breasts (*polymastia*), supernumerary nipples (*polythelia*), or an abnormally enlarged breast or breasts. Even more rarely the nipple or areola may be missing altogether. These conditions are all congenital anomalies. Extra breasts and nipples usually follow the milk line, which starts under the arm, then extends through the breasts and down both sides of the abdomen in a line to the lips of the vulva, terminating in the inner thighs. Plastic surgery can correct these abnormalities once the enlargement has formed (*Dorland's illustrated medical dictionary;* Netter). Any unusual growth, pain, or change in the feel, function, or appearance of the breast should be investigated immediately by a physician.

PART SIX

SEX AND SOCIETY

21 ILLEGITIMACY

In this chapter we shall look at illegitimacy in the United States primarily in the context of an unwanted pregnancy. It is nevertheless well recognized that there have always been members of society—perhaps more visible today than ever before—who reject the concept of traditional marriage yet very genuinely wish to have a child. Whether the pregnancy out of wedlock was unwanted (which is usually the case) or planned, many of the consequences for the parents are the same. And these consequences result from Western society's traditional award of "second-class citizenship" to the illegitimate child and its ostracism of the parents, most particularly the mother.

All societies must perpetuate themselves. The manner in which they do so is always societally and legally regulated, and procreation is generally approved of only within the bonds of matrimony. Illegitimacy has traditionally been regarded as an affront to marriage and social order, and as detrimental to the best interests of the child and its parents. Illegitimacy is therefore almost universally condemned, but the punishment meted out to the "offenders" has varied enormously from culture to culture and from time to time within the same culture (Illegitimacy).

THE SCOPE OF THE PROBLEM

A recent study of birth, pregnancy, and abortion (Gebhard *et al. b*) reveals that over 40 million American women alive today have had or will have premarital sexual intercourse; of this number, one out of five has become or will become pregnant. Of these 8 million premaritally pregnant women, over 1.5 million will marry during their pregnancy; of those who do not marry, about 400,000 will have a miscarriage and about 500,000 will give birth to illegitimate children. The remaining premarital pregnancies —about 5.5 million of them—will end in induced abortion.

Of the more than 10 million divorced, widowed, or separated women presently living in the United States, approximately 75% engage in sexual relations; about 15% of these sexually active women, or almost 1.5 million, will become pregnant, although only about 60,000 of these pregnancies will go to term (Bowman; Christensen and Meissner; Gebhard *et al. b;* Kenkel; Kinsey *et al. c*). It is estimated that 6% of all unmarried women in the United States have been pregnant by the age of 15, and 25% by the age of 40 (Trainer). In 1968, 9.7% of all United States births were illegitimate (United States Bureau of the Census).

Illegitimacy in the United States has historically been considered a moral wrong, for which both mother and child have been subjected to strong social condemnation and legal punishment (Bell *a*). It has long been recognized that American morality is sex-centered (Landis); when the word *morality* is used, for example, most Americans think first of *sexual* self-control. Seldom, unfortunately, do we interpret morality as meaning financial honesty, truthfulness, loyalty to a person or cause, compassion, or unselfishness.

Illegitimacy, however, has not always been viewed in the Western world in such an intolerant manner as in America today. The public's attitude toward premarital pregnancies was rather lenient until the time of the Protestant Reformation and the Catholic Counter-Reformation in the sixteenth century. Both these religious movements attacked what some considered a general moral laxity among the people. One subject for attack was the unmarried mother, against whom severe punishment was levied. Seizing upon the opportunity to turn moral indignation into economic advantage, wives and legitimate children worked toward legislation that would protect their rights to inheritance of money, land, and property against any claims by "natural children" (Beigel *b;* Searle). This legal discrimination against illegitimate children, which continues even today, places them at a great economic disadvantage—to say nothing of the inherent psychological and sociological handicaps.

A common outcry, particularly in the popular press, is that illegitimacy is on the rise in the United States (for whatever reason ascribed). There has been, to be sure, a rather marked rise in recorded illegitimate births in the United States during recent years. However, much of the increase can doubtless be accounted for by the fact that a greater number of women of lower socioeconomic status now have their babies, legitimate or otherwise, in hospitals and maternity homes, where careful records are kept. In the past, women tended to have their illegitimate babies as surreptitiously as possible, and certainly not in a hospital.

This increase in hospital births accounts in part for the jump in recorded illegitimate births among nonwhites from 54,000 a year in the 1940–44 period to 130,000 a year in 1955–59. (This subject will be explored more thoroughly in the next section.) Illegitimate hospital births among whites also increased during the same period—from 43,000 to 71,000 per annum.

Over this 20-year span, the smallest increase, within age groups, was among the 15- to 19-year-olds (89%). The largest increase was in the 25- to 29-year-old group (348%); next highest, among women 30 to 34 years old (316%); followed by those 20 to 24 years old (234%); then those 35 to 39 years old (230%); and finally the 40- to 44-year-old group, with a 131% increase (Vincent *b*; U.S. Bureau of the Census).

The change in incidence of illegitimate births within age groups from the 1955–59 period to 1968 is quite a different story. Here the greatest increase was among the 15- to 19-year-olds (28%); the next greatest, in the 40- to 44-year-old group (27%); then the 35- to 39-year-old group (22%); then those 30 to 34 years old (9%); and, finally, the 20- to 24-year-old group and those 25 to 29 years old, who showed practically no increase in illegitimacy rate (1%) (U.S. Bureau of the Census).

As can be seen from Table 21.1, there were further changes in the illegitimacy rates for the various age groups between 1965 and 1968. These statistics are somewhat misleading, however, because of changes made during this period by the Bureau of the Census in the age categories. Had the age composition of the groups remained unchanged from 1965 to 1968, the illegitimacy rate of the 15- to 19-year-old group—the only group

TABLE 21.1 Estimated Illegitimacy Rates (Illicit Births per 1000 Unmarried Females) for U.S. Women by Age Groups: 1940–1968

	AGE OF WOMEN					
YEAR	15 to 19 years old	20 to 24 years old	25 to 29 years old	30 to 34 years old	35 to 39 years old	40 to 44 years old
1968	19.8	37.3	38.6	28.2	14.9	3.8
1965	16.7	39.9	49.3	37.5	17.4	4.5
1955–59	15.5	37.1	38.1	25.8	12.2	3.0
1940–44	8.2	11.1	8.5	6.2	3.7	1.3

showing an increase—would have evidenced a slight decline (U.S. Bureau of the Census).

The number of illegitimate births continues a rapid rise in the United States, primarily owing to the sharp increase in the number of unmarried women of childbearing age (from 10.3 million in 1960 to 13.9 million in 1968). For example, the actual *number* of illegitimate births among United States women of all races increased slightly over 50% from 1960 (224,000) to 1968 (339,000), yet the illegitimacy *rate* increased only 13% over the same period, from 21.6% to 24.4% per 1000 unmarried females (U.S. Bureau of the Census).

Socioeconomic Implications in Illegitimacy

Much has been written about the high incidence of illegitimate births among blacks. While it is true that the illegitimacy rate among black and other non-Caucasian races has been several times higher than among whites in the past, the margin has narrowed in recent years. For example, the illegitimacy rates for all races nearly tripled between 1940 and 1961. However, between 1961 and 1968, the illegitimacy rate among nonwhite races declined by 14%, while that for whites increased by 3.2% (U.S. Bureau of the Census).

It has already been mentioned that more accurate recording of all illegitimate births in recent years no doubt accounts in part for the high incidence of illegitimacy among blacks. But other factors need also to be examined.

The facts are that 29.5% of all births among blacks in 1967 were illegitimate compared with 4.9% of all white births, and that there is a higher illegitimacy rate among blacks than among whites at all socioeconomic levels. Many researchers nevertheless feel that the problem of illegitimacy in this country is ascribable not to race but to poverty, being directly related to inferior education, poor living conditions in our inner-cities, and insufficient income (Guttmacher c).

But it is interesting to note that, historically, explanations for the who and why of unwed mothers have tended to reflect the social ills or set of social problems prevalent at that particular time. Before 1930, for example, the major causes of illegitimacy were presumed to be mental deficiency, immorality, and bad companions. Investigations made during the 1930s, on the other hand, found that these "wayward" girls were more often than not victims of broken homes, poverty, and disorganized neighborhoods. The conclusions drawn from research done in the 1940s and early 1950s, by contrast, underscored the emotional problems of unwed mothers.

Several reasons for today's illegitimacy rate among the under-privileged can be specified. First, the poor and undereducated make little use of contraceptive methods to prevent unwanted pregnancies. Second, they are often unable to obtain either legal or illegal abortions (the incidence of legal abortions among white women is more than 25 times greater than among black). Third, the high cost of divorce may keep the under-privileged couple from having their unsatisfactory marriage legally dissolved, and any child born after either partner has formed a new permanent rela-tionship without marriage is termed illegitimate. Fourth, there is less social pressure for shotgun marriages among the poor, in whose socioeconomic group illegitimacy does not always carry a grave social stigma. Fifth, poor women cannot obtain falsified birth certificates as readily as more affluent women (Guttmacher c).

Statistics show that the higher the income, the lower the incidence of premarital pregnancies and illegitimate births. In 1969, the average black family's income in the United States was slightly below $6000, while the average white family's income approached $10,000; 31% of all blacks were living below the poverty level, as compared with 10% of all whites. About 50% of all black adults have only a grade-school education, and only about 10% of them have gone to college—factors that are certainly related to income level (Westoff and Westoff). In 1969, more than 37% of girls of families earning less than $3000 per year went to the altar pregnant, while only 8% of those from families with incomes exceeding $10,000 did so (In the news b).

Carefully controlled analyses of multiple samplings, begun in 1950 and continuing to the present time, have shown that unwed mothers are fairly representative of the general population of unmarried females with respect not only to education and intelligence but also to socioeconomic status (Vincent g). If generalizations can be made on the basis of one recent study, most unwed mothers (over 80% of the white sample in the study and 75% of the black sample) believe that they were in love with their partner and were planning to be married at the time of their sexual union; hardly any feel any hatred toward the father (Fink). Furthermore, the girl's relation-ship with her sexual partner was usually a longstanding one, frequently extending back a year or more before the pregnancy (Reiss g). A recent remark by a doctor may sum up the situation aptly. "It is the good girl who gets pregnant," he said. "Genuinely promiscuous girls know better" (Malcolm).

Religious Implications in Illegitimacy

Most authorities are of the opinion that religious devoutness is the chief restraining force upon the premarital sexual experiences of girls. Table 21.2, constructed from Kinsey's findings (Kinsey et al. c), shows that, despite religious affiliation, some very devout girls have premarital sexual intercourse, while some religiously inactive girls will not permit themselves to become involved in any level of petting.

TABLE 21.2   Relationship between Religious Affiliation and Sexual Activity of Girls under the Age of 20

	Pet to Orgasm	Premarital Coitus
Devout Protestants	17%	14%
Inactive Protestants	20%	25%
Devout Catholics	15%	12%
Inactive Catholics	31%	41%
Moderately Religious Jews	27%	11%
Inactive Jews	33%	27%

The question naturally arises: Why would a girl with a high degree of religious commitment engage in premarital sexual intercourse? Rodman has listed some of the more common reasons in his book *Marriage, Family, and Society:*

> She may belong to a particular religious group that does not place an unduly high premium on chastity.
>
> Despite her religious training, she may belong to a gang that expects its members to have sexual intercourse.
>
> She may have a particularly strong physiological sex drive.
>
> She may fall under the influence of a particularly persuasive sex partner.
>
> She may lose her self-control because of alcoholic consumption.
>
> She may use sex in a deliberate attempt to snare a husband.
>
> She may be unconsciously rebelling against her strict religion, or the overly strict religion or moral expectations of her parents.
>
> She may not be intelligent enough to understand all the issues involved in such sexual activity.
>
> She may be so emotionally crippled by marked feelings of inadequacy and insecurity that she bypasses her religious convictions in an attempt to fulfill her emotional needs through coitus.

Many of the foregoing reasons why girls with strong religious convictions engage in premarital sexual intercourse obviously have no connection with religious background; they are therefore equally applicable to all teen-age girls who become so involved. It should be recalled in passing that girls—in contrast to boys—do not as a rule have a strong physical need for sex in their teen-age years.

THE ILLEGITIMATE MOTHER

The choices open to a girl who unintentionally becomes premaritally pregnant are limited (Bowman). She may get married before the baby's birth; she may remain unmarried and have her baby; or she may seek an abortion.

If the girl marries before the birth of her baby, she makes the child legitimate. The prospects of success in such marriages, however, are notoriously poor; the divorce rate is about twice as high among those marriages in which conception occurs before the wedding as it is among those in which conception occurs afterwards (Christensen and Meissner). One or both partners may enter such a marriage with extreme reluctance, thereby producing unconscious—if not conscious—hostility. Furthermore, forced marriage may curtail education and impose financial hardship on the young couple, adding further strain on an already shaky relationship.

The girl who remains unmarried yet has her baby has the choice of keeping the infant and rearing it; or placing the child for adoption through an official agency, an attorney or doctor, or the black market. Or she may turn the baby over to her or the father's parents or relatives to rear. In a society such as ours, which holds in disgrace the child born out of marriage and harshly criticizes its mother, considerable pressure exists to conceal the illegitimacy (Kenkel).

If the girl resorts to an abortion, there are ethical, psychological, legal, religious, and social considerations that she must face, to say nothing of the dangers to life or health that an abortion performed by an untrained person or in an ill-equipped or unsterile setting may pose. The mother, perhaps even more than the child, pays—and pays, and pays—for the sexual misadventure that results in an illegitimate child.

Society applies its traditional double standard of judgment to illegitimate mothers and illegitimate fathers (Vincent e). A woman is judged much more harshly than a man for any form of nonmarital sexual behavior. She is judged especially severely for the ultimate in sexual misadventures—having a child outside marriage. The unwed mother has obviously had "illicit sex" and is often seen as a threat by those women who may doubt their own sexual desirability or whose marriages are shaky.

Popular opinion of the unwed mother, as reflected in utterances from many pulpits and in newspapers, is that she is oversexed and underprincipled. As discussed earlier, however, investigations suggest that unmarried girls become pregnant because of unfortunate environmental influences, such as poverty, ignorance, poor educational facilities, and depressing homes; or because emotional problems drive them into compulsive sexual behavior based on unconscious needs to be accepted and loved (Beigel b).

Middle-class people tend to see illegitimacy as being a problem of the lower social class. Because of this attitude, they frequently make no

effort to try to understand the causes of illegitimacy, and content themselves with viewing the issue as a moral one. In actuality, as was pointed
out, the causes of illegitimacy among the lower classes seem rather to lie in
the basic problems of "second-class citizenship," and in the considerably
greater family and marital instability that appears to exist in lower-class
groups (DeBurger). Relationships between the sexes in the lower-class
group are much more casual, suggesting a willingness to engage in sexual
intercourse even when there is no strong emotional attachment between
the partners (Rodman). The less emotionally involved a man is with a
woman, the less concern he shows for her welfare, and the less likely he
is to protect her from pregnancy (Kirkendall a; Udry). But the fact is important that, although there are more unwed mothers in the lowest socioeconomic class than in any other, premarital pregnancies occur at all levels;
the upper levels are simply better able to hide the pregnancy or to end it
through abortion (Beigel b).

Educational factors are also related to the incidence of illegitimacy.
One study revealed that, of those unmarried girls who became pregnant,
the majority had ended their education with grammar school. Of those
girls who had had some high-school education, 7% became pregnant
before they were 20 years old, while less than half this number of college
girls 20 years of age suffered the same mishap (Beigel b).

It has been estimated that, when a boy and girl who are still in
high school marry, the chances are as high as 80% that the marriage was
precipitated by a premarital pregnancy (Udry). As a matter of fact, 33%
of *all* firstborn children in the United States are conceived out of wedlock
(In the news b). Poorly educated women are the ones most likely to be
ignorant about birth-control matters, and to trust to luck rather than use
some sort of contraceptive protection. Indeed, 11% of those women who
have premarital sexual experiences employ no means whatsoever of birth
control (Beigel b).

Girls from lower socioeconomic levels begin their sexual activity about
five or six years earlier than those from other levels. The dangers of sexual
mishaps stemming from ignorance are therefore greater because of the
girls' age. These young girls—many not yet 15 years old—often engage in
premarital sexual intercourse in order to appear adult and to be able to
attract men. The results are frequently disastrous. About 70% of all babies
born to mothers under 15 years of age are illegitimate, and among the
nonwhite group the percentage rises to 87% (Kenkel).

Of those girls who engage in premarital sexual intercourse by the
age of 25, 25% of the high-school-level girls and 17% of the college-level
girls have been pregnant. Furthermore, of those women who become premaritally pregnant, 13% become so twice, 5% three times, and 2% four
times or more (Bowman; Gebhard *et al. b*).

Campbell and Cooking paint a vivid and accurate picture of what happens to many unmarried girls who have babies:

> The girl who has an illegitimate child at the age of 16 suddenly has 90 percent of her life's script written for her. She will probably drop out of school; even if someone else in her family helps to take care of the baby, she will probably not be able to find a steady job that pays enough to provide for herself and her child; she may feel compelled to marry someone she might not otherwise have chosen. Her life choices are few, and most of them are bad. Had she been able to delay the first child, her prospects might have been quite different, assuming that she would have had opportunities to continue her education, improve her vocational skills, find a job, marry someone she wanted to marry, and have a child when she and her husband were ready for it. Also, the child would have been born under quite different circumstances and might have grown up in a stable family environment.

The personal characteristics and experiences of the unwed mothers who decide to keep their children are of passing interest. More nonwhite mothers than whites—especially those who are older—keep their babies. Those unwed white women who keep their children are less likely than average to have completed high school. They are also more likely to have come from broken or lower-income homes than are those unwed white women who give up their babies for adoption (Festinger).

Most studies of illegitimate births focus on cases in which the mother has never been married. It is estimated, however, that from 20% to 25% of illegitimate births involve women who are married but are impregnated by someone other than their husbands, or who have been married but are not living with their husbands at the time of the sexual union with another man (Vincent *h*). It is next to impossible to know just how many supposedly legitimate babies are actually sired illegitimately, because few women who are impregnated by a man other than their husband would admit to such an act.

THE ILLEGITIMATE FATHER

In comparison with the numerous investigations made concerning the unwed mother, few studies have attempted to uncover the sexual motivations and character of the unwed father. Indeed, for every 30 studies of the unmarried mother, only 1 has been made of the unmarried father (Vincent *d*). To those who seek to evaluate the legal, social, psychological, and economic difficulties involved in illegitimacy, it is obvious that no understanding or realistic solution can be reached until considerably more is known about the fathers of illegitimate babies. Showing more concern over unwed mothers than over the fathers is probably understandable, since the mothers place demands on society that the fathers do not—

prenatal care, maternity homes, and child support—all of which may impose a financial burden on the state and, therefore, on the taxpayer. The fathers, on the other hand, are not a direct economic burden on the taxpayer (Vincent *d*).

The unmarried father carries with him no physical evidence of his unacceptable premarital sexual behavior, and his violation of the moral standards of the community is therefore less obvious than that of the unwed mother. Even within marriage it is the woman rather than the man who is blamed for an unwanted pregnancy. This attitude carries over into public thinking in the matter of illegitimate pregnancies, and is perhaps responsible for laws that in some states suggest, and in other states require, that unmarried women who have had several nonmarital pregnancies be sterilized. These laws make no mention of the fathers (further evidence of the double standard of sexual morality that exists in this country) (Vincent *d*).

In general, unmarried fathers constitute a fairly representative cross section of the American male population. The women whom they impregnate usually come from the same general socioeconomic level of society that they do, although—as is true with married partners—the man is ordinarily slightly older and better educated than his sexual mate (Vincent *a*).

Despite generally held opinion, unwed fathers are not necessarily exploiters of the women whom they impregnate. In fact, any exploitation present in the relationship is as likely to be reciprocal as one-sided. And when it is one-sided, it well may be the woman who is the exploiter and the man who is the victim. The unwed mother tends to use sex as a means to assure herself of dates, expensive outings, upward mobility, companionship, and even marriage. The unwed father, on the other hand, provides the expensive outings and companionship, and gives some degree of love as a means of achieving coitus. His slight superiority in age, education, and socioeconomic status, which is valued in usual men–women relationships, is, however, considered evidence of exploitation in the unwed father–mother alliance.

Despite the fact that illegitimate fathers are usually viewed as being unconcerned about their responsibilities, they actually have strong feelings of conflict about their illegitimate child and its mother. The conflict frequently leads to feelings of guilt and depression, which they attempt to overcome through rationalization. These men often unconsciously hold the unwed mother responsible for their own guilt feelings, and they punish her by labeling all illegitimate mothers as worthless and immoral creatures. These fathers relieve their conscience by such statements as "The kid's not mine"; "She'll go to bed with anything that wears pants"; "She had plenty of fun, the same as I did"; "I spent lots of money on that bitch";

and so forth. Despite such attempts to rid themselves of guilt, these feelings usually persist (Vincent *d*).

THE ILLEGITIMATE CHILD

The child who has been born out of wedlock has, throughout history and literature, been identified as the bastard child, the "natural child," the "love child." Even though the unwed father acknowledges the child as his, the infant's birth is not legitimate unless a marriage takes place between the father and mother. In about 20% of the cases, the man who has fathered the child marries the pregnant woman before the birth of the baby. After the child's birth, however, marriage between the two parents occurs in only 2% of the cases. In about 25% of the cases, the mother appeals to the courts to establish the paternity of her illegitimate child. If a man denies the charges, he has about a 55% chance to prove, through blood tests, that he is falsely accused. If paternity is established, the father is responsible for the support of the child; otherwise, the mother has that responsibility (Beigel *b*). The professed belief of most adult Americans (which is at odds with their actual behavior, according to statistical studies) is that sexual activity should be confined to the marriage bed. It is therefore small wonder that the illegitimate child—the living symbol of his parents' unacceptable sexual behavior—has great difficulty in his efforts to lead a normal life (Landis and Landis).

Other than the unfortunate circumstances already described concerning the child who is identified as illegitimate, little more is known about him. But these questions logically arise (Vincent *c*): How badly would a *legitimate* child be hurt and humiliated if (a) his mother had been continuously belittled, criticized, and shamed by society; (b) his father had refused to acknowledge him as his child, or to assume responsibility for him; and (c) his birth were openly regarded as being the result of lust, accident, force, alcohol, or drugs? How well would the legitimate child have fared physically if his mother had not received adequate prenatal care?

In many states the birth certificate of a child born out of wedlock still contains the information that the child is illegitimate. The child of the unwed mother in the United States has the same inheritance rights to her property that her legitimate children do, although in most states the child may not inherit from her relatives. In 44 states, however, the illegitimate child does not have the right to inherit from his father (although 46 states require the illegitimate father to support his child). In only two states— Arizona and North Dakota—are *all* children considered legitimate and accorded equal rights (Bell *a*; Landis and Landis).

Little can be done to correct society's prejudice against the illegitimate child until the laws of the states are changed to protect that child fully. It seems only fair, and it is certainly sound reasoning insofar as contributing to the mental health of the population is concerned, that the states should establish more adequate laws to protect the illegitimate child (Landis and Landis). These are some of the ways in which this goal might best be accomplished:

Birth certificates should be so worded that the data in them regarding paternity do not reveal illegitimacy. Birth data are public records and in most states are available at the country seat of a baby's birthplace; anyone who cares to look can do so.

The state should be made responsible for attempting to establish paternity, since the mother is often unable (or unwilling) to do so. As matters presently stand, if the mother does not institute legal proceedings, there is no pressure on the father to support the child.

Adequate prenatal care should be available to every expectant mother, regardless of whether her pregnancy is legitimate or illegitimate.

All needy children should be given adequate financial aid by the state.

Most important of all, from the pulpit, home, and school should come sincere efforts to remold the public's view of the illegitimate child. For if blame for illegitimacy must be ascribed, it should be to the parents and not to the child, who is the most innocent of the three people involved.

22 SEX AND THE LAW

If it were not for the tragedy involved, one of the great farces of American history would be its laws designed to control and regulate sexual behavior. Even a cursory examination of legislation attempting to regulate sexual expression reveals amazing vagueness and inconsistency among the various states (and frequently within the same state). In Kentucky, for example, if a 12-year-old girl gives her lawful consent for sexual intercourse, the man is considered to be without legal guilt; the same man could be executed as a rapist in Wyoming. The age of consent ranges from 10 years in Georgia and the Carolinas to 18 years in Colorado, Kansas, and Wyoming (Czinner).

Much of this confusion can be accounted for historically. Over the past 50 years, the nation's laws have in general undergone constant scrutiny and chance, but this flexibility and review have as yet barely touched legislation governing sexual matters (Sherwin a). A short time ago, a man in North Carolina was convicted and sentenced to 30 years' imprisonment for homosexuality, "the abominable and detestable crime against nature, not to be mentioned among Christians." Upon appeal, the United States district judge who heard the case suggested it was time that the state

457

legislature redraft this criminal statute, since the law was first enacted over 300 years ago (Beigel *f*)!

THE PERNICIOUS INFLUENCE OF ANTHONY COMSTOCK

Many of this country's present statutes relating to sexual matters are a direct result of the efforts of Anthony Comstock (1844–1915), a New York State moralist who influenced not only his own but also other states' legislators to enact severe, rigid, and unrealistic laws on sexually associated matters.

Early in his life Comstock developed a hatred for liquor, and for a number of years he directed much of his efforts toward eradication of this "evil" from the world. His hostility toward liquor was mild, however, in comparison with his feelings about sex. On his own initiative he began to investigate violations of the 1868 New York State statutes forbidding "immoral works." He helped form the Committee for the Suppression of Vice to work for national obscenity legislation (Report of Commission on Obscenity and Pornography a).

March 3, 1873, was a black day in the history of individual rights in this country. On that day Comstock succeeded in getting Congress to pass, through his successful lobbying, the infamous Comstock Law. In prohibiting the mailing of obscene material, this statute set forth the most unreasonable restrictions against "obscenity" ever passed in America, while leaving the word open to wide interpretation. Birth-control information, for instance, was classified as pornography, and both the importation of contraceptive supplies from aboard and their interstate shipment were forbidden. The law further stipulated savage penalties for anything that with the slightest imagination could be construed as "obscene."

One wonders how such an unrealistic statute could have gained sufficient support for passage. Perhaps the Congressmen were tired and wanted to go home, for it was 1 a.m. when the law was finally passed. It is at least charitable to assume that if they had had any inkling of what they were signing their names to, or of the hypermoralistic invasion into America's cultural and private life that they were unleashing, Comstock's proposal would probably have been voted down.

With passage of the bill into law Comstock was made a special agent of the Post Office, in charge of enforcing the federal law. He now held the legal right to open other people's mail. He began to employ trickery to entrap people whom he believed to be involved in obscenity (which he defined with considerable latitude) or whom he suspected of disseminating information about, or practicing, birth control. For example, he regularly wrote kindhearted physicians pretending to be a sick and frail mother of many children, begging the doctors for information on contraceptive methods. If the doctors responded, they were apprehended and frequently fined and imprisoned. Worst of all, their careers were usually ruined.

Comstock directed much of his effort against Margaret Sanger, the founder of the planned-parenthood movement in America. He did not succeed in ensnaring Mrs. Sanger in his lifetime, but he did contrive to have her husband, William Sanger, arrested and convicted. A Comstock agent had begged Mr. Sanger for a copy of his wife's pamphlet *Family Limitation*; when he obtained it, he had Mr. Sanger arrested. Sanger refused to pay a fine, serving a 30-day jail sentence for his "crime."

Although Anthony Comstock the man is no longer with us (he died during the course of William Sanger's term in jail), the spirit of his oppressive sexual attitudes lives on in the legislation he influenced and the deprivation of personal liberties for which he established many precedents.

Resistance to changing laws governing sexual behavior stems, of course, from the anxieties of the nation's citizenry when it must deal with anything sexual. It is the result, as well, of every lawmaker's reluctance to do anything that might cause uneasy constituents to view his attitudes on sex, punishment, or morality as libertine. Progress in this realm of legislation thus blocked, such current problems as artificial insemination are virtually untouched by direct legal interpretation, unrelated laws being unrealistically extended and applied to them (Sherwin a).

In addition, the administration and enforcement of laws pertaining to sexual matters are in discord. It is well known that the ratio of enforcement to violation is very low (Ellis e; Ellis and Brancale; Sherwin a). For example, 3 million homosexual acts are performed in America for every one conviction, for, on the whole, homosexual behavior is punished only when it occurs in public (Slovenko a). Yet the laws condemning such behavior both in public and in private remain on the statute books. Oral or anal intercourse between individuals of opposite sex is similarly viewed as a crime in most states (Abominable & detestable crime), but few law-enforcing agencies bother to prosecute. Thirty-three states have statutes making voluntary coition between unmarried adults a criminal act. Yet they license and support a variety of services for unwed mothers, who undeniably have violated the statutes on fornication. Prosecution of these women for their "criminal" act is rare (Vincent j).

Inconsistencies in enforcement of sex laws often relate directly to the religious beliefs and social attitudes of the judge and law-enforcement officers. Incongruities in enforcement also stem from confusion over what specific acts a law is intended to define as being sexual offenses.

The whole enforcement picture is muddied even further (if one can concede the possibility) by the great disparity in penalties assessed for the same offense by various jurisdictions (Caprio c)—and by the application of a double standard of justice within one jurisdiction. A well-documented 1967 study of sentencing practices in the state of Maryland, for instance, revealed that the average sentence of a black man convicted of raping a white woman (not including those receiving a death or life sentence) was 15.4 years; for a black man raping a black woman, the figure fell to 3.18 years. For white men raping a white woman, sentences averaged 3.67 years and for raping a black woman, 4.6 years (From the editor's scrapbook *g*).

PRIVATE SEXUAL PRACTICES

The extent to which some of our present laws are at odds with reality is evidenced by the fact that in all but two states a married couple can, at least theoretically, be arrested and convicted for most sexual acts conducted in the privacy of their bedroom, other than the insertion of the penis into the vagina. (The two states that are exceptions are Illinois, which has attempted to eliminate from its criminal code all sexual acts performed in privacy involving two consenting adults; and New York, which has continued the criminal proscription of such acts but has immunized a husband and wife from criminal prosecution [Sherwin *b*].) According to the fuzzy laws of most states, 95% of adult American men and a large percentage of American women have experienced orgasm in an illegal manner (Beigel *f*; Ellis *e*; Kinsey *et al. c*).

But the constitutionality of this archaic body of legislation is coming more and more under attack. In 1965 the United States Supreme Court (in *Griswold* v. *Connecticut*) declared unconstitutional Connecticut's law prohibiting the use of birth-control devices, holding that married couples have a substantial right to marital privacy (Abominable & detestable crime). The dispensing of contraceptives and their use—by married couples, at least—are now legal in all 50 states (Guttmacher *d*). Statutes that give only physicians and pharmacists the right to prescribe and distribute contraceptives are currently being challenged in the courts of at least one state—on the grounds that such legislation violates the right of sexual privacy and serves no justifiable state interest (ACLU news *a*).

Although the battle has just begun, there are other instances in which the higher courts have acted as agents of reform in regard to repressive laws related to sexual practices conducted privately. In June 1967 the Supreme Court struck down state laws banning interracial marriage (such legislation still remaining at that time on the statute books of at least 16 states). And in 1968 the United States Seventh Circuit Court of Appeals reversed a sodomy conviction in Indiana, citing the 1965 Supreme Court decision mentioned above: "The import of the *Griswold* decision is that private, consensual, marital relations are protected from regulation by the state" (Abominable & detestable crime). Religious leaders too are pushing for reform in this area. In support of legalizing birth-control information and methods in Massachusetts, the late Cardinal Cushing of Boston observed: "It does not seem reasonable to me to forbid in civil law a practice that can be considered a matter of private morality" (Public law and private morality).

OBSCENITY AND PORNOGRAPHY

Another area of sex legislation considered by many to be a matter of private morality concerns laws on obscenity and pornography. Because they are ambiguous, such laws are subject to a variety of interpretations and frequently appear to be used in the course of legal prosecution largely to satisfy the unconscious needs and desires of the accuser rather than to protect society from the accused. The American culture reacts to the subject of sex with such intense emotionality that almost any literary or pictorial representation of sexual interaction is liable to be objectionable to *someone* and hence vulnerable to the charge of being obscene (Honigmann).

Despite the fact that the United States Supreme Court has been called upon several times recently to settle questions of law regarding obscenity, there remains much ambiguity over what is and is not legally obscene and pornographic (Kirkendall c). Such ambiguity, as a matter of fact, has led in the past to the censorship or restriction of sale of such classics as *Alice in Wonderland*, *Huckleberry Finn*, *Adventures of Sherlock Holmes*, *Robinson Crusoe*, *On the Origin of Species*, and *The Scarlet Letter*.

Two 1957 United States Supreme Court rulings indicate the difficulty in defining what is and is not obscene. The Court held that, while the First and Fourteenth Amendments give no one the right to purvey obscene material, the Constitution does not restrict any material "having even the slightest redeeming social importance . . . ," however unpopular the ideas therein contained. The Court did hold as obscene any material "utterly without redeeming social importance . . . in which to the average person, applying contemporary community standards, the dominant theme of the material taken as a whole appeals to prurient interest." One can see the endless possibilities for divergent evaluation of the same piece of material, since it is the responsibility of each township, county, or state to determine the prurience of a particular work. What might not cause an eye to widen in Greenwich Village could cause apoplexy in some small midwestern town.

As a case in point, *Little Red Riding Hood* has recently been banned as being too sexy by some of the kindergarten teachers in Australia. One Melbourne psychiatrist stated, "Little Red Riding Hood is a sexually tempted young girl, with the warning of her mother not to stray from the straight and narrow path ringing in her ears. The big bad wolf does not need much interpretation" (*Indianapolis Star*).

A battle rages continually around the possible dangers of pornography. Admittedly, pornographic matter can be stimulating sexually, but there is no significant empirical or clinical evidence to support the contention that pornography causes sexual deviation or violence. It is well known to psychotherapists that normal, sexually well-adjusted people often enjoy the erotic stimulation of certain written and pictorial matter. It therefore seems logical to consider perusal of such material abnormal only when it is consistently preferred to heterosexual activity.

In 1969 Denmark abolished all laws forbidding the sale of pornography. One notable result was the sharp decline in sales of pornographic materials. But the most significant consequence was a 31% drop during 1969, in comparison with 1968 figures, in the overall number of sex crimes committed in Denmark. The greatest decrease was in homosexual offenses, exhibitionism, and child molestation; rape and attempted rape also decreased, although by a smaller margin (Lipton). Furthermore, Danish school officials state that the relaxation of the law has not increased children's contact with obscene material (Pornography).

The Kinsey researchers' 25-year study of sex offenders may have uncovered an explanation for the results of the Danish experiment insofar as pornography's apparent nonimplication, one way or the other, in violent sex crimes. The Kinsey group asserted that rapists and other sexual aggressors, being motivated by other factors, are unlikely to be affected by sexually stimulating writing. The sexual aggressor is essentially a psychopath, taking whatever he wants when he wants it. A sexual assault, then, is merely part of his general criminality. His is a socially disordered mind, not a sexually variant one upon which pornography might act as a trigger (Gebhard et al. a).

The relationship between the availability of erotic material and the commission of sex crimes in America appears to present a more complex picture than that in Denmark. In recent years, as pornography has become much easier to buy in this country, the incidence of certain sex crimes (e.g., forcible rape) has increased, whereas the incidence of others (e.g., overall juvenile sex-related criminality) has declined. Among juveniles, the number of arrests for sex crimes decreased, although arrest for nonsexual crimes increased by more than 100%. Among adults, arrests for sex offenses increased slightly more than did arrests for other offenses (Commission on Obscenity and Pornography a). The conclusion must be, therefore, that the relationship between freer availability of erotica and current shifts in the incidence of sex crimes can be neither proved nor disproved. But it is known that no massive overall increase in sex-related criminality has occurred as the result of a burgeoning supply of pornography in the market place.

The President's Commission on Obscenity and Pornography, which made its report in August 1970, found no scientific evidence that exposure to pornography operates as a cause of misconduct in either youths or adults. The two sociologists on the Commission—Dr. Otto N. Larsen, Professor of Sociology at the University of Washington, and Dr. Marvin E. Wolfgang, Director of the Center of Criminological Research at the University of Pennsylvania—concluded, in fact, that all existing federal, state, and local statutes regarding obscenity, including those restricting juveniles' access to pornographic materials, should be repealed. In recommending repeal, the sociologists declared: "Advocating repeal is not advocating anarchy, for we believe that informal social controls will work better without the confusion of ambiguous and arbitrarily administered laws. With improvements in sex education and better understanding of human sexual behavior, society can more effectively handle, without legislation, the distribution of material deemed by some to be offensive to juveniles or adults" (Commission on Obscenity and Pornography a).

THE SEX OFFENDER

Psychotherapists speak of sexual variance, deviance, or perversion, but the law considers only offenses. The sex offender is an individual who commits an act designated by law as a sexual offense and hence a crime (Sadoff). Periodic public clamor for stricter laws in the area of sex crimes has received the support of such personages as the late J. Edgar Hoover, who, when testifying before the House Appropriations Subcommittee in January 1962, advocated fingerprinting all teachers; he considered them potentially dangerous sex offenders! (Hoover cited one instance of a child's having been molested by a teacher to support his position [Falk].)

On the other hand, many scientific investigators contend that there has been no drastic increase in sex crimes in recent years, despite an increase in the number of arrests and in public outcry. They say further that what is really needed is a more objective attitude toward sex offenders along the lines of understanding and treatment rather than of punishment (Beigel f; Ellis e; Ellis and Brancale; Falk; Gebhard et al. a; Sherwin a). The news media may on occasion contribute to an imperfect understanding of the problem of sexual criminality by exaggerated or faulty reporting.

In the United States, about 40,000 arrests a year are made for major sexual offenses. New Jersey, for example, made this breakdown of such offenders: rapists, 45%; exhibitionists, 18%; perverts, 14%; those involved in commercial sex, 7%; and unclassified offenses, 16% (Ellis e). It should be noted that approximately 80% of so-called rape convictions in the United States are for statutory rape, which is voluntary coitus between partners, one of whom—almost always the girl—is under the legal age of consent. The essence of this legal concept is the girl's age, not her actual consent or degree of sophistication (Slovenko b).

The sex offender is rarely involved in nonsexual crimes. Rather than progressing through the gamut of paraphilia (unacceptable or illegal sexual acts) to more serious and diversified criminality, he seems to become relatively fixed in his variant erotic behavior (Coleman). Few convicted sex offenders resemble the "sex fiend" of popular fiction, most being rather harmless minor deviates (Ellis e; Ellis and Brancale; Gebhard *et al.* a; Rubin *i*).

A relatively small number (about 20%) of sex offenders use force or duress on their victims, and homicide seldom occurs in conjunction with sexual offenses. In actuality, 90% of homicides occur within the family group or within a close circle of friends. The probability, then, of being murdered by a "sex fiend" is considerably less than that of being murdered by a relative or close friend (Ellis e; Falk). When homicide does occur in sex crimes, the offender is usually insane as well as sexually deviated (Coleman).

The sex offender who is arrested is usually found to be suffering from personality disturbances. In a study of 300 typical sex offenders at a New Jersey diagnostic center, only 14% were psychologically "normal"; 29% were classified as mildly neurotic, 35% as severely neurotic, 8% as borderline psychotic, 5% as organically brain-damaged, 4% as mentally deficient, 3% as psychopathic, and 2% as psychotic (Ellis and Brancale).

The majority of apprehended sex offenders come from low socio-economic backgrounds, are poorly educated, and fall well below average in intellectual capacity. Subnormal intelligence is more typical of offenders convicted of statutory rape, bestiality, incestuous relations, and sexually aggressive acts against little girls than of offenders convicted of forcible rape, exhibitory acts, homosexuality, and the dissemination of "obscene" material (Ellis e; Ellis and Brancale; Gebhard *et al.* c).

Few sex criminals take narcotics or are under the influence of drugs at the time of the sex offense. However, a large percentage (32%) of convicted sex offenders are under the influence of alcohol when they commit their crimes, especially in cases of sexual assaults and incestuous relations with children (Ellis e; Ellis and Brancale; Gebhard *et al.* a).

As already noted, some studies suggest that certain types of imprisoned sex offenders profess strong religious convictions, only a small percentage (10%) claiming to have received no religious training in childhood. They read the Bible regularly, faithfully perform religious rituals, and see themselves as devoted to their religion (Allen, G. H.). The results of other studies—notably the Kinsey group's *Sex Offenders* (Gebhard *et al.* a)—do not agree. They suggest, rather, that the convicted sex offender is generally less religiously devout than the average citizen. The exception is the incest offender, who was found to be especially moralistic, traditional, and religiously devout.

Quite contrary to popular notion, the typical convicted sex offender is undersexed rather than oversexed. He is quite likely to be afraid of sexual contact with the adult female and to be severely inhibited sexually (except when the crime is statutory rape or incestuous acts against minors). The less emotionally disturbed the sex offender, the less sexually inhibited he tends to be (Caprio *c*; Ellis and Brancale; Gebhard *et al. a*).

Although the age of the convicted sex offender varies according to the specific type of sexual act committed, the majority of offenders are rather young—in their late teens or early 20s. Between 50% and 60% are unmarried (Ellis *e*).

A popular and often tragic public misconception is that the sex offender is typically an elderly person. One of the most compassionate statements ever made on this subject—and certainly an accurate one—came from Dr. Frederick E. Whiskin of the Harvard Medical School. He termed the old man alleged to be a sex offender the most maligned person in our society: a "benign and impotent" creature, whose actions typically are not genital in origin but spring from tragic loneliness (Rubin *o*).

There is special pathos in the plight of the older man charged as a sex offender. Many old people, in their loneliness and emotional starvation, reach out to a child for warmth and affection. If an elderly woman caresses a child, the act is regarded as normal and natural. But if an elderly man does so, his simple gesture—which rarely bears any sexual overtones—may well meet with a hysterical cry: "molester!"

Facts exonerating the man past 65 as the chief molester of children were firmly established by the Kinsey researchers in their study of the dynamics and circumstances involved in the various forms of sex offense (Gebhard *et al. a*). It might be noted that the Kinsey group classified anyone under the age of 12 as a child and defined the child molester, or *pedophile*, as an adult having a sexual contact with a child without the use of force or threat.

The Kinsey data flatly disprove the popular image of the sex offender as a "dirty old man." The average age of child molesters is only 35! Only one-sixth of all men arrested on charges of child molestation are past the age of 50. A comparison, according to age groups, of all paroled sex offenders in the state of Pennsylvania in 1960 heaps further discredit on this popular misconception. Only 4.58% of these offenders were past 60, although men in this age group constituted nearly 20% of the state's total male population. The largest number of sex offenders (23%) fell in the age range of 20 to 24 years, yet men in this age group comprised only 8% of the male population of Pennsylvania (Dangerous sex offender).

Most convicted sex offenders are the "losers" of our society. They are usually so inept and severely disturbed emotionally that all their activities, sexual offenses included, are probably executed in a stupid or indiscreet manner. They are, consequently, quite liable to be found out—in contrast to intelligent sex offenders, who are not, and even if discovered, are less likely to be convicted for their offenses (Ellis e; Gebhard et al. a).

Because of his emotional problems, the sex offender may well repeat his offense unless he receives psychotherapy (Ellis e). Even so, the recidivism rate among convicted sex offenders is lower than that of other criminals. During a recent 13-year span, less than 10% of 4000 convicted sex offenders studied and treated at New Jersey's Menlo Park Diagnostic Center were known to become recidivists. Attention centers, unfortunately, on the 10% who do become recidivists rather than on the 90% who never do. The consequent public outcry and newspaper headlines persuade parole boards to the belief that all sex offenders are poor parole risks (Sex offenders good parole risk).

Many psychologists and psychiatrists object to the use of the term *sexual psychopath* to describe the sex offender. True sexual psychopaths (3% of all convicted sex offenders) are unable to control their unacceptable erotic impulses, may use force or serious threat, lack remorse and anxiety over their sexual behavior, may disrupt social organization, and form no close emotional attachments; but they are not psychotic or feebleminded. Indeed, they may give the appearance of being perfectly normal in all respects. The "sexual psychopath," then, is a far cry from the *typical* convicted sex offender, who characteristically is mentally disturbed, suffering from brain damage, or below average in mentality, and who probably does not understand why he committed his offense (Coleman; Ellis e; Ellis and Brancale).

Investigators generally divide sex offenses into two broad categories (Ellis e; Ellis and Brancale; Gebhard et al. a; Rubin i). The first involves more or less normal behavior, which does not deviate very far from that of the general populace. Transgressions falling in this category (for example, the man who occasionally becomes a Peeping Tom) do little or no psychological damage to the people involved, and have no adverse effect on social organization. For various reasons, however, the conduct is considered by society as ·sufficiently inappropriate to warrant punishment. Since society is not harmed by these offenses, as is widely acknowledged, punishment should not be severe. Effort is more appropriately directed toward helping offenders make a better adjustment to their life situation.

The second class of sex offense is uncommon. Here the behavior is truly unacceptable and is motivated by abnormal personality traits. The offenses may constitute a public nuisance, be socially disruptive, and cause psychological damage to those involved. It is toward this category of sex offenders that attention and money should be spent for detection, research, and treatment (Gebhard et al. a; Rubin i).

In some European countries, treatment of sex offenders includes voluntary castration. Removal of the testicles, the major source of male hormones, is performed at the request of the sex criminal to eliminate abnormally intense and perverse sexual urges. According to a study of some 1000 such cases in Germany, castration reduces the likelihood of recidivism among sex offenders from 70% to less than 3%. Similar results have been reported in Switzerland and the Scandinavian countries, where castration of sex criminals is also practiced. Although the laws of several American states permit voluntary castration, it is seldom performed (Legal castration). Recent research suggests that the drug medroxyprogesterone acetate, which has a reversible hormonal castration effect, may offer a less drastic form of treatment in those cases of unacceptable sexual behavior for which the only other alternatives are likely to be a sentence of life imprisonment or death (Money *j*).

HOMOSEXUALITY

Homosexual relations are considered a crime in most American states and are punishable by prison terms ranging from six months to life (Homosexual in America). A recent poll conducted by CBS-TV revealed that the majority of Americans regard homosexuality as a greater menace to society than abortion, prostitution, or adultery (Homosexuality). But many dispute the view that homosexual behavior between consenting adults should be considered a crime.

Is the public justified in its strong distrust of the homosexual? His sexual proclivities notwithstanding, the homophile hardly presents the picture of a man who is in any way a detriment to his community. Of all sex offenders, he has the highest socioeconomic status and is the best educated. Drugs and drink are not factors in his behavior. He is the least likely of all to deny his guilt when faced with legal charges of homosexuality. The number of homophiles convicted of offenses other than the sexual ones is the smallest of all the sex offenders in the Kinsey study (Gebhard *et al. a*). The conclusion of the Kinsey investigators is that homosexuals are neither dangerous nor criminal. "They do not damage society; they merely do not fit into it" (Homosexuality).

Under the sponsorship of the National Institutes of Mental Health, in October of 1969 a 14-member panel (led by Dr. Evelyn Hooker of UCLA, a leading authority on homosexuality) completed a far-reaching investigation into the subject of homosexuality. The panel concluded that the hostility and suspicions harbored by so many Americans toward the homophile are unfounded, that he poses no threat to public morals and decorum. The report said further that the widespread infamy and contempt attached to homosexuality do more social harm than good and go beyond the limits necessary to the preservation of order and decency. The report continuues: "Homosexuality presents a major problem for our society largely because of the amount of injustice and suffering entailed in it, not only for the homosexual, but also for those concerned about him" (Homosexuality).

The NIMH report went on to recommend that the United States follow the example of England, which in 1968 made legal any homosexual act performed discreetly between consenting adults. There have been no discernible ill effects suffered by the British public. (Any forcible homosexual contact or one involving minors remains, of course, a criminal act.)

The implication of the Hooker report is that we have jeopardized the mental health of homophiles by driving them underground into a life shrouded by fear of discovery and the ever-present danger of blackmail. The techniques of entrapment used by the police are often degrading. The homosexual is discriminated against in government and in many private-industry jobs, although most are good citizens and productive members of society. Homosexuality is an undesirable way of life to members of the "straight" world, but this in no way implies that all homosexuals are undesirable members of society—or that heterosexuals are more desirable because they are "straight."

The suggestion that homosexuals in top-level governmental jobs are poor security risks and should therefore be fired upon discovery may be well taken; but, tragically, not for the reasons usually offered to support it. Because his sexual preferences are different from those of the average heterosexual man, the homophile is judged to have a flawed character, and to be lacking in the virtues of trustworthiness and loyalty. It is assumed, therefore, that at the first opportunity—or at least with little pressure—he is ready to betray his country. Knowing that the revelation of his homosexuality will bring shame to his family, loss of his job, and—depending upon what state he resides in—perhaps legal prosecution, the homosexual understandably might yield to threat and commit an act of disloyalty rather than face public exposure. It is the threat of blackmail, then, that makes the homosexual somewhat vulnerable to corrupt pressures, rather than an innate tendency to disloyalty.

PROSTITUTION

Prostitution, the participation in sexual activities for payment, is an age-old practice that continues to flourish despite laws condemning it. Legal efforts to abolish it have largely been ineffective. England's Wolfenden Report recommended that, while prostitution should not be made illegal, legislation should be passed "to drive it off the streets" on the ground that public solicitation is a nuisance. English law now prohibits only open prostitution. The USSR has no law on prostitution, but handles it as a "disturbance of the social order" when it is flagrant (Slovenko a).

As an example of the ineffectiveness of much prostitution legislation, a law passed in Italy in 1958, aimed at stamping out prostitution and "freeing" the habitants of brothels, had precisely the opposite effect. By 1965 the number of Italian prostitutes had increased from 18,000 to an estimated 200,000, the latter figure including part-time practitioners. Within a year of the 1958 legislation, furthermore, the incidence of syphilis in Italy had risen by 25%, and by 1961, the country's VD rate had become the highest in Europe (From the editor's scrapbook *f*).

Other attempts to regulate prostitution officially have met with fairly good results. In legalized prostitution one can hope to control the spread of venereal disease through medical surveillance of prostitutes. Furthermore, these women and their clientele would be protected, at least to an extent, from the exploitation of blackmailers, a frequent correlative of prostitution (Benjamin *b*).

ABORTION

Laws concerning abortion have always varied widely throughout the world. Among European countries, Sweden and Denmark were the first in modern times (in 1938 and 1939, respectively) to pass laws permitting abortion under certain humanitarian and eugenic conditions. In Sweden a special committee of the Royal Medical Board determines eugenic indications for therapeutic abortions, of which there are now 5 for every 95 live births. Denmark uses a special board of two physicians and one Mother's Aid Society representative to review and pass on applications for therapeutic abortions. About 40% of such applications are approved, and the abortions are performed in accredited hospitals. In both Denmark and Sweden, however, illegal abortions still occur (Neumann).

Norway's laws, similar to those of Sweden, are somewhat more liberal in their interpretation of justifications for therapeutic abortion. Socioeconomic factors, as well as the mother's health, are taken into account.

In 1936, Russia repealed legislation enacted 16 years earlier that had made abortion legal. Apparently there was, among other considerations, concern about the low birth rate at that particular time. In 1955, however, therapeutic abortions were again legalized in the USSR. The present law requires the hospitalization of abortion patients in special clinics established for that purpose. They must remain hospitalized for three days—longer, if there are any complications.

Japan legalized abortion in 1948. A survey made eight years later indicated that, while legal abortions numbered 1,159,280 in a one-year period, nearly a million illegal abortions were also performed during the same period. Perhaps the doctors involved in the illegal abortions were avoiding the payment of income tax by performing the operation in their offices rather than going through the formalized procedure of admitting their patients to a hospital; or they may not have been specifically licensed to perform abortions. A physician performing an abortion after the third month of pregnancy must hand over the fetus to a mortician, who sometimes charges a higher fee for his services than the abortionist. An estimated 8000 to 10,000 physicians in Japan are licensed abortionists.

Abortion laws have also varied considerably within the United States. In January 1973, the Supreme Court ruled (7 to 2) that the decision to have an abortion in the first trimester of pregnancy is a personal judgment to be made by the pregnant woman and her physician without interference from the law. This controversial ruling invalidated almost all existing state laws, many of which contradicted one another. Some of this state legislation was written in the 1800s, when abortion was medically hazardous because antibiotics and blood transfusions were not available.

Today, an abortion performed early in pregnancy by a competent physician is safer than childbirth, yet at the time of the Court's decision more than 30 states still prohibited abortion except to save the life of the mother. Only 17 states and the District of Columbia had passed some form of abortion law reflective of the model code governing abortion suggested by the American Law Institute in 1962 (Westoff and Westoff). The code recommends that abortion be permitted in those cases in which the mother's physical or mental health would be impaired by the birth, the child would be born with serious mental or physical defects, or the pregnancy is the result of rape or incest. The American Medical Association endorsed these recommendations in 1967 (thereby altering for the first time its official position on abortion, which had been originally adopted in 1870). Many physicians, however, believe that these guidelines are still far too restrictive.

By the early 1970s, some states had adopted the legal position that abortion is permissible under any circumstance, and that the decision rests solely with the woman and her doctor. The only restriction was that the operation be performed by a licensed physician within the first 24 weeks of pregnancy. In Hawaii and Alaska there were, additionally, residency requirements for the woman, and it was stipulated that the operation be performed in a hospital. Abortion laws continued to be challenged, by those in favor of and those opposed to them. In 1972, for instance, a federal court ruled unconstitutional New Jersey's restrictive statute against abortion.

In those states clinging to restrictive abortion laws, punishment was typically leveled at the abortionist, for whom the penalty ranged from 1 to 14 years in prison, rather than at the woman seeking his services. A few states also assessed penalties against the woman, although there is no record of prosecution under these laws. Death resulting from abortion was branded as murder in 14 states and as manslaughter in 14 others.

Most states punished even the intent to perform an illegal abortion, although 27 states required proof of the woman's pregnancy. In states where legal abortion could be obtained only on grounds that the pregnancy constituted a danger to the mother's life (Guttmacher *b*), doctors were painfully aware that they must prove this danger if prosecution were ever to arise. This awareness accounts for their seeming indifference to the distraught woman seeking their help in an unwanted pregnancy.

For all practical purposes, however, the existence of legislation against abortion was largely academic, because few of the people involved were arrested—and of those who were arrested, few were convicted. Between 1950 and 1965 in Chicago, as an example, fewer than six cases involving abortion were uncovered by the police per annum. Less than half the people concerned were judged guilty of breaking the law, and only 6% of that number received a jail or prison sentence (Ziff).

American society appears to have a double standard of judgment in the matter of abortion—condemning it publicly while condoning it privately —if one can judge from abortion statistics. This hypocrisy is also implicit in the restrictive abortion laws of the past, which in effect discriminated against the poor and made abortion largely the privilege of the rich. Even when the law prohibits most abortions, women who can afford the charges in private wings of hospitals are able to procure many more "therapeutic" abortions than those women lying in charity wards of the same hospitals (Hall). One reason for this inequity may be that the poor frequently wait too long in any pregnancy to seek medical attention, thus making an abortion inadvisable. According to most authorities, however, the more probable explanation is that if a woman can pay for a "therapeutic" abortion, she can very likely procure it. Herein may also rest the explanation for the high death rate from abortion among the poor.

It has long been maintained that if a woman wants an abortion she will get it, even if she has to do so by means of a do-it-yourself kit (Trainer). When legislation prohibits most abortions and a woman cannot pay for an expensive "therapeutic" abortion, she will probably search out illegal, less expensive procedures—and considerably more dangerous ones. In the past, unfortunately, too many of these women have resorted to untrained and irresponsible abortionists. The rich get richer and the poor get babies —or perhaps incur a death sentence.

Psychiatrists have often mistakenly blamed abortions for the mental breakdowns of some of their women patients. The error here would appear to stem from the fact that psychiatrists see only those patients with severe emotional problems. They rarely have contact with any of the numerous women who not only suffer no psychological ill effects from abortion, but actually gain personal strength from the experience (Guttmacher *b*).

Many authorities—including Dr. Alan Guttmacher, long-time president of an organization concerned with finding solutions to problems of the world's population growth—voice strong opposition, in both published works and open discussion, to archaic American laws governing abortion.

They advocate public education in the light of the twentieth-century knowledge. The 1973 Supreme Court ruling has made a reexamination of existing statutes inevitable.

Despite varying opinions on abortion legislation and practice, the moral and legal problems in abortion are clearly profound. They revolve around the question of when the conceptus becomes a human being and hence capable of being murdered. To those who believe that human life begins the moment the sperm enters the ovum, any abortion constitutes murder, no matter how great the therapeutic or eugenic justification may be. Indeed, the zygote does contain the full component of its chromosomal inheritance from the moment of conception. As a human being, this group argues, the fetus comes under the protection of the Constitution and has the right to life.

Others view the embryo as nothing more than a cell mass or an organic part of the mother until it becomes capable of living apart from her (generally considered to be about the twenty-fifth week of prenatal life). A fetus under 20 weeks old usually does not require burial or a death certificate. They argue that an embryo, as a part of the mother, is subject to her will—and that a woman has the fundamental right to choose whether to bear a child.

Because convictions regarding abortion differ vastly, one is left with the doubt that a consensus among doctors, lawyers, lawmakers, and the general public can ever be reached. What, for example, are the legal rights of the unborn child? Certain court rulings in the United States have established the inheritance rights of the unborn child, and its right to recover damages if it receives injuries prior to birth. What about the right of the unborn to be born? How sacred is that right? If a group of lawmakers decrees that the right to birth is not absolute, to what degree is the mother's health, sanity, and well-being superior to the right of the infant? In those cases in which there is good reason to suspect that the child conceived will be born with serious defects, what considerations justify legislation to terminate the pregnancy?

If abortion is right under special circumstances, what are they? At what fetal age does it become wrong? Is it, in fact, a legal question at all, or should the decision be left to the person most vitally concerned in the matter—the woman involved in the unwanted pregnancy?

Despite the incredible advances recently made in techniques of birth control, will it ever be possible to prevent all pregnancies except those a woman desires? Public conscience appears to be moving gradually toward the following view, as expressed in a *Time* magazine essay:

> Along with poverty, ignorance and moral strictures against birth control, the unpredictability of human sexual practices makes unwanted pregnancy inevitable. The way to deal with the problem forthrightly is on terms that

permit the individual, guided by conscience and intelligence, to make a choice unhampered by archaic and hypocritical concepts and statutes (Desperate dilemma of abortion).

STERILIZATION

Sterilization for eugenic reasons is sanctioned in some American states, particularly in tax-supported institutions. In these instances a doctor is free to perform sterilizing operations without concern for any legal consequences. If the operation is done purely for reasons of health, however, the doctor's legal position is less secure. As a consequence, many doctors are reluctant to perform sterilization upon a patient's request.

In this area, too, there are no uniform laws among the various states. In California, malpractice suits resulting from surgery for sterilization are not usually covered by insurance companies. One study (Reiser) revealed that 87% of the physicians sampled who had performed vasectomies had never had suit brought against them because of the surgery, and that only 8% had faced legal action; 5% did not reply. Written consent by the patient affords the physician some measure of safety, but is no guarantee against a subsequent suit or even prosecution in a court of criminal law. However, only one state (Utah) still prohibits sterilization except in cases of severe medical necessity. The other 49 states hold that steriliaztion is legal for socioeconomic reasons as well (Guttmacher *d;* Pilpel).

Sterilization in Japan, though legal, is usually performed only upon women. In India, sterilization is limited to men, who are monetarily compensated for time lost from work following the surgery (Belt). As the result of a governmental program designed to curb India's crippling population growth, some 1.3 million vasectomies were performed in 1968, and officials hope to increase this figure to 3 million a year in the future (Guttmacher *d*).

ARTIFICIAL INSEMINATION

The use of semen from a donor to impregnate a woman whose husband is infertile has an uncertain legal status. Some jurists have declared artificial insemination to be adultery and the children born as a result of it illegitimate. Others have deemed it a legal procedure, producing legitimate children.

At least two states (Georgia and Oklahoma) have taken action to bring order out of this chaos by passing statutes legalizing artificial insemination from a donor, provided that both husband and wife sign their consent. The Supreme Court of California has made a similar decision, pointing out that artificial insemination is actually the antithesis of adultery. It is to be hoped that other states will follow suit in declaring artificial insemination to be a legal procedure (Guttmacher *d*).

MODEL SEX LAWS

It seems reasonable to suppose that the purpose of laws concerning sexual conduct is to protect the individual from coercion, to protect the young against the unwholesome designs of adults who would take advantage of them, to protect the public from flagrant displays of sexual acts that may be disruptive of the peace, and to protect the institutions of family and marriage. The purpose of such laws should not be to determine and enforce standards of morality (Cory and LeRoy). These were the principles set forth recently by the Illinois and Chicago Bar Associations. In their formulation of a legal code governing sexual behavior, they suggested that these principles would adequately and realistically meet the needs of a modern society. The two groups of lawyers propounded and had accepted by the Illinois state legislature what is probably the most sensible and enforceable set of sex laws ever found in America (Cory and LeRoy).

Under the new Illinois code, for example, the legal definition of rape no longer includes "statutory" or "nonviolent" rape. A sexual act is not rape unless the male uses force against the female. If she gives her consent but is not of legal age, the offense is handled under that section of the penal code dealing with "contributing to the sexual delinquency of a child."

Furthermore, no offense is committed under the Illinois code for engaging in bestiality. Acts of sexual gratification involving the sex organs of one person and the mouth or anus of another are no longer punishable, unless such acts are brought about by force, threat, or violence, or unless one participant is underage, or unless the act offends public decency. Such acts performed by consenting adults, whether heterosexual or homosexual, if conducted in private, are not punishable.

Punishment for incest in Illinois now takes into consideration the closeness of the relationship between the parties and their ages. Aggravated incest, which incurs the most severe punishment, is defined as coitus or an act of deviant sexual conduct between a man and his daughter, no matter what her age. Other forbidden sexual contact involves father–stepdaughter and father–foster daughter if the girl is under the age of 18. The strictness of this law is based on the strong position that the father often holds in the family, and the influence that he can exert on a daughter.

Public indecency or public exposure, according to the Illinois law, relates to the place where the sex act is carried out. A public place is "any place where the conduct may reasonably be expected to be viewed by others." Thus, while a boy and a girl may be permitted to engage in light petting on a park bench, two men could not expect to get by with similar activity. However, a man would not be punished for suggesting to another man that they engage in such acts in private.

The Illinois law punishes men and women alike for prostitution, solicitation for a prostitute, operating a place for prostitution, and patronizing a prostitute. While the law defines prostitution as accepting money for sexual intercourse or deviate sexual conduct, it does not define as prostitution the acceptance of nonmonetary gifts (such as jewelry) for sexual favors.

In May 1967, the President's Crime Commission recommended removing from the domain of criminal law many sexual acts now considered crimes, contending that these matters are often social ills and should be treated as such. States other than Illinois are, fortunately, beginning at least to recognize the need for similar revamping of legal codes to cope more realistically with the sexual activity of their citizenry.

The Fourth International Convention on Criminology, held in 1960 at The Hague, Holland, and attended by over 600 governmental representatives and criminal law professors from almost every nation in the world, adopted various resolutions to correct inequities in and misuse of sex laws. They called for (1) removal of fornication and adultery from the list of criminal offenses; (2) more liberal interpretation and lenient punishment of acts of incest; (3) liberalizing laws concerning birth control, abortion, and artificial insemination; (4) granting equal rights and freedom to homosexuals; and (5) the toughening of laws concerning nonsupport of wives and children (Mueller a).

Universal adoption of these legislative principles would be of immense value to both individuals and society. A burden of fear, guilt, and shame would thereby be lifted from the minds of citizens who, because of existing archaic laws, might otherwise be victims of entrapment, blackmail, unfair fines, and even imprisonment (Cory and LeRoy).

Since the first Kinsey reports, the thinking of many experts in the legal, psychological, and sociological fields has been that laws pertaining to sex should be limited to those sex acts that (1) involve the use of force or threat of force, (2) involve minors, or (3) are performed in public. By concentrating on these aspects, many problems are bypassed—especially those problems created by laws that are unenforceable, useless, antiquated, inapplicable, or simply not within the province of law enforcement. In addition to these three basic criteria, other measures geared to prevent potential sex offense and to provide better care and treatment of acknowledged offenders have been suggested by Albert Ellis (e), who has been prominent in the study of the psychology of sex offenders:

All laws pertaining to sexual behavior should be rewritten in more definitive and meaningful terminology.

Before the accused is sentenced, a complete psychological examination should be performed to determine whether he is sexually or psychologically abnormal, or is psychopathic.

Psychological treatment should be provided for offenders in their own community while they are on probation. If confinement is ordered, it should be in a mental hospital or similar institution that affords specific psychotherapy for sex offenders. In the event of institutionalization, protective custody should be maintained for as long as the patient is judged to be a menace to society.

Sex offenders should be offered help and understanding, rather than contempt and punishment.

If a preventive approach to sexual offense is to be effective, there must be wider dissemination of accurate sex information. Through such education, children will gain a more scientific and objective understanding of human sexuality.

When a society refuses to seek improvement of the condition of its sick and downtrodden, and when overly severe punishment is meted out to transgressors, something is assuredly wrong. Psychological evaluation of those members of society who would maltreat the unfortunate will quite likely reveal personal hostilities and conflicts rather than an altruistic desire to protect the community. The prime American example of hostility and sexual conflict masked as public altruism is the aforementioned Anthony Comstock, who has been called "the most aggressive opponent of personal liberties ever to soil the pages of American history" (Berke).

If legislation governing sexual affairs is to be improved, society must gain a clearer understanding of the character of the sex offender. Implicit in this understanding is an insight into the significant roles played by guilt and conflict in sexual difficulties. Guilt regarding sexual matters begins early in childhood when a child engaging in sexual exploration is censured, or when questions concerning sex are avoided by his parents. At such moments, the youngster's sexual acts and desires, such as they are, begin to be tinged with guilt; his ability to respond normally and naturally to his sex drive becomes impaired. Out of this guilt spring almost endless possibilities for psychosexual disturbances. A denial of sexuality and deviant or furtive methods of expressing sexuality are among the potential aberrations that can result from defective sexual training.

Hopefully, we are finding our way out of the morass of sexual ignorance and guilt. Perhaps the next decade will bring a better all-round understanding of human sexuality, and with it more realistic approaches to sexual problems.

SEXUAL MYTHS
AND FALLACIES

When any aspect of the human condition becomes as shrouded in misinformation and superstition as human sexuality has, it is almost inevitable that a welter of myths and fallacies should mushroom. The mythology is perpetuated not only laterally by the peer group among its members, but also vertically by those legitimately in a position to educate.

Scientists have made notable advances in sex research. Yet educators (parents, teachers, clergymen), because of their own faulty sex education or their fears or embarrassment in the matter of sex, ignore modern scientific contributions toward greater understanding of the subject. Thus do illogical and bigoted sexual attitudes become the bequest of one generation to the next.

Beliefs for which there is no conceivable foundation in truth are by no means held only by the uneducated and the unsophisticated. Highly educated professional people, as has been said, can harbor a curious (if not dangerous) collection of sexual misconceptions. If not corrected, this misinformation will almost certainly be handed down as indisputable truth to their children or pupils.

This book has emphasized the vital importance of possessing accurate sex information and the dispensing of that knowledge in an honest, direct manner to those in one's charge. And, indeed, the same approach can be used whenever one encounters anyone caught up in some of the mythology obscuring the realities of sex. One hundred of the most common of these fallacies are listed here. (For a detailed discussion of the most common sexual myths that plague the country today, see *Sexual Myths and Fallacies* by James Leslie McCary.)

SEXUAL PHYSIOLOGY AND FUNCTIONING

Nocturnal emissions ("wet dreams") indicate a sexual disorder.

Women do not experience nocturnal orgasms.

Women ejaculate, as men do.

Ejaculation and orgasm in men are one and the same phenomenon.

Simultaneous orgasms are more satisfactory than those experienced separately and are, moreover, necessary for sexual compatibility in marriage.

Sexologists are in agreement that there is a distinct difference between a vaginal and a clitoral orgasm.

During menstruation, women should not engage in sports; nor should they take a bath, shower, or shampoo their hair.

Menstruation begins earlier in girls living in the tropics than in girls living in cooler climates.

Lower animals menstruate just as humans do.

The absence of the hymen proves that a girl is not a virgin.

The presence of the hymen is ipso facto evidence that a girl is a virgin.

The best health is enjoyed by those who abstain from sex.

Excellence of athletic performance is reduced by sexual intercourse the night before or the day of any athletic competition.

Diminishing function of the sex glands signals the end of the sex life of both men and women.

Impotence in old men is always the result of physical factors.

The size of a man's penis can be judged by the size of his hands and feet.

A large penis is important to a woman's sexual gratification.

The man with a large penis is more sexually potent than the man with a small penis.

The penis of the black male is larger than that of the white male.

A small penis can usually be enlarged by the use of drugs or hormones, or by performing a specific series of exercises.

Sexual intercourse should be avoided during pregnancy.

The older man has no advantages over a younger one insofar as satisfactory coitus is concerned.

The uterus "sucks up" seminal fluid ejaculated into the vagina.

A woman's repeated sexual experiences with one man will leave a mark on a child later fathered by another man.

Humans can get "hung up" (*i.e.,* experience *penis captivus*) during sexual intercourse.

SEX DRIVE

Each individual is allotted just so many sexual experiences; when they are used up, sexual activity is finished for that person.

Blacks have a greater sex drive than whites.

Alcohol is a sexual stimulant.

Marijuana is an aphrodisiac.

Sterilization reduces the sex drive of a man or woman.

Castration always destroys the sex drive completely.

The total or partial removal of the prostate reduces a man's sexual enjoyment, and will ultimately destroy his sexual capabilities.

Menopause or hysterectomy terminates a woman's sex life.

Sex desire and ability decrease markedly after the age of 40 to 50.

The amount of hair on a man's body is an index of his virility.

A poor sexual adjustment in marriage inevitably spells its doom.

REPRODUCTION AND BIRTH CONTROL

There is an absolutely "safe" period for sexual intercourse in which coitus cannot cause impregnation.

Vasectomies are 100% successful as a birth-control technique.

A couple must have simultaneous climaxes if conception is to take place.

A woman can become pregnant only through coitus or artificial insemination.

Urination by the woman after coitus, or having sexual intercourse in a standing position will prevent pregnancy.

Abortion, whether legal or criminal, is always dangerous.

Frigid women, prostitutes, and promiscuous women are not so likely to conceive as women whose sexual response or activity is more normal.

There must be two acts of sexual intercourse to produce twins, three for triplets, and so on.

Sperm from one testicle will produce males, and from the other, females; or the ova from one ovary will produce males, and from the other, females.

Having only one testicle reduces a man's ability to father a child.

The woman determines the sex of the child.

A woman's diet during pregnancy has a bearing on the sex of the child.

The sex of a child to be conceived is a matter of pure chance, and nothing can be done to change the odds.

A fetus sleeps during the day and is awake at night (and kicks).

A seventh-month baby has a better chance of survival than an eighth-month baby.

An unborn child can be "marked."

"Virgin birth" (parthenogenesis) does not occur in humans or animals.

The birth-control pill will eventually cause a wide variety of ills in any woman using it for any length of time.

Taking the Pill will delay a woman's menopause.

Humans and infrahuman animals can crossbreed.

A breast-feeding mother cannot become pregnant again as long as she continues to nurse her baby.

HOMOSEXUALITY

Homosexual offenders are a menace to society.

People are either totally homosexual or totally heterosexual.

Childhood involvement with an adult homophile is an important causative factor in the individual's later becoming a homosexual.

Men (and women) are homosexuals because they were "born that way."

Hormonal imbalance is the chief cause of homosexuality.

Homosexuals are more creative than heterosexuals.

Oral–genital sex between a man and a woman indicates homosexual tendencies.

Because of their sexual tendencies, homosexuals are more likely than heterosexuals to be disloyal to their country or cause.

The man who enjoys having his nipples stimulated has suppressed homosexual desires.

A child conceived through rear-entry coitus will be homosexual.

Any lesbian would prefer a man, if he were a "real man" and if he used the right technique.

Most prostitutes are lesbians.

The typical career woman is a suppressed lesbian.

SEXUAL DISORDERS AND SEXUAL ABNORMALITIES, REAL AND IMAGINED

Frequent masturbation has been known to lead to lunacy.

Masturbation can cause a number of physical manifestations, including warts, hair in the palms of the hands, pimples, acne, and, ultimately, impotence.

Masturbation is a practice restricted almost exclusively to men.

Masturbation is a habit of the young and immature; its practice typically ceases after men and women marry.

Unusual or excessive sexual practices can lead to mental breakdowns.

Vaginal–penile intercourse is the only normal method of sex relations.

Women who have strong sex drives, come to easy climax, and are capable of multiple orgasms are nymphomaniacs.

Nymphomaniacs and satyromaniacs abound in our society.

If one partner desires sex more often than the other, nothing can be done to make the couple sexually more compatible.

People suffering from sexual inadequacy—*i.e.,* impotence, premature ejaculation, frigidity—can expect little help from treatment for their problems.

Premature ejaculation is due to physical circumstances.

Circumcision makes it difficult for a man to control ejaculation.

A transvestite and a transsexualist are the same, and both are homosexuals.

SEX OFFENSES

A sex offender cannot be cured and is likely to continue his unacceptable behavior for the rest of his life.

The person who commits a series of minor sex crimes will quite likely become involved in more serious sex criminality If he is not apprehended.

Being oversexed is a primary characteristic of sex offenders.

The typical sex offender, particularly when the victim is a child, is aggressive and potentially homicidal.

Sex offenders are typically unreligious.

Sexual molesters of children are usually over 65 years of age.

Pornography has a corruptive effect on people's minds and behavior, especially children's.

Pornography stimulates people to commit criminal sex acts.

Pornography and obscenity lead to sexual excess and sexual acting out.

Excessive exposure to pornographic material leads to an ever-increasing craving for pornography.

... AND OTHER FALLACIES

The average physician is well trained and emotionally equipped to deal with his patients' sexual problems.

The virginity of the woman is an important factor in the success of a marriage.

Nature compensates for the number of males killed during a time of war.

If a white woman has a blood transfusion from a black donor, the child she later conceives may be black.

Heart patients need not worry that sexual activity will be detrimental to their health, so long as they remain physically inactive and quiet during coitus.

Today's young adults are "going wild" sexually.

Sex education has no place in our schools, because it is a communist plot to destroy the country from within, and because it leads to: (1) sexual acting-out behavior; (2) a rise in promiscuity; (3) an increase in premarital pregnancy; (4) etc., etc., etc.

GLOSSARY

abdominal pregnancy. A type of displaced or ectopic pregnancy in which the embryo becomes attached to mislocated endometrial tissue in the abdominal wall.

abortifacient. A drug or other agent that causes abortion.

abortion. Premature expulsion from the uterus of the product of conception—a fertilized ovum, embryo, or nonviable fetus.

abstinence. A refraining from the use of or indulgence in certain foods, stimulants, or sexual intercourse.

adolescence. The period of life between puberty (appearance of secondary sex characteristics) and adulthood (cessation of major body growth).

adultery. Sexual intercourse between a married person and an individual other than his or her legal spouse.

afterbirth. The placenta and fetal membranes expelled from the uterus following the birth of a child.

amenorrhea. Absence of the menses (menstruation).

amnion. A thin membrane forming the closed sac or "bag of waters" that surrounds the unborn child within the uterus and contains amniotic fluid in which the fetus is immersed.

amniotic tap. A procedure in which amniotic fluid is drawn from the amniotic sac surrounding the fetus and subjected to microscopic analysis.

ampulla. A flasklike widening at the end of a tubular structure or canal.

anal eroticism. Pleasurable sensations in the region of the anus.

anaphrodisiac. A drug or medicine that allays sexual desire.

androgen. A steroid hormone producing masculine sex characteristics and having an influence on body and bone growth and on the sex drive.

anomaly. An irregularity or defect.

aphrodisiac. Anything, such as a drug or a perfume, that stimulates sexual desire.

areola. The ring of darkened tissue surrounding the nipple of the breast.

artificial insemination. Introduction of male semen into the vagina or womb of a woman by artificial means.

autoerotic.   Pertaining to self-stimulation or erotic behavior directed toward one's self; frequently equated with masturbation.

Bartholin's glands.   Two tiny glands in a female, located at either side of the entrance to the vagina.

bestiality.   A sexual deviation in which a person engages in sexual relations with an animal. Cf. ZOOPHILIA.

birth canal.   See VAGINA.

birth control.   Deliberate limitation of the number of children born—through such means as contraceptives, abstinence, the rhythm method, *coitus interruptus,* and the like.

bisexual.   Literally, having sex organs of both sexes, as in hermaphrodites; having a sexual interest in both sexes.

blastocyst.   The fertilized egg in the early stage of cell division when the cells form a hollow sphere.

blastula.   The embryonic stage of development in which the cells form a single-layered hollow sphere.

body stalk.   A complex connecting structure that attaches the embryo and placenta. It later develops into the umbilical cord.

breech presentation.   A birth position in which the baby is presented and delivered buttocks first.

caesarean birth (also caesarean section).   Delivery of a child through a surgical incision in the abdominal and uterine walls.

carpopedal spasm.   A spastic contraction of the hands and feet.

castration.   Removal of the gonads (sex glands)—the testicles in men, the ovaries in women.

castration complex.   In psychoanalytic theory, unconscious fears centering around injury or loss of the genitals as punishment for forbidden sexual desires; a male's anxiety about his manhood.

celibacy.   The state of being unmarried; abstention from sexual activity.

cervix.   Neck; in the female, the narrow portion of the uterus or womb that forms its lower end and opens into the vagina.

chancre.   The sore or ulcer that is the first symptom of syphilis.

chancroid.   A highly contagious disease characterized by ulcerations at the points of physical contact and typically spread through sexual intercourse.

change of life. See CLIMACTERIC, MENOPAUSE.

chastity.   Abstention from sexual intercourse.

chorion.   The outermost envelope of the growing zygote (fertilized ovum), which later contributes to the formation of the placenta.

chromosome.   One of several small rod-shaped bodies found in the nucleus of all body cells, which contain the genes, or hereditary factors.

circumcision.   Surgical removal of the foreskin or prepuce of the male penis.

climacteric.   The syndrome of physical and psychologic changes that occur at the termination of menstrual function (i.e., reproductive capability) in the woman and reduction in sex-steroid production in both sexes; menopause; change of life.

climax. See ORGASM.

clitoris (adj. **clitoral**). A small, highly sensitive nipple of flesh in the female, located just above the urethral opening in the upper triangle of the vulva.

coitus. Sexual intercourse between male and female, in which the male penis is inserted into the female vagina.

coitus interruptus (also **premature withdrawal**). The practice of withdrawing the penis from the vagina just before ejaculation.

coitus reservatus. Prolonged coitus in which ejaculation is intentionally suppressed.

colostrum. A thin, milky fluid secreted by the female breast just before and after childbirth.

conception. The beginning of a new life, when an ovum (egg) is penetrated by a sperm, resulting in the development of an embryo; impregnation.

condom. A contraceptive used by males consisting of a rubber or gut sheath that is drawn over the erect penis before coitus.

congenital. Existing at birth, but not necessarily inherited.

continence. A state of exercising self-restraint, especially in regard to the sex drive.

contraception. The use of devices or drugs to prevent conception in sexual intercourse.

coprophilia. A sexual deviation in which sexual gratification is associated with the act of defecation; a morbid interest in feces.

copulation. Sexual intercourse; coitus.

corona glandis. The rim surrounding the base of the glans penis in the male.

corpus luteum. A yellow mass in the ovary, formed from a ruptured graafian follicle, that secretes the hormone progesterone.

Cowper's glands. Two glands in the male, one on each side of the urethra near the prostate, which secrete a mucoid material as part of the seminal fluid.

crabs. See PEDICULOSIS PUBIS.

cremaster (adj. **cremasteric**). The muscles that elevate the male testes.

criminal abortion. Illegal termination of a human pregnancy by any type of medical, surgical, or other means of interference, as distinguished from *therapeutic abortion,* which is done to protect the health or life of the mother.

cryptorchidism. See UNDESCENDED TESTICLE.

cul-de-sac. The "blind alley" ending of the female vagina just beyond the opening into the womb (cervix).

cunnilingus. The act of using the tongue or mouth in erotic play with the external female genitalia (vulva).

curettage (also **curettement**). Scraping the lining of the uterus with a *curette,* a spoon-shaped medical instrument.

cystitis. Inflammation of the bladder, usually characterized by a burning sensation during urination.

cystocele. Hernial protrusion of the female bladder through the vaginal wall.

cytogenic. Forming or producing cells.

defloration. The rupture of the hymen in a virgin's first experience of coitus or through vaginal examination.

detumescence. Subsidence of swelling; subsidence of erection in the genitals following orgasm.

diaphragm. A rubber contraceptive, used by women, that is hemispherical in shape and fits like a cap over the neck of the uterus (cervix).

Doderlein's bacilli. The bacteria (germs) normally present in the female vagina.

dorsal. Pertaining to the back (as the back of the hand, of the whole body, or of the upper surface of the penis), as opposed to the *ventral* (front) side.

douche. A stream of water or other liquid solution directed into the female vagina for sanitary, medical, or contraceptive reasons.

dry orgasm. Sexual climax in a male without any apparent ejaculation of semen; usually an instance of retrograde ejaculation, caused by some anomaly within the prostate, in which the semen is ejaculated backward into the posterior urethra and bladder rather than out through the penis. Removal of the prostate prevents production and ejaculation of semen, although capability for orgasm remains.

dysmenorrhea. Painful menstruation.

dyspareunia. Coitus that is difficult or painful, especially for a woman.

eclampsia. A condition of convulsions and coma that can occur in a woman during pregnancy or immediately following childbirth.

ectoderm. The outermost of the three primitive or primary germ layers of the embryo, from which the nervous system, sense organs, mouth cavity, and skin eventually develop.

ectopic. In an abnormal place, *e.g.,* an *ectopic pregnancy*, in which the unborn child develops outside the uterus, either in an ovary, the abdominal cavity, or a fallopian tube.

ejaculatio praecox. Premature ejaculation.

ejaculation. The expulsion of male semen, usually at the climax (orgasm) of the sexual act.

Electra complex. Excessive emotional attachment of a daughter to her father.

emasculate. To castrate; to deprive of manliness or masculine vigor.

embryo. The unborn young in its early stage of development—in man, from one week following conception to the end of the second month.

emission. Discharge of semen from the male penis, especially when involuntary, as during sleep (nocturnal emission).

endemic. Pertaining to or prevalent in a particular district or region; pertaining to a disease that has a low incidence but is constantly present in a given community.

endocrine gland. A gland that secretes its product (hormone) directly into the bloodstream.

endoderm. The innermost of the three primitive or primary germ layers of the embryo, from which the digestive and respiratory systems of the body develop.

endometriosis. The aberrant presence of endometrial tissue (uterine lining) in other parts of the female pelvic cavity, such as in the fallopian tubes or in the ovaries, bladder, or intestines.

endometrium. The mucous membrane that lines the cavity of the uterus in the female.

epididymis. The network of tiny tubes in the male that connects the testicles with the sperm duct.

episiotomy. Incision in a woman's perineum to facilitate the birth of a child.

epispadia. A congenital defect in males in which the opening (meatus) of the urethra is on the upper surface of the penis instead of at its tip. Cf. HYPO-SPADIA.

epithelium (adj. **epithelial**). The outer layer of cells covering the internal and external surfaces of the body.

erection. The stiffening and enlargement of the penis (or clitoris), usually as a result of sexual excitement.

erogenous zone. A sexually sensitive area of the body, such as the mouth, lips, breasts, nipples, buttocks, genitals, or anus.

erotic. Pertaining to sexual love or sensation; sexually stimulating.

estrogen. A steroid hormone producing female sex characteristics and affecting the functioning of the menstrual cycle.

estrus. A recurrent period of sexual receptivity in female animals, marked by intense sexual urge.

eugenics. A science that seeks to improve future generations through the control of hereditary factors.

eunuch. A castrated male.

eunuchoid. Having the physical characteristics of a eunuch without actually being castrated.

excitement phase. The initial stage in the human sexual response cycle that follows effective sexual stimulation.

exhibitionism. A sexual variance in which the individual—usually male—suffers from a compulsion to expose his genitals publicly.

extragenital. Originating or lying outside the genital organs.

extramarital. Literally, outside of marriage; usually used in reference to adulterous sexual intercourse.

fallopian tube. The oviduct or egg-conducting tube that extends from each ovary to the uterus in the female.

fecundity. The ability to produce offspring, especially in a rapid manner and in large numbers.

fellatio. The act of taking the penis into the mouth and sucking it for erotic purposes.

fertility. The state of being capable of producing young; the opposite of *sterility*.

fertilization. The union of egg (ovum) and sperm (spermatazoon), which results in conception.

fetishism. A sexual variance in which sexual gratification is achieved by means of an object, such as an article of clothing, that bears sexual symbolism for the individual.

fetus. In humans, the unborn child from the third month after conception until birth.

fibrillation. Spontaneous contraction of individual muscle fibers no longer under control of a motor nerve.

follicle. The small sac or vesicle near the surface of the ovary in the female that contains a developing egg cell (ovum).

follicle-stimulating hormone (FSH). A hormone secreted by the pituitary gland that stimulates, in the female, the growth and development of the ovarian follicles and, in the male, the production of sperm by the seminiferous tubules.

foreplay.   The preliminary stages of sexual intercourse, in which the partners usually stimulate each other by kissing, touching, and caressing.

foreskin.   The skin covering the tip of the male penis or female clitoris; prepuce.

fornication.   Sexual intercourse between two unmarried persons (as distinguished from *adultery,* which involves a person who is married to someone other than his coital partner).

fourchette.   The fold of mucous membrane at the posterior junction of the labia majora in the female.

fraternal twins.   Two offspring developed from two separate ova (eggs) usually fertilized at the same time.

frenulum.   A delicate, tissue-thin fold of skin that connects the foreskin with the under surface of the glans penis; frenum.

frenulum clitoridis.   The clitoral prepuce.

frenum.   See FRENULUM.

frigidity.   A common term for a form of female sexual dysfunction, implying coldness, indifference, or insensitivity on the part of a woman to sexual intercourse or sexual stimulation; inability to experience sexual pleasure or gratification.

frottage.   A sexual variance in which orgasm is induced by rubbing against an individual of the opposite sex, usually a stranger.

fundus.   The base or part of a hollow organ farthest from its mouth.

gamete.   The mature reproductive cell of either sex—sperm (male) or ovum (female).

gastrula.   The embryonic stage of development in which the cells form a double-layered hollow sphere.

gene.   The basic carrier of hereditary traits, contained in the chromosomes.

genital organs (or **genitals** or **genitalia**).   The sex or reproductive organs.

germ cell.   The sperm (spermatozoon) or egg (ovum).

gerontosexuality.   A sexual disorder in which a young person chooses an elderly person as the subject of his sexual interest.

gestation.   Pregnancy; the period from conception to birth.

glans clitoridis.   The head of the female clitoris.

glans penis.   The head of the male penis.

gonad.   A sex gland; a testicle (male) or ovary (female).

gonadotropin.   A substance having a stimulating effect on the gonads (sex glands).

gonorrhea.   A venereal disease, transmitted chiefly through coitus, that is a contagious catarrhal inflammation of the genital mucous membrane.

graafian follicle.   A small sac or pocket in the female ovary in which the egg (ovum) matures and from which it is discharged at ovulation.

granuloma inguinale.   A disease most often affecting the genitals that is characterized by widespread ulceration and scarring of the skin and underlying tissues.

gynecologist.   A physician specializing in the treatment of the problems of the female sexual and reproductive organs.

gynecomastia.   Femalelike development of the male breasts.

heredity.   The transmission of bodily traits and characteristics or of diseases from parents to offspring.

hermaphrodite. An individual possessing both male and female sex glands (ovary and testicle) or sex-gland tissue of both sexes. Cf. PSEUDOHERMAPHRODITE.

heterogeneous. Consisting of dissimilar elements; the opposite of *homogeneous*.

heterosexuality. Sexual attraction to, or sexual activity with, members of the opposite sex; the opposite of *homosexuality*.

hirsutism. Abnormal hairiness, especially in women.

homologous. Corresponding in position, structure, or origin to another anatomical entity.

homosexuality. Sexual attraction to, or sexual activity with, members of one's own sex; the opposite of *heterosexuality*.

hormone. A chemical substance produced by an endocrine gland that has a specific effect on the activities of other organs in the body.

human chorionic gonadotropin (HCD). A hormone secreted early in pregnancy by the chorionic villi (and later by the placenta); because of its excretion in the urine, it makes possible the biological tests for pregnancy.

hydrocele. An accumulation of fluid in the male scrotum.

hymen. The membranous fold that partly covers the external opening of the vagina in most virgin females; the maidenhead.

hyperplasia. The abnormal multiplication or increase in the number of cells in a tissue. Cf. HYPERTROPHY.

hypertrophy. An excessive enlargement or outgrowth of a bodily part or organ because of enlargement of its constituent elements.

hypospadia. A congenital defect in males in which the opening (meatus) of the urethra is on the underside of the penis instead of at its tip. Cf. EPISPADIA.

hypothalamus. A small portion of the brain that controls such vital bodily processes as visceral activities, temperature, and sleep.

hysterectomy. Surgical removal of the female uterus, either through the abdominal wall or through the vagina.

hysterotomy. Incision into the uterus.

identical twins. Two offspring developed from one fertilized ovum (egg).

implantation. Embedding of the blastocyst (fertilized egg) in the mucous membrane, or endometrium, lining the uterus.

impotence. Disturbance of sexual function in the male that precludes satisfactory coitus; more specifically, inability to achieve or maintain an erection sufficient for purposes of sexual intercourse.

impregnation. The act of fertilization or fecundation; making pregnant.

incest. Sexual relations between close relatives, such as father and daughter, mother and son, or brother and sister.

infanticide. The murder or murderer of an infant.

infectious mononucleosis. A virus-produced disease affecting the lymph glands.

inguinal canal. The passageway from the abdominal cavity to the scrotum in the male through which the testicles descend shortly before birth or just after.

insemination. The deposit of semen within the vagina.

intercourse, anal. A form of sexual intercourse in which the penis is inserted into the partner's anus; sometimes termed *sodomy*.

intercourse, sexual. Sexual union of a male and a female, in which the penis is inserted into the vagina; coitus.

interstitial cells.   Specialized cells in the testicles that produce the male sex hormones.

interstitial cell-stimulating hormone (ICSH).   A harmone secreted by the pituitary gland that stimulates, in the male, the maturation of the sperm cells.

intrauterine device (IUD).   A small plastic or metal device that, when fitted into the uterus, prevents pregnancy. Also termed *intrauterine contraceptive device* (IUCD).

intromission.   The insertion of the male penis into the female vagina.

invert.   A homosexual; one who is sexually attracted to persons of his own sex.

involution.   An inward curvature; a shrinking or return to a former size, as of the uterus after childbirth; the regressive alterations in the body or its parts characteristic of the aging process.

jel, contraceptive.   A nongreasy substance containing an ingredient toxic to sperm that is introduced into the vagina before sexual intercourse to prevent conception.

jock itch.   See TINEA CRURIS.

kleptomania.   An irresistible compulsion to steal, usually without any use for the article stolen.

Klinefelter's syndrome (XXY).   An abnormality, afflicting males, in which the sex-determining chromosomes are XXY, instead of the normal XY, the ovum having somehow contributed an extra X at the time of fertilization. Symptoms of the condition include small testicles, sterility, and often a distinctly feminine physical appearance.

labia majora (sing. **labium majus**).   The outer and larger pair of lips of the female external genitals (vulva).

labia minora (sing. **labium minus**).   The inner and smaller pair of lips of the female external genitals (vulva).

lactation.   The manufacture and secretion of milk by the mammary glands in a mother's breasts.

lesbian.   A female homosexual.

libido.   Sexual drive or urge.

lochia.   The discharge from the uterus and vagina that takes place during the first few weeks after childbirth.

luteinizing hormone (LH).   A hormone secreted by the pituitary gland that stimulates, in the female, the formation of the corpus luteum.

lymphogranuloma venereum.   A virus-produced disease that affects the lymph glands in the genital region.

maculopapular.   Spotted and raised or elevated.

maidenhead.   The hymen.

masochism.   A sexual variance in which an individual derives sexual gratification from having pain inflicted on him.

masturbation.   Self-stimulation of the genitals through manipulation; autoeroticism.

meatus.   An opening, such as at the end of the urethral passage in the male penis.

menarche.   The onset of menstruation in the human female, occurring in late puberty and ushering in the period of adolescence.

menopause. The period of cessation of menstruation in the human female, occurring usually between the ages of 45 and 55; climacteric; change of life.

menstruation. The discharge of blood from the uterus through the vagina that normally recurs at approximately four-week intervals in women between the ages of puberty and menopause.

mesoderm. The middle layer of the three primitive or primary germ layers of the embryo, from which the muscular, skeletal, excretory, circulatory, and reproductive systems of the body develop.

miscarriage. Spontaneous expulsion of a fetus from the onset of the fourth to the end of the sixth month of pregnancy.

Monilia (or **moniliasis**). A yeast-like infective organism (fungus) causing itching and inflammation of the female vagina.

monogamy. Marriage between one man and one woman.

mononucleosis. See INFECTIOUS MONONUCLEOSIS.

mons veneris (or **mons pubis**). A triangular mound of fat at the symphysis pubis of a woman, just above the vulval area.

mucoid. Resembling mucus.

mucosa. A mucous membrane; a thin tissue that has a moist surface from the secreting of mucus.

mucus (adj. **mucous**). The thick, slippery fluid secreted by mucous membranes.

multipara (adj. **multiparous**). A woman who has given birth to two or more children.

myoma (pl. **myomas** or **myomata**). A tumor consisting of muscle tissue that grows in the wall of the uterus; also called *fibroid*.

myotonia. Increased muscular tension.

narcissism. Excessive self-love; sexual excitement through admiration of one's own body.

necrophilia. A sexual variance in which an individual has a morbid sexual attraction to corpses.

neural tube. The epithelial tube that develops from the neural plate to form the embryo's central nervous system and from which the brain and spinal column develop.

neurosyphilis. Syphilitic infection of the nervous system.

nidation. The implantation of the blastocyst (fertilized ovum) in the lining of the uterus in pregnancy.

nocturnal emission. An involuntary male orgasm and ejaculation of semen during sleep; a "wet dream."

nullipara (adj. **nulliparous**). A woman who has never borne a viable child.

nymphomania. Excessive sexual desire in a woman.

obscene. Disgusting, repulsive, filthy, shocking—that which is abhorrent according to accepted standards of morality.

obsession. A neurosis characterized by the persistent recurrence of some irrational thought or idea, or by an attachment to or fixation on a particular individual or object.

obstetrician. A physician specializing in the care of women during pregnancy, labor, and the period immediately following delivery.

Oedipus complex. Excessive emotional attachment, involving conscious or unconscious incestuous desires, of a son in relation to his mother.

onanism. Withdrawal of the male penis from the female vagina before ejaculation; *coitus interruptus.*

oophorectomy. The surgical removal of an ovary or ovaries.

oral eroticism. Pleasurable sensations centered in the lips and mouth.

orgasm. The peak of climax or sexual excitement in sexual activity.

orgasmic phase. The third stage in the human sexual response cycle during which the orgasm occurs.

orgasmic platform. The area comprising the outer third of the vagina and the labia minora, which displays marked vasocongestion in the plateau phase of the female sexual response cycle (term used by Masters and Johnson).

os. A mouth or orifice, as the external os of the cervix (*os externum uteri*).

ovary. The female sex gland, in which the ova are formed.

oviduct. The fallopian or uterine tube through which the egg (ovum) travels from the ovary to the uterus.

ovulation. The release of a mature, unimpregnated ovum from one of the graafian follicles of an ovary.

ovum (pl. **ova**). An egg; the female reproductive cell, corresponding to the male spermatozoon, that after fertilization develops into a new member of the same species.

oxytocin. A hormone secreted by the pituitary gland that stimulates the muscles of the uterus to contract during childbirth.

paraphilia. Sexual deviations; aberrant sexual activity.

paresis. A chronic syphilitic inflammation of the brain and its enveloping membranes, characterized by progressive mental deterioration and a general paralysis that is sometimes fatal.

parthenogenesis. Reproduction by the development of an egg without its being fertilized by a spermatozoon.

parturition. Labor; the process of giving birth.

pathogenic. Causing disease.

pathological. Pertaining to a diseased or abnormal physical or mental condition.

pederasty. Male sexual relations with a boy; also sexual intercourse via the anus.

pediculosis pubis. An itchy skin irritation in the genital area caused by the minute bites of the crab louse.

pedophilia. A sexual variance in which an adult engages in or desires sexual activity with a child.

penile agenesis. Abnormal smallness of the penis; microphallus.

penis. The male organ of copulation and urination.

penis captivus. A condition in humans in which it is alleged that the shaft of the fully introduced penis is tightly encircled by the vagina during coitus and cannot be withdrawn. Most authorities say this condition occurs only in animals, notably the dog.

perineum (adj. **perineal**). The area between the thighs, extending from the posterior wall of the vagina to the anus in the female and from the scrotum to the anus in the male.

peritoneum (adj. **peritoneal**). The strong, transparent membrane lining the abdominal cavity.

perversion. Sexual deviation from normal; paraphilia.

petting. Sexual contact that excludes coitus.

Peyronie's disease. A condition, usually in men of middle age or older, in which the penis develops a fibrous ridge along its top or sides, causing curvature.

phallus. The male penis, usually the erect penis.

phimosis. Tightness of the foreskin of the male penis, so that it cannot be drawn back from over the glans.

pituitary. Known as the "master gland" and located in the head, it is responsible for the proper functioning of all the other glands, especially the sex glands, the thyroid, and the adrenals.

pituitary gonadotropins. Hormones produced by the pituitary gland that stimulate the gonads (sex glands).

placenta. The cakelike organ that connects the fetus to the uterus by means of the umbilical cord, and through which the fetus is fed and waste products are eliminated; the afterbirth.

plateau phase. The fully stimulated stage in the human sexual response cycle that immediately precedes orgasm.

polyandry. The form of marriage in which one woman has more than one husband at one time.

polygamy. The form of marriage in which a spouse of either sex may possess a plurality of mates at the same time.

polygyny. The form of marriage in which one man has more than one wife at the same time.

pornography. The presentation of sexually arousing material in literature, art, motion pictures, or other means of communication and expression.

postpartum. Occurring after childbirth or after delivery.

potent. Having the male capability to perform sexual intercourse; capable of erection.

precocious sexuality. Awakening of sexual desire at a prematurely early age.

precoital fluid. Alkaline fluid secreted by the Cowper's glands that lubricates the urethra for easy passage of semen.

pregnancy. The condition of having a developing embryo or fetus in the body; the period from conception to birth or abortion.

premature ejaculation. Ejaculation prior to, just at, or immediately after intromission; *ejaculatio praecox*.

prenatal. Existing or occurring before birth.

prepuce. Foreskin.

priapism. Persistent abnormal erection of the penis in males, usually without sexual desire.

procreation. The producing of offspring.

progesterone. The female hormone (known as the pregnancy hormone) that is produced in the yellow body or corpus luteum, and whose function is to prepare the uterus for the reception and development of a fertilized ovum.

prolactin. A hormone secreted by the pituitary gland that stimulates the production of milk by the mammary glands in the breasts (lactation).

promiscuous. Engaging in sexual intercourse with many persons; engaging in casual sexual relations.

prophylactic. A drug or device used for the prevention of disease, often specifically venereal disease.

prostate. The gland in the male that surrounds the urethra and the neck of the bladder.

prostatic fluid. A highly alkaline, thin, milky fluid produced by the prostate gland that constitutes a major portion of the male's semen or ejaculatory fluid.

prostatitis. Inflammation of the prostate gland, typically a disease of older men.

prostitute. A person who engages in sexual relationships for payment.

prudish. Extremely or falsely modest.

pseudocyesis. False pregnancy.

pseudohermaphrodite. An individual who has both male and female external sex organs, usually in rudimentary form, but who has the sex glands (ovary or testicle) of only one sex, and is thus fundamentally male or female. Cf. HERMAPHRODITE.

psychogenic. Of psychic or emotional origin; functional.

puberty (or **pubescence**). The stage of life at which a child turns into a young man or young woman: *i.e.*, the reproductive organs become functionally operative and secondary sex characteristics develop.

pudendum (pl. **pudenda**). The external genitalia, especially of the female (the mons pubis, labia majora, labia minora, and the vestibule of the vagina).

pyromania. A compulsion, usually sexually oriented, to start fires.

rape. Forcible sexual intercourse with a person who does not give consent or who offers resistance.

rectocele. A hernia in females in which part of the rectum protrudes into the vagina.

rectum. The lower part of the large intestine, terminating at the anus.

refractory period. A temporary state of psychophysiologic resistance to sexual stimulation immediately following an orgasmic experience (term used by Masters and Johnson).

resolution phase. The last stage in the human sexual response cycle during which the sexual system retrogresses to its normal nonexcited state.

retrograde ejaculation. Backward ejaculation in males into the posterior urethra and bladder, instead of into the anterior urethra and out through the meatus of the penis.

retroversion. The tipping of an entire organ backward.

rhythm method. A method of birth control that relies on the so-called "safe period" or infertile days in a woman's menstrual cycle.

sadism. The achievement of sexual gratification by inflicting physical or psychological pain upon the sexual partner.

"safe period." The interval of the menstrual cycle when the female is presumably not ovulating.

saliromania. A sexual variance, found primarily in men, that is characterized by the desire to damage or soil the body or clothes of a woman or a representation of a woman.

salpingectomy. Surgical removal of a fallopian tube from a woman.

satyriasis. Excessive sexual desire in a man.

scoptophilia (or **scotophilia**).   A sexual variance in which a person achieves sexual gratification by observing sexual acts or the genitals of others. Cf. VO-YEURISM.

scrotum.   The pouch suspended from the groin that contains the male testicles and their accessory organs.

secondary sex characteristics.   The physical characteristics—other than the external sex organs—that distinguish male from female.

seduction.   Luring a female (sometimes a male) into sexual intercourse without the use of force.

semen.   The secretion of the male reproductive organs that is ejaculated from the penis at orgasm and contains, in the fertile male, sperm cells.

seminal emission (or **seminal fluid**).   A fluid composed of sperm and secretions from the epididymis, seminal vesicles, prostate gland, and Cowper's glands that is ejaculated by the male through the penis upon his reaching orgasm.

seminal vesicles.   Two pouches in the male, one on each side of the prostate, behind the bladder, that are attached to and open into the sperm ducts.

seminiferous tubules.   The tiny tubes or canals in each male testicle that produce the sperm.

serology.   The study of antigen and antibody reactions in blood serum tests.

sex drive.   Desire for sexual expression.

sex flush.   The superficial vasocongestive skin response to increasing sexual tensions that begins in the plateau phase (term used by Masters and Johnson).

sex gland.   A gonad; the testicle in the male and the ovary in the female.

sex hormone.   A substance secreted by the sex glands directly into the bloodstream, e.g., androgens (male) and estrogens (female).

sex organs.   Commonly, the organs used in sexual intercourse—namely, the male's penis and the female's vagina.

sex skin.   The skin of the labia minora in the female, which shows a discoloration response in the plateau phase of the sexual response cycle.

sexual inadequacy.   Any degree of sexual response that is not sufficient for the isolated demand of the moment or for a protracted period of time; frequent or total inability to experience orgasm.

sexual intercourse.   See INTERCOURSE, SEXUAL.

sexual outlet.   Any of the various ways by which sexual tension is released through orgasm.

shaft, penile.   The body of the male penis, composed of three cylindrical bodies and a network of blood vessels, which are encircled by a band of fibrous tissue and covered by skin.

smegma.   A thick, cheesy, ill-smelling accumulation of secretions under the foreskin of the penis or around the clitoris.

sodomy.   A form of paraphilia, variously defined by law to include sexual intercourse with animals and mouth-genital or anal contact between humans.

somatic.   Pertaining to the body, as distinct from the psyche or mind: organic, as distinguished from functional or psychosomatic.

sperm (or **spermatozoon**).   The mature reproductive cell (or cells) capable of fertilizing the female egg and causing impregnation.

sperm duct.   The tube or duct in males that conveys the sperm from the epididymis to the seminal vesicles and urethra; the vas deferens.

spermatic cord.   The structure in males, by which the testicle is suspended, containing the sperm ducts, nerves, and veins.

spermatogenesis.   The process of sperm formation.

spermatozoon (pl. **spermatozoa**).   A mature male germ cell.

spermicide.   An agent that destroys sperm.

sphincter.   A ringlike muscle that closes a natural orifice.

spirochete.   A corkscrew-shaped microorganism; one type of spirochete causes syphilis.

sterility.   The inability to produce offspring.

sterilization.   Any procedure (usually surgical) by which an individual is made incapable of reproduction.

stricture.   The abnormal narrowing of a canal, duct, or passage.

"sweating" phenomenon.   The appearance of little droplets of fluid on the walls of the vagina early in the excitement phase of the female sexual response cycle.

symphysis pubis.   The articulation between the pubic bones in the lower abdomen.

syphilis.   Probably the most serious venereal disease, it is usually acquired by sexual intercourse with a person in the infectious stage of the disease and is caused by invasion of the spirochete *Treponema pallidum*.

systemic.   Spread throughout the body; affecting all body systems and organs.

taboo.   An absolute prohibition based on religion, tradition, social usage, or superstition.

telegony.   The alleged appearance in the offspring of one sire of characteristics derived from a previous sire or mate of the female.

testicle.   The testis; the male sex gland.

testis (pl. **testes**).   The male sex gland or gonad, which produces spermatozoa.

testosterone.   The male testicular hormone that induces and maintains the male secondary sex characteristics.

thrombosis.   The clogging of a blood vessal as the result of the formation of a blood clot within the vessel itself.

therapeutic abortion.   Abortion performed when abnormal conditions threaten the well-being of the mother or the unborn child.

tinea cruris.   A fungus infection causing irritation to the skin in the genital region.

transsexualism.   A compulsion or obsession to become a member of the opposite sex through surgical changes.

transvestism.   A sexual variance characterized by a compulsive desire to wear the garments of the opposite sex; cross dressing.

trichomoniasis.   An infection of the female vagina caused by infestation of the microorganism *Trichomonas* and characterized by inflammation, usually resulting in a vaginal discharge and itching and burning.

trimester.   A period of three months; one of the three time divisions of a pregnancy.

troilism (or **triolism**).   A sexual variance in which, ordinarily, three people (two men and a woman or two women and a man) participate in a series of sexual practices.

tubal ligature.   A surgical procedure for sterilizing a female in which the fallopian tubes are cut and tied.

tubal pregnancy. A type of displaced or ectopic pregnancy in which the embryo fails to descend into the womb and instead develops in the fallopian tube.

tumescence. The process of swelling or the condition of being swollen.

Turner's syndrome (XO). An abnormality afflicting females, in which one of the sex-determining pair (XX) of chromosomes is missing, leaving a total of 45 rather than the normal 46 chromosomes. Symptoms of the condition include incomplete development of the ovaries, short stature, and often webbing of the neck.

umbilical cord. The flexible structure connecting the fetus and the placenta; navel cord.

undescended testicle. A developmental defect in males in which the testicles fail to descend into the scrotum; cryptorchidism.

urethra. The duct through which the urine passes from the bladder and is excreted outside the body.

urethrocele. Protrusion of the female urethra through the vaginal wall; a hernia.

urologist. A physician specializing in the treatment of the diseases and disorders of the urinary tract of both sexes, as well as of the genital tract of the male.

uterine tube. The fallopian tube, which extends from each ovary to the uterus in the female.

uterus. The hollow, pear-shaped organ in females within which the fetus develops; the womb.

vagina. The canal in the female, extending from the vulva to the cervix, that receives the penis during coitus and through which an infant passes at birth.

vaginal barrel. The vaginal cavity in women.

vaginal lubrication. A clear fluid (like sweat) that appears on the walls of the vaginal barrel within a few seconds after the onset of sexual stimulation.

vaginal orgasm. A term of ambiguous meaning, apparently referring to an orgasm that a woman allegedly can achieve vaginally without any clitoral stimulation.

vaginismus. Strong muscular contractions within the vagina, preventing intromission of the penis when intercourse is attempted.

vaginitis. Inflammation of the female vagina, usually as a result of infection.

varicocele. A swelling or enlargement of the veins in the male spermatic cord.

vas deferens (or **ductus deferens**). The sperm duct(s) in males, leading from the epididymis to the seminal vesicles and the urethra.

vasectomy. A surgical procedure for sterilizing the male involving removal of the vas deferens, or a portion of it.

vasocongestion. Congestion of the blood vessels, especially the veins in the genital area.

venereal disease. A contagious disease communicated mainly by sexual intercourse, such as syphilis or gonorrhea.

verumontanum. A small mound in the portion of the male urethra passing through the prostate, which contains the openings of the ejaculatory ducts.

vestibule. The area surrounding and including the opening of the vagina in the female.

virgin birth. See PARTHENOGENESIS.

virginity. The physical condition of a girl or woman before first intercourse.

voyeurism. A sexual variance in which a person achieves sexual gratification by observing others in the nude. *Cf.* SCOPTOPHILIA.

vulva. The external sex organs of the female, including the mons veneris, the labia majora, the labia minora, the clitoris, and the vestibule.

Wassermann test. A blood test used to determine whether or not a person has syphilis.

wet dream. See NOCTURNAL EMISSION.

withdrawal. See COITUS INTERRUPTUS.

womb. The uterus in the female.

X chromosome. A sex-determining chromosome present in all of a female's ova and in one-half of a male's sperm; the fertilization of an ovum by a sperm having an X chromosome will result in the conception of a female (XX).

Y chromosome. A sex-determining chromosome present in one-half of a male's sperm; the fertilization of an ovum by a sperm having a Y chromosome will result in the conception of a male (XY).

zoophilia. A sexual variance that involves an abnormal degree of affection for animals. *Cf.* BESTIALITY.

zygote. The single cell resulting from the union of two germ cells (sperm and egg) at conception; the fertilized egg (ovum).

BIBLIOGRAPHY

This bibliography is arranged alphabetically by author. In cases of more than one work by a single author, the works are listed here in chronological order and are designated by letters—*(a)*, *(b)* etc.—which correspond to the references in the text. In the case of articles for which the author is not named, the sources are listed alphabetically here by title.

Abelson, H., Cohen, R., Heaton, E., and Slider, C. Public attitudes toward and experience with erotic materials. *Technical reports of the Commission on Obscenity and Pornography,* Vol. 6. Washington, D.C.: U.S. Government Printing Office, 1970.

Abominable & detestable crime. *Time,* June 28, 1968, p. 39.

Abortion in two minutes. *Family health,* Oct. 1972, p. 8.

Abortion law shows results. *Behavior today,* Aug. 14, 1972, p. 1.

Abou-David, K. T. Epidemiology of carcinoma of the cervix uteri in Lebanese Christians and Moslems. *Cancer* 20(1967):1706.

ACLU news. (a) *Civil liberties,* Dec. 1971. (b) *Civil liberties,* Apr. 1972.

Adams, C. R. An informal preliminary report on some factors relating to sexual responsiveness of certain college wives. In *Sexual behavior and personality characteristics,* ed. M. F. DeMartino. New York: Grove, 1966.

Alcohol and sex. *Parade,* Mar. 1, 1970, p. 5.

Alexander, M. (a) Is the nose a sex organ? *Sexology,* Nov. 1964, pp. 266–268. (b) The overdue baby. *Sexology,* Jan. 1965, pp. 410–412. (c) Sex and stealing. *Sexology,* Apr. 1965, pp. 636–640.

Allen, C. (a) Perversions, sexual. In *The encyclopedia of sexual behavior,* Vol. II, ed. A. Ellis and A. Abarbanel. New York: Hawthorn Bks, 1961. (b) The prostitute's customers. *Sexology,* Aug. 1966, pp. 10–12. (c) Why men read girlie magazines. *Sexology* Mar. 1966, pp. 549–552. (d) The long history of birth control. *Sexology,* Dec. 1968, pp. 276–278.

Allen, G. H. The damaging effects of prudery. *Sexology,* Feb. 1966, pp. 463–464.

Amelar, R. D. *Infertility in men.* Philadelphia: Davis, 1966.

Anderson, E. E. Gonadal failure in the male. *Med. aspects human sexuality,* July 1970, pp. 114–121.

Anderson, W. J. *How to understand sex.* Minneapolis: T. S. Denison, 1966.

Answers to questions. *Sexual behavior,* Feb. 1972, pp. 63–64.

Anthony, R. *The teenager's guide to sexual awareness.* Tucson: Seymour Press, 1963.

Antibody's role in infertility studies. *J.A.M.A.* 189(1964):32.

APHA Western Branch Conference report. *Pub. health rep.* 77(1962):1000–1004.

Arey, L. B. *Developmental anatomy.* Philadelphia: Saunders, 1937.

Armstrong, E. B. The possibility of sexual happiness in old age. In *Advances in sex research,* ed. H. G. Beigel. New York: Harper, 1963.

Associated Press. (a) Pill, cancer link denied. *Houston Post,* Nov. 15, 1970. (b) Abortion is safer than birth. *Houston Chronicle,* Mar. 24, 1971. (c) Abortions reported under liberal law. *Houston Chronicle,* Mar. 24, 1971. (d) German drug may reduce sex offenses. *Houston Chronicle,* Aug. 28, 1971. (e) Researcher links U.S. birth rate drop to major change in contraception methods. *New York Herald Tribune,* Aug. 3, 1972. (f) New reversible sterilization method is used. *Houston Chronicle,* Aug. 18, 1972.

Athanasiou, R., Shaver, P., and Tavris, C. Sex. *Psychol. today,* July 1970, pp. 39–52.

Auerback, A. (a) Satyriasis and nymphomania. *Med. aspects human sexuality,* Sept. 1968, pp. 39–45. (b) Voyeuristic need. *Med. aspects human sexuality,* Dec. 1970, p. 69.

Austerman, W., and Beach, P. D. True hermaphroditism with a report of two cases. *J. urol.* 85(1961):345–351.

Aycock, L. The medical management of premature ejaculation. *J. urol.* 62(1949): 361–362.

Ball, J. C., and Logan, N. Early sexual behavior of lower-class delinquent girls. In *Studies in human sexual behavior: The American scene,* ed. A. Shiloh. Springfield, Ill.: C. C. Thomas, 1970.

Ball, T. L. *Gynecologic surgery and urology.* St. Louis: Mosby, 1957.

Barclay, A. M. Biopsychological perspectives on sexual behavior. In *Sexuality: A search for perspective,* ed. D. L. Grummon and A. M. Barclay. New York: Van Nostrand-Reinhold, 1971.

Bardin, J. Abortion without fear—or surgery. *Sexology,* Feb. 1971, pp. 26–29.

Barfield, M. A study of relationships between sex information scores and selected personality variables, religious commitment, and biographical variables. Doctoral dissertation, University of Houston, 1971.

Barfield, M., and McCary, J. L. Why sex education? Paper delivered at the annual meeting of the Texas Psychological Association, Dallas, Dec. 1969.

Barr, M. L., and Bertram, E. G. A morphological distinction between neurones of the male and female, and the behavior of the nucleolar satellites during accelerated nucleoprotein synthesis. *Nature* 163(1949):676.

Bartell, G. D. (a) Group sex among the mid-Americans. *J. sex research* 6(1970): 113–130. (b) *Group sex.* New York: Wyden, 1971.

Bass-Hass, R. The lesbian dyad. *J. sex research* 4(1968):108–126.

Becker, H. S. *Outsiders.* Glencoe, Ill.: Free Press, 1963.

Beigel, H. G. (a) *Encyclopedia of sex education.* New York: Daye, 1952. (b) Illegitimacy. In *The encyclopedia of sexual behavior,* Vol. I, ed. A. Ellis and

A. Abarbanel. New York: Hawthorn Bks, 1961.   (c) The danger of orgasm worship. *Sexology,* Nov. 1963, pp. 232–234.   (d) False beliefs about reproduction. *Sexology,* Dec. 1964, pp. 334–336.   (e) Imaginary rape. *Sexology,* May 1965, pp. 675–677.   (f) Outmoded sex laws should be changed. *Sexology,* Dec. 1965, pp. 341–343.   (g) *Advances in sex research.* New York: Harper, 1963.

Bell, R. R. (a) *Marriage and family interaction.* Homewood, Ill.: Dorsey Press, 1971.   (b) Sex as a weapon and changing social roles. *Med. aspects human sexuality,* June 1970, pp. 99–111.   (c) Female sexual satisfaction as related to levels of education. *Sexual behavior,* Nov. 1971, pp. 8–14.   (d) "Swinging," the sexual exchange of marriage partners. *Sexual behavior,* May 1971, pp. 70–79.

Bell, R. R., and Bell, P. L. Sexual satisfaction among married women. *Med. aspects human sexuality,* Dec. 1972, pp. 136–144.

Bell, R. R., and Blumberg, L. Courtship stages and intimacy attitudes. *Family life coordinator,* Mar. 1960, pp. 60–63.

Bell, R. R., and Buerkle, J. V. Mother and daughter attitudes to premarital sexual behavior. *Marriage family living* 23(1961):390–392.

Bell, R. R., and Chaskes, J. B. Premarital sexual experience among coeds, 1958 and 1968. *J. marriage family* 32(1970):81–84.

Belliveau, F., and Richter, L. *Understanding human sexual inadequacy.* New York: Bantam, 1970.

Belt, E. Sterilization: Can it be undone? *Sexology,* Dec. 1961, pp. 313–317.

Benjamin, H. (a) Outline of a method to estimate the biological age with special reference to the role of sexual functions. *Intern. j. sexol.,* Aug. 1949, pp. 34–37.   (b) Prostitution. In *The encyclopedia of sexual behavior,* Vol. II, ed. A. Ellis and A. Abarbanel. New York: Hawthorn Bks, 1961.   (c) *The transsexual phenomenon.* New York: Julian Press, 1966.   (d) Transvestism and transsexualism in the male and female. *J. sex research* 3(1967):107–127.

Benjamin, H., and Masters, R. E. L. *Prostitution and morality.* New York: Julian Press, 1964.

Benson, L. *The family bond.* New York: Random House, 1971.

Berger, A. S., Gagnon, J. H., and Simon, W. Urban working-class adolescents and sexually explicit media. *Technical reports of the Commission on Obscenity and Pornography,* Vol. 9. Washington, D.C.: U.S. Government Printing Office, 1970.

Bergler, E. *Counterfeit-sex: Homosexuality, impotence, frigidity.* 2d ed. New York: Grove, 1961.

Berke, J. E. The man who hated sex. *Sexology,* Aug. 1965, pp. 12–14.

Bieber, I. Advising the homosexual. *Med. aspects human sexuality,* Mar. 1968, pp. 34–39.

Bieber, I., et al. *Homosexuality: A psychoanalytic study of male homosexuals.* New York: Basic Bks, 1962.

Bieber, T. The lesbian patient. *Med. aspects human sexuality,* Jan. 1969, pp. 6–12.

Bing, E., and Rudikoff, E. Divergent ways of parental coping with hermaphrodite children. *Med. aspects human sexuality,* Dec. 1970, pp. 73–88.

Blaine, G. B., Jr. Sex and the adolescent. *New York j. med.* 67(1967):1967–1975.

Blank, H., and Rake, G. *Viral and rickettsial diseases.* Boston: Little, 1955.

Blau, S. Venereal diseases, The. In *The encyclopedia of sexual behavior,* Vol. II, ed. A. Ellis and A. Abarbanel. New York: Hawthorn Bks, 1961.

Blazer, J. A. Married virgins—A study of unconsummated marriages. *J. marriage family* 26(1964):213–214.

Bonaparte, M. *Female sexuality.* New York: Grove, 1953.

Botwinick, J. Drives, expectancies, and emotions. In *Handbook of aging and the individual,* ed. J. E. Birren. Chicago: Univ. of Chicago Press, 1960.

Bouvier, L. F. Catholics and contraception. *J. marriage family* 34(1972):514–522.

Bowers, L. M., Cross, R. R., Jr., and Lloyd, F. A. Sexual function and urologic disease in the elderly male. *J. Amer. geriat. soc.* 11(1963):647–652.

Bowman, H. A. *Marriage for moderns.* 4th ed. New York: McGraw, 1960.

Boyd, H. Eleven-year survival of an advanced abdominal pregnancy. *Obstet. gynecol.* 25(1965):128–129.

Branson, H. K. (a) Triolism: Sex on exhibition. *Sexology,* Jan. 1960, pp. 374–376. (b) Where did you learn about sex? *Sexology,* Apr. 1963, pp. 609–610. (c) How to handle pornography. *Sexology,* Dec. 1966, pp. 308–309.

Brayer, F. T., Chiazze, L., Jr., and Duffy, B. J. Calendar rhythm and menstrual cycle range. *Fertility sterility* 20(1969):279–288.

Breasted, M. *Oh! Sex education!* New York: Praeger, 1970.

Brecher, R., and Brecher, E., eds. *An analysis of human sexual response.* New York: New Amer. Lib., 1966.

Briggs, D. K. Chromosomal anomalies in hermaphroditism and other sexual disorders. In *Advances in sex research,* ed. H. G. Beigel. New York: Harper, 1963.

British Council of Churches. *Sex and morality.* London: S.C.M. Press, 1966.

British "sex revolution," The. *Sexology,* June 1964, pp. 733–734.

Broderick, C. B. (a) Preadolescent sexual behavior. *Med. aspects human sexuality,* Jan. 1968, pp. 20–29. (b) Normal sociosexual development. In *The individual, sex, and society,* ed. C. B. Broderick and J. Bernard. Baltimore: Johns Hopkins Press, 1969.

Brown, D. G. (a) Transvestism and sex-role inversion. In *The encyclopedia of sexual behavior,* Vol. II, ed. A. Ellis and A. Abarbanel. New York: Hawthorn Bks, 1961. (b) Female orgasm and sexual inadequacy. In *An analysis of human sexual response,* ed. R. Brecher and E. Brecher. New York: New Amer. Lib., 1966.

Brown, W. J. The national VD problem. *Med. aspects human sexuality,* Feb. 1972, pp. 152–178.

Brown, W. J., Lucas, J. B., Olansky, S., and Norins, L. C. Roundtable: Venereal disease. *Med. aspects human sexuality,* Apr. 1971, pp. 74–97.

Buckley, T. The transsexual operation. *Esquire,* Apr. 1967, pp. 111–205.

Burgess, E. W., and Wallin, P. *Engagement and marriage.* Philadelphia: Lippincott, 1953.

Buxton, C. L., and Engle, E. T. Time of ovulation. *Amer. j. obstet. gynecol.* 60(1950):3.

Calderone, M. S. (a) *Release from sexual tensions.* New York: Random House, 1960. (b) Abortion, disease of society. *Sexology,* Apr. 1964, pp. 604–606. (c) The Sex Information and Education Council of the U.S. *J. marriage family* 27(1965):533–534. (d) Contraception, teenagers, and sexual responsibility. *J. sex research* 2(1966):37–40. (e) Sex education for young people—and for their parents and teachers. In *An analysis of human sexual response,* ed. R. Brecher and E. Brecher. New York: New Amer. Lib. 1966. *(f)* Love, sex, intimacy, and aging as a life style. In *Sex, love and intimacy—whose life styles?* New York: SIECUS, 1971. *(g)* Sex education for children. *Sexology,* Apr. 1971, p. 71.

Calleja, M. A. Homosexual behavior in older men. *Sexology,* Aug. 1967, pp. 46–48.

Campbell, A. A., and Cooking, J. D. The incidence of illegitimacy in the U.S. *Welfare in review,* May 1967, pp. 1–6.

Caprio, F. S. *(a) The sexually adequate male.* New York: Citadel, 1952. *(b) Female homosexuality: A modern study of lesbianism.* New York: Grove, 1954. *(c) Variations in sexual behavior.* New York: Grove, 1955. *(d) The modern woman's guide to sexual maturity.* New York: Grove, 1959.

Caprio, F. S., Mozes, E. B., and Dengrove, E. *Marriage techniques.* Sex education library, sect. 1. New York: Health Publications, 1960.

Carbary, L. J. The fascinating facts about twins. *Sexology,* Feb. 1966, pp. 478–481.

Carolina Population Center. *Laparoscopy.* Chapel Hill, N. Carolina: Univ. of N. Carolina, n.d.

Carrier, J. M. Participants in urban Mexican male homosexual encounters. *Arch. sexual behavior* 1(1971):279–291.

Cavallin, H. Incestuous fathers: A clinical report. *Amer. psychiat.* 122(1966): 1132–1138.

Cavanagh, J. R. Rhythm of sexual desire in women. *Med. aspects human sexuality,* Feb. 1969, pp. 29–39.

Cawood, C. D. Petting and prostatic engorgement. *Med. aspects human sexuality,* Feb. 1971, pp. 204–218.

Charny, C. W. The husband's sexual performance and the infertile couple. *J.A.M.A.* 185(1963):43 of no. 2.

Chase, L. Irrelevant worries. *Women's med. news service,* July 1969.

Chernick, A. B., and Chernick, B. A. Role of ignorance in sexual dysfunction. *Med. aspects human sexuality,* Feb. 1970, pp. 114–121.

Chesser, E. *Love without fear.* New York: Signet, 1949.

Chiazze, L., Jr., Brayer, F. T., Macisco, J. J., Jr., Parker, M. P., and Duffy, B. J. The length and variability of the human menstrual cycle. *J.A.M.A.* 203(1968): 377–380.

Chilman, C. S. Fertility and poverty in the U.S.: Some implications for family-planning programs, evaluation, and research. *J. marriage family* 30(1968): 207–227.

Christensen, H. T., and Carpenter, G. R. Timing patterns in the development of sexual intimacy: An attitudinal report on three modern Western societies. *Marriage family living* 24(1962):30–35.

Christensen, H. T., and Gregg, C. F. Changing sex norms in America and Scandinavia. *J. marriage family* 32(1970):616–627.

Christensen, H. T., and Johnson, K. P. *Marriage and the family.* New York: Ronald, 1971.

Christensen, H. T., and Meissner, H. H. Studies in child spacing: III—Premarital pregnancy as a factor in divorce. *Amer. sociol. rev.* 18(1953):641–644.

Christopherson, W. M., and Parker, J. E. Relation of cervical cancer to early marriage and childbearing. *N. Engl. j. med.* 273(1965):235–239.

Chromosomes & crime, Of. *Time,* May 3, 1968, p. 41.

Churchill, W. Do drugs increase sex drive? *Sexology,* Oct. 1968, pp. 164–167.

Ciociola, G. Eleven kinds of virility. *Sexology,* Dec. 1962, pp. 299–301.

Clark, L. (a) *The enjoyment of love in marriage.* New York: Crest Bks, 1949. (b) *Sex and you.* Indianapolis: Bobbs-Merrill, 1949. (c) Sterility in the female. *Sexology,* Sept. 1959, pp. 308–314. (d) Fluid tumors of the scrotum. *Sexology,* Sept. 1962, pp. 118–121. (e) Your personal questions answered. *Sexology,* Oct. 1963, p. 186. (f) Your personal questions answered. *Sexology,* Nov. 1963, pp. 251–260. (g) Your personal questions answered. *Sexology,* Nov. 1964, p. 255. (h) Painful intercourse. *Sexology,* Oct. 1965, pp. 194–196. (i) Your personal questions answered. *Sexology,* Apr. 1965, p. 614. (j) Your personal questions answered. *Sexology,* July 1965, p. 837. (k) How long to make a baby? *Sexology,* Feb. 1967, pp. 478–481. (l) Your personal questions answered. *Sexology,* Feb. 1967, p. 469. (m) Your personal questions answered. *Sexology,* Nov. 1969, p. 36. (n) Is there a difference between a clitoral and a vaginal orgasm? *J. sex research* 6(1970):25–28. (o) What gives women sex pleasure. *Sexology,* Jan. 1970, pp. 46–49. (p) Your personal questions answered. *Sexology,* Mar. 1970, pp. 43–44. (q) *Illustrated sex atlas.* New York: Health Publications, 1964.

Coleman, J. C. *Abnormal psychology and modern life.* 4th ed. Chicago: Scott, Foresman, 1972.

Comfort, A. *The joy of sex.* New York: Crown, 1972.

Commission on Obscenity and Pornography. (a) *The report of the Commission on Obscenity and Pornography.* New York: Bantam, 1970. (b) Pornography: Patterns of exposure and patrons. In *The social dimension of human sexuality,* ed. R. R. Bell and M. Gordon. Boston: Little, 1972.

Coombs, R. H. (a) Acquiring sex attitudes and information in our society. In *Human sexuality in medical education and practice,* ed. C. E. Vincent. Springfield, Ill.: C. C. Thomas, 1968. (b) Sex education in American medical colleges. In *Human sexuality in medical education and practice,* ed. C. E. Vincent. Springfield, Ill.: C. C. Thomas, 1968.

Corsini, R. J. Pruritus ani: An incident in psychotherapy. *Voices* 1, no. 1 (1965): 103–104.

Cory, D. W. Homosexuality. In *The encyclopedia of sexual behavior,* Vol. I, ed. A. Ellis and A. Abarbanel. New York: Hawthorn Bks, 1961.

Cory, D. W., and LeRoy, J. P. A radically new sex law. *Sexology,* Jan. 1964, pp. 374–376.

Cox, B. J. *Sexual techniques during prescribed continence.* New York: Medical Press, 1968.

Crawley, L. Q., Malfetti, J. L., Stewart, E. I., and Vas Dias, N. *Reproduction, sex, and preparation for marriage.* Englewood Cliffs, N. J.: Prentice-Hall, 1964.

Cuber, J. F. The mistress in American society. *Med. aspects human sexuality,* Sept. 1969, pp. 81–91.

Cuber, J. F., with Hanoff, P. B. *The significant Americans.* New York: Appleton, 1966.

Current research. *Sexology,* Sept. 1961, p. 111.

Curtis, E. M. Oral-contraceptive feminization of a normal male infant. *Obstet. gynecol.* 23(1964):295–296.

Cutter, F. The crime of incest. *Sexology,* June 1963, pp. 744–746.

Czinner, R. The many kinds of rape. *Sexology,* Jan. 1970, pp. 12–15.

Dager, E. Z., and Harper, G. Family life education in Indiana public schools: A preliminary report. *Marriage family living* 21(1959):385–388.

Dager, E. Z., et al. Family life education in public high schools of Indiana: A survey report on course content. *Family life coordinator,* April 1966, pp. 43–50.

Dalton, K. Menstruation and examinations. *Lancet,* Dec. 28, 1968, pp. 1386–1388.

Dalven, J. Bizarre menstrual bleeding. *Sexology,* May 1964, pp. 676–678.

Daly, M. J. Sexual attitudes in menopausal and postmenopausal women. *Med. aspects human sexuality,* May 1968, pp. 48–53.

Dangerous sex offender, The. A report of the panel of medical advisors on health and welfare to the joint state [Pennsylvania] *government commission.* Appendix to the legislative journal, May 1963, pp. 672–683.

Davis, K. Sexual behavior. In *Contemporary social problems,* ed. R. Merton and R. Nisbet. New York: Harcourt, 1966.

Davis, K. B. *Factors in the sex life of twenty-two hundred women.* New York: Harper, 1929.

Davis, K. E. Sex on campus: Is there a revolution? *Med. aspects human sexuality,* Jan. 1971, pp. 128–142.

Davis, M. *The sexual responsibility of woman.* New York: Dial Press, 1956.

Dearborn, L. W. Masturbation. In *Sexual behavior and personality characteristics,* ed. M. F. DeMartino. New York: Grove, 1966.

DeBurger, J. E. Marital problems, help-seeking, and emotional orientation as revealed in help-request letters. *J. marriage family* 29(1967):712–721.

Dedman, J. The relationship between religious attitude and attitude toward premarital sex relations. *Marriage family living* 21(1959):171–176.

DeMartino, M. F. (a) Dominance-feeling, security-insecurity, and sexuality in women. In *Sexual behavior and personality characteristics,* ed. M. F. DeMartino. New York: Grove, 1966. (b) How women want men to make love. *Sexology,* Oct. 1970, pp. 4–7. (c) *Sexual behavior and personality characteristics.* New York: Grove, 1966.

Denfield, D., and Gordon, M. The sociology of mate swapping: Or the family that swings together clings together. *J. sex research* 6(1970):85–100.

Dengrove, E. Myth of the captive penis. *Sexology,* Feb. 1965, pp. 447–449.

Deschin, C. S. (a) Teen-agers and venereal disease. *Pub. health news* 43(1962): 274. (b) Teen-agers and venereal disease: A sociological study of 600 teen-agers in NYC social hygiene clinics. *Amer. j. nurs.* 63(1963):63–67.

Desperate dilemma of abortion, The. *Time,* Oct. 13, 1967, pp. 32–33.

Dickes, R. Psychodynamics of fetishism. *Med. aspects human sexuality,* Jan. 1970, pp. 39–52.

Dickinson, R. L. *Atlas of human sex anatomy.* Baltimore: Williams & Wilkins, 1949

Dorland's illustrated medical dictionary. 23rd ed. Philadelphia: Saunders, 1957.

Duffy, J. (a) Masturbation and clitoridectomy. *J.A.M.A.* 19(1963):246–248. (b) Masturbation and clitoris amputation. *Sexology,* May 1964, pp. 668–671.

Duggan, H. E. Effect of x-ray therapy on patients with Peyronie's disease. *J. urol.* 91(1964):572–573.

Eagle, H. The spirochetes. In *Bacterial and mycotic infections of man,* ed. R. J. Dubos. Philadelphia: Lippincott, 1952.

Eastman, N. J., and Hellman, L. M. *Williams obstetrics.* 12th ed. New York: Appleton, 1961.

Edey, H. Commonly asked questions about vasectomy. *Sexual behavior,* Jan. 1973, pp. 14–16.

Ehrmann, W. (a) *Premarital dating behavior.* New York: Holt, 1959.   (b) Premarital sexual intercourse. In *The encyclopedia of sexual behavior,* Vol. II, ed. A. Ellis and A. Abarbanel. New York: Hawthorn Bks, 1961.

Eichenlaub, J. E. (a) *The marriage art.* New York: Dell, 1961.   (b) Abortions, fact and fancy. *Sexology,* Oct. 1963, pp. 155–157.

Elias, J. E. Exposure to erotic materials in adolescence. *Technical reports of the Commission on Obscenity and Pornography,* Vol. 9. Washington, D.C.: U.S. Government Printing Office, 1970.

Ellis, A. (a) *Sex without guilt.* New York: Lyle Stuart, 1958.   (b) *The art and science of love.* New York: Lyle Stuart, 1960.   (c) *The folklore of sex.* New York: Grove, 1961.   (d) Frigidity. In *The encyclopedia of sexual behavior,* Vol. I, ed. A. Ellis and A. Abarbanel. New York: Hawthorn Bks, 1961.   (e) Sex offenders, The psychology of. In *The encyclopedia of sexual behavior,* Vol. II, ed. A. Ellis and A. Abarbanel. New York: Hawthorn Bks, 1961.   (f) *The American sexual tragedy.* 2d ed., rev. New York: Lyle Stuart, 1962.   (g) Constitutional factors in homosexuality: A re-examination of the evidence. In *Advances in sex research,* ed. H. G. Beigel. New York: Harper, 1963.   (h) *If this be sexual heresy.* New York: Lyle Stuart, 1963.   (i) *The intelligent woman's guide to man-hunting.* New York: Lyle Stuart, 1963.   (j) *Sex and the single man.* New York: Lyle Stuart, 1963.   (k) *The theory and practice of rational-emotive psychotherapy.* New York: Lyle Stuart, 1964.   (l) *Suppressed.* Chicago: New Classics House, 1965.   (m) Masturbation. In *Sexual behavior and personality characteristics,* ed. M. F. DeMartino. New York: Grove, 1966.   (n) The sex revolution. *Sexology,* May 1966, pp. 660–664.   (o) *The civilized couple's guide to extramarital adventure.* New York: Wyden, 1972.   (p) *The sensuous person: Critique and corrections.* Secaucus, N. J.: Lyle Stuart, 1972.

Ellis, A., and Abarbanel, A., eds. (a) *The encyclopedia of sexual behavior,* Vol. I. New York: Hawthorn Bks, 1961.   (b) *The encyclopedia of sexual behavior,* Vol. II. New York: Hawthorn Bks, 1961.

Ellis, A., and Brancale, R. *The psychology of sex offenders.* Springfield, Ill.: C. C. Thomas, 1956.

Ellis, A., and Sagarin, E. *Nymphomania.* New York: Gilbert Press, 1964.

English, O. S. (a) Sexual adjustment in marriage. In *Modern marriage and family living,* ed. M. Fishbein and R. Kennedy. New York: Oxford Univ. Press, 1957.   (b) Positive values of the affair. In *The new sexuality,* ed. H. A. Otto. Palo Alto: Science & Behavior, 1971.

Epidemic gonorrhea (editorial). *Southern med. bull.* 59, no. 2 (1971):4–5.

Erikson, K. T. *Wayward puritans.* New York: Wiley, 1966.

Everett, H. C. Competition in bed. *Med. aspects human sexuality,* Apr. 1971, pp. 4–5.

Falk, G. J. The truth about sex offenders. *Sexology,* Nov. 1965, pp. 271–273.

Farnsworth, D. L. Sexual morality and the dilemma of the colleges. *Med. aspects human sexuality,* Oct. 1970, pp. 64–94.

Feldman, H. Sexual adjustment in early marriage. Address to the annual Groves conference on marriage and the family, Kansas City, Mo., Apr. 1966.

Festinger, T. B. Unwed mothers and their decisions to keep or surrender children. *Child welfare*, May 1971, pp. 253–263.

Finch, B. E., and Green, H. *Contraception through the ages*. Springfield, Ill.: C. C. Thomas, 1963.

Fink, P. J. Dealing with sexual pressures of the unmarried. *Med. aspects human sexuality*, Mar. 1970, pp. 42–53.

Finkle, A. L. (a) The relationship of sexual habits to benign prostatic hypertrophy. *Med. aspects human sexuality*, Oct. 1967, pp. 24–25. (b) Sex after prostatectomy. *Med. aspects human sexuality*, Mar. 1968, pp. 40–41.

Finkle, A. L., Moyers, T. G., Tobenkin, M. I., and Karg, S. J. Sexual potency in aging males: I. Frequency of coitus among clinic patients. *J.A.M.A.* 170(1959): 1391–1393.

Fischer, I. C. Reproduction, Human. In *The encyclopedia of sexual behavior*, Vol. II, ed. A. Ellis and A. Abarbanel. New York: Hawthorn Bks, 1961.

Fischer, S. *The female orgasm: Psychology, physiology, fantasy*. New York: Basic Bks, 1973.

Fisher, C., Gross, J., and Zuch, J. Cycle of penile erection synchronous with dreaming (REM) sleep. *Arch. gen. psychiat.* 12(1965):29–45.

Fiumara, N. J. Gonococcal pharyngitis. *Med. aspects human sexuality*, May 1971, pp. 194–209.

Flanagan, G. L. *Nine months of life*. New York: Simon & Schuster, 1962.

Fleck, S. Some psychiatric aspects of abortion. *J. nervous mental disease* 151 (1970):42–50.

Fletcher, A., and Landes, R. R. Treatment of gonorrhea today. *Med. aspects human sexuality*, Aug. 1970, pp. 50–61.

Ford, C. S., and Beach, F. A. (a) *Patterns of sexual behavior*. New York: Harper, 1951. (b) Self-stimulation. In *Sexual behavior and personality characteristics*, ed. M. F. DeMartino. New York: Grove, 1966.

Frank, L. K. *The conduct of sex*. New York: Grove, 1963.

Frankl, V. E. *Man's search for meaning*. New York: Beacon Press, 1963.

Franklin, R. R., Malinak, L. R., and Dukes, C. D. The infertile man. *Med. aspects human sexuality*, Nov. 1967, pp. 49–57.

Frede, M. C. Sexual attitudes and behavior of college students at a public university in the Southwest. Doctoral dissertation, University of Houston, 1970.

Freedman, A. M. Drugs and sexual behavior. *Med. aspects human sexuality*, Nov. 1967, pp. 25–31.

Freedman, R., Whelpton, P. K., and Campbell, A. A. *Family planning, sterility, and population growth*. New York: McGraw, 1959.

Freeman, J. T. Sexual capacities in the aging male. *Geriatrics* 16(1961):37–43.

Friedfeld, L. Geriatrics, medicine, and rehabilitation. *J.A.M.A.* 175(1961):595–598.

From the editor's scrapbook. (a) *Sexology*, Aug. 1963, p. 34. (b) *Sexology*, Jan. 1964, pp. 408–410. (c) *Sexology*, Mar. 1965, pp. 536–538. (d) *Sexology*, Sept. 1965, pp. 118–120. (e) *Sexology*, Jan. 1966, p. 392. (f) *Sexology*, June 1966, p. 744. (g) *Sexology*, Apr. 1968, p. 588. (h) *Sexology*, June 1968, pp. 753–754. (i) *Sexology*, May 1970, pp. 52–53. (j) *Sexology*, July 1971, p. 60.

Fromm, E. *Sigmund Freud's mission.* New York: Grove, 1963.

Fromme, A. *Sex and marriage.* New York: Barnes & Noble, 1955.

Gadpaille, W. J. (a) Father's role in sex education of his son. *Sexual behavior,* Apr. 1971, pp. 3–10. (b) Research into the physiology of maleness and femaleness. *Arch. gen. psychiat.* 26(1972):193–206.

Gagnon, J. H. (a) Sexuality and sexual learning in the child. *Psychiatry* 28(1965): 212–228. (b) Talk about sex, sexual behavior, and sex research. Address to the annual Groves conference on marriage and the family, Kansas City, Mo., Apr. 1966.

Gagnon, J. H., and Simon, W. Prospects for change in American sexual patterns. *Med. aspects human sexuality,* Jan. 1970, pp. 100–117.

Galton, L. VD: Out of control? *Sexual behavior,* Jan. 1972, pp. 17–24.

Gardner, L. I., and Neu, R. L. Evidence linking an extra Y chromosome to socio-pathic behavior. *Arch. gen. psychiat.* 26(1972):220–222.

Garrett, R. A. Treat undescended testicle by age six. *J.A.M.A.* 188(1964):34.

Gebhard, P. H. (a) Factors in marital orgasm. *J. soc. issues* 22, no. 2(1966):88–95. (b) Misconceptions about female prostitutes. *Med. aspects human sexuality,* Mar. 1969, pp. 24–30.

Gebhard, P. H., Gagnon, J. H., Pomeroy, W. B., and Christenson, C. V. (a) *Sex offenders.* New York: Harper; Hoeber, 1965.

Gebhard, P. H., Pomeroy, W. B., Martin, C. E., and Christenson, C. V. (b) *Pregnancy, birth, and abortion.* New York: Harper, 1958.

Geller, J. Progesterone drug may reduce benign prostatic hypertrophy *J.A.M.A.* 189(1964):32.

Gold, L. N. Psychiatric profile of a firesetter. *J. sci.* 7(1962):404.

Golde, P., and Kogan, N. A sentence completion procedure for assessing attitudes toward old people. *J. gerontol.,* 14(1959):355–363.

Goldfarb, A. F., Daly, M. J., Lieberman, D., and Reed, D. M. Sex and the meno-pause. *Med. aspects human sexuality,* Nov. 1970, pp. 64–89.

Gonads, Disorders of. *Encyclopedia Britannica,* Vol. 10. Chicago: Encyclopedia Britannica, 1963.

Goodall, K. (a) Tie line. *Psychol. today,* Mar. 1972, p. 25. (b) Tie line. *Psychol. today,* Dec. 1972, pp. 10–13.

Goss, D. A. Gonorrhea: Diagnosis, complications and treatment in the female. *Southern med. bull.* 59, no. 2 (1971):35–37.

Green, D. S., and Green, B. Double sex. *Sexology,* Mar. 1965, pp. 561–563.

Green, R. Change-of-sex. *Med. aspects human sexuality,* Oct. 1969, pp. 96–113.

Green, R., and Money, J., eds. *Transsexualism and sex reassignment.* Baltimore: Johns Hopkins Press, 1969.

Greenbank, R. Are medical students learning psychiatry? *Penn. med. j.* 64(1961): 989–992.

Greenblat, B. R. *A doctor's marital guide for patients.* Chicago: Budlong Press, 1962.

Greene, B. L. How valid is sex attraction in selecting a mate? *Med. aspects human sexuality,* Jan. 1970, p. 23.

Greene, G. *Sex and the college girl.* New York: Dial Press, 1964.

Greenhill, J. P. What is the psychological significance of various coital positions? *Med. aspects human sexuality,* Feb. 1971, pp. 8–16.

Growing older—later. *J.A.M.A.* 191(1965):143.

Guttmacher, A. F. (a) The attitudes of 3,381 physicians towards contraception and the contraceptives they prescribe. *Human biol.* 12(1947):1–12. (b) Should our abortion laws be changed? *Sexology,* Feb. 1963, pp. 436–439. (c) How can we best combat illegitimacy? *Med. aspects human sexuality,* Mar. 1969, pp. 48–61. (d) Who owns fertility: the church, the state, or the individual? In *Sexuality: A search for perspective,* ed. D. L. Grummon and A. M. Barclay. New York: Van Nostrand-Reinhold, 1971.

Hall, R. E. Therapeutic abortion, sterilization, and contraception. *Amer. j. obstet. gynecol.* 91(1965):518–532.

Hamilton, E. Emotions and sexuality in the woman. In *The new sexuality,* ed. H. A. Otto. Palo Alto: Science & Behavior, 1971.

Hamilton, G. V. *Research in marriage.* New York: Boni, 1929.

Hanes, M. V. Ectopic pregnancy following total hysterectomy: Report of a case. *Obstet. gynecol.* 23(1964):882–884.

Hardin, G. *Birth control.* New York: Pegasus, 1970.

Haring, B. Conjugal love. Lecture presented at the conference on theology and sexuality, Yale University, New Haven, May 1967.

Harlow, H. F., and Harlow, M. K. (a) The effect of rearing conditions on behavior. In *Sex research: New developments,* ed. J. Money. New York: Holt, 1965. (b) Social deprivation in monkeys. In *Human development,* ed. M. L. Haimowitz and N. R. Haimowitz. New York: Crowell, 1966.

Harper, R. A. (a) Extramarital sex relations. In *The encyclopedia of sexual behavior,* Vol. I, ed. A. Ellis and A. Abarbanel. New York: Hawthorn Bks, 1961. (b) Overcoming impotence. *Sexology,* May 1965, pp. 680–682.

Hartman, W. E., Fithian, M. A., and Johnson, D. Sex in nudist camps. *Sexology,* Apr. 1969, pp. 580–586.

Has a real aphrodisiac been found? *Sexology,* June 1970, pp. 7–9.

Henry, L. Some data on natural fertility. *Eugenics quart.* 8(1961): 81–91.

Herrick, E. H. (a) Telegony. *Sexology,* Dec. 1959, pp. 316–319. (b) Is virgin birth possible? *Sexology,* Apr. 1962, pp. 590–594.

Higgins, J. W., and Katzman, M. B. Determinants in the judgment of obscenity. *Amer. j. psychiat.* 125(1969):1733–1738.

Himes, N. E. *Medical history of contraception.* New York: Gamut Press, 1963.

Hirsch, E. W. *How to improve your sexual relations.* Chicago: Zeco, 1951.

Hoffman, M. (a) Homosexual. *Psychol. today,* July 1969, pp. 43–45, 70–71. (b) The male prostitute. *Sexual behavior,* Aug. 1972, pp. 16–21.

Hollender, M. H. Women's wish to be held: Sexual and nonsexual aspects. *Med. aspects human sexuality,* Oct. 1971, pp. 12–26.

Hollingshead, A. B. *Elmtown's youth.* New York: Wiley, 1949.

Holmes, K. K., Johnson, D. W., and Trostle, H. J. An estimate of the risk of men acquiring gonorrhea by sexual contact with infected females. *Amer. j. epidemiol.* 37(1970):170–174.

Homosexual in America, The. *Time,* Jan. 21, 1966, p. 40–41.

Homosexuality: Coming to terms. *Time,* Oct. 24, 1969, p. 82.

Honigmann, J. J. A cultural theory of obscenity. In *Sexual behavior and personality characteristics,* ed. M. F. DeMartino. New York: Grove, 1963.

Hooker, E. (a) The adjustment of the male overt homosexual. *J. proj. tech.* 21 (1957):18–31.   (b) An empirical study of some relations between sexual patterns and gender identity in male homosexuals. In *Sex research: New developments,* ed. J. Money. New York: Holt, 1965.

Hospital Tribune, Oct. 4, 1971, p. 1.

Hotchkiss, R. S. How will an operation on the prostate affect a man's sex life? *Sexual behavior,* Aug. 1971, p. 14.

Houdek, P. K. Potentials in peanuts. *Sex news,* Sept. 1971, p. 1.

Houston Chronicle, (a) Oct. 16, 1968.   (b) Feb. 11, 1972.   (c) Mar. 3, 1972.   (d) Aug. 25, 1972.

Houston Post, July 25, 1971.

Husband's pregnancy symptoms. *Sexology,* Feb. 1965, p. 457.

Hutton, L. *The single woman.* London: Barrie & Rockliff, 1960.

Illegitimacy. *Encyclopaedia Britannica,* Vol. 12. Chicago: Encyclopaedia Britannica, 1963.

In the news. (a) *Med. aspects human sexuality,* Dec. 1968, p. 55.   (b) *Med. aspects human sexuality,* May 1970, p. 114.   (c) *Med. aspects human sexuality,* July 1970, p. 130.   (d) *Med. aspects human sexuality,* Sept. 1971, p. 147.

Indianapolis Star, Nov. 17, 1968.

Intelligence report. *Parade,* July 25, 1971.

"J." *The sensuous woman.* New York: Lyle Stuart, 1969.

James, W. H. The incidence of spontaneous abortion. *Population studies* 24(1970): 245.

Javert, C. T. Role of the patient's activities in the occurrence of spontaneous abortion. *Fertility sterility* 11(1960):550–558.

Johnson, V. E., and Masters, W. H. A product of dual import: Intravaginal infection control and conception control. *Pac. med. surg.* 73(1965):267–271.

Johnson, W. R. *Human sex and sex education.* Philadelphia: Lea, 1963.

Jones, H. E. Adolescence in our society. In *The adolescent,* ed. J. M. Seidman. New York: Holt, 1960.

Kaats, G. R., and Davis, K. E. The dynamics of sexual behavior of college students. *J. marriage family* 32(1970):390–399.

Kahn, E. REM sleep and sexuality in the aged. Paper delivered before Boston Society for Gerontologic Psychiatry, Boston, Sept. 1967.

Kanin, E. J. Premarital sex adjustments, social class, and associated behaviors. *Marriage family living* 22(1960):258–262.

Kanin, E. J., and Howard, D. H. Postmarital consequences of premarital sex adjustment. *Amer. sociol. rev.* 22(1957):197–204.

Kaplan, H. S., and Sager, C. J. Sexual patterns a different ages. *Med. aspects human sexuality,* June 1971, pp. 10–23.

Kardiner, A. *Sex and morality.* Indianapolis: Bobbs-Merrill, 1954.

Karlen, A. *Sexuality and homosexuality.* New York: Norton, 1971.

Karpman, B. *The sexual offender and his offenses.* New York: Julian Press, 1954.

Katzman, M. Obscenity and pornography. *Med. aspects human sexuality,* July 1969, pp. 77–83.

Kaye, H. E. Lesbian relationships. *Sexual behavior,* Apr. 1971, pp. 80–87.

Kegel, A. H. Letter to the editor. *J.A.M.A.* 153(1953):1303–1304.

Kelly, G. L. (a) *Sex manual.* Augusta, Ga.: Southern Medical Supply Co., 1959 (b) Impotence. In *The encyclopedia of sexual behavior,* Vol. I, ed. A. Ellis and A. Abarbanel. New York: Hawthorn Bks, 1961.

Kenkel, W. F. *The family in perspective.* 2d ed. New York: Appleton, 1966.

Ketterer, W. A. Homosexuality and venereal disease. *Med. aspects human sexuality,* Mar. 1971, pp. 114–129.

Keys, A. Experimental induction of psychoneuroses by starvation. In *Biology of mental health and disease: 27th annual conference of the Milbank Memorial Fund.* New York: Harper, 1952.

Kiev, A., and Hackett, E. The chemotherapy of impotency and frigidity. *J. sex research* 4(1968):220–224.

Kinsey, A. C., Pomeroy, W. B., and Martin, C. E. (a) *Sexual behavior in the human male.* Philadelphia: Saunders, 1948. (b) Concepts of normality and abnormality in sexual behavior. In *Psychosexual development in health and disease,* ed. P. H. Hoch and J. Zubin. New York: Grune, 1949. (c) and Gebhard, P. H. *Sexual behavior in the human female.* Philadelphia: Saunders, 1953.

Kirkendall, L. A. (a) *Premarital intercourse and interpersonal relations.* New York: Julian Press, 1961. (b) Sex drive. In *The encyclopedia of sexual behavior,* Vol. II, ed. A. Ellis and A. Abarbanel. New York: Hawthorn Bks, 1961. (c) Obscenity and the U.S. Supreme Court. *Sexology,* Nov. 1965, pp. 242–245. (d) Using a student panel in teacher education on sex standards. *J. marriage family* 28(1966):521–523. (e) Sex education. In *Human sexuality in medical education and practice,* ed. C. E. Vincent. Springfield, Ill.: C. C. Thomas, 1968.

Kirkendall, L. A., and Libby, R. W. (a) Interpersonal relationships: Crux of the sexual renaissance. *J. soc. issues* 22, no. 2(1966):45–59. (b) Sex and interpersonal relationships. In *The individual, sex, and society,* ed. C. B. Broderick and J. Bernard. Baltimore: Johns Hopkins Press, 1969.

Kirkpatrick, C. *The family: As process and institution.* 2d ed. New York: Ronald, 1963.

Kirsch, F. M. *Sex education and training in chastity.* New York: Benziger, 1930.

Kiser, C. V., Grabill, W. H., and Campbell, A. A. *Trends and variations in fertility in the United States.* Cambridge: Harvard Univ. Press, 1968.

Kleegman, S. J. (a) Frigidity. *Quart. rev. surg. obstet. gynecol.* 16(1959):243–248. (b) Female sex problems. *Sexology,* Nov. 1964, pp. 226–229.

Kleegman, S., Amelar, R. D., Sherman, J. K., Hirschhorn, K., and Pilpel, H. Round-table: Artificial donor insemination. *Med. aspects human sexuality,* May 1970, pp. 84–111.

Kolodny, R. C., Masters, W. H., Hendryx, B. S., and Toro, G. Plasma testosterone and semen analysis in male homosexuals. *N. Engl. j. med.* 285(1971):1170–1174.

Kopp, S. B. The character structure of sex offenders. *Amer. j. psychother.* 16 (1962):64–70.

Kronhausen, P., and Kronhausen, E. *The sexually responsive woman.* New York: Ballantine, 1965.

Kutner, S. J. Sex guilt and the sexual behavior sequence. *J. sex research* 7 (1971):107–115.

Lachenbruch, P. A. Frequency and timing of intercourse: Its relation to the probability of conception. *Population studies* 21(1967):23–31.

Landis, J. T., and Landis, M. G. *Building a successful marriage.* 4th ed. Englewood Cliffs, N. J.: Prentice-Hall, 1963.

Landis, P. H. *Making the most of marriage.* 3d ed. New York: Appleton, 1965.

Lash, H. Silicone implant for impotency. *J. urol.* 100(1968):709–710.

Lear, H. Little ejaculatory sensation. *Med. aspects human sexuality,* Aug. 1972, p. 106.

Lederer, W. J., and Jackson, D. D. *The mirages of marriage.* New York: Norton, 1968.

Legal castration. *Newsweek,* Feb. 23, 1970, pp. 87–88.

Legman, G. An encyclopaedic outline of oral technique in genital excitation. Quoted by "M," *The sensuous man.* New York: Lyle Stuart, 1971, p. 111.

Lehfeldt, H. (a) Artificial insemination. In *The encyclopedia of sexual behavior,* Vol. I, ed. A. Ellis and A. Abarbanel. New York: Hawthorn Bks, 1961. (b) Contraception. In *The encyclopedia of sexual behavior,* Vol. I, ed. A. Ellis and A. Abarbanel. New York: Hawthorn Bks, 1961.

Lehrman, N. *Masters and Johnson explained.* Chicago: Playboy Press, 1970.

Leiman, A. H., and Epstein, S. Thematic sexual responses as related to sexual drive and guilt. *J. abnorm. soc. psychol.* 63(1961):169–175.

Lenz, W., Pfeiffer, R. A., and Tünte, W. Supernumerary chromosomes (trisomies) and maternal age. *Germ. med. monthly* 12(1967):27–30.

Levene, H. I., and Rigney, F. J. Law, preventive psychiatry, and therapeutic abortion. *J. nervous mental disease* 151(1970):51–59.

Levie, L. H. Phimosis. *J. sex research* 1(1965):189–200.

Levine, M. I. Sex education in the public elementary and high school curriculum. In *Human sexual development,* ed. D. L. Taylor. Philadelphia: Davis, 1970.

Levinger, G. Husbands' and wives' estimates of coital frequency. *Med. aspects human sexuality,* Sept. 1970, pp. 42–57.

Levitt, E. E., and Brady, J. P. Sexual preferences in young adult males and some correlates. *J. clin. psychol.* 21(1965):347–354.

Lewis, G. M. *Practical dermatology for medical students and general practitioners.* Philadelphia: Saunders, 1955.

LeWitter, M., and Abarbanel, A. Aging and sex. In *The encyclopedia of sexual behavior,* Vol. I, ed. A. Ellis and A. Abarbanel. New York: Hawthorn Bks, 1961.

Licklider, S. Jewish penile carcinoma. *J. urol.* 86(1961):98.

Lief, H. I. Sex education of medical students and doctors. In *Human sexuality in medical education and practice,* ed. C. E. Vincent. Springfield, Ill.: C. C. Thomas, 1968.

Lief, H. I., Israel, S. L., Garcia, C. R., and Charny, C. W. Roundtable: Sex after 50. *Med. aspects human sexuality,* Jan. 1968, pp. 41–47.

Lion, E. G., et al. *An experiment in the psychiatric treatment of promiscuous girls.* San Francisco: Dept. of Public Health, 1945.

Lipton, M. A. The "power" of pornography. *Psychiatry 1971.* New York: Medical World News, 1971.

Lisk, R. D. Mechanisms regulating sexual activity in mammals. *J. sex research* 6(1970):220–228.

Lloyd, C. W. *Human reproduction and sexual behavior.* Philadelphia: Lea, 1964.

Locke, H. J. *Predicting adjustment in marriage.* New York: Holt, 1951.

Louria, D. B. Sexual use of amyl nitrite. *Med. aspects human sexuality,* Jan. 1970, p. 89.

Lowry, T. P. First coitus. *Med. aspects human sexuality,* May 1969, pp. 91–97.

Luttge, W. G. The role of gonadal hormones in the sexual behavior of the rhesus monkey and human: A literature survey. *Arch. sexual behavior* 1(1971):61–88.

"M." *The sensuous man.* New York: Lyle Stuart, 1971.

MacDougald, D., Jr. Aphrodisiacs and anaphrodisiacs. In *The encyclopedia of sexual behavior,* Vol. I, ed. A. Ellis and A. Abarbanel. New York: Hawthorn Bks, 1961.

Mace, D. R. *(a)* The danger of sex innocence. *Sexology,* Nov. 1970, pp. 50–52. *(b)* The physician and marital sexual problems. *Med. aspects human sexuality,* Feb. 1971, pp. 50–62. *(c)* Sex and marital enrichment. In *The new sexuality,* ed. H. A. Otto. Palo Alto: Science & Behavior, 1971.

MacLean, P. D. New findings relevant to the evolution of psychosexual functions of the brain. In *Sex research: New developments,* ed. J. Money. New York: Holt, 1965.

Malcolm, A. H. Sex goes to college. *Today's health,* Apr. 1971, pp. 26–29.

Mann, T. *The biochemistry of semen.* London: Methuen, 1954.

Marmor, J. *(a)* "Normal" and "deviant" sexual behavior. *J.A.M.A.* 217(1971): 165–170. *(b) Sexual inversion.* New York: Basic Bks, 1965.

Marmor, J., Finkle, A. L., Lazarus, A. A., Schumacher, S., Auerbach, A., Money, J., and Morris, N. Viewpoints: Why are some orgasms better than others? *Med. aspects human sexuality,* Mar. 1971, pp. 12–23.

Martinson, F. M. *Marriage and the American ideal.* New York: Dodd, Mead, 1960.

Maslow, A. H. *(a) Motivation and personality.* New York: Harper, 1954. *(b)* Critique and discussion. In *Sex research: New developments,* ed. J. Money. New York: Holt, 1965. *(c)* Love in self-actualizing people. In *Sexual behavior and personality characteristics,* ed. M. F. DeMartino. New York: Grove, 1966. *(d)* Self-esteem (dominance-feeling) and sexuality in women. In *Sexual behavior and personality characteristics,* ed. M. F. DeMartino. New York: Grove, 1966.

Masters, R. E. L. *Patterns of incest.* New York: Julian Press, 1963.

Masters, W. H. *(a)* The sexual response cycle of the human female: II. Vaginal lubrication. *Ann. N.Y. acad. sci.* 83(1959):301–317. *(b)* The sexual response cycle of the human female: I. Gross anatomic considerations. *Western j. surg., obstet gynecol.* 68(1960):57–72.

Masters, W. H., and Johnson, V. E. *(a)* The human female: Anatomy of sexual response. *Minn. med.* 43(1960):31–36. *(b)* Vaginal pH: The influence of the male ejaculate. In *Report of the thirty-fifth Ross conference, endocrine dysfunction and infertility.* Columbus, Ohio: Ross Laboratories, 1960. *(c)* Intravaginal environment: I. A lethal factor. *Fertility sterility* 12(1961):560–580. *(d)* Orgasm, anatomy of the female. In *The encyclopedia of sexual behavior,* Vol. II, ed. A. Ellis and A. Abarbanel. New York: Hawthorn Bks, 1961. *(e)* The physiology of the vaginal reproductive function. *Western j. surg., obstet.*

gynecol. 69(1961):105–120.   (f) Treatment of the sexually incompatible family unit. *Minn. med.* 44(1961):466–471.   (g) The sexual response cycle of the human female: III. The clitoris: Anatomic and clinical considerations. *Western j. surg., obstet. gynecol.* 70(1962):248–257.   (h) The clitoris: An anatomic baseline for behavioral investigation. In *Determinants of human sexual behavior,* ed. G. W. Winokur. Springfield, Ill.: C. C. Thomas, 1963.   (i) The sexual response of the human male: I. Gross anatomic considerations. *Western j. surg., obstet. gynecol.* 71(1963):85–95.   (j) Sexual response: Part II. Anatomy and physiology. In *Human reproduction and sexual behavior,* ed. C. W. Lloyd. Philadelphia: Lea, 1964.   (k) Counseling with sexually incompatible marriage partners. In *Counseling in marital and sexual problems (A physician's handbook),* ed. R. H. Klemer. Baltimore: Williams & Wilkins, 1965.   (l) The sexual response cycle of the human female: 2. The clitoris: Anatomic and clinical considerations. In *Sex research: New developments,* ed. J. Money. New York: Holt, 1965.   (m) The sexual response cycles of the human male and female: Comparative anatomy and physiology. In *Sex and behavior,* ed. F. A. Beach. New York: Wiley, 1965.   (n) *Human sexual response.* Boston: Little, 1966. (o) Major questions in human sexual response. Lecture presented to the Harris County Medical Society, Houston, Mar. 1967.   (p) *Human sexual inadequacy.* Boston: Little, 1970.   (q) Sexual values and sexual function. A paper delivered at the fortieth anniversary meeting of the Marriage Council of Philadelphia, Philadelphia, Dec. 1971.

Masterson, J. F. Adolescents and the sexual evolution. *Sexual behavior,* June 1971, pp. 3–9.

Mathis, J. L. (a) What doctors don't know about sex. *Med. economics* 43 (Dec. 12, 1966):110–115.   (b) The exhibitionist. *Med. aspects human sexuality,* June 1969, pp. 89–101.   (c) The sexual tease. *Med. aspects human sexuality,* Dec. 1970, pp. 21–25.

Mayer, J. Better-educated mothers lead trend toward breast feeding. *Houston Post,* Aug. 20, 1972.

McCaghy, C. H. Child molesting. *Sexual behavior,* Aug. 1971, pp. 16–24.

McCary, J. L. (a) *An introduction to sexology, a neglected subject.* Houston: Pierre St. Le Macs, 1966.   (b) What I would tell my daughter about premarital sex. *Sexology,* Apr. 1966, pp. 583–586.   (c) What I would tell my son about premarital sex. *Sexology,* Nov. 1969, pp. 26–29.   (d) *Sexual myths and fallacies.* New York: Van Nostrand-Reinhold, 1971.

McCary, J. L., and Flake, M. H. The role of bibliotherapy and sex education in counseling for sexual problems. *Professional psychol.* 2(1971):353–357.

McCary, J. L., and McElhaney, M. *The abbreviated Bible.* New York: Van Nostrand-Reinhold, 1971.

McGuire, T. F., and Steinhilber, R. M. Frigidity, the primary female sexual dysfunction. *Med. aspects human sexuality,* Oct. 1970, pp. 108–123.

McRoberts, J. W. Vasectomy repair. *Med. aspects human sexuality,* May 1972, p. 189.

Mead, M. *Coming of age in Samoa.* New York: Morrow, 1928.

Medical science notes. (a) *Sexology,* June 1961, p. 790.   (b) *Sexology,* July 1961, p. 862.   (c) *Sexology,* Aug. 1961, p. 70.   (d) *Sexology,* Oct. 1961, p. 214.

Melody, G. F. Role of the clitoris. *Med. aspects human sexuality,* June 1970, p. 116.

Melzack, R. The perception of pain. *Sci. Amer.*, Feb. 1961, pp. 41–49.

Menaker, J. S. "Engagement" ovaries. *Sexology*, Aug. 1961, pp. 49–53.

Ministers and sex. *Sexology*, May 1959, p. 663.

Money, J. (a) Phantom orgasm in the dreams of paraplegic men and women. *Arch. gen. psychiat.* 3(1960):373–382. (b) Psychosexual differentiation. In *Sex research: New developments*, ed. J. Money. New York: Holt, 1965. (c) Judging teenage mores. *J. sex research* 2(1966):41–42. (d) The strange case of the pregnant hermaphrodite. *Sexology*, Aug. 1966, pp. 7–9. (e) Influence of hormones on psychosexual differentiation. *Med. aspects human sexuality*, Nov. 1968, pp. 32–42. (f) *Sex errors of the body.* Baltimore: Johns Hopkins Press, 1968. (g) Earlier maturation. *Med. aspects human sexuality*, Dec. 1969, p. 77. (h) Clitoral size and erotic sensation. *Med. aspects human sexuality*, Mar. 1970, p. 95. (i) Phantom orgasm in paraplegics. *Med. aspects human sexuality*, Jan. 1970, pp. 90–97. (j) Use of an androgen-depleting hormone in the treatment of male sex offenders. *J sex research* 6(1970):165–172.

Money, J., and Brennan, J. G. Heterosexual vs. homosexual attitudes: Male partners' perception of the feminine image of male transsexuals. *J. sex research* 6(1970): 193–209.

Money, J., and Yankowitz, R. The sympathetic-inhibiting effects of the drug Ismelin on human male eroticism, with a note on Mellaril. *J. sex research* 3(1967): 69–82.

Montagu, A. (a) Myths about birthmarks. *Sexology*, June 1963, pp. 734–736. (b) Smoking, pregnancy and sex. *Sexology*, Nov. 1963, pp. 220–222. (c) Sex made to order. *Sexology*, Jan. 1964, pp. 384–386.

Moore, J. E. Problematic sexual behavior. In *The individual, sex, and society*, ed. C. B. Broderick and J. Bernard. Baltimore: Johns Hopkins Press, 1969.

Mosher, D. L., and Cross, H. J. Sex guilt and premarital sexual experiences of college students. *J. consult. clin. psychol.* 36(1971):27–32.

Mozes, E. B. (a) The technique of wooing. *Sexology*, July 1959, pp. 756–760. (b) Premature ejaculation. *Sexology*, Nov. 1963, pp. 274–276. (c) Stone babies. *Sexology*, Jan. 1964, pp. 411–413.

Mueller, G. O. W. (a) Sex law reform. *Sexology*, June 1965, pp. 742–744. (b) Seduction and the law. *Med. aspects human sexuality*, Jan. 1972, pp. 14–20.

Murdock, G. P. (a) *Our primitive contemporaries.* New York: Macmillan, 1934. (b) *Social structure.* New York: Macmillan, 1949.

Nadler, R. P. Approach to psychodynamics of obscene telephone calls. *Med. aspects human sexuality*, Aug. 1968, pp. 28–33.

Need for reform, A. *Sexology*, Aug. 1965, p. 70.

Neiger, S. (a) Increasing your sex pleasure. *Sexology*, May 1968, pp. 656–659. (b) Sex potions. *Sexology*, June 1968, pp. 730–733. (c) Mate-swapping: Can it save a marriage? *Sexology*, Jan. 1971, pp. 8–12.

Netter, F. H. *Reproductive system.* Summit, N.J.: CIBA Pharmaceutical Products, 1961.

Neubardt, S. *Contraception.* New York: Pocket Bks, 1968.

Neubeck, G. *Extra-marital relationships.* Englewood Cliffs, N.J.: Prentice-Hall, 1969.

Neumann, G. Abortion. In *The encyclopedia of sexual behavior*, Vol. I, ed. A. Ellis and A. Abarbanel. New York: Hawthorn Bks, 1961.

New pornography, The. *Time,* Apr. 16, 1965, pp. 28–29.

Newman, G., and Nichols, C. R. Sexual activities and attitudes in older persons. *J.A.M.A.* 173(1960):33–35.

News of the month. (a) *Sexology,* Oct. 1961, p. 197.   (b) *Sexology,* Nov. 1961, p. 269.   (c) *Sexology,* Dec. 1961, p. 342.

Newsweek, Apr. 13, 1970.

Nonatuplets in Pakistan. *Sexology,* Nov. 1966, p. 270.

O'Conner, L. R. *The photographic manual of sexual intercourse.* New York: Pent-R Bks, 1969.

Oliver, B. J., Jr. What the rapist is like. *Sexology,* July 1965, pp. 849–851.

Ottenheimer, L., Rosenbaum, S., Seidenberg, R., and Chernick, N. B. Should women ever pretend to climax? *Sexual behavior,* Apr. 1971, pp. 11–13.

Otto, H. A. The new sexuality: An introduction. In *The new sexuality,* ed. H. A. Otto. Palo Alto: Science & Behavior, 1971.

Ovesey, L., and Meyers, H. Retarded ejaculation. *Med. aspects human sexuality,* Nov. 1970, pp. 98–119.

Packard, V. *The sexual wilderness.* New York: McKay, 1968.

Panagoras, N. Pregnancy by proxy. *Houston Post,* June 13, 1971.

Parkes, A. S., and Bruce, H. M. Olfactory stimuli in mammalian reproduction. *Science* 134(1961):1049–1054.

Pauly, I. B., and Goldstein, S. G. Prevalence of significant sexual problems in medical practice. *Med. aspects human sexuality,* Nov. 1970, pp. 48–63.

Pearlman, C. K. Frequency of intercourse in males at different ages. *Med. aspects human sexuality,* Nov. 1972, pp. 92–113.

Peretti, P. O. Premarital sexual behavior between females and males of two middle-sized midwestern cities. *J. sex research* 5(1969):218–225.

Pereyra, A. J. Relationship of sexual activities to cervical cancer. *Obstet. gynecol.* 17(1961):154–159.

Perrin, N. *Dr. Bowdler's legacy: A history of expurgated books in England and America.* New York: Atheneum, 1969.

Personality mailbag, Texas magazine section. *Houston Chronicle,* May 24, 1970.

Pilpel, H. F. The voluntary approach: Population control. *Civil liberties,* Nov. 1971.

Pineo, P. C. Disenchantment in the later years of marriage. *Marriage family living* 23(1961):3–11.

Platt, R. Reflections on aging and death. *Lancet,* Jan. 5, 1963, pp. 1–6.

Playboy interview: Timothy Leary. *Playboy,* Sept. 1966, p. 93.

Poffenberger, T. (a) Family life education in this scientific age. *Marriage family living* 21(1959):150–154.   (b) Individual choice in adolescent premarital sex behavior. *Marriage family living* 22(1960):324–330.

Pohlman, E. Premarital contraception: Research reports and problems. *J. sex research* 5(1969):187–194.

Polsky, N. *Hustlers, beats and others.* Chicago: Aldine, 1967.

Pomeroy, W. B. (a) The sexual non-conformist. *Sexology,* Dec. 1965, pp. 295–296. (b) Why we tolerate lesbians. *Sexology,* May 1965, pp. 652–654.   (c) The Masters-Johnson report and the Kinsey tradition. In *An analysis of human sexual response,* ed. R. Brecher and E. Brecher. New York: New Amer.

Lib., 1966. (*d*) Parents and homosexuality: I. *Sexology*, Mar. 1966, pp. 508–511. (*e*) Parents and homosexuality: II. *Sexology*, Apr. 1966, pp. 588–590. (*f*) Homosexuality, transvestism, and transsexualism. In *Human sexuality in medical education and practice*, ed. C. E. Vincent. Springfield, Ill.: C. C. Thomas, 1968.

Pornography: What is permitted is boring. *Time*, June 6, 1969, p. 47.

Posner, L. B., Chidiac, J. E., and Posner, A. C. Pregnancy at age forty and over. *Obstet. gynecol.* 17(1961):194–198.

Prince, V. "C." *The transvestite and his wife*. Los Angeles: Argyle Bks, 1967.

Psychiatrist looks at the problem of obscenity, A. *Sexology*, Sept. 1960, p. 93.

Public law and private morality. *Sexology*, July 1965, p. 862.

Pund, E. R., and Von Haam, E. Spirochetal and venereal diseases. In *Pathology*, ed. W. A. D. Anderson. St. Louis: Mosby, 1957.

Quality Educational Development, Inc. Sex education programs in the public schools of the United States. *Technical reports of the Commission on Obscenity and Pornography*, Vol. 10. Washington, D.C.: U.S. Government Printing Office, 1970.

Quinn, R. W. Epidemiology of gonorrhea. *Southern med. bull.* 59, no. 2 (1971): 7–12.

Raboch, J. (*a*) Penis size: An important new study. *Sexology*, June 1970, pp. 16–18. (*b*) Will hormones increase your sex power? *Sexology*, May 1970, pp. 9–12.

Rainwater, L. (*a*) Some aspects of lower class sexual behavior. *J. soc. issues* 22, no. 2 (1966):96–108. (*b*) Some aspects of lower class sexual behavior. *Med. aspects human sexuality*, Feb. 1968, pp. 15–25.

Ramsey, G. The sex information of younger boys. *Amer. j. orthopsychiat.* 13(1943): 347–352.

Rector, F. The unusual case of breast-feeding fathers. *Sexology*, July 1970, pp. 33-34.

Reevy, W. R. Child sexuality. In *The encyclopedia of sexual behavior*, Vol. I, ed. A. Ellis and A. Abarbanel. New York: Hawthorn Bks, 1961.

Reichlin, S. Relationship of the pituitary gland to human sexual behavior. *Med. aspects human sexuality*, Feb. 1971, pp. 146–154.

Reik, T. *Psychology of sex relations*. New York: Grove, 1966.

Reiser, C. Vasectomy: Medical and legal aspects. *J. urol.* 79(1958):138–143.

Reiss, I. L. (*a*) How and why America's sex standards are changing. *Trans-action*, Mar. 1960, pp. 26–32. (*b*) *Premarital sexual standards in America*. Glencoe, Ill.: Free Press, 1960. (*c*) Sexual codes in teen-age culture. *The annals*, Nov. 1961, pp. 53–62. (*d*) Standards of sexual behavior. In *The encyclopedia of sexual behavior*, Vol. II, ed. A. Ellis and A. Abarbanel. New York: Hawthorn Bks, 1961. (*e*) Premarital sex permissiveness among Negroes and whites. *Amer. socio. rev.* 29(1964):688–698. (*f*) Premarital sexual standards. In *Human sexuality in medical education and practice*, ed. C. E. Vincent. Springfield, Ill.: C. C. Thomas, 1968. (*g*) The influence of contraceptive knowledge on premarital sexuality. *Med. aspects human sexuality*, Feb. 1970, pp. 71–86. (*h*) Premarital coitus and marital happiness. *Med. aspects human sexuality*, Oct. 1970, p. 165. (*i*) Critique of Psychodynamics of seduction by L. Salzman. *Sexual behavior*, Aug. 1971, p. 57. (*j*) Premarital sex codes: The old and the new. In *Sexuality: A search for perspective,* ed. D. L. Grummon and A. M. Barclay. New York: Van Nostrand-Reinhold, 1971.

Revitch, E., and Weiss, R. G. The pedophiliac offender. *Diseases nervous system* 23(1962):73–78.

Riedman, S. R. Change of life. *Sexology,* July 1961, pp. 808–813.

Rizzo, J. M. How guilt got into sex. *Sexology,* Aug. 1968, pp. 64–67.

Robbins, E. S., Herman, M., and Robbins, L. Sex and arson: Is there a relationship? *Med. aspects human sexuality,* Oct. 1969, pp. 57–64.

Robinson, I. E., and King, K. Sex attitudes and the fear of venereal disease among college students. *J. sex research* 5(1969):195–198.

Rodgers, D. A., Ziegler, F. J., Prentiss, R. J., and Martin, P. L. Comparisons of nine contraceptive procedures by couples changing to vasectomy or ovulation suppression medication *J. sex research* 1(1965):87–96.

Rodman, H. *Marriage, family, and society.* New York: Random House, 1965.

Rorvik, D. M. (a) Beyond the pill. *Look,* June 15, 1971, pp. 17–19.   (b) The test-tube baby is coming. *Look,* May 18, 1971, pp. 83–88.

Rosato, D. J., and Kleger, B. Is cervical cancer a venereally transmitted disease? *Med. aspects human sexuality,* Mar. 1970, pp. 82–92.

Rosen, H. S. A survey of the sexual attitudes and bevahior of mate-swappers in Houston, Texas. Master's thesis, University of Houston, 1971.

Rosenbaum, S. Pretended orgasm. *Med. aspects human sexuality,* Apr. 1970, pp. 84–96.

Rosenberg, B., and Bensman, J. Sexual patterns in three ethnic subcultures of an American underclass. *Ann. Amer. acad. pol. soc. sci.* 376(1968):61–75.

Rosengard, I. S. (a) Are men becoming obsolete? *Sexology,* May 1970, pp. 19–21.   (b) How the pill affects your sex life. *Sexology,* Mar. 1971, pp. 20–22.

Rosenthal, Jack. *Houston Chronicle,* Mar. 3, 1972.

Rotkin, I. D. Epidemiology of cancer of the cervix: III. Sexual characteristics of a cervical cancer population. *Amer. j. public health* 57(1967):815.

Rowan, R. L. "Honeymoon cystitis" and other bladder problems. *Sexology,* Sept. 1964, pp. 118–120.

Rubin, I. (a) Birth control pills for men. *Sexology,* Aug. 1961, pp. 12–15.   (b) Sex over 65. In *Advances in sex research,* ed. H. G. Beigel. New York: Harper, 1963.   (c) The electric vibrator and frigidity. *Sexology,* Oct. 1964, pp. 156–158.   (d) Sex needs after 65. *Sexology,* June 1964, pp. 769–771.   (e) Should students learn birth control? *Sexology,* Feb. 1964, pp. 449–451.   (f) Is there a sex revolution? *Sexology,* Nov. 1965, pp. 220–222.   (g) *Sexual life after sixty.* New York: Basic Bks, 1965. (h) Transition in sex values—Implications for the education of adolescents. *J. marriage family* 27(1965):185–189.   (i) The new Kinsey report. *Sexology,* Feb. 1966, pp. 443–446.   (j) Sex after forty—and after seventy. In *An analysis of human sexual response,* ed. R. Brecher and E. Brecher. New York: New Amer. Lib., 1966.   (k) Changing college sex: New Kinsey report. *Sexology,* June 1968, pp. 780–782.   (l) New sex findings. *Sexology,* Nov. 1969, pp. 65–66.   (m) The prostitute and her customer. *Sexology,* June 1969, pp. 785–787.   (n) New sex findings. *Sexology,* Jan. 1970, pp. 67–68.   (o) *Sexual life in the later years.* SIECUS study guide no. 12. New York: SIECUS, 1970.   (p) New sex findings: Some trends and implications. In *The new sexuality,* ed. H. A. Otto. Palo Alto: Science & Behavior, 1971.

Russell, M. Sterilization. In *The encyclopedia of sexual behavior*, Vol. II, ed. A. Ellis and A. Abarbanel. New York: Hawthorn Bks, 1961.

Rutledge, A. L. Sex during pregnancy. *Sexology*, Feb. 1964, pp. 483–485.

Sadoff, R. L. Myths regarding the sex criminal. *Med. aspects human sexuality*, July 1969, pp. 64–74.

Safest abortion time calculated. *Houston Post*, Dec. 19, 1971.

Safier, B. *A psychiatric approach to the treatment of promiscuity*. New York: Amer. Social Hygiene Assoc., 1949.

Salzman, L. (a) Recently exploded sexual myths. *Med. aspects human sexuality*, Sept. 1967, pp. 6–11. (b) Psychodynamics of seduction. *Sexual behavior*, Aug. 1971, pp. 57–62.

Scheinfeld, A. *You and heredity*. New York: Garden City Pub. Co., 1945.

Schering Corporation. *Sex endocrinology: A handbook for the medical and allied professions*. Bloomfield: Schering Corporation, Medical Research Division, 1944.

Schofield, M. G., et al. *The sexual behavior of young people*. London: Longmans, Ltd., 1965.

Schur, E., ed. *The family and the sexual revolution: Selected readings*. Bloomington: Indiana Univ. Press, 1964.

Science notes. (a) *Sexology*, Oct. 1962, p. 214. (b) *Sexology*, Nov. 1964, p. 281. (c) *Sexology*, Feb. 1965, p. 199. (d) *Sexology*, May 1965, p. 715. (e) *Sexology*, Dec. 1965, p. 356. (f) *Sexology*, Jan. 1966, p. 428. (g) *Sexology*, Mar. 1968, p. 572. (h) *Sexology*, Sept. 1969, p. 14. (i) *Sexology*, Feb. 1970, p. 32. (j) *Sexology*, Nov. 1970, p. 20.

Searle, G. D., and Co. *A prescription for family planning: The story of Enovid*. New York: G. D. Searle and Co., 1964.

Secondary syphilis. *Med. aspects human sexuality*, July 1971, pp. 82–101.

Segal, S. J., and Tietze, C. Contraceptive technology: Current and prospective methods. *Rep. population family planning*, Oct. 1969.

Sentnor, M., and Hult, S. Erotic zones—Facts and superstitions. *Sexology*, Sept. 1961, pp. 76–81.

Sex and sin in Sweden. *Sexology*, May 1970, p. 71.

Sex behavior of older women. *Sexology*, June 1966, p. 734.

Sex education and the "latency period." *Sexology*, Nov. 1969, p. 71.

Sex in the news. (a) *Sexology*, Oct. 1963, p. 209. (b) *Sexology*, Mar. 1965, p. 569. (c) *Sexology*, Aug. 1966, p. 67. (d) *Sexology*, Jan. 1967, p. 421. (e) *Sexology*, June 1970, p. 69. (f) *Sexology*, Nov. 1970, p. 7. (g) *Sexology*, Sept. 1971, p. 25.

Sex offenders good parole risk. *Sexology*, June 1963, p. 768.

Sex scene, The. *Sexology*, Feb. 1970, p. 58.

Sexual maturity and climate. *Sexology*, June 1961, p. 773.

Shader, R. I., and Ohly, J. I. Premenstrual tension, femininity, and sexual drive. *Med. aspects human sexuality*, Apr. 1970, pp. 42–49.

Shafer, N. (a) Vaginal discharges. *Sexology*, Mar. 1966, pp. 531–533. (b) Catch prostate cancer early! *Sexology*, July 1968, pp. 823–826.

Shaffer, J. W. Masculinity–femininity and other personality traits in gonadal aplasia

(Turner's syndrome). In *Advances in sex research,* ed. H. G. Beigel. New York: Harper, 1963.

Shainess, N. The formation of gender identity. *J. sex research* 5(1969):75–85.

Shaw, W. *Operative gynaecology.* Baltimore: Williams & Wilkins, 1954.

Shearer, L. Intelligence report. *Parade,* Mar. 21, 1971, p. 17.

Sherman, J. K. Freezing human sperm. *Sexology,* July 1965, pp. 812–815.

Sherwin, R. V. (a) Laws on sex crimes. In *The encyclopedia of sexual behavior,* Vol. II, ed. A. Ellis and A. Abarbanel. New York: Hawthorn Bks, 1961. (b) Sexual problems and marital dissolution. *Med. aspects human sexuality,* Apr. 1970, pp. 16–17.

Shettles, L. B. (a) Observations on human spermatozoa. *Bull. sloan hosp. women* 6(1960):48. (b) The great preponderance of human males conceived. *Amer. j. obstet. gynecol.* 89(1964):130–133. (c) Predetermining children's sex. *Med. aspects human sexuality,* June 1972, p. 172.

Shiloh, A. Introduction: The problem. In *Studies in human sexual behavior: The American scene,* ed. A. Shiloh. Springfield, Ill.: C. C. Thomas, 1970.

Shope, D. F. (a) Orgasm in college girls. *Sexology,* May 1968, pp. 711–715. (b) The orgastic responsiveness of selected college females. *J. sex research* 4(1968): 206–219.

SIECUS. *Sexuality and man.* New York: Scribner, 1970.

Sikes, O. J. If not the pill, what? *Sexology,* Aug. 1970, pp. 22–25.

Slovenko, R. (a) Sex laws: Are they necessary? In *Sexuality: A search for perspective,* ed. D. L. Grummon and A. M. Barclay. New York: Van Nostrand-Reinhold, 1971. (b) Statutory rape. *Med. aspects human sexuality,* Mar. 1971, pp. 155–167.

Smartt, W. H., and Lighter, A. G. The gonorrhea epidemic and its control. *Med. aspects human sexuality,* Jan. 1971, pp. 96–115.

Smith, G. P. For unto us a child is—legally. *Amer. bar assoc. j.* 56(1970):143–145.

Smith, J. R., and Smith, L. G. Co-marital sex and the sexual freedom movement. *J. sex research* 6(1970):131–142.

Smoking deters pregnancy. *Sexology,* Apr. 1968, p. 643.

Sonenschein, D. The ethnography of male homosexual relationships. *J. sex research* 4(1968):69–83.

Speidel, J. J. Knowledge of contraceptive techniques among a hospital population of low socio-economic status. *J. sex research* 6(1970):284–306.

Steen, E. B., and Montagu, A. *Anatomy and physiology,* Vol. 2. New York: Barnes & Noble, 1959.

Steinhaus, A. H. *Toward an understanding of health and physical education.* Dubuque, Iowa: W. C. Brown, 1963.

Stiller, R. (a) Wife swapping. *Sexology,* May 1961, pp. 652–656. (b) Electrically caused ejaculation. *Sexology,* Dec. 1962, pp. 321–322. (c) Common prostate problems. *Sexology,* July 1963, pp. 817–819. (d) The firebug and sex. *Sexology,* Nov. 1964, pp. 236–238. (e) Drinking and sex. *Sexology,* Mar. 1965, pp. 519–521. (f) Why girls get pregnant. *Sexology,* Oct. 1966, pp. 162–165. (g) *Illustrated sex dictionary.* New York: Health Publications, 1966.

Stokes, W. R., Montagu, A., Money, J., Rutledge, A. L., and Yoder, H. W. Is pornography harmful? *Sexology,* Aug. 1963, pp. 16–19.

Stone, A. *The practice of contraception.* Baltimore: Williams & Wilkins, 1931.

Stone, A., and Stone, H. *A marriage manual.* New York: Simon & Schuster, 1952.

Storr, A. *Sexual deviation*. Baltimore: Penguin, 1964.

Story of the sperm. *Sexology*, Jan. 1965, pp. 379–381.

Sullivan, H. S. *Conceptions of modern psychiatry*. New York: Norton, 1947.

Sullivan, P. R. What is the role of fantasy in sex? *Med. aspects human sexuality*, Apr. 1969, pp. 79–89.

Sullivan, W. Boys and girls are now maturing earlier. *New York Times*, Jan. 24, 1971.

Sutker, P. B., and Kilpatrick, D. G. Religious preference, practice and personal sexual attitudes and behavior. *Psychol. rep.* 26(1970):835–841.

Swift, P. Keeping up with youth. *Parade*, Aug. 6, 1972, p. 16.

Tagliamonte, A., Tagliamonte, P., Gessa, G. L., and Brodie, B. B. Compulsive sexual activity induced by p-chlorophenylalanine in normal and pinealectomized male rats. *Science* 166(1969):1433–1435.

Tarail, M. Sex over 65. *Sexology*, Feb. 1962, pp. 440–443.

Tarr, J. D. F., and Lugar, R. R. Early infectious syphilis: Male homosexual relations as a mode of spread. *Calif. med.* 93(1960):35–37.

Teen-age extramarital conception. *Sexology*, Oct. 1961, p. 178.

Teen-age sex: Letting the pendulum swing. *Time*, Aug. 21, 1972, pp. 34–38.

TeLinde, R. W. *Operative gynecology*. Philadelphia: Lippincott, 1953.

Terman, L. M. *Psychological factors in marital happiness*. New York: McGraw, 1938.

Thornburg, H. D. Age and first sources of sex information as reported by 88 college women. *J. sch. health* 40(1970):156–158.

Thorne, F. C. Ejaculatio praecox. *Diseases nervous system* 4(1943):273–275.

Thorpe, L. P., Katz, B., and Lewis, R. T. *The psychology of abnormal behavior*. New York: Ronald, 1961.

Tietze, C. (a) Probability of pregnancy resulting from a single unprotected coitus. *Fertility sterility* 11(1960):485–488. (b) History of contraceptive methods. *J. sex research* 1(1965):69–85. (c) Fertility while breast feeding. *Med. aspects human sexuality*, Nov. 1970, p. 90.

Trainer, J. B. *Physiologic foundations for marriage counseling*. St. Louis: Mosby, 1965.

Trice, E. R., Gayle, S., Jr., and Clark, F. A., Jr. The transmission of early infectious syphilis through homosexual practices. *Virginia med. monthly* 87(1960): 132–134.

Turner, H. H. A syndrome of infantilism, congenital webbed neck and cubitus valgus. *Endocrinology* 23(1938):566.

Ubell, E. *New York Herald Tribune*, June 17, 1962.

Udry, J. R. (a) *The social context of marriage*. Philadelphia: Lippincott, 1966. (b) Sex and family life. *Med. aspects human sexuality*, Nov. 1968, pp. 66–82.

Ueno, M. The so-called coition death. *Jap. j. legal med.* 17(1963):535.

United Press International. (a) Marijuana, impotency linked. *Houston Post*, Mar. 2, 1971. (b) N.Y.C. pregnancy deaths decline. *Houston Post*, Apr. 27, 1971.

U.S. Bureau of the Census. *Fertility indicators: 1970*. Current population reports, Series P-23, No. 36. Washington, D.C.: U.S. Government Printing Office, 1971.

U.S. Department of Health, Education, and Welfare. Public Health Service. *Morbidity and mortality annual supplement summary 1969*. Public Health Service Vol. 18, No. 54. Atlanta, Ga.: Center for Disease Control, 1970.

Van Dellen, T. R. Babies are born at random. *Houston Chronicle,* Aug. 16, 1971.

Van de Velde, T. H. *Ideal marriage: Its physiology and technique.* New York: Random House, 1957.

Vatsyayana. *The Kama sutra.* New York: Dutton, 1962.

VD: The epidemic. *Newsweek,* Jan. 24, 1972, pp. 46–50.

Villee, C. A. *Biology.* 5th ed. Philadelphia: Saunders, 1967.

Vincent, C. E. (a) Unmarried fathers and the mores: "Sexual exploiter" as an ex post facto label. *Amer. sociol. rev.* 25(1960):40–46.   (b) *Unmarried mothers.* Glencoe, Ill.: Free Press, 1961.   (c) Seven million illegitimates. *Sexology,* Oct. 1962, 178–181.   (d) Spotlight on the unwed father. *Sexology,* Mar. 1962, pp. 538–542.   (e) Unmarried mothers: Society's dilemma. *Sexology,* Feb. 1962, pp. 450–455.   (f) The physician as counselor in postmarital and extramarital pregnancies. *Med. aspects human sexuality,* Nov. 1967, pp. 34–41.   (g) Illegitimacy as an introductory topic for the teaching of human sexuality in medical schools. In *Human sexuality in medical education and practice,* ed. C. E. Vincent. Springfield, Ill.: C. C. Thomas, 1968.   (h) Illicit pregnancies among married and divorced females. In *Human sexuality in medical education and practice,* ed. C. E. Vincent. Springfield, Ill.: C. C. Thomas, 1968.   (i) Sexual interest in someone older or younger. *Med. aspects human sexuality,* Nov. 1968, pp. 6–11.   (j) Unmarried mothers and pregnant brides. In *Human sexuality in medical education and practice,* ed. C. E. Vincent. Springfield, Ill.: C. C. Thomas, 1968.   (k) Sex and the young married. *Med. aspects human sexuality,* Mar. 1969, pp. 13–23.

Vizinczey, S. *In praise of older women.* London: Barrie & Rockliff, 1966.

Wake, F. R. Attitudes of parents towards the premarital sex behavior of their children and themselves. *J. sex research* 5(1969):170–177.

Walker, C. More abortions than babies in Eastern Europe. *Parade,* Feb. 13, 1972, p. 31.

Walker, K. Erection disorders. *Sexology,* May 1963, pp. 696–698.

Waller, W., and Hill, R. *The family.* New York: Dryden, 1951.

Walsh, R. H. The generation gap in sexual beliefs. *Sexual behavior,* Jan. 1972, pp. 4–10.

Ward, D. A., and Kassebaum, G. G. Homosexuality: A mode of adaptation in a prison for women. *Soc. problems* 12(1964):159–177.

Weaver, R. G. Scrotum and testes. *Med. aspects human sexuality,* Oct. 1970, pp. 124–143.

Weinberg, J. Sexuality in later life. *Med. aspects human sexuality,* Apr. 1971, pp. 216–227.

Weinberg, M. S. Nudists. *Sexual behavior,* Aug. 1971, pp. 51–55.

Wershub, L. P. Male genital abnormalities which interfere with intercourse. *Med. aspects human sexuality,* Sept. 1968, pp. 53–58.

Westoff, C. F., Bumpass, L., and Ryder, N. B. The pill and coital frequency. *Med. aspects human sexuality,* Mar. 1971, pp. 72–79.

Westoff, L. A., and Westoff, C. F. *From now to zero: Fertility, contraception and abortion in America.* Boston: Little, 1971.

Whiskin, F. E. The geriatric sex offender. *Med. aspects human sexuality,* Apr. 1970, pp. 125–129.

Wiener, D. N. Sexual problems in clinical experience. In *The individual, sex, and society*, ed. C. B. Broderick and J. Bernard. Baltimore: Johns Hopkins Press, 1969.

Williamson, P. The erotic zones. *Sexology*, June 1961, pp. 740–743.

Winick, C. A study of consumers of explicitly sexual materials: Some functions served by adult movies. *Technical reports of the Commission on Obscenity and Pornography*, Vol. 4. Washington, D.C.: U.S. Government Printing Office, 1970.

Winick, C., and Kinsie, P. M. Prostitution. *Sexual behavior*, Jan. 1973, pp. 33–43.

Wolbarst, A. L. The gynecic factor in the causation of male impotency. *N.Y. state j. med.* 47(1947):1252–1255.

Wolfenden, J. *Report of the Committee on Homosexual Offenses and Prostitution*. London: Her Majesty's Stationery Office, 1957.

Wood, R. Popular sex superstitions. *Sexology*, June 1963, pp. 752–754.

Wright, M. R., and McCary, J. L. Positive effects of sex education on emotional patterns of behavior. *J. sex research* 5(1969):162–169.

Wright, R. C. The relief of cervical dyspareunia by transvaginal paracervical uterine denervation. *Amer. j. obstet. gynecol.* 87(1963):963–967.

Zarem, H. A. Breast augmentation. *Med. aspects human sexuality*, May 1970, p. 145.

Zehv, W. (a) How men and women differ in sex. *Sexology*, May 1968, pp. 666–668. (b) Trying new positions in intercourse. *Sexology*, Jan. 1969, pp. 364–367.

Ziegler, F. J., Rodgers, D. A., and Kriegsman, S. A. Effect of vasectomy on psychological functioning. *Psychosomat. med.* 28(1966):50–63.

Ziegler, F. J., Rodgers, D. A., and Prentiss, R. J. Psychosocial response to vasectomy. *Arch. gen. psychiat.* 31(1969):46–54.

Ziff, H. L. Abortion law enforcement in Chicago. *J. sex research* 6(1970):235–239.

INDEX